UNDERSTAND
SECURITIES LAW

UNDERSTANDING SECURITIES LAW

FIFTH EDITION

Marc I. Steinberg
Radford Professor of Law
Southern Methodist University
Dedman School of Law

 LexisNexis®

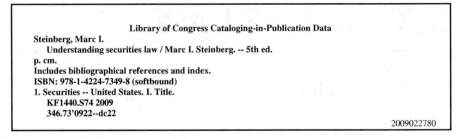

Library of Congress Cataloging-in-Publication Data

Steinberg, Marc I.
    Understanding securities law / Marc I. Steinberg. -- 5th ed.
    p. cm.
    Includes bibliographical references and index.
    ISBN: 978-1-4224-7349-8 (softbound)
    1. Securities -- United States. I. Title.
        KF1440.S74 2009
        346.73'0922--dc22

2009022780

ISBN: 978-1-4224-7349-8

NOTE TO USERS

To ensure that you are using the latest materials available in this area, please be sure to periodically check the LexisNexis Law School web site for downloadable updates and supplements at www.lexisnexis.com/lawschool.

Editorial Offices
121 Chanlon Rd., New Providence, NJ 07974 (908) 464-6800
201 Mission St., San Francisco, CA 94105-1831 (415) 908-3200
www.lexisnexis.com

MATTHEW◆BENDER

ACKNOWLEDGMENTS— FIRST EDITION

I wish to thank a number of individuals for their help regarding this project. In particular, my thanks to Professors Alan Bromberg, Dennis Honabach, and Mark Sargent for their comments. I thank Ralph Ferrara, Robin Goldman, Sam Gruenbaum, Will Kaulbach, Joe Kempler and Richard Starr, all of whom were my coauthors for certain publications, portions of which appear herein. My thanks also to Callaghan & Co., publishers of my treatise on Securities Practice: Federal and State Enforcement (1985) (updated annually) (coauthored with Ralph Ferrara), and to Law Journal Seminars-Press, publisher of my treatise on Securities Regulation: Liabilities and Remedies (1984) (updated annually) for granting their permission for me to use excerpts from the respective treatises. I also thank several law reviews in which I authored articles for granting their permission to use certain portions thereof herein, including the Cornell Law Review (67 Cornell L. Rev. 557 (1982), 66 Cornell L. Rev. 27 (1980)) and Fred B. Rothman & Co., the Emory Law Journal (30 Emory L.J. 169 (1981)), the Journal of Corporation Law (11 J. Corp. L. 1 (1985)), the Loyola of Los Angeles Law Review (13 Loyola Univ. (L.A.) L. Rev. 247 (1980) (coauthored with Samuel Gruenbaum), the University of Maryland Law Review (46 Md. L. Rev. 923 (1987)) (coauthored with Robin Goldman), the University of Pennsylvania Law Review (129 U. Pa. L. Rev. 263 (1980)) (coauthored with Ralph Ferrara) and Fred B. Rothman & Co., and the Vanderbilt Law Review (40 Vand. L. Rev. 489 (1987)) (coauthored with Will Kaulbach).

From the University of Maryland Law School, I thank Bob Krusen for his research assistance, Anne Rollins for her comments, and LuAnn Marshall, Gwen Davis, and Eileen Gretes for their expert secretarial help. This book was written while I was a member of two faculties, the faculties of the University of Maryland Law School and the Southern Methodist University School of Law. I thank both institutions and their respective deans, Mike Kelly at Maryland and Paul Rogers at SMU, for their support of this project.

I wish to dedicate this book to my friends at The University of Maryland School of Law. I've been fortunate to teach during the past six years at this superb institution with wonderful colleagues and students. As I enthusiastically join the SMU Law faculty on a more permanent basis, I will miss my friends at the Maryland Law School.

June 1989

ACKNOWLEDGMENTS— SECOND EDITION

The Second Edition to this reference text comes during my seventh year at SMU. It has been a fine seven years and I thank the university and my colleagues.

This project was funded by summer research grants (including the William Hawley Atwell Fund) from SMU Law School. I thank Dean Paul Rogers and the Atwell Fund for their support.

I owe many thanks to several individuals for helping this project become reality. I certainly thank the contribution of all those mentioned in the acknowledgments to the First Edition as well as the publishers who granted permission for me to use excerpts from my other books and articles.

For the Second Edition, I thank my secretary, Ms. Kathleen Vaughan, for her significant assistance. I also thank Professor Alan Bromberg, Mr. Ralph Janvey, Mr. Daryl Lansdale, Mr. Bruce Mendelsohn, Mr. Chris Olive and Mr. Buddy Reece as well as my research assistants, Mr. Cory Farley, Ms. Julie Herzog, and Mr. Cliff Murray, for their meaningful input. My thanks as well to The International Lawyer granting permission for me to use excerpts from my article that appeared in 29 Int'l Law. 43 (1995). I again thank Law Journal Seminars-Press for granting permission for me to use excerpts from my treatise, Securities Regulation: Liabilities and Remedies.

I dedicate this Second Edition to my good friend and colleague Professor Alan R. Bromberg. Professor Bromberg truly is the preeminent scholar in the United States in the areas of the law relating to securities fraud and partnership law. He also is a wonderful and generous individual. His help and guidance through my years at the University of Maryland and here at SMU have meant so very much to me. I thank you Alan.

August 1995

ACKNOWLEDGMENTS— THIRD EDITION

Fifteen years have elapsed since the publication of the First Edition of *Understanding Securities Law*. As this reference text undergoes modification due to securities law developments and the author's prerogative, I thank the contribution of all those mentioned in the acknowledgments to the First and Second Editions as well as the publishers who have granted permission for me to use excerpts from my other books and articles.

This project was funded by summer research grants from the SMU School of Law. I thank Dean John Attanasio and the Law School for their generous support.

For the Third Edition, I thank my secretary, Ms. Judy Parsley, for her significant assistance. I also thank my research assistants Mr. Jeff Brown, Mr. Noah Hansford, Mr. Barrett Howell, and Mr. Jason Myers for their meaningful input.

I dedicate this Third Edition to my parents Gerald and Phyllis Steinberg in honor of their fifty-ninth wedding anniversary. I am a lucky man to have two wonderful and loving parents. Mom and Dad, thanks so very much for your love, support, and guidance.

September 2000

ACKNOWLEDGMENTS—
FOURTH EDITION

Twenty years have elapsed since the publication of the First Edition of Understanding Securities Law. As this reference text undergoes modification due to securities law developments and the author's prerogative, I thank the contribution of all those mentioned in the acknowledgments to the First, Second and Third Editions as well as the publishers who have granted permission for me to use excerpts from my other books and articles.

This project was funded by a summer research grant from the SMU Dedman School of Law. I thank Dean John Attanasio and the Law School for their generous support.

For the Fourth Edition, I particularly thank my administrative assistant, Ms. Jan Spann, for her significant contribution. I also express my gratitude to Ms. Michele Oswald and Ms. Carolyn Yates for their secretarial assistance.

I thank Mr. Gregory Ivy, Associate Director of the Underwood Law Library, for his contribution of "Selected Securities Law Research Sources" contained in Chapter 1 of the book. My thanks also to my research assistants, a number of whom are now practicing lawyers-Mr. Chris Claasen, Ms. Karen Crenshaw, Ms. Shanna Nugent, Ms. Andrea Petersen and Mr. Tabor Pittman-for their meaningful input.

I dedicate this Fourth Edition to my wonderful family-my wife Laurie, my daughter Alexandra (Alex), and my sons Avram (Avi) and Phillip (Bear)-with all my love.

November 2006

ACKNOWLEDGMENTS— FIFTH EDITION

This project was funded by a summer research grant from the SMU Dedman School of Law. I thank Dean John B. Attanasio and the Law School for their generous support. I also thank my research assistants Mr. Dustin Appel and Mr. Ignacio Hirigoyen as well as my administrative assistant Ms. Jan Spann for their assistance. In addition, I wish to extend my appreciation to those persons mentioned in the acknowledgments to the First, Second, Third and Fourth Editions as well as the publishers who have granted permission for me to use excerpts from my other books and articles.

I dedicate this Fifth Edition to my terrific aunt and uncle, Frances and Fred Marblestone. Aunt Frances and Uncle Fred — this is a "small" way for me to say thank you for being so wonderful to my Mom and Dad, my sister Nancy, and me.

December 2008

Table of Contents

Table of Contents

Table of Contents

Table of Contents

Table of Contents

Table of Contents

Table of Contents

Table of Contents

Table of Contents

Table of Contents

Table of Contents

Chapter 1

INTRODUCTION

§ 1.01 PURPOSE OF TEXT

The purpose of this reference text is to provide a general understanding of the key issues that a student will face in the basic securities regulation course. As a consequence, the text's scope principally focuses on the Securities Act of 1933 (hereinafter called the "Securities Act" or "1933 Act") and the Securities Exchange Act of 1934 (hereinafter called the "Exchange Act" or "1934 Act"). In this respect, the text addresses pertinent Congressional amendments to these Acts as well as Securities and Exchange Commission regulatory developments. State securities statutes (also known as "blue sky" laws) also are covered. For students wishing a broader subject matter treatment or more intense coverage of a particular issue (such as tender offers or SEC enforcement), the sources cited in § 1.03 of this chapter should be consulted.

Securities regulation is a difficult course. At the same time, it is intellectually challenging and generates provocative policy issues. It thus has the potential of being one of the more interesting yet demanding courses in the law school curriculum. This text hopefully will stimulate student interest and help make the course's subject matter more understandable.

§ 1.02 OVERVIEW

Enacted in the aftermath of "The Great Crash," the Securities Act of 1933 (hereinafter the "Securities Act" or "1933 Act") and the Securities Exchange Act of 1934 (hereinafter the "Exchange Act" or "1934 Act") have become the principal governors of federal securities law regulation. Basically, the 1933 Act deals with the initial offer and sale of securities while the 1934 Act primarily concerns trading and regulation in the secondary markets. Both Acts also prohibit manipulative and deceptive practices. Undoubtedly, the central focus of the federal securities laws is that of disclosure, thereby providing shareholders and the marketplace with sufficient information to make relevant decisions and to be apprised of significant developments. Congress thus sought to promote investor protection and the maintenance of fair and orderly markets. Generally, in enacting these Acts, Congress declined to adopt a merit approach. Rather, irrespective of the value or fairness of a transaction or other corporate action, the investor may decide for him or herself *after* receiving disclosure of pertinent information.

It would be a mistake, however, to assume that disclosure does not affect substantive conduct. As Justice Brandeis wisely stated: "Publicity is justly commended as a remedy for social and industrial diseases. Sunlight is said to be the best of disinfectants.[1] Or, as more contemporaneously phrased in this context, "[t]oday the disclosure requirements of the securities laws are used, in a variety of ways, for the explicit purpose of influencing a wide range of corporate primary behavior."[2]

It bears mentioning that the Exchange Act addresses a number of other matters, including oversight of brokers, dealers, and the stock exchanges, as well as proxy and tender offer regulation. In addition, the Exchange Act directs the Securities and Exchange Commission to facilitate the establishment of a national market system.

In 2002, in the wake of major financial debacles, such as Enron, WorldCom, Tyco, Adelphia and Global Crossings, Congress enacted the Sarbanes-Oxley Act (SOX). Going beyond disclosure, this Act federalizes state corporation law in significant respects. For example, the composition and functions of audit committees are statutorily prescribed. Chief executive officers and chief financial officers must "certify" the accuracy of disclosures in periodic reports filed by subject companies with the Securities and Exchange Commission. In order to help ensure the accuracy of these certifications, reasonably effective internal controls must be implemented. Moreover, accounting firms auditing publicly-held companies now are subject to far greater regulation and oversight.

In addition to the foregoing legislation, Congress has enacted other securities legislation: the Public Utility Holding Company Act of 1935, the Trust Indenture Act of 1939, the Investment Company Act of 1940, the Investment Advisers Act of 1940, and the Securities Investor Protection Act of 1970. Also, the individual states have passed their own securities statutes, called "Blue Sky" laws.[3] A number of these statutes, depending on the particular state, provide for significant investor protection and substantive regulation.

The Securities and Exchange Commission (hereinafter called the "SEC" or the "Commission") is the agency which administers and enforces the federal securities laws. Not surprisingly, the Commission during the years has had both its ardent supporters and outspoken critics, including during the 2008 financial crisis.[4] Nonetheless, as described in the New York Times, "the agency

---

[1] L. Brandeis, Other People's Money 92 (1914).

[2] R. Stevenson, Corporations and Information — Secrecy, Access & Disclosure 81–82 (1980). *See* M. Steinberg, Corporate Internal Affairs — A Corporate and Securities Law Perspective 28–29 (1983); Weiss, *Disclosure and Corporate Accountability*, 34 Bus. Law. 575 (1979).

[3] This term came into being due to the original purpose of the "blue sky" laws which was to prevent "speculative schemes which have no more basis than so many feet of blue sky." *Hall v. Geiger-Jones Co.*, 242 U.S. 539, 550 (1917).

[4] *See* R. Karmel, Regulation by Prosecution — The Securities and Exchange Commission versus Corporate America (1982); H. Kripke, The SEC and Corporate Disclosure: Regulation in Search of a Purpose (1979); J. Seligman, The Transformation of Wall Street — A History of the Securities and Exchange Commission and Modern Corporate Finance (1982); M. Steinberg, Corporate Internal Affairs — A Corporate and Securities Law Perspective (1983); Scannell, *SEC Faulted for Missing Red Flags at Bear Stearns*, Wall St. J., Sept. 27, 2008, at A3. *Compare* Macey, *Administrative Agency Obsolescence and Interest Group Formation: A Case Study of the SEC at Sixty*, 15 Cardozo L. Rev. 909 (1994), *and* Pritchard, *The SEC at 70: Time for Retirement?*, 80

created in 1934 to enforce [the securities] laws, the Securities and Exchange Commission, is still widely regarded as the nation's finest independent regulatory agency."[5] It is clear, however, that the recent financial debacles have adversely impacted the SEC's reputation. As a *New York Times* article stated, the Commission "is plagued by problems that go deeper than its leadership difficulties and have undermined its ability to police companies and markets."[6]

Turning to state securities regulation, the first such statute was enacted in Kansas nearly a century ago. Today, all the states have enacted some form of "blue sky" law designed to apply to securities activities within their individual borders. In general, these statutes seek to regulate such activities by one or more of the following routes: "(1) to prohibit fraud in the offer and sale of securities; (2) to require and regulate licensing of investment advisors, broker-dealers, and their agents; (3) to require the registration of securities, and (4) to determine that the securities meet certain standards which are often referred to as 'merit' or 'fair, just, and equitable' standards."[7]

§ 1.03   SELECTED SECURITIES LAW RESEARCH SOURCES[8]

There are a number of useful securities law research sources. These sources include:

Legislative History

Lexis contains the Senate and House committee reports prepared in connection with the 1933 and 1934 Acts. Lexis also offers Congressional Information Service (CIS) legislative history materials for some federal securities statutes.

Westlaw provides the Federal Securities — Legislative History database (Westlaw database identifier 'fsec-lh'), which contains the "legislative history of the federal securities statutes beginning with 1933. This history includes

---

Notre Dame L. Rev. 1073 (2005), *with* Goldshmid, *The SEC at 70: Let's Celebrate Its Reinvigorated Golden Years*, 80 Notre Dame L. Rev. 825 (2005), *and* Ratner, *The SEC at Sixty: A Reply to Professor Macey*, 16 Cardozo L. Rev. 1765 (1995). *See also* Hicks, *Securities Regulation: Challenges in the Decades Ahead*, 68 Ind. L.J. 791 (1993); Goshen & Parchomovsky, *The Essential Role of Securities Regulation*, 55 Duke L.J. 711 (2006); Karmel, *Realizing the Dream of William O. Douglas — The Securities and Exchange Commission Takes Charge of Corporate Governance*, 30 Del. J. Corp. L. 79 (2005).

   [5] Miller, *S.E.C.: Watchdog 1929 Lacked*, N.Y. Times, Oct. 31, 1979, at D1; *see also* D. Vise & A. Coll, Eagle on the Street (1991); *The SEC at 60*, Nat'l L.J., July 18, 1994, at Sec. C (articles contained therein).

   [6] Labaton, *S.E.C. Facing Deeper Trouble*, N.Y. Times, Dec. 1, 2002, at D1; *see also* sources cited note 4 *supra*.

   [7] Walker & Hadaway, *Merit Standards Revisited*, 7 J. Corp. L. 651, 653 (1982); *see generally* Macey & Miller, *Origin of the Blue Sky Laws*, 70 Tex. L. Rev. 347 (1991); J. Long, Blue Sky Law (2008); L. Loss, Commentary on the Uniform Securities Act (1976).

   [8] This section was prepared by Gregory Ivy, Esq., Associate Director, Underwood Law Library, Southern Methodist University. I thank Mr. Ivy for his contribution to this Project as well as his expert assistance with respect to my scholarly pursuits for the past several years.

congressional committee reports as reprinted in U.S. Code Congressional and Administrative News beginning with 1948. From 1990 forward, FSEC-LH contains all securities-related congressional committee reports, including reports on bills that did not become law. Presidential signing statements, issued at the time the President signed a bill into law, are also available."

Other sources providing legislative history of the federal securities statutes include:

Corporate Fraud Responsibility: A Legislative History of the Sarbanes-Oxley Act of 2002 (William H. Manz ed. 2003).

Federal Bar Association, Federal Securities Laws: Legislative History, 1933–1982 (1983).

_____, Federal Securities Laws: Legislative History, 1983–1987, *Supplement* (1988).

_____, Federal Securities Laws: Legislative History, 1987–1990, *Supplement* (1991).

Government Securities Law: A Legislative History of the Government Securities Act of 1986, Pub. Law No. 99-571 (Bernard D. Reams, Jr. & Carol J. Gray eds. 1989).

Insider Trading and Securities Fraud: A Legislative History of the Insider Trading and Securities Fraud Enforcement Act of 1988, Pub. Law No. 100-704, With Related Materials on Corporate Takeovers (Bernard D. Reams, Jr. ed. 1989).

Insider Trading and the Law: A Legislative History of the Insider Trading Sanctions Act of 1984, Pub. Law. No. 98-376 (Bernard D. Reams, Jr. ed. 1989).

Legislative History of the Securities Act of 1933 and Securities Exchange Act of 1934 (J.S. Ellenberger & Ellen P. Mahar eds. 1973).

Securities Primary Law Sourcebook (A.A. Sommer, Jr. ed. 1996). Contains the legislative history of the Acts of 1933 and 1934, among many other things.

SEC Issuances

Categories of SEC documents available on the SEC website www.sec.gov) are below. Many of these documents are also available on Lexis, Westlaw, and in CCH's Federal Securities Law Reporter.

- *Forms and Filings ('EDGAR')*

    The SEC's EDGAR (Electronic Data Gathering, Analysis, and Retrieval) system "performs automated collection, validation, indexing, acceptance, and forwarding of submissions by companies and others who are required by law to file forms with the U.S. Securities and Exchange Commission (SEC). Its primary purpose is to increase the efficiency and fairness of the securities market for the benefit of investors, corporations, and the economy by accelerating the receipt, acceptance, dissemination, and analysis of time-sensitive corporate information filed with the agency." EDGAR is accessible for free on the SEC's website. Commercial services such as Livedgar, 10-K Wizard, Lexis, and Westlaw provide the same information with value-adding enhancements.

- *Regulatory Actions*

  - Proposed Rules
  - Final Rules
  - Concept Releases
  - Interpretive Releases
  - Policy Statements
  - PCAOB Rulemaking
  - SRO Rulemaking and NMS Plans
  - Exchange Act Exemptive Applications
  - Exemptive Orders
  - Other Commission Orders and Notices
  - Public Petitions and Rulemaking

- *Staff Interpretations*

  - Staff Accounting Bulletins
  - Staff Legal Bulletins
  - Telephone Interpretations
  - Staff No-Action Letters, Interpretive and Exemptive Letters

- *News and Public Statements*

  - News Digest
  - Press Releases
  - Special Studies
  - Speeches and Public Statements
  - Testimony
  - Investor Complaint Data

- *Litigation*

  - Litigation Releases
  - Administrative Proceedings
  - ALJ Initial Decisions & Orders
  - Reports of Investigations
  - Commission Opinions
  - Trading Suspensions
  - Investor Claims Funds
  - Briefs

Court Decisions

Litigation in the federal district courts involving federal securities laws generally arises when the SEC or investors file civil actions, or when the Department of Justice files criminal actions. The resulting court opinions, orders, and other documents may be published in federal court reports such as the *Federal Supplement, Federal Reporter*, and *United States Reports*, as well as Lexis, Westlaw, court websites, CCH's *Federal Securities Law Reporter*, and securities law newsletters.

Secondary Sources

Services

Federal Securities Law Reporter (Commerce Clearing House (CCH)). This Reporter provides extensive treatment of the federal securities laws. It contains the text of statutes, proposed statutes, regulations, proposed regulations, annotations, court decisions, SEC releases, SEC staff no-action letters, SEC forms, and other SEC-issued pronouncements, as well as CCH editorial explanations.

Blue Sky Law Reporter (Commerce Clearing House (CCH)). This Reporter contains U.S. state (and territorial, e.g., Guam) laws, regulations, decisions, and pronouncements relating to securities at the state (and territorial) level.

Treatises

Bader, W. Reece, Securities Arbitration.

Bainbridge, Stephen M., Securities Law: Insider Trading.

Bialkin, Kenneth & Grant, William, Securities Underwriting.

Bloomenthal, Harold S., Going Public and the Public Corporation.

——————————, Securities Law Handbook (annual).

——————————, Securities and Federal Corporate Law.

——————————, & Wolff, Samuel, International Capital Markets and Securities Regulation.

——————————, Emerging Trends in Securities Law.

Borden, Arthur M. & Yunis, Joel A., Going Private.

Bostelman, John T., The Sarbanes-Oxley Deskbook.

Branson, Douglas M., Corporate Governance.

Brodsky, David M. & Kramer, Daniel J., Federal Securities Litigation: Commentary and Forms.

Bromberg, Alan R. & Lowenfels, Lewis D., Bromberg and Lowenfels on Securities Fraud and Commodities Fraud.

Brown, Gary M., Soderquist on the Securities Laws.

Brown, J. Robert, Jr., Regulation of Corporate Disclosure.

Cane, Marilyn Blumberg & Shub, Patricia A., Securities Arbitration: Law and Procedure.

Cohn, Stuart R., Securities Counseling for New and Developing Companies.

Fanto, James A., Directors' and Officers' Liability.

Fleischer, Arthur & Sussman, Alexander R., Takeover Defense.

Frankel, Tamar, The Regulation of Money Managers.

_____, Securitization: Structured Financing, Financial Assets Pools, and Asset-Backed Securities.

Friedman, Howard M., Securities Regulation in Cyberspace.

Garner, Bryan A., Securities Disclosure in Plain English.

Glaser, Donald, FitzGibbon, Scott & Weise, Steven, Legal Opinions.

Goldwasser, Dan L. & Arnold, M. Thomas, Accountants' Liability.

Haft, Robert J., Liability of Attorneys and Accountants for Securities Transactions.

Hazen, Thomas Lee, Treatise on the Law of Securities Regulation.

Hicks, J. William, Civil Liabilities: Enforcement and Litigation Under the 1933 Act.

_____, Exempted Transactions Under the Securities Act of 1933.

Jacobs, Arnold S., Disclosure and Remedies Under the Securities Laws.

_____, Manual of Corporate Forms for Securities Practice.

_____, Opinion Letters in Securities Matters: Text, Clauses, Law.

_____, Section 16 of the Securities Exchange Act.

Janvey, Ralph S., Regulation of the Securities and Commodities Markets.

Johnson, Charles J. & McLaughlin, Joseph, Corporate Finance and the Securities Laws.

Johnson, Philip McBride & Hazen, Thomas Lee, Commodities Regulation.

Karmel, Roberta S., Regulation by Prosecution — The Securities and Exchange Commission Versus Corporate America.

Kaufman, Michael J., Securities Litigation: Damages.

Kirsch, Charles E., Investment Adviser Regulation.

Langevoort, Donald C., Insider Trading: Regulation, Enforcement, and Prevention.

Lederman, Scott J., Hedge Fund Regulation.

Lee, Ruben, What is an Exchange?: The Automation, Management, and Regulation of Financial Markets.

Lemke, Thomas P. et al., Regulation of Investment Companies.

Lipton, David A., Broker-Dealer Regulation.

Lipton, Martin & Steinberger, Erica H., Takeovers and Freezeouts.

Long, Joseph C., Blue Sky Law.

Lorne, Simon M., Acquisitions and Mergers: Negotiated and Contested Transactions.

Loss, Louis & Seligman, Joel, Fundamentals of Securities Regulation.

_____, Securities Regulation.

Mahoney, Colleen P. et al., The SEC Enforcement Process: Practice and Procedure in Handling an SEC Investigation After Sarbanes-Oxley.

Perino, Michael A., Securities Litigation After the Reform Act.

Poser, Norman S., Broker-Dealer Law and Regulation.

_____, International Securities Regulation.

Richter, Scott E., Securities Litigation: Forms and Analysis.

Robbins, David E., Securities Arbitration Procedure Manual.

Romeo, Peter J. & Dye, Alan L., Section 16 of the Securities Exchange Act of 1934: Treatise and Reporting Guide.

Russo, Thomas A., Regulation of the Commodities Futures and Options Markets.

Sargent, Mark A., & Honabach, Dennis R., Proxy Rules Handbook.

Securities Law Techniques: Transactions, Litigation (A.A. Sommer, Jr. ed.).

Seligman, Joel, The SEC and the Future of Finance.

_____, The Transformation of Wall Street: A History of the Securities and Exchange Commission and Modern Corporate Finance.

Soderquist, Larry D., Understanding the Securities Laws.

Steinberg, Marc I., Attorney Liability After Sarbanes-Oxley.

_____, International Securities Law: A Contemporary and Comparative Analysis.

_____, Securities Regulation: Liabilities and Remedies.

_____ & Ferrara, Ralph C., Securities Practice: Federal and State Enforcement.

Thomas, Randall S. & Dixon, Catherine T., Aranow & Einhorn on Proxy Contests for Corporate Control.

Wang, William K. S. & Steinberg, Marc I., Insider Trading.

Waters, Michael D., Proxy Regulation.

Journals, Newsletters, and Other Periodicals

Andrews Securities Litigation and Regulation Reporter (Andrews Publications). This Reporter contains "selected court documents, including petitions, complaints, briefs, motions, trial court memoranda and other documents from state and federal courts." Available on Westlaw.

Insights: The Corporate and Securities Law Advisor (Aspen Publishers). Available on Lexis.

Mealey's Emerging Securities Litigation (Mealey Publications). Covers "evolving and dynamic areas of securities litigation." Available on Lexis.

The Review of Securities & Commodities Regulation (Thomson/West). Available on Westlaw.

SEC News Digest (Securities and Exchange Commission). This publication "provides daily information on recent Commission actions, including enforcement proceedings, rule filings, policy statements, and upcoming Commission meetings." Available on the SEC website at http://www.sec.gov/news/digest.shtml and on Lexis.

Securities Class Action Alert (Investor's Research Bureau).

Securities Regulation and Law Report (Bureau of National Affairs) (BNA). Available on Westlaw.

Securities Law Review (Thomson/West). Available on Westlaw.

Securities Regulation Law Journal (Thomson/West). Available on Westlaw.

Periodicals Index: Legal Resource Index (1980-present). This is a nearly comprehensive tool for locating legal periodical articles dating from 1980 to the present. The *Legal Research Index* is available on Lexis and Westlaw and currently indexes approximately 1,000 English-language periodicals.

Continuing Legal Education (CLE) Publications

ALI-ABA Course of Studies Materials. Available on Lexis and Westlaw.

Practising Law Institute, *Commercial Law and Practice* course handbook series. Available on Lexis and Westlaw.

Forms

Regulatory Forms. The SEC's regulatory forms are available from many sources, among the best of which are the SEC's website and CCH's *Federal Securities Law Reporter.* Numerous treatises and CLE publications provide instructions and examples for completing these forms, such as: Weinstein, et al., SEC Compliance: Financial Reporting and Forms.

Andrews Securities Litigation and Regulation Reporter. This Reporter contains "selected court documents, including petitions, complaints, briefs, motions, trial court memoranda and other documents from state and federal courts." Available on Westlaw beginning in 2000.

Brodsky, David M. & Kramer, Daniel J., Federal Securities Litigation: Commentary and Forms.

Richter, Scott E., Securities Litigation: Forms and Analysis.

Updating Research

KeyCite. Covers SEC decisions and releases, as well as statutes, cases, law reviews, etc. Available on Westlaw.

Shepard's Citations. Coverage includes SEC decisions, reports, and releases, as well as statutes, cases, law reviews, etc. Available on Lexis.

Chapter 2

DEFINITION OF A "SECURITY"

§ 2.01   INTRODUCTION

Failure on counsel's part to recognize that a "security" is present can be disastrous. As will be seen in the following chapters, absent an exemption, no sale of a security can take place unless a registration statement is in effect. Because the requirements for meeting any particular exemption may be complex, failure on counsel's part to perceive that his or her client's "deal" involves a security often means that the securities are being sold in violation of the securities laws. Under such circumstances, the Securities and Exchange Commission (SEC), state securities commissioner(s), and private parties may bring suit. Even criminal liability, depending on the circumstances, may be imposed. Hence, many deals have been scuttled, parties held liable, and lawyers sued for failure on counsel's part to recognize that a "security" was present.

The definition of "security" in the Securities Act of 1933 and the Securities Exchange Act of 1934[1] ("the Acts") covers a broad range of transactions. Although the term includes familiar instruments such as stock, notes, bonds, and "in general, any instrument commonly known as a 'security,' " the statutory definition also encompasses a wide variety of novel and unique instruments. Such instruments have included, for example, interests in "pyramid" sales schemes, chinchillas, whiskey warehouse receipts, and beavers. Ordinarily, these rather novel types of instruments come within the securities laws because they are held to be "investment contracts."

The term "security" is defined in Section 2(a)(1) of the Securities Act of 1933 and Section 3(a)(10) of the Securities Exchange Act of 1934. Although the language of these statutes somewhat differs, they have been construed in an identical manner. Fairly broad at first glance, the instruments set forth in the statutory definitions are only the starting point. This is due to the phrase *"unless the context otherwise requires"* which precedes each of the provisions. This phrase, as will be seen, focuses on the economic reality of the transaction, and hence, is very significant.

---

[1] Securities Act of 1933 § 2(a) (1), 15 U.S.C. § 77b(a)(1); Securities Exchange Act of 1934 § 3(a)(10), 15 U.S.C. § 78c(a)(10).

§ 2.02   OVERVIEW OF KEY U.S. SUPREME COURT DECISIONS

The Supreme Court has construed the definition of a "security" several times in an attempt to clarify the statutory definitions contained in the securities acts.[2] In its decisions, the Court has rejected a literal interpretation of the statutes, adopting instead a more flexible view which looks to the economic reality of the particular plan or scheme addressed.

In the first such case, *SEC v. C.M. Joiner Leasing Corp.*,[3] the Court recognized that, although the statutory definition makes specific reference to a number of "standardized" investment devices, "the reach of the [Securities] Act does not stop with the obvious and commonplace."[4] Therefore, as the Court suggested, other "[n]ovel, uncommon, or irregular devices" may fall within one of the definition's more descriptive categories, such as "investment contract," if the facts so warrant.[5]

In *SEC v. W.J. Howey Co.*[6] the Supreme Court subsequently explained that the term "investment contract" had been employed in previously enacted state "blue sky" laws and had come to signify "a contract or scheme for 'the placing of capital or laying out of money in a way intended to secure income or profit from its employment.' "[7] The transaction in *Howey* involved the offering of small parcels of land in a citrus grove in Florida, coupled with a service contract for cultivating and marketing the produce. The prospective purchasers were informed that the venture was not economically feasible without arranging for a service contract. In holding that the instrument offered was an "investment contract" and, hence, a security, the *Howey* Court emphasized that "investment contract" embodies a "flexible rather than a static principle" and that the term had been broadly construed by state courts as a means of protecting the investing public. "Form was disregarded for substance and emphasis was

---

[2] *See SEC v. Edwards*, 540 U.S. 389 (2004); *Reves v. Ernst & Young*, 494 U.S. 56 (1990); *Gould v. Ruefenacht*, 471 U.S. 681 (1985); *Marine Bank v. Weaver*, 455 U.S. 551 (1982); *International Bhd. of Teamsters v. Daniel*, 439 U.S. 551 (1979); *United Hous. Found., Inc. v. Forman*, 421 U.S. 837 (1975); *Tcherepnin v. Knight*, 389 U.S. 332 (1967); *SEC v. United Benefit Life Ins. Co.*, 387 U.S. 202 (1967); *SEC v. Variable Annuity Life Ins. Co. of Am.*, 359 U.S. 65 (1959); *SEC v. W.J. Howey Co.*, 328 U.S. 293 (1946); *SEC v. C.M. Joiner Leasing Corp.*, 320 U.S. 344 (1943). Cases not discussed in the following discussion include *SEC v. Variable Annuity Life Insurance Co. of America*, 359 U.S. 65 (1959) (holding variable annuity contracts to be securities), and *SEC v. United Benefit Life Insurance Co.*, 387 U.S. 202 (1967) (holding that a "flexible fund annuity contract" was a security).

[3] 320 U.S. 344 (1943) (holding that the sale of assignments of oil leasehold subdivisions constituted a sale of securities).

[4] *Id.* at 351.

[5] *Id.* The Court looked to such factors as "what character the instrument is given in commerce by the terms of the offer, the plan of distribution and the economic inducements held out to the prospect." *Id.* at 352–353.

[6] 328 U.S. 293 (1946) (holding that the sale of units in a citrus grove development together with service contracts for cultivating and marketing the produce constituted a sale of securities).

[7] *Id.* at 298 (quoting *State v. Gopher Tire & Rubber Co.*, 146 Minn. 52, 56, 177 N.W. 937, 938 (1920)).

placed upon economic reality."[8] Reasoning that Congress was aware of prior judicial interpretation of "investment contract" when it employed the term in defining "security" and noting that a broad construction was consistent with the federal securities laws' remedial intent, the *Howey* Court devised a standard to comport with this background.[9] Under what has become known as the "*Howey* test*," the term "investment contract" means "an investment of money in a common enterprise with profits to come solely from the efforts of others."[10] This test has been elaborated upon by both the Supreme Court and lower federal courts. These decisions are discussed later in this chapter.

In *Tcherepnin v. Knight*,[11] the Court reiterated that "remedial legislation should be construed broadly to effectuate its purposes" and that "[e]ven a casual reading of [Section] 3(a)(10) of the 1934 Act reveals that Congress did not intend to adopt a narrow or restrictive concept of security in defining that term."[12] Therefore, in its early post-*Howey* decisions construing the Acts, the Court adopted a flexible, expansive interpretation of the three-part *Howey* test. The lower courts, expanding on the *Howey* test, followed suit.[13] By the mid-1970s, however, the Supreme Court retreated from this remedial approach.

The decision that signaled the Court's retreat was *United Housing Foundation, Inc. v. Forman.*[14] In *Forman* the Court held that shares of stock in a cooperative housing project purchased by individuals who were residents of the apartment complex were not securities. The Court assessed the economic realities of the transaction: the shares purchased did not confer the attendant rights that ordinarily accompany stock, were not transferable to a non-tenant, could not be pledged or encumbered, carried no voting rights in relation to the shares owned, and had to be offered back to the cooperative housing corporation at their initial selling price. In determining whether such shares of stock constituted securities, the Court rejected a literal approach and refused to require that the transaction, evidenced by the sale of "stock," be considered a security transaction merely because the statutory definition of a security contains the words "any stock." Instead, the Court stressed that "*economic*

---

[8] 328 U.S. at 298.

[9] *Id.* at 299 (defining the term "investment contract" to encompass "a flexible rather than a static principle, one that is capable of adaptation to meet the countless and variable schemes devised by those who seek the use of the money of others on the promise of profits").

[10] *Id.* at 301.

[11] 389 U.S. 332 (1967).

[12] *Id.* at 336–339 (also stating that "form should be disregarded for substance and the emphasis should be on economic reality").

[13] *See, e.g., SEC v. Koscot Interplanetary, Inc.*, 497 F.2d 473 (5th Cir. 1974) (holding that a franchise-like "pyramid" promotion scheme involved securities even though the investors exerted some effort, provided that the promoters' efforts were the undeniably significant ones); *SEC v. Glenn W. Turner Enters., Inc.*, 474 F.2d 476, 482 (9th Cir. 1973) (looking to "whether the efforts made by those other than the investor are the undeniably significant ones, those essential managerial efforts which affect the failure or success of the enterprise"); *infra* notes 46–51 (and accompanying text).

[14] 421 U.S. 837 (1975).

reality," not form, should control: "Because securities transactions are economic in character Congress intended the application of these statutes to turn on the economic realities underlying a transaction, and not on the name appended thereto."[15] Hence, the context of the transaction demanded that the interests purchased, although labeled "stock," were not to be treated as "stock" under the federal securities laws.[16]

After finding that the shares of stock in *Forman* lacked the attributes of ordinary stock, the Court also declined to view the instruments as investment contracts. The Court reasoned that the federal securities laws are inapplicable when the purchaser is "motivated by a desire to use or consume the item purchased," rather than by the anticipation of receiving a return on his or her investment.[17] In *Forman*, the purchasers of stock sought adequate and affordable housing to live. Accordingly, they were not investors and did not purchase a "security."

Similarly, in *International Brotherhood of Teamsters v. Daniel,*[18] the Supreme Court applied the "economic reality" concept to constrict, rather than to broaden, the definition of "investment contract." Specifically, the Court held that interests in a noncontributory, compulsory pension plan is not an investment contract and, hence, not a security. In a noncontributory, compulsory pension plan, the employer contributes the necessary payments, not the employee who ultimately benefits from the plan. The Court applied the *Howey* test for an investment contract. Concentrating on the economic reality of the plan, the Court observed that "an employee is selling his labor primarily to obtain a livelihood, not making an investment" and, therefore, concluded that the *Howey* test's "investment of money" element was not satisfied.[19] Moreover, the employer's contributions to the fund were not the equivalent of an "investment" by the employee because no fixed relationship existed between the employer's contributions and the employee's potential benefits. The Court also found that the pension fund's assets did not depend on profits yielded by the efforts of others. To the contrary, the vast majority of the income generated derived from the employer's contributions and thus was independent from the efforts of the fund's managers. In addition, actual receipt of benefits from the fund depended on whether employees met certain individual eligibility requirements, not on the financial success of the fund itself.[20]

---

[15] *Id.* at 849.

[16] *Id.*; *see Seger v. Federal Intermediate Credit Bank of Omaha*, 850 F.2d 468 (8th Cir. 1988) (interpreting *Forman*, class B stock held not a security).

[17] 421 U.S. at 852–853; *see Rice v. Branigar Organization, Inc.*, 922 F.2d 788, 790–791 (11th Cir. 1991) (holding that purchases of beach front lots and equity memberships in adjacent country club were not securities and stating that "where those who purchase something [have] the primary desire to use it or consume it, the security laws do not apply").

[18] 439 U.S. 551 (1979).

[19] *Id.* at 560–561.

[20] *Id.* at 561–562.

The *Daniel* Court further supported its holding by concluding that the enactment of ERISA, which expressly regulates pension plans,[21] eliminated the need for coverage under the securities laws:

> The existence of this comprehensive legislation governing the use and terms of employee pension plans severely undercuts all arguments for extending the Securities Acts to noncontributory, compulsory pension plans. Congress believed that it was filling a regulatory void when it enacted ERISA, a belief which the SEC actively encouraged. Not only is the extension of the Securities Acts . . . not supported by the language and history of those Acts, but in light of ERISA it serves no general purpose. . . . Whatever benefits employees might derive from the effect of the Securities Acts are now provided in more definite form through ERISA.[22]

Thus, in both *Forman* and *Daniel* the Supreme Court employed the language, if not quite the spirit, of the *Howey* "economic reality" test to exclude transactions that otherwise might fall within the literal definition of "investment contract." This trend was further evidenced by the Court's decision in *Marine Bank v. Weaver*.[23] At the outset of its analysis, the *Marine Bank* Court paraphrased the prefatory language to Section 3(a)(10) of the Exchange Act, stating that the instruments included in the Act's definitional section are not to be considered securities if "the context otherwise requires." The Court then asserted that "Congress, in enacting the securities laws, did not intend to provide a broad federal remedy for all fraud."[24] It concluded that neither a conventional certificate of deposit nor an agreement given as consideration for pledging the certificate of deposit to guarantee a bank loan constituted a security under the federal securities laws.

In addressing the certificate of deposit issue, the *Marine Bank* Court elevated the presence of other comprehensive regulation, a factor of inferential importance in *Daniel*, to paramount significance. The Court commenced its analysis by distinguishing the withdrawable capital shares in *Tcherepnin v. Knight* on the ground that the *Tcherepnin* purchasers received dividends based on the savings and loan association's profits, rather than at a fixed rate of interest, and also received voting rights. The *Marine Bank* Court observed that the withdrawable capital shares in *Tcherepnin* "were much more like ordinary shares of stock and 'the ordinary concept of a security,' . . . than a certificate of deposit."[25] Then, looking to the context of the transaction, the Court turned

---

[21] *See* Employee Retirement Income Security Act of 1974 (ERISA), 29 U.S.C. §§ 1001–1461.

[22] 439 U.S. at 569–570 (citations omitted). On the other hand, interests in voluntary contributory pension plans may be securities. *See Uselton v. Commercial Lovelace Motor Freight, Inc.*, 940 F.2d 564 (10th Cir. 1991); Securities Act Release Nos. 6188 (1980), 6281 (1981). *But see Matassarin v. Lynch*, 174 F.3d 549 (5th Cir. 1999) (interest in a mandatory employer-funded employee option plan held not a security); *Conrad v. Colgate-Palmolive Co.*, 686 F.2d 1230 (7th Cir. 1982) (interests in contributory voluntary pension plans are not securities). *See generally* Bromberg, *The Employee Investor & ESOPS and Other Employee Benefit Plans as Securities*, 19 Sec. Reg. L.J. 325 (1992).

[23] 455 U.S. 551 (1982).

[24] *Id.* at 556.

[25] *Id.* at 557.

to the differences it perceived between a certificate of deposit and other long-term debt obligations. The Court focused not so much on the particular attributes of these instruments, but rather on the existence of comprehensive federal regulation governing the banking industry. Moreover, unlike the holder of a long-term debt obligation who assumes the risk of the borrower's insolvency, the purchaser of a certificate of deposit is almost assured of repayment due to the availability of depositor insurance. Accordingly, the Court concluded that "[i]t is unnecessary to subject issuers of bank certificates of deposit to liability under the antifraud provisions of the federal securities laws since the holders of bank certificates of deposit are abundantly protected under the federal banking laws."[26]

Likewise, with respect to investment contract analysis, the Court observed that the profit-sharing agreement present in *Marine Bank* was not the type of transaction that "comes to mind when the term 'security' is used" and concluded that the agreement differed in several respects from other unusual arrangements found to involve securities. Specifically, the Court noted that: the agreement was a private transaction, negotiated one-on-one, with no prospectus distributed to potential investors; the agreement was unique (as evidenced by the provisions allowing the Weavers to use the barn and pasture), lacked "equivalent value" to other investors, and was not designed to be traded publicly; and the Weavers' "veto" power over future loans gave them a measure of control over the business. Therefore, although the Court did not apply the *Howey* test expressly, it held that the agreement was not a security despite the profit-sharing provision.[27]

On the other hand, in *Landreth Timber Co. v. Landreth*[28] and *Gould v. Ruefenacht*,[29] the Supreme Court held that common stock having the attributes normally associated with this instrument is a security. In so holding, the Court rejected the approach embodied by the sale of business doctrine. That doctrine stood for the proposition that the incidental transfer of stock to manifest the sale of a closely-held business is not a security with respect to those who are entrepreneurs (namely, those who exercise control over critical entrepreneurial or managerial decisions of the corporation).[30] In refusing to adopt the doctrine, the Supreme Court indicated that scrutiny of a transaction's economic substance is necessary only when the instruments involved are "unusual . . . not easily characterized as 'securities.' "[31] Hence, the Court distinguished *Forman* by reasoning that the stock involved in the cases at bar bore all the characteristics traditionally associated with common stock, which the Court described as follows: "(i) the right to receive dividends contingent upon an

---

[26] *Id.* at 558–559.

[27] *Id.* at 559–560; *see Mace Neufeld Productions, Inc. v. Orion Pictures Corp.*, 860 F.2d 944 (9th Cir. 1988) (agreement between two parties which "was unique, private, and never intended to be publicly traded" held not to be a security).

[28] 471 U.S. 681 (1985).

[29] 471 U.S. 701 (1985).

[30] *See, e.g., Christy v. Cambron*, 710 F.2d 669 (10th Cir. 1983); *King v. Winkler*, 673 F.2d 342 (11th Cir. 1982); *Canfield v. Rapp & Son, Inc.*, 654 F.2d 459 (7th Cir. 1981).

[31] *Landreth*, 471 U.S. at 690.

apportionment of profits; (ii) negotiability; (iii) the ability to be pledged or hypothecated; (iv) the conferring of voting rights in proportion to the number of shares owned; and (v) the capacity to appreciate in value."[32]

Looking to the "plain meaning" of the statutory definition of a "security," the Supreme Court held that traditional stock necessarily falls within the Acts' coverage. Reconciling this approach with the economic reality test, the Supreme Court in a subsequent case reasoned: "*Landreth Timber* does not signify a lack of concern with economic reality; rather it signals a recognition that stock is, as a practical matter, always an investment if it has the economic characteristics traditionally associated with stock."[33]

In *Reves v. Ernst & Young*,[34] the Court rejected the *Landreth Timber* rationale in the note context. Unlike "stock" which by its nature (if it has the attributes typically associated with such an instrument) is within the class of instruments Congress intended to regulate under the securities laws, the same cannot be said of "notes" which are used in a variety of settings, some of which are commercial and others of which involve investments. Hence, since "notes" are not necessarily securities, the Court, after searching for a proper standard to be applied, opted for the "family resemblance" test.[35] As elaborated upon later in this chapter,[36] this test (in ascertaining whether a "note" is a "security") encompasses the "motivations" of a reasonable buyer and seller to engage in the transaction, the plan of distribution, the reasonable expectations of the investing public, and the presence of a risk reducing factor.[37] Applying the family resemblance test, the Court held that the notes at issue were securities.[38]

---

[32] *Id.* at 686; *see Gould*, 471 U.S. at 704–706.

[33] *Reves v. Ernst & Young*, 494 U.S. 56, 62 (1990) (also stating that "[e]ven if sparse exceptions to this generalization can be found, the public perception of common stock as the paradigm of a security suggests that stock, in whatever context it is sold, should be treated as within the ambit of the Acts"). Subsequent cases continue to address the issue concerning the security law status of instruments called stock. *See, e.g., Great Rivers Cooperative of Southeast Iowa v. Farmland Industries, Inc.*, 198 F.3d 685 (8th Cir. 1999) (equity interests in capital credits issued by agricultural cooperative association held not a security); *Seger v. Federal Intermediate Credit Bank of Omaha*, 850 F.2d 468 (8th Cir. 1988) (applying *Forman* criteria, lender's Class B "stock" did not have characteristics normally associated with such an instrument and, hence, was not a security); *One-O-One Enterprises, Inc, v. Caruso*, 848 F.2d 1283 (D.C. Cir. 1988) (option to purchase stock deemed a security relying on *Landreth*); *McVay v. Western Plains Service Corporation*, 823 F.2d 1395 (10th Cir. 1987) (interpreting *Forman*, loan participation certificates held not to be "stock" within scope of the securities laws because such certificates "lack[ed] any of the basic attributes of true stock"); *B. Rosenberg & Sons, Inc. v. St. James Sugar Coop., Inc.*, 447 F. Supp. 1 (E.D. La. 1976), *aff'd*, 565 F.2d 1213 (5th Cir. 1977) (applying *Forman*, common stock in sugar coop held not a security).

[34] 494 U.S. 56 (1990).

[35] *Id.* at 64–67.

[36] *See infra* notes 98–125 (and accompanying text).

[37] 494 U.S. at 66–67.

[38] *Id.* at 67–73.

More recently, in *SEC v. Edwards*,[39] the Supreme Court held that a contractual entitlement to a fixed (rather than variable) rate of return in a payphone package investment[40] satisfied the "expectation of profit" prong of the *Howey* test.[41] In so holding, the Court distinguished language contained in two of its earlier decisions[42] that the "profit" component of *Howey* was confined to "capital appreciation resulting from the development of the initial investment" or a "participation in earnings resulting from the use of investors' funds."[43] The Court accordingly held that a contractual entitlement to a fixed return met *Howey's* "solely from the efforts of others" prong. As the Court observed, "[t]he fact that investors have bargained for a return on their investment does not mean that the return is not also expected to come solely from the efforts of others."[44] Indeed, to rule otherwise, "would conflict with our holding that an investment contract was offered in *Howey* itself, [namely, that the] service contract entitled [the *Howey*] investors to [an] allocation of net profits."[45]

§ 2.03   KEY ISSUES FOR "INVESTMENT CONTRACT" ANALYSIS

The discussion that follows addresses three key issues (i.e., "solely from the efforts of others," "expectation of profits" and the "common enterprise" requirement) that arise in determining whether an ownership interest satisfies the *Howey* investment contract test. They are analyzed at this point for ease of organization and understanding. Emphasis is made that these three issues surface when analyzing whether any interest in an enterprise (such as an

---

[39] 540 U.S. 389 (2004).

[40] Edwards owned and controlled ETS Payphones, Inc., through which the company sold "payphone packages." The packages included a payphone, a leasing agreement with ETS and an agreement for ETS to repurchase the payphone at the buyer's request. Through the "payphone package," an investor purchased a payphone from ETS which ETS then leased from the investor for five years at an annualized return of 14% to the investor. Under the buyback agreement, ETS agreed to repurchase the payphone from the investor at the end of the five-year lease, or at the investor's request with 180 days notice. ETS filed for bankruptcy protection after six years of operation. The SEC brought an enforcement action against ETS and Edwards claiming that the "payphone packages" were "investment contracts" subject to the federal securities laws. The SEC alleged that Edwards and ETS had violated the registration requirements of the Securities Act and the antifraud provisions of the 1933 and 1934 Acts. *Id.*

[41] *Id.* at 394 (stating that the term "profit" includes, for example, "dividends, other periodic payments, or the increased value of the investment" and that, for purposes of the *Howey* test, "[t]here is no reason to distinguish between promises of fixed returns and promises of variable returns").

[42] *Id.* at 395–396 (distinguishing *Reves v. Ernst & Young*, 494 U.S. 56, 61 n. 4 (1990) (viewing *Reves'* language that a fixed rate of return does not satisfy *Howey's* "profit" prong as "passing dictum") and *United Housing Foundation v. Forman*, 421 U.S. 837, 852 (1975) (viewing *Forman's* setting forth of capital appreciation and participation in earnings as examples and not an exclusive list).

[43] 540 U.S. at 395 (quoting 421 U.S. at 852).

[44] 540 U.S. at 397.

[45] *Id.*

interest in a limited partnership, general partnership, limited liability company, or joint venture) meets the *Howey* investment contract test, and, hence, is a security under federal law.

[A]   "Solely from the Efforts of Others"

The Supreme Court in *Howey* stated that one of the requirements for an instrument to be an investment contract is that the investor must expect to derive "profits *solely* from the efforts of the promoter or a third party."[46] One of the issues often present in determining whether limited partnership interests, limited liability company (LLC) interests, and "similar" interests are securities under the *Howey* test is how strictly the term *solely* from the efforts of others should be construed. A number of federal appellate court decisions have addressed the issue.

Two leading cases are the Fifth Circuit's decision in *SEC v. Koscot Interplanetary, Inc.*[47] and the Ninth Circuit's ruling in *SEC v. Glenn W. Turner Enterprises, Inc.*[48] As enunciated in these cases, the critical inquiry is "whether the efforts made by those other than the investor are the undeniably significant ones, those essential managerial efforts which affect the failure or success of the enterprise."[49] This *Koscot/Turner* test rejects a literal interpretation of "solely" and has been widely followed.[50] Stated in somewhat different terms, the inquiry in this context is "whether the investor has meaningfully participated in the management of the [venture] in which it has invested such that it has more than minimal control over the investment's performance."[51]

The Supreme Court, although not expressly adopting a more flexible formulation of this aspect of the *Howey* test, appears to have acquiesced in such a formulation. For example, in *United Housing Foundation, Inc. v. Forman*, the Court opined that "profits [must] be derived from the entrepreneurial or managerial efforts of others."[52]

---

[46] 328 U.S. at 298 (emphasis added).

[47] 497 F.2d 473 (5th Cir. 1974).

[48] 474 F.2d 476 (9th Cir. 1973).

[49] *Id.* at 482; *see* 497 F.2d at 483.

[50] *See, e.g., United States v. Leonard*, 529 F.3d 83 (2d Cir. 2008); *SEC v. Merchant Capital, LLC*, 483 F.3d 747 (11th Cir. 2007); *Goodman v. Epstein*, 582 F.2d 388 (7th Cir. 1978).

[51] *Steinhardt Group, Inc. v. Citicorp*, 126 F.3d 144, 152 (3d Cir. 1997).

[52] 421 U.S. at 852 n.16. For other cases applying the "efforts of others" standard, *see, e.g., United States v. Leonard*, 529 F.3d 83 (2d Cir. 2008) (interests in limited liability company held to be an investment contract due to the investors' passive role in the LLC's management and operation); *Robinson v. Glynn*, 349 F.3d 166 (4th Cir. 2003) (interests in limited liability company deemed not an investment contract due to investor's active managerial input); *Webster v. Omnitriton Int'l, Inc.*, 79 F.3d 776 (9th Cir. 1996) (fact that investors exerted some efforts does not preclude securities law coverage); and *Steinhardt Group, Inc. v. Citicorp*, 126 F.3d 144 (3d Cir. 1997) (holding that due to limited partner's retention of "pervasive control over its investment in the limited partnership," no investment contract present).

With respect to whether fractional interests in viatical settlements are securities, compare *SEC*

On a related point, note the following important principle: namely, that the party exerting the significant efforts need not be owned or controlled by the seller-promoter.[53] Such a result makes a great deal of sense. Otherwise, even though investors may be unable to exercise meaningful control over the enterprise, promoters could avoid securities law coverage merely by contracting with a non-affiliated third party to perform the necessary acts. Application of *Howey's* economic reality test prevents this consequence.

[B]   "Expectation of Profits"

In *Forman* the Supreme Court identified two forms of "profit" that meet the *Howey* investment contract test: (1) "capital appreciation resulting from the development of the initial investment," and (2) "a participation in earnings resulting from the use of investors' funds."[54] More recently, in *SEC v. Edwards*, the Supreme Court elaborated that "profit" includes, "for example, dividends, other periodic payments, or the increased value of the investment."[55] Hence, a contractual entitlement to a fixed return meets the *Howey* expectation of profit prong.

In *Forman* the Court rejected the plaintiffs' argument that their tax deductions were a form of profit. Nonetheless, lower courts have held that an investor's desire for favorable tax consequences may not prevent the instrument from being a security so long as there was also an expectation of profit in real terms.[56]

Another key point is that the securities laws generally do not apply where the purchaser is principally motivated by a desire to use or consume the interest acquired. For example, because the plaintiffs in *Forman* were motivated mainly by the desire to obtain affordable and decent housing, rather than seeking a return on the acquisition, the securities laws were not applicable.[57] As a more recent example, in *Rice v. Branigar Organization, Inc.*[58] Justice Powell, sitting by designation on the Eleventh Circuit, opined that purchases of beach front lots and equity memberships in an adjacent country club were not securities. The court reasoned that the purchasers acquired the beach front lots and country club memberships "primarily to use

---

v. Life Partners, Inc., 87 F.3d 536 (D.C. 1996) (holding that "[t]he combination of [the promoter's] pre-purchase services and its largely ministerial post-purchase services is not enough to satisfy the third requirement in *Howey*" [that] the investors' profits were generated predominantly from the efforts of others), with *SEC v. Mutual Benefits Corp.*, 408 F.3d 737 (11th Cir. 2005) (disagreeing with the D.C. Circuit's rationale in *Life Partners* and opining that "[s]ignificant pre-purchase managerial activities undertaken to insure the success of the investment may also satisfy *Howey*"). *See generally* Deeley, *Viatical Settlements Are Not Securities: Is It Law or Sympathy?*, 66 Geo. Wash. L. Rev. 382 (1998); Lann, *An Exploration of Viatical Settlements as Securities*, 46 Drake L. Rev. 923 (1998).

[53] *See, e.g., Continental Marketing Corp. v. SEC*, 387 F.2d 466 (10th Cir. 1967).

[54] 421 U.S. at 852.

[55] 540 U.S. at 394; *see supra* notes 39–45 (and accompanying text).

[56] *See, e.g., Goodman v. Epstein*, 582 F.2d 388 (7th Cir. 1978).

[57] *See* 421 U.S. at 853–854.

[58] 922 F.2d 788 (11th Cir. 1991).

them, not to derive profits from the entrepreneurial efforts of the developers."[59] Moreover, "[t]he overall emphasis in the promotional material was clearly placed on enjoying the beauty . . . and the amenities of the club and community." Hence, the court held: "where those who purchase something [have] the primary desire to use or consume it, the security laws do not apply."[60]

[C]   The "Common Enterprise" Requirement

As the Supreme Court pointed out in *Howey*, an essential ingredient for the finding of an investment contract is that there be a "common enterprise." Generally, there are two types of common enterprise: horizontal commonality and vertical commonality. All courts hold that horizontal commonality is sufficient to meet this aspect of the *Howey* test. Generally, horizontal commonality looks to the relationships which exist between an individual investor and the pool of other investors. Under this standard, a pooling of the interests of the investors is essential to finding the existence of an investment contract. Hence, "no horizontal common enterprise can exist unless there . . . exists between [the investors] themselves some relationship which ties the fortunes of each investor to the success of the overall venture."[61]

The lower courts widely disagree, however, on whether "vertical commonality" (*i.e.*, the relationship between the investor(s) and the promoter) satisfies the *Howey* common enterprise element. A number of courts hold that only horizontal commonality (and not vertical commonality) satisfies the common enterprise requirement.[62] On the other hand, other courts deem "vertical commonality" to be sufficient. As explained by one court, there are two types of vertical commonality:

> There is a split in the courts that have applied the "vertical commonality" approach regarding precisely what is necessary to satisfy this standard. The courts applying the more restrictive defini-tion state that "vertical commonality" exists where "the fortunes of the investor are interwoven with and dependent upon the efforts and success of those seeking the investment or third parties." . . . Thus,

---

[59] *Id.* at 790.

[60] *Id.* at 790–791. For another decision on this point, see *Teague v. Bakker*, 1998 U.S. App. LEXIS 7079, [1998 Transfer Binder] Fed. Sec. L. Rep. (CCH) ¶ 90,182 (4th Cir. 1998) (holding that jury was properly instructed for *Howey* investment contract test to inquire whether the purchasers acquiring lodging in a vacation park were primarily attracted by the prospective financial return or by enjoyment of the lodging).

Note, however, if an instrument has the usual characteristics of traditional stock, the federal securities laws will apply. This is so even if the purchaser intends to be an active entrepreneur who seeks to "use or consume" the business acquired. *See Gould v. Ruefenacht*, 471 U.S. 701 (1985); *Landreth Timber Co. v. Landreth*, 471 U.S. 681 (1985). These cases are discussed earlier in this chapter, *supra* notes 28–33 and accompanying text.

[61] *Curran v. Merrill Lynch, Pierce, Fenner & Smith, Inc.*, 622 F.2d 216, 224 (6th Cir. 1980), *aff'd on other grounds*, 456 U.S. 353 (1982).

[62] *See, e.g., Salcer v. Merrill Lynch, Pierce, Fenner & Smith, Inc.*, 682 F.2d 459 (3d Cir. 1982); *Milnarik v. M.S. Commodities, Inc.*, 457 F.2d 274 (7th Cir. 1972).

[one view] appears to require . . . that there be a "direct relation between the success or failure of the promoter and that of his investors."

A broader definition of "vertical commonality" seems to have been articulated by [some courts holding] that "the requisite commonality is evidenced by the fact that the fortunes of [the investor(s)] are inextricably tied to the efficacy of the [promoter's efforts]". . . . Thus, the broader definition merely requires a link between the fortunes of the investors and the efforts of the promoters.[63]

§ 2.04 APPLICATION OF THE *HOWEY* TEST TO SPECIFIC VENTURES

[A] Limited Partnerships

The judicial analysis of whether partnership interests fall within the definition of a security has proceeded along the lines of whether a partnership interest is an "investment contract."

Since state law governing the operation of limited partnerships traditionally prohibited limited partners from performing significant managerial functions, courts usually held that these interests met the *Howey* requirement that profits be derived essentially from the efforts of others. Analysis often focused upon both the terms of the partnership agreement and on the actual extent of managerial participation by the limited partners.[64]

It should be emphasized, however, that a court still must make an independent examination of whether the limited partnership interest meets the *Howey* investment contract test. Whether or not a partnership interest is "limited" for state law purposes is significant but not determinative. This is illustrated by *Gordon v. Terry.*[65] In that case, a limited partnership was formed for the purposes of buying and selling undeveloped land. The limited partners had explicit voting power on whether or not specific pieces of land should be sold and at what time. The Eleventh Circuit held that these interests

---

[63] *Mechigian v. Art Capital Corp.*, 612 F. Supp. 1421, 1427 (S.D.N.Y. 1985) (citations omitted); *see Dooner v. NMI Limited*, 725 F. Supp. 153, 159 (S.D.N.Y. 1989) ("The limited partnership interest here satisfies the common enterprise element of the investment contract test because it meets the requirement of narrow vertical commonality: the fortunes of the [investor] and [promoter] are linked so that they rise and fall together."). For further discussion, see Chang, *Meaning, Reference and Reification of a Security*, 19 U.C. Davis L. Rev. 403 (1986); Gordon, *Common Enterprise and Multiple Investors: A Contractual Theory for Defining Investment Contracts and Notes*, 1988 Colum. Bus. L. Rev. 635; McDonald, *Toward Consistent Investor Protection Under the Federal Securities Laws: The Solution to the Conflict Among the Circuits Regarding the So-Called "Commonality" Requirement for an Investment Contract*, 32 Sec. Reg. L.J. 68 (2004); Monaghan, *An Uncommon State of Confusion: The Common Enterprise Element of Investment Contract Analysis*, 63 Fordham L. Rev. 2135 (1995).

[64] *See, e.g., L&B Hospital Ventures, Inc. v. Healthcare International, Inc.*, 894 F.2d 150 (5th Cir. 1990); *Mayer v. Oil Field Systems Corp.*, 721 F.2d 59 (2d Cir. 1983).

[65] 684 F.2d 736 (11th Cir. 1982).

did not pass the *Howey* test and, hence, were not securities. Similarly, in a more recent decision, the Third Circuit in *Steinhardt Group, Inc. v. Citicorp*,[66] concluded that "the limited partner retained pervasive control over its investment in the limited partnership such that it cannot be deemed a passive investor under *Howey* and its progeny."[67]

This issue has become more prevalent. Pursuant to applicable limited partnership statutes, limited partners may engage in extensive activities yet retain their limited liability status.[68] For example, under Section 303(b) of the Revised Uniform Limited Partnership Act (RULPA), a limited partner may engage in such actions as "consulting with and advising a general partner" regarding the partnership business, serving as an officer or director of a corporation which is a general partner of the limited partnership, and voting on a number of important subjects, such as "a change in the nature of the business" and "the admission or removal of a general partner."[69] Moreover, if the limited partnership agreement so provides, the limited partner may enjoy a right of approval over *any* matter related to the partnership's business.[70] Even more expansive is the 2001 Uniform Limited Partnership Act which generally insulates a limited partner from personal liability "even if the limited partner participates in the management and control of the limited partnership."[71]

In sum, interests in a limited partnership generally are securities because limited partners ordinarily rely on the general partners to exercise the essential managerial efforts. However, in those situations where limited partners have the capability to exert meaningful efforts, the *Howey* investment contract test may not be met.[72]

[B]   General Partnerships

Since general partnerships do not possess the same restrictions on participation in management as limited partnership interests, they normally fail to satisfy the *Howey* "solely from the efforts of others" standard. Several

---

[66] 126 F.3d 144 (3d Cir. 1997).

[67] *Id.* at 145.

[68] *See* Revised Uniform Limited Partnership Act (RULPA) § 303 (1985); Uniform Limited Parternership Act § 303 (2001).

[69] RULPA § 303(b).

[70] *Id.* § 303(b)(6)(ix).

[71] Uniform Limited Partnership Act § 303 (2001). *See* Comment to § 303 ("The shield established by this section protects only against liability for the limited partnership's obligations and only to the extent that the limited partner is claimed to be liable on account of being a limited partner.").

[72] *See Steinhardt Group, Inc. v. Citicorp*, 126 F.3d 144, 155 (3rd Cir. 1997) (concluding that limited partner's adherence to safe harbor provided by Delaware Revised Uniform Limited Partnership Act "not controlling" for investment contract analysis); Everhard, *The Limited Partnership Interest: Is It a Security? Changing Times*, 17 Del. J. Corp. L. 441 (1992) (asserting that in those situations where "the powers retained by the limited partners are so pervasive that they are in a position to adequately protect themselves, . . . the protections of the federal securities laws are neither appropriate nor necessary").

courts in the 1960s and 1970s applied *Howey* in a fairly literal manner and held that general partnership interests were not securities.[73]

In *Williamson v. Tucker*,[74] the Fifth Circuit may have "rescued" general partnership interests from being declared outside the scope of the securities laws as a matter of law. That case involved a series of joint ventures each of which owned an undivided interest in certain real estate. The participants in each joint venture retained substantial control over the prospect pursuant to the joint venture agreements that they signed. The Fifth Circuit stated that, in spite of the form which the investment took, if the investor was in fact unable to exercise meaningful management powers because of his or her dependence on the promoter or a third party, then the general partnership or joint venture interest could be designated a security under federal law. The court went on to delineate three sets of circumstances where this could happen: First, an interest could be a security if the agreement between the parties leaves so little power in the hands of the investor that power is distributed as it would be in a limited partnership. Second, a security also could be present if the investor is so inexperienced and unknowledgeable in business affairs as to be incapable of intelligently exercising his or her partnership powers. Finally, the *Williamson* court stated that a security could be present if the investor is so dependent on some unique "entrepreneurial or managerial" ability of the promoter or manager that he or she cannot in all practicality replace the manager or otherwise exercise meaningful partnership powers.[75]

The *Williamson* decision appears to be an expansion of the circumstances under which general partnership or joint venture interests will be found to be securities. A number of cases in other circuits have examined general partnership interests under the analysis set forth in *Williamson*.[76] On the other hand, some courts have rejected its application as being too expansive.[77] One such view posits that each general partner as a matter of law enjoys the right of ultimate control over the venture, hence signifying that each such general power may exert meaningful managerial efforts and thus negating securities law coverage.[78] Another approach, broader than the preceding standard but narrower than *Williamson*, solely focuses on the terms of the general partnership agreement. Applying this approach, irrespective of a particular general partner's financial unsophistication or lack of control actually exercised, the general partnership agreement's inclusion of "real power" in the general partners signifies that the securities laws do not apply. As stated by the Tenth Circuit: "[R]egardless of the control actually exercised,

---

[73] *See, e.g., Hirsch v. du Pont*, 396 F. Supp. 1214 (S.D.N.Y. 1975), *aff'd*, 553 F.2d 750 (2d Cir. 1977) ("substantial 'legal rights to a voice in partnership matters' inhered in the general partnership interests: [thus] those interests were not securities, irrespective of the degree to which [the partners] actually chose to exercise their rights.").

[74] 645 F.2d 404 (5th Cir. 1981).

[75] *Id.* at 417–425.

[76] *See, e.g., Koch v. Hankins*, 928 F.2d 1471 (9th Cir. 1991); *Bailey v. J.W.K. Properties, Inc.*, 904 F.2d 918 (4th Cir. 1990).

[77] *See, e.g., Goodwin v. Elkins & Co.*, 730 F.2d 99 (2d Cir. 1984).

[78] *Id.* at 103–105 (Garth, J., opinion announcing judgment of the court).

if a partnership agreement retains real power in the general partners, then an investment in the general partnership is not a security. Thus, our determination of whether a general partnership interest can be characterized as a security turns on the partnership agreement."[79]

[C]   Limited Liability Partnerships (LLPs)

With respect to (registered) limited liability partnership (LLP or RLLP) interests, on the other hand, these interests, depending on the circumstances, may be deemed investment contracts. LLPs are general partnerships. By registering with the applicable state regulator and meeting certain other criteria, partners in a LLP are not vicariously liable for the LLP's debts and obligations. Due to this more limited liability exposure, LLP partners are more likely to be passive investors. As stated by the Eleventh Circuit:

> An RLLP partner is liable only for the amount of his or her capital contribution, plus the partner's personal acts, and is not exposed to vicarious liability for the acts of other partners or the acts of the partnership as a whole. This limitation on liability means that RLLP partners have less of an incentive to preserve control than general partners do. While general partners normally wish to preserve control because their personal assets are at risk, RLLP partners have only their investment at risk if they remain passive, and risk personal liability only if they become active.[80]

Likening the powers held by the LLP partners to those of limited partners, the court held that the LLP partners did not exercise essential managerial efforts. Hence, the LLP interests were held to be investment contracts.[81]

[D]   Limited Liability Companies (LLCs)

Depending on the applicable circumstances and organizational structure, interests in a limited liability company (LLC) may be securities. An LLC, a creature of statute, is a flexible form of non-corporate business organization that allows a planner to choose pass-through taxation without classification as an S corporation. The Internal Revenue Service (IRS) recognizes LLCs as partnerships for tax purposes, thus legitimizing the LLC's pass-through tax structure. Thus, the LLC avoids double taxation and corporate formalities and allows a pass-through of income and loss to its members for tax purposes. Further, LLC investors (referred to as "members") may take an unrestricted role in management without sacrificing limited liability. The LLC also need not

---

[79] *Banghart v. Hollywood General Partnership*, 902 F.2d 805, 808 (10th Cir. 1990). *See generally* Callison, *Changed Circumstances: Eliminating the Williamson Presumption That General Partnership Interests Are Not Securities*, 58 Bus. Law. 1373 (2003).

[80] *SEC v. Merchant Capital*, 483 F.3d 747 (11th Cir. 2007).

[81] *Id.* at 755–756. *See generally* Welle, *When Are Limited Liability Partnership Interests Securities?*, 27 J. Corp. L. 63 (2001).

have any member subject to unlimited liability as is required in limited partnerships.[82]

The *Howey* investment contract test applies to determine whether LLC interests are securities. If the LLC operating agreement vests managerial authority in the board of managers, then the LLC interests may be treated for definition of security purposes like limited partnership interests and will more likely invoke securities law coverage. In this context, a key issue is whether the efforts exerted by the LLC members are significant enough so as to preclude the presence of a "security." On the other hand, when managerial power rests with the LLC members (rather than with a board of managers), it may be argued that such LLC members are not relying essentially on the efforts of others. Under this approach, LLC interests may be viewed as similar to interests in a general partnership and, therefore, ordinarily are not investment contracts.[83] Nonetheless, depending on the provisions contained in the LLC operating documents and the surrounding circumstances (such as the subject member's degree of influence and the expertise required to operate the business), application of the *Williamson* factors may result in such LLC interests satisfying the *Howey* test.

Note, moreover, that a number of courts, pointing to the limited liability protection afforded to LLC members, hold that the *Williamson* analysis has no application in the LLC setting. For example, one court opined:

> In *Williamson*, the court cited a general partner's liability for the obligations of the partnership and his right to control the business . . . as being the "critical factors" to distinguishing a general partnership interest from an investment contract. Because limited liability companies ordinarily do not share these characteristics, there is no justification for a broad presumption against interests in limited liability companies being investment contracts. Extending the *Williamson* presumption for general partnership interests to interests in limited liability companies is not appropriate, given the essential distinctions between the two business forms. We eschew a presumption that interests in limited liability companies are not investment contracts, within the meaning of the securities laws.[84]

More recently, upon examining the economic realities of the underlying transaction, the Second Circuit held that the LLC members in fact were passive investors, thereby signifying that the LLC interests were securities.[85]

---

[82] *See generally* M. Sargent, Limited Liability Company Handbook (updated annually).

[83] *See Robinson v. Glynn*, 349 F.3d 166 (4th Cir. 2003) (purchaser of LLC interests had sufficient managerial control to preclude securities law coverage under *Howey*).

[84] *AKs Daks Communications, Inc. v. Maryland Securities Division*, 771 A. 2d 487, 498 (Md. Ct. Sp. App. 2001).

[85] *Leonard v. United States*, 529 F.3d 83, 89–91 (2d Cir. 2008); *see SEC v. Friendly Power Company*, 49 F. Supp. 2d 1363 (S.D. Fla. 1999). *See generally* Goforth, *Why Limited Liability Company Membership Interest Should Not Be Treated as Securities and Possible Steps to Encourage This Result*, 45 Hastings L.J. 1223 (1994); McGinty, *Are Interests In Limited Liability Companies Securities?*, 25 Sec. Reg. L.J. 121 (1997); Ribstein, *Form and Substance in the*

[E] Property Interests Combined with Service Contracts

The factual setting presented to the Supreme Court in *Howey* has been repeated numerous times in a variety of contexts. Courts repeatedly have looked beyond a strict statutory construction and have examined the economic reality of the transaction to determine whether a property interest combined with some form of service contract constitutes a security (termed the "aggregation" approach). The *Howey* analysis applied by the courts in these cases usually can be broken down into three issues: First, are the investors dependent on other investors and/or the promoter for a return on their investment ("common enterprise")? Second, is the interest bought in order to obtain a financial return or for other reasons ("expectation of profits")? Third, do the investors participate in the venture to such a degree that they are not dependent "solely on the efforts of others" for their profits?[86]

The applicability of the securities laws in this context may arise where there is the offer and sale of condominium units, or other units in a real estate development, coupled with an arrangement for the promoter or its designee to perform certain rental services for the purchaser. Such agreements may be held to involve the offer and sale of an investment contract or a participation in a profit sharing arrangement within the meaning of the securities acts. On this subject, the SEC has expressed the following view:

> [T]he offering of condominium units in conjunction with any one of the following will cause the offering to be viewed as an offering of securities in the form of investment contracts:
>
> 1. The condominiums, with any rental arrangement or other similar service, are offered and sold with emphasis on the economic benefits to the purchaser to be derived from the managerial efforts of the promoter, or a third party designated or arranged for by the promoter, from rental of the units;
>
> 2. The offering of participation in a rental pool arrangement; [or]
>
> 3. The offering of a rental or similar arrangement whereby the purchaser must hold his unit available for rental for any part of the year, must use an exclusive rental agent or is otherwise materially restricted in his occupancy or rental of his unit.
>
> In all of the above situations, investor protection requires the application of the federal securities laws.[87]

Definition of a "Security": The Case of Limited Liability Companies, 51 Wash. & Lee L. Rev. 807 (1994); Sargent, *Are Limited Liability Company Interests Securities?*, 19 Pepperdine L. Rev. 1069 (1992); Steinberg & Conway, *The Limited Liability Company as a Security*, 19 Pepperdine L. Rev. 1105 (1992); Welle, *Limited Liability Company Interests as Securities: An Analysis of Federal and State Actions Against Limited Liability Companies Under the Securities Laws*, 73 Den. U.L. Rev. 425 (1996).

[86] *See, e.g., Westchester Corp. v. Peat Marwick Mitchell & Co.*, 626 F.2d 1212 (5th Cir. 1980); *Continental Marketing Corp. v. SEC*, 387 F.2d 466 (10th Cir. 1967).

[87] Securities Act Release No. 5347 (1973). Continuing, the SEC stated:

Note that a security may exist in additional situations other than the three classified above in the SEC release. For example, in *Hocking v. Dubois*,[88] the Ninth Circuit expansively applied the *Howey* test to a condominium *resale* coupled with a rental agreement between the purchaser and a rental agent recommended by but not affiliated with the real estate broker. The decision raised concerns among real estate brokers that their recommendation of a leasing agent (even if not affiliated with such broker) in connection with the sale as well as resale of a vacation-type condominium may trigger application of the securities laws.[89]

[F]   Franchises

Conventional franchising agreements (which also may take such forms as dealerships, distributorships, or leasing arrangements) generally have been held not to constitute "investment contracts." The rationale is that pursuant to these arrangements, the franchisee exerts meaningful efforts.[90] Nonetheless, it is important to emphasize that the label "franchise" is not determinative. Where the franchisee has not been granted realistic authority to exercise significant managerial rights and responsibilities with respect to the

---

> If the condominiums are not offered and sold with emphasis on the economic benefits to the purchaser to be derived from the managerial efforts of others, and assuming that no plan to avoid the registration requirements of the Securities Act is involved, an owner of a condominium unit may, after purchasing his unit, enter into a non-pooled rental arrangement with an agent not designated or required to be used as a condition to the purchase, whether or not such agent is affiliated with the offeror, without causing a sale of a security to be involved in the sale of the unit. Further, a continuing affiliation between the developers or promoters of a project and the project by reason of maintenance arrangements does not make the unit a security.

Id. For a more recent SEC staff interpretation, see *Intrawest Corp.*, SEC No-Action Letter, avail. Nov. 8, 2002, discussed in, 34 Sec. Reg. & L. Rep. (BNA) 1978 (2002) (SEC Staff acquiescing in the view that "mere disclosure of the existence of a rental program as one of the many services offered to unit owners does not involve the offer of a security").

[88] 885 F.2d 1449 (9th Cir. 1989) (en banc); *see SEC v. Kelly*, [2007–2008 Transfer Binder] Fed. Sec. L. Rep. (CCH) ¶ 94,642 (N.D. Ill. 2008); *SEC v. Kirkland*, 521 F. Supp. 2d 1281 (M.D. Fla. 2007); *Hodges v. H&R Investments Ltd.*, 668 F. Supp. 545 (N.D. Miss. 1987).

[89] *See* Rumsey, *Resort Condominiums and the Federal Securities Laws*, 18 Colo. Lawyer 229 (1989); Comment, *Hocking v. Dubois: Applying the Securities Laws to Condominium Resales*, 58 Fordham L. Rev. 1121 (1990).

[90] *See, e.g., Meyer v. Dans un Jardin*, 816 F.2d 533 (10th Cir. 1987), where the court reasoned:

> It is undeniable that the product, the reputation, and the promotional and managerial expertise developed by the franchisor are material to the success of its franchisees. Benefits expected from the franchisor provide incentives for entering into a franchise agreement rather than undertaking a wholly independent business. But that does not mean the typical franchisee can expect to profit from the investment without regard to the franchisee's own business skills.

> Under the franchise agreement here, the plaintiffs were responsible for constructing the franchise store, paying rent, salaries, and advertising expenses, hiring and firing employees, maintaining customer relationships, ordering inventory, and devoting their full time and best efforts to the day-to-day management of the franchise store. The defendants' role was essentially limited to providing merchandise and promotional materials at plaintiffs' expense, conducting training seminars, and assisting plaintiffs in the commencement of their operation. . . .

Id. at 535.

enterprise, an investment contract may be held to exist.[91] Moreover, where a franchise agreement is really a pyramid scheme, in which profits are sought from the sale of other "franchises" through the main efforts of the promoter and/or third parties (rather than from the sale of products), an investment contract normally will be recognized.[92]

§ 2.05 THE RISK CAPITAL TEST

The *Howey* test is the prevalent standard for ascertaining the existence of an investment contract under both federal and state law. Nonetheless, the risk capital test remains an important state law alternative to the *Howey* standard. Although not generally adopted by the federal courts, the risk capital test has been embraced by a number of states by statute or case law. Importantly, application of the risk capital test may lead to a finding of a "security" under the applicable state law where the *Howey* test would hold that no security interest is present.

The risk capital test was first recognized by the California Supreme Court in *Silver Hills Country Club v. Sobieski*[93] in an opinion written by Justice Traynor. There, the California Commission of Corporations successfully argued that the offer and sale of memberships in a country club to be operated for profit were securities under California law. The proceeds from such memberships were to be used for club improvements; members and their immediate families were entitled to use club facilities. Even though the benefits to be received were non-pecuniary, the court, applying the risk capital test, held that the membership interests were securities. Justice Traynor stated:

> We have here nothing like the ordinary sale of a right to use existing facilities. Petitioners are soliciting the risk capital with which to develop a business for profit. The purchaser's risk is not lessened merely because the interest he purchases is labeled a membership. Only because he risks his capital along with other purchasers can there be any chance that the benefits of club membership will materialize.[94]

The risk capital test has been adopted by a number of state courts and legislatures.[95] It is important to note that generally under the risk capital test: (1) there is no horizontal common enterprise required; (2) similar to the *Howey* line of cases, non-pecuniary benefits are sufficient; and (3) the *Howey* "solely" from the efforts of others standard is relaxed.

---

[91] *See, e.g., SEC v. Aqua-Sonic Products Corp.*, 687 F.2d 577 (2d Cir. 1982); Securities Act Release No. 5211 (1971).

[92] *See Piambino v. Bailey*, 610 F.2d 1306 (5th Cir. 1980); Johnson & Campbell, *Securities Law and the Franchise Agreement*, 1980 Utah L. Rev. 311.

[93] 55 Cal. 2d 811, 13 Cal. Rptr. 186, 361 P.2d 906 (1961).

[94] 361 P.2d at 908.

[95] *See, e.g., State, Commissioner of Securities v. Hawaii Market Center, Inc.*, 52 Haw. 642, 485 P.2d 105 (1971); Ga. Code Ann. § 97-102(a)(16); Mich. Stat. Ann. § 19.776(401)(1). *See generally* Coffey, *The Economic Realities of a "Security": Is There a More Meaningful Formula?*, 18 Case W. Res. L. Rev. 367 (1967).

Irrespective of whether the risk capital or the *Howey* test is employed, it may be argued that some courts have not adequately focused on the prospective investor's position at the time that the offer and negotiation occur. Instead, such courts too often may concern themselves with the investor's anticipated position after the deal is struck. Yet, because the critical decisions are made at the offer and negotiation stages, it is at these stages that courts should assess whether the interests at stake warrant invocation of the securities laws. Hence, the time of the applicable "offer" and "sale" should be determinative.[96]

§ 2.06   DEBT SECURITIES

A substantial portion of case law has addressed whether certain debt instruments are securities under federal and state law. One threshold issue is that the definitions pertaining to debt securities in Section 2(a)(1) of the Securities Act and Section 3(a)(10) of the Exchange Act are not precisely the same. Further, the Securities Act definition, although exempting notes of less than nine months maturity from the registration requirement, specifically includes "evidence(s) of indebtedness". The Exchange Act definition of security (§ 3(a)(10)), on the other hand, specifically excludes notes of less than nine months maturity. Nonetheless, the coverage of the two Acts, as the Supreme Court has so held, "may be considered the same."[97]

[A]   Notes

Prior to the Supreme Court's decision in *Reves v. Ernst & Young*,[98] the lower federal courts were sharply divided on the applicable criteria to be employed in determining the security law status of "notes". The tests utilized included the "family resemblance" approach,[99] the "commercial/investment" standard,[100] the "risk capital" test,[101] and the *Howey* criteria.[102] Given the

---

[96] On this point, see Carney & Fraser, *Defining a "Security: Georgia's Struggle With the Risk Capital Test*, 30 Emory L.J. 73 (1981). *See generally* Branson & Okamoto, *The Supreme Court's Literalism and the Definition of "Security" in the State Courts*, 50 Wash. & Lee L. Rev. 1043 (1993).

[97] *Reves v. Ernst & Young*, 494 U.S. 56, 61 n.1 (1990).

[98] 494 U.S. 56 (1990).

[99] *See, e.g., Exchange National Bank of Chicago v. Touche Ross & Co.*, 544 F.2d 1126 (2d Cir. 1976).

[100] *See, e.g., Baurer v. Planning Group, Inc.*, 669 F.2d 770 (D.C. 1981). As set forth in this text's first edition:

> Several courts have adopted the commercial/investment test where the focus is on the underlying character of the transaction. Applying the "unless the context otherwise requires" language of Sections 2(1) and 3(a)(10) as well as the economic reality concept, courts adhering to this view hold that a note is not a security where it arises from a commercial transaction even when its terms are literally within the Acts' coverage. In making this determination, the courts have focused on such factors as the use of the funds (to fund current expenses rather than long-term projects), whether the note is collateralized (and, hence, less "risky"), the number of purchasers (limited to few or marketed to many), the level of sophistication of the purchasers (is the purchaser a bank or an uninitiated investor), and whether the note has a short maturity.

M. Steinberg, Understanding Securities Law 25–26 (1989).

divergent approaches, the Supreme Court's decision in *Reves*, although far from being a model of clarity, helps to resolve ambiguities in this area.

The instruments in *Reves* were demand notes, such notes being uncollateralized and uninsured, paying a variable rate of interest adjusted monthly to be higher than that paid by local financial institutions but not being linked to the earnings of the business. In determining the proper standard to adopt, the Court declined to adhere to the *Howey* test in the "note" context. The *Reves* Court reasoned: "To hold that a 'note' is not a 'security' unless it meets a test designed for an entirely different variety of instrument 'would make the Acts' enumeration of many types of instruments superfluous,' and would be inconsistent with Congress' intent to regulate the entire body of instruments sold as investments."[103] On the other hand, the Court rejected the *Landreth Timber* formula in the note context. Unlike "stock" which by its nature (if it has the attributes typically associated with such an instrument) is within the class of instruments Congress intended to regulate under the securities laws, the same cannot be said of "notes" which are used in a variety of settings, some of which are commercial and others of which involve investments. Hence, since "notes" are not necessarily securities, the Court, after searching for a proper standard to be applied, opted for the "family resemblance" test.[104]

Under the family resemblance test, a "note" exceeding nine months duration is presumed to be a security.[105] The presumption may be rebutted by a showing that the note bears a strong resemblance (by looking to the four-factor "family resemblance" test) to an instrument that has been excluded from the reach of the securities laws or that application of the "family resemblance" evidences that the note ought to be excluded. As stated by the Supreme Court:

> We conclude that in determining whether an instrument denomi-nated a "note" is a "security," courts are to apply the version of the "family resemblance" test that we have articulated here: a note is presumed to be a "security," and that presumption may be rebutted only by a showing that the note bears a strong resemblance (in terms of the four factors we have identified) to one of the enumerated categories of instrument. If an instrument is not sufficiently similar to an item on the list, the decision whether another category should be added is to be made by examining the same factors.[106]

---

[101] *See, e.g., Great Western Bank & Trust v. Kotz*, 532 F.2d 1252 (9th Cir. 1976) (looking at such factors as the length of the note's maturity, whether the note is collateralized, the relative size of the debt in relation to the size of the borrower's business, and the use of the proceeds).

[102] *See supra* notes 6–10, 46–63 (and accompanying text).

[103] 494 U.S. at 62–63.

[104] *Id.* at 65.

[105] For notes having a duration of nine months or less, the Court declined to address whether this presumption applied. *Id.* at 65 n.3.

[106] *Id.* at 65. Although a number of states follow the family resemblance test enunciated in *Reves*, other standards may be applicable. These include the risk capital test, the investment versus

Prior application of this test reveals that the following notes are *not* securities:

1. The note delivered in consumer financing;

2. The note secured by a mortgage on a home;

3. The short-term note secured by a lien on a small business or some of its assets;

4. The note evidencing a "character" loan to a bank customer;

5. Short-term notes secured by an assignment of accounts receivable;

6. A note formalizing an open-account debt incurred in the ordinary course of business; and

7. Notes evidencing loans by commercial banks for current operations.[107]

Hence, the *Reves'* "family resemblance" test consists of the following four factors:

(1) *The motivations that would prompt a reasonable buyer and seller to enter into the transaction.* "If the seller's purpose is to raise money for the general use of a business enterprise or to finance substantial investments and the buyer is interested primarily in the profit the note is expected to generate, the instrument is likely a 'security.'" On the other hand, if the note is exchanged to promote some commercial or consumer purpose, it is less likely to be a security.[108]

(2) *The plan of distribution of the instrument.* If there exists "common trading for speculation or investment," the note more likely will be viewed as a security. To establish such common trading, it must be shown that the notes were "offered and sold to a broad segment of the public." The notes need not be traded on an exchange.[109]

(3) *The investing public's reasonable expectations.* Where, for example, notes are advertised and otherwise marketed as an "investment" and no countervailing factors would lead a reasonable person to doubt this characterization, a security may be recognized. Accordingly, "[t]he Court will consider instruments to be 'securities' on the basis of such public expectations, even where an economic analysis of the particular transaction might suggest that the instruments are not

---

commercial test, and the *Howey* test. *See* Warren, *The Treatment of Reves "Notes" and Other Securities Under State Blue Sky Law*, 47 Bus. Law. 321, 325–329 (1991).

[107] 494 U.S. at 65 (citing *Chemical Bank v. Arthur Andersen & Co.*, 726 F.2d 930 (2d Cir. 1984)); *Exchange National Bank v. Touche Ross & Co.*, 544 F.2d 1126 (2d Cir. 1976).

[108] 494 U.S. at 67.

[109] *Id.* at 67–68.

'securities' as used in that transaction."[110]

(4) *The existence of a risk reducing factor.* For example, securities law application may well be deemed unnecessary when another regulatory framework significantly reduces the risk.[111]

Applying the "family resemblance" test to the case at bar, the Supreme Court in *Reves* held that the notes came within the purview of the securities laws. The notes were sold in an effort to raise capital for general business operations and were purchased by investors in order to earn a profit, the plan of distribution was widespread, the public's reasonable expectations were that the notes were securities as they were advertised as investments, and there was no risk-reducing factor (such as the presence of other comprehensive regulation) that minimized the risk of loss. Moreover, the "demand" nature of the notes did not take them outside the reach of the federal securities laws as this feature did not significantly lessen the investment's risk (as phrased by the Court, "demand only eliminates risk when and if payment is made"). Accordingly, the Court held that such promissory notes are securities.[112]

In light of the Supreme Court's decision in *Reves* and lower court application post-*Reves*, the following points are set forth:

(1) *Rejection of the* Howey *Test.* The Court's rejection of the *Howey* test in the "note" context seemingly is significant. With the exception of "stock," some lower courts had advocated that the *Howey* test be applied, irrespective of the nature of the instrument. The Supreme Court's rejection of this interpretation may signal that *Howey's* relevance is confined to investment contract analysis.

(2) *Definition of "Profit."* The "demand" notes in *Reves* paid a fixed rate of interest, not being keyed to revenues or earnings. The Court held that payment of interest in this context constituted "profit." According to the Court, in the "note" setting, "profit" means an investment having a valuable return "which undoubtedly includes interest."[113] As a result, it may be asserted that in order for a note to have a "valuable" return, it must pay interest to the holder above the generally prevailing rate offered by instruments that are deemed "safe." Such "safe" instruments would include notes that are adequately insured and other instruments where the rate of default (both from a prospective and historical view) is practically nil. Generally, an investor purchases a note not having these more secure characteristics for the purpose of receiving a return that may be deemed "substantial," and hence, "valuable." At the same time, when an investor seeks a more valuable return, the risk of loss is magnified.[114]

---

[110] *Id.* at 66.

[111] *Id.* at 67.

[112] *Id.* at 67–73.

[113] *Id.* at 68 n.4.

[114] *See, e.g., Financial Security Assurance, Inc. v. Stephens, Inc.,* 500 F.3d 1276 (11th Cir. 2007) (municipal bonds at issue were not "notes" under the federal securities laws because the subject

(3) *Application of Four-Prong Test.* In adopting the four-prong "family resemblance" test, the Supreme Court declined to state whether all factors must be met or whether the standard calls for balancing the various factors. The Court's language in *Reves* is somewhat ambiguous. After *Reves,* a number of lower court decisions have suggested that a note may be a security even though all four factors have not been met.[115]

(4) *Plan of Distribution.* After *Reves,* it was uncertain whether the inquiry as to plan of distribution focused on whether the notes *in fact* were distributed to a broad segment of the public or whether this prong would be satisfied if the notes were *capable* of being so distributed. Although the *Reves* Court did not refer to the "capability" of mass distribution, the cases relied on by the Court support this proposition.[116] Nonetheless, post-*Reves,* lower court decisions generally have looked to the distribution that occurred *in fact* rather than to the capability of distribution.[117]

(5) *Risk-Reducing Factors.* After *Reves,* a number of lower court decisions have relied on the fact that the notes at issue were collateralized as a basis for excluding such notes from securities law coverage.[118] Hence, along with the presence of another regulatory framework that significantly reduces the risk of loss,[119] lower courts view collateralization of notes as a key risk-reducing factor.

(6) *Notes Not Exceeding Nine Months.* The Supreme Court's holding articulates that a "note" is presumed to be a "security" unless the note bears a strong resemblance (by looking to the four-factor "family resemblance" test) to an instrument that has been excluded

---

bonds did not have the potential to generate profit for complainant) (for an article analyzing this decision, *see* Fendler, *Municipal Bonds as "Non-Securities": Financial Security Assurance, Inc. v. Stephens, Inc.,* 36 Sec. Reg. L.J. 22 (2008)); *McNabb v. SEC,* 298 F.3d 1126 (9th Cir. 2002) (applying *Reves'* family resemblance test and holding promissory notes were securities); *Stoiber v. SEC,* 161 F.3d 745 (D.C. Cir. 1998) (applying *Reves,* court held that notes were securities, reasoning in part that purchasers of notes were motivated to earn a profit from loan interest); *National Bank of Yugoslavia v. Drexel Burham Lambert, Inc.,* 768 F. Supp. 1010, 1015 (S.D.N.Y. 1991) (stating that "a fixed interest rate is a feature of many notes undoubtedly covered by the federal securities laws").

[115] *See* Kerr & Eisenhauer, *Reves Revisited,* 19 Pepperdine L. Rev. 1123, 1157 (1992) (stating that "[m]ost courts seem to have adopted a balancing approach") (citing cases at 1157 n. 296).

[116] *See* 494 U.S. at 66, 68 (relying on *Landreth Timber,* 471 U.S. at 687, 693 (1985) (stock of closely held corporation not traded on any exchange held to be a "security")); *Tcherepnin v. Knight,* 389 U.S. 332, 337 (1967) (nonnegotiable but transferable "withdrawable capital shares" in savings and loan association held to be a "security"); *Howey,* 328 U.S. 293, 295 (1946) (units of citrus grove and maintenance contract held to be "securities" although not traded on an exchange).

[117] *See, e.g., Pollack v. Laidlaw Holdings, Inc.,* 27 F.3d 808 (2d Cir. 1994); *Banco Espanol de Credito v. Security Pacific National Bank,* 973 F.2d 51 (2d Cir. 1992).

[118] *See, e.g., Resolution Trust Corporation v. Stone,* 998 F.2d 1534 (10th Cir. 1993).

[119] *See Reves,* 494 U.S. at 67; *Trust Company of Louisiana v. N.N.P., Inc.,* 104 F.3d 1478 (5th Cir. 1997) (applying "family resemblance" test and holding notes at issue were securities, court pointed to lack of other regulatory framework to protect the investors).

from the securities laws' reach or unless application of the "family resemblance" test indicates that the note ought to be excluded. The Court, however, declined to address whether this presumption applies to securities with a maturity not exceeding nine months. Chief Justice Rehnquist, writing for a four member dissent, would exclude notes of nine months or less duration from the scope of the securities laws as a matter of law.[120] While a literal interpretation of the nine-month exemption contained in Section 3(a)(10) of the Exchange Act would exclude such instruments from that Act's reach all together, the exclusion in Section 3(a)(3) of the Securities Act would exclude such instruments from the registration provisions. The antifraud provisions of the 1933 Act would still apply to such instruments. Irrespective of the difference in this statutory language, the Court has consistently held, reaffirmed in *Reves*, that the coverage of the two Acts is the same. Moreover, each definition is prefaced by the term "unless the context otherwise requires." Employing this language, courts have applied an approach rooted in economic reality to determine whether a particular instrument is a security.[121]

Justice Stevens, concurring in *Reves*, stated that the nine-month exclusion applies to "commercial paper, not investment securities."[122] Hence, only short-term high quality commercial paper issued to fund current operations and offered to sophisticated investors should qualify for exclusion. For support, Justice Stevens relied on lower court case law and the position of the SEC.[123] Case law post-*Reves* mainly adheres to this approach.[124]

Also, there can be little question that, from a general perspective, the shorter time period one's money is in another's hands, the less the risk of loss. It also can be stated with confidence, however, that such a time period is far from a guarantee of repayment. Other factors are equally, if not more, important, such as the solvency of the seller of the note, the intended use of the

---

[120] 494 U.S. at 77–81 (Rehnquist, C.J., dissenting in part).

[121] *See, e.g., Reves*, 494 U.S. at 61 n. 1; *Forman*, 421 U.S. at 849.

[122] 494 U.S. at 74 (Stevens, J., concurring). Justice Stevens also joined the opinion issued by the five-member majority. *Id.* at 58.

[123] *See, e.g., Zeller v. Bogue Electric Mfg. Corp.*, 476 F.2d 795 (2d Cir. 1973); *Sanders v. John Nuveen & Co.*, 463 F.2d 1075 (7th Cir. 1972); Securities Act Release No. 4412 (1961). Hence, commercial paper is not a security if it is:

　　(1) prime quality negotiable commercial paper;

　　(2) of a type not ordinarily purchased by the general public;

　　(3) is paper issued to facilitate well recognized types of current operational business requirements; and

　　(4) of a type eligible for discounting by Federal Reserve banks.

463 F.2d at 1079 (quoting Securities Act Release No. 4412 (1961)).

[124] *See, e.g., SEC v. Wallenbrock*, 313 F.3d 532 (9th Cir. 2002) (concluding that nine-month exclusion is limited to commercial paper sold to sophisticated investors); *SEC v. Better Life of America*, 995 F. Supp. 167 (D.D.C. 1998) (notes having maturity periods of less than nine months not of prime quality and offered to small-scale investors were securities). *See generally* Couture, *The Securities Acts' Treatment of Notes Maturing in Less Than Nine Months: A Solution to the Enigma*, 31 Sec. Reg. L.J. 496 (2003).

proceeds, general market conditions, and the rate of interest required to be paid to service the debt. Indeed, certain financings extended in leveraged buyouts evidence that fairly short-term debt can be at risk of default. Hence, a note's duration, although relevant, should not be determinative for securities law coverage.

As another point, the significance of the *Reves* dissent that notes of less than nine months duration as a matter of law are not "notes" within federal securities law coverage takes on less significance in light of the Supreme Court's 2004 decision in *SEC v. Edwards*. Even assuming that the dissent's approach eventually "wins" on this issue, such debt instruments, nonetheless, may well be "investment contracts" under the expanded definition of "profit" embraced in *Edwards* to encompass the receipt of "periodic payments".[125] Accordingly, short-term notes paying an attractive rate of interest that are mass marketed to individual investors likely are investment contracts under the *Howey* test.

[B]   Certificates of Deposit

The definitive case in this area is *Marine Bank v. Weaver*[126] where the Court focused on the existence of depositor insurance and the pervasive federal regulation over banking. Accordingly, the Court held that a certificate of deposit (CD) purchased from a federally regulated bank is not a security. Given the widespread impact of the Federal Deposit Insurance Co. and other federal insurance, the *Marine Bank* holding would in practical terms seem to have very wide impact. Note, however, that application of the federal securities laws to a CD issued by a state chartered non-federally insured bank or a foreign bank may not be foreclosed by *Marine Bank*.

A number of post-*Marine Bank* decisions help highlight the questions involved. For example, in *Wolf v. Banco Nacional de Mexico*,[127] the Ninth Circuit was faced with the issue of whether *Marine Bank's* analysis applies to CDs issued by a foreign bank. More precisely, the issued presented in *Wolf* was whether a certificate of deposit in Mexican pesos in a Mexican bank was a security under U.S. law. The district court, relying on *Marine Bank's* emphasis on the protection given to depositors by the federal banking laws, held that, since the Mexican deposits were outside the U.S. banking regulatory system, *Marine Bank* did not control. Reversing, the Ninth Circuit held that

---

[125] *SEC v. Edwards*, 540 U.S. 389 (2004) (discussed *supra* notes 39–45, 55 (and accompanying text)). For articles addressing *Reves* and its ramifications, *see, e.g.*, Brown & Breckinridge, *Notes Qualifying as Securities In the Wake of Reves: Recent Developments*, 31 Rev. Sec. & Comm. Reg. 1 (1998); Couture, *supra* note 124; Fendler, *supra* note 114; Gordon, *Interplanetary Intelligence About Promissory Notes as Securities*, 69 Texas L. Rev. 383 (1990); Kerr & Eisenhauer, *supra* note 115; Steinberg, *Notes as Securities: Reves and Its Implications*, 51 Ohio St.L.J. 675 (1990); Warren, *supra* note 106; Comment, *Bank Loans as Securities: A Legal and Financial Economic Analysis of the Treatment of Marketable Bank Assets Under the Securities Act*, 40 UCLA L.Rev. 799 (1993).

[126] 455 U.S. 551 (1982); *see supra* notes 23–27 (and accompanying text).

[127] 739 F.2d 1458 (9th Cir. 1984); *see West v. Multibanco Comermex*, 807 F.2d 820 (9th Cir. 1987).

the Mexican CD was not a security in that the issuing bank was sufficiently regulated and repayment in full was virtually guaranteed. The court stated: "When a [domestic or foreign] bank is sufficiently well regulated that there is virtually no risk that insolvency will prevent it from repaying the holder of one of its certificates of deposit in full, the certificate is not a security for purposes of the federal securities laws."[128]

In *Tafflin v. Levitt*,[129] the Fourth Circuit applied *Marine Bank* to state regulation. There, the Fourth Circuit held that Maryland's regulatory and insurance system with respect to state-chartered savings and loans compelled the conclusion that the certificates of deposit were not securities.

Not all courts agree with the foregoing cases. For example, the Tenth Circuit in *Holloway v. Peat, Marwick, Mitchell & Co.*,[130] rejected *Marine Bank's* functional regulation approach to state regulation. In holding passbook savings accounts and thrift certificates (issued by a financial institution subject to state oversight) to be securities, the court asserted that "under the supremacy clause [of the U. S. Constitution] our focus must be on federal regulation; *state regulatory schemes cannot displace the [Securities] Acts.*"[131]

---

[128] 739 F.2d at 1463.

[129] 865 F.2d 595 (4th Cir. 1989).

[130] 900 F.2d 1485 (10th Cir. 1990).

[131] *Id.* at 1488 (emphasis added); *see also Olson v. E.F. Hutton & Co.*, 957 F.2d 622 (8th Cir. 1992) (construing *Marine Bank* so as not to bar securities law coverage when the certificates of deposit were not guaranteed); *Riedel v. Bancam, S.A.*, 792 F.2d 587 (6th Cir. 1986) (holding certificates of deposit issued by Mexican bank to be securities under Ohio law); *Meason v. Bank of Miami*, 652 F.2d 542 (5th Cir. 1982) (holding that certificates of deposit issued by bank situated in the Grand Cayman Islands may be a security).

In addition to the sources cited previously in this chapter, for further coverage on definition of "security," see generally Arnold, *The Definition of a Security Under the Federal Securities Laws Revisited*, 34 Cleve. St. L. Rev. 249 (1986); Bradford, *Expanding the Investment Company Act: The SEC's Manipulation of the Definition of Security*, 60 Ohio St. L.J. 995 (1999); Chappinelli, *Reinventing a Security: Arguments for a Public Interest Definition*, 49 Wash. & Lee L. Rev. 957 (1992); Corgill, *Securities as Investments at Risk*, 67 Tulane L. Rev. 861 (1993); Gabaldon, *A Sense of a Security: An Empirical Study*, 25 J. Corp. L. 307 (2000); Lowenfels & Bromberg, *What Is a Security Under the Federal Securities Laws?*, 56 Albany L. Rev. 473 (1993); McGinty, *What Is A Security?*, 1993 Wisc. L. Rev. 1033; Rosin, *Historical Perspectives on the Definition of a Security*, 28 S. Tex. L. Rev. 575 (1987); Sherrard, *What Is A Security — Revisited*, 37 Rev. Sec. & Comm. Reg. 227 (2004); and Steinberg & Kaulbach, *The Supreme Court and the Definition of "Security": The "Context" Clause, "Investment Contract" Analysis, and Their Ramifications*, 40 Vand. L. Rev. 489 (1987).

Chapter 3

ISSUER EXEMPTIONS FROM REGISTRATION

§ 3.01 EXEMPT SECURITIES FROM REGISTRATION

The general rule is that, absent an exemption, all sales of securities must be registered pursuant to Section 5 of the Securities Act of 1933 ("Securities Act" or "1933 Act"). Note, importantly, that the securities law antifraud provisions apply irrespective of whether an exemption from registration exists.

There are two general types of exemptions: transactional exemptions and securities exempt from registration. The latter covers specific securities or categories of securities which are never required to be registered under Section 5, largely due to the intrinsic character or nature of the issuer itself. These exempt securities include, for example: certain short-term promissory notes or bills of exchange; securities issued or guaranteed by municipalities, state or federal governments; and securities issued by nonprofit, religious, educational or charitable organizations.[1]

Moreover, some securities, although exempt from the 1933 Act's registration requirements, come under the supervision of another federal or state governmental authority. For example, with respect to securities issued by national banks, the Comptroller of the Currency has developed a regulatory framework somewhat similar, yet many feel not as rigorous, as that developed by the Securities and Exchange Commission ("SEC"). On the other hand, the securities of bank holding companies are not exempt securities from registration under the federal securities laws.[2]

Significantly, it is the transactional exemptions from registration which play the important role in this context. As a consequence, the chapter will focus on these exemptions.

§ 3.02 WHY PERFECT A TRANSACTIONAL EXEMPTION?

As stated above, unless an exemption is available, any sale of a subject security must be made pursuant to a duly effective registration statement. Given this consequence, one may ask "why perfect a transactional exemption from registration rather than registering the offering of securities under Section 5 of the 1933 Act?" There are several reasons why a transactional

---

[1] See Securities Act § 3(a)(2)–(8), 15 U.S.C. § 77c(a)(2)–(8), for a listing of the exempt securities from registration.

[2] *See generally* L. Loss & J. Seligman, Securities Regulation 1142–1210 (3d ed. 1989).

exemption often is the preferred route. Keep in mind that the following discussion somewhat simplifies the pertinent requirements.

Generally, in order to register an offering of securities under Section 5 and have what is called a "public offering" or "to go public,"[3] a registration statement must be filed with the Securities and Exchange Commission. In addition, the final prospectus, which is part of the registration statement, must be timely provided to the purchaser. The registration statement (the prospectus which is a part thereof) is no ordinary document. The disclosures required are detailed and complex, the document's length is massive, and the costs of preparing the registration statement, including accountant, attorney, investment banker and printer fees, easily can run into the hundreds of thousands of dollars.

The costs and nature of the registration statement are due largely to Section 11 of the 1933 Act which, in practical effect, imposes strict liability upon a subject issuer as well as a "due diligence" requirement upon specified parties, including the issuer's directors and certain executive officers, the underwriters, and the experts, including the accountants (with respect to those portions of the registration statement which an accountant has "expertised"). Attorneys, unless they act as experts,[4] are not subject to Section 11 liability. Counsel, nonetheless, is integrally involved in the registration process. He or she frequently is delegated by the issuer, underwriter, or other parties potentially liable under Section 11 to perform the requisite "due diligence" on their behalf. Other fundamental aspects of counsel's role in this process involve the drafting of the language contained in the registration statement, advising whether certain disclosures should or must be made, and acting as informal mediator between the various parties involved.

The concept of "due diligence," its significance, and the steps that must be taken to fulfill this mandate are addressed in Chapter 7. In theory, "due diligence" is a defense that may be asserted by the subject party rather than an affirmative obligation. It is certainly true that if the statements made in the registration statement are true or if no lawsuit is ultimately brought, no liability will be incurred for failure to exercise due diligence. If an action is instituted and a material misstatement or omission is shown, however, liability often may be avoided under Section 11 only by proving the performance of due diligence. In the realities of corporate practice, therefore, due diligence is a necessity rather than a discretionary function.

Hence, the "due diligence" requirement is given "teeth" by the liability consequences. In general, if there is a material misrepresentation or nondisclosure in the nonexpertised portion of the registration statement, parties

---

[3] The terms "public offering" and "going public" are often not synonymous. In short, the initial public offering ("IPO") made by an enterprise constitutes "going public." On the other hand, a successful corporation which has gone public decades ago may make public offerings of its securities on a periodic basis.

[4] Counsel acts as an expert, for example, if he or she proffers an opinion contained or referred to in the registration statement. An accountant, by certifying financial statements contained in the registration statement, is the party who frequently is sued as an expert under Section 11.

subject to Section 11 liability, except experts and the issuer (which is strictly liable), often can avoid such liability only by showing that they had conducted a reasonable investigation and, after such investigation, had no reason to believe and did not believe that the registration statement contained any materially false or misleading statement.

With respect to expertised portions of the registration statement, nonexperts are not required to investigate. They need show only that they had no reason to believe and did not believe that the expertised portions of the registration statement contained any materially false or misleading statement. Moreover, experts are potentially liable under Section 11 only for those portions of the registration statement which they "expertised." They can avoid Section 11 liability by showing that, with respect to the expertised portions of the registration statement, they had conducted a reasonable investigation and, after such investigation, had no reason to believe and did not believe that such expertised portions of the registration statement contained any materially false or misleading statement.

While the issuer is the only party which has no "due diligence" defense under Section 11 and is subject to strict liability, it may well be insolvent. The result is that aggrieved plaintiffs seek redress against the "deep pockets," frequently the underwriters and the accountants. Because of the severe financial ramifications that can amount to several million dollars, parties potentially subject to Section 11 liability seek to ensure that meaningful due diligence is performed and extensive disclosure made, including the potentially negative consequences and risks of the venture.

Accordingly, the costs of having a "registered" offering under the Securities Act frequently will be substantial. For a start-up venture or a business in severe financial difficulty, the costs of a public offering normally will prove prohibitive. Moreover, it is next to impossible successfully to consummate a registered offering unless receptive investment bankers can be retained to underwrite the offering and the financial markets are favorable. These conditions are exacerbated in cases where enterprises with little or no previous earnings history seek to "go public." However, as some of the "high-tech" and "research" companies illustrated in the 1990's bull market, these problems are not insurmountable.[5]

Even if a financially successful registered offering can be made, it may be advisable for the client nonetheless to perfect a transactional exemption. By refraining from "going public," the enterprise essentially is keeping its financial affairs and related matters private among its various participants. By "going public," however, the enterprise, pursuant to the disclosure requirements of the

---

[5] *See, e.g.*, Kelly & Hennessey, *Finally, an IPO! But It Surely Isn't a Mania*, Wall St. J., Feb. 15, 2003, at C1 (The year's first IPO closed just below the offering price, "a far cry from the routine 'pops' of 50%, 100% and more when IPOs were hot — and the deal outlook for the rest of the year is still the worst it has been in more than a decade."). *Cf.* Cowan, *Visa's Debut Pops 28% — Record U.S. IPO Nabs $19.65 Billion*, Wall St. J., Mar. 20, 2008, at C3 (stating that VISA's IPO "closed at $56.50 a share, up $12.50 from the offer price of $44").

securities laws, will be hanging its dirty linen out for public viewing.[6] The enterprise, pursuant to certain provisions of the Securities Exchange Act, such as Section 13(a) or Section 15(d), will be required to file annual, quarterly, and other periodic reports with the SEC as well as to provide periodic reports to its shareholders and the pertinent self regulatory organizations. Other sections of the Exchange Act, such as Section 13(b)'s recordkeeping and internal accounting control provisions, will become applicable. Moreover, the certification, internal control, and the other mandates of the Sarbanes-Oxley Act of 2002 must be implemented.[7] Hence, the enterprise, by having a registered offering, will be faced not only with public scrutiny but saddled with high accounting and legal fees as well as the persistent threat of litigation due to the consequences of public disclosure.

For the above reasons as well as others (such as, by taking the corporation public, the insiders may potentially risk loss of control through a hostile takeover), it may be advisable and indeed necessary to procure a transactional exemption from registration. It should not be surprising that, given the above, the vast majority of offerings are made under a transactional exemption rather than by a registered offering. In many instances, therefore, counsel will seek the viability of a transactional exemption before advising that a registered offering go forward. Hence, an examination of the offering process begins with the transactional exemptions.

§ 3.03   TRANSACTIONAL EXEMPTIONS — INTRODUCTORY POINTS

Prior to turning to a discussion of the transactional exemptions from 1933 Act registration, certain introductory points should be made:

First, the following material in this chapter addresses exemptions from Securities Act registration that are transactionally based. Hence, for each separate *transaction*, an exemption from registration must be perfected.

Second, the relevant parties for the purposes of this chapter who are seeking to come within the transactional exemptions are primary issuers of securities. For example, a corporation issuing authorized but unissued stock or a limited partnership issuing interests to its participants would each be viewed as a primary issuer while a shareholder who seeks to transfer his or her shares to another would not be so viewed.

Third, accordingly, individuals reselling their stock must register any offer or sale unless they likewise perfect an exemption.[8] The exemption that normally would be invoked in this context is Section 4(1) of the Securities Act

---

[6] *Cf. Schlick v. Penn-Dixie Cement Corp.*, 507 F.2d 374, 384 (2d Cir. 1974); Kilman, *Giant Cargill Resists Pressure to Go Public As It Pursues Growth*, Wall St. J., Jan. 9, 1997, at A1 (stating that "Cargill is the nation's largest closely held company, generating annual revenues approaching $60 billion . . . , and it perhaps best demonstrates the benefits of being private").

[7] The Sarbanes-Oxley Act is covered throughout this text, including in Chapter 5.

[8] *See, e.g., Pennaluna & Company v. SEC*, 410 F.2d 861 (9th Cir. 1969).

(and SEC rules thereunder) which exempts from the registration requirements of Section 5 offers or sales made by any person "other than an issuer, underwriter, or dealer." The subject of resales is addressed in Chapter 6.

Fourth, the party seeking the exemption has the burden of proving that it has perfected the exemption by establishing that it has satisfied the necessary conditions for invoking the exemption. Failure to carry this burden signifies that no transactional exemption has been perfected, resulting in liability under the Securities Act for failure to register the offer or sale in question.[9]

Such failure to register gives rise to SEC and perhaps criminal liability for violation of Section 5 and to private recovery under Section 12(a)(1) of the 1933 Act. Generally, Section 12(a)(1) grants to the purchaser the right to rescind the transaction in an action brought against the seller for violation of Section 5. In effect, the provision imposes strict liability upon the seller for failure to comply with Section 5's registration requirements. Generally, the state securities laws have similar provisions.

Fifth, consistent with the federal securities laws in general, the interstate commerce requirement must be met in order for federal jurisdiction to be invoked in the transactional exemption context. This requirement normally is shown without difficulty. Use of the mail or any means or instrumentality of interstate commerce is sufficient. An intrastate telephone call, for example, satisfies the federal jurisdictional requirement.[10]

Sixth, even if a transactional exemption has been perfected, thereby obviating the need to register the offering, the antifraud provisions of the securities acts nonetheless fully apply. The antifraud provisions most frequently invoked are Section 17(a) of the Securities Act, Section 10(b) of the Exchange Act, and Rule 10b-5 promulgated by the SEC pursuant to its Section 10(b) rulemaking authority.

Seventh, as a final important point, federal law is not the only source of regulation in this setting. The state "blue sky" laws also frequently apply and present additional dilemmas for the corporate practitioner and his or her client. With certain exceptions, to perfect an exemption, in addition to satisfying the requirements of federal law, the securities regulations of *each* state (or territory) where *any* offer or sale is made also must be satisfied. To the credit of the SEC and the states, significant progress has been made in coordinating the federal and state transactional exemption scheme, thereby alleviating much of the burden in complying with this multi-faceted regulatory framework. Moreover, as discussed later in this chapter, federal legislation enacted in 1996 preempts state regulation of certain exempt offerings.

---

[9] *See, e.g., SEC v. Ralston Purina Co.*, 346 U.S. 119 (1953).

[10] *See, e.g., Lennerth v. Mendenhall*, 234 F. Supp. 59 (N.D. Ohio 1964).

§ 3.04   THE BURDEN OF PROOF FILE, SEC STAFF NO-ACTION LETTERS AND RESCISSION OFFERS

[A]   Burden of Proof File

Questions frequently arise, particularly in the litigation setting, regarding an issuer's compliance with an exemption from registration. As the law stands, the issuer (as the party seeking to perfect an exemption) has the burden to prove that it has satisfied the requirements for invoking an applicable exemption from registration. To satisfy this criteria, the attorney or the issuer or its designee (with the assistance of counsel) should maintain a "burden of proof" file. Such a file, if properly maintained, goes a long way toward showing that the issuer conducted the offering in compliance with the conditions for invoking the exemption.[11]

The importance of properly maintaining a burden of proof file is illustrated by the Sixth Circuit's decision in *Mark v. FSC Securities Corporation.*[12] Holding that the defendants had failed to perfect the Rule 506 exemption, the court alluded to the inadequate procedures utilized:

> [T]he documents [introduced at trial] offered no evidence from which a jury could conclude [that] the issuer reasonably believed each purchaser was suitable so as to warrant a Rule 506 exemption. Instead, all that was proved was the sale of twenty-eight limited partnerships, and the circumstances under which those sales were *intended* to have been made. The mere fact that the limited partnership interests were sold cannot support a conclusion that they were sold in compliance with the conditions contemplated by the Rule 506 exemption. The blank subscription document and offeree questionnaire simply do not amount to probative evidence, when it is the answers and information received *from* purchasers that determines whether the conditions of the Rule 506 exemption have been met. Because there was no evidence from which a jury could conclude that the issuer had the requisite belief, nor from which a jury could determine the reasonableness of any such belief, [the issuer] FSC has failed to sustain its burden of proving an exemption under Rule 506 of Regulation D.[13]

[B]   SEC Staff No-Action Letters

Although not specifically related to transactional exemptions from registration, this is a good point to mention the SEC "no-action" letter process. Under this process, counsel advises the SEC staff (not the Commission itself) in writing of his or her client's contemplated conduct. Such contemplated conduct may involve, for example, questions related to a Regulation D offering,

---

[11] *See* L. Wertheimer, Securities and Partnership Law for MLPs and Other Investment Limited Partnerships § 7.01 (1988).

[12] 870 F.2d 331 (6th Cir. 1989).

[13] *Id.* at 337 (emphasis in original).

resales of stock, or proxy statements. The staff generally responds by either issuing a no-action letter or by refusing to issue such a letter. At times, the staff's response communicates solely an enforcement posture — namely, whether the staff would recommend to the Commission that an enforcement action be initiated if the contemplated conduct were undertaken in the manner set forth in the written request. In other staff responses, in addition to the enforcement position taken, the staff may articulate interpretations of applicable SEC rules and regulations as they pertain to the proposed conduct. In either situation, the staff's views are not those of the Commission and are not binding in any manner. Notwithstanding the informal status of SEC no-action letters, they unquestionably have great significance and are relied upon by market participants and their attorneys.[14]

Not surprisingly, the SEC staff's refusal to approve a no-action request normally results in the affected parties not engaging in the contemplated conduct. Even if the staff issues a no-action letter, however, that does not ensure that the client's conduct will not be challenged. Private parties are not bound by an SEC no-action letter and may sue irrespective of the issuance of such a letter. Moreover, although very unlikely to happen, the SEC retains its discretion to institute an enforcement action even though its staff has issued a no-action letter covering the very same conduct.[15]

[C]   Rescission Offers

An ever present fear for securities counsel and his or her client is that a securities law violation has occurred that is material to the transaction. For example, in a Rule 506 offering, suppose that either before or after the transaction "closes" counsel discovers that there are 36 non-accredited purchasers rather than the allotted maximum of 35 or that there was general solicitation in connection with the offering. Is there any curative action that the issuer may take? Insofar as purchasers are concerned, the issuer may make a "rescission offer" that fully informs the purchasers of all material facts and provides such purchasers with the right to rescind.

Needless to say, counsel who is responsible for the transaction will be in an uncomfortable position. If counsel does nothing, permitting the "deal" to go forward and the issuer to use the funds, he or she may be liable under the securities laws. Alternatively, if the mistake happens to be counsel's doing, he or she may be liable to the client for malpractice. Moreover, even if a rescission offer may cut off a purchaser's right to sue (although it may not), the SEC and state authorities retain their prerogative to bring an enforcement action.

Rescission offers may occur in the private or public offering context. If a rescission offer is made in the private offering setting, an exemption from

---

[14] *See* Nagy, *Judicial Reliance on Regulatory Interpretations in SEC No-Action Letters: Current Problems and a Proposed Framework*, 83 Cornell L. Rev. 921, 924 (1998).

[15] *See New York City Employees' Retirement System v. SEC*, 45 F.3d 7 (2d Cir. 1995); *In re Morgan Stanley & Co.*, Securities Exchange Act Release No. 28990 (1991). *See generally* R. Haft, *Analysis of Key No-Action Letters* (2008); Lemke, *The SEC No-Action Letter Process*, 42 Bus. Law. 1019 (1987); Nagy, *supra* note 14.

registration must be perfected. Otherwise, compliance with the Securities Act registration requirements may be necessary.[16]

§ 3.05   THE SECTION 4(2) PRIVATE OFFERING EXEMPTION

Section 4(2) of the Securities Act exempts from the registration requirements "transactions by an issuer not involving any public offering." There is no monetary limit to the amount of funds that can be raised under this exemption. The provision's legislative history expresses Congress' intent to exempt those transactions from registration "where there is no practical need for [such] application . . . [or] where the public benefits are too remote."[17] As subsequently construed, courts have looked to a number of factors in determining the availability of the Section 4(2) private offering exemption.

A good starting point in ascertaining the requirements of the Section 4(2) private offering exemption is the Supreme Court's decision in *Securities and Exchange Commission v. Ralston Purina Co.*[18] In that case, the company made purported private offerings to scores of "key" employees, many of whom held non-managerial positions. The Supreme Court, observing that the burden of proving the perfection of an exemption from registration is upon the party relying upon the availability of such an exemption, held that the company had not satisfied this burden. The availability of the Section 4(2) private offering exemption, according to the Court, should turn upon "whether the particular class of persons affected needs the protection of the [Securities] Act."[19] Accordingly, the private offering exemption, among other things, requires that all persons to whom offers are made have the requisite financial sophistication (or be advised by one who has such sophistication) and are provided with or have access to the type of information that would be contained in a registration statement.[20]

The lower federal courts subsequent to *Ralston Purina* have had numerous occasions to construe the Section 4(2) exemption.[21] Although the principles emerging from these cases are not crystal clear, the following points can be made:

First, as construed by some courts, the Section 4(2) exemption turns on whether *all offers* (rather than actual purchases) are made in accordance with the exemption. A single noncomplying offer may invalidate the entire offering. For example, the Fifth Circuit has stated: "[W]e have held that the defendant

---

[16] *See* Bromberg, *Curing Securities Violations: Rescission Offers and Other Techniques*, 1 J. Corp. L. 1 (1975); Rowe, *Rescission Offers Under Federal and State Securities Law*, 12 J. Corp. Law 383 (1987).

[17] H.R. Rep. No. 85, 73d Cong., 1st Sess. 5 (1933).

[18] 346 U.S. 199 (1953).

[19] *Id.* at 124.

[20] *Id.* at 124–27.

[21] *See, e.g., SEC v. Murphy*, 626 F.2d 633 (9th Cir. 1980); *Seenson v. Engelstad*, 626 F.2d 421 (5th Cir. 1980); *Lawler v. Gilliam*, 569 F.2d 1283 (4th Cir. 1978).

must establish that each and every offeree either had the same information that would have been available in a registration statement or had access to such information."[22]

Second, although the courts and the SEC have not placed a finite number on how many offers can be permissibly made under the Section 4(2) exemption, it is clear that certain limits, depending on the circumstances, apply.[23]

Third, related to the above point, is that, pursuant to the Section 4(2) exemption, the issuer cannot engage in general solicitation or advertising. The precise limits of what conduct constitutes general solicitation so as to make unavailable the Section 4(2) exemption (as well as the Rule 505 and Rule 506 exemptions of Regulation D) are unclear. For example, a seminar held for an offering where twenty-five existing clients of adequate sophistication attend should be permitted while a seminar for a particular offering open to all clients of a major broker-dealer (e.g., Merrill Lynch) should be deemed general solicitation.[24]

Fourth, an issuer should take certain precautions against resales, such as obtaining written commitments by purchasers that they are acquiring for investment purposes (called an investment letter), placing appropriate legends on the certificates, and issuing stop transfer instructions. These procedures help the issuer perfect the Section 4(2) exemption in the event that purchasers subsequently resell their stock. It may well be, however, that the absence of these steps does not nullify an otherwise valid Section 4(2) exemption if no distribution in fact takes place.[25]

Fifth, all offerees must be financially sophisticated or be advised by someone who has the requisite acumen (called an offeree representative). Under case law, individual wealth (unlike the Rule 506 exemption) does not make one sophisticated for Section 4(2) private placement purposes.[26]

Sixth, irrespective of whether an offeree (or offeree representative) has financial acumen, "[s]ophistication is not a substitute for access to the [type of] information that a registration statement would disclose."[27] In short, if offerees have not received the type of information that registration would elicit, they cannot bring any alleged "sophistication" to bear in deciding whether or not to

---

[22] *Swensen v. Engelstad,* 626 F.2d 421, 425–426 (5th Cir. 1980); *see Mark v. FSC Securities Corp.,* 870 F.2d 331, 334 (6th Cir. 1989).

[23] *See Ralson Purina,* 346 U.S. at 125.

[24] The SEC has issued no-action letters in this context. *See supra* § 3.04[B], *infra* § 3.08; *see also* Cohn, *Securities Markets for Small Issuers: The Barrier of Federal Solicitation and Advertising Prohibitions,* 38 U. Fla. L. Rev. 1 (1986).

[25] *See Livens v. William D. Witter, Inc.,* 374 F. Supp. 1104, 1110 (D. Mass. 1974); Schneider, *The Statutory Law of Private Placements,* 14 Rev. Sec. Reg. 870, 881 (1981).

[26] *See Doran v. Petroleum Management Corp.,* 545 F.2d 893, 903 (5th Cir. 1977). For a more relaxed standard, *see Acme Propane, Inc. v. Tenexco, Inc.,* 844 F.2d 1317, 1321 (7th Cir. 1988). The Rule 506 exemption is discussed *infra* § 3.06.

[27] *Doran,* 545 F.2d at 902; *see United States v. Custer Channel Wing Corp.,* 376 F.2d 675, 678 (4th Cir. 1967).

invest.[28] Hence, all offerees must be provided with the type of information (not necessarily identical) that would be contained in a registration statement or have access to such information.

Ascertaining which offerees have "access" to registration-type information may be problematic. Relevant factors include high level executive status in the enterprise, family ties, a privileged relationship based upon prior business dealings between the parties, and economic bargaining power that enables an offeree effectively to obtain the registration-type information.[29]

Moreover, some courts have looked to two additional factors in determining whether the Section 4(2) exemption has been perfected: the number of units offered and the size of the offering.[30] These factors, however, often are irrelevant. For example, the offer and sale by an issuer of one million corporate debentures for $500 million to five sophisticated institutional investors (such as insurance companies), having effective access to registration-type information, normally should be within the Section 4(2) private offering exemption.

Note that, with respect to Section 4(2) offerings, state regulation also applies. In addition, states have authority to prosecute or to provide redress for fraud. Interestingly, enactment of the National Securities Markets Improvement Act of 1996 preempts state regulation of SEC "rules or regulations issued under section 4(2)."[31] Nonetheless, states may continue to impose their own requirements for private offerings that are exempt under the statute itself (namely, the Section 4(2) *statutory* exemption).

§ 3.06   RULE 506 OF REGULATION D

As seen from the preceding discussion, perfecting a Section 4(2) exemption is no easy matter. In addition, the alleged vagueness of judicial decisions, setting forth relevant Section 4(2) criteria, resulted in the securities bar clamoring for an SEC "safe harbor" rule. In 1974, the Commission responded by adopting Rule 146. As stated by the SEC in a subsequent release:

> Section 4(2) of the Securities Act of 1933 provides that offers and sales of securities by an issuer not involving any public offering are exempt from the registration provisions of the Act. Rule 146 provides objective standards for determining when the exemption is available. The main conditions of the rule require that (1) there be no general advertising or soliciting in connection with the offering; (2) offers be made only to persons the issuer reasonably believes have the requisite knowledge and experience in financial and business matters or who can bear the economic risk; (3) sales be made only to persons as described above

---

[28] *See Hill York Corp. v. American International Franchises, Inc.*, 448 F.2d 680, 690 (5th Cir. 1971).

[29] *See Doran v. Petroleum Management Corp.*, 545 F.2d 893, 903 (5th Cir. 1977); Schneider, *supra* note 25, at 877.

[30] *See, e.g., SEC v. Continental Tobacco Co.*, 463 F.2d 137, 158 (5th Cir. 1978).

[31] *See* § 18(b)(4)(D) of the Securities Act, discussed *infra* § 3.06.

except that persons meeting the economic risk test must also have an offeree representative capable of providing the requisite knowledge and experience; (4) offerees have access to or be provided information comparable to that elicited through registration; (5) there be no more than 35 purchasers in the offering; and (6) reasonable care be taken to ensure that the securities are not resold in violation of the Act's registration provisions.[32]

Rule 146 was severely criticized by the securities bar. Indeed, the rule was viewed as more restrictive than the case law construing the Section 4(2) statutory exemption.[33] Responding to this criticism and in an effort to facilitate capital formation, the SEC promulgated Regulation D in 1982. Rule 506, one of the rules promulgated by the Commission pursuant to Regulation D, is a "safe harbor" to the Section 4(2) exemption and supersedes Rule 146. Compliance with Rule 506 thus may be viewed as an alternative method to perfect the Section 4(2) private offering exemption. Moreover, federal legislation enacted in 1996 preempts state regulation of Rule 506 offerings (but does not preempt Section 4(2) offerings).

Generally, Rule 506 is available to any issuer. There is no limit to the aggregate price of the securities offered. Although Rule 506 does not limit the number of offerees, no advertising or general solicitation is permitted under the rule. Hence, depending on the circumstances, offers to a large number of offerees may be viewed as general solicitation, resulting in loss of the exemption.[34] The number of nonaccredited purchasers is limited to thirty-five plus an unlimited number of accredited investors. If any of the purchasers are not accredited, then specified disclosure must be made to all nonaccredited purchasers (see chart in § 3.10). As addressed later, a substantial compliance standard applies to Rule 506 offerings (see § 3.07).

Unlike prior Rule 146, there is no requirement under Rule 506 that the issuer determine that the purchaser can bear the economic risk of the investment. Suitability determinations, however, must be made for all nonaccredited purchasers. Except for accredited investors, the issuer prior to sale must "reasonably believe" that each nonaccredited purchaser either alone or with his or her "purchaser" representative has such knowledge and experience in financial and business matters that he or she is capable of evaluating the merits and risks of the prospective investment. (See the Appendix for this chapter.) Moreover, the issuer must take certain actions to guard against resales (*e.g.*, obtaining purchaser investment letters) in order to help ensure that a "distribution" does not occur.[35] In addition, the issuer is required to provide written disclosure to all nonaccredited purchasers regarding limita-

---

[32] Securities Act Release No. 5913 (1978).

[33] *See, e.g., Woolf v. S.D. Cohen & Co.*, 515 F.2d 591, 612 n.14 (5th Cir. 1975), *vacated and remanded on other grounds*, 426 U.S. 944 (1976).

[34] *See supra* note 24 (and accompanying text), *infra* § 3.08.

[35] *See* Securities Act Release Nos. 6389 (1982), 6758 (1988); *supra* note 25 (and accompanying text). *See generally* J.W. Hicks, Limited Offering Exemptions: Regulation D (2006).

tions on resale.[36] And, as discussed in § 3.15, principles of "integration of offerings" generally apply to Regulation D offerings.

An important concept under Rule 506 (as well as under Rule 505) is that of an "accredited investor." Under Regulation D, accredited investors irrebuttably are deemed to have access to registration-type information and to possess investment sophistication. Under Rule 501, accredited investors include not only certain institutional investors but also "fat cat" individual investors. These persons include those whose net worth at the time of the purchase exceeds $1 million (including the value of one's residence) and those who had an individual income exceeding $200,000 in each of the two most recent years (or $300,000 joint income with one's spouse) and who reasonably anticipate such an income for the current year.[37] Significantly, in a Rule 505 or 506 offering involving accredited investors, there is no mandated delivery of information to such accredited investors as Regulation D irrebuttably presumes that these investors can fend for themselves.

It is noteworthy that Rule 506 expands the Section 4(2) private offering exemption in at least two ways. First, unlike Section 4(2) which applies to both offers and sales, Rule 506 focuses on purchaser (rather than offeree) qualification. Hence, for example, Rule 506, unlike Section 4(2), requires that only purchasers meet the sophistication standards. Second, institutions and purportedly wealthy individuals irrebuttably are deemed under Regulation D to be sophisticated and to have access to the type of information that a registration statement would provide. Case law under Section 4(2), particularly with respect to wealthy individual investors, disagrees with the SEC's position.[38]

Significantly, federal legislation enacted in 1996 preempts state regulation of offerings coming within Rule 506 (*see* Securities Act § 18(b)(4)(D)). States nonetheless may set forth notice filing requirements and collect fees with respect to such offerings. States also retain their authority to bring enforcement actions for fraudulent conduct in connection with such offerings. However, with respect to the requisite parameters of the Rule 506 exemption, once

---

[36] *See* Rule 502(d) of Regulation D.

[37] *See* SEC Releases, *supra* note 35. In 2007, the SEC proposed that an individual (with his or her spouse) having $750,000 in investments (not counting the value of one's personal residences and places of business) would also qualify as an accredited investor. *See* Securities Act Release No. 8828 (2007).

The monetary levels for accredited investor status have remained the same since Regulation D's adoption in 1982. In the Regulation D amendments proposed in 2007, the SEC set forth "a mechanism to adjust the dollar-amount thresholds in the definition of 'accredited investor' to reflect future inflation." Securities Act Release No. 8828 (2007). Thus far, the 2007 proposed Regulation D amendments have not been adopted by the SEC.

This author has criticized the SEC for not increasing these levels in view of inflation. One million dollars in 1982 is worth roughly $500,000 today. The Commission's inaction is detrimental to investor protection. *See* Steinberg, *The "Accredited" Individual Purchaser Under SEC Regulation D: Time to Up the Ante*, 29 Sec. Reg. L.J. 93 (2001).

[38] *See, e.g., Lawler v. Gilliam*, 569 F.2d 1283 (4th Cir. 1978). Note that in the SEC 2007 Release proposing amendments to Regulation D, the Commission stated that over 8% of U.S. households qualify as "accredited investors." *See* Securities Act Release No. 8828 (2007); *see also* Kripke, *Has the SEC Taken All the Dead Wood Out of Its Disclosure System?*, 38 Bus. Law. 833 (1983).

an issuer shows that it has met the requirements for this exemption, the states no longer have any role.

As discussed above, federal legislation enacted in 1996 (NSMIA) preempts state regulation of Rule 506 offerings. The question arises whether preemption is triggered upon a mere assertion that the subject offering was made pursuant to Rule 506 or that "something more" is required, such as a showing that the Rule 506 exemption indeed was perfected. A minority of courts broadly preempt state law regulation of Rule 506 offerings irrespective of whether the substantive requirements of Rule 506 actually were satisfied.[39] On the contrary, the only federal appellate court to address this question held that the Rule 506 exemption in fact must be met in order to preempt state regulation of such offerings.[40] Similarly, the Alabama Supreme Court in this context requires a subject defendant (such as the issuer) to submit evidence that the Rule 506 exemption was complied with before shifting the burden of proof to the plaintiff to show the existence of a genuine issue of material fact sufficient to preclude summary judgment.[41]

Irrespective of the Rule 506 exemption, Section 4(2) still is the key exemption in certain contexts. For example, under Rule 506, disclosure of specified information must be provided to all purchasers who are not accredited. On the other hand, Section 4(2) allows an offeree's access to the applicable information to substitute for the providing of such information. In view of the costs expended in supplying such information, particularly in offerings of relatively small financial amounts, Section 4(2) may provide an attractive alternative. However, with respect to offerings made pursuant to the Section 4(2) *statutory* exemption (unlike the Rule 506 exemption), the states may continue to impose their own requirements.[42]

---

[39] *See, e.g., Temple v. Gorman*, 201 F. Supp. 2d 1238 (S.D. Fla. 2002).

[40] *Brown v. Earthboard Sports USA, Inc.*, 481 F.3d 901, 910 (6th Cir. 2007) ("We now agree with those courts that have held that offerings must actually qualify for a valid federal securities registration exemption in order to enjoy NSMIA preemption."); *see Hamby v. Clearwater Concepts*, 428 F. Supp. 915, 921 (E.D. Ark. 2006) (stating that "the only way to assert preemption is to first show that an exemption from federal registration actually applies").

[41] *Buist v. Time Domain Corporation*, 926 So. 2d 290 (Ala. 2005); *see Risdall v. Brown-Wilbert, Inc.*, 753 N.W. 2d 723 (Minn. 2008) (holding that Rule 506 exemption must be met in order to preempt state registration exemption requirements). *See generally* Rapp & Berckmueller, *Testing the Limits of NSMIA Preemption: State Authority to Determine the Validity of Covered Securities and to Regulate Disclosure*, 63 Bus. Law. 809 (2008).

[42] Note that in 2007 the SEC proposed the adoption of a new exemption, Rule 507. The Commission stated:

> We propose to create a new exemption to the registration requirements of the Securities Act for offers and sales of securities to a new category of investors called "large accredited investors." The exemption would permit limited advertising of these offerings. Large accredited investors would consist of the same categories of entities and individuals that qualify for accredited investor status under existing Rule 506, but with significantly higher dollar-amount thresholds for investors subject to such thresholds. Legal entities that are considered accredited investors if their assets exceed $5 million would be required to have $10 million in investments to qualify as large accredited investors. Individuals generally would be required to own $2.5 million in investments or have annual income of $400,000 (or $600,000 with one's spouse) to qualify as large accredited investors, as compared to the current accredited investor standard of $1

§ 3.07   RULES 507 AND 508 — SUBSTANTIAL COMPLIANCE STANDARD AND FILING OF FORM D

After the SEC's adoption of Regulation D, additional criticism was heard. Two major points were: (1) the unduly technical requirement that the Form D must be filed with the Commission as a condition of a Regulation D exemption; and (2) the need for a "substantial compliance" standard so that minor and inadvertent errors would not result in loss of a Regulation D exemption. After consideration, the SEC responded to these assertions by adopting a "substantial compliance" standard in Rule 508 and by eliminating the Rule 507 disqualification provisions.

In adopting Rule 507, thereby deleting the Form D filing requirement as a condition to the pertinent Regulation D exemption, the Commission stated:

> The proposals to eliminate the Form D filing requirement as a condition to every Regulation D exemption and the Rule 507 disqualification provisions were favorably received by the public commenters. These revisions have been adopted without change. The Rule 503 requirement to file a Form D [electronically] within 15 days of the first sale of securities remains, but will no longer be a condition to the establishment of any exemption under Regulation D. Rule 507 will serve as a disqualification to the use of Regulation D for future transactions by any issuer, if it, or a predecessor or affiliate, has been enjoined by a court for violating the filing obligation established by Rule 503. The Commission has the authority to waive a disqualification upon a showing of good cause.[43]

In other words, the timely filing of the Form D with the SEC is not a condition for perfecting a Regulation D exemption. The issuer nonetheless is required to file a Form D electronically, and, if such issuer is enjoined for failing to file the Form D, the failure to do so acts as a disqualification for such issuer to use a Regulation D exemption in the future. In its discretion, the SEC may waive any such disqualification upon a showing of good cause.

---

million in net worth or annual income of $200,000 (or $300,000 with one's spouse). Legal entities that are not subject to dollar-amount thresholds to qualify as accredited investors, generally government-regulated entities, would not be subject to dollar-amount thresholds to qualify as large accredited investors.

Securities Act Release No. 8828 (2007). Thus far, the SEC has not adopted this proposed exemption. *See generally* J. W. Hicks, Limited Offering Exemptions: Regulation D (2008); Bagnell & Cannon, *The National Securities Markets Improvement Act of 1996: Summary and Discussion*, 25 Sec. Reg. L.J. 3 (1997); Donahue, *New Exemptions from Registration Requirements of the Securities Act of 1933: Regulation D*, 10 Sec. Reg. L.J. 235 (1982); Warren, *A Review of Regulation D: The Present Exemption Regimen for Limited Offerings Under the Securities Act of 1933*, 33 Am. U. L. Rev. 355 (1984); Sargent, *The New Regulation D: Deregulation, Federalism and the Dynamics of Regulatory Reform*, 68 Wash. U.L.Q. 225 (1990); Note, *Regulation D: Coherent Exemptions for Small Business Under the Securities Act of 1933*, 24 Wm. & Mary L. Rev. 121 (1982).

[43] Securities Act Release No. 6825 (1989). The electronic filing of the Form D was adopted by the SEC in Securities Act Release No. 8891 (2008).

As discussed above, the SEC promulgated a "substantial compliance" standard for offerings pursuant to the Rule 504–506 exemptions. As set forth by the Commission, the "substantial compliance" standard contained in Rule 508 may be explained as follows:

> Rule 508 provides that an exemption from the registration require-ments will be available for an offer or sale to a particular individual or entity, despite failure to comply with a requirement of Regulation D, if the requirement is not designed to protect specifically the complaining person; the failure to comply is insignificant to the offering as a whole; and there has been a good faith and reasonable attempt to comply with all requirements of the regulation. Rule 508 specifies that the provi-sions of Regulation D relating to general solicitation, the dollar limits of Rules 504 and 505 and the limits on non-accredited investors in Rules 505 and 506 are deemed significant to every offering and therefore not subject to the Rule 508 defense. Further, the rule specifies that any failure to comply with a provision of Regulation D is actionable by the Commission under the Securities Act.[44]

Accordingly, in order to invoke the Rule 508 substantial compliance defense in private litigation, the subject defendant must show that: *first*, the particular requirement is not intended to specifically protect the complainant (*e.g.*, a complainant who is an accredited investor who does not receive information that was required to be but was not provided to a nonaccredited purchaser); *second*, the compliance defect was not significant to the offering as a whole (*e.g.*, only one nonaccredited purchaser failed to receive the requisite information); *and third*, there was a good faith and reasonable effort to adhere to all of Regulation D's mandates (*e.g.*, despite implementing a reasonably effective procedure for compliance, a ministerial error resulted in one nonaccredited purchaser not being provided the requisite information). Nonetheless, even if the above three conditions are met, the substantial compliance defense may not be invoked if: (1) there is general solicitation (*e.g.*, one newspaper advertise-ment is placed for one day by the issuer in the locale's major newspaper); (2) the dollar limits in a Rule 504 or Rule 505 offering are violated (*e.g.*, in a Rule 505 offering $5,000,001 is raised); *or* (3) the number of nonaccredited purchasers in a Rule 505 or Rule 506 is exceeded (*e.g.*, in a Rule 506 offering, there are thirty-six nonaccredited purchasers). Moreover, irrespective of the foregoing, any Regulation D violation, no matter how technical, may result in the SEC bringing suit.[45]

§ 3.08   THE MEANING OF "GENERAL SOLICITATION"

In order to satisfy several of the exemptions from Securities Act registra-tion, there must not be any advertising or general solicitation. This ban on general solicitation is a necessary condition to such exemptions as those

---

[44] *Id.*

[45] *See* Sargent, *The New Regulation D: Deregulation, Federalism, and the Dynamics of Regulatory Reform*, 68 Wash. U.L.Q. 225 (1990).

provided by Section 4(2), Rule 505, Rule 506, and Section 4(6).[46] Note, moreover, that as discussed above, Rule 508 (substantial compliance) provides no defense for violation of the general solicitation prohibition in Regulation D offerings. Unfortunately, the meaning of general solicitation at times remains elusive. To gain a general understanding of what type of conduct violates the ban on general solicitation, such as under Rule 502(c) of Regulation D, a number of no-action letters issued by the SEC's Division of Corporate Finance are helpful.

According to the Commission, analysis of Rule 502(c) focuses on two separate inquiries:

> First, is the communication in question a general solicitation or general advertisement? Second, if it is, is it being used by the issuer or by someone on the issuer's behalf to offer or sell the securities? If either question can be answered in the negative, then the issuer will not be in violation of Rule 502(c).[47]

The former inquiry is generally regarded as the more difficult. In general, to avoid general solicitation in Regulation D offerings, the no-action letters issued by the SEC staff frequently require a *preexisting relationship* between the issuer (or its agents) and the prospective investors which is of some substance and duration or which allows the issuer to evaluate the prospective investor's financial standing and sophistication. Note that the number of prospective investors solicited is not controlling. However, it is apparent that certain conduct, such as the use of the media to offer securities, is prohibited by the general solicitation ban of Rule 502(c).[48]

The first no-action letter addressing general solicitation under Rule 502(c) was *Woodtrails-Seattle, Ltd.*,[49] wherein the SEC staff found that the mailing of written offers to 330 prospective investors who had previously invested with the issuer over the last three years did not constitute general solicitation. The staff reasoned that the general solicitation ban had not been violated because of the *preexisting relationships* between the general partner and the prospective investors, as evidenced by the general partner's determination that the proposed investment was suitable for each of the prospective investors.[50]

In the staff's view, a key basis underlying the preexisting relationship requirement is to aid the issuer in assessing investor suitability, namely, that a potential investor is capable of evaluating the merits and risks of a proposed investment prior to it being offered.[51] Nonetheless, even if a potential investor possesses some degree of financial sophistication and/or wealth, if no preexisting relationship exists between the potential investor and the issuer, the issuer

---

[46] For the circumstances where general solicitation is permitted in Rule 504 offerings, *see infra* § 3.09[B][1].

[47] Securities Act Release No. 6455 (1983).

[48] *Id.*

[49] *See Woodtrails-Seattle, Ltd.*, 1982 SEC No-Act. LEXIS 2662.

[50] *See id.* at *1–2.

[51] *See Mineral Lands Research & Marketing Corp.*, 1985 SEC No-Act. LEXIS 2811.

may not solicit such prospective investor without violating the general solicitation ban.[52]

Subsequent no-action letters issued by the SEC staff focus on the *substance* of the relationship between the issuer and the solicitees and the importance of a *"cooling-off"* period between the beginning of a substantive relationship and the point in time at which that investor may be solicited to invest in a particular offering. For example, in *E.F. Hutton & Co*,[53] and *Bateman Eichler, Hill Richards, Inc.*,[54] the staff addressed the use of "questionnaire" materials by broker-dealers to pre-qualify potential investors for future private offerings. These letters were generic questionnaires that were to provide relevant information for each potential client, including the respondent's personal financial circumstances and investment sophistication. Bateman Eichler also proposed to have an account executive follow up on the questionnaire's responses for the purpose of procuring additional financial information about the respondents.[55]

In addressing the use of questionnaires to establish a substantive preexisting relationship, the SEC staff stated in *E.F. Hutton* that "substantive relationships may be established with persons who provide satisfactory responses to questionnaires that provide [the broker-dealer] with sufficient information to evaluate the prospective offerees' sophistication and financial circumstances."[56] However, the staff believed that the responses to both the E.F. Hutton and Bateman Eichler questionnaires in fact were inadequate to determine the level of sophistication and financial circumstances of the prospective offerees.[57]

In light of the staff's position in *Woodtrails-Seattle, E.F. Hutton*, and *Bateman Eichler*, one may conclude that a "substantive" preexisting relationship may be established by showing that the subject party (such as a broker-dealer) was sufficiently aware of the potential investor's financial circumstances and sophistication because: (1) the potential investor had previously invested with the broker-dealer and the offeree's relationship with

---

[52] *See In the Matter of Kenman Corp. and Kenman Sec*, 1985 SEC LEXIS 1717, n. 6; *see also* Interpretive Release on Regulation D, Securities Act Release No. 33-6455, 1983 SEC LEXIS 2288, Q. 60 ("The mere fact that a solicitation is directed only to accredited investors will not mean that the solicitation is in compliance with Rule 502(c). [Rule 502(c)] relates to the nature of the offering, not the nature of the offerees.").

[53] *See E.F. Hutton & Co.*, 1985 SEC No-Act. 2917.

[54] *See Bateman Eichler, Hill Richards, Inc.*, 1985 SEC No-Act. 2918.

[55] *See id.* at *4–5.

[56] *E.F. Hutton, supra* note 53, at *1–2.

[57] Unfortunately, the SEC did not specifically explain why the E.F. Hutton and Bateman Eichler questionnaires were inadequate. *See E.F. Hutton, supra* note 53, at *2; *Bateman Eichler, supra* note 54, at *2. Furthermore, the SEC did not address the fact that Bateman Eichler account executives would follow up to receive additional information from the prospective offerees. *See id.* However, in reference to the E.F. Hutton Letter, a former Associate Director of the SEC Division of Corporation Finance suggested that "a form designed to establish sophistication for purposes of Rule 506 would generally be sufficient." McCoy & Aalbregtse, *Partnership Disclosure and Regulation D Developments*, Thirteenth Ann. Sec. Reg. Institute, U. Cal. S. D., Dec. 1985, at 6.

the broker-dealer had existed for some duration; or (2) the potential investor had been effectively pre-screened. It is important to note the distinction between the two situations: the former involves a relationship with a *previous* investor, while the latter involves a recently established relationship with a *new* customer. That is, a previous investor would be one who the issuer would have good reason to know was suited to invest in the proposed offering because the investor had similarly invested with the issuer in the past. This is distinct from a new customer whose financial background and sophistication is known by the issuer because of the prescreening process, thus enabling the issuer to determine that the proposed offering is a suitable investment for the new customer.

Of equal importance to the SEC staff in determining whether certain contact with *new* customers constitutes general solicitation is whether "sufficient time" elapsed between the pre-qualification of the new customer and the participation by the issuer or its agents in the particular offering under consideration.[58] This "cooling-off" period has been underscored in a number of no-action letters issued by the staff in determining whether the relationship between the broker-dealer and the customer is, in fact, "preexisting." For instance, the no-action letter issued in *H.B. Shaine & Co.*[59] illustrates the interplay between the "substantive" and "cooling-off" period requirements of the general solicitation ban set forth by the Commission, and provides an example of how broker-dealers can avoid violating the ban on general solicitation while still soliciting new investors for private offerings.

In *H.B. Shaine*, the broker-dealer intended to send pre-qualifying questionnaires to both established Shaine clients and individuals with whom Shaine had no previous relationship in order to determine which potential customers were accredited within the meaning of Regulation D or sophisticated within the meaning of Section 4(2) of the Securities Act (if the investor is accredited under Regulation D, it is presumed that such investor is sophisticated for purposes of Rule 506).[60] The H.B. Shaine questionnaire also sought other information to inform the broker-dealer about the respondent's ability to evaluate the risks and merits of potential offerings, including the respondent's own opinion about his or her ability to do so.[61] In response, the Commission stated:

> We understand that the proposed questionnaire is generic in nature and that sufficient time will have elapsed between the respondent's completion of the questionnaire and the completion or inception of any particular offering. The Division is of the view that the procedure outlined in your letter would establish a preexisting substantive relationship with a respondent provided that the respondent furnishes complete responses to the questionnaire. We take no position as to whether the information obtained from the questionnaire is sufficient

---

[58] *See E.F. Hutton, supra* note 53, at *1–2; *Bateman Eichler, supra* note 54, at *1–2.

[59] *See H. B. Shaine & Co., Inc.*, 1987 SEC No-Act. LEXIS 2004.

[60] *See id.* at *4.

[61] *See id.*

to form a reasonable basis for believing an individual to be accredited or sophisticated.[62]

This same analysis was extended to Internet solicitations in subsequent SEC staff no-action letters, such as the IPONET no-action letter.[63] In general, the IPONET letter provides an example of the SEC staff's position regarding general solicitation in private offerings. IPONET proposed the posting of private offerings in a password-protected page.[64] In order to receive a password to view the posted offerings, W.J. Gallagher & Co. (through the IPONET website) would "solicit individuals who meet the 'accredited investor' or sophisticated investor standards of Regulation D," as determined by a questionnaire to be completed on-line and verified by W. J. Gallagher & Co.[65] Once the investor receives its password, the "IPONET site will only allow an Accredited Investor access to those private offerings which are posted subsequent in time to the Accredited Investor qualification with IPONET."[66] First, because IPONET involves the use of an Internet website, it is clear that the number of potential investors that view the IPONET website plays no part in the determination of whether the ban on general solicitation has been violated. Second, in order to receive a password the potential investor must be sophisticated or accredited under Regulation D. This ensures that the Commission's underlying objective of the substantive preexisting relationship standard is met, i.e., the issuer is aware of the potential investor's financial circumstances and level of sophistication. Further, because the issuer must have adequate information to make that determination, the relationship between the potential investor and the issuer is considered to be "substantive." Finally, because the potential investor is not able to view any offerings that were initiated or under consideration at the time the potential investor was under pre-qualification review, the requisite "cooling-off" period is met and the relationship is considered "preexisting" according to the Commission.

Another key SEC staff no-action letter in the general solicitation context is *Lamp Technologies, Inc.*[67] There, a prospective subscriber through use of the Internet completed a questionnaire that enabled Lamp Technologies (which was engaged in the creation and maintenance of websites but did not provide investment advisory services) to have a reasonable basis for ascertaining whether the prospective subscriber was deemed an accredited investor. Upon

---

[62] *Id.* at *1. *But see Agristar Global Networks, Ltd.*, 2004 SEC No-Act. LEXIS 203 (staff declined no-action request when requester sought to create accredited investor database through use of generic questionnaire).

[63] *See IPONET*, 1996 SEC No-Act. LEXIS 642.

[64] *See id.* at *2.

[65] *Id.* at *7.

[66] *Id.* at *9.

[67] *Lamp Technologies, Inc.*, 1998 SEC No-Act. LEXIS 615, 1997 SEC No-Act. LEXIS 638. The private funds in *Lamp Technologies* were made available only on a quarterly basis. This persuaded the SEC staff that investors would not subscribe to the service with the objective of investing in a specific fund. Moreover, a subscriber could not invest in any posted fund for a thirty day period after such subscriber's qualification. *See* Killingsworth, *A History of General Solicitation Under the 1933 Act*, 33 Sec. Reg. L.J. 47 (2005).

being qualified, such subscriber was provided access to information relating to investing in certain private funds on Lamp Technologies' websites, including information relating to offerings posted prior to the subject accredited investor being granted access (which could be purchased after a thirty-day waiting period). Nonetheless, even though seemingly more expansive than the IPO-NET situation where investors could view only those offerings posted after their qualification review, the SEC staff granted the no-action request.

The second inquiry in the two-step analysis of what conduct falls within the scope of Rule 502(c) is whether the general solicitation is being used by the issuer or by someone on the issuer's behalf (*e.g.*, a broker-dealer) to offer or sell securities. This second inquiry can be broken into two elements: (1) by the issuer or by someone on the issuer's behalf; and (2) to offer or sell securities. Cases in which the use of general solicitation is "by the issuer" are often straightforward. In general, if a communication is in an issuer's name or such issuer's management solicits a potential investor, it is clearly "by the issuer." However, what is meant by Rule 502 (c)'s language "any person acting on [the issuer's] behalf" is more difficult to determine. The Commission apparently deems third party communications *not* on the issuer's behalf if the issuer has not influenced the content of the communication in any way and the communication bears no direct connection to a current or pending offer by the issuer.[68]

Focusing on the issue of whether a particular communication relates to an offer to sell securities,[69] the Commission staff takes the position that communications connected to a particular offering that occur after that offering has closed and have no "immediate or direct bearing on contemporaneous or subsequent offers or sales of securities" are not part of an offer or sale.[70] However, communications that occur before or during a particular offering require an analysis of the circumstances surrounding the communication to determine if an offer or sale of a security has occurred. For example, the "questionnaire" no-action letters discussed above did not constitute offers to sell securities because the questionnaires did not mention any specific offerings under consideration that were currently being offered.[71] However, in *Gerald F.*

---

[68] *See Richard Daniels*, 1984 SEC No-Act. LEXIS 2874 (SEC finding that proposed newsletter setting forth public information concerning all limited partnerships in Arizona, making no mention of any issuer or offerings, and prepared completely independent of contact with any issuer not in violation of the ban on general solicitation); *Tax Investment Information Corp.*, 1983 SEC No-Act. LEXIS 1737 (finding lack of facts concerning any issuer's connection with proposed newsletter analyzing Regulation D offerings in Louisiana to preclude SEC staff's judgment that proposed activity not general solicitation). *See generally* Martin & Parsons, *The Preexisting Relationship Doctrine Under Regulation D: A Rule Without Reason?*, 45 Wash. & Lee L. Rev. 1031, 1038–1039 (1988).

[69] *See* R. Haft, *supra* note 15, at § 3.05; L. Loss & J. Seligman, Securities Regulation, 1437–1445 (3d ed. 1995). *See generally* Daugherty, *Rethinking the Bank of General Solicitation*, 38 Emory L.J. 67, 115–123 (1989).

[70] *Alma Securities Corp.*, 1982 SEC No-Act. LEXIS 2647, *2.

[71] In *Bateman Eichler*, it was proposed that the account executives would not send any offering materials for at least 45 days following the "questionnaire" mailing. *See Bateman Eichler*, *supra* note 54, at *5.

Gerstenfeld,[72] the SEC found that an institutional advertisement relating to a syndicator that sold securities in private placements and invited potential investors to contact the syndicator for additional information to be general solicitation because "the primary purpose of the advertisement is to sell securities and to condition the market for future sales ? if the syndicator expects in the near future to offer and sell securities."[73] Hence, the analysis employed by the SEC staff in *Gerstenfeld* is similar to the approach used by the Commission to address "gun-jumping" concerns for unseasoned issuers in the pre-filing period of registration.[74]

§ 3.09   THE LIMITED OFFERING EXEMPTIONS

The statutory limited offering exemptions are contained in Sections 3(b) and 4(6) of the Securities Act. These exemptions reflect Congressional concern that small enterprises should not be unduly burdened in raising capital. Note, moreover, that Congress' enactment of Section 28 of the Securities Act in 1996 gives the SEC broad exemptive authority to create additional exemptions from registration. Generally with the exception of the "California" exemption,[75] the SEC thus far has declined to invoke this authority.

[A]   The Section 4(6) Exemption

Generally, Section 4(6) exempts from registration under the 1933 Act offers and sales by any issuer solely to one or more "accredited investors" if the total offering price does not exceed the amount permitted under Section 3(b) of the Act (currently $5 million). No advertising or public solicitation is permitted in connection with a Section 4(6) offering, and the issuer must file a notice of such sales made pursuant to the exemption with the SEC.[76]

[B]   The Section 3(b) Exemptions

Generally, Section 3(b) contains an exemption for small offerings, empowering the Commission to exempt from registration any offering of securities where the aggregate amount of such offering does not exceed $5,000,000. The most significant rules that the SEC has promulgated pursuant to this authority are Regulation A and Rules 504, 505, and 701. Note that although the National Securities Market Improvement Act of 1996 (NSMIA) preempts state regulation of Rule 506 offerings, state regulation continues to

---

[72] *Gerald F. Gerstenfeld,* 1985 SEC No-Act. LEXIS 2790.

[73] *Id.* at *2. Thus, in contrast to *Bateman Eichler,* the fact that investors could receive additional information concerning current or pending offers as soon as it was requested from the syndicator represented an "offer for securities" according to the SEC. *See* Killingsworth, *supra* note 67, at 68y70.

[74] *See* Chapter 4.

[75] *See infra* § 3.11. Note that the SEC relied upon Section 28 of the Securities Act in its proposed adoption of Rule 507. *See* Securities Act Release No. 8828 (2007). Thus far, this proposed exemption has not been adopted by the Commission.

[76] *See* Securities Act Release No. 6256 (1980).

apply to these exempt offerings under Section 3(b).

[1]   Rule 504

The SEC adopted Rule 504 to facilitate the capital raising needs for the small start-up company. The exemption is not available for investment companies and reporting entities under the Exchange Act (i.e. those registrants which must file periodic reports with the SEC). In a Rule 504 offering, the issuer need not determine whether the purchaser is sophisticated; nor does the issuer need to provide a purchaser representative for the unsophisticated. There are no specified federal disclosure requirements in a Rule 504 offering and there is no express limit on the number of offerees and purchasers. Generally, offerings made pursuant to the Rule 504 exemption during any twelve-month period have a ceiling of $1 million.[77]

In fact, the Rule 504 offering exemption permits the issuer to conduct, in essence, a "mini-public" offering where general solicitation is permitted and purchasers in such offerings acquire freely transferable securities. In order for general solicitation to be permitted and the securities acquired to be freely transferable, one of two conditions must be met:

- the offering is registered under a state law requiring public filing and delivery of a substantive disclosure document before sale. For sales to occur in a state that does not mandate such a disclosure document, the offering must be registered in another state with such a provision and the disclosure document filed in that state must be delivered to all purchasers before sale in both states; *or*
- the securities are issued under a state law exemption that permits general solicitation and general advertising so long as sales are made only to "accredited investors" as that term is defined in Regulation D.[78]

Where neither of these conditions is satisfied, Rule 504 prohibits advertising and general solicitation and deems the securities acquired restricted. Imposing these limitations, according to the SEC, was necessary in order to curb abuse of the Rule 504 exemption in the markets for "microcap" enterprises.[79]

---

[77] *See* Securities Act Release Nos. 6389 (1982), 6758 (1988).

[78] Securities Act Release No. 7644 (1999).

[79] *Id.* Offerings involving securities of microcap enterprises often are associated with low prices per share, limited public information, thin capitalization, and little, if any, analyst coverage. In the 1999 Release, the SEC stated:

Recent market innovations and technological changes, most notably, the Internet, have created the possibility of nationwide Rule 504 offerings for securities of non-reporting companies that were once thought to be sold locally.

In some cases, Rule 504 has been used in fraudulent schemes to make prearranged "sales" of securities under the Rule to nominees in states that do not have registration or prospectus delivery requirements. As a part of this arrangement, these securities are then placed with broker-dealers who use cold-calling techniques to sell the securities at ever-increasing prices to unknowing investors. When their inventory of shares is exhausted, these firms permit the artificial market demand created to collapse, and

Thus, except for the conditions set forth above, Rule 504 may be viewed as a blanket federal exemption from registration for offerings not exceeding $1 million. The SEC believes that the remedial provisions of the federal securities laws, in conjunction with state regulation, are sufficient protection in these smaller offerings.

[2]   Rule 505

Rule 505 provides any issuer that is not an investment company with an exemption from registration under Section 3(b) of the Securities Act for sales of securities to (what the issuer reasonably believes are) not more than thirty-five nonaccredited purchasers and to an unlimited number of accredited investors. In aggregation with other offerings made pursuant to exemptions available under Section 3(b) (or sold in violation of Section 5), an issuer pursuant to Rule 505 may raise up to $5 million during any twelve-month period. In a Rule 505 offering, general solicitation or advertising is prohibited and restrictions on resale apply. As in Rule 506 offerings, issuers under the Rule 505 exemption must provide written disclosure to all nonaccredited purchasers regarding limitations on resale (*see* Rule 502(d)).[80] And, as set forth in § 3.07, a substantial compliance standard applies to offerings made pursuant to the Rule 505 exemption.

The availability of the Rule 505 exemption is conditioned upon the disclosure of specified information to nonaccredited purchasers. Unlike Rule 506, however, the issuer need not make a determination that the purchaser is sophisticated. If unsophisticated, there is no requirement that the investor have a purchaser representative.[81] Finally, the Rule 505 exemption is unavailable to issuers that have engaged in certain misconduct ("bad boy" disqualifiers). For example, an issuer subject to an SEC injunction within the previous five years may not avail itself of the Rule 505 exemption.[82]

Note that today the Rule 505 exemption is not frequently used. The reason is that issuers prefer to seek the Rule 506 exemption where state regulation of the subject offering is preempted. In Rule 505 offerings, many states elect to impose additional requirements, such as, for example, that the purchase not

---

investors lose much, if not all, of their investment. This scheme is sometimes colloquially referred to as a "pump and dump."

See generally Bradford, *Securities Regulation and Small Business: Rule 504 and the Case for an Unconditional Exemption,* 5 J. Small & Emerging Bus. L. 1 (2001); Cohn, *The Impact of Securities Laws on Emerging Companies: Would the Wright Brothers Have Gotten Off the Ground?,* 3 J. Sm. & Emer. Bus. Law 315 (1999); Haas, *Small Issue Public Offerings Conducted Over the Internet: Are They "Suitable" for the Retail Investor?,* 72 S. Cal. L. Rev. 67 (1998).

[80] *See* Securities Act Release No. 6389 (1982).

[81] For further discussion on this point, see Friedman, *On Being Rich, Accredited, and Undiversified: The Lacunae in Contemporary Securities Regulation,* 47 Okla. L. Rev. 291 (1994); Warren, *A Review of Regulation D: The Present Exemption Regimen for Limited Offerings Under the Securities Act of 1933,* 33 Am. U. L. Rev. 355 (1984). *See also* Bradford, *Transaction Exemptions in the Securities Act of 1933: An Economic Analysis,* 45 Emory L.J. 591 (1996).

[82] For a complete listing of the disqualifiers, see Rule 262 of Regulation A, 17 C.F.R. § 230.262. In 2007, the SEC proposed the application of uniform disqualification provisions throughout Regulation D. *See* Securities Act Release No. 8828 (2007).

exceed ten percent of the investor's net worth.

[3] **Rule 701**

In 1988, the SEC adopted Rule 701 pursuant to Section 3(b) of the 1933 Act. In 1999, the Commission increased the monetary amount that may be raised under Rule 701 by invoking its exemptive authority under Section 28 of the Securities Act. Generally, Rule 701 provides an exemption from registration for offers and sales of securities for certain compensation benefit plans adopted for the participation of employees, officers, directors, consultants, and advisers of an eligible company. Rule 701's availability is limited due to that companies eligible to use the exemption must not be subject to the periodic reporting requirements of the Exchange Act. As a preliminary note to the rule makes clear, Rule 701 is designed to facilitate the issuance of securities for compensation. As a consequence, the rule does not exempt offers and sales which are intended to raise capital.[83]

So long as the offering is made solely to eligible purchasers, Rule 701 permits such offerings to be public in nature, thereby permitting general solicitation. In a Rule 701 offering, unless more than $5 million of securities are to be sold, there are no specific disclosure requirements.[84] Limitations on resales, however, do apply. The monetary amount of securities that can be offered and sold pursuant to Rule 701 during any twelve-month period is the greatest of the following:

(1) $1 million, (2) 15 percent of the company's total assets, or (3) 15% of the outstanding securities of the class of securities issued.[85]

Importantly, because of the exemption's compensatory (rather than capital raising) purpose, offerings made pursuant to Rule 701 are not aggregated with offerings made pursuant to the other Section 3(b) exemptions. Nor are the monetary ceilings for other offerings made pursuant to the other Section 3(b) exemptions affected by Rule 701 offers and sales. Moreover, "integration of offering" problems are minimized because Rule 701 "specifically state[s] that all offers and sales pursuant to its rubric are deemed to be a part of a single, discrete offering; consequently, Rule 701 transactions need not be integrated into any other offering made by the issuer or vice versa."[86]

---

[83] *See* Securities Act Release No. 6768 (1988). *See generally* Robbins, *Securities Offerings to Employees, Consultants, and Advisers Under Rule 701*, 31 Rev. Sec. & Comm. Reg. 51 (1998).

[84] Securities Act Release No. 7645 (1998); *see SEC v. Phan*, 500 F.3d 895 (9th Cir. 2007). Where sales exceed the $5 million threshold, the required disclosure consists of:
- a copy of the compensatory benefit plan or contract;
- a copy of the summary plan description required by the Employee Retirement Income Security Act of 1974 ("ERISA") or, if the plan is not subject to ERISA, a summary of the plan's material terms;
- risk factors associated with investment in the securities under the plan or agreement; and
- the financial statements required in an offering statement on Form 1-A under Regulation A.

[85] *Id.*

[86] For restrictions on resales regarding securities issued in Rule 701 offerings, see Chapter 6.

[4] Regulation A

In 1992, the SEC amended Regulation A in an effort to enhance capital formation by small business.[87] Although Regulation A is an exemption from registration for non-reporting companies, it in fact permits generalized interstate public offerings of up to $5 million during any 12-month period, including up to $1.5 million in non-issuer resales. The Regulation imposes no limit on the number of offerees or purchasers and authorizes the use of broker-dealers to advertise and distribute the securities. Purchasers of securities acquired in a Regulation A offering generally may resell such securities without being subject to restrictions on resale imposed by such SEC rules as 147 and 505–506. In addition, like Rule 508 in Regulation D, Regulation A contains a "substantial compliance" standard.

An offering pursuant to Regulation A may very much resemble a "mini-public" offering. Indeed, the filing with the SEC of an "offering statement" (like a registration statement in a registered offering) is required. There, however, are some important differences, including:

— Because Regulation A offerings are exempt from registration, there is no Section 11 liability (for materially false or misleading statements contained in the registration statement) and no requirement for the issuer to file with the SEC periodic reports under the Exchange Act.

— The Regulation A exemption is not available for any issuer if it or its affiliated persons, executive officers, or other like persons have been subject to certain discipline in the recent past, including a criminal conviction relating to the sale of securities and the imposition of an SEC injunction (see Rule 262 — "bad boy" disqualifications).

— Prior to conducting a Regulation A offering, a prospective issuer may "test the waters" for potential investor interest by means of oral and written communications.

— The information required to be contained in a Regulation A offering statement generally is not as extensive as that mandated in a registration statement. For example, a registration statement must contain audited financial statements.

— Unlike the Rule 505, 506, and 701 exemptions, purchasers in a Regulation A offering are not subject to limitations on resale.

A relatively frequent use of the Regulation A offering exemption is by privately-held (nonreporting) issuers for employee stock option and purchase plans. Note that this remains true in many circumstances even after the SEC's adoption of Rule 701 for the following reason: while stock purchased under the Rule 701 exemption is subject to limitations on resale, securities acquired

---

[87] Securities Act Release No. 6949 (1992). *See generally* Bradford, *Regulation A and the Integration Doctrine: The New Safe Harbor,* 55 Ohio St. L.J. 255 (1994); Campbell, *Regulation A: Small Business' Search for "A Moderate Capital,"* 31 Del. J. Corp. L. 77 (2006). Note that Regulation A also is available to certain Canadian companies.

pursuant to the Regulation A exemption are not restricted. As discussed in Chapter 6, limitations on resale may pose undue burdens upon those who wish to freely resell their stock into the market.

The state securities regulators have expressed grave reservations regarding the SEC's Regulation A amendments, particularly the "test the waters" provision. For example, one prominent state regulator opined that the SEC was "embarking on an attempt to facilitate the sale of the riskiest securities in the market to the least sophisticated of buyers" and predicted that the states would reject the SEC's amendments. Without such state cooperation, it is clear that any simplification of the federal requirements is illusory. Hence, because an issuer must perfect exemptions from both state and federal registration, the SEC small business initiatives will only become significant if a sufficient number of states adopt coordinated exemptive regulations.[88]

Nonetheless, a number of states have adopted modified versions of "testing the waters." Although generally not as broad as the SEC's Regulation A, these state versions provide some flexibility for assessing potential investor interest prior to incurring the major expenses associated with a public offering.[89]

§ 3.10 COMPARATIVE CHART

Given the complexity of the various requirements for perfecting the issuer transactional exemptions from registration discussed in §§ 3.05–3.09, the following chart may prove helpful. Remember, however, that the chart may simplify certain of the requirements. Reference should be made to the pertinent SEC rules, releases, and the preceding discussion in this chapter.

---

[88] *See* 24 Sec. Reg. & L. Rep. (BNA) 1139, 1297 (1992). *See generally* Campbell, *Blue Sky Laws and the Recent Congressional Preemption Failure*, 22 J. Corp. L. 175 (1997); Cohn and Yadley, *Capital Offense: The SEC's Continuing Failure to Address Small Business Financing Concerns*, 4 N.Y.U. J. Law & Bus. 1 (2007); Steinberg, *The Emergence of State Securities Laws: Partly Sunny Skies for Investors*, 62 U. Cin. L. Rev. 395 (1993).

[89] *See* Ariz. Rev. Stat. Ann. § 44-1845; 70 Pa. Cons. Stat. Ann. §§ 1-203, 1-205; NASAA Proposed Statement of Policy on Solicitation of Interest (Test the Waters), NASAA (CCH) ¶ 4141 (1993).

Chart of Selected Securities Act Exemptions

Item	Rule 504	Rule 505	Rule 506	Rule 701	Reg. A	§ 4(2)	§ 4(6)
Aggregate Offering Price Limitation	$1,000,000 (12 mos.)	$5,000,000 (12 mos.)	Unlimited	Depending on certain factors, at least $1,000,000 (12 mos.)	$5,000,000 (12 mos.)	Unlimited	$5,000,000
Number of investors	Unlimited	35 plus an unlimited number of accredited investors	35 plus an unlimited number of accredited investors	Unlimited but must be an eligible purchaser	Unlimited	Uncertain but evidently a finite number of offerees depending on the circumstances	An unlimited number of accredited investors only
Investor Qualification	None required	No sophistication requirements	Purchaser must be sophisticated (alone or with representative); accredited investors presumed to be qualified	Purchaser must be employee, officer, director, consultant or advisor of an eligible company who has acquired the securities as compensation	None required	Exact requirements uncertain; offeree must receive or have access to the type of information that registration would disclose; also, sophistication standards apply – offeree must be financially sophisticated (alone or with representative)	Accredited investors only
Commissions	Permitted	Permitted	Permitted	Permitted	Permitted	Permitted	Permitted
Limitations on Manner of Offering	General solicitation and advertising permitted if state registered or sold only to accredited purchasers	No general solicitation or advertising permitted	No general solicitation or advertising permitted	General solicitation and advertising permitted	General solicitation and advertising permitted	No general solicitation or advertising permitted	No general solicitation or advertising permitted
Limitations on Resale	Not restricted if state registered or sold only to accredited purchasers	Restricted	Restricted	Restricted	Not Restricted	Restricted	Restricted
Issuer Qualifications	Among others, no reporting or investment companies	No investment companies or issuers disqualified under Regulation A	None	No reporting companies	Among others, no reporting or investment companies; "bad boy" disqualifiers apply	None	None
Filing with SEC	Form D required but not as a condition of exemption	Form D required but not as a condition of exemption	Form D required but not as a condition of exemption	No notice of sales required	Filings required	No notice of sales required	Form 4(6) required
Information Requirements	No information specified	In either a Rule 505 or 506 offering, see SEC Rule 502(b) for information requirements	In either a Rule 505 or 506 offering, see SEC Rule 502(b) for information requirements	No information specified except if greater than $5 million sold	Information specified in Regulation A	Investors receive or have access to the type of information that registration would disclose	No information specified

§ 3.11   RULE 1001 — THE "CALIFORNIA" EXEMPTION

Showing its administrative flexibility, the SEC adopted Rule 1001 to provide a federal exemption from registration in order to coordinate with a California exemption from state registration for small business issuers. Rule 1001 exempts from registration "offers and sales up to $5,000,000 that are exempt from state qualification under paragraph (n) of Section 25102 of the California Corporations Code."[90] The Rule 1001 exemption was promulgated by the SEC under Section 3(b) of the Securities Act to enhance capital raising by small

---

[90] Securities Act Release 7285, [1996 Transfer Binder] Fed. Sec. L. Rep. (CCH) ¶ 85,803, at 88,807 (SEC 1996).

businesses, while seeking to maintain adequate investor protection. A closer look at the requirements of Rule 1001 reveals that this exemption is broader than the exemptions provided by Rules 505 and 506 of Regulation D.

California Section 25102(n) limits the exemption to issuers that are California corporations or other business entities that are formed under California law, including partnerships and trusts.[91] In addition, a non-California corporation may use the exemption if more than 50 percent of its outstanding voting securities are held by California residents and at least 50 percent of its property, payroll, and sales, as determined for state tax purposes, can be attributed to California.[92] The California exemption is not available to investment companies subject to the Investment Company Act of 1940.[93]

To perfect the exemption, an eligible issuer must be able to show that "sales of securities are made only to qualified purchasers or other persons the issuer reasonably believes, after reasonable inquiry, to be qualified purchasers."[94] Section 25102(n) sets forth its own definitions of qualified purchasers that are similar, but not the same as, accredited purchasers under Regulation D. Examples of qualified purchasers under the "California" exemption include:

- any person purchasing more than $150,000 of securities in the offering; or
- a natural person whose net worth exceeds $500,000, or a natural person whose net worth exceeds $250,000 if such purchaser's annual income exceeds $100,000 — in either case the transaction must involve:

    (a) only one-class voting stock (or preferred stock establishing the same voting rights),

    (b) an amount limited to no more than 10 percent of the purchaser's net worth, and

    (c) a purchaser able to protect his or her own interests (alone or with the guidance of a professional advisor).[95]

The solicitation permitted under California Section 25102(n) is less restrictive than that of Rules 505 and 506 of Regulation D (which prohibit general solicitation). An eligible issuer under Rule 1001 is permitted to "test the waters" by distributing to qualified and non-qualified purchasers a written general announcement that contains certain specified information.[96] The SEC

---

[91] See Cal. Corp. Code § 25102(n)(1).

[92] See Cal. Corp. Code §§ 25102(n)(1), 2115.

[93] See Cal. Corp. Code § 25102(n)(1).

[94] Cal. Corp. Code § 25102(n)(2).

[95] Securities Act Release, *supra* note 90, at 88,007–88,008.

[96] For example, such specified information includes:

    (i) The name of the issuer of the securities,

    (ii) The full title of the security to be raised, [and]

    (iii) The anticipated suitability standards for prospective purchasers.

Cal. Corp. Code § 25102(n)(5)(A). The issuer also has the option of providing additional information, such as the nature of the issuer's business, its geographic location, and/or the probable price range

has previously accepted this general announcement process in connection with a "mini-public" offering pursuant to a Regulation A exemption, discussed earlier in this chapter. However, telephone solicitation is specifically prohibited until it can be determined that the prospective purchaser is deemed qualified.[97] As a general rule, all offers, oral and written, are limited to qualified purchasers.[98]

The California exemption sets forth further requirements. For example, issuers are required to "provide certain purchasers who are natural persons a disclosure document as specified in [SEC] Rule 502 of Regulation D five days prior to any sale or commitment to purchase."[99] In addition, securities issued pursuant to the exemption are "restricted."[100] This resale restriction and the $5,000,000 offering limitation are the only two federal requirements that are imposed independent of California Section 25102(n).

The SEC has stated that any state enacting a transaction exemption similar to California's is eligible to receive the same exemption.[101] To date, the SEC has not formally received any request from a state other than California.[102]

§ 3.12   NASAA — MODEL ACCREDITED INVESTOR EXEMPTION

In an effort to stimulate capital formation for small companies and promote greater uniformity in state securities regulations, the North American Securities Administrators Association (NASAA)[103] approved the Model Accredited Investor Exemption. In those states in which the Accredited Investor Exemption is adopted, issuers may avoid state registration requirements if securities are sold only to persons "who are or the issuer reasonably believes are accredited investors."[104] The model exemption incorporates by reference the SEC definition of accredited purchaser set forth in Rule 501 of Regulation D. The model exemption is regarded as a simpler version of the "California Exemption" and the SEC's corresponding Rule 1001. Importantly, however, the SEC has not promulgated a federal exemption from registration that coordinates with NASAA's model exemption. Thus, issuers that rely on the model exemption to avoid state registration requirements must also register the offering under the federal securities laws or perfect a federal exemption (such as pursuant to the intrastate offering exemption — Section 3(a)(11) or

---

of the security being offered. *See* Cal. Corp. Code § 25102(n)(5)(B).

[97] *See* Cal. Corp. Code § 25102(n)(6).

[98] *See* Securities Act Release 7285, *supra* note 90, at 88,008.

[99] *Id.*

[100] 17 C.F.R. § 230.1001(c).

[101] *See* Securities Act Release 7285, *supra* note 90, at 88,009.

[102] *See id.*; *see also* Bradford, *The SEC's New Regulation CE Exemption: Federal-State Coordination Run Rampant*, 52 U. Miami L. Rev. 429 (1998); *infra* § 3.12.

[103] NASAA is a voluntary organization comprised of securities regulatory authorities of the fifty states, the Commonwealth of Puerto Rico, Guam, Mexico, and the provinces of Canada.

[104] Model Accredited Investor Exemption § A.

Rule 147 — or the Rule 504 limited offering exemption). Note, however, if ultimately adopted, SEC proposed Rule 507 (discussed in § 3.06 at n. 42) to a significant degree would coordinate with the NASAA model exemption.

In order to sell securities pursuant to NASAA's model exemption, the issuer must reasonably believe that the purchaser is accredited as defined in SEC Rule 501(a). For example, an issuer offering securities under the model exemption may sell such securities to any person that has a net worth (or the issuer reasonably believes has a net worth) at the time of purchase of $1 million or greater. In contrast, the California exemption requires sales to be made only to "qualified purchasers" which are distinguished from accredited investors under Regulation D. By utilizing the accredited investor definition promulgated by the SEC, the model exemption enhances federal-state uniformity in this respect.

The model exemption is not available to an issuer that is "in the development stage that either has no specific business plan or purpose or has indicated that its business plan is to engage in a merger or acquisition with an unidentified company or companies, or other entity or person."[105] In addition, subject to certain exceptions, the model exemption disqualifies an issuer from using the exemption if the issuer or any of its affiliated persons (such as an officer, director, or general partner) have been subject to certain disciplinary action ("bad boy" disqualifiers).[106] Similar to SEC Rules 505 and 506, restrictions on resale apply.[107]

Importantly, the model exemption allows the issuer to use a general advertisement to "test the waters" if such advertisement contains specified information mandated by the model exemption.[108] Note that an issuer is not

---

[105] Model Accredited Investor Exemption § B.

[106] Model Accredited Investor Exemption § D(1)(a)-(d). Hence, a "bad boy" disqualifier exists if such person is subject to, or has been in the last five years subject to, a state, federal or judicial order, judgment, or decree, or "has been convicted of any criminal offense in connection with the offer, purchase, or sale of security, or involving fraud or deceit." However, the model exemption lifts the disqualification of the issuer in any of the aforementioned situations if: (1) the subjected party is licensed or registered in the state in which the disqualifying order, judgment or decree was entered; (2) the court or regulatory agency issuing the order, judgment or decree waives the disqualification before any offer is made; or (3) the issuer demonstrates that, in the exercise of reasonable care, that it did not know of the existing disqualification. *See* Model Accredited Exemption § D(2)(a)-(c).

[107] Model Accredited Investor Exemption § C.

[108] *See* Model Accredited Investor Exemption § E(2)(a)-(f). Information required in the general advertisement includes:
  (a)   the name, address and telephone number of the issuer of the securities;
  (b)   the name, a brief description and price (if known) of any security to be issued;
  (c)   a brief description of the business of the issuer in 25 words or less;
  (d)   the type, number and aggregate amount of securities being offered;
  (e)   the name, address and telephone number of the person to contact for additional information; and
  (f)   a statement that:
      (i)   sales will only be made to accredited investors;
      (ii)   no money or other consideration is being solicited or will be accepted by way of this general announcement; and
      (iii) the securities have not been registered with or approved by any state securities agency or

required to use a general advertisement.[109] Similar to the California exemption, the permitted use of a general advertisement under the model exemption is a departure from the general solicitation ban imposed by Rules 505 and 506 of Regulation D. An issuer is not disqualified from using the model exemption should a non-accredited investor receive the general advertisement.[110]

In addition to the use of a general advertisement, an issuer under the model exemption has the option to provide additional information to offerees. Such additional information is to be provided pursuant to one of two delivery requirements. First, the model exemption allows the additional information to be delivered via "an electronic database that is restricted to persons who have been prequalified as accredited investors."[111] This approach appears consistent with the SEC staff's *IPONET* no-action letter,[112] wherein the staff agreed that prequalifying an investor as accredited and allowing a "cooling off" period between the potential investor's prequalification and the point in time in which that investor is offered a particular security creates a "substantive preexisting relationship" and therefore does not violate the ban on general solicitation imposed by Rules 505 and 506 of Regulation D, as well as Sections 4(2) and 4(6) of the Securities Act. Second, the issuer may deliver additional information after the issuer reasonably believes that the recipient of such additional information is an accredited investor.[113]

Finally, telephone solicitation is permitted if the issuer reasonably believes that the solicited investor is accredited prior to placing the call.[114] This provision grants to issuers considerable leeway to solicit investors under the model exemption. As of July 2008, 32 states have adopted the model exemption.[115]

§ 3.13   INTRASTATE OFFERINGS

Section 3(a)(11) of the Securities Act provides an exemption from registration with respect to "[a]ny security which is a part of an issue offered and sold only to persons resident within a single State or Territory, where the issuer of such security is a person resident and doing business, or, if a corporation, incorporated by and doing business within, such State or Territory." The rationale underlying the intrastate offering exemption is based on "the probability that investors in local enterprise will have adequate familiarity with [such enterprises] and an acknowledgment that [local] issuers will be relatively

---

the U.S. Securities and Exchange Commission and are being offered and sold pursuant to an exemption from registration.

[109] *See* Model Accredited Investor Exemption § E(1).

[110] *See* Model Accredited Investor Exemption § H.

[111] Model Accredited Investor Exemption § F(1).

[112] *See supra* § 3.08.

[113] *See* Model Accredited Investor Exemption § F(2).

[114] *See* Model Accredited Investor Exemption § G.

[115] *See* J.W. Hicks, Limited Offering Exemptions: Regulation D § 10:15 (2008) (stating that as of July 2008, 32 states have adopted the model exemption); *supra* § 3.08.

small and thus less able to bear the burden of federal registration,"[116] thereby leaving the respective states as the principal regulators in such offerings. In 1974, the SEC, in order to establish more definitive standards regarding the intrastate exemption, promulgated Rule 147 to serve as a safe harbor.[117] If the conditions of the rule have not been met, the party still may assert the availability of the Section 3(a)(11) statutory exemption. Unlike the exemption provided by Rule 147 and unlike those exemptions provided by Rules 504–506 of Regulation D as well as Section 4(2) of the Securities Act which are available only to the issuer, the Section 3(a)(11) exemption also may be used under certain circumstances by shareholders seeking to resell their stock.

[A]   The Section 3(a)(11) Exemption

The Section 3(a)(11) exemption, as well as the Section 3(a)(9) and Section 3(a)(10) exemptions (addressed in § 3.13 of this chapter), are categorized in the Securities Act as exempt securities rather than transactional exemptions from registration. In practical effect, however, these exemptions come into play only where there is a transaction which meets the criteria of the applicable exemption. For example, the Section 3(a)(11) exemption, concerning securities which are offered and sold pursuant to an intrastate offering, is invoked only where there is an offering which meets the exemptive requirements of the statute.

Generally, the principal issues that come into play concerning the Section 3(a)(11) exemption deal with the concepts of "resident," "doing business within the state," and restrictions on resale. For purposes of the statutory intrastate exemption, offers only can be made to persons "resident" in a single state or territory. An offer to a single nonresident evidently voids the exemption, thereby giving rise to liability if no other exemption is perfected. Moreover, the SEC historically has defined "residence" to be similar to that of "domicile" which looks to the state of mind of the offeree. This subjective standard has been criticized for its uncertainty.[118]

Second, under the Section 3(a)(11) exemption, the issuer must be a person resident and "doing business" within the state in which the offering takes place. From the statutory definition, it is clear that the issuer must be incorporated in that state. Generally, the term "doing business" has been interpreted to mean that a "substantial," though not necessarily "exclusive," portion of the issuer's business must be conducted in that state. How much business is sufficiently substantial to validate use of the exemption seems unclear.[119]

---

[116] Deaktor, *Integration of Securities Offerings*, 31 U. Fla. L. Rev. 465, 481 (1979).

[117] *See* Securities Act Release No. 5450 (1974). *See generally* Morrissey, *Think Globally, Act Locally: It's Time to Reform the Intrastate Exemption*, 20 Sec. Reg. L.J. 59 (1992).

[118] *See* Securities Act Release Nos. 4434 (1961), 5450 (1974); Thomforde, *Exemptions from SEC Registration for Small Businesses*, 47 Tenn. L. Rev. 1, 28–29 (1979).

[119] *See, e.g., Chapman v. Dunn*, 414 F.2d 153 (6th Cir. 1969); Thomforde, *supra* note 118, at 29.

With respect to restrictions on resale, a purchaser of securities offered under either the Section 3(a)(11) or Rule 147 exemption may resell without restriction to another bona fide resident of that state. For an offer or sale by a purchaser to a nonresident to be permitted, however, the issue of the securities offered must have "come to rest." While the SEC historically is said to have taken the position that a one-year holding period normally is necessary under Section 3(a)(11) before there is a resale to a nonresident,[120] courts may adopt a shorter resale period. In this regard, one court held that a seven-month holding period, although not within the Rule 147 safe harbor, nonetheless was of sufficient duration for Section 3(a)(11) purposes:

> The Court is of the opinion that the seven month period from the time of initial sale to the time of resale [to an out-of-state resident] is sufficient for the offering to come to rest. Plaintiffs argue that Rule 147 requires nine months before a resale can be made. The Court concludes that Rule 147 provides only a safe harbor [to the Section 3(a)(11) exemption]; compliance with [Rule 147's] provisions ensures that the SEC will take no action. But it does not follow that, as plaintiffs argue, that non-compliance necessarily means that the statute and its policies have been violated. . . . Accordingly, defendants have complied with Section 3(a)(11). . . .[121]

[B]   The Rule 147 Exemption

In an effort to minimize the uncertainty surrounding the scope of the Section 3(a)(11) intrastate exemption, the SEC promulgated Rule 147 as a safe harbor. In the release adopting Rule 147, the Commission stated:

> Section 3(a)(11) was intended to allow issuers with localized operations to sell securities as part of a plan of local financing. Congress apparently believed that a company whose operations are restricted to one area should be able to raise money from investors in the immediate vicinity without having to register the securities with a federal agency. In theory, the investors would be protected both by their proximity to the issuer and by state regulation. Rule 147 reflects this Congressional intent and is limited in its application to transactions where state regulation will be most effective. The Commission has consistently taken the position that the exemption applies only to local financing provided by local investors for local companies. To satisfy the exemption, the entire issue must be offered and sold exclusively to residents of the state in which the issuer is resident and doing business. An offer or sale of part of the issue to a single non-resident will destroy the exemption for the entire issue.[122]

---

[120] *See In re Brooklyn Manhattan Transit Corp.*, 1 S.E.C. 147 (1935); Thomforde, *supra* note 118, at 29–30.

[121] *Busch v. Carpenter*, [1984–1985 Transfer Binder] Fed. Sec. L. Rep. (CCH) ¶ 91,810 (D. Utah 1984).

[122] Securities Act Release No. 5450 (1974).

Rule 147 sets forth more objective criteria in defining the parameters of the intrastate exemption. Similar to Section 3(a)(11), Rule 147 has no monetary ceiling on the amount of funds that can be raised or on the number of offerees or purchasers. Offers and sales can only be made to residents of the state where the offering occurs. A single offering to a non-resident invalidates the exemption. Rule 147 defines "residence" to mean principal residence at the point in time that the offer and sale occur, thereby rejecting the subjective concept of "domicile."

With respect to the issuer's qualifications to use Rule 147, the enterprise must be incorporated or organized in the offering state and must be "doing business" within that state. The rule enumerates four specific criteria for defining the term "doing business within a state": (1) the enterprise must have its principal office within that state, (2) the enterprise must derive at least eighty percent of its gross revenues "from the operation of a business . . . or from the rendering of services within such state;" (3) the enterprise must have at least eighty percent of its assets situated within the state, and (4) the enterprise must use at least eighty percent of the funds raised by the offering for operations within the state.[123]

To come within Rule 147's safe harbor, while resales to residents can immediately be transacted, a period of nine months from the date of the last sale by the issuer must transpire before resales to non-residents are permitted. Issuers must take certain precautions to guard against illicit resales. These measures include disclosing in writing the resale limitations to all offerees, placing legends on the certificates describing the resale limitations, issuing stop transfer instructions to the transfer agent, and receiving a written representation from each purchaser declaring bona fide residence in the state of the offering.[124]

[C]   ALI Federal Securities Code

It has been asserted that the Section 3(a)(11) and Rule 147 intrastate exemptions are unduly restrictive. If so, criticism should be directed toward Congress and not the Commission which is bound by Section 3(a)(11)'s scope when adopting a safe harbor rule pursuant to that statute. The approach taken by the American Law Institute's (ALI) Federal Securities Code may be more appropriate. The ALI Code labels such offerings "local offerings" and does not confine them to a single state (§ 514). Section 514 of the ALI Code focuses solely on purchasers of securities rather than offerees. State lines under Section 514 no longer are necessarily controlling as the SEC is given authority, after evaluating economic characteristics and population, to define contiguous areas encompassing a number of states or a state and a contiguous foreign country. Moreover, Section 514 permits up to five percent of the securities in

---

[123] *Id.*; *see* Thomforde, *supra* note 118, at 31–32.

[124] *See* Rule 147(f), 17 C.F.R. § 230.147(f). Note that, pursuant to SEC staff no-action letters, sales to foreign citizens residing outside the United States will not destroy the exemption. *See, e.g., Scientific Manufacturing, Inc.*, [1983–1984 Transfer Binder] Fed. Sec. L. Rep. (CCH) ¶ 77,505 (SEC staff no-action letter 1983) (offering sold to Hong Kong and California residents).

such an offering to be sold to no more than five percent of all purchasers who neither work nor reside in the localized area.

Prior to consultation with and determination by the SEC to support the ALI Code, Section 514 permitted up to twenty percent of the securities in a "local offering" to be sold to no more than five percent of "non-local" purchasers. In view of the provision's objective of facilitating local financing for local business, the SEC believed that the percent of securities sold "non-locally" should be decreased. The change to five percent was subsequently made.

In 1980 the SEC announced its support for congressional enactment of the ALI Code, provided that revisions it sought and obtained from the ALI Reporter and his group of advisers were not significantly amended during the legislative process.[125] The ALI Code, however, has not been introduced in either the U.S. House of Representatives or the Senate and its prospects for enactment are dim.

§ 3.14   THE SECTION 3(a)(9) AND 3(a)(10) EXEMPTIONS

Section 3(a)(9) of the Securities Act exempts from the registration requirements certain bona fide recapitalizations, namely, "[a]ny security exchanged by the issuer with its existing security holders exclusively where no commission or other remuneration is paid or given directly or indirectly for soliciting such exchange." Section 3(a)(10) generally exempts from registration securities which are issued in exchange for bona fide legal claims, securities, or property interests when a court or other specified tribunal, after conducting an adversary proceeding on the transaction's fairness, grants such approval. Traditionally, the Section 3(a)(10) exemption has been invoked in three situations: (1) settlement of private lawsuits; (2) reorganization of insolvent business organizations outside of bankruptcy litigation; and (3) reorganization of solvent business organizations.

In a recent release, the SEC staff set forth the following conditions for compliance with the Section 3(a)(10) exemption:

[1]   The securities must be issued in exchange for securities, claims, or property interests; they cannot be offered for cash.

[2]   A court or authorized governmental entity must approve the fairness of the terms and conditions of the exchange.

[3]   The reviewing court or authorized governmental entity must:

[a]   find, before approving the transaction, that the terms and conditions of the exchange are fair to those to whom securities will be issued; and

[b]   be advised before the hearing that the issuer will rely on the Section 3(a)(10) exemption based on the court's or authorized governmental entity's approval of the transaction.

[4]   The court or authorized governmental entity must hold a hearing

---

[125] *See* Securities Act Release No. 6242 (1980); *see also* Morrissey, *supra* note 117.

before approving the fairness of the terms and conditions of the transaction.

[5] A governmental entity must be expressly authorized by law to hold the hearing, although it is not necessary that the law require the hearing.

[6] The fairness hearing must be open to everyone to whom securities would be issued in the proposed exchange.

[7] Adequate notice must be given to all those persons.

[8] There cannot be any improper impediments to the appearance by those persons at the hearing.[126]

While both the Section 3(a)(9) and 3(a)(10) exemptions reflect Congress' concern for the financially troubled enterprise which seeks internal readjustment without having to comply with the 1933 Act's costs of registration, an issuer may have a number of motives for utilizing these exemptions. Indeed, the financial status of an issuer does not affect the availability of these exemptions. For example, in practice the Section 3(a)(10) exemption "has been availed of almost exclusively by financially sound issuers involved in reorganization or other exchanges for a variety of legitimate ongoing business purposes."[127]

§ 3.15 INTEGRATION OF OFFERINGS

Under the concept of integration of offerings, what apparently may seem to be separate offerings instead are construed as one integrated offering. Because of the fairly distinct requirements for each exemption, otherwise exempt offerings are unlikely to qualify for an exemption once they are integrated,

---

[126] Staff Legal Bulletin 3A (CF) (issued by the SEC Division of Corporation Finance), Fed. Sec. L. Rep. (CCH) ¶ 60,003 (2008). With respect to the resale status of securities received pursuant to the Section 3(a)(10) exemption, the SEC staff stated:

[I]t is the Division's view that securities received in a Rule 145(a) transaction not involving a shell company that was exempt under Section 3(a)(10) may generally be resold without regard to Rule 144 if the sellers are not affiliates of the issuer of the Section 3(a)(10) securities and have not been affiliates within 90 days of the date of the Section 3(a)(10)-exempt transaction, as such securities would not constitute "restricted securities" within the meaning of Rule 144(a)(3) under the Securities Act. In the event that the securities are held by affiliates of the issuer, those holders may be able to resell the securities in accordance with the provisions of Rule 144.

When a Rule 145(a) transaction is exempt from Securities Act registration under Section 3(a)(10) and any party to that transaction is a shell company, other than a business combination related shell company, then the Rule 145(c) and (d) resale limitations apply to any party to that transaction (other than the issuer of the Section 3(a)(10) securities) and to any person who is an affiliate of such party at the time such transaction is submitted for vote or consent. In those situations, holders who are deemed to be underwriters under Rule 145(c) may resell their securities without registration in the manner permitted by Rule 145(d).

Id. See generally J. W. Hicks, Exempted Transactions Under the Securities Act of 1933 ¶ 3.02 (rev. ed. 2008); Glanzer, Schiffman & Packman, *Settlement of Securities Litigation Through the Issuance of Securities Without Registration: The Use of Section 3(a)(10) in SEC Enforcement Proceedings*, 50 Fordham L. Rev. 533 (1981); Mann, *The Section 3(a)(10) Exemption: Recent Interpretations*, 22 UCLA L. Rev. 1247 (1975).

[127] Ash, *Reorganizations and Other Exchanges Under Section 3(a)(10) of the Securities Act of 1933*, 75 Nw. U. L. Rev. 1, 10 (1980); *see* Hicks, *Recapitalization Under Section 3(a)(9) of the Securities Act of 1933*, 61 Va. L. Rev. 1057, 1060–1061 (1975).

thereby resulting in a violation of the Securities Act's registration requirements. Moreover, if a purported exempt offering is integrated with a registered
offering, the exemption will be destroyed, again resulting in liability.

In determining whether offers and/or sales should be integrated, the SEC
has set forth a five factor analysis:

(1)   Whether the offerings are part of a single plan of financing;
(2)   Whether the offerings involve issuance of the same class of securities;
(3)   Whether the offerings have been made at or about the same time;
(4)   Whether the same type of consideration is received; and
(5)   Whether the offerings are made for the same general purposes.[128]

The SEC and the courts continue to apply this analysis.[129]

In order to provide greater certainty for issuers, the SEC, pursuant to its
rulemaking authority, has adopted integration "safe harbor" rules. For example, Rule 502(a) of Regulation D in part provides:

> Offers and sales that are made more than six months before the
> start of a Regulation D offering or are made more than six months
> after completion of a Regulation D offering will not be considered part
> of that Regulation D offering, so long as during those six month periods
> there are no offers or sales of securities by or for the issuer that are of
> the same or a similar class as those offered or sold under Regulation D.
> . . .[130]

Rule 147(b)(2), as another example, has a similar "safe harbor" from
integration with respect to the intrastate offering exemption.

Remember that Rules 147(b)(2) and 502(a) are "safe harbor" provisions. If
the issuer engages in offers or sales during the six month period prior to
commencement or after completion of the purportedly exempt offerings, the
five factor analysis outlined above will be applied to determine whether the
apparently separate offerings should be integrated.[131]

SEC Rules 152 and 155 also are relevant in the integration of offering
setting. Rule 152 provides that the Section 4(2) exemption is still available
"although subsequently . . . the issuer decides to make a public offering and/or

---

[128] Securities Act Release No. 4552 (1962).

[129] *See, e.g., Donohoe v. Consolidated Operating & Production Corporation*, 982 F.2d 1130 (7th
Cir. 1992); *SEC v. Murphy*, 626 F.2d 633 (9th Cir. 1980).

[130] See also the discussion of integration of offerings with respect to Rule 701, *supra*
§ 3.09[B][3]. In 2007, the SEC proposed to decrease this six-month "safe harbor" period to 90 days.
See Securities Act Release No. 8828 (2007).

[131] *See generally* Bradford, *Regulation A and the Integration Doctrine: The New Safe Harbor*,
55 Ohio St. L.J. 255 (1994); Deaktor, *Integration of Offerings*, 31 U. Fla. L. Rev. 465 (1979);
Morrissey, *Integration of Securities Offerings — The ABA's "Indiscrete" Proposal*, 26 Ariz. L.
Rev. 41 (1984); Shapiro & Sachs, *Integration Under the Securities Act: Once an Exemption, Not
Always* . . . , 31 Md. L. Rev. 3 (1971); Wallace, *Integration of Securities Offerings: Obstacles to
Capital Formation Remain for Small Businesses*, 45 Wash. & Lee L. Rev. 883 (1988).

files a registration statement."[132] More recently, the SEC adopted Rule 155 which provides under certain circumstances "safe harbors" from Securities Act integration "for a registered offering following an abandoned private offering, or a private offering following an abandoned registered offering."[133] In the Rule 155 adopting release, the SEC stated:

> The new integration safe harbors that we adopt today as new Rule 155 provide clarity and certainty regarding two common situations, and do not otherwise affect traditional integration analyses. Under Rule 155, we provide conditions under which an issuer that begins a private offering but sells no securities will be able to abandon it and begin a registered offering. Any private offering that relies on this integration safe harbor will need to satisfy the conditions of a private offering exemption, so that the private offering is bona fide. In addition, the issuer and any person acting on its behalf will need to terminate all offering activity with respect to the private offering. Any prospectus filed as part of the registration statement will need to include disclosure regarding abandonment of the private offering. The issuer also will need to wait 30 days after abandoning the private offering before filing the registration statement unless securities were offered in the private offering only to persons who were (or who the issuer reasonably believes were) accredited investors or sophisticated.
>
> New Rule 155 also provides an integration safe harbor that will permit an issuer that started a registered offering to withdraw the registration statement before any securities are sold and then begin a private offering. To use the safe harbor, the issuer and any person acting on its behalf will need to wait 30 days after the effective date of withdrawal of the registration statement before commencing the private offering. The issuer must provide each offeree in the private offering with information concerning withdrawal of the registration statement, the fact that the private offering is unregistered and the legal implication of its unregistered status. In addition, any disclosure document used in the private offering must disclose any changes in the issuer's business or financial condition that occurred after the issuer filed the registration statement that are material to the investment decision in the private offering.[134]

---

[132] Securities Act Release No. 305 (1935); *see* Securities Act Release No. 4761 (1965); *In re JAI*, Inc., [1990 Transfer Binder] Fed. Sec. L. Rep. (CCH) ¶ 79,505 (SEC staff no-action letter 1990) (applying Rule 152, SEC staff states that the making of a registered offering after an otherwise exempt private offering under Section 4(2) would not nullify the Section 4(2) exemption); Johnson & Patterson, *The Reincarnation of Rule 152: False Hope on the Integration Front*, 46 Wash. & Lee L. Rev. 539 (1989); Securities Act Release No. 4761 (1965).

[133] Securities Act Release No. 7943 (2001).

[134] *Id.* Note that Rule 152 remains viable after the adoption of Rule 155. As stated by Professor Hicks:

> An important exception to the integration doctrine is found in Rule 152. . . . Rule 152 applies to an issuer that sells securities privately under Section 4(2) and then shortly thereafter sells additional securities in a public offering. Technically, Rule 152 is only

As a final point, the principle of *integration* of offerings must be distinguished from that of *aggregation* of offering price used for purposes of the Section 3(b) exemptions. The following example provided by the SEC serves aptly to distinguish the two concepts:

> The Commission is aware that in computing the aggregate offering price [for offerings made pursuant to the Section 3(b) exemptions] issuers frequently misunderstand the interaction of the concepts of aggregation and integration as applicable under Rules 504(b)(2)(i) and 505(b)(2)(i). Aggregation is the principle by which an issuer determines the dollar worth of exempt sales available directly under Section 3(b) of the Securities Act. Integration is a principle under which an issuer determines overall characteristics of its offering. The following examples illustrate the application of these concepts. An issuer that has conducted an offering under Rule 505 in May [2008] must aggregate the proceeds from that offering with the proceeds of a Rule 505 offering conducted in December [2008]. [On the other hand,] if the May offering had been under Rule 506 [which is a "safe harbor" to the § 4(2) exemption], it would not need to be aggregated with the December offering. In either case, the May offering should be exempt from principles of integration by virtue of the safe harbor provision in Rule 502(a). If a Rule 506 offering had been conducted in July [2008], the integration safe harbor would not be available as to a subsequent Rule 505 offering in December. Although the proceeds from the July [Rule] 506 offering would not be added to the December [Rule] 505 aggregate offering price under aggregation principles, they would have to be included if the two offerings [were] integrated. Assuming the two offerings were integrated, then the issuer would have to evaluate all characteristics of the combined transactions, e.g., number of investors, aggregate offering price, etc., when determining the availability of an exemption.[135]

§ 3.16   STATE "BLUE SKY" LAW EXEMPTIONS

With certain exceptions and subject to the preemptive provisions of the National Securities Markets Improvement Act of 1996 (NSMIA), unless an exemption from state registration is perfected, any offer or sale within a particular state must be registered. The result is that perfecting a federal exemption from registration frequently is only half the battle. Exemptions often must be found on the state level in any state where the security is offered or sold.

Until recently, there was little uniformity between the federal and state exemption framework. The promulgation of the Uniform Limited Offering

---

applicable where the issuer's decision to make a public offering is formed after the completion of the Section 4(2) offering. . . .

J.W. Hicks, Limited Offering Exemptions: Regulation D § 3:9 (2008); *see* Jones, *The Doctrine of Securities Act "Integration,"* 29 Sec. Reg. L.J. 320 (2001).

[135] Securities Act Release No. 6389 (1982). For further discussion, *see supra* §§ 3.05–3.10.

Exemption by the North American Securities Administrators Association (NASAA) and its subsequent adoption (in whole or substantial part) by several states eased this uniformity problem. With qualifications, the Uniform Limited Offering Exemption exempts offerings sold in compliance with Rules 501–503 and 505 of SEC Regulation D.[136] In certain respects, however, the NASAA Exemption is more protective of investor interests than Regulation D. For example, investor sophistication or suitability standards may apply in Rule 505 offerings (unlike the SEC's 505).

After the adoption of Regulation D and ULOE, corporations, financial intermediaries and their legal counsel voiced their criticisms. Two of the more significant points concerned the unnecessarily technical requirement that the Form D be filed with the applicable agency as a condition of the exemption and the desirability for the adoption of a "substantial compliance" standard so that minor and inadvertent mistakes would not cause the exemption to be lost. The Commission's release responding to the foregoing criticisms was viewed by a number of state administrators as overly broad. For example, the Maryland Securities Division registered its strong opposition to the SEC proposals. In addition to viewing the Form D filing requirement as critical to its investigatory efforts, Maryland perceived that the availability to issuers and related parties of a "good faith and reasonable defense" would be unduly burdensome to its overall enforcement program.[137]

Due to the input by NASAA and the individual states, the Regulation D and ULOE changes were more modest than otherwise would have occurred. Pursuant to SEC Rule 507, the timely filing of the Form D is no longer a condition for perfecting a Regulation D exemption. The issuer nonetheless is required to file a Form D, and if such issuer is enjoined for failing to file the Form D, the failure to do so acts as a disqualification for such issuer to use a Regulation D exemption in the future. In its discretion, the SEC may waive any such disqualification upon a showing of good cause.[138]

A substantial compliance standard was added to both Regulation D and ULOE. The standard's reach, however, is far less encompassing than proponents had advocated. As stated by the Commission in the 1989 adopting release:

> Rule 508 [of Regulation D] provides that an exemption from the registration requirements will be available for an offer or sale to a particular individual or entity, despite failure to comply with a requirement of Regulation D, if the requirement is not designed to protect specifically the complaining person; the failure to comply is insignificant to the offering as a whole; and there has been a good faith and reasonable attempt to comply with all requirements of the regulation.

---

[136] Securities Act Release No. 6389 (1982). Rule 504, discussed *supra* § 3.09[B][1], leaves solely to the individual states the authority to prescribe disclosure of specified information and certain other requirements with respect to offerings made within the parameters of that exemption. State regulation of offerings under Rule 506 generally is preempted by the 1996 federal legislation.

[137] Letter from Ellyn L. Brown, Esq., Maryland Securities Commissioner, to the SEC (May 12, 1988) (on file with the author).

[138] *See supra* § 3.07.

Rule 508 specifies that the provisions of Regulation D relating to general solicitation, the dollar limits of Rules 504 and 505 and the limits on non-accredited investors in Rules 505 and 506 are deemed significant to every offering and therefore not subject to the Rule 508 defense.[139]

Nonetheless, both Rule 508 and the ULOE counterpart provide that such "inadvertent" failures to comply are subject to enforcement actions by the SEC and the respective states.[140]

Critics assert that, as adopted, the substantial compliance defense leaves unsettled far too many questions and subjects issuers and their associates to a continuing saga of astronomical liability exposure. When merely technical rather than fraud violations are at issue, one may contend that public policy should call for greater flexibility in the enforcement regimen, particularly given our country's need to foster capital-raising activities. Moreover, the failure to include matters relating to general solicitation within the substantial compliance defense without clearly delineating what constitutes such conduct plays havoc upon all those associated with the raising of capital in the private markets.[141]

The above points, although meritorious, did not sway a number of the state administrators who viewed their primary mission as safeguarding the interests of unsophisticated investors in their respective jurisdictions. Faced with this situation, the SEC elected to coordinate the Regulation D changes with NASAA, presumably due to the Commission's perception that the states' acquiescence was necessary to make the exemption process function in an efficient manner.[142]

The attitude of certain states in favor of strong investor protection provisions is intriguing when compared to the "race to the bottom" approach[143] taken by some of these very same states under the applicable corporation laws. Perhaps one response is that the state securities laws are designed in part to protect the individual investor against so-called speculative shady promoters while enabling corporation laws favoring management hopefully will induce publicly-held companies to incorporate within the respective states, thereby

---

[139] Securities Act Release No. 6825 (1989).

[140] Rule 508(b) of Regulation D; Uniform Limited Offering Exemption, 33 NASAA Rep. (CCH) ¶ 6201, at 6104 (1989); *see supra* § 3.07.

[141] *See* Cohn, *Securities Markets for Small Issuers: The Barriers of Federal Solicitation and Advertising Prohibitions*, 38 U. Fla. L. Rev. 1 (1986); Daugherty, *Rethinking the Ban on General Solicitation*, 38 Emory L.J. 69 (1989); Martin & Parsons, *The Preexisting Relationship Doctrine Under Regulation D: A Rule Without Reason?*, 45 Wash. & Lee L. Rev. 1031 (1988); Sargent, *The New Regulation D: Deregulation, Federalism and the Dynamics of Regulatory Reform*, 68 Wash. U.L.Q. 225 (1990).

[142] *See generally* Maynard, *The Uniform Limited Offering Exemption: How "Uniform" is "Uniform?" — An Evaluation and Critique of the ULOE*, 36 Emory L.J. 357 (1987); Rossi, *The Uniform Limited Offering Exemption*, 16 Rev. Sec. Reg. 875 (1983); Sargent, *Blue Sky Law: The SCOR Solution*, 18 Sec. Reg. L.J. 93 (1990); sources cited *supra* note 141.

[143] *See, e.g.*, Cary, *Federalism and Corporate Law: Reflection Upon Delaware*, 83 Yale L.J. 663 (1974).

bringing in a welcome source of revenues in the form of franchise fees.

This supposed state-SEC accommodation did not entirely persuade the U.S. Congress. In an effort to reduce overlapping regulation and simplify the regulatory framework, Congress enacted the National Securities Markets Improvement Act of 1996 (NSMIA). This reallocation of regulatory authority, including the preemption of state regulation of certain exempt offerings, and in particular Rule 506 offerings, represents a major change in the federal-state relationship in the securities law setting.[144] In addition to preempting Rule 506 offerings, the 1996 federal legislation defines the following as "covered" securities, thereby providing the SEC with exclusive authority over the registration of such securities:

> (1) securities issued by investment companies registered with the Commission under the Investment Company Act of 1940 (Investment Company Act); (2) securities offered or sold to "qualified purchasers," as that term will be defined by Commission rule; (3) all securities that are listed or authorized for listing on the New York Stock Exchange (NYSE), the American Stock Exchange (AMEX), or quoted on the Nasdaq National Market System (NMS), or listed or authorized for listing on any other national securities exchange that the Commission finds has listing standards that are "substantially similar" to these exchanges or Nasdaq, including securities of an issuer that rank senior to listed securities, and (4) securities issued in connection with certain specified transactions that are exempt under the Securities Act.[145]

§ 3.17   EXTRATERRITORIAL APPLICATION — REGULATION S

Although not an exemption from Securities Act registration, adherence to the provisions of Regulation S signifies that the registration mandates of Section 5 are not applicable. Regulation S represents an attempt by the SEC to clarify the extraterritorial application of the 1933 Act's registration requirements.[146] This effort seeks to ease undue regulatory burdens on issuers and those seeking to resell, thereby fostering a more efficient international

---

[144] *See* Bagnell & Cannon, *The National Securities Markets Improvement Act of 1996: Summary and Discussion*, 25 Sec. Reg. L.J. 3 (1997).

[145] *Id.* at 5–6; *see* Campbell, *The Impact of NSMIA on Small Issuers*, 53 Bus. Law. 575 (1998); Friedman, *The Impact of NSMIA on State Regulation of Broker-Dealers and Investment Advisers*, 53 Bus. Law. 511 (1998); Miller & O'Brien, *The National Securities Markets Improvement Act of 1996*, 30 Rev. Sec. & Comm. Reg. 23 (1997); Sargent, *The National Securities Improvement Act — One Year Later*, 53 Bus. Law. 507 (1998).

Pursuant to the 1996 legislation, the SEC has authority to preempt state regulation with respect to offerings made to "qualified purchasers" who, due to their wealth and sophistication, are deemed not to need state registration. *See* Securities Act § 18(b)(3). *See generally* Campbell, *Blue Sky Laws and the Recent Congressional Preemption Failure*, 22 J. Corp. L. 175 (1997).

[146] *See* Securities Act Release No. 6863 (1990). The adoption of Regulation S superseded Securities Act Release No. 4708 (1964) and the interpretive and no-action letters relating thereto.

securities market.[147]

In Regulation S, the SEC embraced a territorial approach to the extraterritorial application of registration under the Securities Act. This approach is based on the notion that the registration requirements of the Securities Act are intended to protect the U.S. capital markets and all investors in such markets, whether U.S. residents or foreign nationals. Regulation S represents a change in emphasis, from attempting to protect U.S. persons irrespective of where they are located, to protecting the integrity of the U.S. capital markets. For registration purposes, the Commission decided to rely upon the laws in the jurisdictions in which the transactions occur rather than the U.S. Securities Act. The Commission stated: "The territorial approach recognizes the primacy of the laws in which a market is located. As investors choose their markets, they choose the laws and regulations applicable in such markets." Adherence to this approach is premised on the principles of comity and the expectations of participants in the global markets. The territorial approach thus forms the basis of the Regulation S regulatory framework.[148]

It bears emphasis that Regulation S is directed at Securities Act registration. The extraterritorial application of the U.S. securities laws has a broader reach with respect to the antifraud provisions, such as Section 10(b) of the Exchange Act.[149]

Regulation S comprises five rules: Rules 901, 902, 903, 904 and 905. Rule 901 contains a general statement that reflects the SEC's new territorial approach. Rule 901 states that only offers and sales of securities inside the United States are subject to Section 5. This statement reflects a shift from previous SEC policy (namely, that Section 5 was to protect all U.S. citizens no matter where such persons lived or invested) to a basically geographical approach under Regulation S.[150]

The primary inquiry under the new regulatory scheme, as stated in Rule 901, is whether the offer and sale of securities occurs "outside the United States." If the offer and sale are outside the United States within the meaning of Rule 901, the registration provisions of Section 5 are not applicable; if the offer or sale occurs within the United States, the registration provisions (absent the perfection of an exemption) are applicable. However, determining whether an

---

[147] *See* Wolff, *Offshore Distributions Under the Securities Act of 1933: An Analysis of Regulation S*, 23 L. & Pol'y Int'l Bus. 101 (1991–1992).

[148] *See* Securities Act Release No. 6863 (1990); Thalacker, *Reproposed Regulation S*, 683 PLI/Corp. 799 (1990).

[149] For case law, see, for example, *Robinson v. TCI/US West Communications, Inc.*, 117 F.3d 900 (5th Cir. 1997); *Consolidated Gold Fields PLC v. Minorco, S.A.*, 871 F.2d 252 (2d Cir. 1989); *Zoelsch v. Arthur Andersen & Co.*, 824 F.2d 27 (D.C. Cir. 1987); *Bersch v. Drexel Firestone, Inc.*, 519 F.2d 974 (2d Cir. 1975). As the Second Circuit stated in *Consolidated Gold Fields*, "the antifraud provisions of American securities laws have broader extraterritorial reach than American filing requirements." 871 F.2d at 262. Note, moreover, that the state blue sky laws remain applicable. *Id.* For further discussion, see *infra* § 8.13.

[150] *See* Securities Act Release No. 6863 (1990), *superseding*, Securities Act Release No. 4708 (1964); *supra* note 146.

offer and sale have occurred outside the United States is not necessarily an easy matter to resolve.

The SEC provides that whether an offer and sale are made outside the United States is to be determined on an ad hoc basis. To clarify when an offer and sale will be considered outside the United States, Regulation S provides two nonexclusive safe harbor provisions in Rules 903 and 904. If the offer and sale satisfy the conditions of either of the safe harbor provisions, such transaction will be deemed to have occurred outside the United States and outside the reach of Section 5. Hence, perfecting a safe harbor provides assurance that the registration provisions of the Securities Act will not apply.

Regulation S comprises two safe harbor provisions: (1) an issuer safe harbor (Rule 903) and (2) a safe harbor for resales (Rule 904). All offers and sales, whether made in reliance on the issuer or the resale safe harbor, must satisfy two general conditions. In addition, the issuer must satisfy specific conditions that are set out in each safe harbor provision.[151]

[A]   General Conditions

The general conditions applicable to all offers and sales, whether based on the issuer or resale safe harbor, are that: (1) the offer or sale is made in an "offshore transaction;"[152] and (2) there are no "direct selling efforts"[153] in the United States in connection with the distribution or resale of the securities.[154] To engage in an "offshore transaction" there can be no offer or sale to a person in the United States[155] and either of two additional requirements must be satisfied.[156] The first of the alternative requirements is that the buyer is outside the United States, or the seller reasonably believes that the buyer is outside of the United States, at the time the buy order is originated.[157] If an employee of an entity formed under the laws of the United States places the buy order while abroad, the requirement that the buyer be outside the United States is satisfied.[158] The second alternative means of satisfying the "offshore transaction" requirement is to execute the transaction on a designated offshore

---

[151] *See* Securities Act Release No. 6863 (1990).

[152] Rule 902(h).

[153] Rule 902(c).

[154] Rule 903(a), (b); *see* McLaughlin, *"Directed Selling Efforts" Under Regulation S and the U.S. Securities Analyst*, 24 Rev. Sec. & Comm. Reg. 117 (1991). These two conditions are herein referred to as "general conditions."

[155] Reversing the approach in Securities Act Release 4708, Regulation S defines "U.S. Person" as "any natural person resident in the United States," rather than a U.S. citizen regardless of location. Rule 902(k). Therefore, selling to a U.S. citizen living abroad will not automatically prevent the transaction from being considered an offshore transaction. However, Rule 902(h)(2) makes clear that offers and sales specifically targeted at identifiable groups of U.S. citizens abroad, such as members of the armed forces, will not be offshore transactions. The phrase "offshore transaction" is defined in Rule 902(h). *Id.*

[156] Rule 902(h).

[157] *Id.*, Rule 902(h)(1)(ii).

[158] Securities Act Release No. 6863 (1990). This holds true when the buyer is an investment company or its investment advisor. *Id.*

securities market.[159] However, if the seller or its agent knows that the transaction has been pre-arranged with a buyer in the United States, the second alternative will not be satisfied.[160]

The second general condition that must be satisfied in order for an offer and sale to be considered "outside the United States" is that there be no "direct selling efforts" in the United States. For purposes of the issuer safe harbor, neither the issuer, distributors, nor their respective affiliates may engage in direct selling efforts in the United States. Failure to adhere to this condition will result in loss of the safe harbor for all participants in the offering.[161]

"Directed selling efforts" are defined as any activity that could reasonably be expected to have the effect of conditioning the market in the United States for any of the securities being offered in reliance on Regulation S.[162] Specifically, placing advertisements with television or radio stations reaching the United States or in publications with a general circulation[163] in the United States, mailing printed material to U.S. investors, or conducting promotional seminars in the United States are considered "direct selling efforts."[164] Rule 902(b), however, excludes certain types of advertising from the definition of "direct selling efforts." These exceptions include advertisements that are required under either U.S. or foreign law and "tombstone" advertisements[165] that are placed in publications that have less than twenty percent of their total circulation in the United States. Additionally, sellers are permitted to visit and inspect real estate and other facilities located in the United States without engaging in "direct selling efforts."[166]

[B]   Issuer Safe Harbor — Rule 903

The "issuer" safe harbor is applicable not only to the actual issuer but also to the issuer's distributors, their respective affiliates, and persons acting on behalf of the foregoing.[167] The safe harbor may be utilized by both U.S. and foreign issuers offering securities outside the United States. Similar to the previous SEC policy, the conditions that must be satisfied to meet the issuer safe harbor differ depending on the type of securities being offered. For purposes of Regulation S, the SEC separates securities into three categories:

---

[159] Rule 902(b) specifically identifies the markets that the SEC considers to be "designated offshore securities markets."

[160] Rule 902(h)(1)(ii).

[161] Rule 903(a)-(b).

[162] Rule 902(c).

[163] A definition of publications with a general circulation in the United States is provided in Rule 902(c)(2).

[164] Rule 902(c).

[165] In order to qualify as a "tombstone" ad that will not be considered conditioning the U.S. market for a foreign offering, the ad must meet the specific requirements set forth in Rule 902(c)(3)(iii).

[166] Rule 902(c)(3)(iv).

[167] Rule 903. Therefore, references to the term "issuer" hereinafter will refer to the issuer, its distributors, and any of their respective affiliates, or any person acting on behalf of the foregoing.

Category I, Category II and Category III. The categorization of securities is based on the likelihood that the securities will flow back to the United States. As the probability that the securities will flow back to the United States increases, the procedural requirements necessary to avoid registration become more difficult. Under the Regulation S regulatory scheme, Category I securities are subject to the least regulatory restraints and Category III securities are subject to the most.[168]

Category I securities are securities of "foreign issuers"[169] for which there is no "substantial U.S. market interest,"[170] securities offered and sold in "overseas directed offerings,"[171] securities which are backed by the full faith and credit of a "foreign government,"[172] and securities sold pursuant to certain employee benefit plans.[173] Because the SEC concluded that these securities were the least likely to flow back to the United States, it put only minimal procedural requirements upon them.[174] Accordingly, to satisfy the issuer safe harbor, an issuer of Category I securities need only satisfy the general conditions described above: (1) an "offshore transaction;" and (2) no "direct

---

[168] *See* SEC Release No. 6863 (1990); Cogan & Kimbrough, *Regulation S Safe Harbors for Offshore Offers, Sales and Resales*, 4 Insights No. 8, at 3 (1990).

[169] The definition of "foreign issuer" is contained in Rule 902(e). Basically, a foreign issuer may be a foreign government, a national of any foreign government, or a corporation or other entity formed under the laws of a foreign country.

[170] Whether a "substantial U.S. market interest" exist depends on the type of security being offered. Generally, if the foreign issuer is offering equity securities, a substantial U.S. market interest is deemed to exist at the commencement of the offering if: (1) the securities exchanges and inter-dealer quotation systems in the United States in the aggregate constitute the single largest market for such securities; or (2) twenty percent or more of the trading of the class of securities took place on a securities exchange or inter-dealer quotation system located in the United States and less than fifty-five percent of such trading took place in a foreign securities market. Rule 902(j)(1).

A substantial U.S. market interest in a foreign issuer's debt securities is deemed to exist upon commencement of the offering if: (1) 300 or more U.S. persons are the aggregate record holders of the issuer's debt securities, its non-participating preferred stock and its asset-backed securities; (2) U.S. persons hold $1 billion or more of the outstanding indebtedness of the foreign issuer; or (3) U.S. persons hold twenty percent or more of the outstanding debt securities of the foreign issuer. Rule 902(j)(2).

Definitions for U.S. market interest in warrants, non-participating preferred stock and asset-backed securities are provided in Rule 903. The other members in the issuer's chain of distribution, such as the underwriter and its affiliates, may rely on the written representation of the issuer that it has a reasonable belief that there is no substantial U.S. market interest in its securities. *See* SEC Release No. 6863 (1990).

[171] Two types of offerings, for example, can qualify as "overseas directed offerings." *See* Rule 903(b)(ii). One is an offering of a foreign issuer's securities directed to residents of a single country other than the United States. The other includes an offering of nonconvertible debt securities of a domestic (U.S.) issuer directed to a single foreign country. Under this latter type of offering, the principal and interest of the securities must be denominated in non-U.S. currency.

[172] Rule 903(b)(iii).

[173] Rule 903(b)(iv). An offering made to employees of either a domestic or foreign issuer pursuant to a qualified employee benefit plan may be made under Category I as long as certain conditions are met. The specific conditions set forth in Rule 903(b)(iv) are similar to those contained in no-action letters relating to Release 4708. *See* SEC Release No. 6863.

[174] Securities Act Release No. 6863 (1990).

selling efforts" in the United States. Under the Category I issuer safe harbor, sales to U.S. investors overseas are permissible.[175] Nonetheless, participants should be cognizant of Preliminary Note 2 to Regulation S which excludes from the Regulation's protection any plan or scheme to evade the registration provisions of the Securities Act.[176] In sum, prior to the promulgation of Regulation S, the applicability of the federal securities laws to offerings falling under Category I was unclear. Today, Regulation S clarifies the reach of the Securities Act's registration requirements in this context and sets forth relatively minimal regulatory burdens with respect to such offerings.

Offerings falling within the second issuer safe harbor, Category II, are those not eligible under Category I and that "are equity securities of a reporting foreign issuer, or debt securities of a reporting issuer or of a nonreporting foreign issuer."[177] To qualify for the Category II issuer safe harbor, the issuer must satisfy not only the general conditions but must also comply with certain selling restrictions.[178]

There are two types of selling restrictions applicable to offerings of securities falling within Category II: (1) "transactional restrictions" and (2) "offering restrictions." The transactional restrictions prohibit offers and sales of such securities in the United States or to a "U.S. person"[179] during a restricted period lasting forty days.[180] Additionally, a distributor selling the securities prior to the end of the restricted period to certain securities professionals (such as dealers) is required to send a "confirmation or other notice"[181] to such professionals advising them that they are subject to the same restrictions on offers and sales that are applicable to the distributor.[182]

In addition, the issuer and its entire distribution syndicate must adhere to certain "offering restrictions" (which basically are procedures) to meet the Category II and Category III issuer safe harbors.[183] These offering restrictions are procedures that impact the entire offering process and that

---

[175] *See* Rule 903.

[176] *See* Regulation S Preliminary Note 2.

[177] Rule 903(b)(2). This category also includes foreign issuers offering nonparticipating preferred stock and asset-backed securities.

[178] The SEC placed these selling restrictions on Category II securities offerings due to the Commission's belief that Category II securities are more likely to flow back to the United States than are the securities included in Category I. *See* SEC Release No. 6863 (1990).

[179] A "U.S. person" as defined in Rule 902(k) focuses not on U.S. citizenship, but on U.S. residency. SEC Release No. 6863 (1990). Therefore, U.S. investors, distributors and the like residing overseas may engage in their respective activities without the issuer losing the Regulation S safe harbor protection.

[180] Rule 903(b)(2)(ii).

[181] "Confirmation or other notice," as used in Rule 903(b)(2)(iii), allows various types of notice to fulfill the distributors' notice requirement. *See* SEC Release No. 6863 (1990). This confirmation includes notice given over the telephone or computer generated notice given on a screen, provided the seller keeps written records that notice was provided. *Id.*

[182] *Id.*

[183] Securities Act Release No. 6863 (1990).

seek to ensure compliance with the conditions imposed.[184] Generally, as currently formulated, the procedures require that all distributors[185] agree in writing that all offers and sales during the applicable restricted period be made only in accordance with a Regulation S safe harbor or pursuant to registration under the Securities Act or an exemption therefrom.[186] Furthermore, the issuer, distributors and their respective affiliates must include statements in all offering materials that the securities have not been registered under the Securities Act and may not be offered or sold in the United States or to U.S. persons unless the securities are registered or an exemption from registration is perfected.[187]

The final safe harbor category, Category III, applies to all securities not within Categories I or II. This category includes, for example, offerings of equity securities of U.S. reporting issuers, offerings of equity and debt securities of non-reporting U.S. issuers, and equity securities of non-reporting foreign issuers when there is a substantial U.S. market interest in such securities. The SEC imposes the most rigorous restrictions on offerings falling within this category due to the Commission's position that these securities have the highest probability of flowing back to the United States.[188]

As is the case in the first two categories of securities, the general conditions that the offer and sale be made in an "offshore transaction" and that there be no "direct selling efforts" in the United States or to a U.S. person are applicable to Category III securities. Moreover, the offering restrictions applicable to Category II offerings discussed above also are applicable to offerings under Category III. However, the transactional restrictions applicable to Category III offerings are more demanding than those required under Category II.[189]

The transactional restrictions applicable to Category III offerings are similar to the restrictions existing (under SEC Securities Act Release 4708) prior to the promulgation of Regulation S. Due to the Commission's belief that debt offerings of Category III securities are less likely to flow back to the United States, the SEC imposes less stringent transactional restrictions upon them than it does upon equity securities.[190]

Debt securities offered pursuant to Category III are subject to a forty day restricted period.[191] During this period the securities may not be sold to U.S.

---

[184] *Id.*

[185] "Distributor" is defined as "any underwriter, dealer, or other person who participates, pursuant to a contractual arrangement, in the distribution of the securities. . . . " Rule 902(d).

[186] Rule 902(g).

[187] Rule 902(g)(2).

[188] Securities Act Release No. 6863 (1990); *see* Bai, *U.S. Registration Requirements for Multi-National Offerings* (Pts. 1 & 2), 25 Rev. Sec. & Comm. Reg. 131, 144 (1992), 25 Rev. Sec. & Comm. Reg. 151, 157 (1992).

[189] Securities Act Release No. 6863 (1990).

[190] *Id.*

[191] Rule 903(b)(3)(ii).

persons or for the account (or benefit) of U.S. persons.[192] The debt securities must be represented by a temporary global security which is not exchangeable for definitive securities until the forty day restricted period has expired. When the global security is exchanged for the definitive security, certification must be effected that a non-U.S. person owns the security or that a U.S. person purchased securities in a transaction that was exempt from the registration requirements of the Securities Act.[193] If a distributor or other person receiving a selling concession sells prior to the expiration of the forty day restricted period, it must send a "confirmation or other notice" to the purchaser stating that the purchaser is subject to the same restrictions on offers and sales that apply to the distributor.[194]

The transactional restrictions applicable to equity offerings under the third issuer safe harbor — Category III — are even more demanding than the restrictions applicable to debt securities in the same category. Rule 903(b)(3)(iii) prohibits equity securities offered under Category III from being sold to a U.S. person or for the account (or benefit) of a U.S. person for a period of one year (except for reporting issuers who are subject to a six-month distribution compliance period).[195]

Furthermore, the purchaser of the security must certify that it is not a U.S. person and is not acquiring the securities for the account (or benefit) of any U.S. person.[196] In addition, the purchaser must agree to resell only if it adheres to one of three conditions, namely, that such resale is made in accordance with Regulation S, pursuant to a registration statement, or under an exemption from registration.[197] If a U.S. issuer is utilizing the Category III safe harbor, it must place a legend on the securities offered stating that all transfers are prohibited except as set forth above.[198] Finally, the issuer is required, either by contract or pursuant to a provision in its bylaws, articles or charter, to refuse to register any transfer not in accordance with the foregoing.[199]

[C]   Resale Safe Harbor

The resale safe harbor generally is available only to security holders who are not issuers, affiliates of an issuer, distributors, or affiliates of a distributor. Nonetheless, under certain circumstances, officers and directors of an issuer and securities professionals may use the resale safe harbor.[200] By satisfying all

---

[192] Rule 903(b)(3)(ii)(A).

[193] Rule 903(b)(3)(ii)(B).

[194] Rule 903(b)(3)(iv); *see* Securities Act Release No. 6863 (1990).

[195] *See* Securities Act Release No. 8869 (2007).

[196] Rule 903(b)(3)(iii)(B)(1).

[197] Rule 903(b)(3)(iii)(B)(2).

[198] Rule 903(b)(3)(iii)(B)(3).

[199] Rule 903(b)(3)(iii)(B)(4).

[200] Without this exception, officers and directors would be considered affiliates and therefore would be unable to utilize the resale safe harbor.

conditions of the resale safe harbor, the registration requirements of the Securities Act can be avoided.[201] In general, other than securities professionals[202] and certain officers and directors of an issuer, persons may sell in reliance on the resale safe harbor simply by satisfying the general conditions applicable to Regulation S transactions — (1) a resale in an offshore transaction and (2) without direct selling efforts in the United States.[203]

An officer or director may rely on the resale safe harbor if, in addition to meeting the general requirements, the officer or director is an affiliate solely by virtue of his or her position and there is paid no special selling compensation in the resale transaction.[204] With respect to securities professionals, they may not knowingly offer or sell securities to U.S. persons during the applicable restricted period.[205] If the securities professional is selling to another securities professional, a trade confirmation or other notice must be sent to such purchaser reciting the applicable restrictions.[206]

[D]   The 1998 Regulation S Amendments

In 1998 and 2007, the SEC adopted amendments to Regulation S. The 1998 amendments reflect the Commission's concern with certain abusive and problematic practices in connection with offers, sales, and resales of securities made in offshore transactions purportedly pursuant to Regulation S.[207] The 1998 Regulation S amendments accordingly focus on market participants who purport to conduct legitimate offshore Regulation S placements but actually place the securities offshore in an effort to evade registration requirements.[208]

---

[201] *See* Rule 904.

[202] Persons who are considered securities professionals include: "dealers and persons receiving a selling concession, fee or other remuneration in respect of the securities offered or sold, which may include subunderwriters." Securities Act Release No. 6863 (1990).

[203] Rule 904(a).

[204] Rule 904(b)(2).

[205] Rule 904(b)(1).

[206] Rule 904(b)(1)(ii). The applicable restrictions are that the securities may be offered and sold during the restricted period only in accordance with the provisions of Regulation S, if the securities are registered, or pursuant to an available exemption from the registration requirement. *Id.* For discussion on Rule 144A, see *infra* § 6.07. *See generally* Berger, *Offshore Distributions of Securities: The Impact of Regulation S*, 3 Transn'l Law. 578 (1990); Bloomenthal, *Distributions Outside the U.S. — Regulation S*, 10 Sec. & Fed. Corp. L. Rep. 161 (1988); Bradley, *Regulation S: Tempest in a Safe Harbor*, 25 Rev. Sec. & Comm. Reg. 185 (1992); Karmel, *SEC Regulation of Multijurisdictional Offerings*, 16 Brook. J. Int'l L. 3 (1990); Longstreth, *Global Securities Markets and the SEC*, 10 U. Pa. J. Int'l Bus. L. 183 (1988); Steinberg & Lansdale, *Regulation S and Rule 144A: Creating A Workable Fiction in an Expanding Global Securities Market*, 29 Int'l Law. 43 (1995); Thalacker, *supra* note 148; Wolff, *supra* note 147.

[207] *See* Securities Act Release No. 7505, [1997–1998 Transfer Binder] Fed. Sec. L. Rep. (CCH) ¶ 86,006 (SEC 1998). The SEC also adopted amendments to Regulation S in 2007. *See* Securities Act Release No. 8869 (2007); Barron, *The SEC Acts to Slam the Door on Regulation S Advisers*, 26 Sec. Reg. L.J. 211 (1998); Lewis, *Offers Under Regulation S: How Safe is the Harbor?*, 30 Rev. Sec. & Comm. Reg. 205 (1997).

[208] Securities Act Release No. 7505, [1997–1998 Transfer Binder] Fed. Sec. L. Rep. (CCH) ¶ 86,006 (SEC 1998). See the SEC's release proposing amendments to Regulation S, Securities Act

The amendments seek to impede abusive practices in connection with placements of equity securities by U.S. issuers,[209] while "promot[ing] capital formation and efficient, competitive markets."[210] Hence, the amendments "should prevent further abuses . . . but also allow continuous reliance on Regulation S in legitimate offshore offerings."[211]

Thus, the 1998 Regulation S amendments:

1.   Classify the equity securities of all U.S. issuers (both reporting and nonreporting companies) placed offshore under Regulation S as "restricted securities" within the meaning of Rule 144;[212]

2.   Align the Regulation S restricted period for these equity securities issued by all U.S. enterprises with the Rule 144 holding periods by lengthening from 40 days to one year for non-reporting issuers and (pursuant to the 2007 SEC amendments) to six months for reporting issuers the period during which persons relying on the Regulation S safe harbor may not sell these securities to U.S. persons, unless pursuant to registration or an exemption therefrom (termed the "distribution compliance period");[213]

3.   Impose certification, legending, stop transfer, and other requirements for sales of equity securities by all U.S. (reporting and non-reporting) issuers;[214]

4.   Require purchasers of these equity securities sold by U.S. issuers to agree not to engage in hedging transactions with regard to such securities unless such transactions are in compliance with the Securities Act;[215]

5.   Unless certain conditions are satisfied, prohibit the use of promissory notes as payment for these equity securities;[216] and

6.   Clarify that offshore resales under Rule 901 or Rule 904 of equity securities of U.S. issuers, classified as "restricted securities" as defined in Rule 144, will not affect the restricted status of those securities or

---

Release No. 7392, [1997 Transfer Binder] Fed. Sec. L. Rep. (CCH) ¶ 85,909 (SEC 1997).

[209]   *See* Securities Act Release No. 7505, [1997–1998 Transfer Binder] Fed. Sec. L. Rep. (CCH) ¶ 86,006 (SEC 1998). Note that the Commission declined to address potentially abusive practices in Regulation S equity offerings of foreign issuers.

[210]   Securities Act Release No. 7392, [1997 Transfer Binder] Fed. Sec. L. Rep. (CCH) ¶ 85,909, at 89,292 (SEC 1997).

[211]   *See* SEC Release No. 7505, *supra* note 207, at 80,157. These abuses occurred especially with respect to "the securities of thinly capitalized or microcap companies. These types of securities are particularly vulnerable to fraud and manipulation because little information about them is available to investors." *Id.*

[212]   *See* Rules 903, 905 of Regulation S, 17 C.F.R. §§ 230.903, 230.905.

[213]   *Id.*; *see* Rule 144(a)(3), 17 C.F.R. § 230.144(a)(3) (defining "restricted securities to include" equity securities of all domestic issuers acquired in a transaction or chain of transactions subject to the conditions of . . . Regulation S"); Securities Act Release No. 8869 (2007); *see also supra* notes 206–07.

[214]   Rule 903(b)(3)(iii)(B) of Regulation S. *See* SEC Release No. 7505, *supra* note 207, at 80,162.

[215]   Rule 903(b)(3)(iii)(B)(2).

[216]   SEC Release No. 7505, *supra* note 207, at 80,164.

otherwise cleanse the securities of their restricted status.[217]

[E]   Facilitating Global Trading

By promulgating Regulation S the SEC has acknowledged the existence of a global economy and the important role of international securities transactions. While not a panacea, Regulation S establishes a uniform U.S. framework with respect to international securities offerings. Moreover, Regulation S decreases some of the ambiguity that existed under the prior regulatory regimen. Regulation S, aside from creating a more flexible approach with fewer regulatory burdens, has been used in conjunction with Rule 144A to increase investment in foreign issuers and to expand international securities trading in general (*see infra* § 6.07).

---

[217] M. Steinberg, International Securities Law — A Contemporary and Comparative Analysis 194–198 (1999); *see* Rule 905 of Regulation S, 17 C.F.R. § 230.905.

Ch. 3 APPENDIX

LIMITED OFFERING MATERIALS

PURCHASER SUITABILITY QUESTIONNAIRE

INVESTOR:

_____

Name

THE FOLLOWING PURCHASER SUITABILITY QUESTIONNAIRE IS TO ENSURE THAT THIS PRIVATE OFFERING IS CONDUCTED IN FULL COMPLIANCE WITH RULE 506 OF REGULATION D PROMULGATED UNDER THE SECURITIES ACT OF 1933, AS AMENDED. THE QUESTIONNAIRE WILL REMAIN ON FILE IN ABSOLUTE CONFIDENCE IN THE OFFICE OF _____, AND, IF APPLICABLE, YOUR BROKER-DEALER AND YOUR REGISTERED REPRESENTATIVE WITH THE FOLLOWING EXCEPTION: THAT THIS QUESTIONNAIRE MAY BE PRESENTED TO SUCH PARTIES AS DEEMED APPROPRIATE OR NECESSARY TO ESTABLISH THAT THE SALE OF THE INTERESTS TO A PURCHASER WILL NOT RESULT IN VIOLATION OF THE EXEMPTION FROM REGISTRATION UNDER THE SECURITIES ACT OF 1933, AS AMENDED, AND APPLICABLE STATE SECURITIES LAWS WHICH ARE BEING RELIED UPON IN CONNECTION WITH THE SALE OF THE INTERESTS.

Instructions: Please complete each question fully and attach additional information, if necessary. If the answer to any question is "None" or "Not Applicable", please so state.

TO: _____

          _____

          _____

RE: Purchaser Suitability Questionnaire

          _____

Ladies and Gentlemen:

In order to induce you to permit me to purchase the Interests in _____, a Texas Limited Partnership

(the "Partnership"), I hereby acknowledge and understand that:

      1.   I am submitting this Purchaser Suitability Questionnaire (the "Questionnaire") in

connection with a proposed purchase of an Interest(s) in the Partnership;

      2.   I understand that this Questionnaire is not an offer to sell securities and that the

completion of this Questionnaire will not constitute a purchase of securities;

      3.   The Interests heretofore offered to me in the Partnership will not be registered under the

Securities Act of 1933, as amended (the "Act"), and applicable state securities statutes and regulations (the

"State Acts");

      4.   In order to endure that the offering and sale of the Interests (the "Offering") is exempt

from registration under the Act and the State Acts, you are required to have reasonable grounds to believe,

and must actually believe, after making reasonable inquiry and prior to making any sale, that all purchasers

meet the suitability standards set forth in the Confidential Private Placement Memorandum dated

_____ (the "Memorandum");

      5.   The information provided herein will be relied upon in connection with the determination

as to whether I meet the standards imposed by Rule 506 promulgated under the Act, because the Interests

offered hereby have not been and will not be registered under the Act and are being sold in reliance upon

the exemptions from registration afforded issuers of securities provided by Section 4(2) of the Act, as well

as other limited offering exemptions from the securities and broker-dealer registration provisions of

applicable state securities statutes and regulations; and

6.   All information supplied will be treated in confidence, except that this Questionnaire may be presented to such parties as deemed appropriate or necessary to establish that the sale of the Interests to me will not result in violation of the exemption from registration under the Act and the State Acts which is being relied upon in connection with the sale of the Interests.

PART I.   BIOGRAPHICAL INFORMATION

A.   Name:_____ Date of Birth:_____

         Business Name:_____

         Business Address:_____

         Business Telephone Number:_____ Business Fax Number:_____

         Business email:_____

         Residence Address:_____

         Residence Telephone Number:_____

         Spouse Tax Identification Number:_____

         Spouse Name:_____ Date of Birth:_____

         Business Name:_____

         Business Address:_____

         Business Telephone Number:_____ Business Fax Number:_____

         In which state (i.e., TX) do you hold your:

                (i) DRIVER'S LICENSE:_____:

                (ii) VOTER'S REGISTRATION:_____;

         Please submit copy of unexpired driver's license or passport.

B.   *Education:*

         1.   College or University (Field(s) of Study):

                Doctorate:_____

                Masters:_____

                Bachelors:_____

2.   Other Specialized Education or Instruction:_____

Spouse Education:

1.   College or University (Field(s) of Study):

     Doctorate:_____

     Masters:_____

     Bachelors:_____

2.   Other Specialized Education or Instruction:_____

C.   *Professional Memberships or Licenses: (Please List)*

_____

D.   *History of Occupation:*

1.   Present occupation (with number of years) and employer:

_____

2.   Prior occupations (with number of years for each) and employer:

_____

_____

3.   Are you currently associated with, or do you own more than 10% of the stock of a registered FINRA member firm: (Check as appropriate)   YES_____   NO_____

If YES, please provide below the name, address and telephone number of such firm.

_____

4.   Is the Account Holder(s), or any of his/her immediate family members, a control person of any publicly traded corporation (examples of control persons are policy making officers, directors, or 10% shareholders)?   YES_____   NO_____

5.   Is the Account Holder(s) an employee or related to an employee of the firm, its subsidiaries, or affiliates?   YES:_____   NO:_____

E.   *Investor Knowledge and Experience*

     1.   Do you have sufficient knowledge and experience in financial and business matters so as to be capable of evaluating the merits and risks associated with investing in the Partnership?

            YES:_____ NO: _____

     2.   Have you read the Memorandum of the Partnership, including all exhibits, appendices supplements (if any) thereto?

            YES:_____NO: _____

     3.   Do you understand the nature of an investment in the Partnership and the risks associated with such an investment?

            YES:_____ NO:_____

     4.   Do you understand that there is no guarantee of any financial return on this investment and that you run the risk of losing your entire investment?

            YES:_____NO:_____

     5.   Do you understand that this investment provides limited liquidity since the Interests are not freely transferable and the Partners have limited rights to withdraw capital from or to withdraw as Partners of the Partnership?

            YES:_____NO:_____

     6.   Do you or the entity proposing to invest in the Partnership have adequate means of providing for your or its current needs and personal contingencies in view of the fact that this investment provides limited liquidity?

            YES:_____ NO:_____

     7.   Are you purchasing these securities for investment and not with the intent to resell them?

            YES:_____ NO:_____

8.   You have the right, will be afforded an opportunity, and are encouraged to investigate the Partnership and review relevant records and documents pertaining to the General Partner and the Partnership and its business and to ask questions of a qualified representative of the Partnership regarding this investment and the operations and methods of doing business with the partnership.

Have you conducted any such investigation, sought such documents or asked questions of a qualified representative of the Partnership regarding this investment and the operations and methods of doing business of the Partnership?

YES:_____ NO:_____

     a.   If the answer to question 8 is yes, have you completed such investigation and/or received satisfactory answers to any questions posed?

YES:_____ NO:_____

9.   a.   Have you ever invested in securities:

YES:_____ NO:_____

     b.   Have you ever invested in investment partnerships, venture capital funds, or other nonmarketable or restricted securities?

YES:_____ NO:_____

10.   Indicate the frequency of your investments or, if the prospective purchaser is a corporation, partnership, or other entity, your investments on behalf of such entity, in nonmarketable securities (circle appropriate answer):

Often   Occasional   Seldom

PART II.   Individuals Only

(This part must be completed by primary investor even if investing as an entity.)

A.   *Accredited Investor Status*

1.   _____ I am a director or executive officer of _____ or its Affiliates.

2. _____ I am a natural person whose individual net worth, or joint net worth with my spouse, exceeds $1,000,000.

3. _____ I am a natural person whose individual income was in excess of $200,000 in each of the two most recent years or joint income with my spouse was in excess of $300,000 in each of those years and I reasonably expect to reach the same income level in the current year.

B. *Accredited Investor Status – Joint Accounts Combine Financial Information*

1. My net worth, excluding home, furnishings, automobiles, and other assets which are not readily marketable, is in excess of: (Please Check One)

$100,000 _____	$400,000 _____	$800,000 _____
$200,000 _____	$500,000 _____	$900,000 _____
$250,000 _____	$600,000 _____	$1,000,000 _____
$300,000 _____	$700,000 _____	$1,000,000+ _____

2. The current market value of my assets which are liquid (readily convertible to cash) exceeds $_____.

3. PERSONAL INCOME TAX INFORMATION:

(a) Two Years Ago: Annual Gross Income $_____

(b) Last Year: Annual Gross Income $_____

(c) Current Year (estimated): Annual Gross Income $_____

4. Describe any other experience you have in accounting or financial matters:

_____

5. Have you previously participated in other private placement investments?

YES:_____ NO:_____ (Check as appropriate). If so, with whom?_____

_____

6. Indicate the types of investments in which you have previously participated (either direct ownership, limited partnerships, etc.) (check applicable):

☐ Real Estate   ☐ Bonds   ☐ Options

☐ Oil & Gas Drilling   ☐ Equipment Leasing   ☐ Futures
  and/or Lease Acquisition
                        ☐ Agriculture   ☐ Mutual
                                           Funds
☐ Oil & Gas Production ☐ Commodities   ☐ Annuities

☐ Stocks   ☐ Other (please specify)_____

7. Cash and cash equivalents and liquid securities (includes stock, bonds, government obligations, etc. at fair market value): (Please Check One)

$100,000 _____ $400,000 _____ $800,000 _____

$200,000 _____ $500,000 _____ $900,000 _____

$250,000 _____ $600,000 _____ $1,000,000 _____

$300,000 _____ $700,000 _____ $1,000,000+ _____

8. Equity in all real estate, net of mortgages: (Please Check One)

$100,000 _____ $400,000 _____ $800,000 _____

$200,000 _____ $500,000 _____ $900,000 _____

$250,000 _____ $600,000 _____ $1,000,000 _____

$300,000 _____ $700,000 _____ $1,000,000+ _____

9. Other investments: (Please Check One)

$100,000 _____ $500,000 _____ $1,000,000 _____

$250,000 _____ $750,000 _____ $1,000,000+ _____

10. State your investment objectives by checking the following where applicable:

☐ Income – generate income from investments

☐ Appreciation – increase in the value of an asset

    ☐   Tax Shelter – legally avoid or reduce tax liabilities

    ☐   Other:_____

PART III.   *Entities Only*

A.   1.   Name of Entity:_____

        2.   Address of Principal Office:_____

        3.   Type of Organization:_____

            If a Partnership, what states are the principal residences of each of the partners:_____

           _____

        4.   Date and Place of Organization:_____

        5.   Total assets:_____

B.   *Accredited Investor Status*

The undersigned is an entity qualifying as an Accredited Investor as: (Check those that apply)

    1.   (a)   whether acting in its individual or fiduciary capacity:

               (i) _____   a bank as defined in Section 3(a)(2) of the Act;

               (ii) _____   a saving and loan association or other institution as defined in Section 3(a)(5)(A) of the Act;

        (b)   _____   a broker-dealer registered pursuant to Section 15 of the Securities Exchange Act of 1934;

        (c)   _____   an insurance company as defined in Section 2(a)(13) of the Act;

        (d)   (i)_____   an investment company registered under the Investment Company Act of 1940;

               (ii)_____   a business development company as defined in Section 2(a)(48) of the Investment Company Act of 1940;

(e) _____ a Small Business Investment Company licensed by the U.S. Small Business Administration under Section 301(c) or (d) of the Small Business Investment Act of 1958;

(f) _____ a plan established and maintained by a state, its political subdivision, or any agency or instrumentality of a state or its political subdivisions for the benefit of employees, if such plan has total assets in excess of $5,000,000;

(g) _____ an employee benefit plan within the meaning of the Employee Retirement Income Security Act of 1974, if the investment decision is made by the undersigned as a plan fiduciary, as defined in Section 3(21) of such act, which is either a:

    (i) _____ bank;

    (ii) _____ saving and loan association;

    (iii) _____ insurance company; or

    (iv) _____ registered investment advisor;

(h) _____ an employee benefit plan with total assets in excess of $5,000,000;

(i) _____ a self directed plan, with investment decisions made solely by persons that are accredited investors;

2. _____ a private business development company as defined in Section 202(a)(22) of the Investment Advisors Act of 1940;

3. _____ an organization described in Section 501(c)(3) of the Internal Revenue Code, corporation, Massachusetts or similar business trust, or partnership not formed for the specific purpose of acquiring the securities offered, with total assets in excess of $5,000,000;

4.   _____   any trust, with total assets in excess of $5,000,000, not formed for the specific purpose of acquiring the securities offered, whose purchase is directed by a sophisticated person as described in Rule 506 of Regulation D;

5.   _____   an entity in which *all* of the equity owners are Accredited Investors as defined in Regulation D.

PART IV. Representations and Warrants

(To Be Completed By All Prospective Participants)

In order to induce you to permit the undersigned to purchase the Interests in the Partnership, I hereby warrant and represent to you that:

1. I have received, carefully read and understood a copy of that certain Confidential Private Placement Memorandum dated _____ (the "Memorandum"), and all exhibits thereto setting forth information relating to the Partnership and the terms and conditions in the Interests, as well as any other information I deemed necessary or appropriate to evaluate the merits and risks of an investment in the Interests;

2. I have had the opportunity to ask questions of and to receive answers from, representatives of the General Partner concerning the terms and conditions of the Offering and the information contained in the Memorandum;

3. I have such knowledge and experience in financial and business matters, that I am capable of evaluating the merits and risks of an investment decision in the program and am capable of making an informed decision;

4. I DO/DO NOT (circle one) intend to utilize the services of a Purchaser Representative to evaluate the merits and risks of an investment;

5.   The information contained in this Questionnaire is accurate, true, complete and correct and may be relied upon by you;

6.   I will notify you immediately of any material change in any of such information occurring prior to any purchase of Interests by me.

*Dated:*_____

Individual   *Entity*

_____   _____
Signature   *Print Name*

_____   *By:*_____
Print Name   *Signature of Individual Completing Questionnaire*

_____   _____
Social Security Number   *Print Name of Individual Completing Questionnaire*

*Its:*_____
Title

_____
Taxpayer Identification Number

SUBSCRIPTION AGREEMENT

The undersigned hereby subscribes for a Limited Partner Interest in _____, a Texas limited partnership (the "Partnership"), in the amount set forth below.

1. *Subscription.* Subject to the terms and conditions hereof, the undersigned hereby irrevocably subscribes for a Limited Partnership interest (the "Partnership Interest") in the Partnership for a total purchase price of $_____. The undersigned hereby tenders with this Subscription Agreement a check payable to the order of _____ or wire transfer, in the amount of $_____.

2. *Closing.* The undersigned understands the General Partner intends to make an initial closing of the Partnership Interests on _____, 2008 and thereafter will open the partnership on a quarterly basis for additional capital contributions from existing or new Limited Partners. If you do not accept this subscription, this Subscription Agreement, together with the funds and other documents delivered to the Partnership, shall be promptly returned to the undersigned with interest, if any.

3. *Determination of Compliance.* The undersigned agrees that this subscription is subject to the following terms and conditions:

(a) You shall have the right, in your sole discretion, to accept or reject all or part of this subscription and to determine whether the Subscription Agreement has been properly completed and whether all suitability requirements have been satisfied. If you find this subscription to be defective, deficient or noncomplying, the subscription price will be promptly returned without interest or deduction.

(b) This subscription is not transferable or assignable.

4. *Receipt of Information.* The undersigned hereby acknowledges receipt of the _____ Private Placement Memorandum, and a copy of the Limited

Partnership Agreement which governs the rights of Limited Partners and the operation of the Partnership, and the undersigned acknowledges that he has had reasonable time and opportunity to examine those documents. The undersigned further acknowledges that the Partnership is a suitable investment only for sophisticated investors; that the Partnership Interests are being offered and sold under an exemption from registration under the Securities Act of 1933, as amended, and appropriate state securities laws; and that the offering has not been submitted to or reviewed by the Securities and Exchange Commission, the State Securities Board of Texas, the securities regulation agency of any other state or any other governmental agency.

5. *Representation of Purchaser.* The undersigned hereby makes the following representations, declarations, and warranties to you, with the intent that the same be relied upon in determining the suitability of the undersigned to invest in the Partnership:

    (a)   *Individual Investor*:   I am of legal age and a resident of the State of _____; or

    (aa) *Partnership, Trust or other Entity:* The investor has been organized in compliance with applicable law of the State of _____, is presently in existence, and has the power to invest in the Partnership.

    (b) The undersigned understands that an investment in the Partnership is an illiquid investment, which means that:

        (i) The undersigned must bear the economic risk of investment in the Partnership for an indefinite period of time, since the Partnership Interests have not been registered under the Securities Act of 1933 nor any state securities laws and cannot be sold unless the Partnership Interests are either subsequently registered under said Act and applicable state laws (which is neither contemplated by nor required of the Partnership) or an exemption from such registration is available; and

(ii) There is no established market for the Partnership Interests and that it is not anticipated that any public market for the Partnership Interests will develop in the near future.

(c) The undersigned represents that this investment is being made for the account of the undersigned; the undersigned has not offered or sold any portion of the Partnership Interest for which the undersigned hereby subscribes to any other person and has no present intention of dividing such Partnership Interest with others or reselling or otherwise disposing of any portion of such Partnership Interest, either currently or after the passage of a fixed or determinable period of time, or upon the occurrence or nonoccurrence of any predetermined event or circumstance.

(d) The undersigned represents that none of the following has been represented, guaranteed, or warranted to the undersigned by any broker, the Partnership, their agents or employees, or any other person, expressly or by implication:

(i) The length of time that the undersigned will be required to remain as the owner of the Partnership Interest;

(ii) The profit to be realized, if any, as a result of investment in the Partnership; or

(iii) The past performance or experience on the part of the Partnership, or any partner or affiliate, their partners, salesmen, associates, agents, or employees or of any other person, will in any way indicate the predicted results of the ownership of the Partnership Interest.

(e) The undersigned has adequate means of providing for current needs and possible personal contingencies and has no need for liquidity in the investment in the Partnership. The undersigned is either (i) an "accredited investor" (as indicated in the Private Placement Questionnaire), or (ii) has a personal net worth in excess of three (3) times the amount to be invested in the Partnership and could afford to sustain a loss of the entire investment in the Partnership in the event such loss should occur.

(f) The undersigned has made an independent examination of the investment and has depended on the advice of counsel and accountants to the undersigned and agrees that you have no responsibility with respect to such matters and such advice.

(g) The undersigned understands that the Partnership is newly formed and has no operating history; the undersigned has carefully reviewed and relied solely upon the Private Placement Memorandum and independent investigations made by the undersigned or by representative(s) of the undersigned, if any, in making the decision to purchase the Partnership Interest hereby subscribed for, and the undersigned has a full understanding and appreciation of the risks involved.

(h) The undersigned understands that any offering literature used in connection with this offering has not been prefiled with the Attorney General or Securities Commission of any state and has not been reviewed by the Attorney General or Securities Commission of any state.

(i) The undersigned understands that any and all documents, records and books pertaining to this investment have been made available for inspection by the undersigned, his attorney and/or accountant, and that the books and records of the Partnership will be available, upon reasonable notice, for inspection by investors during reasonable hours at the principal place of business of the Partnership. The undersigned represents that he has had an opportunity to ask questions of and receive answers from the General Partner, or a person or persons acting on its behalf, concerning the terms and conditions of this investment.

6. *Indemnification of the Partnership and the General Partner.* The undersigned understands the meaning and legal consequences of the representations and warranties contained herein, and hereby agrees to indemnify and hold harmless the Partnership, the General Partner, and their agents and employees from

and against any and all loss, damage or liability due to or arising out of a breach of any representation or warranty of the undersigned contained in this Subscription Agreement. Notwithstanding any of the representations, warranties, acknowledgments or agreements made herein, the undersigned does not in any manner waive any rights granted to the undersigned under United States Federal or state securities laws.

7. *Power of Attorney.* In order to induce the General Partner to accept the subscription of the undersigned, and in consideration of the General Partner's agreement to serve as General Partner of the Partnership, the undersigned hereby irrevocably constitutes and appoints the General Partner, with full power of substitution, his true and lawful attorney for him and in his name, place and stead for his use and benefit, to execute:

(a) the Partnership Agreement in the form provided to the undersigned or as the same may be thereafter amended;

(b) all amendments to the Certificate of Limited Partnership and Partnership Agreement regarding a change in name of the Partnership, its address, or that of the General Partner or any Partner, or the admission or withdrawal of a Partner;

(c) all amendments adopted in accordance with Section 11.04 of the Partnership Agreement;

(d) all certificates and other instruments necessary to qualify or continue the Partnership in the states where the Partnership may be doing business;

(e) all conveyances or other instruments or documents necessary, appropriate or convenient to effect the dissolution and termination of the Partnership.

The undersigned hereby agrees to be bound by any representations made by the General Partner or its substitutes acting pursuant to this Power of Attorney, and the undersigned hereby waives any and all defenses which may be available to him to contest, negate or disaffirm its actions or the actions of his substitutes under this Power of Attorney. The powers herein granted are granted for the sole and exclusive benefit of the undersigned and not on behalf of any other person, in whole or in part. This Power of

Attorney is hereby declared to be irrevocable and a power coupled with an interest which will survive the death, disability, dissolution, bankruptcy or insolvency of the undersigned.

8. *Subscription Not Revocable.* The undersigned hereby acknowledges and agrees that the undersigned is not entitled to cancel, terminate or revoke this Subscription Agreement or any agreements of the undersigned hereunder and that this Subscription Agreement shall survive the dissolution, death or disability of the undersigned.

9. *Representative Capacity.* If an investment in the Partnership is being made by a corporation, partnership, trust or estate, I, the person signing on behalf of the undersigned entity, represent that I have all right and authority, in my capacity as an officer, general partner, trustee, executor or other representative of such corporation, partnership, trust or estate, as the case may be, to make such decision to invest in the Partnership and to execute and deliver this Subscription Agreement on behalf of such corporation, partnership, trust or estate as the case may be, enforceable in accordance with its terms. I also represent that any such corporation, partnership or trust was not formed for the purpose of buying the Partnership Interest hereby subscribed.

10. *Restrictions on Transferability.* The undersigned understands and agrees that the purchase and resale, pledge, hypothecation or other transfer of the Partnership Interest is restricted by certain provisions of the Limited Partnership Agreement of _____ and that the Partnership Interest shall not be sold, pledged, hypothecated or otherwise transferred unless the Partnership Interest is registered under the Securities Act of 1933, as amended, and applicable state securities laws or an exemption from such registration is available.

11. *Number and Gender.* In this Agreement the masculine gender includes the other two genders and the singular includes the plural, where appropriate to the context.

IN WITNESS WHEREOF, the undersigned has executed this Subscription Agreement on the date set forth below.

Date of Execution: _____

IF INDIVIDUAL INVESTOR:

_____
(Signature)

_____
(Printed Name)

IF CORPORATION, PARTNERSHIP, TRUST,
ESTATE OR REPRESENTATIVE:

_____
Name of Investor

By:_____

Name:_____

Title:_____

APPROVED THIS _____ DAY
of _____, 2008.

By:_____
General Partner

PURCHASER REPRESENTATIVE QUESTIONNAIRE

The information contained herein is being furnished for consideration by the General Partners in determining whether the sale of Limited Partnership interests in _____, a Texas Limited Partnership (the "Partnership") may be made to:

_____

(Printed or typed name of potential Limited Partners)

The undersigned understands that (i) the General Partners will rely upon the information contained herein for purposes of such determination, (ii) the Limited Partnership interests will not be registered under the Securities Act and may not be registered under the securities laws of the Limited Partner's state of residence in reliance upon exemptions from the registration provisions thereof and (iii) this Questionnaire is not an offer of the Limited Partnership interests or any other securities to the undersigned or to the above-named prospective Limited Partner.

The undersigned is acting as Purchaser Representative for the above-named Limited Partner(s) and is furnishing the following representations and information:

1.   The undersigned is not an affiliate of the Partnership (as defined hereafter), except as set forth below. (Write "No Exceptions" or set forth exceptions and give details.)

_____

_____

The only permitted exceptions are those stated below: A Purchaser Representative may not be an affiliate of the Partnership (director, officer, or other employee of the Partnership or of the General Partners or beneficial owner of 10% or more of any class of equity interest in the Partnership or of the General Partners), except where the purchaser is:

(a)   related to the purchaser representative by blood, marriage or adoption, no more remotely than as a first cousin;

(b)   any trust or estate in which the purchaser representative and any persons related to him or her, as specified in subparagraph (a) or (c), collectively have more than 50% of the beneficial interest (excluding contingent interests) or of which the purchaser representative serves as trustee, executor or in any similar capacity; or

(c)   any corporation or other organization in which the purchaser representative and any persons related to him or her, as specified in subparagraph (a) or (b), collectively are the beneficial owners of more than 50% of the equity securities (excluding directors' qualifying shares) or equity interests.

2.   The undersigned believes that he/she has sufficient knowledge and experience in financial and business matters to be capable of evaluating, alone or together with other Purchaser Representatives of the purchaser, or together with the purchaser, the relative merits and risks of an investment in the Partnership. Such opinion is based upon the following information; if the undersigned has relied upon, in part, the expertise of additional Purchaser Representatives or others, their names and addresses are indicated below. (Please describe personal investment experience, business experience, profession and education.)

_____

_____

_____

3.   There is no material relationship or agreement between the undersigned or any of his/her affiliates and the Partnership or its affiliates which now exists or is mutually understood to be contemplated or which has existed at any time during the previous two years, nor has the undersigned or any of his/her affiliates received any compensation from the Partnership or its affiliates as a result of any such relationship, except as set forth below. *If you and your firm are participating in the solicitation of purchasers in connection with this private placement or any prior offerings by the General Partners or their affiliates, please (a) so state, (b) separately indicate the total*

compensation to be received and (c) make sure that the purchaser reads, answers and signs the statements at the end of this Purchaser Representative Questionnaire. (Write "No Exceptions" or set forth exceptions and give details.)

_____

_____

_____

      The foregoing information is complete, correct and may be relied upon by the General Partners and the Partnership. The undersigned agrees to promptly advise of any changes in the foregoing information which may occur prior to the termination of the offering.

Signed this _____ day of _____, 2008, at _____

                                             (City and State)

_____   _____

Firm Name   Signature

_____   _____

Street Address   Type or Print Name

_____   _____

City, State and Zip Code   (Area Code) Telephone Number

IMPORTANT NOTE TO PURCHASER:

If the answer to question 3 above is anything other than "No Exceptions," it means that your Purchaser Representative may at some future date have, presently has, or within the past two years had, a material relationship with the Partnership or its affiliates and will receive or has received compensation therefor. Accordingly, you should understand that such person may have a conflict of interest between such Purchaser Representative's impartial representation of you as a purchaser representative and such Purchaser Representative's past, present, or future relationship with the Partnership or its affiliates. After consideration of the effects such a conflict of interest may have upon such Person's acting as your Purchaser Representative and, if such Person is to so act, you should acknowledge that you have been advised in writing by the Purchaser Representative, prior to completion of the Subscription Agreement, of such potential conflict of interest and that you desire such person to act as your Purchaser Representative. I have been advised in writing by my Purchaser Representative, prior to my completion of the Subscription Agreement, of the potential conflict of interest described in question 3 above.

Yes _____   No _____

I desire the above named person to act as my Purchaser Representative.

Yes _____   No _____

Signed this _____ day of _____, 2008, at _____
                                                           (City and State)

IF INDIVIDUAL INVESTOR:

_____
(Signature)

_____
(Printed Name)

IF CORPORATION, PARTNERSHIP,
TRUST, ESTATE OR
REPRESENTATIVE:

_____
Name of Investor

By:_____

Name:_____

Title:_____

Chapter 4

THE REGISTRATION PROCESS

§ 4.01   OVERVIEW OF THE REGISTRATION PROCESS

To protect investors and the integrity of the securities markets, the Securities Act of 1933 (Securities Act or 1933 Act) has two basic objectives: (1) to provide investors with adequate and accurate material information concerning securities offered for sale and (2) to prohibit fraudulent practices in the offer or sale of securities. The registration framework of the Securities Act seeks to meet these goals by imposing certain obligations and limitations upon persons engaged in the offer or sale of securities. For the Securities Act's registration framework to apply, the interstate commerce requirement must be met. This normally is satisfied without difficulty.

Pursuant to Section 5, a public offering of securities requires that a registration statement must be filed with the Securities and Exchange Commission (SEC). As a general matter, with certain key exceptions, before the registration statement is filed, there can be no offers to sell or offers to buy the securities in question. After the filing of the registration statement, oral offers and certain written offers are permitted. Until the registration statement becomes effective, however, there can be no sale of the securities. Moreover, unless preempted, the registration requirements of the applicable state securities laws must be met. Note that SEC registered offerings of securities that are listed (or will be listed such as pursuant to an IPO) on a national securities exchange are preempted from state registration regulation.

Under federal law, the main purpose of registration is to provide adequate and accurate disclosure of material information concerning the issuer (as well as affiliates and certain other parties) and the securities the issuer (which, for example, may be common stock in a corporation or interests in a limited partnership) proposes to offer. The disclosure of this information, largely in the form of statutory and free writing Section 10 prospectuses, enables investors to evaluate the securities offered and thus make informed investment decisions.

The registration of a securities offering with the SEC does not mean that the offering is considered to be a good risk. The Commission does not have the authority to prevent an offering from going to market because it considers the investment to be of a speculative nature. Rather, the main role of the federal securities laws in this setting is to require the accurate disclosure of material information.

On the other hand, a number of states apply "merit" regulation to certain securities offerings. Under this standard, the pertinent state securities administrator can prevent an offering from going forward because it is not "fair, just and equitable." Under merit regulation, therefore, adequate disclosure is not the only criterion. The substantive fairness of the offering also may be scrutinized.

It also should be pointed out that neither the SEC nor the states verify the truthfulness of the disclosures made in the registration statement. That a registration statement becomes effective in no way vouches for the veracity of the information contained therein. In this regard, both federal and state law prohibit materially false and misleading statements, with civil and criminal remedies available to redress such violations. For example, as discussed in Chapter 7, provided certain conditions are met, Section 11 of the 1933 Act imposes civil monetary liability against certain persons who fail to establish "due diligence" (except the issuer which is strictly liable) for any misstatement or omission of a material fact contained in a registration statement; Section 12(a)(1) provides that a purchaser may rescind, or alternatively, recover damages against any person who offers or sells a security in violation of Section 5; Section 12(a)(2) likewise grants the purchaser the right to rescind or to recover damages against any person who sells a security by means of a prospectus or oral communication which includes a materially false or misleading statement if such seller fails to establish the exercise of reasonable care; Section 17(a), as addressed in Chapter 9, provides a remedy to the SEC (or the U.S. Department of Justice in a criminal proceeding) for redressing any fraudulent or deceptive conduct committed in the offer or sale of securities; and Section 24 of the Securities Act provides for criminal penalties for the willful violation of any provision of the Securities Act or any rule or regulation promulgated by the SEC thereunder. Moreover, as discussed in Chapter 8, under certain circumstances, suit also may be brought under Section 10(b) of the Securities Exchange Act for any materially false or misleading statement contained in a registration statement.

Section 5 of the Securities Act may be viewed as the central provision of the federal registration framework. *Subject to certain key exceptions*, the provision prohibits any person from using the mails or any means of interstate commerce to offer a subject security for sale unless a registration statement has been filed with the SEC and, with respect to any written communication, unless such communication meets the prospectus requirements.[1] Section 5 also prohibits any sale of a subject security unless a registration statement is effective.

Generally, disclosure pursuant to a Section 10 statutory prospectus encompasses the issuer, affiliated persons, and the securities to be offered. The Section 10 statutory prospectus, among other things, may be viewed as being both a selling and a disclosure document. As a selling document, it is used by underwriters and dealers for the purpose of helping to persuade investors to purchase the securities. Another commonly-held view is that the Section 10 statutory prospectus, as a disclosure document, serves to protect the various parties from liability. From this perspective, information placed in the statutory prospectus traditionally has been conservative, focusing on historically-

---

[1] There are a number of exceptions to this general principle. *See infra* § 4.02.

based information and clearly warning prospective investors of any material risks involved.

In the 1970s and 1980s, the SEC's promulgation of Rule 175 and Item 303 of Regulation S-K signaled a new era for facilitating the disclosure of forward-looking statements and other "soft" (rather than historical) information in the Section 10 prospectus. Enactment of the Private Securities Litigation Reform Act of 1995 (PSLRA) also induced Exchange Act reporting issuers in public offerings to engage in disclosure of "forward-looking" or "soft" information. The "free writing" prospectus adopted by the SEC pursuant to the 2005 reforms further encourages issuer use of forward-looking information.[2]

§ 4.02　FRAMEWORK OF SECTION 5

When speaking of making a public offering, the concept of *"in registration"* is sometimes heard. Generally, the term refers to the entire registration period, commencing at least from the time that the issuer reaches an understanding with the managing underwriter prior to the filing of the registration statement to the time that the prospectus delivery requirements terminate in the post-effective period.[3]

From a structural perspective having legal ramifications, Section 5 covers three basic time periods for making offers and sales of securities during a registered offering: (1) the pre-filing period, (2) the waiting period, and (3) the post-effective period.

Generally, the offering rules will turn on two factors: (1) the time period, taken into consideration with, (2) the issuer's reporting status. Thus to understand which offering activities are permitted by a particular issuer at a given point in time, it is important to understand not only how the SEC defines each time period, but also the Commission's issuer classification framework.

[A]　Issuer Classifications

Generally, the SEC has categorized issuers into four tiers consisting of (1) non-reporting issuers, (2) unseasoned issuers, (3) seasoned issuers, and (4) well-known seasoned issuers:

> (1) A *non-reporting issuer* is an issuer that is not required to file reports pursuant to Section 13 or Section 15(d) of the Securities Exchange Act (Exchange Act). Such issuers include, for example, a privately-held company that is conducting an initial public offering (IPO) as well as a voluntary filer (namely a non-reporting issuer that elects to voluntarily file periodic reports).

---

[2] The "free writing" prospectus is discussed *infra* § 4.02[C][2]. Rule 175, Item 303 of Regulation S-K, and the treatment of forward-looking information by the Private Securities Litigation Reform Act are addressed in Chapters 5, 8, and 11 of this text.

[3] *See* Securities Exchange Act Release No. 5180 (1971).

(2) An *unseasoned issuer* is an issuer that is required to file Exchange Act reports, but does not satisfy the requirements for Form S-3 (or Form F-3) for a primary offering of its securities (*e.g.*, such unseasoned issuer has a public float (those securities held by nonaffiliates) of less than $75 million). Unseasoned issuers typically register offerings on Form S-1.[4]

(3) A *seasoned issuer* is an issuer that qualifies to use Form S-3 (or Form F-3) to register primary offerings of its common stock, but does not meet the well-known seasoned issuer criteria. Generally, a seasoned issuer is one that has timely filed Exchange Act reports for a twelve-month period and that has a public float (representing the aggregate market value of the company's voting stock held by non-affiliates) of at least $75 million.[5]

(4) The last category of issuer is the *well-known seasoned issuer*.[6] Such issuers represent the largest amount of capital raised and traded in the U.S. public capital markets. Because well known seasoned issuers have such a wide following by market participants, institutional investors and the media, the SEC has determined that these issuers merit the greatest flexibility in regard to their activities during the public offering process.

There are four requirements that must be satisfied in order for an issuer to qualify as a *well-known seasoned issuer*. First, the issuer is required to file reports pursuant to Section 13(a) or Section 15(d) of the Exchange Act. Second, the issuer must meet the registrant requirements of Form S-3 (or Form F-3), which includes the requirement that the issuer be current and timely in its Exchange Act reporting obligations for at least a twelve-month period. Third, the issuer must not be an ineligible issuer.[7] And finally, the issuer must either (1) have a worldwide common equity (*e.g.*, common stock) market capitalization ("public float") of at least $700 million, or (2) have issued at least $1 billion of non-convertible securities, other than common equity, in registered primary offerings for cash (not exchange offers) in the last three years.

---

[4] An issuer that is filing Exchange Act reports voluntarily accordingly is considered a non-reporting issuer for purposes of the rules.

[5] *See* Securities Act Release Nos. 6964 (1992), 6383 (1982).

[6] This category of issuer was added as a part of the 2005 offering reform initiative to ease the public offering burden on well-known issuers with widely disseminated financial information available to the public. Whether an issuer qualifies as a well-known seasoned issuer is determined annually. Well-known issuer status is determined on the latter of the date the issuer files its most recent shelf registration statement or its most recent amendment thereto, or the date the issuer files its most recent annual report. *See* Securities Act Release No. 8591 (2005).

[7] Ineligible issuers include those issuers who: are not current in their periodic reporting; have filed for bankruptcy or insolvency during the past three years; have been subject to a refusal or stop order under the Securities Act during the past three years; have been convicted of a felony or a misdemeanor or have been found to have violated the anti-fraud provisions of the federal securities laws during the past three years; have been blank check companies, shell companies, or issuers of penny stock during the past three years; or are limited partnerships offering securities other than through a firm commitment underwriting.

If an issuer is a well-known seasoned issuer based on its public float (namely, common stock held by nonaffiliates), that issuer can use automatic shelf registration to register any offering of securities (other than an offering in connection with a business combination). On the other hand, an issuer that has attained well-known seasoned issuer status based on its registered non-convertible securities can register any offering for cash with an automatic shelf registration statement if it is eligible to register primary offerings of securities on Form S-3 (or Form F-3). If it is not eligible to use Form S-3 (or Form F-3), such an issuer is limited to using automatic shelf registration for offerings of non-convertible securities (other than common equity) for cash.[8] The subject of automatic shelf registration is discussed in Chapter 5 (§ 5.02).

The following discussion will address how the offering rules vary depending on the status of the issuer and the time period(s) in which a subject communication occurs.

[B]　　The Pre-Filing Period

[1]　　Overview

The *pre-filing* period is the time period before a registration statement has been filed with the SEC.[9] During this time period, with certain exceptions, Section 5(c) prohibits the use of the mails or any means of interstate commerce to offer to sell or offer to buy the securities to be offered.[10]

Certain activities, however, are not deemed to be an offer to sell or an offer to buy. For example, Section 2(a)(3) exempts negotiations and agreements between the issuer and any underwriter or among underwriters who are or will be in privity of contract with the issuer. Rule 135 permits an issuer to make an announcement of a proposed public offering, provided that only the information specified in the Rule is released. Moreover, pursuant to Rules 137–139, brokers or dealers may publish certain information about specified issuers in the pre-filing period (as well as in the waiting and post-effective periods).

As a general proposition, however, during the pre-filing period, the concept of "making an offer to sell" is given a relatively broad interpretation. Depending on the classification of the subject issuer and the underlying circumstances, publication of information about the issuer or its securities, (even where such information does not refer to a forthcoming offering), *prior to the filing of a registration statement*, may be considered an "offer to sell." Although the publication is not an express offer, it may be viewed as

---

[8] *See* Securities Act Release No. 8591 (2005).

[9] Note that as a result of certain offering rules adopted by the SEC in 2005, pre-filing period communications may be treated differently depending on whether they occurred within the thirty day period leading up to the filing of the registration statement or more than thirty days prior to such filing. *See* Securities Act Release No. 8591 (2005); *infra* § 4.02[B][3] (discussion of Rule 163A).

[10] Note also that Section 5(a) prohibits the use of the mails or any instrument or means of interstate commerce to sell or to deliver securities for purposes of sale before the effective date of the registration statement.

conditioning the public market or stimulating interest in the securities to be registered (more colorfully referred to as "gun-jumping"). Hence, during the pre-filing period, *absent certain exceptions*, the issuer and other participants must be cautious regarding the publication of information. Nonetheless, the SEC's 2005 amendments, as discussed later in this chapter, permit certain issuers to engage in a wide range of solicitation activities prior to the filing of the registration statement.

[2]   Conditioning the Market ("Gun-Jumping")

A major concern in the pre-filing period is that statements made by the issuer and others (even when such statements do not refer to a forthcoming offering) will be construed as "conditioning the market" ("gun-jumping"), and, hence, constitute an "offer to sell" in violation of Section 5(c). The SEC has issued a number of releases on this issue. In this regard, the Commission has asserted that "the publication of information and statements, and publicity efforts, made in advance of a proposed financing which have the effect of conditioning the public mind or arousing public interest in the issuer or in its securities constitutes an offer in violation of the Act."[11] Nonetheless, the SEC has provided four non-exclusive safe harbors from the Section 5 gun-jumping prohibitions for specified issuers:

First, as discussed later in this chapter, well known seasoned issuers are exempt entirely from the "gun-jumping" prohibitions (see Rule 163). These issuers may make "offers to sell" the subject securities in the pre-filing period without violating the registration mandates of Section 5.[12]

Second, also as elaborated upon later in this chapter, by rule, the SEC excludes all communications made by or on behalf of any issuer (other than those communications directed at the contemplated offering or made by an underwriter) made more than thirty days prior to the filing of the registration statement from the Section 5 gun-jumping prohibitions (so long as the subject issuer takes reasonable steps to prevent further dissemination of the information during the thirty-day period prior to the filing of the registration statement — Rule 163A).[13]

Third, subject to certain conditions, Rule 168 provides a safe harbor to Section 5's gun-jumping prohibitions by allowing Exchange Act reporting issuers to continue to publish any regularly released factual business information and forward-looking information without restriction, subject to the antifraud provisions. The purpose of these types of communications is to keep the market informed about the subject company's financial condition rather than to condition the market for new issuances. A Rule 168 communication must be made by or on behalf of the issuer. This means that the issuer or an agent or

---

[11] Securities Exchange Act Release No. 5180 (1971).

[12] Rule 163 is discussed *infra* § 4.02[B][3].

[13] Rule 163A is discussed in *infra* § 4.02[B][3].

representative of the issuer (other than an offering participant who is an underwriter or dealer) must authorize the release of the communication before it is made. In addition, under Rule 168, information will only be considered "regularly released" if the issuer has previously released the same type of information by substantially the same method of release in the ordinary course of its business.[14] Excluded from the safe harbor of Rule 168 is the subject issuer's disclosure of information about the registered offering itself. Note, however, as discussed later in this chapter, disclosure of information by the issuer about the registered offering nonetheless may be protected under Rule 135. Moreover, if the subject issuer is a well known seasoned issuer, then Rule 163 allows communications that focus on the contemplated offering in the pre-filing period.[15]

Importantly, the Rule 168 safe harbor rule, providing insulation from Section 5 liability with respect to forward-looking information, affords Exchange Act reporting issuers with significant relief from the competing pressures of making full disclosure in Exchange Act reports while simultaneously complying with the gun-jumping provisions. Prior to the adoption of Rule 168, registrants planning a prospective public offering were required to disclose forward-looking information as part of their periodic Exchange Act filings with such disclosure possibly being viewed as conditioning the market. Rule 168 should lay to rest reporting issuer concerns over Section 5 liability stemming from publication of regularly released forward-looking information.[16]

Pursuant to Rule 169, the fourth safe harbor, all issuers including non-reporting issuers (such as voluntary filers or IPO issuers) may continue to publish, prior to the filing of the subject registration statement, any regularly released factual business information intended for use by persons other than in their capacity as investors or potential investors (such as information directed for the use of customers or suppliers). A communication intended for non-investors and disseminated under this safe harbor is still protected, even if it inadvertently reaches investors. Further, similar to information disseminated under Rule 168, a release in compliance with Rule 169 is not a Section 2(a)(10) prospectus and does not violate the general prohibition against pre-filing offers. And, as with Rule 168, the communication must be made by or on behalf of the subject issuer (other than by a participant underwriter or dealer). However, in contrast to Rule 168, non-reporting issuers under Rule 169 may not publish forward-looking information. And, similar to Rules 163A and 168, the Rule 169 safe harbor cannot be used to communicate any information about the registered offering itself.[17]

---

[14] One previous release or dissemination may establish the requisite "regularly released" track record. Note, moreover, that Rule 168 does not extend to voluntary filers.

[15] *See* Securities Act Release No. 8591 (2005).

[16] *See Chris-Craft Industries, Inc. v. Bangor Punta Corporation*, 426 F.2d 569 (2d Cir. 1970); Securities Act Release No. 8591 (2005).

[17] Prior to the adoption of Rules 168 and 169, the Commission took a similar position regarding regularly released factual information. *See* Securities Act Release Nos. 5180 (1971); 7856 (2000).

[3] Rules 163 and 163A

As the foregoing discussion provides, there are important safe harbors to the Section 5(c) prohibition against pre-filing offers. Generally, the safe harbor rules vary depending on the status of the issuer. For example, under Rule 163, well-known seasoned issuers (*e.g.*, companies that have a public float of $700 million and have timely filed their Exchange Act reports for the past twelve months[18]) are completely exempt from restrictions on offers during the pre-filing period. Hence, these issuers are completely free of the gun-jumping prohibitions. They may communicate in compliance with Section 5 at any time by means of unrestricted oral and written communications. Nonetheless, these communications, when considered offers to sell, may be subject to liability under other securities law provisions based on misrepresentation or omission.[19] As discussed later in this chapter, a written offer made by a well-known seasoned issuer pursuant to Rule 163 will constitute a "free writing prospectus."[20]

Issuers that are not well known seasoned issuers remain subject to the gun-jumping prohibitions. Importantly, Rule 163A provides protection for these issuers with respect to their communications that occur more than thirty days prior to the filing of the subject registration statement. Effectively, the Rule 163A safe harbor exempts these communications from the definition of "offer" for Section 5(c) purposes. However, unlike Rule 163 communications, a Rule 163A communication has several stipulations:

> *First*, a Rule 163A communication cannot reference the offering itself; *second*, only communications made by or on behalf of the issuer come within the safe harbor (accordingly, underwriters and participating dealers may not claim the safe harbor); and *third*, the burden is on the issuer to take reasonable steps to prevent circulation of the communication in the thirty day period leading up to the filing of the registration statement.[21] Key challenges facing the SEC in the interpretation of Rule 163A include determining what constitutes an impermissible 'reference' to the contemplated public offering in a pre-filing communication, and determining what actions the issuer must take to corral previously released communications during the thirty-day period immediately prior to the filing of the registration statement. Nonetheless, as discussed below, an issuer's disclosure of information about the contemplated registered offering in the pre-filing period may be protected under Rule 135.

---

[18] The definition for "well known seasoned issuer" is discussed *supra* § 4.02[A].

[19] A written offer made in connection with a public offering is deemed a prospectus under Section 2(a)(10) of the Securities Act. If materially inadequate, such communication may render the issuer liable under Section 12(a)(2) and Section 17(a) of the Securities Act as well as Section 10(b) of the Exchange Act and Rule 10b-5 promulgated thereunder.

[20] *See infra* § 4.02[C][2].

[21] *See* Securities Act Release No. 8591 (2005). Note that Rule 163A may not be used in offerings made by a blank check company, shell company, or penny stock issuer. Also, note that separate rules apply to business combination transactions. *See* Rules 165, 424, 425.

[4] Effect of Rule 135

Rule 135 allows an issuer, subject to certain conditions, to make a public announcement relating to a contemplated public offering of its securities. In this respect, Rule 135 exempts from Section 5(c) a notice given by an issuer in the pre-filing period that complies with its provisions. Hence, an issuer notice that adheres to Rule 135 is not deemed to constitute an "offer to sell." Generally, a Rule 135 notice, in addition to containing only certain specified information, must include a legend stating that the notice does not constitute an offer to sell. Note that the Rule prohibits the underwriters from being named in the notice and that judicial authority has interpreted the Rule as setting forth an exclusive list.[22] Accordingly, an issuer notice that:

(1) goes beyond the parameters of Rule 135,
(2) that cannot invoke the umbrella of another safe harbor provision (such as Rule 163 for well known seasoned issuers), and
(3) where the information set forth in the notice is not otherwise required by another SEC regulation.

likely will constitute an "offer to sell" in the pre-filing period, thereby violating Section 5(c). In this regard, the Second Circuit has opined:

> When it is announced that securities will be sold at some date in the future and, in addition, an attractive description of these securities and of the issuer is furnished, it seems clear that such an announcement provides much the same kind of information as that contained in a prospectus. Doubtless the line drawn between an announcement containing sufficient information to constitute an offer and one which does not must be to some extent arbitrary. A checklist of features that may be included in an announcement which does not also constitute an offer to sell serves to guide the financial community and the courts far better than any judicially formulated "rule of reason" as to what is or is not an offer. Rule 135 provides just such a checklist, and if the Rule

---

[22] *See Chris-Craft Industries, Inc. v. Bangor Punta Corporation*, 426 F.2d 569 (2d Cir. 1970) (en banc). Generally, Rule 135 provides that only the following may be set forth in the "notice":

(1) The notice includes a statement to the effect that it does not constitute an offer of any securities for sale; and

(2) The notice otherwise includes *no more than* the following information:

(i) The name of the issuer;

(ii) The title, amount and basic terms of the securities offered;

(iii) The amount of the offering, if any, to be made by selling security holders;

(iv) The anticipated timing of the offering;

(v) A brief statement of the manner and the purpose of the offering without naming the underwriters;

(vi) Whether the issuer is directing its offering to only a particular class of purchasers;

(vii) Any statements or legends required by the laws of any state or foreign country of administrative authority. . . .

Id. (emphasis added). Additional information may be provided pursuant to Rule 135 for certain types of offerings, including, for example, an exchange offer, a rights offering to existing security holders, and an offering to the subject issuer's employees. *See* Rule 135(a)(2)(viii)(A)-(D).

is not construed as setting forth an exclusive list, then much of its value as a guide is lost.[23]

Importantly, note that the safe harbors contained in Rules 168, 169, and 163A cannot reference the contemplated public offering. Therefore, issuers that are not well known seasoned issuers must continue to exercise caution with respect to public announcements in the pre-filing period of contemplated public offerings.

[5]   **Transactions Between Market Professionals**

In addition to Rule 135, certain other actions are exempt from constituting an offer to sell or an offer to buy, and, hence, are permitted in the pre-filing period. For example, under Section 2(a)(3) of the Securities Act, negotiations and agreements between the underwriter and the issuer or among underwriters who are (or will be) in privity with the issuer are allowed in the pre-filing period.

Importantly, unless otherwise exempted, the prohibitions of Section 5 apply to transactions and discussions between market professionals. For example, an "offer to buy" in the pre-filing period by a dealer not in privity with the issuer to an underwriter who is in privity with the issuer constitutes a violation of Section 5(c). The prohibitions of Section 5 in the waiting and post-effective periods also apply to transactions and discussions between market professionals, unless otherwise exempted.[24]

Turning to another point, an individual investor who contacts his/her broker-dealer in the pre-filing period to buy a few shares of a company's stock to be issued in the public offering normally does not violate Section 5. That is because the individual, unless he/she is deemed to be engaged in a "distribution," has the Section 4(1) exemption which exempts from the Section 5 registration requirements "transactions by any person other than an issuer, underwriter, or dealer."[25]

[6]   **Rules 137, 138, and 139**

Rules 137, 138, and 139 permit broker-dealers to engage in specified "safe harbor" activities in the pre-filing period without violating Section 5. Rules 137–139 apply as well to the waiting and post-effective periods. The availability and scope of these rules may be contingent on the reporting status of the issuer as discussed below and in § 4.02[A].[26]

Generally, Rules 137, 138 and 139 establish standards for ascertaining the circumstances under which broker-dealers without violating Section 5 may

---

[23] 426 F.2d at 574.

[24] *See, e.g., Byrnes v. Faulkner, Dawkins & Sullivan*, 550 F.2d 1303 (2d Cir. 1977).

[25] *See* Chapter 6 for further discussion of the Section 4(1) exemption.

[26] References will hereafter generally be made only to U.S. issuers who register their Securities Act offerings on such Forms as S-1 or S-3.

publish research reports concerning issuers that propose to conduct a registered public offering.

Rule 137 is directed at brokers or dealers who are not participating in the public offering — in other words, those broker-dealers who are not in privity of contract either with the issuer or with any underwriter or other participant of the offering (for example, such broker-dealers are not purchasing the securities offered from the issuer or from any of the underwriters). The Rule may be invoked for any eligible issuer irrespective of the subject issuer's Exchange Act reporting status. Generally, Rule 137 allows a nonparticipating broker-dealer in the regular course of its business to publish and distribute research reports containing information, recommendations, and opinions concerning the securities of an issuer that intends to file (or has filed) a Securities Act registration statement without such broker-dealer being deemed an underwriter.[27]

Rule 138 permits brokers or dealers who are (or will be) participating in a distribution of an issuer's common stock (or convertible preferred stock or convertible debt securities) to publish or distribute research reports that are confined specifically to the issuer's non-convertible fixed income securities (or vice versa). A research report complying with Rule 138 is deemed not to constitute an offer to sell for purposes of: Section 2(a)(10) (defining the term "prospectus"); or Section 5(c) (prohibiting offers to sell in the pre-filing period by, among others, underwriters and dealers). Any such research report must be disseminated in the regular course of the broker-dealer's business. Unlike Rule 137, Rule 138 applies only to eligible issuers current in their Exchange Act reporting obligations (or to certain non-reporting foreign private issuers that have either equity securities traded on a designated offshore market or that have a worldwide market value of at least $700 million in outstanding common equity held by nonaffiliates).[28]

Provided that its requirements are met, *Rule 139* permits a broker or dealer participating in a distribution of securities that is the subject of a Securities Act registration statement to publish research reports concerning the issuer or any class of its securities. A research report adhering to Rule 139 is not an offer to sell under Section 2(a)(10) (defining the term "prospectus") and is not viewed as "gun-jumping" under Section 5(c), namely, an illegal offer to sell in the pre-filing period by a participant in the contemplated public offering. Any such research report under Rule 139 must be published or distributed in the regular course of the broker-dealer's business.

With respect to issuer-specific research reports, use of Rule 139 for U.S. issuers generally requires that a seasoned (or well known seasoned) issuer be current in its Exchange Act reporting and is either eligible to file (or has filed) a registration statement on Form S-3 (or Form F-3) based on Form S-3's $75

---

[27] Note that Rule 137 cannot be used for offerings by ineligible issuers — ineligible issuers include those issuers that are (or during the past three years have been) a blank check company, shell company, or penny stock issuer. Rule 137(d).

[28] Like Rule 137, Rule 138 cannot be used for blank check companies, shell companies, and penny stock issuers. Rule 138(a)(ii)(C)(4).

million minimum public float eligibility provision. Rule 139 requires that for such issuer-specific research reports, any such publication or distribution by the broker or dealer must "not represent the initiation of publication of research reports about such issuer or its securities or reinitiation of such publication following discontinuation."[29]

In addition, the Rule provides a safe harbor for industry reports covering the securities of an Exchange Act reporting issuer. Such industry report as is the case with issuer-specific research reports may upgrade the opinion regarding the subject security (*e.g.*, from "hold" to "buy"). Moreover, such industry report must "includ[e] similar information about the issuer or its securities [as contained] in similar reports." Moreover, the report must include similar information for a substantial number of companies in the issuer's industry (or sub-industry), or, alternatively, contain a comprehensive list of securities that the broker or dealer currently recommends. Last, for such industry reports, Rule 139 mandates that "[t]he analysis regarding the issuer or its securities is given no materially greater space or prominence in the publication than that given to other securities or issuers."[30]

[C]   The Waiting Period

[1]   Overview

After the registration statement is filed with the Commission, the *waiting period* commences. In this time period, subsections (a) and (b) of Section 5 are applicable. Section 5(b)(1) prohibits the use of the mails or any means of interstate commerce to transmit any prospectus, unless such prospectus meets the requirements of Section 10. Since Section 2(a)(10) defines a prospectus to include any written offer, there is no prohibition against verbal offers during the waiting period. However, the contents and form of written offers are limited by Section 2(a)(10) and Section 10 as well as SEC rules.

Stated generally, during the waiting period (as well as the post-effective period), written offers may be made by means of a statutory Section 10 prospectus, a Section 10 free writing prospectus, as well as the tombstone ad (or Rule 134 public notice). Moreover, pursuant to Section 5(a), the securities may not be sold nor may offers to buy be accepted unless the registration statement has become effective.

---

[29] Rule 139(a)(iii). Note that under certain conditions, issuer-specific research reports may be issued pursuant to Rule 139 for foreign private issuers. *See* Rule 139(a)(1)(B).

[30] Rule 139(a)(2). Like Rules 137 and 138, Rule 139 cannot be used for blank check companies, shell companies, or penny stock issuers. *See* Morrissey, *Rhetoric and Reality: Investor Protection and the Securities Regulation Reform of 2005*, 56 Cath. U. L. Rev. 561, 579 (2007) (asserting that pursuant to Rule 139, "it seems that a financially interested broker or dealer will be able to take advantage of this revised [Rule 139] safe harbor to inflate its rating of [a subject] security despite having great financial incentive to condition the market to increase the price of the securities being offered").

[2] Free Writing Prospectus

A free writing prospectus is a writing that offers for sale the registered offering of securities. Not meeting the detailed disclosure requirements of a statutory Section 10(a) final prospectus, *the free writing prospectus generally may be used by the issuer or any other offering participant.* The free writing prospectus may contain information not set forth in the registration statement but must not conflict with such registration statement. Note that the SEC forbids the use of legends in a free writing prospectus that disclaim liability based on the contents of such free writing prospectus.

To begin, under Rule 163, well-known seasoned issuers may use free writing prospectuses during any phase of an offering, including the pre-filing period,[31] without violating Section 5. Such prospectuses must be filed with the SEC and must contain a legend notifying the recipient where the registration statement (in the waiting and post-effective periods) can be located.

Eligible seasoned issuers (*e.g.*, S-3 issuers, those that have a $75 million float and that have timely reported under the Exchange Act for a twelve-month period but are not well known seasoned issuers) may use a free writing prospectus only if a registration statement containing a preliminary statutory prospectus has been filed. Such a free writing prospectus must contain a legend identifying where the investor can access the statutory prospectus, a hyperlink to the statutory prospectus, or the URL for the SEC website where the investor can locate the statutory prospectus. Thus, a seasoned (including a well known seasoned) issuer's use of a free writing prospectus is not conditioned on delivery to the investor of the most recent statutory prospectus.[32]

Moreover, under Rule 164 eligible non-reporting issuers and eligible unseasoned issuers,[33] may use a free writing prospectus if a registration statement has been filed with the SEC and the free writing prospectus is accompanied or preceded by the most recent statutory prospectus.[34] One form of "accompaniment" is a hyperlink to the statutory prospectus in an electronic free writing prospectus which makes it feasible for these types of issuers to use broadly disseminated free writing prospectuses. Once the required

---

[31] Note that during the *pre-filing period*, the free writing prospectus may be used by (or on behalf of) a well known seasoned issuer but may not be used during this period by an offering participant who is an underwriter or dealer. *See* Rule 163(a), (c).

[32] The legend may contain, for example, an email address through which the statutory prospectus may be requested. *See* Rules 164, 433; Securities Act Release No. 8591 (2005).

Rule 164 provides a cure for unintentional or immaterial failure to include a proper legend in a free writing prospectus so long as the issuer has made a good faith, reasonable effort to comply and the free writing prospectus is amended as soon as possible. After amendment, the free writing prospectus must be retransmitted by substantially the same means and to substantially the same investors as was the original free writing prospectus.

[33] Thus, eligible Exchange Act reporting companies that, for example, have a public float of less than $75 million, as well as companies conducting initial public offerings (IPOs) may use free writing prospectuses during the waiting and post-effective periods subject to the conditions set forth in Rules 164 and 433.

[34] *See* Rules 164, 433.

statutory prospectus has been provided, an issuer is not required to provide subsequent preliminary statutory prospectuses to an investor unless there has been a material change to the most recent such statutory prospectus. In other words, absent a material change in the most recent statutory preliminary prospectus, a subject issuer is allowed to send an investor who has received a prior statutory prospectus additional free writing prospectuses unaccompanied by the most recent statutory prospectus. However, after the registration statement becomes effective and the "final" statutory prospectus is available, delivery of an earlier "preliminary" prospectus will not suffice. The final statutory Section 10(a) prospectus must precede or accompany any free writing prospectus thereafter disseminated, even if a preliminary statutory prospectus had already been provided to the investor.[35]

Last, ineligible issuers also may use free writing prospectuses during the waiting and post-effective periods but such prospectuses may provide only a description of the terms of the offering and the securities offered.[36] Use of such a free writing prospectus by an ineligible issuer is subject to the statutory prospectus delivery requirements set forth above.[37]

As a general proposition, free writing prospectuses (or the information contained in such prospectuses) must be filed with the SEC.[38] Importantly, free writing prospectuses, unlike Section 10(a) statutory prospectuses, are not part of the registration statement and as such are not subject to Section 11 liability; however, free writing prospectuses are subject to Section 12(a)(2) disclosure liability and the anti-fraud provisions of the federal securities laws, including Section 10(b) of the Exchange Act. Furthermore, pursuant to Rule 159A, an issuer meets the definition of "seller" in a primary securities offering for Section 12(a)(2) liability purposes in the context of various underwriting arrangements, including firm commitment underwritings. Under this rule, an issuer is deemed a seller and subject to Section 12(a)(2) liability regardless of the underwriting method employed to sell such issuer's securities when, for example, any free writing prospectus or other prospectus required to be filed with the SEC is prepared by (or on behalf of) or is used by the subject issuer.[39]

Under Rule 433, an offer of securities on an issuer's website or hyperlinked from an issuer's website to another website is considered a written offer by the

---

[35] *See* Rule 433(b)(2).

[36] An ineligible issuer, for example, is an issuer that has not filed the required Exchange Act reports, has filed for bankruptcy, or has been convicted of a felony. Moreover, blank check companies, shell companies and penny stock issuers are excluded and cannot use any type of free writing prospectus. *See* Rule 164(e)(2).

[37] *See* Securities Act Release No. 8591 (2005).

[38] *See* Rule 433(d)(1). Rule 433(g) requires issuers using free writing prospectuses to retain for three years any free writing prospectuses that have not been filed with the SEC. This condition allows the SEC to review such free writing prospectuses used in reliance on Rules 164 and 433. Note that Rule 164 provides a cure for the immaterial or unintentional failure to retain a free writing prospectus so long as a good faith, reasonable effort was made to comply with the prospectus retention requirement.

[39] *See* Rule 159A for a complete listing of communications that come within the scope of this Rule.

issuer and, unless exempt from registration, is deemed a free writing prospectus. Nonetheless, the Rule allows an issuer to publish historical information on its website that is considered neither an offer to sell nor a free writing prospectus, if the information is identified as historical information and is located on a separate section of the issuer's website that contains historical information.

In most cases, underwriters and dealers are not required to file a free writing prospectus that they prepare, use, or to which they refer.[40] However, there is an exception to this Rule: a free writing prospectus used or referred to by an underwriter or other offering participant, and distributed by or on behalf of an offering participant in a manner that is reasonably designed to lead to its broad unrestricted dissemination, must be filed with the SEC before use.[41]

One last point regarding free writing prospectuses is in the context of Regulation FD (discussed in Chapter 11). The Commission has exempted from the operation of Regulation FD certain communications that are made as part of a registered offering, including free writing prospectuses, issued after the filing of a registration statement. In effect, the Commission has determined that such communications suffice for public notice purposes and are an adequate substitute for the prescribed Regulation FD procedures.[42]

[3] Media

Issuers and offering participants often use the media to deliver information about themselves to the general public through press releases and interviews. Recognizing that the media is a viable instrument for providing information about issuers and offerings to the public, the Commission has adopted certain rules in this setting. Specifically, where information (oral or written) about an issuer or an offering is provided by the issuer or any offering participant to the media and the information is subsequently published and constitutes an offer to sell, it will be considered a free writing prospectus. As such, these communications are allowed, but the issuer is required to file with the SEC such written communications within four business days of their first publication. In order to satisfy this filing requirement, the issuer may file the actual media publication (or all the information provided to the media in lieu of the publication itself), or a transcript of the interview or similar materials that were provided to the media.[43] Any further obligations imposed on the issuer for a media publication free writing prospectus will depend on whether the issuer prepared or paid for the publication (be it a written publication or a

---

[40] *See* Securities Act Release No. 8591 (2005).

[41] *See* Rule 433(d)(l)(ii).

[42] These exceptions focus on communications directly related to the registered offering. Importantly, as the SEC pointed out, "[c]ommunications not contained in our enumerated list of exceptions from Regulation FD — for example, the publication of regularly released factual business information or regularly released forward-looking information or pre-filing communications — are subject to Regulation FD." Securities Act Release No. 8591 (2005).

[43] *See* Rule 433(f).

television or radio broadcast).[44]

If an issuer prepares, pays for, or gives other consideration for the preparation or dissemination of a published article, advertisement, or broadcast, or if an issuer uses or refers to such communication, then the issuer must satisfy all of the conditions (discussed above) for that type of issuer using a free writing prospectus. Put another way, non-reporting issuers and reporting unseasoned issuers that have prepared or paid for the article, advertisement, or broadcast must precede or accompany the communication with a statutory prospectus and file the media piece with the SEC. A seasoned issuer that prepared or paid for the communication only needs to have filed a registration statement with the SEC and to file the media piece. A well known seasoned issuer, not subject to the gun-jumping prohibition due to Rule 163, may use such a media piece at any time, subject to filing the free writing prospectus with the SEC.

If, on the other hand, the free writing prospectus is prepared and published or broadcast by media persons unaffiliated with the issuer, and the issuer has participated but has not prepared or paid for the publication of such media piece, the issuer's (other than a well known seasoned issuer[45]) obligation under Section 5 is to have filed a registration statement and thereby a statutory prospectus with the SEC (otherwise, publication of such media piece within the thirty-day period prior to the filing of the registration statement with the SEC may constitute gun-jumping — see Rule 163A; § 4.02[B][2]). Under such circumstances, accompaniment of the statutory prospectus with the publication is not required.[46]

[4]   The Rule 134 Public Notice

Another avenue available to issuers looking to publish information about a forthcoming public offering after the filing of a registration statement is to disseminate a tombstone ad[47] or the more expansive Rule 134 public notice. Under Rule 134 an issuer, for example, may release general information about: its business; the terms of the securities being offered; the underwriter(s) of the offering; details on the offering process; the anticipated schedule of the offering; a description of marketing events; indications of interest and conditional offers to buy; and the security rating that is reasonably expected to be assigned. The principal purpose behind the public notice is to enable the

---

[44] *Id.*; *see* Securities Act Release No. 8591 (2005).

[45] Well-known seasoned issuers, of course, are not required to have filed a registration statement prior to using a free writing prospectus, including a media piece. *See* Rule 163. Within thirty days of filing a registration statement, issuers (other than well-known seasoned issuers) using a media publication that is a free writing prospectus may be engaged in gun-jumping. *Cf.* Rule 163A.

Note also that there exists a limited exception for issuers that are in the media business, allowing such issuers to rely on the unaffiliated media condition under certain circumstances. *See* Rule 433(f)(3).

[46] *See* Securities Act Release No. 8591 (2005).

[47] The tombstone ad is exempt from the definition of "prospectus" pursuant to Section 2(a)(10)(b) of the Securities Act.

issuer to gauge the level of financial intermediary and investor interest in the prospective offering. Notably, although the availability of Rule 134 is contingent upon the issuer filing a registration statement (which includes a prospectus), the Commission permits use of the Rule prior to ascertaining a bona fide price range of the securities to be offered. Note, however, that Rule 134 does not permit the issuer to set forth a detailed description of the securities being offered pursuant to the registration statement. If a term sheet is used by the issuer, for example, such communication, although not allowed under Rule 134, will be treated as a free writing prospectus subject to the requirements for free writing prospectuses that are addressed above.[48]

[5]   Roadshows

During the waiting period, in addition to oral communications, tombstone ads, Rule 134 public notices and Section 10 prospectuses, issuers and underwriters customarily conduct "roadshows" to prospective institutional investors, securities professionals and others as a means to present the issuer and the securities offered in a favorable light. These "performances" are used to ascertain what parties are interested in the securities and the extent of such interest.

Recall that during the thirty days leading up to the filing of the registration statement, except for well known seasoned issuers, no written sales literature (so-called "free writing") is allowed (see Rule 163A). During the waiting period, depending on the status of the issuer, written offering materials that generally may be used include a Section 10 prospectus (such as a statutory or free writing prospectus), a tombstone ad, or a Rule 134 public notice. Because roadshows frequently occur during the waiting period and involve the use of the Internet and other electronic media, it is important to determine how the Commission treats such media in light of the restrictions against written offers.

Historically, through a number of no-action letters, the SEC staff had acquiesced in the view that roadshow media did not constitute a Section 2(a)(10) prospectus and allowed the use of electronic media by issuers and underwriters to conduct roadshows for audiences consisting of sophisticated investors and securities professionals.[49] However, recognizing that roadshows have evolved from live, real-time productions made primarily to institutional investors to, at times, recorded media reproductions to larger, less sophisticated audiences, the Commission has taken a more detailed approach as to what constitutes written offers and prospectuses.

Pursuant to SEC rules, the conducting of real-time roadshows to live audiences that also are transmitted graphically in real-time (such as in real-time by means of the Internet) are not deemed written communications or free

---

[48] *See* SEC Securities Act Release 8591 (2005).

[49] *See, e.g., In re Charles Schwab & Co.*, 1999 SEC No-Act. LEXIS 903; *In re Private Financial Network*, [1997 Transfer Binder] Fed. Sec. L. Reg. (SEC) ¶ 77,332 (March 12, 1997).

writing prospectuses.[50] On the other hand, "[r]oadshows that do not originate live, in real-time to a live audience and are graphically transmitted [such as by being retransmitted by electronic mail] are electronic roadshows that will be considered written communications and, therefore, free writing prospectuses."[51] With one exception,[52] these electronic roadshows that constitute free writing prospectuses are not required to be filed with the SEC.[53]

[6]   SEC's Power of Acceleration

Under Section 8(a) of the Securities Act, a registration statement becomes effective the twentieth day after it is filed with the SEC. Significantly, the filing of any amendment commences the twenty day waiting period anew. Moreover, customarily, an issuer, particularly in an initial public offering, files its registration statement with a legend (referred to as the "delaying amendment" pursuant to Rule 473) voluntarily waiving this twenty-day period in favor of waiting until the SEC elects to clear the registration statement. Note that an exception to this general rule is that well known seasoned issuers may opt for automatic shelf registration (discussed in Chapter 5) whereby such registration statement becomes effective immediately upon filing with the SEC.[54]

Pursuant to Section 8(a), the Commission has the power of acceleration, meaning, for example, that it can determine to have the registration statement become effective immediately after the last amendment is filed. In practice, this power of acceleration along with the issuer's waiver of the twenty-day period referred to above may give the Commission a good deal of leverage. Imagine if an issuer, after filing its last amendment, would have to wait twenty days before being able to have the registered securities sold. In many situations, given the volatile nature of the financial markets, the offering, twenty days later, no longer may find a receptive audience. The end result is that the Commission staff may be able to "persuade" the issuer and affiliated parties to disclose more information than they otherwise would prefer.

The SEC has reduced its leverage in this context by adopting Rule 430A. Under Rule 430A, issuers engaging in offerings of securities for cash no longer are required to file a pre-effective "pricing" amendment (i.e., information relating to price and the underwriting syndicate). Today, specified changes can

---

[50]   Note that, if visual aids (such as slides) are used as part of a live in real-time roadshow, such visual aids are not a free writing prospectus. However, such a roadshow is an offer to sell the securities subject to Section 12(a)(2) and other liability provisions. *See* Securities Act Release No. 8591 (2005).

[51]   *Id.*; *see* Rule 433(d)(8)(ii).

[52]   Such an electronic roadshow must be filed with the SEC by a nonreporting issuer (such as an issuer conducting an IPO) "unless the issuer . . . makes at least one version of [the] roadshow available without restriction by means of graphic communication to any person, including any potential investor in the securities. . . ." Rule 433(d)(8).

[53]   *See* Rule 433(d)(8)(i); Securities Act Release No. 8591 (2005).

[54]   *See* Rule 415(a)(5)(i); Securities Act Release No. 8591 (2005).

be made with respect to such matters as price and volume information after the registration statement's effective date, provided that such changes do not materially alter the disclosure contained in the registration statement.

With respect to Rule 430A, the SEC has pointed out that the Rule does not alter an issuer's disclosure obligations. According to the Commission, Rule 430A is intended to "minimize the risk of disruption of a registrant's marketing schedule caused by the need to file a pricing amendment and wait until the registration statement is declared effective."[55] Note, moreover, that pursuant to the 2005 amendments, registration statements filed by well known seasoned issuers pursuant to the SEC's automatic shelf registration process (discussed in Chapter 5) become effective immediately upon filing with the Commission.

Significantly, as a condition to granting acceleration, the SEC may require the respective parties to undertake certain actions. For example, under Item 512(h) of Regulation S-K, in order to request acceleration of the effective date of the registration statement, the issuer must disclose, inter alia, any arrangement to indemnify any director, officer or controlling person of the issuer against liabilities arising under the Securities Act. Moreover, a subject issuer, pursuant to Item 510 of Regulation S-K, also must disclose that such indemnification with respect to a director, officer, or controlling person of the issuer, "in the opinion of the Securities and Exchange Commission . . . is against public policy as expressed in the [Securities] Act and is, therefore, unenforceable."

[D]   The Post-Effective Period

[1]   Overview

After the registration statement becomes effective, the *post-effective* period commences. Sales of the subject securities now may be made. Written offers continue to be regulated by the SEC offering rules discussed above, such as use of the free writing prospectus.[56]

The contents of the final statutory prospectus are specified in Section 10(a). Unlike the preliminary prospectus which is used in the waiting period (see Rule 430), the statutory final prospectus is used after the registration statement becomes effective. This is because the preliminary prospectus has certain incomplete information. During the post-effective period, the Section 10(a) final statutory prospectus must be provided or be accessible to purchasers of the subject securities.[57]

---

[55] Securities Act Release No. 6714 (1987); *see* Securities Act Release No. 6964 (1992).

[56] *See* discussion *supra* § 4.02[C][2].

[57] *See* Rules 172, 173; Securities Act Release No. 8591 (2005).

[2]   Access Equals Delivery

As part of its effort to modernize the offering process, and in acknowledgment of the vast availability of internet access to the investing public, the SEC adopted an "access equals delivery" framework to the Section 5 prospectus delivery requirement in the post-effective period.[58] Under the access equals delivery approach, and subject to certain exceptions,[59] investors are presumed to have access to the Internet. Accordingly, issuers and other offering participants, such as dealers, may satisfy the prospectus delivery requirement by posting the final statutory prospectus on a readily accessible website. Thus, the Section 5 requirement that a final statutory prospectus precede or accompany the delivery of the securities for sale or accompany a sale confirmation has been eliminated provided that the final statutory prospectus is timely filed with the Commission and is posted on a readily accessible website.[60] Moreover, in recognition that actual physical delivery aided investors in tracing their purchase to a specific registration statement, thereby preserving their Section 11 right of action for any material disclosure deficiency in such registration statement, the SEC adopted a notification rule requiring dealers or underwriters to provide a notice to purchasers that their purchase was pursuant to a registration statement.[61]

[E]   Chart of Time Periods

The following chart hopefully will help clarify the conduct permitted as well as prohibited during the pre-filing, waiting, and post-effective periods. Note that the Chart simplifies a number of the requirements and should be used for ease of reference purposes.

---

[58] Rule 172.

[59] Rule 172 does not apply to tender offers or business combination transactions, and is unavailable to registered investment and business development companies.

[60] *See* Securities Act Release No. 8591 (2005).

[61] *See* Rule 173(a) (providing that "each underwriter or dealer . . . shall provide to each customer from it, not later than two business days following the completion of such sale, a copy of the final prospectus or, in lieu of such prospectus, a notice to the effect that the sale was made pursuant to a registration statement or in a transaction in which a final prospectus would have been required to have been delivered in the absence of Rule 172"). For further discussion, *see* Morrissey, *Rhetoric and Reality: Investor Protection and the Securities Regulation Reform of 2005*, 56 Cath. U.L. Rev. 561 (2007); Pena, *The Free-Writing Prospectus: A Six Question Approach for Issuers*, 33 Sec. Reg. L.J. 36 (2006).

Time Period Chart

Pre-Filing	Waiting	Post-Effective
Offers to sell as well as offers to buy are prohibited – see §§ 2(a)(3), 5(c). Exception for well-known seasoned issuers – see Rule 163.	Oral offers and written offers by means of a § 10 prospectus are permitted – see §§ 2(a)(10), 5(b)(1), 10(b), Rules 164, 430, 431, 433.	Sales may be made only if a statutory § 10(a) prospectus has been provided or is accessible to the purchaser – see §§ 2(a)(10), 5(b), 10(a), Rules 172, 173.
More than 30 days before filing date: Written and oral communications are permitted as long as they do not reference the offering and subject to certain other restrictions – see Rule 163A.	May make written offers under Rule 164 using a free writing prospectus as long as Rule 433 is complied with and the issuer satisfies applicable "accompaniment" requirements – see Rules 164, 433.	Final prospectus requirements may be satisfied by providing "access" to the statutory prospectus in lieu of actual delivery – see Rule 172.
Sales are prohibited – see §§ 2(a)(3), 5(a). Negotiations and agreements between the issuer and any underwriter or among underwriters who are or will be in privity with the issuer are permitted – see § 2(a)(3).	For seasoned and well-known seasoned issuers, no requirement that use of free writing prospectus is conditioned on actual delivery of preliminary statutory prospectus; rather, a legend must be used stating where the preliminary statutory prospectus can be accessed – see Rules 164, 433.	Use of free-writing prospectuses in the post-effective period permitted under certain circumstances – see §§ 2(a)(10), 5(b)(1), 10(a), Rules 164, 172, 173, 430A, 433. Both the "tombstone ad" and the "public notice" may be used – see § 2(a)(10), Rule 134.
All issuers may make an announcement of a proposed public offering in compliance with Rule 135.	Securities may be sold and offers to buy may be accepted only in the post-effective period – see §§ 2(a)(3), 5(a).	
All issuers may continue to publish regularly released factual information (including as well in the Waiting and Post-Effective Periods) – see Rules 168, 169.	Both the "tombstone ad" and the "public notice" may be used – see § 2(a)(10), Rule 134.	
Exchange Act Reporting Issuers may continue to publish forward-looking information (including as well in the Waiting and Post Effective Periods) – see Rule 168.		
Pursuant to Rules 137-139, a broker or dealer may publish certain information about specified issuers. This is also the case in the waiting and post-effective periods.		
Well known Seasoned Issuers may make offers to sell and may use free writing prospectuses – see Rule 163.		

§ 4.03   THE "MISLEADING" PROSPECTUS

In *SEC v. Manor Nursing Centers, Inc.*,[62] the Second Circuit considered whether material misrepresentations or nondisclosures contained in a statutory prospectus signified that, in addition to incurring antifraud liability, the prospectus failed to meet the requirements of Section 10(a) of the 1933 Act and,

---

[62] 458 F.2d 1082 (2d Cir. 1972).

hence, violated Section 5(b)(2) of that Act. In that case, the violations were premised on the defendants' failure to amend or supplement the prospectus to reflect changes which occurred in the post-effective period that made the previous information furnished materially false and misleading. The Second Circuit held that Section 5(b)(2) had been violated, stating:

> We hold that implicit in the statutory provision that the prospectus contain certain information is the requirement that such information be true and correct. A prospectus does not meet the requirements of § 10(a), therefore, if information required to be disclosed is materially false and misleading. Appellants violated § 5(b)(2) by delivering Manor securities for sale accompanied by a prospectus which did not meet the requirements of § 10(a) in that the prospectus contained materially false and misleading statements with respect to information required by § 10(a) to be disclosed.[63]

The *Manor Nursing* analysis is subject to criticism because it imposes essentially strict liability, thereby nullifying the due diligence and reasonable care defenses contained in Sections 11 and 12(a)(2) of the Securities Act (see Chapter 7). For this reason, a number of courts have limited its holding to apply only where the prospectus or a like document is egregiously incomplete or permeated with misrepresentations.[64] Other courts, in analogous situations, have completely rejected *Manor Nursing*'s rationale.[65]

One such case is *SEC v. Southwest Coal & Energy Company*.[66] There, the SEC relied by analogy on *Manor Nursing*, arguing that the issuer had never properly qualified for a Regulation B exemption since its Schedule D offering sheets were materially false and misleading. Such materially defective offering sheets, the SEC asserted, did not meet Regulation B's initial filing requirements, thereby violating Section 5(a) and 5(c). The Fifth Circuit rejected this contention, reasoning that such an interpretation would impose strict liability and vitiate the defenses available under other provisions of the securities laws (*e.g.*, Sections 11, 12(a)(2), and 17(a) of the Securities Act and Section 10(b) of the Exchange Act). The court stated:

> That an offering sheet which formally complies with the disclosure requirements of Schedule D is misleading in some respect, should not automatically render void *ab initio* a Regulation B exemption obtained on the basis of that offering. Rather, representations and material nondisclosures may be adequately dealt with under the pertinent antifraud provisions expressly designed for that purpose, instead of under § 5(a), (c) which is more appropriately focused upon failures to adhere to the prescribed formal mechanisms or procedures.[67]

---

[63] *Id.* at 1098.

[64] *See, e.g., Byrnes v. Faulkner Dawkins & Sullivan*, 413 F. Supp. 453 (S.D.N.Y. 1976), *aff'd on other grounds*, 550 F.2d 1303 (2d Cir. 1977).

[65] *See, e.g., SEC v. Blazon Corp.*, 609 F.2d 960 (9th Cir. 1979).

[66] 624 F.2d 1312 (5th Cir. 1980).

[67] *Id.* at 1319 (citations omitted).

The view expressed above, on balance, is correct. To hold that a Section 5 violation occurs whenever a security is sold pursuant to a materially false or misleading statement in the registration statement or like document (such as the prospectus which comprises part of the registration statement) would negate the defenses that would otherwise be available. Such a result is one that Congress could not have intended.

On the other hand, confining the thrust of *Manor Nursing* to issuers of registered offerings, then the decision may be viewed as compatible with Section 11. Because Section 11 holds issuers strictly liable for the making of a materially false or misleading statement in a registration statement, the *Manor Nursing* rationale may be viewed as consistent with the framework of Section 11, provided that it is limited only to issuers.[68]

§ 4.04   "GOING PUBLIC" — PROS AND CONS

Briefly, the *advantages* of an enterprise going public and having its initial public offering (IPO) include:

    1. The funds obtained from the offering may be used for capital formation purposes as well as for retiring existing indebtedness.

    2. The insiders may sell a substantial portion of their stock and thereby become (if they are not already) millionaires.

    3. A public offering, by improving the company's financial position, will enable the company to have access to capital on more favorable terms.

    4. The funds desired from the offering may enable the company to expand by acquiring other businesses.

    5. By offering stock remuneration packages tied to a public market, the enterprise will be in a better position to hire and retain quality personnel.

    6. By having a public market for its stock, the company may become better known, thereby possibly resulting in improved profits.

On the other hand, perceived *disadvantages* of going public include:

    1. The costs of an IPO, particularly when compared to other methods of procuring funds, are high.

    2. Due to shareholder concern for the short-term, management may discount long-term strategies in order to put emphasis on the company's stock price.

---

[68] In this regard, the Commission has certain enforcement powers if the registration statement is materially false or misleading. The most significant such power is the "stop order" pursuant to Section 8(d) of the Securities Act. *See* McLucas, *Stop Order Proceedings Under the Securities Act of 1933: A Current Assessment*, 40 Bus. Law. 515 (1980).

3. Management, through its sale of stock, may lose control of the enterprise and become subject to a hostile takeover.

4. By going public, the enterprise becomes a reporting company under the Securities Exchange Act. Such a consequence may be viewed as having several disadvantages to insiders including:

a. The company now must file periodic and annual reports, comply with the internal accounting controls and recordkeeping mandates of the Foreign Corrupt Practices Act (even if all of the company's operations are domestic), be subject to the federal proxy provisions, as well as a number of other requirements.

b. The company becomes subject to the rigors of the Sarbanes-Oxley Act (SOX). For example, SOX: requires chief executive officer and chief financial officer certification of the subject company's periodic reports with the SEC; mandates the implementation of sufficient internal controls; delineates the composition and functions of audit committees; bars company loans to directors and executive officers; and bars an auditor from performing certain non-audit services for a corporate audit-client.

c. The expenses of complying with Exchange Act and SOX requirements will be substantial.

d. Insiders lose some of their privacy as their salaries, perquisites, and transactions with the issuer must be disclosed pursuant to SEC rules.

e. Due to such mandated disclosure, there is a greater risk of shareholder litigation.

f. Insiders are subject to the short-swing six-month trading provisions of Section 16 of the Exchange Act, thereby resulting in some loss of liquidity and potential liability.

Given the above, the decision to go public may not be an easy one. Moreover, the registration process, including the planning, preparation, structuring, and timing of a public offering, is a major undertaking for all parties concerned.

§ 4.05 A BRIEF LOOK AT THE PROCESS OF A PUBLIC OFFERING

The advantages and disadvantages of going public are addressed in § 4.04. In addition, the process of the initial public offering and the ramifications thereof are described in excerpts from articles contained in the textbook.[69]

---

[69] *See* M. Steinberg, Securities Regulation 182–189 (5th ed. 2008) (containing excerpts from, Schneider, Manko & Kant, *Going Public: Practice, Procedure, and Consequences*, 27 Vill. L. Rev. 1 (1981); Schneider & Shargel, *"Now That You Are Publicly Owned . . . ",* 36 Bus. Law. 1631 (1981)).

In brief, and put simplistically, the process of a public offering may be analogized to the sale of commercial goods. In a public offering, the distribution chain normally is as follows: Issuer — Underwriters — Participating Dealers — Investors/Purchasers (who may be individuals or institutions). Generally speaking, the larger in dollar size and the greater the geographical area where the selling activity takes place, the larger the number of underwriters and dealers who will comprise the distribution chain to effectuate the offering. Note the similarity to the sale of commercial goods: Manufacturer — Wholesalers — Retailers — Consumers. As with the sale of commercial goods where wholesalers may sell directly to the public, underwriters also may bypass the "dealer-link" and sell the securities directly to investors. This may occur, for example, when an underwriter (such as Merrill Lynch) has a national retail brokerage capacity with which to market the securities directly to investors.

Underwriting agreements for the most part are on a "firm commitment" basis. This means that the underwriters agree to purchase the securities from the issuer (at a discount) with the intent to resell them to participating dealers and/or investors. Although the underwriters incur the risk of "being stuck" with the securities if there is insufficient buyer interest, this risk is minimized due to that, during the "waiting" period (when, regardless of the status of the subject issuer, offers can be made[70]), purchaser interest can be estimated with a fair degree of accuracy. And, importantly, the underwriters' obligations normally are subject to several conditions, including various "outs" to not close should certain adverse developments arise prior to the closing date. Thus, the underwriters customarily are not obligated until the "eve" of the offering's effective date when the underwriting agreement is finalized to, inter alia, determine the desired number of shares to be offered and fix the offering price per share. By that time, there exists a strong indication of the market's likely response to the offering.[71]

Another type of underwriting agreement is on a "best efforts" basis. In this situation, the underwriters act as agents for the issuer. Rather than purchasing the securities outright from the issuer and incurring the risk of insufficient investor interest in such securities or the specter of a "bear" market, the underwriters, acting as agent for the issuer, locate buyers utilizing their "best efforts." These types of offerings may be used for start-up or financially troubled enterprises where there is a substantial degree of uncertainty regarding the offering's, as well as the company's, ultimate success. Because investors may wish some degree of comfort when they part with their money in these types of offerings, such offerings frequently may be made on "a part or none" or "an all or nothing" basis. This means that, unless the requisite number of shares as stated in the registration statement are sold to bona fide purchasers and the proceeds are received by a specified date, all funds must be returned to the prospective investors.[72]

---

[70] See supra § 4.02[C].

[71] See C. Johnson & J. McLaughlin, Corporate Finance and the Securities Laws 65-117 (3d ed. 2004); Schneider, Manko & Kant, Going Public: Practice, Procedure and Consequences, 27 Vill. L. Rev. 1, 24 (1981).

[72] See Rule 10b-9, 17 C.F.R. § 240.10b-9; Securities Exchange Act Release No. 11532 (1975). See

In either a "firm commitment" or "best efforts" underwriting arrangement, the obligations of the underwriters normally are subject to various contractual conditions, called "outs." Pursuant to such an arrangement, for example, underwriters may have the right not to close the "deal" if specified adverse developments arise before the closing date (such as the presence of adverse market conditions) or if the issuer fails to comply with its specified representations and warranties. Moreover, the underwriters condition their obligations by bargaining for the receipt of certain legal opinions and/or representations from counsel for the issuer.[73]

A word should be said about the underwriting syndicate and dealer group. The syndicate is headed by the main underwriter or main underwriters (there, for example, may be three main underwriters in a fairly large offering). These underwriters generally are the ones to negotiate with the issuer and are delegated by the other underwriters in the syndicate to perform the due diligence functions. To effectuate the desired distribution, the main underwriter(s) will locate and bring in other underwriters which desire to take part in the offering. Generally, these "lower-tier" underwriters in the offering will purchase a significantly smaller number of shares from the issuer than the main underwriter(s). Although all underwriters are jointly and severally liable for material misstatements in the registration statement, Section 11(e) mitigates this potentially harsh effect somewhat by limiting an underwriter's damages to the dollar amount of the securities offered by such underwriter to the public. Moreover, Section 11(f) expressly permits a party to recover contribution.[74]

Members of the dealer group ("participating" dealers), as discussed earlier in this chapter, are not in privity with the issuer. These are broker-dealers who for one reason or another (such as inability or a conscious desire not to commit the necessary funds) are not members of the underwriting syndicate but who nonetheless deem it in their financial interests to become a "participant" in the offering. Hence, they purchase from underwriters an allocated number of shares offered and resell them to their customers, their profit being the difference between the purchase price from the underwriters and the price of resale to their customers. Although dealers are not subject to Section 11 liability, they may incur liability under other provisions by, for example, making material misstatements (or omissions), violating the registration requirements, or being held responsible for material misrepresentations (or nondisclosures) that are contained in a prospectus.

---

generally Frelich & Janvey, *Understanding "Best Efforts" Offerings*, 17 Sec. Reg. L.J. 151 (1989).

[73] *See* Schneider, Manko & Kant, *Going Public: Practice, Procedure and Consequences*, 27 Vill. L. Rev. 1, 24 (1981). *See generally* L. Loss & J. Seligman, Securities Regulation 315-595 (3d ed. 1989). Such opinions, representations, or statements from counsel raise serious liability concerns. *See infra* Glossary (defining the term "Comfort Opinion"). *See generally* D. Glaser, S. FitzGibbon & S. Weise, Legal Opinions (2d. ed. 2001 & supp.); *Statement on the Role of Customary Practice in the Preparation and Understanding of Third-Party Legal Opinions*, 63 Bus. Law. 1277 (2008); Rice & Steinberg, *Legal Opinions in Securities Transactions*, 16 J. Corp. L. 375 (1991).

[74] Such contribution is allowed "unless the person who has become liable was, and the other [person] was not, guilty of fraudulent misrepresentation." § 11(f)(1).

§ 4.06 STATE "BLUE SKY" LAW

Generally, under state Blue Sky law, as under the federal securities laws, every security offered to be sold in the applicable state must be registered or exempt from registration. Note one important caveat: If the securities offered are or will be listed on such national securities markets as the New York or American Stock Exchange or traded on the NASDAQ National Market System, offerings of such securities are exempt from state registration requirements. Hence, companies whose stock, for example, is or will be listed on a major stock exchange or traded on the NASDAQ National Market System are exempt from the states' registration requirements.[75]

Traditionally, there are three types of registration which states may require. The first type, registration by coordination, is available to the issuer when a registered offering is being made under the Securities Act of 1933. This method of registration only requires the filing of three copies of the current federal prospectus as well as any additional information required by the state securities administrator. A second type of registration, registration by notification, requires the filing of a short-form registration statement and is available generally only when an issuer and its predecessors have had a seasoned business history for at least five years (*e.g.*, no default and average net earnings). The third type of registration, registration by qualification, goes further than mandating full disclosure and authorizes the state securities administrator to engage in merit regulation. Under merit regulation, the state securities administrator can prevent an offering from going forward because it is not "fair, just and equitable."[76]

Although many states reject merit regulation, a number of others adhere to this approach. In states adopting merit regulation, full and fair disclosure alone is not enough. Rather, the offering also must be deemed "fair, just, and equitable." The debate over merit regulation generally has focused on whether full disclosure of material information concerning an offering is sufficient to protect investors, the propriety of paternalistic government regulation, and the economic costs versus benefits of such a system of regulation.[77] Generally, merit regulation is used to describe the securities laws of those states which, "in addition to requiring full disclosure, have granted their administrators power to analyze the securities to be offered, the terms of the offering, and the business of the issuer for purposes of determining, according to certain formal and informal rules, whether the securities are too speculative for public sale."[78]

---

[75] *See* Securities Act § 18(b)(1), enacted as part of the National Securities Markets Improvement Act of 1996. *See generally* Manning, *The Status of the Marketplace Exemption from State Securities Registration*, 41 Bus. Law. 1511 (1986).

[76] *See* T. Hazen, The Law of Securities Regulation § 8.2 (5th ed. 2005). *See generally* J. Long, Blue Sky Law § 1.04 (2008).

[77] *See generally* Campbell, *An Open Attack on the Nonsense of Blue Sky Regulation*, 10 J. Corp. L. 553 (1985); Sargent, *The Challenge to Merit Regulation*, 12 Sec. Reg. L.J. 276, 367 (1984); Tyler, *More About Blue Sky*, 39 Wash. & Lee L. Rev. 899 (1982); American Bar Association, *Report on State Regulation of Securities Offerings*, 41 Bus. Law. 785 (1986).

[78] J. Mofsky, *Blue Sky Restrictions on New Business Promotions* 7–8 (1971); *see* authorities cited *supra* note 77.

In general, "tough" merit regulation states may deny registration or impose conditions (such as requiring escrow of insider proceeds for a certain period of time or until specified contingencies are met) where insiders or promoters have invested relatively little in relation to the amount of capital sought by the offering or if the promoters or insiders have received "cheap stock" (namely, stock received at significantly lower prices than the proposed public offering price). Further, registration may be denied in such states if the proposed offering price is deemed too high (*e.g.*, the issuer's earnings history is not reflected in the proposed offering price), if the voting rights sought to be issued to the public are inequitable, or if the underwriter's commissions are unreasonable for the proposed offering.[79]

---

[79] *See* J. Long, *supra* note 76, at § 1.05.

Chapter 5

DISCLOSURE, MATERIALITY AND SARBANES-OXLEY

§ 5.01 INTRODUCTION

This chapter examines key issues underlying concepts of disclosure and materiality under the federal securities laws. Issues addressed encompass the SEC's integrated disclosure framework, "plain English" principles, the policies underlying the mandatory disclosure system, disclosure of forward-looking information, as well as the application of materiality principles, including what is called qualitative materiality. In addition, this chapter focuses on key provisions of the Sarbanes-Oxley Act of 2002.

§ 5.02 THE INTEGRATED DISCLOSURE FRAMEWORK

The SEC's integrated disclosure system was adopted to ameliorate the expenses and duplication that were prevalent as a result of two different reporting mandates under the 1933 Act and the 1934 Act. In seeking to make disclosure as uniform as practicable under the two Acts, the SEC promulgated Regulation S-K and Regulation S-X (accounting rules) which act as the key sources for ascertaining the disclosures required to be made.

This is not to imply, however, that the disclosures contained in the various documents prepared pursuant to SEC mandates are identical. For example, with respect to the annual report on Form 10-K and the annual report to shareholders, the SEC took the following position:

> The Commission has determined to require only portions of the Form 10-K and the annual report to security holders to have equivalent disclosure because these documents are not necessarily used in an identical manner. Disclosure requirements in annual reports evolved in the context of shareholders making voting decisions. The [disclosure in the] Form 10-K . . . has been more detailed.[1]

Hence, under the Commission's integrated disclosure framework, registrant reporting is simplified in three ways: "(1) disclosure requirements are made uniform under the Securities Act and the Exchange Act; (2) Exchange Act periodic reporting is used to satisfy much of the disclosure necessary in Securities Act registration statements; and (3) the use of informal shareholder communications is encouraged, but not required, to satisfy formal statutory requirements under both Acts."[2]

---

[1] Securities Act Release No. 6231 (1980).

[2] SEC Securities Act Release No. 6331 (1981). Note that, under the Electronic Data Gathering,

This emphasis on Exchange Act periodic disclosure under the integrated disclosure system induced the SEC to require that a majority of the registrant's directors sign the annual Form 10-K. Such a signature requirement was necessary, according to the Commission, in order to encourage directors "to devote the needed attention in reviewing the Form 10-K and to seek the involvement of other professionals to the degree necessary to give themselves sufficient comfort."[3]

The integrated disclosure process, although calling for meaningful non-duplicative information, has evoked important liability concerns. These liability issues, related to the concept of "due diligence," are addressed in Chapter 7.

[A]   Registration Forms

To implement the integrated disclosure system, the Commission has in place two registration forms, Form S-1 and Form S-3.[4] These forms serve as the basic framework for registered offerings under the Securities Act. Incorporation by reference from 1934 Act reports is permitted in varying degrees on both Forms.

The registration statement for the first category is Form S-1. Form S-1 is to be used by enterprises engaging in an initial public offering (IPO), registrants in the Exchange Act reporting system that are ineligible to use Form S-3, and other registrants who choose to utilize Forms S-1.[5] An eligible Form S-1 issuer may incorporate by reference from Exchange Act reports into its Securities Act registration statement when it: (1) has filed at least one annual report; (2) is current in its Exchange Act reporting obligations; and (3) has made its Exchange Act reports readily accessible on a website maintained by or for such registrant. This access may be achieved by means of the registrant having on its website a hyperlink to the reports filed on EDGAR, with such reports being accessible through the SEC's website or through a third-party website.[6]

With respect to Form S-3, the SEC has explained:

Analysis, and Retrieval System (EDGAR), subject registrants must submit to the SEC virtually all documents (such as filings) electronically. *See generally* Westerberg, *EDGAR*, 26 Rev. Sec. & Comm. Reg. 173 (1993).

[3] SEC Securities Act Release No. 6231 (1980); *infra* § 7.06; *see* Brown, *Deregulation and the Annual Report to Shareholders*, 15 Sec. Reg. L.J. 423 (1988). Moreover, chief executive officers and chief financial officers are subject to certification requirements. *See infra* § 5.08[B].

[4] The SEC eliminated a third form, Form S-2, as part of its 2005 initiative to streamline the registration process. Prior to the 2005 offering reform, incorporation by reference was only allowed on Forms S-2 and S-3. *See* Securities Act Release No. 8591 (2005).

[5] The SEC expanded the Form S-3 eligibility requirements for primary offerings of equity securities to now permit issuers that have timely filed their Exchange Act reports and whose equity securities are listed on a national securities exchange (and that are not shell companies) to use Form S-3. *See* Securities Act Release No. 8878 (2007).

[6] *See* Securities Act Release No. 8591 (2005). Note that incorporation by reference may not be used by blank check companies, shell companies, or issuers conducting penny stock offerings.

Form S-3, in reliance on the efficient market theory, allows maximum use of incorporation by reference of Exchange Act reports [into Securities Act registration statements] and requires the least disclosure to be presented in the prospectus. . . . Generally, the Form S-3 prospectus [which can be used in primary offerings of common stock by an issuer which has timely filed in the Exchange Act reporting system for twelve months, has a class of common stock (or similar equity security) traded on a national securities exchange, and is not (and has not been for the past twelve months) a shell company] will present the same transaction-specific information as will be presented in a Form S-1 prospectus. Information concerning the registrant will be incorporated by reference from its Exchange Act reports. The prospectus will not be required to present any information concerning the registrant unless there has been a material change in the registrant's affairs which has not been reported in an Exchange Act filing or unless the Exchange Act reports incorporated by reference do not reflect certain restated financial statements or other financial information.[7]

To emphasize, the use of the Form S-3 registration statement has been greatly expanded by the SEC pursuant to the 2007 revisions (see Securities Act Release No. 8878 (2007)). Today, for primary offerings of equity securities (such as common stock), Form S-3 generally can be used by issuers that have timely filed Exchange Act reports for the prior twelve months, have a class of equity security traded on a national securities exchange (such as the New York Stock Exchange, American Stock Exchange or Nasdaq), and are not (and have not been for at least twelve months) a shell company. For those issuers that meet the foregoing conditions but have less than $75 million of voting stock outstanding held by non-affiliates ("public float"), no more than one-third of the public float may be offered by such issuers in primary offerings during any twelve-month period.

The rationale largely underlying incorporation by reference of Exchange Act reports into 1933 Act registration statements is that information regularly furnished to the securities markets through 1934 Act periodic reports is digested by the marketplace and reflected in the price of the issuer's securities, thereby eliminating the need to reiterate such information in the public offering context. Hence, this theory postulates that the securities markets, by analyzing the available information and accurately valuing the information in setting the price for the security, are efficient. The efficient market theory has received Supreme Court approbation with respect to the issue of "reliance" in Section 10(b) litigation,[8] discussed in Chapter 8.

Note that the SEC's 2007 amendments expanding the scope of the Form S-3 contradicts the Commission's principal rationale for the Form's adoption. In promulgating the Form S-3 in 1982, the SEC "reli[ed] on the efficient market

---

[7] SEC Securities Act Release No. 6383 (1982). *See* Securities Act Release No. 6964 (1992). For mergers and certain other reorganizations, the Form S-4 registration statement may be used. The Form S-4 is discussed in Chapter 6.

[8] *See Basic, Inc. v. Levinson*, 485 U.S. 224 (1988).

theory, allow[ing] a maximum use of incorporation of Exchange Act reports and requir[ing] the least disclosure to be presented in the prospectus and delivered to investors."[9] As then adopted, the Form S-3 could be used in primary at the market offerings of common stock only if the subject issuer had filed its Exchange Act reports for at least a 36-month period and had a public float of $150 million (or alternately a public float of $100 million and three million share trading volume on an annual basis). In 1992, still adhering to the efficient market rationale, the Commission lowered the Form S-3 criteria for issuers having such equity offerings to a 12-month reporting history and $75 million public float.[10]

The U.S. Supreme Court has given its approbation to the efficient market theory in the securities litigation context.[11] In ascertaining whether a subject security trades in an efficient market, lower courts view Form S-3 eligibility as a key criterion.[12] Given this history underlying the Form S-3's adoption and implementation, the SEC's expansion of Form S-3 to encompass issuers that may not be traded in an efficient market is a significant departure. Indeed, the Commission's 2007 amendments may be viewed as an effort to facilitate capital raising while rationalizing implicitly that any security listed on a national securities exchange is by definition traded in a efficient market. This rationalization, however, contravenes established doctrine that the critical inquiry is the market for that particular stock, not the location where such stock trades.[13]

---

[9] Adoption of Integrated Disclosure System, Securities Act Release No. 6383, Exchange Act Release No. 18524 (1982).

[10] Securities Act Release No. 6964 (1992). This rule change allowed approximately 450 additional issuers to use the Form S-3 for such equity offerings. *Id.*

[11] *Basic v. Levinson*, 485 U.S. 224 (1988). The Supreme Court stated:

The presumption [of reliance] is . . . supported by common sense and probability.

Recent empirical studies have tended to confirm Congress' premise that the market price of shares traded on well-developed markets reflects all publicly available information, and hence, any material misrepresentations. It has been noted that "it is hard to imagine that there ever is a buyer or seller who does not rely on market integrity. Who would knowingly roll the dice in a crooked crap game?" *Schlanger v. Four-Phase Systems Inc.*, 555 F. Supp. 535, 538 (S.D.N.Y. 1982). Indeed, nearly every court that has considered the proposition has concluded that where materially misleading statements have been disseminated into an impersonal, well-developed market for securities, the reliance of individual plaintiffs on the integrity of the market price may be presumed. Commentators generally have applauded the adoption of one variation or another of the fraud-on-the-market theory. An investor who buys or sells stock at the price set by the market does so in reliance on the integrity of that price. Because most publicly available information is reflected in market price, an investor's reliance on any public material misrepresentations, therefore, may be presumed for purposes of a Rule 10b-5 action.

Id. at 247. The fraud on the market theory is discussed further *infra* § 8.06.

[12] *See, e.g., Freeman v. Laventhol and Horwath*, 915 F.3d 193, 199 (6th Cir. 1995) (eligibility to use Form S-3 key factor); *Cammer v. Bloom*, 711 F. Supp. 1264, 1275–87 (D.N.J. 1989) (stating that companies entitled to use SEC Form S-3 would almost by definition encompass stocks traded in a "special developed market"); *Harman v. Lymphomed, Inc.*, 122 F.R.D. 522, 525 (N.D. Ill. 1988) (stating that Form S-3 status is perhaps the "most significant" factor that the market for the stock was efficient).

[13] *See Harman v. Lymphomed, Inc.*, 122 F.R.D. at 525; *In re Polymedica Corp. Securities Litigation*, 432 F.3d 1 (1st Cir. 2005); *In re Xcelera.Com Securities Litigation*, 430 F.3d 503 (1st Cir. 2005); *Unger v. Amedysys, Inc.*, 401 F.3d 316 (5th Cir. 2005).

With respect to Small Business Initiatives, the SEC in 1992 adopted Regulation S-B to provide more simplied disclosure, thereby facilitating access of small business issuers to the public securities markets.[14] In 2007, the SEC, while rescinding Regulation S-B, adopted additional amendments to the disclosure and reporting requirements under the 1933 and 1934 Acts to expand the number of issuers that qualify for "scaled" disclosure accommodations for "smaller" reporting companies. The Commission estimated that nearly 5,000 companies are eligible to use "scaled" disclosure, representing about 13% of the Exchange Act reporting companies.[15] As stated by the SEC, the "scaled" disclosure 2007 amendments:

- Establish a category of "smaller reporting companies" eligible to use our scaled disclosure requirements. The primary determinant for eligibility will be that the company have less than $75 million in public float. When a company is unable to calculate public float, however, such as if it has no common equity outstanding or no market price for its outstanding common equity exists at the time of the determination, the standard will be less than $50 million in revenue in the last fiscal year. [Note that investment companies and asset-backed issuers are not eligible to use "scaled" disclosure];

- Move 12 non-financial scaled disclosure items from [former] Regulation S-B into Regulation S-K. The 12 scaled item requirements are: (1) Description of Business (Item 101); (2) Market Price of and Dividends on Registrant's Common Equity and Related Stockholder Matters (Item 201); (3) Selected Financial Data (Item 301); (4) Supplementary Financial Information (Item 302); (5) Management's Discussion and Analysis of Financial Condition and Results of Operations (Item 303); (6) Quantitative and Qualitative Disclosures about Market Risk (Item 305); (7) Executive Compensation (Item 402); (8) Transactions with Related Persons, Promoters and Certain Control Persons (Item 404); (9) Corporate Governance (Item 407); (10) Prospectus Summary, Risk Factors, and Ratio of Earnings to Fixed Charges (Item 503); (11) Use of Proceeds (Item 504); and (12) Exhibits (Item 601). These scaled requirements will be available only for smaller reporting companies. The remaining 24 item requirements of [former] Regulation S-B are substantially the same as their corresponding Regulation S-K item requirements . . . ;

- Move [certain] scaled financial statement requirements in . . . [former] Regulation S-B into . . . Regulation S-X, and amend these requirements to provide a scaled disclosure option for smaller reporting companies . . . ;

- Permit smaller reporting companies to elect to comply with scaled financial and non-financial disclosure on an item-by-item or "a la carte" basis. As adopted, eligible companies may elect to follow scaled financial statement requirements or to provide the larger company financial

---

[14] Securities Act Release No. 6949 (1992).

[15] Securities Act Release No. 8876 (2007). This total amounts to an additional 1,581 companies that now can take advantage of "scaled" disclosure than was the case prior to the 2007 amendments.

statement presentation on a quarterly basis, rather than require companies to elect the full fiscal year's financial presentation in the first quarterly report of the fiscal year . . . ;

- Eliminates our "SB" forms [that had been adopted by the SEC in 1992 for registered offerings that could be used by such "smaller" companies]; [and]

- Permit all foreign companies to qualify as "smaller reporting companies" if they otherwise qualify and choose to file on domestic company forms and provide financial statements prepared in accordance with U.S. Generally Accepted Accounting Principles ("U.S. GAAP"). . . .[16]

[B]   Shelf Registration

One of the Commission's significant actions with respect to the integrated disclosure framework is its adoption of Rule 415, the "shelf" registration rule. Generally, Rule 415 focuses on the Securities Act registration of securities to be offered or sold on a delayed or continuous basis in the future. The thrust of shelf registration is that it allows qualified issuers to raise capital in an expedited manner to capture favorable market conditions while benefitting from significant cost savings in the form of reduced legal, accounting, and other fees. In a shelf registered offering, information from Exchange Act reports is incorporated by reference into the subject registration statement.

Currently, only issuers qualified to register securities on Form S-3 (or Form F-3) are eligible to conduct primary at the market offerings of equity securities by means of shelf registration. Other issuers that may use Form S-3 for other types of offerings include those that make: "offerings on a continuing basis of securities issued on exercise of outstanding options or warrants or conversion of other securities; [certain debt offerings,] offerings on a continuous basis under dividend reinvestment plans; offerings on a continuous basis under employee benefit plans; and offerings solely on behalf of selling security holders."[17]

Generally, there is no limit on the amount of securities that can be registered pursuant to a shelf registration statement.[18] The underwriters of the offering are not required to be identified in the shelf registration statement. Such a registration statement can be used for up to three years (subject to limited extension). Moreover, the Commission has made shelf registration even more useful for well known seasoned issuers by way of "automatic" shelf registration under which the shelf registration statement becomes effective immediately upon filing with the SEC. As will be addressed in Chapter 7, shelf registration raises significant liability concerns.

---

[16] *Id.*

[17] *See* Securities Act Release Nos. 6499 (1983), 8591 (2005). *See generally* Banoff, *Regulatory Subsidies, Efficient Markets and Shelf Regulation — An Analysis of Rule 415*, 70 Va. L. Rev. 135 (1984).

[18] As discussed earlier in this chapter, eligible issuers that do not have a $75 million float may register on Form S-3 in primary offerings no more than one-third of their public float during any twelve-month period. *See* Securities Act Release No. 8878 (2007).

§ 5.03   THE MANDATORY DISCLOSURE SYSTEM DEBATE

The propriety of Congress' enactment of a mandatory securities law disclosure system has generated much debate over the last four decades. As discussed throughout this text, issuers must disclose certain material and other specified information when publicly offering securities pursuant to the Securities Act's registration framework. Moreover, once an issuer engages in a public offering, it is required under the Exchange Act to provide the SEC and its shareholders with annual and other periodic reports. Whether such a mandatory disclosure system is appropriate and the type of information that should be subject to compelled disclosure have been subject to debate.

Critics of the mandatory disclosure system argue that the system produces considerable costs yet few benefits.[19] As stated two decades ago by Professor Homer Kripke:

> [T]he Commission's disclosure system cannot be given high marks either for performance or on a cost/benefit basis. . . . The system was founded not on disclosure of "all material facts," but on disclosure of events in the past which the Commission could objectively verify. This historical perspective was assumed for the inefficient purpose of preventing blatant securities fraud and for the less apparent purpose of protecting the Commission from criticism for issues that turn sour. In recent years, while the Commission has shown commendable willingness to try to modernize the system, development and economic theory have outrun adaptation of the system.[20]

Today, some of the sting of Professor Kripke's rebuke has been lessened by the SEC's increasing support for enhanced disclosure of "soft" or "forward-looking" information.[21] Nonetheless, it may be asserted that undue reliance on mandatory disclosure is not without costs and weaknesses. Indeed, one authority, assessing whether disclosure should give way to more substantive regulation that impacts normative conduct more directly, opines that "[o]ne of the most significant problems with relying on a disclosure-based system to protect securities markets and investors is the flawed assumption that investors are purely rational actors who can utilize the disclosure effectively to make optimal investment decisions."[22]

Proponents of a mandatory disclosure system assert that, in the absence of such a system: (1) some registrants would engage in fraudulent disclosure practices, (2) insider perquisites and salaries as well as underwriter costs would

---

[19] See, e.g., H. Manne, Insider Trading and the Stock Market (1966); Benston, *The Value of the SEC's Accounting Disclosure Requirements*, 44 Acct. Rev. 515 (1969); Stigler, *Public Regulation of the Securities Markets*, 37 J. Bus. 117 (1964).

[20] Kripke, *Fifty Years of Securities Regulation in Search of a Purpose*, 21 San Diego L. Rev. 257 (1984).

[21] See, e.g., discussion *infra* § 5.05.

[22] Ripken, *The Dangers and Drawbacks of the Disclosure Antidote: Toward a More Substantive Approach to Securities Regulation*, 58 Baylor L. Rev. 139, 147–148 (2006).

be excessive, (3) current state laws and self-regulatory oversight by themselves would be inadequate for enforcement purposes, (4) the threat of civil and criminal actions would not induce the appropriate level of disclosure, and (5) investors would lose confidence in the integrity of the securities markets.[23]

Additionally, it is argued that mandatory disclosure obligations comprise an economically efficient mechanism for achieving information discovery. As stated by one source:

> Absent mandatory disclosure duties, information traders would engage in duplicative efforts to uncover nonpublic information. The cost of these efforts would be extremely high because information traders, as outsiders, lack access to the management of the firm. Disclosure duties pass these costs to the individual firm. For the firm, the cost of obtaining firm-specific information is rather minimal; indeed, it is a mere by-product of managing the firm.[24]

A further point that should be raised is the role that disclosure under the federal securities laws has on normative corporate conduct. As this author has stated:

> Although the rationale underlying disclosure is not based primarily on influencing corporate internal affairs but rather on providing shareholders and the marketplace with sufficient information to make intelligent decisions and to be apprised of significant developments, there is little question that disclosure has a substantial impact on the normative conduct of corporations. In this regard, the Commission's disclosure policies . . . have not only had an effect of deterring unlawful or questionable conduct but have played a positive role in influencing the establishment of improved standards of conduct.[25]

---

[23] *See* Seligman, *The Historical Need for a Mandatory Corporate Disclosure System*, 9 J. Corp. L. 1, 9 (1979).

[24] Goshen & Parchomovsky, *The Essential Role of Securities Regulation*, 55 Duke L.J. 711, 738 (2006) (also opining that the specific disclosure format, as mandated by SEC rule, further decreases the costs of analyzing information and comparing such information to the data provided by other enterprises). *See generally* Brown, *Corporate Governance, the Securities and Exchange Commission and the Limits of Disclosure*, 57 Cath. U.L. Rev. 45 (2007); Coffee, *Market Failure and the Economic Case for a Mandatory Disclosure System*, 70 Va. L. Rev. 717 (1984); Easterbrook & Fischel, *Mandatory Disclosure and the Protection of Investors*, 70 Va. L. Rev. 669 (1984); Fanto, *The Absence of Cross-Cultural Communications: SEC Mandatory Disclosure and Foreign Corporate Governance*, 17 Nw. J. Int'l L. & Bus. 119 (1996); Fox, *Retaining Mandatory Securities Disclosure: Why Issuer Choice Is Not Investor Empowerment*, 85 Va. L. Rev. 1335 (1997); Hannes, *Comparisons Among Firms: (When) Do They Justify Mandatory Disclosure?*, 29 J. Corp. L. 699 (2004); Palmiter, *Toward Disclosure Choice in Securities Offerings*, 1991 Colum. Bus. L. Rev. 1; Romano, *Empowering Investors: A Market Approach to Securities Regulation*, 107 Yale L.J. 2359 (1998).

[25] M. Steinberg, Corporate Internal Affairs: A Corporate and Securities Law Perspective 29 (1983); *see* R. Stevenson, Corporations and Information — Secrecy, Access and Disclosure 81–82 (1980) ("Today the disclosure requirements of the securities laws are used, in a variety of ways, for the explicit purpose of influencing a wide range of corporate primary behavior. . . . "); Ripken, *supra* note 22, at 152 (arguable that disclosure rules serve to indirectly affect corporate decisionmaking); Weiss, *Disclosure and Corporate Accountability*, 34 Bus. Law. 575 (1979) ("[O]ne

§ 5.04　"PLAIN ENGLISH" DISCLOSURE

In 1998, the SEC adopted the "plain English" disclosure rules primarily to address concerns that disclosure documents were too complicated to be effectively used by many individual investors. The principal focus of these rules is clarity of prospectus disclosure. Because prospectuses are drafted in significant part to avoid liability that may ensue from a public offering, language used in prospectuses traditionally has often been highly technical and legalistic. This complexity, in turn, impairs the ability of investors to make knowledgeable judgments regarding the merits of the securities being offered. Under the plain English disclosure rules, the Commission requires issuers to write the cover pages, summary, and risk factors sections of prospectuses in plain English.[26] Note that risk factor disclosure in Exchange Act reports also must be written in plain English.[27] Further, the SEC has provided specific guidance on how to make the entire prospectus clear, concise, and understandable.[28]

The plain English rule (Rule 421) sets forth requirements with respect to the front and back cover pages, the summary, and the risk factors sections of the prospectus. These requirements include:

- Short sentences;
- Definite, concrete, everyday language;
- Active voice;
- Tabular presentation or bullet lists for complex material, whenever possible;
- No legal jargon or highly technical business terms; and
- No multiple negatives.[29]

In addition to the specific portions of the prospectus discussed above, Rule 421(b) mandates that the entire prospectus be "clear, concise, and understandable." Pertinent standards to be followed in prospectus preparation include:

- Present information in clear, concise sections, paragraphs, and sentences . . . ;
- Use descriptive headings and subheadings;
- Avoid frequent reliance on glossaries or defined terms as the primary means of explaining information in the prospectus . . . ; and
- Avoid legal and highly technical business terminology.[30]

---

of the central themes of the system by which large corporations are governed [is] that corporate decisionmaking be regulated through mandatory disclosure requirements rather than direct government intervention.").

[26] Securities Act Release No. 7497 (1998). *See generally* B. Garner, Securities Disclosure in Plain English (1999).

[27] *See* Securities Act Release No. 8591 (2005); Robbins & Rothenberg, *Writing Risk Factor Disclosure in Exchange Act Reports*, 39 Rev. Sec. & Comm. Reg. 87 (2006).

[28] *See* Rule 421; Securities Act Release No. 7497 (1998).

[29] Securities Act Release No. 7497 (1998); *see* Rule 421(d)(2).

[30] Rule 421(b). Further, Rule 421(b) and Securities Act Release No. 7497 (1998) list the following drafting styles that the SEC believes make the prospectus harder to understand:

The SEC makes clear, however, that certain business terms are often necessary to describe companies in certain industries (*e.g.*, high-tech enterprises). Therefore, the Commission suggests that, if certain technical terms are necessary, prospectuses attempt to clearly define the meaning of those terms the first time that they are used. Further, the SEC recognizes that sophisticated investors may want to read certain documents relating to the company in their entirety. For example, such investors may wish to read the specific language of a contract that is highly pertinent to the company's future. In these situations, the Commission sets forth that information relating to such documents must be presented and explained in a clear fashion.[31]

§ 5.05   DISCLOSURE OF "FORWARD-LOOKING" INFORMATION

Although continuing to strongly support the need for a mandatory disclosure system, the Commission has responded to Professor Kripke and other critics by taking certain actions. Perhaps the most important is the adoption of the integrated disclosure system. A second is the Commission's promulgation of Securities Act Rule 175 (and Exchange Act Rule 3b-6) providing a "safe harbor" for projections.[32] A third is the SEC's adoption of Item 303 of Regulation S-K focusing on Management Discussion and Analysis (MD&A).[33] In this regard, the area encompassing issuer affirmative disclosure obligations (including such subjects as disclosure of "soft" information, merger negotiations, and adverse information) is addressed at length in Chapter 11. And a fourth major development is the enactment of the Private Securities Litigation Reform Act of 1995 (PSLRA). A key aspect of the PSLRA is the providing of a safe harbor from liability in private actions for certain forward-looking statements made by publicly-held companies (for further discussion, see § 11.05).

Whereas "hard" information emphasizes historical data, "soft" information often focuses on forward-looking statements, such as projections, forecasts, and predictions. Until the mid 1970s, the SEC and the courts discouraged and even prohibited the disclosure of soft information. The major concern had been that investors, particularly the unsophisticated, might attach too much significance to information that is of perhaps questionable reliability.[34]

- Legalistic or overly complex presentations that make the substance of the disclosure difficult to understand;
- Vague "boilerplate" explanations that are imprecise and readily subject to differing interpretations;
- Complex information copied directly from legal documents without any clear and concise explanation of the provision(s); and
- Disclosure repeated in different sections of the document that increases the size of the document but does not enhance the quality of the information.

[31] Securities Act Release No. 7497 (1998).

[32] *See* Securities Act Release No. 6084 (1979).

[33] *See* SEC Financial Reporting Release No. 36 (1989).

[34] *See, e.g., Gerstle v. Gamble-Skogmo, Inc.*, 478 F.2d 1281, 1294 (2d Cir. 1973).

[A]   Rule 175

With the adoption of Rule 175 under the Securities Act, the SEC recognized that the flow of "soft" information to the marketplace may enable more informed investment decisions to be made. Generally, Rule 175 (as well as Rule 3b-6 under the Exchange Act) encourages issuer use of financial projections in 1933 Act registration statements, 1934 Act reports, annual reports to shareholders, and other documents filed with the SEC. The rule establishes a "safe harbor" from liability for parties who invoke the rule.

Under Rule 175, "a safe harbor [is recognized] from the applicable liability provisions of the federal securities laws for statements [made by or on behalf of an issuer or by an outside reviewer retained by such issuer] relating to or containing (1) projections of reserves, income (loss), earnings (loss) per share or other financial items, such as capital expenditures, dividends, or capital structure, (2) management plans and objectives for future company operations, and (3) future economic performance included in management's statements."[35] In providing this "safe harbor," Rule 175 precludes liability for the making of issuer forward-looking statements unless the plaintiff establishes that any such statement was made or reaffirmed without a reasonable basis or was disclosed other than in good faith.[36]

It may be argued that the SEC went too far in permitting first-time public issuers to include "safe harbor" projections in their registration statements. Indeed, pursuant to the Commission's 1992 Small Business Initiatives, non-reporting issuers in Regulation A offerings also are entitled to invoke Rule 175.[37] Unlike reporting companies, many such issuers are start-up companies with no previous substantial earnings history. Moreover, normally such issuers have not been followed in the market. Nonetheless, it may be argued (not necessarily successfully) that, if such first-time issuers make projections with no previous earnings history, such projections are not within Rule 175's "safe harbor" because they are not made in "good faith" and "with a reasonable basis."[38]

The above argument, however, is unlikely to succeed. Projections for issuers engaged in IPOs or Regulation A offerings clearly are permitted within the confines of the safe harbor rule. Moreover, pursuant to legislation enacted by Congress in 1995, the safe harbor provisions have been broadened to encompass certain oral and written statements, even if not filed with the SEC, by an Exchange Act reporting company and those acting on its behalf (*see infra* § 11.05). Nonetheless, perhaps in recognition that abuses may be

---

[35] Securities Act Release No. 6084 (1979).

[36] *Id.*

[37] *See* Securities Act Release No. 6949 (1992); *see also supra* § 3.09[B][4].

[38] *See generally* Fiflis, *Soft Information: The SEC's Former Exogenous Zone*, 26 UCLA L. Rev. 95 (1978); Poole, *Improving the Reliability of Management Forecasts*, 14 J. Corp. L. 547 (1989); Comment, *The Safe Harbor for Forecasts — A Step in the Right Direction?* 1980 Duke L.J. 607; Note, *Disclosure of Future-Oriented Information Under the Securities Laws*, 88 Yale L.J. 338 (1978).

rampant under an expansive safe harbor rule, Congress excluded issuers of speculative securities, such as penny stocks, from being entitled to invoke such safe harbor provisions.[39]

[B]   The PSLRA Safe Harbor

Disclosure of forward-looking information by Exchange Act reporting issuers has been greatly facilitated by enactment of the Private Securities Litigation Reform Act of 1995 (PSLRA). In this respect, the PSLRA amends both the Securities Act and the Exchange Act to provide an expansive safe harbor from liability in private actions for certain forward-looking statements made by such reporting issuers. The provisions and ramifications of this safe harbor are addressed in Chapter 11.

[C]   Management Discussion and Analysis ("MD&A")

Responding further to critics that the Commission slights the importance of forward-looking information, the SEC adopted Item 303 of Regulation S-K. Item 303 pertains to "Management Discussion and Analysis of Financial Condition and Results of Operation" (MD&A). This provision plays a significant role in the mandatory disclosure of forward-looking information in certain situations. As stated by one source, "the MD&A has become a major, if not the major, item of narrative disclosure that is studied, together with the financial statements, for investment decision and analysis purposes."[40]

Pursuant to the MD&A, the SEC has taken the position that a disclosure obligation exists "where a trend, demand, commitment, event or uncertainty is both presently known to management and reasonably likely to have material effects on the registrant's financial condition or results of operation."[41] In circumstances where a trend, demand, commitment, event or uncertainty is known, the subject company's management must consider the following:

> 1. Is the known trend, demand, commitment, event or uncertainty likely to come to fruition? If management determines that it is not reasonably likely to occur, no disclosure is required.

> 2. If management cannot make that determination, it must evaluate objectively the consequences of the known trend, demand, commitment, event or uncertainty, on the assumption that it will come to fruition.

> Disclosure is then required unless management determines that a material effect on the registrant's financial condition or results of operations is not reasonably likely to occur.[42]

---

[39] *See* discussion *infra* § 11.05[D].

[40] Schneider, *MD&A Disclosure*, 22 Rev. Sec. & Comm. Reg. 149, 150 (1989); *see* SEC Financial Reporting Release No. 36 (1989).

[41] SEC Financial Reporting Release No. 36, 6 Fed. Sec. L. Rep. (CCH) ¶ 73,193, at 62,842 (1989).

[42] *Id.* at 62,843; *see* Securities Exchange Act Release No. 8350, [2003–2004 Transfer Binder]

Clearly, the SEC will bring enforcement actions when it deems the MD&A deficient.[43] In view of these significant liability concerns, preparation of the MD&A demands careful planning, adequate time for reflection, and communication among the participants of the disclosure "team."[44]

§ 5.06 DISCLOSURE OF INFORMATION FOCUSING ON DIRECTOR/OFFICER INTEGRITY OR COMPETENCY

Purely qualitative information focusing on management integrity or competency, unlike quantitative information, does not ordinarily impact significantly on the earnings, assets, or economic viability of the registrant. Under the Commission's rules and judicial decisions, disclosure is required, for example, of certain self-dealing transactions engaged in by management as well as adjudicated illegalities and certain other events (such as the imposition of an SEC injunction).[45] Absent self-dealing, an adjudicated illegality, or mandated disclosure called for by a specific SEC rule, courts often are reluctant to require an issuer to disclose qualitative information that is not economically material.[46]

In this context, as well as others, where liability is premised on the failure to disclose, the information omitted in order to be actionable must be material (or called for by an SEC rule) and there must exist a disclosure obligation.[47] For example, in the insider trading context, the Supreme Court has made it clear that silence when trading on material nonpublic information is not actionable under Section 10(b) of the Exchange Act unless there exists a duty to disclose such information.[48]

Fed. Sec. L. Rep. (CCH) ¶ 87,127 (2003) (setting forth guidelines to assist registrants and issuers in "preparing MD&A disclosure that is easier to follow and understand; and in providing information that more completely satisfies our previously enumerated principal objectives of MD&A").

[43] *See, e.g., In the Matter of Caterpillar, Inc.*, Administrative Proceeding No. 3-7692 (SEC 1992). *See generally* Seamons, *Requirements and Pitfalls of MD&A Disclosure*, 25 Sec. Reg. L.J. 239, 240 (1997) (stating that "the SEC scrutinizes MD&A compliance closely and institutes actions not only against registrants, but also against personnel responsible for preparing such disclosure").

[44] *See generally* Hiler & Freeman, *Management's Discussion and Analysis: Known Trends in SEC Enforcement*, 8 Insights No. 12, at 11 (Dec. 1994); Schneider, *supra* note 40, at 155–156.

[45] *See, e.g., Maldonado v. Flynn*, 597 F.2d 789 (2d Cir. 1979); Regulation S-K, Items 402, 404; Securities Act Release No. 8732 (2006) (adoption of regulations updating disclosure of executive compensation).

[46] *See, e.g., Greenhouse v. MCG Capital Corp.*, 392 F.3d 650 (4th Cir. 2004); *Gaines v. Haughton*, 645 F.2d 761 (9th Cir. 1981). *See generally* Symposium, *Corporate Disclosure and its Impact on Corporate Morality/Efficiency*, 48 Cath. U. L. Rev. No. 1 (1998); Ferrara, Starr & Steinberg, *Disclosure of Information Bearing on Management Integrity and Competency*, 76 Nw. U.L. Rev. 555 (1981); Williams, *The Securities and Exchange Commission and Corporate Social Transparency*, 112 Harv. L. Rev. 1199 (1999).

[47] *See, e.g., Roeder v. Alpha Industries*, 814 F.2d 22 (1st Cir. 1987). For an expansive decision under state securities law, see *Bridwell v. State*, 804 S.W.2d 900 (Tex. Ct. Crim. App. 1991).

[48] *See, e.g., Chiarella v. United States*, 445 U.S. 222 (1980); Chapter 12. *See generally* W. Wang & M. Steinberg, Insider Trading (2d ed. 2005 & 2008 supp.).

As a general matter, Regulation S-K is the central source for determining a publicly-held company's disclosure obligations under the federal securities laws.[49] It is not, however, the only source. For example, in the securities offering setting, Rule 408 of Regulation C provides:

> In addition to the information expressly required to be included in a registration statement, there shall be added such further material information, if any, as may be necessary to make the required statements, in the light of the circumstances under which they are made, not misleading.

Rule 12b-20 promulgated under the 1934 Act contains a similar requirement with respect to reports filed with the SEC pursuant to the Exchange Act.

Moreover, it may be argued that because the issuer itself is selling securities in the offering context, a fiduciary duty triggering a disclosure obligation arises between the issuer and purchasers of the securities. Although this view is not held by all courts, it may be posited that in the Securities Act registration setting, if the information is material, it must be disclosed.[50]

§ 5.07   QUALITATIVE ECONOMIC MATERIALITY

Materiality under the federal securities laws signifies that the misstated or omitted fact, if accurately disclosed, would have been considered important by a reasonable investor in making his/her voting or investment decision.[51] At times, a subject event or circumstance may give rise to difficult materiality determinations. For example, the probability and magnitude in regard to the consummation of certain corporate developments, such as the successful completion of merger negotiations, may be "contingent or speculative in nature."[52] To ascertain whether such contingent developments are material, the probability/magnitude test is utilized. This test postulates that materiality "will depend at any given time upon a balancing of both the indicated probability that the event will occur and the anticipated magnitude of the event

---

[49] See supra § 5.02.

[50] See Chiarella v. United States, 445 U.S. 222, 230 (1980). Nonetheless, as a general proposition, materiality alone does not trigger a duty to disclose. See, e.g., Roeder v. Alpha Industries, Inc., 814 F.2d 22 (1st Cir. 1987). For discussion on this issue, see infra § 11.01.

[51] Basic, Inc. v. Levinson, 485 U.S. 224, 232 (1988); TSC Industries, Inc. v. Northway, Inc., 426 U.S. 438, 449 (1976). As stated by the Supreme Court:

> An omitted [or misstated] fact is material if there is a substantial likelihood that a reasonable shareholder would consider it important in deciding how to [invest or] vote. . . . It does not require proof of a substantial likelihood that disclosure of the [misstated or] omitted fact would have caused the reasonable investor to change his [mind]. What the standard does contemplate is a showing of a substantial likelihood that, under all circumstances, the [misstated or] omitted fact would have assumed actual significance in the deliberations of the reasonable shareholder. . . . [T]here must be a substantial likelihood that the disclosure of the [misstated or] omitted fact would have been viewed by the reasonable investor as having significantly altered the total mix of the information available.

426 U.S. at 449. The concept of materiality is discussed at numerous points in this text.

[52] Basic, 485 U.S. at 232.

in light of the totality of the company activity."[53]

During the past decade, attention has focused on whether materiality is based on solely quantitative valuations. For example, one traditionally followed approach is that if a misrepresentation or omission is less than five percent of the value being assessed, then such disclosure deficiency is not material, absent the presence of self-dealing or similar misconduct.[54] A number of courts continue to adopt this approach.[55] Nonetheless, the prevailing view today embraces the concept of qualitative economic materiality. For example, the SEC staff in Staff Accounting Bulletin (SAB) 99 set forth the following list of considerations that may result in a quantitatively "small" misstatement of a financial statement item being deemed "material":

- Whether the misstatement arises from an item capable of precise measurement or whether it arises from an estimate and, if so, the degree of imprecision inherent in the estimate;
- Whether the misstatement masks a change in earnings or other trends;
- Whether the misstatement hides a failure to meet analysts consensus expectations for the enterprise;
- Whether the misstatement changes a loss into income or vice versa;
- Whether the misstatement concerns a segment or other portion of the registrant's business that has been identified as playing a significant role in the registrant's operations or profitability;
- Whether the misstatement affects the registrants' compliance with regulatory requirements;
- Whether the misstatement affects the registrant's compliance with loan covenants or other contractual requirements;
- Whether the misstatement has the effect of increasing management's compensation, for example, by satisfying requirements for the award of bonuses or other forms of incentive compensation; and
- Whether the misstatement involves concealment of an unlawful transaction.[56]

Several courts have applied qualitative economic materiality principles to both narrative and financial statement disclosure, thereby rejecting a rigid numerical formula (e.g., less than five percent).[57] According to this view, "[a]ny approach that designates a single fact or occurrence as always determinative of an inherently fact-specific finding, such as materiality, must necessarily be overinclusive or underinclusive."[58] Hence, today most courts hold that the

---

[53] *Id.* at 238 (citing *SEC v. Texas Gulf Sulphur Co.*, 401 F.2d 833 (2d Cir. 1968)).

[54] As discussed in Staff Accounting Bulletin (SAB) 99, 64 Fed. Reg. 45,150 (1999).

[55] *See, e.g., In re SCB Computer Technology, Inc. Securities Litigation*, 149 F. Supp. 2d 334 (W.D. Tenn. 2001) (holding misstatements of revenue of less than three percent not material); *SEC v. Hoover*, 903 F. Supp. 1135 (S.D. Tex. 1995) (holding misstatement of three percent not material).

[56] SAB 99, *supra* note 54.

[57] *See, e.g., Helwig v. Vencor, Inc.*, 251 F.3d 540 (6th Cir. 2001); *Ganino v. Citizens Utilities Co.*, 228 F.3d 154 (2d Cir. 2000); *Holmes v. Baker*, 166 F. Supp. 2d 1362 (S.D. Fla. 2001).

[58] *Ganino*, 228 F.3d at 162 (quoting *Basic*, 485 U.S. at 236).

pertinent inquiries with respect to materiality are both qualitative and quantitative.[59]

§ 5.08 THE SARBANES-OXLEY ACT

[A]   Introduction

After the enactment of three major acts of federal legislation in 1995,[60] 1996[61] and 1998,[62] seeking to foster capital formation and redress perceived abuses associated with class actions, the election of President George W. Bush portended the continued deregulation of the securities markets and affected players in the process. Instead, at the outset of President Bush's first term, the very opposite occurred: After the revelation of major financial debacles that impaired the very foundation of the U.S. capital markets, Congress enacted the most pro-regulatory securities legislation since the passage of the Securities Exchange Act in 1934.

The Sarbanes-Oxley Act of 2002 (SOX) federalizes state corporation law in several ways, going far beyond the disclosure framework that serves as the foundation of federal securities regulation.[63] Regulation of auditors now is at a level never envisioned even in the worst nightmares of the accounting profession. Moreover, chief executive and chief financial officers must "certify" with prudence, taking care to have effective controls in place to help assure the accuracy of their assessments. Overlooked to some degree, yet a surprising mandate in light of previous law, is Congress' direction for the SEC to oversee a continuous issuer disclosure regime.[64]

The U.S. securities markets traditionally have been viewed as premier, serving a vital role in the stability of our economy. Hopefully, the enactment of the Sarbanes-Oxley Act as well as vigorous implementation and enforcement of its provisions will help restore investor confidence in the integrity of our

---

[59] See the cases cited *supra* note 57. *See generally* M. Steinberg, Securities Regulation: Liabilities and Remedies § 1.11 (2008); Hodges, *The Qualitative Considerations of Materiality: The Emerging Relationship Between Materiality and Scienter*, 30 Sec. Reg. L.J. 4 (2002).

[60] The Private Securities Litigation Reform Act of 1995 (PSLRA).

[61] The National Securities Markets Improvement Act of 1996 (NSMIA).

[62] The Securities Litigation Uniform Standards Act of 1998 (SLUSA).

[63] For example, directors who serve on an audit committee must be independent (Sarbanes-Oxley Act § 301(m)(3)), CEOs and CFOs must forfeit bonuses if an issuer financial restatement is prepared under certain circumstances (Sarbanes-Oxley Act § 304), and company loans to directors and executive officers are generally prohibited (Sarbanes-Oxley Act § 402).

[64] *See* Sarbanes-Oxley Act § 409, *amending* § 13(l) of the Exchange Act (requiring publicly-held companies to "disclose to the public on a rapid and current basis such additional information concerning material changes in the financial condition or operations of the issuer in plain English . . . as the Commission determines, by rule. . . . ") This provision is a marked contrast to the previously established periodic disclosure framework. *See* Securities Act Release No. 8090 (2002); Steinberg, *Insider Trading, Selective Disclosure, and Prompt Disclosure: A Comparative Analysis*, 22 U. Pa. J. Int'l L. 635 (2001). For further discussion, see Chapter 11.

financial markets. In view of the 2008 financial debacles, however, more extensive government regulation may be warranted.[65]

[B]   CEO and CFO Certifications

The Sarbanes-Oxley Act (SOX) enhanced senior corporate management's responsibility to the investing public by requiring that the chief executive officer (CEO) and the chief financial officer (CFO) each certify, among other items, that the company's financial disclosures are a fair and accurate representation of such company's financial position.[66] Under the Act, the CEO and the CFO of all publicly-held companies each must provide two separate certifications (pursuant to SOX Sections 302 and 906). Section 302 of the Act covers each registrant's annual (Form 10-K) and quarterly (Form 10-Q) report required to be filed under the Exchange Act. The Section 302 certification mandates that the CEO and CFO each certify as follows:

1. I have reviewed this annual report on Form 10-K [or periodic report on Form 10-Q] of the Registrant;

2. Based on my knowledge, this report does not contain any untrue statement of a material fact or omit to state a material fact necessary to make the statements made, in light of the circumstances under which such statements are made, not misleading with respect to the period covered by this report;

3. Based on my knowledge, the financial statements, and other financial information included in this report, fairly present in all material respects the financial condition, results of operations and cash flows of the Registrant as of, and for, the periods presented in this report;

4. The Registrant's other certifying officer and I are responsible for establishing and maintaining disclosure controls and procedures and internal control over financial reporting for the Registrant and have:

(a) Designed such disclosure controls and procedures, or caused such disclosure controls and procedures to be designed under our supervision, to ensure that material information relating to the Registrant, including its consolidated subsidiaries, is made known to us by others within those entities, particularly during the period in which this report is being prepared;

(b) Designed such internal control over financial reporting, or caused such internal control over financial reporting to be designed

---

[65] *See* Scannel, *SEC Faulted for Missing Red Flags at Bear Stearns*, Wall St. J., Sept. 27, 2008, at A3 (referring to the "Inspector General's scathing report [that the SEC] failed to require the investment bank to rein in its risk-taking"). *See generally* J. Bostelman, The Sarbanes-Oxley Deskbook (2005); Symposium, 3 J. Bus. & Tech. L. Rev. No. 2 (2008); Symposium, 39 Loy. U. (Chi) L. J. No. 3 (2008); Symposium, 105 Mich. L. Rev. No. 8 (2007); Morrissey, *Catching the Culprits: Is Sarbanes-Oxley Enough?*, 2003 Colum. Bus. L. Rev. 801.

[66] Sarbanes-Oxley Act § 302(a).

under our supervision, to provide reasonable assurance regarding the reliability of financial reporting and the preparation of financial statements for external purposes in accordance with generally accepted accounting principles;

(c) Evaluated the effectiveness of the Registrant's disclosure controls and procedures and presented in this report our conclusions about the effectiveness of the disclosure controls and procedures, as of a date within 90 days preceding this report; and

(d) Disclosed in this report any change in the Registrant's internal control over financial reporting that occurred during the Registrant's most recent fiscal quarter (the Registrant's fourth fiscal quarter in the case of an annual report) that has materially affected, or is reasonably likely to materially affect, the Registrant's internal control over financial reporting; and

5. The Registrant's other certifying officer and I have disclosed, based on our most recent evaluation of internal control over financial reporting, to the Registrant's auditors and the audit committee of the Registrant's board of directors (or persons performing the equivalent functions):

(a) All significant deficiencies and material weaknesses in the design or operation of internal control over financial reporting which are reasonably likely to adversely affect the Registrant's ability to record, process, summarize and report financial information; and

(b) Any fraud, whether or not material, that involves management or other employees who have a significant role in the Registrant's internal control over financial reporting.[67]

The Section 906 certification, adding Section 1350 to the criminal statutes,[68] applies to each Exchange Act report containing financial statements and provides for significant criminal penalties for knowingly false certification. Pursuant to Section 906, the CEO and CFO certification each must state "that the periodic report containing the financial statements fully complies with the [Exchange Act periodic reporting] requirements and that information contained in the [subject] periodic report fairly presents, in all material respects, the financial condition and results of operations of the issuer."[69]

These provisions in SOX place CEOs and CFOs in a potentially precarious situation, such as where a company restates its audited financials. Clearly, a CEO or CFO who, with knowledge, falsely certifies any such report is subject to severe penalties. As a defense, the officer may claim that he/she did not know

---

[67] Rule 13a-14(a)/15d-14(a) Certification. *See* Sarbanes-Oxley Act § 302(a)(1)-(6).

[68] 18 U.S.C. § 1350.

[69] *Id.*; *see United States v. Scrushy*, 2004 U.S. Dist. LEXIS 23820 (N.D. Ala. 2004) (upholding constitutionality of section 906 of SOX). *See generally* Hogan, *The Enron Legacy: Corporate Governance Requirements for a New Era*, 31 Sec. Reg. L.J. 142, 143–144 (2003) (interpreting 18 U.S.C. § 1350).

that a statement in the report was materially incorrect. Even assuming that this defense is meritorious, the officer nevertheless is subject to other civil liability based on SOX's mandate that the certifying officer engage in specified affirmative conduct for the establishment and implementation of reasonably effective disclosure controls and procedures. Such liability may arise, for example, in a private Section 10(b) action (where recklessness is sufficient scienter); in an SEC enforcement action (where depending on the provision violated, negligence is sufficient); or in a state court suit for breach of fiduciary duty.[70]

[C]   Audit Committee

Under the Sarbanes-Oxley Act, the audit committee is defined as a committee established by the board of directors for the purpose of overseeing the accounting and financial reporting processes of the company and the audits of such company's financial statements. Under SOX, if no such committee exists, then the entire board of directors is considered the audit committee; however, all members of the audit committee must be independent.[71] The audit committee is given the direct responsibility of engaging the auditing firm, preapproving audit as well as non-audit services, and overseeing the auditor's work. Under SOX, the independent auditor is required to directly report to the audit committee. In addition, the audit committee must establish procedures for dealing with internal corporate "whistle-blower" complaints concerning accounting or auditing matters. The audit committee also is vested with the power to employ its own legal counsel and other advisers as the committee deems is necessary to carry out its duties.[72]

[1]   Audit Committee Independence

The Act requires that the members of the audit committee be independent, thus precluding a member from being affiliated with the company or its subsidiaries other than his/her membership on the board of directors. This requirement of independence prohibits an audit committee member from

---

[70] See the discussion in Chapters 8, 9, and 15. For example, negligence suffices for violations of Section 17(a)(2) or 17(a)(3) of the Securities Act and Section 13(a) of the Exchange Act. Note that a false certification, without more, is not indicative of the subject officer's scienter. *See Central Laborers' Pension Fund v. Integrated Electrical Services, Inc.*, 497 F.3d 546 (5th Cir. 2007); *Garfield v. NDC Healthcare Corp.*, 466 F.3d 1255 (11th Cir. 2006). *See generally* Alverson, *Sarbanes-Oxley §§ 302 and 906: Corporate Reform or Legislative Redundancy?*, 33 Sec. Reg. L.J. 15 (2005); Brockett, *The Sarbanes-Oxley Act of 2002: What It Means For Business Litigators*, 30 Sec. Reg. L.J. 360 (2002). For an SEC enforcement action based on an allegedly false Section 302 certification, *see, e.g., SEC v. Rica Foods, Inc.*, 35 Sec. Reg. & L. Rep. (BNA) 1427 (S.D. Fla. 2003). For a private securities action premised on an allegedly false Section 302 certification, *see, e.g., In re Ramp Corp. Securities Litigation*, [2006 Transfer Binder] Fed. Sec. L. Rep. (CCH) ¶ 93,914 (S.D.N.Y. 2006).

[71] Sarbanes-Oxley Act § 205(a)(58)(A)-(B), *amending* §§ 3(a)(58)(A)-(B), 10A(m)(3) of the Exchange Act; Securities Act Release No. 8220 (2003).

[72] Sarbanes-Oxley Act §§ 201(h), 202(i), 301(m), *amending* § 10A(h), (i), (m) of the Exchange Act. Note that the auditors are precluded from engaging in specified non-audit services. SOX §§ 201–203. *See infra* § 5.08[O].

receiving consulting or similar fees. Thus, an independent director may receive compensation only for serving as a director and as a board committee member.[73]

The SEC has implemented this aspect of SOX, precluding the self-regulatory organizations (SROs) from listing the security of any company that fails to comply with the SEC mandates. The SEC requirements, in conjunction with the mandates of SOX, signify that listed companies must adhere to the following standards:

- each member of the listed company's audit committee must be independent from the company and its management;
- the audit committee must have direct responsibility for the appointment, compensation, retention and oversight of the company's independent auditor, and the independent auditor must report directly to the audit committee;
- the audit committee must establish procedures for handling complaints regarding the company's accounting practices;
- the audit committee must have authority to engage advisors as it determines necessary to carry out its duties;
- the company must provide appropriate funding for the audit committee to pay the fees of the independent auditor, any outside advisers engaged by the audit committee, and the committee's administrative expenses.[74]

[2] Audit Committee Financial Expert

Under Section 407 of SOX, disclosure is required as to whether any member of the audit committee qualifies as a "financial expert." If an audit committee does not have a financial expert, management must explain the reasons for the absence thereof in applicable SEC filings. In charging the SEC with formulating rules to implement this provision, Congress gave some clear guidance. Under SOX, a financial expert must have an understanding of General Accepted Accounting Principles (GAAP), experience with respect to the auditing or preparation of financial statements, an understanding of audit committee functions, and experience with internal accounting controls.[75]

Under the rules adopted by the SEC pursuant to the Act's mandate, the term "financial expert" is replaced with the term "audit committee financial expert." In order to be classified as an "audit committee financial expert," an individual must have the knowledge and experience described in the Act, as well as the ability to apply generally accepted accounting principles with respect to the accounting for estimates, accruals and reserves. A person can acquire the status of financial expert through education or through experience

---

[73] *Id.* § 301(m)(3), *amending* § 10A(m)(3) of the Exchange Act.

[74] Akin Gump Strauss Hauer & Feld, LLP Corporate Governance Alert, dated May 2, 2003 (on file with the author); *see* Securities Act Release No. 8220 (2003); Securities Exchange Act Release No. 48745 (2003).

[75] Sarbanes-Oxley Act § 407.

as a financial officer, accounting officer, or auditor (or through supervising such person). Significantly, according to the SEC, the designation of an audit committee member as a financial expert does not impose more obligations on that individual than those placed on other audit committee members.[76]

[D] Improper Influence on Audits

The Sarbanes-Oxley Act makes it illegal for any person, whether director, officer, or an individual working on behalf thereof, to fraudulently influence, manipulate, coerce, or mislead any accountant who is engaged in the performance of an audit of the subject registrant's financial statements.[77] Exercising its regulatory authority, the SEC has promulgated the following rule with respect to this provision:

> No officer or director of an issuer, or any other person acting under the direction thereof, shall directly or indirectly take any action to coerce, manipulate, mislead, or fraudulently influence any independent public or certified public accountant engaged in the performance of an audit or review of the financial statements of that issuer that are required to be filed with the Commission . . . if that person knew or should have known that such action, if successful, could result in rendering the issuer's financial statements materially misleading.[78]

[E] Forfeiture of Bonuses and Profits

In the event that a publicly-held company must prepare an accounting restatement due to the material noncompliance of such registrant, as a result of misconduct, the CEO and the CFO must reimburse the company for any bonus or other incentive-based compensation. Moreover, under such circumstances, any profits realized from the sale of the registrant's securities received by the subject officer within the twelve-month period following the filing with the SEC of the misleading report(s) must be disgorged to the company.[79] Unfortunately, the statute does not explain when an accounting restatement is considered to be "as a result of misconduct." Therefore, determination of the meaning of this term will be left to judicial resolution.[80]

[F] Officer and Director Bars

SOX lowers the standard for barring individuals from being officers and directors of publicly-held companies. Previously, a court had authority to bar a securities law violator from serving as a director or officer of a publicly-held

---

[76] Securities Act Release No. 8177 (2003); *see* Regulation S-K, Item 401(h).

[77] Sarbanes-Oxley Act § 303.

[78] Exchange Act Rule 13b2-2(b)(1); *see* Securities Exchange Act Release No. 47890 (2003). Note that the SEC rule renders negligent conduct actionable.

[79] Sarbanes-Oxley Act § 304.

[80] *See* Kelsh, *Section 304 of the Sarbanes-Oxley Act of 2002: The Case for a Personal Culpability Requirement*, 59 Bus. Law. 1005 (2004).

enterprise who was found liable for securities fraud and held to be "substantially unfit." SOX lowers that standard to "unfitness." Accordingly, upon a finding that the subject violator engaged in securities fraud and is deemed unfit to serve as a director or officer of a publicly-held company, a bar order is to be entered.[81]

[G]   Insider Trading During Blackout Periods

Under the Sarbanes-Oxley Act, executive officers and directors are prohibited from trading any equity security of the issuer, acquired through the scope of employment, during a blackout period, when at least half of the issuer's individual account plan participants are not permitted to trade in the equity security for more than three consecutive business days. Stated generally, SOX also requires that the issuer must deliver notice of blackout periods at least thirty days prior to the blackout period, giving proper notice to employees, executives, and the SEC.[82] The SEC has adopted rules governing this prohibition against trading during blackout periods. Under Regulation Blackout Trading Restriction (BTR), a director or executive officer of a publicly-held issuer is prohibited from trading during a blackout period equity securities that were acquired in connection with such director's or officer's service to the subject issuer.[83]

A violation of Section 306(a) of the Act is deemed a violation of the Exchange Act and is subject to SEC enforcement action. Furthermore, an issuer or a security holder may bring on behalf of such issuer an action against the director or officer who violated the blackout period, and seek disgorgement of all profits from the sale of such securities acquired in connection with the director's or officer's service to the issuer. The amount disgorged will be calculated, under Regulation BTR, as the difference between the amount paid for the equity security on the date of the transaction and the amount that would have been received for the security if the transaction had taken place outside of the blackout period.[84]

[H]   Disclosure of Off-Balance Sheet Transactions

SOX requires reporting companies to disclose in their financial statements any off-balance sheet transaction, arrangement or obligation that may have a material effect on the financial condition of the corporation. The Act also mandates that the subject financial report must reflect all material correcting adjustments that have been identified by the public accountant. Further, the Act requires the SEC to promulgate rules providing that subject companies must present pro forma financial information included in an SEC filing or

---

[81] Sarbanes-Oxley Act § 305, *amending* §§ 20(e) of the Securities Act, 21(d)(2) of the Exchange Act; *see* Barnard, *Rule 10b-5 and the "Unfitness" Question*, 47 Ariz. L. Rev. 9 (2005). For further discussion, see Chapter 15.

[82] Sarbanes-Oxley Act § 306.

[83] *See* Securities Exchange Act Release No. 47225 (2003).

[84] *Id.*; *see* Sarbanes-Oxley Act § 306; Regulation BTR; W. Wang & M. Steinberg, Insider Trading §§ 12:1–12:5 (2d ed. 2005); *infra* § 12.09.

other public disclosure (such as a press release) in a nonmisleading manner and must reconcile such pro forma financial information with the subject company's financial condition and results of operation under GAAP.[85] Subsequently, the SEC adopted implementing rules, including Regulation G, pursuant to this legislative directive. These rules "address public companies' disclosure or release of certain financial information that is calculated and presented on the basis of methodologies other than in accordance with generally accepted accounting principles (GAAP)."[86]

[I] Prohibition of Loans to Directors and Officers

The Sarbanes-Oxley Act prohibits loans by a publicly-held company to its executive officers and directors. Certain limited types of loans are permitted if they are extended in the ordinary course of business by the company and are granted to the fiduciary on the same basis as loans provided to the general public.[87]

[J] Reporting of Insider Transactions

The Sarbanes-Oxley Act expedites disclosures of sales or purchases of equity securities by directors, officers, and ten percent shareholders of publicly-held registrants. Under SOX, a change in beneficial ownership, with certain exceptions, must be reported by the end of the second business day following the execution of the transaction. Under the statute, the SEC must allow the filing to be electronic, and make the information contained in such filing to be publicly accessible. The company must also provide this information in a timely manner by placing the information on the company website not later than the business day after the SEC filing.[88] Subsequently, the SEC promulgated rules requiring mandatory electronic filing of beneficial ownership reports under Section 16(a).[89]

[K] Management Assessment of Internal Controls

SOX requires management to create, maintain, and assess internal controls. Management also must report on the effectiveness of the internal controls. In addition, the Act requires the independent auditor to report on whether the company has adequate internal controls.[90] Subsequently, the SEC adopted rules mandating that each Exchange Act reporting company include in its Form 10-K a report of management addressing the subject company's internal control over financial reporting. The Commission stated:

---

[85] Sarbanes-Oxley Act § 401, *amending* § 13(i)-(j) of the Exchange Act.

[86] Securities Act Release No. 8176 (2003); *see* Regulation G; Regulation S-K, Item 10.

[87] Sarbanes-Oxley Act § 402, *amending* § 13(k) of the Exchange Act. For an SEC enforcement based on the loan prohibition of Section 402, see *In the Matter of Goodfellow and Molaris*, Securities Exchange Act Release No. 52865 (2005).

[88] Sarbanes-Oxley Act § 403(a).

[89] Sarbanes-Oxley Act Release No. 8230 (2003).

[90] Sarbanes-Oxley Act § 404.

As directed by Section 404 of the Sarbanes-Oxley Act of 2002, we are adopting rules requiring companies subject to the reporting requirements of the Securities Exchange Act of 1934, other than registered investment companies, to include in their annual reports a report of management on the company's internal control over financial reporting. The internal control report must include: a statement of management's responsibility for establishing and maintaining adequate internal control over financial reporting for the company; management's assessment of the effectiveness of the company's internal control over financial reporting as of the end of the company's most recent fiscal year; a statement identifying the framework used by management to evaluate the effectiveness of the company's internal control over financial reporting; and a statement that the registered public accounting firm that audited the company's financial statements included in the annual report has issued an attestation report on management's assessment of the company's internal control over financial reporting. Under [these] rules, a company is required to file the registered public accounting firm's attestation report as part of the annual report. Furthermore, . . . management [must] evaluate any change in the company's internal control over financial reporting that occurred during a fiscal quarter that has materially affected, or is reasonably likely to materially affect, the company's internal control over financial reporting.[91]

[L]   Senior Financial Officer Code of Ethics

Under SOX, a publicly-held company is required to disclose whether or not it has a code of ethics applicable to its senior financial officers. A code of ethics contains standards that set forth ethical behavior. The code of ethics envisioned by SOX should seek to ensure fair and accurate disclosure of financial data, and compliance with governmental rules and regulations. If a company does not have a code of ethics, it is required to explain the reason for such absence in the applicable periodic reports required to be filed pursuant to the Securities Exchange Act.[92]

Implementing this statute, the SEC has mandated that a subject registrant disclose in its annual report whether the company has a written code of ethics for its chief executive officer, chief financial officer, chief accounting officer or comptroller, or individuals performing like functions. The failure by a company to adopt such a written code of ethics and the reasons explaining such failure

---

[91] Securities Act Release No. 8238 (2003). In 2007, the SEC adopted amendments with respect to management's report on internal control over financial reporting. Securities Act Release No. 8808 (2007). The SEC staff also has issued an interpretive release. *See* Securities Act Release No. 8810 (2007). In general, the SEC has undertaken the task of redesigning Section 404 implementation with the goal of making this process more efficient and cost effective. *See* Securities Act Release Nos. 8730, 8731 (2006); Fed. Sec. L. Rep. (CCH) No. 2239, at 3–4 (2006).

[92] Sarbanes-Oxley Act § 406.

must be disclosed. Moreover, registrants must disclose any waiver or amendment of its Code of Ethics on either a Form 8-K or on its Internet website.[93]

[M]   Real-Time Disclosure

SOX requires publicly-held companies, as set forth by SEC rules, to make rapid and current disclosure of material changes in their financial condition or operations. These disclosures must be in plain English.[94] Under this provision, as discussed in Chapter 11, the Commission has added several items to be promptly disclosed pursuant to Form 8-K.[95] The SEC also approved rules accelerating the filing date for Form 10-K and 10-Q reports for certain issuers.[96]

[N]   Accounting Oversight Board

The Sarbanes-Oxley Act established the Public Accounting Oversight Board (PCAOB or Board). The Board's fundamental purpose is to oversee the auditing of public companies in order to help ensure accurate and independent financial reporting by public companies subject to the federal securities laws. The PCAOB is not an agency of the federal government; it is a non-profit corporation formed under the laws of the District of Columbia. The Board has sweeping powers to establish quality control, ethical, and auditing standards for accounting firms. The PCAOB also has the power and authority to inspect, investigate, and bring disciplinary proceedings against public auditing firms.[97]

The SEC has oversight authority over the Board.[98] Such oversight helps to ensure that the policies and rules of the PCAOB are consistent with the objectives of the federal securities laws. The Board is subject to a similar degree and control by the SEC as is the Financial Industry Regulatory Authority (FINRA).[99] The Board must file its proposed rules with the SEC, and the Commission will publish the proposals for public comment. A rule proposed by the PCAOB will not become effective until the SEC has approved such rule. Also, any disciplinary actions taken by the PCAOB are subject to review by the SEC. The SEC has the power to reduce or modify the sanctions imposed by the PCAOB if the SEC finds that the sanctions are not

---

[93] *See* Regulation S-K, Item 406; Securities Act Release No. 8177 (2003).

[94] Sarbanes-Oxley Act § 409, *amending* § 13(l) of the Exchange Act.

[95] *See* Securities Exchange Act Released No. 49424 (2004); *infra* § 11.07. *See generally* Horwich, *New Form 8-K and Real-Time Disclosure*, 37 Rev. Sec. & Comm. Reg. 109 (2004).

[96] *See* Securities Exchange Act Release No. 47226 (2003).

[97] Sarbanes-Oxley Act § 101(a)-(b). The constitutionality of the PCAOB was upheld in *Free Enterprise Fund v. Public Company Accounting Oversight Board*, 537 F.3d 667 (D.C. Cir. 2008).

[98] Sarbanes Oxley Act § 107.

[99] *See* J. Hamilton & T. Trautmann, Sarbanes-Oxley Act of 2002, 41 (2002) (citing S. Rep. No. 107-205 (2002)).

appropriate.[100] After such SEC review, the U.S. Court of Appeals has authority to review the sanctions ordered.[101] In addition, the SEC has the power to censure the PCAOB and its members, and also has the power to limit the Board's activities.[102]

[O]   Auditor Independence

[1]   Non-Audit Services

The Sarbanes-Oxley Act focuses on the issue of auditor independence. The Act prohibits a registered public accounting firm that is auditing a publicly-held enterprise from engaging in specified non-audit services.[103] These specified prohibited non-audit services include, for example, (1) bookkeeping, (2) appraisal services, (3) actuarial services, (4) management functions or human resources work, (5) broker-dealer, investment adviser or investment banking services, (6) legal services and other expert services unrelated to auditing, (7) internal audit outsourcing, (8) financial information systems design and implementation, and (9) any other service that the PCAOB determines is impermissible.[104]

[2]   Audit Committee Pre-Approval of Permitted Non-Audit Services

SOX generally requires pre-approval by the audit committee for any allowable non-audit functions performed by the accounting firm. As long as the auditing firm complies with the Act's mandate for audit committee pre-approval, the subject firm may provide tax services and other allowable non-audit services to its audit clients. Further, SOX provides for a de minimus exception to the pre-approval of non-audit functions.[105]

[3]   Audit Partner Rotation

SOX requires the lead or coordinating audit partner (but not the firm itself) to rotate off of an audit engagement every five years, with at least a five-year cooling off period before a lead auditor may return to a given audit client.[106]

---

[100] Sarbanes-Oxley Act § 107(b)(2), (b)(4), (c)(1), (c)(3); *see* J. Hamilton & T. Trautmann, *supra* note 94, at 41.

[101] Securities Exchange Act § 25(a).

[102] Sarbanes-Oxley Act § 107(d).

[103] *Id.* § 201(a), *amending* § 10A(g) of the Exchange Act.

[104] *Id.*; *see* Securities Act Release No. 8183 (2003) (adopting rules relating to auditor independence, including prohibition of certain non-audit services).

[105] *See* Sarbanes-Oxley Act § 202(A); Securities Act Release No. 8183 (2003). The de minimus exception arises when the total of non-audit services does not exceed five percent of the revenues paid by the registrant to such auditor, the services were not recognized as non-audit services at the time of the engagement, the services are promptly brought to the audit committee's attention, and such non-audit services are approved by the audit committee (or a duly authorized member of the audit committee) prior to the completion of the audit. Sarbanes-Oxley Act § 202(B).

[106] Sarbanes-Oxley Act § 203, *amending*, § 10A(j) of the Exchange Act.

Also, the SEC has issued rules requiring that other audit partners rotate every seven years, with a minimum cooling-off period of at least two years.[107] If certain conditions are met, "small" firms with fewer than ten partners and fewer than five SEC audit clients are exempt from the rule.[108]

[4] Report to the Audit Committee

SOX requires the independent public auditor to make timely reports to the audit committee.[109] These reports must include all critical accounting policies and practices to be used, all alternative treatments of financial information within GAAP that have been discussed with management and the ramifications of the use of each such alternative, and any other material written communication between the auditor and management. The audit committee is ultimately responsible for deciding any accounting methodology disagreements between management and the independent public accountants.[110]

[5] Cooling-Off Period

Under SOX, an auditor cannot perform an audit of a company if the registrant's chief executive officer, chief financial officer, controller, or chief accounting officer was employed by the subject auditor during the one-year period prior to the initiation of the audit and participated in any capacity in an audit of such issuer.[111]

[P] Attorney Professional Responsibility

Sarbanes-Oxley Act requires an attorney who is practicing before the SEC to report evidence of a material violation of the securities laws or breach of fiduciary duty to the company's CEO or chief legal counsel (CLC). If the CEO or CLC does not respond appropriately, adopting appropriate remedial measures, the attorney is required to report evidence of the violation to the audit committee, another committee comprised entirely of outside directors, or the board of directors.[112] The statute also directs the SEC to formulate rules setting forth minimum standards of attorney professional conduct. Subsequently, the SEC promulgated minimum standards of professional conduct (Standards) for attorneys practicing before the Commission.[113] These Standards also are addressed in Chapter 15 of this text.

---

[107] Securities Act Release No. 8183 (2003). The term "audit partner" is defined by SEC rule and does not encompass all of the firm's partners on the audit engagement team.

[108] *Id.* In order for such an audit firm to qualify for this exemption, the PCAOB "must conduct a review of all of the firm's engagements subject to the rule at least once every three years." *Id.*

[109] Sarbanes-Oxley Act § 204, *amending* § 10A(k) of the Exchange Act.

[110] Sarbanes-Oxley Act §§ 204, 301(B)(2), *amending* § 10A(k), (m) of the Exchange Act.

[111] Sarbanes-Oxley Act § 206, *amending* § 10A(l) of the Exchange Act.

[112] Sarbanes-Oxley Act § 307.

[113] Securities Exchange Act Release No. 47276 (2003).

[1]   "Up-the-Ladder" Reporting

Under the SEC's Standards, attorneys who practice before the Commission and are aware of evidence of a material violation (by the issuer, director, officer, employee or agent of such issuer) of the securities laws or breach of fiduciary duty that has occurred, is ongoing, or will occur, are required to report such evidence to the CEO or the CLC. If the attorney reasonably believes that the CEO or CLC has taken appropriate measures to address the situation, then the attorney has complied with the SEC Standards. However, if the CEO or CLC has not taken appropriate corrective measures, the attorney is required to report such evidence to the audit committee, or another committee comprised of independent directors or, if none exists, then the attorney must report evidence of the violation to the entire board of directors.[114]

[2]   Qualified Legal Compliance Committee

The SEC Standards establish an alternative reporting procedure. If implemented, this alternative requires the issuer to establish a qualified legal compliance committee (QLCC). A qualified legal compliance committee must be comprised of at least one member from the audit committee and at least two other outside directors. By referring a report of evidence of a material violation to the QLCC, the CLC has complied with the SEC Standards.[115]

[Q]   Financial Analysts' Conflicts of Interest

SOX addresses securities analysts and possible conflicts of interest arising from their duties. The Act directs the SEC to formulate rules that enhance the objectivity of analyst research reports and increase investor confidence in analyst research.[116] Responding to this directive, the SEC promulgated Regulation AC. Regulation AC requires, for example, that research analysts: certify the truthfulness of the views expressed in public appearances as well as contained in their research reports; and disclose in such certification any compensation received that is directly or indirectly related to the specific recommendations or views set forth in public appearances or their research reports. Regulation AC contains a number of exemptions, such as excluding from the Regulation's mandates foreign securities analysts, non-registered investment advisers, and the media.[117] In this regard, the Commission also approved extensive self-regulatory rules that, for example, prohibit tying a research analyst's remuneration to the firm's procurement of specific banking transactions, that forbid a research analyst to provide favorable analysis on a company in return for investment banking engagements, and that prohibit a

---

[114] *See* SEC Standards of Professional Conduct Rule 3(b).

[115] *Id.* Rule 3(b)(2), 3(c) (2); *see* Securities Exchange Act Release No. 47276 (2003). For further discussion, see Chapter 15.

[116] Sarbanes-Oxley Act § 501(a); *see* Hilgers, *Analyzing Wall Street Research Analyst Conflicts of Interest*, 31 Sec. Reg. L.J. 427 (2003).

[117] *See* Securities Act Release No. 8193 (2003).

firm from retaliating against a research analyst who publishes a research report that is detrimental to the firm's present or prospective investment banking relationship with a subject corporation.[118]

[R] Remedies and Criminal Penalties

The following discussion highlights key remedies and civil penalties that were enacted pursuant to the Sarbanes-Oxley Act.

[1] Statute of Limitations

As addressed in Chapter 8, SOX extends the statute of limitations for pursuing a private claim based on fraud, deceit, or manipulation to two years after discovery of the relevant facts constituting the violation and in no event more than five years after the violation occurs.[119] The previous statute of limitations was that suit had to be brought within one year after discovery of the facts constituting the violation and in no event more than three years after such violation.[120]

[2] Whistleblower Civil Remedy

SOX creates a private cause of action for an employee of a publicly-held company who has been discharged or incurred retaliatory treatment because he/she has been a whistleblower by providing information regarding conduct reasonably believed to violate a rule or regulation of the SEC, or provision of federal law relating to fraud, including but not limited to mail fraud, wire fraud, bank fraud, and securities fraud. An employee so situated is entitled to all necessary relief, including reinstatement, back pay, interest, compensation for any special damages, litigation costs, attorney's fees and expert fees.[121]

[3] Insider Trading During Blackouts — Disgorgement of Profits

As discussed earlier in this chapter,[122] SOX forbids an executive officer or director of a publicly-held company from trading subject securities during any mandatory blackout period applicable to a registrant's employee pension plan. If this provision is violated, the Act authorizes the company or shareholders of the company (by derivative suit) to procure the disgorgement of any profit realized by the officer or director.[123]

---

[118] *See* Securities Exchange Act Release Nos. 45908 (2002), 48252 (2003); *see also infra* § 13.04.

[119] 28 U.S.C. § 1658.

[120] *See infra* § 8.08.

[121] Sarbanes-Oxley Act § 806, *amending* 18 U.S.C. § 1514A; *see* Steinberg & Kaufman, *Minimizing Corporate Liability Exposure When the Whistle Blows in the Post Sarbanes-Oxley Era*, 30 J. Corp. L. 445 (2005).

[122] *See supra* § 5.08[G].

[123] Sarbanes-Oxley Act § 306.

[4]   No Discharge of Securities Fraud Debts in Bankruptcy

SOX amends the Bankruptcy Code to prohibit individuals from receiving a discharge of debts attributable to a judgment or settlement of federal or state securities fraud claims.[124] The statute seeks to prevent corporate insiders "from sheltering their assets under the umbrella of bankruptcy and protecting [such assets] from judgments and settlements arising from federal and state securities law violations."[125]

[5]   Court Order Freezing Certain Extraordinary Payments

SOX grants to the SEC the authority to seek and procure a court order freezing extraordinary payments made to a corporate officer or director during a Commission investigation involving possible violation of the federal securities laws.[126] According to the Ninth Circuit, the statute "gives the SEC authority to ensure that assets of an issuer of securities which have been fraudulently obtained are not dissipated [by the subject insider(s)] during the investigation and litigation of securities fraud cases."[127] At this point, neither the statute nor the SEC has defined the term "extraordinary payments."

[6]   Fair Funds Provision

SOX authorizes the SEC, when disgorgement and a civil money penalty are ordered against a subject party in an enforcement action, to establish a fund for the benefit of investors that will help offset their losses due to the illegalities committed.[128] For example, in the *WorldCom* matter, the Second Circuit affirmed the district judge's approval of the Commission's proposal to distribute, pursuant to the SOX "Fair Fund" provision, $750 million to aggrieved WorldCom investors.[129]

[7]   SEC Equitable Relief

Prior to Sarbanes-Oxley, the SEC largely relied on the inherent equitable authority of the federal courts to procure equitable relief in its enforcement actions.[130] Types of equitable relief obtained by the Commission have included,

---

[124] Sarbanes-Oxley Act § 803, *amending* § 523(a) of the Bankruptcy Code.

[125] J. Hamilton & T. Trautmann, *supra* note 94, at 83 (citing remarks of Sen. John McCain, Cong. Rep., July 10, 2002, at S6529).

[126] Sarbanes-Oxley Act § 1103, *amending* § 21C(c) of the Exchange Act.

[127] *SEC v. Genstar TV Guide International*, 367 F.3d 1087, 1090–1091 (9th Cir. 2004).

[128] Sarbanes-Oxley Act § 308.

[129] *See Official Committee of Unsecured Creditors of WorldCom Inc. v. SEC*, 467 F.3d 73 (2d Cir. 2006).

[130] *See, e.g., Deckert v. Independent Shares Corp.*, 311 U.S. 282 (1940); *SEC v. Posner*, 16 F.3d 500 (2d Cir. 1994); *SEC v. Wencke*, 622 F.2d 1363, 1369 (9th Cir. 1980) (stating that "[t]he federal courts have inherent equitable authority to issue a variety of 'ancillary relief' measures in actions brought by the SEC to enforce the federal securities laws").

for example, disgorgement, ordering of an accounting, appointment of a receiver, asset freeze and restructuring of the board of directors.[131] Any question as to the propriety of such relief[132] has been resolved by the Sarbanes-Oxley Act. Section 21(d)(5) of the Exchange Act, as amended by SOX, provides: "In any action or proceeding brought or instituted by the Commission under any provision of the securities laws, the Commission may seek, and any Federal court may grant, any equitable relief that may be appropriate or necessary for the benefit of investors."[133]

[8]   Criminal Sanctions

SOX enhances several criminal sanctions under Title VIII (Corporate Fraud and Accountability Act of 2002), Title IX (the White Collar Crime Penalty Enhancement Act of 2002), and Title XI (the Corporate Fraud Accountability Act of 2002). Under these enhancements, it is a crime, punishable for up to twenty years, to "knowingly alter, destroy, mutilate, conceal, cover-up or make a false entry in any record, document, or tangible object with the intent to impede, obstruct or influence the investigation or proper administration of any matter within the jurisdiction of any department or agency of the United States. . . . "[134] Another enhancement makes securities fraud a separate criminal offense, punishable for up to twenty-five years imprisonment. This statute encompasses any person who "knowingly executes or attempts to execute a scheme . . . to defraud any person in connection with any security of an [Exchange Act reporting] issuer or to obtain by false or fraudulent . . . representations . . . any money or property in connection with the purchase or sale of any security of an [Exchange Act reporting] issuer. . . . "[135] The Sarbanes-Oxley Act also sets forth that attempts and conspiracies to commit such offenses as mail fraud, wire fraud, and the new securities fraud are criminally punishable.[136] Lastly, SOX increases the punishment for mail and wire fraud from imprisonment of the previous five years to twenty years.[137]

---

[131] *See, e.g., SEC v. Interlink Data Network of Los Angeles Inc.*, 77 F.3d 1201 (9th Cir. 1996); *SEC v. Commonwealth Chemical Securities, Inc.*, 574 F.2d 90 (2d Cir. 1978); *SEC v. Current Financial Services, Inc.*, 783 F. Supp. 1441 (D.D.C. 1992); *SEC v. Mattel, Inc.*, 1974 U.S. Dist. LEXIS 6489 (D.D.C. 1974).

[132] A number of sources questioned the propriety of certain types of such relief. *See, e.g.*, Dent, *Ancillary Relief in Federal Securities Law: A Study in Federal Remedies*, 67 Minn. L. Rev. 865 (1983).

[133] Sarbanes-Oxley Act § 305(b), *amending* § 21(d)(5) of the Exchange Act.

[134] 18 U.S.C. § 1519.

[135] 18 U.S.C. § 1348.

[136] 18 U.S.C. §§ 1341, 1343, 1344, 1347, 1348.

[137] 18 U.S.C. § 1349.

Chapter 6

RESALES AND REORGANIZATIONS

§ 6.01 INTRODUCTION

As seen from the foregoing materials, the Securities Act of 1933 was enacted in large part to help promote the dissemination of adequate and reliable information to the investing public in the distribution process. To achieve this objective, Section 5 requires registration for any sale of a security unless such sale is exempt from the registration provisions. The party seeking to invoke an exemption from registration has the burden of proving that such exemption has been perfected.[1]

We have examined the exemptions for issuers in Chapter 3. Attention now turns to exemptions for resales by persons other than an issuer. We begin by addressing Section 4(1) which provides the most important exemption in this context. By its terms, Section 4(1) exempts from the registration requirements of Section 5 "transactions by any person other than an issuer, underwriter or dealer." Hence, as a general proposition, the Section 4(1) exemption permits individual investors to resell their securities without registration, provided such resales are viewed as "transactions" (rather than as part of a "distribution") and such persons are not deemed underwriters.

Because Section 4(3) and Section 4(4) exempt most transactions by broker-dealers, the problems that arise under Section 4(1) generally involve underwriters. Underwriter status necessarily renders the Section 4(1) exemption unavailable.

This chapter focuses on the federal provisions relating to resales and reorganizations. Significantly, the National Securities Markets Improvement Act of 1996 preempts state regulation of Section 4(1), 4(3), and 4(4) of the Securities Act. Note, however, that state regulation is federally preempted with respect to the Section 4(1) and 4(3) exemptions only if the issuer of the subject security is an Exchange Act reporting company (see § 18(b)(4) of the Securities Act).

§ 6.02 THE CONCEPT OF "UNDERWRITER"

The concept of underwriter is fundamental to the framework of the 1933 Act. Congress contemplated that underwriters would play an integral role in both the initial and secondary distribution process. Underwriter status subjects

---

[1] *See, e.g.*, *SEC v. Cavanagh*, 445 F.3d 105, 114 (2d Cir. 2006); *Pennaluna & Co. v. SEC*, 410 F.2d 861, 865 (9th Cir. 1969); *SEC v. Culpepper*, 270 F.2d 241, 246 (2d Cir. 1959).

applicable parties to the provisions of Section 5 and results in liability exposure for material misrepresentations and nondisclosures contained in the registration statement.

Section 2(a)(11) of the Securities Act defines an "underwriter" as "any person who has purchased from an issuer with a view to, or offers or sells for an issuer in connection with, the distribution of any security, or participates or has a direct or indirect participation in any such undertaking, or participates or has a participation in the direct or indirect underwriting of any such undertaking, but such term shall not include a person whose interest is limited to a commission from an underwriter or dealer not in excess of the usual and customary distributors' or sellers' commission." The term "distribution" has been described as "the entire process by which in the course of a public offering the block of securities is dispersed and ultimately comes to rest in the hands of the investing public."[2]

In this regard, see SEC Rules 141 and 142 which, in effect, exclude from underwriter status: (1) distributors and dealers not in privity with the issuer who receive a commission from an underwriter or dealer not in excess of the usual and customary distributors' or sellers' commissions (Rule 141); and (2) those persons who, under the circumstances delineated in the rule, purchase for investment purposes all or a specified portion of the securities remaining unsold after the lapse of a defined period of time (Rule 142).

For the purposes of Section 2(a)(11) only (i.e., who should be regarded as an "underwriter"), the term "issuer" is defined to include a person who controls the issuer. SEC Rule 405 defines "control" as "the possession, direct or indirect, of the power to direct or cause the direction of the management and policies of a person, whether through the ownership of voting securities, by contract, or otherwise." Significantly, the inclusion of control persons within the definition of "issuer" for Section 2(a)(11) purposes signifies that sales by directors and executive officers create the risk that some party involved in the transaction is an "underwriter."

An examination of Section 2(a)(11) reveals that a person can become an underwriter in the following ways:

(1) By purchasing from the issuer with a view towards distribution;

(2) By offering or selling for an issuer in connection with a distribution;

(3) By participating, directly or indirectly, in the distribution or underwriting effort;

(4) By selling securities of the issuer on behalf of a control person in connection with the distribution of any security; and

(5) By purchasing securities of the issuer from a control person with a view towards distribution.

---

[2] *SEC v. Kern*, 425 F.3d 143, 153, (2d Cir. 2005) (quoting *In re Lewisohn Copper Corp.*, 38 SEC 226, 234 (1958)).

If a person falls within one of these categories, he/she will be deemed to be an underwriter. Note the lack of guidance Section 2(a)(11) provides. For example: What evidence shows intent to distribute? What circumstances constitute participation? What power must a person possess to be in control? The answers to these questions are necessarily based on the individual circumstances of each case. Judicial decisions are relatively scarce, and not surprisingly, have not eliminated fears of inadvertent underwriter status. Moreover, beyond Rule 144 (which will be examined in § 6.04), the SEC has promulgated few rules or regulations in this area.

[A]   The Presumptive Underwriter Doctrine

In a registered offering of securities, an individual, a few investors, or an institution may purchase a substantial portion of the offering and thereafter resell the securities to the public. At least two problems may arise: First, the purchasers may hold the securities until the information in the registration statement becomes outdated (but note that this concern is minimal when the issuer timely files its periodic reports, such as its Form 10-Ks and Form 10-Qs, pursuant to the Exchange Act); and second, the purchasers, perhaps seeking to take advantage of the rapid price increase normally associated with a "hot issue" (that is, an issue that, shortly after the registration statement has gone effective is trading in the aftermarket at a substantially higher price than the registered offering price), may sell large quantities of the subject securities (for substantial profit) within a short time period. If the Section 4(1) exemption were to apply, these sales would be free of the registration requirements. Concerned with the lack of disclosure in this context, the SEC formulated (*and later abandoned*) the presumptive underwriter doctrine.[3]

Under the presumptive underwriter doctrine, one who purchases more than ten percent of the securities offered in a registered offering may be deemed an underwriter unless such person establishes sufficient investment intent. The doctrine was subject to criticism by institutional investors. In fear of the doctrine, a number of institutional investors significantly limited their purchases of securities in registered public offerings.

Comments made by the SEC staff evidence that the presumptive underwriter doctrine has been abandoned. As stated by the Commission's then Director of the Division of Corporation Finance:

> For many years, a concept known as the "presumptive underwriter" doctrine existed. That doctrine assumed that a purchaser of a relatively large amount of securities covered by a registration statement (at one point 10 percent) was buying with a view to distribution and, therefore, should be deemed a statutory underwriter. The theory was most subjective, most difficult of explanation, and presented considerable problems both in compliance, as well as administration. In 1983, in the

---

[3] *See* Ahrenholz & Van Valkenberg, *The Presumptive Underwriter Doctrine: Statutory Underwriter Status for Investors Purchasing a Substantial Portion of a Registered Offering*, 1973 Utah L. Rev. 773.

American Council of Life Insurance letter, the "presumptive under-writer" doctrine was for all intents and purposes abandoned. . . . Nothing in the Securities Act compelled the view that a person acquiring a substantial part of an offering should be treated differently from any other investor with a large position in the issuer, unless the purchaser becomes an affiliate as a result of the purchases.[4]

[B]   Participating in the Underwriting Effort

Based on the Second Circuit's decision in *SEC v. Chinese Consolidated Benevolent Association*,[5] the making of continual solicitations resulting in a distribution of securities renders the Section 4(1) exemption unavailable, irrespective of a party's motive or relationship with the issuer. This is so even if the party is a volunteer and receives no compensation for its efforts.

The above principle is not always literally applied, creating uncertainty in this area. For example, in one case, the court found that the defendant bank purchased shares on behalf of its customers in a public offering, acted as an important link in the chain of distribution, and issued reports touting the shares to its customers at the time it was buying and selling securities for its customers' accounts. Nevertheless, the court found that, as a matter of law, the bank was not an underwriter. It reasoned that in no manner did [the bank] have a relationship with [the issuer], [the principal underwriter], or the underwriting itself. Plaintiff, therefore, must properly plead some greater nexus between the investment management department of [defendant] Bankers Trust and this underwriting of securities before such liability can attach.[6]

§ 6.03   DISTRIBUTIONS BY CONTROLLING PERSONS OR AFFILIATES

The concept of "control" is crucial to the understanding of secondary distributions. For the purposes of determining who is an "underwriter," Section 2(a)(11) defines the term "issuer" to include a controlling person. Therefore, underwriter status may be accorded to any person who sells securities on behalf of a controlling person in connection with the distribution of any security.

The possibility of inadvertent underwriter status is ever present because of the ambiguities associated with the meaning of "control." Moreover, the inclusion of control persons within the definition of "issuer" for Section 2(a)(11) purposes signifies that sales of securities by directors and executive officers

---

[4] Address by Linda C. Quinn, Esq. Before the ABA's Federal Regulation of Securities Committee (Nov. 22, 1986), *discussed in*, Barron, *The SEC Staff Finally Abandons the "Presumptive Underwriter" Doctrine*, 15 Sec. Reg L.J. 296 (1987). Note that an *"affiliate"* of an issuer generally is one who controls, is controlled by, or is under common control with, either directly or indirectly, such issuer.

[5] 120 F.2d 738 (2d Cir. 1941); *see In re State Bank of Pakistan*, [1991–1992 Transfer Binder] Fed. Sec. L. Rep. (CCH) ¶ 84,946 (SEC 1992).

[6] *Zicklin v. Breuer*, 534 F. Supp. 745, 747 (S.D.N.Y. 1982).

create the risk that some party involved in the transaction is an "underwriter," irrespective of whether the securities are restricted or unrestricted. Indeed, control person status has been found to exist based on such factors as percentage of stock ownership, director or officer position held, and relationships with insiders. Because directors and executive officers frequently are shareholders and have relatively close relationships with other key insiders, this problem of potential underwriter status is a very practical and widespread one.

The lack of a precise definition for control frustrates counselors and corporate planners.[7] The Commission, in an effort to alleviate some of the uncertainty, promulgated Rule 405 which defines "control."

Rule 405 defines "control" as "the possession, direct or indirect, of the power to direct or cause the direction of the management and policies of a person, whether through the ownership of voting securities, by contract, or otherwise." Rule 405 focuses on a person's ability to direct the management and policies of the corporation. Use of Rule 405 to define "control" in the Section 2(a)(11) context, however, has been criticized by commentators. These commentators suggest that an appropriate definition of "control" should stress a person's ability to compel the issuer to register an offering. They assert that Congress never intended a person to be deemed an issuer for Section 2(a)(11) purposes when that person did not possess the power to effect registration. Moreover, they argue that the SEC's use of Rule 405 to define "control" fails to relieve uncertainty.[8]

[A]   Effecting a "Distribution"

The Securities Act does not explicitly hold the conduct of controlling persons illegal when they effect a distribution of unregistered shares through an underwriter. Of course, what a statute fails expressly to do, a court can accomplish through construing the statute's pertinent language, legislative history, and policy rationales. In *United States v. Wolfson*,[9] the Second Circuit held that a group of controlling persons (Wolfson and his cohorts) violated Section 5 because they effected an unregistered distribution of securities through several unwitting brokerage houses. As the court observed, Section 4(1) "by its terms exempts only transactions." Hence, because Wolfson and his cronies were effecting a "distribution," they could not avail themselves of the Section 4(1) exemption. As the Seventh Circuit more recently stated:

> Section 4(1) provides an exemption for *transactions, not individuals.* It was created to exempt routine trading *transactions* with respect to securities already issued and *not to exempt* distributions by issuers

---

[7] *See* Sommer, *Who's "In Control"?* — *S.E.C.*, 21 Bus. Law. 559 (1966).

[8] *See Pennaluna & Company v. SEC*, 410 F.2d 861 (9th Cir. 1969); 7B J. W. Hicks, Exempted Transactions Under the Securities Act of 1933 § 9.03[2][a] (2008); Campbell, *Defining Control in Secondary Distributions*, 18 B.C. Ind. & Comm. L. Rev. 37 (1976).

[9] 405 F.2d 779 (2d Cir. 1968).

or acts of others who engage in steps necessary to such distributions.[10]

As an additional point from the *Wolfson* case, the six brokerage houses, although unable to invoke the Section 4(1) exemption, were not subject to the Section 5 requirements due to the Section 4(4) exemption. The court supported this conclusion by finding that each of the unwitting brokerage houses effected only "transactions" (unaware of the "distribution"), the "transactions" were solicited by Wolfson, and the "transactions" were executed in the over-the-counter market.

An earlier case, *Ira Haupt & Co.*,[11] had the effect of making brokers wary of selling a controlling person's shares. There, an individual Schulte controlled Park & Tilford, Inc. He gave a series of sell orders, involving around 200 shares per order, to his broker Haupt. During a six-month period, 93,000 shares were sold pursuant to these orders. Haupt was charged with violating Section 5 for its role in effecting the unregistered offering. Haupt offered two defenses. First, Haupt argued that its sales of Park & Tilford shares were not a "distribution" because there was no plan to sell a specified number of shares. The Commission rejected this defense, finding that the facts and circumstances clearly put Haupt on notice that a distribution was anticipated.

Second, the broker Haupt claimed the Section 4(4) exemption, which, *inter alia*, exempts "brokers' transactions executed upon customers' orders on any exchange. . . . " In rejecting this defense, the SEC reasoned that the Section 4(4) exemption does not exempt brokers from Section 5 when they act as underwriters in a "distribution." The SEC defined a "distribution" as "[t]he entire process by which in the course of a public offering the block of securities is dispersed and ultimately comes to rest in the hands of the investing public." Here, *Haupt* was effecting a "distribution" rather than engaging in a "transaction." As will be discussed later in the chapter, to alleviate some of the concern generated by the *Haupt* decision, the SEC promulgated Rule 144.

[B]   Contractual Agreements to Sell

As the foregoing discussion suggests, in order to effect a "distribution," a registered offering must take place. Irrespective of whether the offering is on behalf of an issuer or for the benefit of a control person, only the issuer can register a public offering. This consequence is not unduly onerous, according to proponents, because a controlling person has the leverage to induce the issuer to file a registration statement and to elicit adequate disclosure on the part of such an issuer. Because of the ambiguities associated with the concept of control, a person who may be viewed as an affiliate may contract with the issuer when he/she acquires the stock for the right of demand registration,

---

[10] *SEC v. Holschuh*, 694 F.2d 130, 137–138 (7th Cir. 1982) (emphasis added); *accord SEC v. M & A West, Inc.*, 538 F.3d 1043 (9th Cir. 2008); *SEC v. Kern*, 425 F.3d 143, 152 (2d Cir. 2005); *SEC v. Cavanagh*, 445 F.3d 105, 114 (2d Cir. 2006); *SEC v. Kern*, 425 F.3d 143, 152 (2d Cir. 2005); *SEC v. Murphy*, 626 F.2d 633, 648 (9th Cir. 1980); *In re DG Bank (Schweiz) AG*, [1991–1992 Transfer Binder] Fed. Sec. L. Rep. (CCH) ¶ 84,945 (SEC 1992).

[11] 23 SEC 589 (1946); *see In re Paulson Investment Co.*, [1991–1992 Transfer Binder] Fed. Sec. L. Rep. (CCH) ¶ 84,917 (SEC 1991).

thereby granting the control person the contractual right to demand that the issuer file a 1933 Act registration statement when the person wishes to dispose of his/her stock. If the purported "control person" does not have such leverage, he/she may settle for the right of "piggy-back" registration. This right, looking to the terms of the covenant negotiated, authorizes the control person to sell ("piggy-back") his/her stock or a portion thereof at the time that the issuer elects to file a registration statement.[12]

In any event, such "control person" should insist that the issuer covenant to provide Rule 15c2-11 information. Generally, Rule 15c2-11 prohibits broker-dealers from publishing a quotation for any security unless specified information is available with respect to the issuer and the security. In effect, the Rule prevents the widespread distribution of securities without certain minimal information being publicly available. Hence, Rule 15c2-11(a)(5) calls for certain mandated information to be reasonably current and to be made reasonably available by the subject broker or dealer upon the request of a prospective purchaser.[13] Importantly, if the control person induces the issuer to disseminate Rule 15c2-11 information, the "current information" requirement of Rule 144, which provides a safe harbor in the resale context, will be satisfied (*see infra* § 6.05[B]).

Note, moreover, that when restricted securities are involved, the securities will contain a restrictive legend or stop transfer instructions. To have the

---

[12] *See generally* Jacob, et al., *Key Considerations in Drafting a Registration Rights Agreement from the Company's Perspective*, 41 Rev. Sec. & Comm. Reg. 113 (2008); O'Hare, *Institutional Investors, Registration Rights, and the Specter of Liability Under Section 11 of the Securities Act of 1933*, 1996 Wisc. L. Rev. 217.

[13] Hence, Rule 15c2-11 calls for the following information to be made available upon request to a prospective purchaser:

   (i)   the exact name of the issuer and its predecessor (if any);

   (ii)   the address of its principal executive offices;

   (iii)   the state of incorporation, if it is a corporation;

   (iv)   the exact title and class of the security;

   (v)   the par or stated value of the security;

   (vi)   the number of shares or total amount of the securities outstanding as of the end of the issuer's most recent fiscal year;

   (vii)   the name and address of the transfer agent;

   (viii)   the nature of the issuer's business;

   (ix)   the nature of products or services offered;

   (x)   the nature and extent of the issuer's facilities;

   (xi)   the name of the chief executive officer and members of the board of directors;

   (xii)   the issuer's most recent balance sheet and profit and loss and retained earnings statements;

   (xiii)   similar financial information for such part of the two preceding fiscal years as the issuer or its predecessor has been in existence;

   (xiv)   whether the broker or dealer or any associated person is affiliated, directly or indirectly with the issuer;

   (xv)   whether the quotation is being published or submitted on behalf of any other broker or dealer, and, if so, the name of such broker or dealer; and

   (xvi)   whether the quotation is being submitted or published directly or indirectly on behalf of the issuer, or any director, officer or any person, directly or indirectly the beneficial owner of more than 10 percent of the outstanding units or shares of any equity security of the issuer, and, if so, the name of such person, and the basis for any exemption under the federal securities laws for any sales of such securities on behalf of such person.

securities transaction consummated, including removal of the legends or "stops," "the issuer's securities law counsel (or other designated 'point person' for the issuer) [must] authorize the transfer agent to transfer the stock into the 'street name' of the selling securities broker-dealer firm, free of legends and free of stops."[14]

As a final point, even where the control person in a secondary distribution induces the issuer to file a registration statement, there remain significant pitfalls. One particular concern is disclosure. For example, where all or a part of the proceeds of the offering will be paid to selling shareholders rather than to the issuer, the registration statement must carefully disclose this consequence.[15] Another problem is that shareholders effecting a secondary registered offering may be tempted to manipulate the price of the stock. The SEC, aware of the potential for abuse, has brought enforcement actions in this context and has promulgated a number of rules designed to curtail such manipulative activity.[16]

[C] PIPEs

A relatively recent development with respect to the registration of secondary offerings concerns "PIPEs" (Private Investment in Public Equity). Generally, PIPEs involve the purchase of securities in an issuer private placement (such as pursuant to § 4(2) or Rule 506), the issuer's subsequent registration of the restricted stock with the SEC, and, upon effectiveness of the registration statement, the ability of the PIPE investors to resell immediately their stock into the public markets. PIPEs frequently are priced at a discount to the then current public market price (such as that quoted on the Nasdaq Stock Market). As an additional "sweetener," PIPE investors may receive "warrants" priced attractively that may be exercised at some point in the future.

If structured improperly, PIPEs can cause significant shareholder dilution. Moreover, because the price of a subject issuer's stock often drops once a PIPE transaction becomes known, insider trading concerns have developed. Nonetheless, PIPEs may be viewed as providing a useful means for obtaining capital for smaller publicly-held companies that experience difficulty raising funds due to their inability of undertaking traditional private or public offerings or procuring loans from financial institutions.[17]

---

[14] Barron, *Control and Restricted Securities*, 28 Sec. Reg. L.J. 74, 75 (2000).

[15] *See, e.g.*, SEC Regulation S-K, Item 507; *In the Matter of Universal Camera Corp.*, 19 S.E.C. 648 (1945).

[16] *See e.g.*, SEC Regulation M; *In the Matter of Hazel Bishop, Inc.*, 40 S.E.C. 718 (1961).

[17] *See SEC v. Lyon*, 529 F. Supp. 2d 444 (S.D.N.Y. 2008). In 2006, approximately $28 billion of PIPE deals were consummated. However, the SEC is becoming more vigorous in scrutinizing the disclosures made in these arrangements, thereby signifying that PIPEs may become less popular. *See* Burns, *SEC Slows Flow of PIPE Deals to a Trickle*, Wall St. J., Dec. 27, 2006; Lerner, *Disclosing Toxic PIPEs*, 55 Bus. Law. 655 (2003); Sjostrom, *PIPES*, 2 Entre. Bus. L.J. 381 (2007); Steinberg & Obi, *Examining the Pipeline: A Contemporary Assessment of Private Investments in Public Equity ("PIPES")*, 11 U. Pa. J. Bus. & Emp. L. 1 (2008).

§ 6.04 PURCHASING FROM AN ISSUER WITH A VIEW TOWARDS DISTRIBUTION

A person who has acquired "restricted securities" from an issuer often has obtained the securities pursuant to Section 4(2) of the Securities Act or pursuant to Rule 506 of Regulation D. One problem is that when an issuer sells unregistered securities to one or more persons in a non-public transaction, it is possible that the transfer is in reality a public offering in disguise — a two-step, indirect distribution in which the transferees function as "underwriters" for the issuer.

An affiliate of the issuer selling either restricted or nonrestricted securities faces a similar problem — because of his/her close connection with the issuer, an affiliate, absent the exercise of utmost care, may be unable to invoke the Section 4(1) exemption in any resale transaction involving securities of the issuer.

As discussed earlier in this chapter, if a person is deemed to be an "underwriter," he/she cannot rely on the exemption from registration provided by Section 4(1) of the Act to protect the resale transaction. Generally, although Section 4(1) exempts ordinary transactions such as a private resale of securities, it does so only with respect to *"transactions by any person other* than an issuer, *underwriter,* or dealer." The dilemma for persons holding *restricted securities* of an issuer and for affiliates of an issuer (regardless whether such affiliates seek to sell restricted or nonrestricted securities) comes into focus upon examining the statutory definition of "underwriter." Section 2(a)(11) of the Act defines an "underwriter" to include any person who "has purchased" securities from the issuer "with a view to . . . the *distribution* of any security."

Section 2(a)(11) does not provide an objective standard for determining whether a person acquiring securities from an issuer is taking with a view toward investment or with a view toward resale. For a non-affiliate holding *restricted securities*, a resale in purported reliance upon Section 4(1) carries the risk that such seller will be deemed to be an "underwriter" within the meaning of Section 2(a)(11), and therefore, unable to claim the desired exemption. For an affiliate who intends to sell any securities of the issuer, *restricted or not*, the same risk is present. As will be discussed in § 6.05, provided that the requirements of Rule 144 are met, the Rule provides a safe harbor to persons holding restricted securities of an issuer and to affiliates of an issuer who seek to resell either restricted or nonrestricted securities.[18]

[A]   Holding Period

In determining whether a person has purchased from the issuer with a view to distribution, the amount of time that the person held the security prior to resale is deemed a relevant factor. In this regard, a "rule of thumb" for ascertaining investment intent under the Section 4(1) exemption provides that the SEC normally should not initiate an enforcement action against a party

---

[18] *See* J.W. Hicks, *supra* note 8, at § 10.01[1]; discussion *infra* § 6.05.

who is not a "control" person and who held the securities for at least two years prior to resale. As discussed in § 6.05, Rule 144 significantly shortens this time period if certain criteria are met.

On the other hand, compared to noncontrol persons, affiliates (or control persons) are more likely to be engaged in a distribution (rather than a transaction) when they resell their securities. If that indeed is the situation, such affiliates may not avail themselves of the Section 4(1) exemption, irrespective of their stock holding period.[19]

[B]   Restrictive Legends — Change in Circumstances

Restrictive legends normally are placed on securities acquired in an unregistered (*e.g.*, Rule 506) offering of restricted securities. Subject parties may claim that these restrictive legends establish their investment intent at the time of purchase. Not surprisingly, the courts have rejected this contention, holding that the purchase of stock from an issuer under an investment restriction is by no means a conclusive defense to underwriter status.[20] In certain situations, however, "change in circumstances" may serve as a valid defense to underwriter status. When invoking the change in circumstances doctrine, the subject party asserts that it bought the stock with investment intent but that subsequent unforeseen changes compelled the earlier than planned sale of the stock.[21]

When the SEC adopted Rule 144 (discussed in § 6.05 *infra*), the Commission stated that "the 'change in circumstances' concept should no longer be considered as one of the factors in determining whether a person is an underwriter . . . since the circumstances of the seller are unrelated to the need of investors for the protections afforded by the registration [requirement] and other provisions of the Act."[22] Hence, at least according to the SEC, the change in circumstances doctrine no longer retains its validity. On the other hand, it may be asserted that, to the extent that the change in circumstances defense is a valid test in terms of statutorily defining one who purchases with an intent to redistribute, the Commission cannot by administrative fiat change the meaning of the statute.[23]

---

[19] *See SEC v. Kern*, 425 F.3d 143 (2d Cir. 2005); *United States v. Sherwood*, 175 F. Supp. 480 (S.D.N.Y. 1959).

[20] *See G. Eugene England Foundation v. First Federal Corporation*, [1976–1977 Transfer Binder] Fed. Sec. L. Rep. (CCH) ¶ 95,837 (10th Cir. 1973); *Gilligan, Will & Co. v. SEC*, 267 F.2d 461 (2d Cir. 1959).

[21] *See, e.g., Lectmor v. VTR, Inc.*, [1969–1970 Transfer Binder] Fed. Sec. L. Rep. (CCH) ¶ 92,707 (S.D.N.Y. 1970).

[22] Securities Act Release No. 5223 (1972).

[23] *See* T. Hazen, The Law of Securities Regulation 217 (5th ed. 2005).

[C] Sales by Pledgees

The inadvertent underwriter problem (with the prospect of rendering the Section 4(1) exemption unavailable) also arises in connection with sales by pledgees (*e.g.*, banks) of securities pledged by control persons (as well as sales by such pledgees of restricted securities pledged by either control persons or nonaffiliates).[24] For example, if the pledgor control person defaults on a bank loan secured by the pledge, can the bank sell the securities pledged without being deemed an underwriter? In *SEC v. Guild Films Co.*,[25] the pledgor, a controlling shareholder, pledged as collateral for a bank loan a substantial block of securities which bore a restrictive legend on the face of the securities. After the shareholder defaulted on the loan, the bank, knowing of the restrictive legend, sold some of the securities without a registration statement being filed. The Second Circuit held that the bank was an underwriter. Even though the bank may have taken the securities as collateral and had not directly dealt with the issuer, "the bank knew that [it] had been given unregistered stock and that the issuer had specifically forbidden that the stock be sold."[26] Hence, to avoid Section 5 liability, the bank had to retain the securities pledged, invoke an exemption (*e.g.*, Section "4(1½)", Rule 144, Rule 144A), or induce the issuer to file a registration statement.

Language contained in the *Guild Films* case may be criticized as being unduly onerous upon good faith pledgees. By asserting that a good faith pledgee participates in a distribution or takes with the view to distribute whenever a pledgor defaults, it may be asserted that the Second Circuit's rationale unfairly hampers legitimate commercial activity. On the other hand, it may be argued that the key issue is not the pledgee's culpability in facilitating the sale of unregistered securities to the investing public but rather whether such sales by the pledgee should be permitted where the effect is to place into the hands of uninformed investors securities which have never been part of a registered offering. To purchasers of such securities who have not received adequate disclosure, the pledgee's good faith is of little solace.[27]

In this regard, the potentially harsh result of the *Guild Films* decision on legitimate commercial activity may be mitigated in practice by a pledgee bank's use of: (1) a covenant by the pledgor to effect registration of the securities ("a registration covenant") in the event of the pledgor's default (in all likelihood, such a covenant would not be worth the paper it was written on); (2) the invocation of an exemption from registration, such as the Section "4(1½)" exemption (see § 5.06 *infra*); and (3) a more circumspect approach to accepting pledgor securities as collateral.

---

[24] Note that a "pledge" is itself a "sale" under the Securities Act. *See Rubin v. United States*, 449 U.S. 424 (1981).

[25] 279 F.2d 485 (2d Cir. 1960).

[26] 279 F.2d at 490.

[27] *See generally* Rice, *The Effects of Registration on the Disposition of Pledged Securities*, 21 Stan. L. Rev. 1607 (1969); Sargent, *Pledgees and Foreclosure Rights Under the Securities Act of 1933*, 45 Va. L. Rev. 885 (1959).

The thrust of the *Guild Films* decision evidently remains good law. The continued vitality of the court's broad language as it relates to good faith pledgees, however, is open to question. As the First Circuit opined, "[t]here is considerable support for the . . . view that a good faith pledgee who sells unregistered shares at a foreclosure sale is not an 'underwriter.' "[28] Nonetheless, the SEC continues to adhere to the view that, under certain circumstances, the pledgee's sale of the securities pledged creates underwriter status.[29]

§ 6.05   RULE 144

[A]   Background

Historically, that a non-affiliate acquired securities pursuant to a Section 4(2) private placement exemption did not thereafter preclude such person from reselling the securities. For example, as discussed earlier, a non-affiliate holding restricted securities (*e.g.*, securities acquired pursuant to offerings made under Section 4(2) or Rule 506) normally could resell such securities after a substantial holding period, such as two years. Moreover, in certain situations, such non-affiliates, who acquired restricted securities allegedly for investment, could resell them pursuant to Section 4(1), notwithstanding a relatively recent acquisition date, if the seller could demonstrate a "change of circumstances." Nonetheless, given that the burden of proving the perfection of an exemption is upon the seller,[30] prudent parties exercised utmost caution when disposing of their securities without registration.

The situation for affiliates, and broker-dealers that executed orders to sell securities for the account of affiliates, was even more onerous. As a result of the SEC's 1946 administrative proceeding in *Ira Haupt*,[31] discussed in § 6.03[A], it was difficult for the broker to determine whether an affiliate, when disposing of stock, was engaging in a "distribution" of the issuer's securities. The confusion that broker-dealers faced in attempting to determine whether a distribution would occur led the SEC to adopt Rule 154 in 1951.[32] Unfortunately, Rule 154 was of limited value because it was designed for brokers, but offered no protection to those persons on behalf of whom the sale was executed.[33]

---

[28] *A.D.M. Corporation v. Thompson*, [1982–1983 Transfer Binder] Fed. Sec. L. Rep. (CCH) ¶ 99,206 (1st Cir. 1983) (SEC "no-action" letters cited therein).

[29] *See In re DG Bank (Schweiz) AG*, [1991–1992 Transfer Binder] Fed. Sec. L. Rep. (CCH) ¶ 84,945 (SEC 1992); T. Hazen, *supra* note 23, at 214–215; Hueter, *The Plight of the Pledgee Under Rule 144*, 3 Sec. Reg. L.J. 111 (1975).

[30] *See, e.g., SEC v. Ralston Purina Co.*, 346 U.S. 119 (1953).

[31] 23 S.E.C. 589 (1946).

[32] *See* Securities Act Release No. 3421 (1951), *as amended by*, Securities Act Release No. 3525 (1954).

[33] *See* S. Goldberg, Private Placements and Restricted Securities § 7.1 (rev. ed. 1982); J.W. Hicks, *supra* note 8, at § 10.02[1].

After extensive analysis, the "Wheat Report" was issued in 1969.[34] The Report recommended a series of rules that sought to clarify the circumstances under which an affiliate or a non-affiliate could rely upon Section 4(1) for resale transactions. In 1970, the SEC set forth a single proposed rule as an alternative to the series recommended by the Wheat Report.[35] It was called Proposed Rule 144 and was designed to continue the SEC's efforts towards providing objective standards with respect to the availability of the Section 4(1) exemption. Finally, after lively debate and extensive public comments and suggestions, the final version of Rule 144 was adopted in 1972.[36]

Generally, Rule 144 acts as a safe harbor from incurring liability under the registration provisions of the Securities Act. It permits the public sale in ordinary trading transactions of supposedly limited amounts of securities owned by persons controlling, controlled by, or under common control with the issuer (i.e., "affiliates"), and by other persons who have acquired "restricted securities" of the issuer. Hence, Rule 144 protects certain resale transactions from the Securities Act's registration mandates when such transactions are engaged in by: (1) "non-affiliated" persons who have acquired securities from either the issuer or an affiliate of the issuer in a transaction not involving a public offering ("restricted securities"), (2) persons who are deemed to be "affiliates" of the issuer at the time they propose to resell any securities of the issuer (irrespective whether such securities are restricted or unrestricted), and (3) brokers who effect transactions in compliance with the Rule.

The safe harbor derived from Rule 144 is important to the functioning of the securities markets. Absent the availability of an exemption, all sales of securities must be registered under Section 5 of the Act. The exemptions normally available in the resale context are Section 4(1) for sellers and Section 4(4) for brokers. Their application under a given set of conditions, however, may be problematic. By creating a safe harbor for perfecting these exemptions, Rule 144 seeks to provide greater clarity in this area.[37]

[B]   Provisions of the Rule — Overview

Since its adoption in 1972, Rule 144 has been amended several times and substantially liberalized. The basic purpose of Rule 144, however, has remained the same. Generally, with certain caveats, Rule 144 provides a safe harbor under the Section 4(1) exemption for investors (*e.g.*, institutional as well as individual investors) who are selling their securities without registration, and for brokers under the Section 4(4) exemption who are effecting sales of such securities. Rule 144 provides this safe harbor through an objective set of provisions, premised on the rationale that some relaxation of Securities Act disclosure and registration requirements is appropriate with respect to

---

[34] *See* Disclosure to Investors — A Reappraisal of Federal Administrative Policies Under the '33 and '34 Acts (1969) ("Wheat Report").

[35] *See* Securities Act Release No. 5087 (1970).

[36] Securities Act Release No. 5223 (1972); *see* J.W. Hicks, *supra* note 8, at § 10.02[2].

[37] *See* M. Pollock, *Resale of Restricted Securities*, Corporate Practice Series (BNA) No. 46 (1986); Fogelson, *Rule 144 — A Summary Overview*, 37 Bus. Law. 1519 (1981).

relatively small secondary transactions. If the investor and the broker make the sales in compliance with the conditions set forth in Rule 144, they will not be deemed to be "underwriters" or engaged in a "distribution."[38]

An understanding of certain terms is crucial to an understanding of Rule 144. Rule 144 defines an "affiliate" of an issuer as a "person that directly, or indirectly through one or more intermediaries, controls, or is controlled by, or is under common control with, such an issuer." In addition, Rule 144 defines "restricted" securities as those "securities that are acquired directly or indirectly from the issuer, or from an affiliate of the issuer, in a transaction or chain of transactions not involving any public offering, or securities acquired from the issuer that are subject to the resale limitations of Regulation D under the Act, or securities that are subject to the resale limitations of Regulation D and are acquired in a transaction or chain of transactions not involving any public offering." Hence, such restricted securities include those acquired in offerings pursuant to Section 4(2), Rule 505, Rule 506, and Rule 701.

The foregoing definitions are important. In certain situations, Rule 144 treats affiliates and non-affiliates differently. For example, only non-affiliates can resell restricted securities of a nonreporting issuer free of Rule 144 requirements after holding the securities for one year.[39] In addition, Rule 144's holding requirements pertain only to restricted securities. Or, stated differently, affiliates holding nonrestricted securities may resell their securities pursuant to Rule 144 without being subject to a holding period. Note that Rule 144 does not expressly address the area of non-affiliates selling nonrestricted securities.

To utilize Rule 144 a person must meet five general requirements, some of which have been eliminated or substantially modified by the SEC in certain circumstances.

First, there must be adequate current information concerning the issuer (see Rule 144(c)). This requirement is in accord with the underlying policy of the Securities Act which is to protect investors through adequate and fair disclosure. The information requirement can be satisfied in either of two ways: (1) the issuer can be subject to and be currently complying with the reporting requirements of the Exchange Act; or (2) if the issuer is not a 1934 Act reporting company, the issuer can publicly make information available pursuant to Exchange Act Rule 15c2-11 (see § 6.03[B] which sets forth the Rule 15c2-11 information requirements). If the purchaser has sufficient leverage, he/she may contract with the issuer that it be required to furnish the Rule 15c2-11 information.

---

[38] *See* D. Goldwasser, A Guide to Rule 144 (2d ed. 1978); L. Loss & J. Seligman, Securities Regulation 1474–1575 (3d ed. 1989); Ash *in* 11 H. Sowards, Federal Securities Act § 6B.01 (1987); Gilroy & Kaufman *in* 3 A.A. Sommer, Securities Law Techniques § 38.01 (1987).

[39] *See* Securities Act Release No. 8869 (2007). Note that under Rule 144, if non-affiliates of such nonreporting issuer continuously have held the subject securities for at least one year, then the current non-affiliated holder may resell such securities under Rule 144 even if such holder has held such securities for a shorter time period (*i.e.*, less than one year). *See infra* note 45 (and accompanying text).

A second requirement is that the person seeking to sell the restricted securities (*e.g.*, stock acquired in a private offering) must meet the holding period established by Rule 144 (*see* Rule 144(d)). This holding period is six-months for restricted securities of Exchange Act reporting issuers and one-year for restricted securities of non-reporting issuers. The holding period seeks to ensure that the person assumed an investment stake in the prior purchase(s) and has not acted merely as the issuer's conduit for a sale to the public of unregistered securities. Note that the holding period runs from the date of purchase from the issuer or from an affiliate of the issuer. Hence, a subsequent purchaser's acquisition of stock from a control person will trigger the start of the holding period as will an initial purchase from the issuer.[40]

Third, Rule 144 places restrictions on the amount of sales of common stock or similar equity security an affiliate can make during a given period of time in reliance on the Rule (see Rule 144(e)). This requirement is designed to ensure that a "distribution" does not take place and to lessen the impact of these sales on the trading markets. Generally, *with certain exceptions* (see Rule 144(b)(1) discussed later in this section), sales of such equity securities by a person under Rule 144(e) during any three-month period cannot exceed the greater of: (1) 1% of the shares of that class outstanding as shown by the most recent statement of the issuer; or (2) the average weekly trading volume reported on all exchanges (and/or "reported through the automatic quotation system of a registered securities association") for the four weeks preceding the filing of notice as specified in Rule 144(h). Note that the volume limitation for the resale of debt securities (as well as non-convertible preferred stock and asset-backed securities) is set at a higher level. Pursuant to amended Rule 144(e), resales are permitted of such securities "in an amount that does not exceed ten percent of a tranche (or class when the securities are non-participatory, preferred stock) together with all sales of securities of the same tranche sold for the account of the selling security holder within a three-month period."[41]

The fourth requirement under Rule 144 is that equity securities must be resold in ordinary brokerage transactions within the meaning of Section 4(4) or in transactions directly with a market maker, without solicitation, or through riskless principal transactions. Hence, a person seeking to rely on Rule 144 must not "solicit or arrange for the solicitation of orders to buy securities in anticipation of or in connection with such transactions."[42] Moreover, the broker must receive no more than the usual and customary broker's commission. Finally, with respect to sales during a three-month period that

---

[40] *See* Securities Act Release No. 7390 (1997). In reducing the Rule 144 holding periods, the SEC asserted that this reduction will decrease "compliance burdens and costs without significant impact on investor protection. . . . [A]lso the [amendments] will promote market efficiency, investment and capital formation by reducing the liquidity costs of holding restricted securities and reducing issuers' cost of raising capital through the sale of restricted securities." *Accord* Securities Exchange Act Release No. 8869 (2007).

[41] Securities Act Release No. 8869 (2007).

[42] Rule 144(f), 17 C.F.R. § 230.144(f).

exceed 5,000 shares or have a sales price greater than $50,000, notice of each such sale must be filed with the SEC.[43]

The "brokers' transactions" requirement referred to above (see Rule 144(f)) must be distinguished from the requirements with the same name in Rule 144(g). Rule 144(f) is one of the conditions that must be met by a seller intending to rely on the Rule. The broker also must find an exemption for its role in the transaction. Rule 144(g), by defining the term "brokers' transactions" and by delineating aspects of "reasonable inquiry" to be conducted by the broker, greatly assists the broker in meeting Rule 144's safe harbor and thereby perfect the Section 4(4) exemption.[44]

As will be discussed later in this section, Rule 144(b)(1) is the major exception to the foregoing requirements. Provided that the non-affiliate holder has held the restricted securities for the requisite amount of time (for example, one year with respect to restricted securities of a non-reporting issuer), such holder may resell such securities free of Rule 144's many restrictions. The time period is measured from the date of acquisition from the issuer or from an affiliate of the issuer.

To invoke the exemption from Securities Act registration provided by Rule 144, all conditions of the rule must be satisfied. Rule 144 is a "safe harbor" and, hence, is nonexclusive. Accordingly, even though a person has not met the conditions of Rule 144, he/she still may seek to invoke another exemption, such as the statutory Section 4(1) exemption.[45]

[C]   Certain Sales by Non-Affiliates

[1]   Restricted Stock

Paragraph (b)(1) of Rule 144 eliminates the current public information, volume limitation, manner of sale, and notice requirements for non-affiliates who have not been affiliated with the issuer for the preceding three months and where the restricted securities of a non-reporting issuer have been beneficially owned by non-affiliates for at least one year prior to the resale. Note that, with respect to restricted securities of an Exchange Act reporting

---

[43] Rule 144(h), 17 C.F.R. § 230.144(h).

[44] *See* Securities Act Release Nos. 4445 (1962), 5168 (1972); *In re Transactions in Securities of Laser Arms Corporation by Certain Broker-Dealers*, [1990–1991 Transfer Binder] Fed. Sec. L. Rep. (CCH) ¶ 84,724 (SEC 1991). In the *Laser Arms* proceeding, the Commission reaffirmed its position with respect to the appropriate level of a broker's diligence in this setting:

> [A] dealer who offers to sell, or is asked to sell a substantial amount of securities must take whatever steps are necessary, to be sure that this is a transaction not involving an issuer, person in a control relationship with an issuer, or an underwriter. For this purpose, it is not sufficient for him merely to accept self-serving statements of his sellers and their counsel without reasonably exploring the possibility of contrary facts.

[45] Securities Act Release No. 5223 (1972). In the Rule 144 adopting release, however, the SEC asserted that "persons who offer or sell restricted securities without complying with Rule 144 are hereby put on notice by the Commission that . . . they will have a substantial burden of proof that an exemption from registration is available. . . ."). *Accord SEC v. Cavanagh*, 445 F.3d 105, 114 (2d Cir. 2006).

issuer, a non-affiliate may resell all of his/her securities after a six-month holding period, with the condition that the subject issuer adhere to the current public information requirement for an additional six months. As stated by the SEC in its 2007 adopting release:

> In the 2007 Proposing Release, we proposed to permit non-affiliates to resell their restricted securities freely after meeting the applicable holding period requirement (i.e., six months with respect to a reporting issuer and one year with respect to a non-reporting issuer), except that non-affiliates of reporting issuers still would be subject to the current public information requirement in Rule 144(c) for an additional six months after the end of the initial six-month holding period.
>
> . . . .
>
> We are adopting the amendments for the sale of restricted securities by non-affiliates after the holding period, as proposed. Under the amendments, after the applicable holding period requirement is met, the resale of restricted securities by a non-affiliate under Rule 144 will no longer be subject to any other conditions of Rule 144 except that, with regard to the resale of securities of a reporting issuer, the current public information requirement in Rule 144(c) will apply for an additional six months after the six-month holding period requirement is met. Therefore, a non-affiliate will no longer be subject to the Rule 144 conditions relating to volume limitations, manner of sale requirements, and filing Form 144.[46]

Generally, in determining the requisite holding period, a non-affiliate may "tack" to his/her own holding period those of prior holders unaffiliated with the issuer.[47] Thus, Rule 144(b)(1) effectively removes all restrictions when non-

---

[46] Securities Act Release No. 8869 (2007); *see also SEC v. Kern*, 425 F.3d 143 (2d Cir. 2005) (holding that the defendants did not comply with Rule 144(k) (now Rule 144(b)(1)) or the Section 4(1) exemption, thereby violating § 5 of the Securities Act); *accord SEC v. M & A West, Inc.*, 538 F.3d 1043 (9th Cir. 2008).

[47] *See* Securities Act Release No. 6862 (1990). In expanding the "tacking" periods for non-affiliates owning restricted securities, the Commission explained:

> Under Rule 144, as previously in effect, restricted securities generally were required to be held for at least two years before the holder could sell the securities in reliance upon the safe-harbor provisions of Rule 144. Except in limited instances, the holding period of predecessor owners was not combined with, or "tacked" to, the holding period of the person wishing to sell in reliance on Rule 144.
>
> As a result of its reexamination of the tacking concept embodied in Rule 144, the Commission today is amending the Rule to permit holders of restricted securities acquired in a transaction or series of transactions not involving any public offering to add to their own holding period those of prior holders unaffiliated with the issuer. No such tacking will be permitted, however, where the seller has purchased from an affiliate of the issuer whose presence in the chain of title will trigger the commencement of a new holding period. . . .
>
> . . . .
>
> Rule 144(k) [now Rule 144(b)(1)] is amended to permit a non-affiliate, who has been a non-affiliate for at least three months, to resell restricted securities free of the restrictions imposed by paragraphs (c), (e), (f), and (h) of Rule 144 if a period of at least three [now significantly less than] years, as computed in accordance with amended

affiliates have held restricted securities for the applicable holding period and allows such non-affiliates to freely resell such securities. Rule 144(b)(1) accordingly eases the burdens that were placed on the liquidity of restricted securities.

Consider this result with the SEC's assertion when it adopted Rule 144 in 1972:

> [T]he purpose and underlying policy of the [Securities] Act to protect investors requires . . . that there be *adequate current information concerning the issuer,* whether the resales of securities by persons result in a distribution or are effected in trading transactions. Accordingly, the availability of [Rule 144] is conditioned on the existence of adequate current public information.[48]

The SEC, with its amendments to Rule 144, essentially has nullified the above rationale. One justification proffered is the deregulatory assertion that "[t]he purpose of the amendments is to relax restrictions on resales of securities that are more burdensome than necessary."[49] But nowhere does the Commission adequately explain why such restrictions are "more burdensome than necessary," particularly in view of the investor protection concerns that are highlighted throughout the 1972 Rule 144 adopting release. Hence, Rule 144, as revised, may be viewed as inconsistent with a major objective of the 1933 Act, which is to protect investors by ensuring that their decisions are informed, and also as incompatible with a fundamental premise underlying the rule's adoption.

There is, of course, another side to this issue. In order to promote capital formation and induce investors to take a stake in start-up and similar enterprises, a non-affiliate who holds restricted securities must have a way to resell those securities if he or she chooses. Rule 144 now provides such shareholders with an opportunity to resell their restricted securities after holding them for a minimal time period (six months for a reporting issuer and twelve months for a non-reporting issuer). In this way, the revised Rule meets prospective sellers' expectations and facilitates the flow of venture capital into the economy. The prospective purchaser is adequately protected, it may be asserted, by the application of the antifraud provisions. And, if a trading market for the subject issuer's securities should develop, then broker-dealers are required to have available Rule 15c2-11 information.[50] Moreover, a prospective buyer is not compelled to purchase the restricted securities. The determination whether to acquire the securities if adequate current issuer information is unavailable should be left to the prospective purchaser, and not foreclosed by government intervention.

---

paragraph (d) of the Rule, has elapsed since the later of the date the securities originally were acquired from the issuer or the date they were acquired from an affiliate of the issuer.

[48] Securities Act Release No. 5223 (1972) (emphasis supplied).

[49] Securities Act Release No. 6286 (1981); *see* Securities Act Release Nos. 6488 (1983), 8869 (2008).

[50] Generally, Rule 15c2-11 prohibits broker-dealers from publishing a quotation for any security unless specific information is available with respect to the issuer and the security. *See supra* note 13 (and accompanying text).

Nonetheless, it may be asserted that the SEC revisions to Rule 144 unduly liberalize certain restrictions, while other overly burdensome limitations of the Rule have been virtually ignored by the SEC. If comprehensive information is not available concerning the issuer, a prospective non-affiliated seller should not be permitted to unload unlimited quantities of restricted securities into the market. The prospective seller should only be allowed to resell the restricted securities in limited volumes over a period of time. In this way, the prospective seller will not have to rely on the unwilling, nonreporting issuer for public information and will not be locked into the investment, while at the same time, he/she will not be able to dump unlimited amounts of restricted securities into the market. In other words, paragraph (b)(1) should permit a prospective non-affiliated seller to avoid the information requirements of Rule 144(c) only if that seller is willing to conform to the volume limitation restrictions of paragraph (e) of the Rule.

By promulgating Rule 144(b)(1), the SEC appears to take the position that the unloading of all of a non-affiliate's restricted securities stock after the requisite six-month (for reporting issuers) and twelve-month (for non-reporting issuers) holding period will never constitute a "distribution." Such a position in questionable. Given the substantial amount of restricted stock that a non-affiliate can unload in the marketplace under certain conditions, the SEC's blanket exemption spreads too far. A more sensible approach that would accommodate the competing interests would be to require a nonaffiliate to adhere to the volume limitations of Rule 144(e).

Moreover, the SEC's amendments to Rule 144 are inconsistent with the disclosure approach of Rules 505 and 506 of Regulation D. If the Commission's objective is to ensure the provision of adequate information to "unsophisticated" investors of restricted securities, it should be irrelevant whether the investor purchased the securities from the issuer (pursuant to Regulation D) or from a shareholder who is not affiliated with the issuer (by means of Rule 144). In either case, the prospective purchaser's need for sufficient information to make an intelligent investment decision remains the same. Only in the Rule 505 or 506 Regulation D offering context, however, is the investor entitled to such information.[51] In the Rule 144 setting, by contrast, there is minimal or no mandated disclosure when the investor purchases restricted securities from a non-affiliated party (who has met the requisite holding requirement) of an issuer that fails to provide current public information.

[2] Nonrestricted Stock

Rule 144 does not expressly cover a non-affiliate's disposition of nonrestricted stock. Nonetheless, the SEC, by its promulgation of Rule 144(b)(1), appears to take the position that the sale of a non-affiliate's stock is not a separate distribution. Moreover, the assumption of underwriter status may no longer be a pitfall for non-affiliates selling nonrestricted stock due to the SEC staff's apparent abandonment of the presumptive underwriter doctrine (*see supra* § 6.02[A]). These developments may lead to the conclusion

---

[51] *See supra* §§ 3.06, 3.09[B][2].

that a non-affiliate can freely resell nonrestricted stock without limitation pursuant to the Section 4(1) exemption. The Commission, however, has declined to expressly address this issue.

If the above represents the SEC's position, it is misplaced. In certain circumstances, a non-affiliate can hold a substantial percentage of nonrestricted stock. Permitting such nonaffiliates to freely liquidate their positions conflicts with both the definition of underwriter under Section 2(a)(11) and the rationale underlying the Section 4(1) transactional exemption. In short, persons who dispose of large percentages of securities in the public markets are, in actuality, engaging in a distribution rather than a transaction and, when they do so after a short holding period, are purchasing from an issuer with a view towards distribution. Support for this assertion may be premised on the fact that, if a substantial security holder were an affiliate, he/she would be subject to the volume limitation requirements of Rule 144(e). Yet, status as an affiliate in this context should not be determinative. At times, an affiliate may have more leverage to induce the issuer to file a registration statement for the securities such affiliate wishes to sell. Nevertheless, the detrimental effect on the capital trading markets and the investing public are identical, irrespective of whether one has affiliate status when reselling large quantities of stock.

The foregoing assertions are reinforced by the following scenario: Company X, for investment purposes, purchases 12% of Company Y's "unrestricted" stock over a six-month period on the New York Stock Exchange. Insiders of Company Y, who still retain 51% ownership of the public company's stock and are able to elect the entire board of directors, have no desire to share control. Company X, pleased with its investment, increases its ownership interest in Company Y's "unrestricted" stock during a three-year period to 19%. One year later, after the insiders reject Company X's request to have a seat on Company Y's board of directors, Company X elects to sell all of its stock in Company Y on the New York Stock Exchange during a ninety-day period.

Under the above scenario, Company X is not an "affiliate" of Company Y. It is neither in a "control" relationship nor can it compel Company Y to file a registration statement. Being a non-affiliate, its sales, by analogy to Rule 144(b)(1), do not constitute a "distribution." Moreover, again in reference to Rule 144(b)(1) and Rule 144(d), a four-year holding period, as reflected in the illustration, indicates that Company X, not being a control person, acquired and held the securities with investment intent, hence mitigating against the assumption of underwriter status. The policies of the Securities Act, however, demand that Company X, absent registration, should not be able within a fairly short time period to unload its securities on the investing public.

With the promulgation of Rule 144(b)(1) and the apparent abandonment of the presumptive underwriter doctrine, the SEC appears to have given the impression that non-affiliates can resell nonrestricted stock without limitation. Non-affiliates and their counsel, however, should not act with the certainty as other parties and transactions that clearly come within Rule 144's scope. Because unlimited sales by non-affiliates should not be permitted for the reasons provided, the SEC should prescribe a safe harbor volume limitation under the Section 4(1) exemption for non-affiliates selling nonrestricted stock. This pronouncement may be effected either by amending Rule 144 or by promulgating a separate rule.[52]

[D]   Chart

The following chart from the SEC's 2007 adopting release (Securities Act Release No. 8869 (2007)) seeks to clarify the various requirements that a seller must comply with in order to come within the Rule 144 safe harbor. Remember, however, that the chart may simplify some of the pertinent requirements. Attention therefore should be directed to the relevant SEC releases, the discussion contained herein, and the text of the Rule itself.

---

[52] For further discussion, *see* Steinberg & Kempler, *The Application and Effectiveness of SEC Rule 144*, 49 Ohio State L.J. 473 (1988). *See also* Campbell, *Resales of Securities Under the Securities Act of 1933*, 52 Wash. & Lee L. Rev. 1333 (1995); Hicks, *The Concept of Transaction as a Restraint on Resale Limitations*, 49 Ohio St. L.J. 417 (1988).

RULE 144
REQUIREMENTS FOR AFFILIATES AND
NONAFFILIATES OF THE ISSUER

	Affiliate or Person Selling on Behalf of an Affiliate	Non-Affiliate (and Has Not Been an Affiliate During the Prior Three Months)
Restricted Securities of Reporting Issuers	*During six-month holding period –* no resales under Rule 144 permitted. *After six-month holding period –* may resell in accordance with all Rule 144 requirements including: • Current public information, • Volume limitations, • Manner of sale requirements for equity securities, and • Filing of Form 144	*During six-month holding period* – no resales under Rule 144 permitted. *After six-month holding period but before one year* – unlimited public resales under Rule 144 except that the current public information requirement still applies. *After one-year holding period* – unlimited public resales under Rule 144; need not comply with any other Rule 144 requirements.
	Affiliate or Person Selling on Behalf of an Affiliate	Non-Affiliate (and Has Not Been an Affiliate During the Prior Three Months)
Restricted Securities of Non-Reporting Issuers	*During one-year holding period –* no resales under Rule 144 permitted. *After one-year holding period –* may resell in accordance with all Rule 144 requirements, including: • Current public information, • Volume limitations, • Manner of sale requirements for equity securities, and • Filing of Form 144.	*During one-year holding period –* no resales under Rule 144 permitted. *After one-year holding period –* unlimited public resales under Rule 144; need not comply with any other Rule 144 requirements.

§ 6.06　THE SECTION "4(1-1/2)" EXEMPTION

One exemption thus far not discussed is the so-called Section "4(1-1/2)" exemption. This exemption, based largely on SEC no-action letters and other SEC pronouncements, seeks to fill a gap in the statutory exemptive scheme. Upon examining this framework, it appears that none of the statutory or regulatory exemptions expressly cover unlimited sales of securities by affiliates (as well as sales of restricted securities by non-affiliates) who desire to sell such securities in a *private transaction* after a short holding period. By way of example, Rule 144 neither helps a "control" person who wishes to sell all of his/her stock in a private transaction nor a non-affiliate who has not held restricted securities for a sufficient time period to invoke the Rule. Such sales frequently occur and the SEC, provided that certain conditions are met, appears not to be especially troubled by their presence. This should continue to be the case even in view of the Commission's adoption of Rule 144A. As will become evident (*see infra* § 6.07), the Rule 144A exemption is unavailable in numerous situations.

Focusing on the Section "4(1-1/2)" exemption, the SEC has stated:

> In making such private sales, the affiliates presumably would rely on the so-called Section "4(1-1/2)" exemption. This is a hybrid exemption not specifically provided for in the 1933 Act but clearly within its intended purpose. The exemption basically would permit affiliates to make private sales of securities held by them so long as some of the established criteria for sales under both Section 4(1) and Section 4(2) of the Act are satisfied.[53]

Unfortunately, the Commission has declined to identify the pertinent "established criteria" of Section 4(1) and Section 4(2) which must be satisfied in order for a party successfully to invoke the Section "4(1-1/2)" exemption. However, certain criteria relevant for perfecting the exemption may be as follows:

— While the source of the Section "4(1-1/2)" exemption is Section 4(1), the determination of appropriate standards to govern the exemption is primarily derived from Section 4(2) authority.

— Advertising and general solicitation are not permitted.

— Although no finite number has been established, there is some limit on the number of offerees and purchasers.

— Whether the prospective seller must hold the securities for a certain length of time (such as two years) is uncertain. The holding period may be more relevant where there is no public information available concerning the issuer or where a large number of shares are sought to be sold to several unsophisticated investors.

— The purchasers' access to registration-type information (or the actual providing of such information) as well as purchaser sophistication are relevant, though not necessarily determinative, factors.[54]

§ 6.07   RULE 144A

Rule 144A is a non-exclusive safe harbor from the Securities Act registration requirements with respect to the resale of restricted securities to qualified institutional buyers (QIBs) by persons other than the issuer of such restricted securities.[55]

---

[53] Securities Act Release No. 6188 (1980); *see Ackerberg v. Johnson*, 892 F.2d 1328 (8th Cir. 1989).

[54] *See* Olander & Jacks, *The Section 4(1-1/2) Exemption — Reading Between the Lines of the Securities Act of 1933*, 15 Sec. Reg. L.J. 339 (1988); Schneider, *Section 4(1-1/2) — Private Resales of Restricted or Control Securities*, 49 Ohio State L.J. 501 (1988); ABA Committee Report, *The Section "4(1-1/2)" Phenomenon: Private Resales of "Restricted" Securities*, 34 Bus. Law. 1961 (1979).

[55] *See* Securities Act Release No. 6862 (1990).

Rule 144A is directed at providing resale markets in generally three different settings: (1) the sale of debt securities from underwriters to QIBs; (2) resales of restricted securities originally sold pursuant to private or limited offerings, such as pursuant to Rule 505 or 506 of Regulation D; and (3) resales of securities of foreign enterprises or of securities originally offered outside of the United States, such as pursuant to Regulation S (*see supra* § 3.17). Rule 144A's objective generally has been achieved insofar as helping to attract foreign companies to the U.S. capital markets.

Rule 144A is being used by a number of issuers to avoid the federal registration requirements. For example, a company seeking to issue debt securities will place such securities with an underwriter pursuant to the Section 4(2) exemption who in turn will sell them to QIBs under Rule 144A. Rule 144A is deemed advantageous because such offerings can be effected almost instantaneously and without the rigorous disclosure requirements mandated in registered offerings.[56]

Another approach being utilized is to have the Rule 144A offering followed shortly thereafter by a Securities Act registered exchange offering. Such a registered exchange offering, called an "A/B exchange," involves the issuance of the securities offered pursuant to the SEC registration statement to the Rule 144A holders in exchange for their securities that were acquired by means of Rule 144A.[57]

[A]   Requirements

The requirements of Rule 144A may strike the reader as being complicated. The following is a Summary that hopefully will make the conditions of the Rule more understandable.

REQUIREMENTS

(1) Resales of Restricted Securities to Qualified Institutional Buyers (e.g., eligible insurance companies, investment companies, employee benefit plans, venture capital firms)

Such qualified institutional buyer ("QIB") must have $100 million invested in securities (of issuers that are not affiliated with such buyer) at the conclusion of its most recent fiscal year (goes to amount invested in securities, *not* assets).

(a) In addition to $100 million invested in securities, banks and savings and loan associations must have a net worth of at least $25 million.

---

[56] *See* Raghaven, *Private Placement Market Is Proving Popular*, Wall St. J., April 1, 1997, at C14.

[57] Bodner & Welsh, *Institutional Buyer Beware: Recent Decisions Reinforce Narrow Range of Remedies Available to QIBs in Rule 144A Offerings*, 36 Rev. Sec. & Comm. Reg. 1728 (2004) (also stating that "[r]oughly two-thirds to three quarters of high yield offerings are now accomplished by a Rule 144A private placement, often followed by an A/B exchange").

(b) Broker-Dealers are not required to meet the $100 million invested in securities standard. Rather, an eligible broker-dealer must own and invest on a discretionary basis at least $10 million of securities of issuers that are not affiliated with such broker-dealer. In addition, a broker-dealer who acts solely in a riskless principal transaction on behalf of a qualified institutional purchaser is itself treated as a QIB, regardless of whether it meets the $10 million invested in securities standard mentioned above.

(2) Qualifying the Prospective Purchaser

It is the seller's responsibility to qualify the prospective purchaser. In other words, the seller or its agent must "reasonably believe" that such purchaser is a QIB. The rule enumerates a number of non-exclusive means to satisfy this requirement, including such purchaser's most recent publicly available annual financial statements and the most recent information appearing in documents publicly-filed by such prospective purchaser.

(3) Exclusion of Fungible Securities from Rule 144A

The "nonfungibility" condition arose due to concern that Rule 144A would result in the development of side-by-side public and private markets for the same class of securities, thereby resulting in loss of liquidity to the established trading markets. Hence, as adopted, Rule 144A is not available for securities that, at the time of their issuance, are of the same class (i.e., fungible) as securities trading on a U.S. exchange. Today, Rule 144A securities are traded on a "fully automated web-based platform, . . . [a] centralized electronic system [of the Nasdaq Stock Market] for displaying and accessing trading interest in [Rule] 144 issuers."[58] Note that convertible securities, having an effective conversion premium at the time of issuance of less than ten percent, are treated as securities of both the convertible and the underlying securities.

(4) Provision of Information

Upon request to the issuer, such issuer must provide to the holder and to the prospective purchaser certain basic information concerning the issuer's business and its financial statements (if the issuer is not a 1934 Act reporting company or is otherwise exempt from such reporting). Information ordinarily would be obtained by the holder from the issuer pursuant to contractual rights negotiated at the time of issuance.

(5) Notice requirement

The rule requires that the seller take reasonable steps to notify the QIB that the seller is relying on Rule 144A as an exemption from registration.

---

[58] *Nasdaq's New 144A Platform Approved by SEC for Launch Aug. 15*, 39 Sec. Reg. & L. Rep. (BNA) 1214 (2007).

[B]   Criticism

The "provision of information" condition of Rule 144A raised the ire of former SEC Commissioner Edward Fleischman. He contended that the delivery of information requirement will adversely affect "that class of business enterprises most needy of the benefits promised by the rule and most capable of magnifying those benefits to the advantage of the entire American economy, namely smaller domestic privately-owned issuers also known as 'emerging growth companies.' "[59]

On the other hand, Rule 144A has raised concerns that it will adversely impact individual investors. To such critics, the SEC's promulgation of Rule 144A represents yet another example of the Commission's solicitousness toward capital formation and institutional investors to the detriment of ordinary investors. In a letter to then SEC Chairman David Breeden, two influential Congressmen, John D. Dingell and Edward J. Markey, asserted that Rule 144A may be invalid as exceeding the scope of the Commission's authority in this area (namely, that the exemption, Rule 144A, exceeds the scope of the statutes, Section 4(1) and Section 4(4), upon which the Rule 144A exemption is based).[60] The Congressmen also expressed their concern on a policy level:

> We strongly endorse what we understand to be policy goals underlying the Commission's adoption of Rule 144A. The Commission staff is to be commended for its creativity, hard work, and the high quality of its efforts in seeking to enhance the competitiveness of the U.S. in today's global markets. Nonetheless, we are concerned about the specific mechanism established to achieve these goals. In particular, we are concerned about the possible development of a two-tiered securities market for U.S. investors, one public and one private, and the serious negative implications of such a development; the diminished availability of many quality investments to smaller investors and, conversely, the greater likelihood that poor investments will be passed on to unwitting investors through mutual and pension funds or other avenues of leakage, and the rule's diminution of the amount and type of disclosure, particularly with regard to foreign companies about which U.S. investors have historically had little information.[61]

Rule 144A thus far has been most successful in attracting foreign companies to the U.S. capital markets. According to a report authored by the SEC staff, 69 of the first 95 issuers whose securities were sold by means of Rule 144A were foreign entities. The rule, however, has failed to stimulate a resale market in

---

[59] Securities Act Release No. 6862 (1990) (Fleischman, Comm'r, dissenting in part).

[60] Note that this assertion was made prior to the enactment of Section 28 of the Securities Act (as part of the Sarbanes-Oxley Act of 2002) which grants to the SEC broad exemptive authority.

[61] Excerpts of the letter are contained and discussed in Barron, *Some Comments on SEC Rule 144A*, 18 Sec. Reg. L.J. 400 (1991); *see also* Norris, *The SEC and the Death of Disclosure*, N.Y. Times, June 9, 1991, at C5 (offering a critical view that, due to Rule 144A, "institutional investors can buy privately placed securities and trade them freely with other institutions . . . [a]fter minimal financial disclosure").

Regulation D and similar types of offerings. On the other hand, as discussed earlier in this Section, Rule 144A is being used extensively by companies marketing their debt securities to QIBs.[62] Indeed, the Nasdaq Stock Market has implemented a centralized automated trading system for Rule 144A securities. In 2006, for example, the amount of debt and equity capital raised pursuant to Rule 144A exceeded $1 trillion and approximately 2,700 Rule 144A equity and debt securities were designated for trading.[63]

§ 6.08 CORPORATE REORGANIZATIONS

[A]   In General

Corporations as well as other entities frequently engage in reorganizations. State corporation statutes, corporate charters, and similar controlling instruments normally require shareholder approval or consent of mergers, consolidations, transfer of assets and reclassifications of stock. These reorganizations normally result in the exchange of shares or the issuance of new stock. Rule 145(a) makes it clear that when such plans of reorganization are submitted to shareholders for approval, the corporation makes an "offer to sell" within the meaning of Section 2(a)(3) of the Securities Act. Rule 145, therefore, has several ramifications.

[B]   Rule 145 — Ramifications

Absent an exemption from registration, the sale of securities pursuant to Rule 145 triggers the registration requirements of Section 5 as well as due diligence obligations (including the rigorous culpability standards of Section 11). Rule 145 transactions may be registered pursuant to the Securities Act on Form S-4. The Form S-4 framework improves the effectiveness of the business reorganization prospectus by requiring that information be presented in a more accessible and meaningful format.[64]

By triggering the registration requirements, Rule 145 also implicates Section 5's "gun-jumping" prohibition.[65] Thus, with certain exceptions (*see* Chapter 4), communications designed to influence shareholders' votes may be viewed as constituting offers to sell in the pre-filing period and, hence, violations of Section 5(c). Rule 145(b) provides certain exceptions in this

---

[62] *See* 23 Sec. Reg. & L. Rep. (BNA) 1589 (1991); *supra* note 56 (and accompanying text). For discussion on Regulation S, *see supra* § 3.17. *See generally* Bradford, *Rule 144A and Integration*, 20 Sec. Reg. L.J. 37 (1992); Rumsey, *Rule 144A and Other Developments in the Resale of Restricted Securities*, 19 Sec. Reg. L.J. 157 (1991); Steinberg & Lansdale, *Regulation S and Rule 144A: Creating a Workable Fiction in an Expanding Global Securities Market*, 29 Int'l Law. 43 (1995).

[63] *Nasdaq's New 144A Platform Approved by SEC for Launch Aug. 15*, 39 Sec. Reg. & L. Rep. (BNA) 1214 (2007).

[64] *See* Securities Act Release No. 6578 (1985); *see generally* Campbell, *Rule 145: Mergers, Acquisitions and Recapitalizations Under the Securities Act of 1933*, 56 Fordham L. Rev. 277 (1987).

[65] For discussion on conditioning the market ("gun-jumping"), see *supra* § 4.02[B][2].

respect, authorizing the corporation to communicate basic information, including the issuer's name, a brief description of the business of the parties, and a brief description of the transaction. Compliance with the provisions of Rule 145(b) has the effect of protecting the communication from constituting an "offer to sell" under Section 2(a)(3) or from being deemed a "prospectus" under Section 2(a)(10). In this regard, the pre-filing publicity notice permitted under Rule 135 is also available for such transactions.[66]

[C]   "Downstream Sales"

The ramifications of Rule 145 do not end after the shareholders approve a plan of reorganization. Rule 145(c) addresses the problem of "downstream sales." Depending on the circumstances, parties to a Rule 145 transaction who publicly sell or publicly offer to sell their securities may be deemed to be engaged in a distribution as well as being deemed underwriters within the meaning of Section 2(a)(11).[67] These parties can avoid underwriter status, however, by meeting the criteria contained in Rule 145(d).

As an initial point, for parties who neither are affiliates of the acquired company nor affiliates of the acquiring company, the securities received in a Rule 145 transaction are nonrestricted securities, thereby having no restrictions on resale.

In regard to parties who are affiliates of an entity *acquired* pursuant to a Rule 145 transaction, the SEC, consistent with its Rule 144 modifications, has substantially relaxed the "resale" provisions of Rule 145. As a result, such parties (who are affiliates of the acquired, but not of the acquiring, entity) today have much greater leeway in reselling their securities without fear of assuming underwriter status. Accordingly, persons who are affiliates of the acquired entity that receive securities in registered business combinations and who subsequently transfer such securities will not be deemed underwriters if:

    i. The securities are sold in compliance with the provisions of paragraphs (c), (e), (f), and (g) of Rule 144 and at least 90 days have

---

[66] Rule 135 is addressed in *supra* § 4.02[B][4]. Two promulgated rules, Rules 165 and 166, also exempt certain communications regarding business combination transactions from Section 5 of the Securities Act. Rule 165 is not limited to offerors and may be used by "any other participant that may need to rely on and complies with [Rule 165] in communicating about the transaction." Rule 166 permits communications by participants in a registered offering involving a business combination transaction before the first public announcement of the offering upon a showing that "all reasonable steps within their control [were taken] to prevent further distribution or publication of the communication until either the first public announcement is made or the registration statement related to the transaction is filed [with the Commission.]" *See* Securities Act Release No. 42055, [1999–2000 Transfer Binder] Fed. Sec. L. Rep. (CCH) ¶ 86,215 (SEC 1999).

[67] The 2007 amendments to Rule 145 provide that underwriter status will no longer be presumed unless the covered transaction involves a shell company, other than a business combination shell company, as those terms are defined by Rule 405. Rule 405 defines a shell company as a registrant that has either no or nominal assets, or whose assets consist primarily of cash and cash equivalents, while a business combination shell company is a shell company formed solely for the purpose of changing corporate domicile or to complete certain business combination transactions. *See* Securities Act Release No. 8869 (2007).

elapsed since the time that such securities were acquired in connection with the transaction; or

ii. The person is a non-affiliate of the issuer (*i.e.*, a non-affiliate of the acquiring company), has been a non-affiliate of the issuer for at least three months, has held the securities for at least a six-month period, and the issuer has complied with the current public reporting requirements of Rule 144(c) (by either being an Exchange Act reporting company or by making adequate information available); or

iii. The party is a non-affiliate of the issuer, has been a non-affiliate of the issuer for at least three months, and has held the securities for at least one year.[68]

Consider the effect of the SEC's amendments to Rule 145 (with respect to persons who were affiliates of an entity acquired in a Rule 145 transaction, who are not affiliates of the acquiring entity, and who have been such non-affiliates for at least three months). First, such non-affiliates of the issuer (*i.e.*, non-affiliates of the acquiring company) can dispose of all of their securities after six months if the issuer has maintained adequate current public information. Second, such non-affiliates, after a one-year holding period, can sell all of their shares even if the issuer is not making adequate current information available. Note that the holding period is measured from the date of acquisition from the issuer or from an affiliate of the issuer. "Tacking" of the applicable holding period is permitted when transactions take place between non-affiliates.[69]

The public policy assessments made by the Commission in adopting these revisions can be questioned on much the same basis as was made with respect to the amendments to Rule 144 (*see supra* § 6.05[C]). Undoubtedly, the Commission's amendments to Rule 145 are a victory for deregulation and capital formation. Some may claim, however, that the costs are too great: By permitting non-affiliates of the issuer to "dump" their securities on the investing public with little or no information being available about the issuer deals a blow to two fundamental purposes underlying the federal securities laws, namely, to ensure the integrity of the financial marketplace and to enable investors to have adequate information before them so that they can make informed investment decisions.

[D]   "Spin-Offs"

Spin-offs have many variations. The "classical" spin-off occurs when a parent corporation distributes shares of a privately-held subsidiary as a stock dividend to its current shareholders. In such event, it is only a matter of time before these shares becomes publicly traded. Absent the availability of an exemption, "spin-offs" thereby may have the effect of evading the registration requirements. Due to this concern, the SEC and the courts have held that this

---

[68] *See* Securities Act Release Nos. 6508 (1984), 7390 (1997), 8869 (2007).

[69] *See* Securities Act Release Nos. 7390 (1997), 6862 (1990); *supra* note 47 (and accompanying text).

technique, depending on the circumstances, calls for Securities Act registration. Moreover, parent corporations that cause their subsidiaries to engage in such practices may be deemed to be "underwriters."[70]

Defendants, charged with failing to register a "spin-off" offering, have asserted that the stock dividend distributed to shareholders was not an "offer to sell" or "sale" within the meaning of Section 2(a)(3) of the Securities Act because it was not "for value," and hence, was not in violation of Section 5. The SEC and the courts frequently have rejected this argument, reasoning that the creation of a public market for the spun-off securities constitutes value to the parent corporation when the stockholders dispose of these securities.[71]

In 1997, the SEC's Division of Corporation Finance opined that a spin-off does not require Securities Act registration if the following five conditions are met: (1) shareholders of the parent corporation do not provide any consideration for the spun-off shares, (2) the shares spun-off are distributed pro rata to the parent corporation's shareholders, (3) adequate information about the subsidiary and the spin-off must be provided by the parent corporation to both the stockholders and the securities trading markets, (4) the parent corporation has a valid business purpose justifying the spin-off, and (5) if the parent corporation elects to spin-off restricted securities, it must have held such securities for a requisite period of time.[72] Note, moreover, that SEC Rule 15c2-11 effectively thwarts public trading of securities acquired in unregistered spin-offs by prohibiting broker-dealers from either initiating or continuing to provide price quotations for a security unless adequate public information is available with respect to both the issuer and the security.[73]

---

[70] *See SEC v. Datronics Engineers, Inc.*, 490 F.2d 250 (4th Cir. 1973); *SEC v. Harwyn Industries Corp.*, 326 F. Supp. 943 (S.D.N.Y. 1971). *But see Isquith v. Caremark International, Inc.*, 136 F.3d 531 (7th Cir. 1998).

[71] *See supra* note 70 (cases cited therein).

[72] *See* SEC Legal Bulletin No. 4 (Sept. 16, 1997).

[73] *See* T. Hazen, *supra* note 23, at 251–253; Bloomenthal, *Market-Makers, Manipulators and Shell Games*, 45 St. John's L. Rev. 597 (1971); Long, *Control of the Spin-Off Device Under the Securities Act of 1933*, 25 Okla. L. Rev. 317 (1972); Lorne, *The Portfolio Spin-Off and Securities Registration*, 52 Texas L. Rev. 918 (1974); Note, *Registration of Stock Spin-offs Under the Securities Act of 1933*, 1980 Duke L.J. 965; *supra* note 70 (cases cited therein); Rule 15c2-11, *supra* note 13 (and accompanying text).

Chapter 7

DUE DILIGENCE AND SECURITIES ACT LIABILITY

§ 7.01 INTRODUCTION

This chapter addresses due diligence, liability consequences, and other ramifications in both registered and unregistered offerings. The chapter begins with a discussion of Section 11's statutory framework. A number of key concepts under the statute are reviewed, including persons subject to liability under Section 11, requirements for invoking the right of action, defenses (particularly the due diligence defenses), damages, contribution, and indemnification.

Concerning due diligence in the registered offering context, the *BarChris*[1] case still serves as the most appropriate vehicle for focusing on this concept. As *BarChris* illustrates, although technically a defense, due diligence is a necessary function to be performed. The discussion thereafter addresses the various parties who may assert the due diligence defense and the degree of investigation required for each such party, including: directors ("inside" as well as "outside"), signatories of the registration statement, underwriters, accountants (who serve as "experts"), and attorneys (who are not liable under Section 11 unless they "expertise" a portion of the registration statement, serve as a director, or act in some other capacity that brings them within the provision's reach).

After analyzing *BarChris* and its ramifications, the chapter discusses the controversial issue, particularly for underwriters, of due diligence in the integrated disclosure framework. These concerns, as the materials in § 7.07 point out, are accentuated in the shelf registration context. Many critics claim that the SEC's response, principally the adoption of Rule 176, is inadequate. The ultimate resolution reached should accommodate the legitimate concerns of underwriters yet be consistent with investor protection.

The last portion of the chapter focuses on Section 12(a)(2) of the Securities Act which contains a "reasonable care" defense that, depending on the circumstances, may be similar to Section 11's "due diligence" defense. Importantly, Section 12(a)(2) may be Section 11's remedial counterpart where an *unregistered* offering takes on the characteristics of a public offering. Also, Section 12(a)(2) may be invoked in the context of registered offerings.[2]

---

[1] *Escott v. BarChris Construction Corporation*, 283 F. Supp. 643 (S.D.N.Y. 1968).

[2] *See Gustafson v. Alloyd Company*, 513 U.S. 561 (1995) (discussed *infra* § 7.09[D]). Note that Section 12(a)(2) may be invoked in the context of a materially false or misleading statement contained in a free writing prospectus. *See* Securities Act Release No. 8591 (2005).

Moreover, in either the registered or unregistered offering setting, plaintiffs always can seek to invoke Section 10(b) of the Securities Exchange Act.[3]

§ 7.02   THE REGISTERED OFFERING — FRAMEWORK OF SECTION 11

As discussed in the foregoing materials (you may wish to review the discussion in §§ 3.01 and 4.01 at this time), a registered offering under the Securities Act requires that a registration statement be utilized. A key policy underlying this requirement is to enable prospective purchasers to make informed investment decisions based upon the disclosure of adequate and truthful information regarding the issuer, its associated persons, and the offering. This policy is frustrated when a registration statement (including the statutory prospectus which comprises part of the registration statement) contains materially false or misleading statements.

In view of the above, investors under certain conditions may recover their losses if they purchase securities pursuant to a registration statement which contains a material misrepresentation or nondisclosure. The federal law provision most likely to be invoked in this context is Section 11 of the Securities Act.

[A]   Parties Subject to Section 11 Liability

Section 11(a) of the Securities Act specifies the classes of persons who may be subject to liability for material misstatements or omissions contained in the registration statement (including the statutory prospectus which is part of the registration statement). Parties subject to Section 11 liability include: (1) all persons who sign the registration statement (including, pursuant to Section 6(a) of the Securities Act, the "issuer, its principal executive officer or officers, its principal financial officer, its controller or principal accounting officer, and the majority of its board of directors or persons performing similar functions"); (2) every director (or person performing similar functions) or general partner of the issuer; (3) every person named with his/her consent in the registration statement as being or about to become a person stated in (2) above; (4) every expert "who has with his consent been named as having prepared or certified any part of the registration statement, or as having prepared or certified any report or valuation which is used in connection with the registration statement, with respect to the statement in such registration statement, report, or valuation which purports to have been prepared or certified by him;"(5) every underwriter of the offering; and (6) pursuant to Section 15, every control person of a party liable under Section 11.

Due to the statutory language and the exhaustive enumeration of those parties subject to suit under Section 11, courts refuse to impose "aiding and abetting" liability pursuant to that provision. For example, in *In re Equity*

---

[3] *See Herman & MacLean v. Huddleston,* 459 U.S. 375 (1983) (discussed *infra* § 8.07).

Funding Corp. of America Securities Litigation,[4] the court observed: "[W]here a statute specifically limits those who may be held liable for the conduct described by the statute, the courts cannot extend liability, under a theory of aiding and abetting, to those who do not fall within the categories of potential defendants described by the statute."[5] The Supreme Court's decision in *Central Bank of Denver*, holding that aiding and abetting liability may not be imposed under Section 10(b) of the Exchange Act, further evidences that such liability is improper under Section 11.[6]

[B]   Elements of the Section 11 Right of Action

Generally, provided that the interstate commerce requirement has been met and upon proof of a material misstatement or nondisclosure, a private action for damages under Section 11(a) may be brought by "any person acquiring such security" unless it can be shown that, at the time of purchase, the purchaser knew of the misstatement or omission. Privity between the purchaser and the defendant is not required for recovery. Moreover, as held by most courts, the Section 11 right of action is available in the initial offering setting as well as when those shares (subject to the "tracing" requirement) are subsequently traded in the aftermarket.[7] In practical effect, however, with respect to shares traded in the aftermarket, the "tracing" requirement often may have the effect of nullifying the Section 11 right of action. For example, in one such case, stockholders purchasing in the aftermarket were held to lack standing under Section 11 with respect to those shares that they were unable affirmatively to establish were purchased in the public offering.[8] Hence, pursuant to the tracing requirement, plaintiffs must show not that they "might" have purchased shares by means of a deficient registration statement in a particular offering, but that they in fact did purchase such shares pursuant

---

[4]   416 F. Supp. 161 (D.C. Cal. 1976).

[5]   *Id.* at 181.

[6]   *Central Bank of Denver v. First Interstate Bank of Denver*, 511 U.S. 164 (1994) (discussed *infra* §§ 10.01–10.02, 15.05[B]).

[7]   The majority of courts allow Section 11 to be invoked in the aftermarket by allegedly aggrieved purchasers. However, based on the U.S. Supreme Court's decision in *Gustafson v. Alloyd Co.*, 513 U.S. 561 (1995) (discussed *infra* § 7.09[D]), which limited Section 12(a)(2)'s scope to public offerings, some courts have confined Section 11's coverage to those securities purchased in the public offering itself. *Compare Hertzberg v. Dignity Partners, Inc.*, 191 F.3d 1076 (9th Cir. 1999) (holding purchasers who traced shares acquired in the aftermarket to the allegedly false registration statement had standing under § 11) *and Schwartz v. Celestial Seasonings, Inc.*, 178 F.R.D. 545 (D. Colo. 1998) (same), *with Brosious v. Children's Place Retail Stores*, [1999–2000 Transfer Binder] Fed. Sec. L. Rep. (CCH) ¶ 90,651 (D.N.J. 1999) (tracing not recognized to confer § 11 standing) *and Gould v. Harris*, 929 F. Supp. 353 (C.D. Cal. 1996) (same).

[8]   *See Krim v. PCOrder.com*, 402 F.3d 489, 495–496 (5th Cir. 2005). For other cases raising the "tracing" issue, *see, e.g., Barnes v. Osofsky*, 373 F.2d 269 (2d Cir. 1967); *In re Newbridge Networks Securities Litigation*, 767 F. Supp. 275 (D.D.C. 1991); *Guenther v. Cooper Life Sciences, Inc.*, 759 F. Supp. 1437 (N.D. Cal. 1990); *Kirkwood v. Taylor*, 590 F. Supp. 1375 (D. Minn. 1984); *McFarland v. Memorex Corp.*, 493 F. Supp. 631 (N.D. Cal. 1980); *supra* note 7 (cases cited therein). *See generally* Murray, *Aftermarket Purchaser Standing Under § 11 of the Securities Act of 1933*, 73 St. John L. Rev. 633 (1999); Sale, *Disappearing Without a Trace: Sections 11 and 12(a)(2) of the Securities Act*, 75 Wash. L. Rev. 429 (2000).

to that specific offering (and registration statement). As stated by the Fifth Circuit: "[A]ftermarket purchasers seeking standing [under Section 11] must demonstrate the ability to 'trace' their shares to the faulty registration [statement]."[9] Given the practical difficulties of "tracing," this requirement frequently is a burdensome one for "aftermarket" Section 11 plaintiffs.

In addition, a plaintiff bringing suit under Section 11 normally need not show reliance upon the misstatement or omission. In fact, he/she need not even have read the prospectus. Pursuant to Section 11(a), however, where the plaintiff acquired the securities more than twelve months after the effective date of the registration statement and if the issuer has made generally available an "earnings statement" covering this twelve-month period, such plaintiff must prove reliance on the misstatement or omission. This showing of reliance may be made by means other than the actual reading of the prospectus.[10]

Another important point is that a plaintiff seeking to recover under Section 11 need not prove that the material misrepresentation or nondisclosure "caused" the loss. In this regard, however, Section 11(e), supported by case law, permits the defendant to reduce (either in part or totally) the plaintiff's monetary recovery by showing that the loss (or portion thereof) was attributable to factors other than the material misrepresentation(s) or nondisclosure(s) contained in the registration statement.[11]

Section 11's seemingly broad express right of action also is limited by a relatively short statute of limitations. Section 13 of the Securities Act provides that an action pursuant to Section 11 must be brought "within one year after the discovery of the untrue statement or the omission, or after such discovery should have been made by the exercise of reasonable diligence . . . [but] in no event shall any such action be brought . . . more than three years after the security was offered to the public."

To recap, under Section 11, *a plaintiff*:

> — must have purchased the security where a means or instrumentality of interstate commerce was used in connection with the offer or sale;

> — at the time of purchase, must not have known of the misrepresentation or nondisclosure;

> — must show that the misrepresentation or nondisclosure was "material," meaning that reasonable investors would have considered the pertinent information important in making their investment decisions;

---

[9] *Krim*, 402 F.3d at 495–496.

[10] *See* SEC Rule 158 (defining the terms: "earning statement," "made generally available to its security holders," and "effective date of the registration statement" for the purposes of the reliance requirement as set forth in the final paragraph of § 11(a)).

[11] *See, e.g., Akerman v. Oryx Communications, Inc.*, [1984 Transfer Binder] Fed. Sec. L. Rep. (CCH) ¶ 91,680 (S.D.N.Y. 1984), *aff'd*, 810 F.2d 344 (2d Cir. 1987).

— need not establish privity;

— as held by most courts, can recover for aftermarket purchases but subject to the often difficult "tracing" requirement;

— normally need not show reliance upon the disclosure deficiency;

— need not prove that the misrepresentation or nondisclosure "caused" the loss (in other words, causation is presumed, but may be rebutted by the defendant);

— must bring the action within the time period set forth by Section 13's statute of limitations.

[C]   Defenses

[1]   General

Section 11(b) provides a number of due diligence defenses for persons other than the issuer. Generally, the only defenses available to the issuer, who otherwise is strictly liable, are the purchaser's knowledge of the misstatement or omission, lack of materiality, lack of causation, equitable defenses (such as in pari delicto), and expiration of the statute of limitations. These defenses, of course, are available to any defendant.

In addition to the above defenses and the "due diligence" defense (which will be addressed shortly), a non-issuer defendant, who discovers a material misstatement or omission in the registration statement, may avoid liability by taking the action specified in Section 11(b)(1) or (2), namely:

(1) *Before* the effective date of the registration statement or part thereof in question, he or she (1) resigns from or takes such steps as are permitted by law to resign from, or ceases or refuses to act in, every office, capacity or relationship ascribed to him or her in the registration statement, and (2) advises the SEC and the issuer in writing of the action taken and disavowing responsibility for such part of the registration statement.

(2) *After* such part of the registration statement has become effective, (1) if he or she was unaware that it had become effective, and (2) upon becoming aware of such fact, acts forthwith, (3) advises the SEC in writing as set forth above, and (4) gives reasonable public notice that such part of the registration statement had become effective without his or her knowledge.

[2]   Due Diligence — Overview

The "due diligence" defenses are contained in Section 11(b)(3). As regards the *unexpertised portion* of the registration statement, a subject defendant must show that, *after* reasonable investigation he/she had reason to believe and did believe at the time such part of the registration statement became effective, there was no material misstatement or omission. As regards the *expertised part*, a defendant (other than the responsible expert) need show only that he/she had no reasonable ground to believe and did not believe that the expertised portion of the registration statement was defective. While a non-expert is not required to make an investigation of expertised information, he/she must "have no reasonable ground to believe" such information is inaccurate.[12]

An expert, on the other hand, is required to show that after reasonable investigation, he/she had reasonable ground to believe and did believe his/her "expertised" statement to be accurate. In other words, an expert is required to exercise the same standard of care regarding the part expertised by him/her as a non-expert is required to exercise regarding the non-expertised portion of the registration statement. Experts are not subject to liability under Section 11 for misstatements or omissions in the unexpertised part of the registration statement merely by reason of their involvement as experts. Note, however, that depending on the facts and circumstances, an expert may incur liability under another statutory provision, such as Section 10(b), if the non-expertised portion of the registration statement is materially deficient.

[3] Due Diligence Standard

Section 11(c) provides that the standard of reasonableness by which the concept of "reasonable investigation" is to be measured is that required of "a prudent man in the management of his own property." In this regard, the "prudent man" standard applies not only to the reasonableness of one's investigation but also to the reasonableness of one's belief.

While opinions may differ as to whether the standard is unitary or elastic, the *BarChris* decision, which is discussed in § 7.04, unequivocally indicates that the degree of responsibility, and a fortiori the extensiveness of the investigation required to establish due diligence, largely will depend upon the type of person and the nature of his/her relationship with the issuer. While *BarChris* let it be known that the statutory due diligence obligations are not to be treated lightly, the decision did not resolve many of the problems inherent in the vague "reasonable investigation" standard. Subsequently, the SEC adopted Rule 176 which lists a number of factors to be taken into account as "circumstances affecting the determination of what constitutes reasonable investigation." These factors are:

(a)   The type of issuer;
(b)   The type of security;
(c)   The type of person;
(d)   The office held when the person is an officer;
(e)   The presence or absence of another relationship to the issuer when the person is a director or proposed director;
(f)   Reasonable reliance on officers, employees, and others whose duties should have given them knowledge of the particular facts (in light of

---

[12] The same standard applies under Section 11(b)(3)(D) to statements in the registration statement purporting to have been made by a public official or purporting to be a copy or extract from a public official document.

the functions and responsibilities of the particular person with respect to the issuer and the filing);

(g)   When the person is an underwriter, the type of underwriting arrangement, the role of the particular person as an underwriter and the availability of information with respect to the registrant; and

(h)   Whether, with respect to a fact or document incorporated by reference, the particular person had any responsibility for the fact or document at the time of the filing from which it was incorporated.

Critics contend that these guidelines do little to provide meaningful content to the "reasonable investigation" standard. Rule 176 and the ramifications of due diligence in the integrated disclosure framework will be addressed in §§ 7.05-7.07.

§ 7.03   CONTRIBUTION AND INDEMNIFICATION

Under Section 11, violators generally are subject to joint and several liability. Accordingly, a plaintiff is entitled to recover the entire judgment against any violator. An exception to this framework exists with respect to outside directors who are liable only in proportion to their fault unless they had actual knowledge of the falsity.

In order to distribute judgment and settlement costs among joint violators, the two common techniques used are contribution and indemnification. While indemnification involves a shifting of the entire loss from one defendant to another person, contribution involves a sharing of the damages among the tortfeasors.

Section 11(f) of the Securities Act clearly provides for a right to *contribution*.[13] The provision, however, leaves unsettled the extent to which losses are to be shared among the parties. The traditional view is that the parties share the entire loss on a pro rata basis (i.e., equally among the joint tortfeasors irrespective of individual fault). The emerging view is that apportionment of damages should be premised upon a proportionate fault or pro tanto basis.[14] The subjects of contribution and methods of allocating contribution in securities litigation are addressed in § 8.10. The right to *indemnification* is far less certain. Neither Section 11 nor any other provision of the securities laws provides for such a right. The SEC's position, as contained in Item 512(h) of Regulation S-K, is that indemnification of officers, directors, and controlling

---

[13] Where a culpable party engaged in fraudulent misrepresentation and the other culpable defendants acted negligently, the fraudulent violator does not have a right to contribution. Securities Act § 11(f)(1); *see also Musick, Peller & Garrett v. Employers Insurance of Wausau*, 508 U.S. 286 (1993) (implied right to contribution recognized under Exchange Act § 10(b)).

[14] "The pro taeto method mandates that plaintiffs receive the full amount of damages awarded and that the non-settling defendants receive a judgment reduction in the amount paid to the plaintiffs in settlement." Steinberg & Olive, *Contribution and Proportionate Liability Under the Federal Securities Laws in Multidefendant Securities Litigation After the Private Securities Litigation Reform Act of 1995*, 50 SMU L. Rev. 337, 363 (1996). *See generally* Ruder, *Multiple Defendants in Securities Law Fraud Cases: Aiding and Abetting, Conspiracy, In Pari Delicto, Indemnification and Contribution*, 120 U. Pa. L. Rev. 597 (1972).

persons of the registrant for liability arising under the Securities Act is against public policy, and, hence, unenforceable. Interestingly, however, the SEC has no such hostility to the procurement of insurance. Rule 461(c) of Regulation C provides that normally "[i]nsurance against liabilities arising under the [Securities] Act, whether the cost of insurance is borne by the registrant, the insured or some other person, will not be considered a bar to acceleration [of the effective date of the registration statement]."[15]

Another question concerns whether an underwriter, pursuant to an indemnity agreement with the issuer or its controlling persons, may thereby avoid liability. With respect to intentional securities law violations by an underwriter, the courts have denied indemnification. Generally, the courts reason that, permitting a party to avoid monetary liability for its own reckless or willful misconduct, is contrary to the securities acts' objective of inducing parties to be scrupulous about their disclosure obligations. Moreover, the issuer's indemnification of the underwriter is suspect in that the funds ultimately come out of the shareholders' pockets, the very individuals who were damaged by the misconduct.[16] The foregoing reasons also apply for prohibiting indemnification where the underwriter has been negligent. As stated by the Third Circuit:

> [I]ndemnification runs counter to the policies underlying the 1933 and 1934 Acts. In addition, there is no indication that Congress intended that indemnification be available under the Acts. . . . In drafting the Acts, Congress was not concerned with protecting the underwriters, but rather it sought to protect investors. Here, it is the underwriters, not the victims, who seek indemnification. We agree with those courts that have held that there is no implied right to seek indemnification under the federal securities laws.
>
> . . . .
>
> In order to successfully assert a due care or a due diligence defense, an underwriter must prove that it conducted a reasonable investigation and had a reasonable belief that the information relating to an offering was accurate and complete. These defenses encourage an underwriter to act reasonably; they are not available to a negligent underwriter. Unlike indemnification, the statutory defenses support the policies of the Act. Underwriters will be more likely to act diligently in an effort to assert the defenses.[17]

---

[15] *See generally* Griffith, *Uncovering a Gatekeeper: Why the SEC Should Mandate Disclosure of Details Concerning Directors' and Officers' Liability Insurance Policies*, 154 U. Pa. L. Rev. 1147 (2006).

[16] *See, e.g., Globus v. Law Research Serv., Inc.*, 418 F.2d 1276 (2d Cir. 1969).

[17] *Eichenholtz v. Brennan*, 52 F.3d 478, 483–485 (3d Cir. 1995) (not permitting right to indemnification when underwriter was negligent); *Globus*, 418 F.2d at 1288; L. Loss & J. Seligman, Securities Regulation 4632 (3d ed. 1988); Comment, *Allocation of Damages Under the Federal Securities Laws*, 60 Wash. U. L.Q. 211 (1982) (and cases cited therein). For discussion of contribution and indemnification under Section 10(b) of the Securities Exchange Act, see *infra* § 8.11.

§ 7.04 DUE DILIGENCE IN THE REGISTERED OFFERING CONTEXT

As an initial matter, it should be pointed out (*see supra* § 3.01) that, strictly speaking, due diligence is a defense that may be asserted by the subject party rather than an affirmative obligation. If the statements made in the registration statement are true or, alternatively, if no lawsuit is brought, no liability will be incurred for an individual's failure to exercise due diligence. On the other hand, if an action is instituted and a material misstatement or omission is shown, liability often may be avoided under Section 11 only by proving the performance of due diligence. For this reason, as a practical matter, due diligence is a necessity.

Although not a recent decision, the seminal case on due diligence in the Section 11 context is *Escott v. BarChris* Construction Corporation.[18] In *BarChris*, convertible debentures of BarChris Construction Corporation, the issuer, were sold to the public by means of a registration statement filed with the SEC. Plaintiffs, who were purchasers of these debentures, alleged that the registration statement contained material misstatements. Relief was sought against various defendants, including the directors, the persons who signed the registration statement, the underwriters, and the auditors. In imposing liability against the various parties, the *BarChris* court set forth several key principles.

[A] Directors

In analyzing the due diligence defense raised by the defendant directors, *BarChris* draws a distinction between inside and outside directors, and between directors based upon the extent of their knowledge of or access to the pertinent facts. Certainly one would expect a director who also serves as the principal executive officer to be required to perform more diligently than an outside director who otherwise has no relationship with the issuer. As another example, many corporations have established executive committees, comprised of three directors who, in many cases, make decisions that otherwise would be within the province of the entire board of directors. Depending upon the circumstances, an inordinate hardship would be imposed upon directors not serving on those committees if they were held to the same degree of responsibility.

BarChris indicates that, while less may be required of certain outside directors in order to meet their due diligence obligations, reasonable investigation still requires affirmative action. Hence, outside directors must endeavor to make some type of an independent verification of the information contained in the registration statement. Clearly, a director who makes no effort to investigate will not be able to sustain his/her burden of establishing that he/she acted with due diligence. As stated by the court in *WorldCom*,

---

[18] 283 F. Supp. 643 (S.D.N.Y. 1968). See also *Feit v. Leasco Data Processing Equip. Corp.*, 332 F. Supp. 544 (E.D.N.Y. 1971), for an extensive discussion of liability under Section 11 of the Securities Act.

"directors are not excused from performing a meaningful due diligence investigation due to the involvement of professionals, such as underwriters and auditors."[19]

In one case, for example, an outside director met his due diligence defense under Section 11. In *Weinberger v. Jackson*, the district court stated:

> Since Valentine was an outside director, he was not obliged to conduct an independent investigation into the accuracy of all the statements contained in the registration statement. He could rely upon the reasonable representations of management, if his own conduct and level of inquiry were reasonable under the circumstances. He was reasonably familiar with the company's business and operations. He regularly attended board meetings at which the board discussed every aspect of the company's business. And he reviewed the company's financial statements. He was familiar with the company's development of its new product lines. He was involved with various company decisions. He reviewed six drafts of the registration statement and saw nothing suspicious or inconsistent with the knowledge that he had acquired as a director. And he discussed certain aspects of the registration statement with management. . . .
>
> Plaintiffs argue that Valentine did not make specific inquiries of the company's management with respect to the representations contained in the prospectus. But he had no duty to do so as long as the prospectus statements were consistent with the knowledge of the company which he had reasonably acquired in his position as director. He was also given comfort by the fact that the prospectus and the information in it were reviewed by underwriters, counsel and accountants. This met the standards of due diligence and reasonable inquiry. . . .[20]

It may be argued that an outside director should: seek to attend board of director meetings regarding the offering; review the registration statement with care (probing relevant corporate personnel and counsel on the factual contents and representations made therein); review the Exchange Act filed documents that are incorporated by reference into the registration statement; with the aid of competent advisers, assess the abilities of management as well as the company's reputation; ask questions and follow up if necessary. Although the performance of the foregoing actions may not guarantee absolution from liability, it should provide persuasive evidence that the outside director met

---

[19] *In re WorldCom, Inc. Securities Litigation*, [2005–2006 Transfer Binder] Fed. Sec. L. Rep. (CCH) ¶ 93,137, at 95,781 (S.D.N.Y. 2005).

[20] [1990–1991 Transfer Binder] Fed. Sec. L. Rep. (CCH) ¶ 95,693, at 98,256 (N.D. Cal. 1990). *See generally* Hamilton, *Reliance and Liability Standards for Outside Directors*, 24 Wake Forest L. Rev. 5 (1989); Silverman & Fisher, *Director Due Diligence After WorldCom*, 39 Rev. Sec. & Comm. Reg. 1 (2006).

An SEC Advisory Committee has proposed that an issuer establish a disclosure committee comprised of outside directors to oversee the integrity of the company's disclosures. *See Report of the Advisory Committee on the Capital Formation and Regulatory Processes*, [1996–1997 Transfer Binder] Fed. Sec. L. Rep. (CCH) ¶ 85,834 (1996). Implementation of such disclosure committees raises a host of due diligence concerns.

his/her due diligence obligations. Note, moreover, that if held liable, an outside director under Section 11(f)(2) will incur liability only in proportion to his/her fault unless such outside director had actual knowledge of the misrepresentation.

[B] Signatories

Persons who sign the registration statement (a majority of the directors and certain high level officers of the issuer) may be held to stringent due diligence obligations. This is despite the fact that, had they not signed, their respective duties of investigation, particularly in the case of officers not holding directorships, may have differed. The rationale for holding signatories, particularly those who are inside directors or who otherwise hold principal corporate offices (even if not directors), to a strict standard of due diligence is that prospective investors reasonably may assume that, by signing the registration statement, such signatories represent that it is an accurate statement of the information contained therein.

To a large extent, *BarChris* may be viewed as treating "inside" signatories in effect as guarantors of the accuracy of the registration statement (indeed the court may have said as much). Interestingly, however, Congress specifically rejected a proposal that would have made directors guarantors in this context. On the other hand, it may be said that *BarChris* "does not deny the [due diligence] defense [to such inside signatories], but recognizes the obvious difficulty of establishing it."[21]

[C] Attorneys

Due diligence is a concern for lawyers who are involved in a registered offering. For example, counsel may: (1) serve as a director of the issuer, (2) act as an expert within the meaning of Section 11(a)(4) (*e.g.*, by rendering a tax opinion that is contained in the registration statement), (3) draft narrative portions of the registration statement; and (4) perform the due diligence investigation on behalf of a client (*e.g.*, an underwriter) in its stead.

With respect to assuming "expert" status, it is clear that an attorney whose role is to render legal advice or assist in the preparation of the registration statement does not thereby become an expert within the meaning of Section 11. As the Supreme Court has observed: "[C]ertain individuals who play a part in preparing the registration statement generally cannot be reached by a § 11 action. These include . . . lawyers not acting as experts."[22] Further, because Section 11 limits the class of potential defendants, attorneys cannot be held liable under Section 11 on an aiding and abetting theory.[23] Depending on the

---

[21] Folk, *Civil Liabilities Under the Federal Securities Acts: The BarChris Case*, 55 Va. L. Rev. 1, 22 (1969); *see* H.R. Rep. No. 85, 73d Cong., 1st Sess. 5 (1933); H.R. Rep. No. 152, 73d Cong., 1st Sess. 26 (1933); Landis, *The Legislative History of the Securities Act of 1933*, 28 Geo. Wash. L. Rev. 29, 48 (1959).

[22] *Herman & MacLean v. Huddleston*, 459 U.S. 375, 386 n. 22 (1983).

[23] *See Central Bank of Denver v. First Interstate Bank of Denver*, 511 U.S. 164 (1994); *Herman*

circumstances, lawyers can be held liable as primary violators under Section 10(b) of the Securities Exchange Act, as "sellers" under Section 12 of the Securities Act, as "control persons" under both the 1933 and 1934 Acts, and under state law.[24]

In *BarChris*, the young attorney, Birnbaum, while not a director at the time the registration statement originally was filed, was a director when he signed the later amendments. He thereby subjected himself to Section 11 liability as a director and as a signatory. Unfortunately, Birnbaum made no investigation whatsoever and relied on the statements of others. The court noted that, while Birnbaum was not an executive officer in any real sense, he was named as such in the prospectus. Further, by virtue of his duties as in-house counsel and keeper of the corporate minutes, he had considerable information about the corporation's affairs. While not aware of many of the inaccuracies in the prospectus, as a lawyer, he must have appreciated some of them. He should have known his statutory obligations and made a reasonable investigation.

The court's opinion indicates that, even if he were not a signatory to the registration statement, Birnbaum nevertheless would have been subject to Section 11 liability. In this regard, note that his liability would have been based upon his status as a director and not as an attorney. However, the fact that Birnbaum was an attorney was taken into consideration in determining whether he conducted a reasonable investigation.

Grant, the issuer's outside counsel, was held liable in *BarChris* both as a director and as a signatory. The court in *BarChris* took into account his role of being primarily responsible for drafting the registration statement, reasoning that "more was required of him in the way of reasonable investigation than could fairly be expected of a director who had no connection with this work." The court indicated that, by its holding, it was not seeking to establish an unduly onerous standard for outside counsel who also serves as a director. Rather, each case must turn on its own facts. Here, even taking into account that BarChris' officers had misled Grant, "there . . . [were] too many instances in which Grant failed to make an inquiry which, if pursued, would have put him on his guard."[25]

As noted above, counsel who renders a formal legal opinion which is included in the registration statement with his/her consent is considered an "expert" within the ambit of Section 11. For example, counsel may proffer an opinion that (1) the company and its subsidiaries are duly incorporated, (2) licenses are in order, and (3) the company's securities are validly issued under state law and are non-assessable. Such opinions rarely are problematic. More difficult issues arise when counsel proffers an opinion that is critical to the

---

& *McLean v. Huddleston*, 459 U.S. 375, 386 n.22 (1983).

[24] *See, e.g., Molecular Technology Corp. v. Valentine*, 925 F.2d 910 (6th Cir. 1991); *In re Rospatch Securities Litigation*, [1992 Transfer Binder] Fed. Sec. L. Rep. (CCH) ¶ 96,939 (W.D. Mich. 1992); *Zendell v. Newport Oil Corp.*, 544 A.2d 878 (N.J. 1988); M. Steinberg, Attorney Liability After Sarbanes-Oxley (2008).

[25] 283 F. Supp. at 690–692.

"deal" such as an opinion by counsel concerning the pertinent federal tax implications.[26]

A different question is presented where an attorney, acting as counsel for either the issuer or the underwriter, furnishes a "comfort opinion." A comfort opinion essentially is a statement that, based on counsel's participation in the preparation of the registration statement and conferences with representatives of the issuer, underwriters and public accountants, he/she has no reason to believe that the registration statement violates Section 11. In order not to be subject to Section 11 liability, counsel should ensure that neither the opinion nor its contents appear in the registration statement.

[D]   Delegation of Due Diligence

In practice, the issuer, directors and underwriters frequently delegate their due diligence investigations to counsel. Such delegation, as *BarChris* makes clear, is appropriate. In effect, while counsel seeks to perform an adequate investigation on behalf of his/her client, it is the client, and not counsel, who will be held liable under Section 11 if counsel fails to meet the requisite standard of care. In such instances, however, counsel may be faced with a legal malpractice suit under state law.[27]

When counsel performs due diligence on behalf of a client, counsel should stand in the client's "shoes." The scope of the due diligence obligation depends on such factors as the client's position, its relationship with the issuer, and its involvement in the preparation of the registration statement. The extensiveness of the investigation appropriate may range from that required of an outside director who has no other affiliation with the issuer to the extensive verification required of underwriters in the traditional public offering setting.[28]

[E]   Underwriters

The court in *BarChris* imposed a rigorous due diligence degree of investigation upon the underwriters. The court reasoned that the underwriters to a public offering are uniquely situated to verify the accuracy of the registration statement's contents. Underwriters not only have access to the necessary information; they have the leverage in the traditional registration context to compel the issuer to fulfill its disclosure duties. Moreover, the investing public relies upon the underwriters' reputations and upon their participation in the offering as an endorsement of the registration statement's accuracy. As stated by the SEC:

---

[26] *See* D. Glaser, S. FitzGibbon & S. Weise, Legal Opinions (2d ed. 2004); McCallum & Young, *Ethical Issues in Opinion Practice*, 62 Bus. Law. 417 (2007); Rice & Steinberg, *Legal Opinions in Securities Transactions*, 16 J. Corp. L. 375 (1991).

[27] *See supra* note 24 (sources cited therein).

[28] *See* L. Loss & J. Seligman, Securities Regulation 4246–4278 (3d ed. 1992); Spanner, *A Litigation Perspective on the Prospectus Preparation Process for an Initial Public Offering*, 16 Sec. Reg. L.J. 115 (1988).

An underwriter . . . occupies a vital position in an offering. The underwriter stands between the issuer and the public purchasers, assisting the issuer in pricing and, at times, in structuring the financing and preparing disclosure documents. Most importantly, its role is to place the offered securities with public investors. By participating in an offering, an underwriter makes an implied representation about the securities. Because the underwriter holds itself out as a securities professional, and especially in light of its position vis-à-vis the issuer, this recommendation itself implies that the underwriter has a reasonable basis for belief in the truthfulness and completeness of the key representations made in any disclosure documents used in the offerings.[29]

However, an underwriter is not expected to have the intimate knowledge of corporate affairs that inside directors normally possess, and consequently its duty to investigate should be considered in view of its more limited access. The *BarChris* court emphasized, nonetheless, that an underwriter is expected to exercise a high degree of care in the course of its investigation. Not only must underwriters make an independent verification of management's representations, they must play the devil's advocate.[30] Hence, as stated recently by the *WorldCom* court, "underwriters must exercise a high degree of care in investigation and independent verification of the company's representations."[31] As discussed in depth later in this chapter, in recognition of possible limitations on the underwriter's ability to investigate in certain circumstances, the SEC adopted Rule 176.[32]

---

[29] Securities Exchange Act Release No. 26100 (1988); *see Feit v. Leasco Data Processing Equipment Corp.*, 332 F. Supp. 544, 581 (E.D.N.Y. 1971) (stating that "courts must be particularly scrupulous in examining the conduct of underwriters since they are supposed to assume an opposing posture with respect to management").

[30] *See BarChris*, 283 F. Supp. at 697; *see also In re Software Toolworks Inc. Securities Litigation*, 38 F.3d 1078, 1086 (9th Cir. 1994); *Feit v. Leasco Data Processing Equipment Corp.*, 332 F. Supp. 544, 581–582 (E.D.N.Y. 1971).

[31] *In re WorldCom, Inc. Securities Litigation*, 346 F. Supp. 2d 628, 662 (S.D.N.Y. 2004); *see In re Software Toolworks Inc. Securities Litigation*, 38 F.3d 1078 (9th Cir. 1994) (reversing grant of summary judgment that underwriters met their due diligence defense); *In re International Rectifier Securities Litigation*, [1997 Transfer Binder] Fed. Sec. L. Rep. (CCH) ¶ 99,469 (C.D. Cal. 1987) (holding underwriters met due diligence defense); *Weinberger v. Jackson*, [1991 Transfer Binder] Fed. Sec. L. Rep. (CCH) ¶ 95,693 (N.D. Cal. 1990) (same).

[32] *See infra* §§ 7.05–7.07. *See generally* Chapman, *Underwriters' Due Diligence Revisited*, 35 Rev. Sec. & Comm. Reg. 207 (2002); Freilich & Janvey, *Understanding "Best Efforts" Underwritings*, 17 Sec. Reg. L.J. 151 (1989); Greene, *Determining the Responsibilities of Underwriters Distributing Securities Within an Integrated Disclosure System*, 56 Notre Dame Lawyer 755 (1981); Horwich, *Section 11 of the Securities Act: The Cornerstone Needs Some Tuckpointing*, 58 Bus. Law. 1 (2002); O'Hare, *Institutional Investors, Registration Rights and the Specter of Liability Under Section 11 of the Securities Act of 1933*, 1996 Wisc. L. Rev. 217.

[F]   Accountants

When the court in *BarChris* turned to consider the liability of the accountants, it did so with respect to that "part of the registration statement purporting to be made upon the authority of [the accountant] as an expert."[33] The only part of the registration statement made on the authority of the accountants in *BarChris* was, as is usually the case, the certified financial statements. In considering the defense that the accountants acted with due diligence, the court stated that this defense must be assessed at the time that the part of the registration statement containing the allegedly false and misleading financial statements became effective. To accomplish this task, the court scrutinized the audit as well as the accountants' review of events which occurred after the date of the certified balance sheet contained in the registration statement but before the effective date of the registration statement.

The most blatant error found by the court was the accountants' failure to discover that a bowling alley constructed by the registrant, which had been recorded on the books as having been sold, had not been sold. In determining whether the accountants should be held liable for the resulting misstatements in the financial statements, the court carefully considered the various internal documentary evidence examined by the accountants during the course of their audit. In addition, the court considered certain accounting records which had not been examined but which, if examined, would have put the accountants on notice of the impropriety. After reviewing the audit procedures in this context, the court concluded that the accountants failed to prove that they had conducted a reasonable investigation and consequently, their ignorance of the true facts was unjustified.[34]

In scrutinizing the accountants' review of events subsequent to the date of the certified financial statements but prior to the effective date of the registration statement, the court concluded that the written work program utilized for the review conformed to generally accepted auditing standards (GAAS) and would have provided the accountants with the due diligence defense had it been properly executed. The program, with limited exceptions, only required a cursory review of the financial statements and certain specific accounts. Significantly, however, the court criticized the accountants for obtaining answers which they considered satisfactory without attempting to verify them. Thus, while limited review procedures may suffice as to "subsequent events," the court added the gloss that information obtained and examined in the course of such a review must be independently verified. As such, although accountants need not perform a complete audit when conducting a subsequent events review, any danger signals must be pursued and answers must be verified.[35]

---

[33] 283 F. Supp. at 698.

[34] *Id.* at 703; *see also United States v. Benjamin*, 328 F.2d 854 (2d Cir. 1964).

[35] *See* 283 F. Supp. at 700–703; *see also In re Software Toolworks Inc. Securities Litigation*, 38 F.3d 1078 (9th Cir. 1994).

From an overall perspective, the court in *BarChris* believed that accountants "should not be held to a standard higher than that recognized in their profession."[36] Similarly, the Seventh Circuit's decision in *Hochfelder v. Ernst & Ernst*[37] is instructive on the standards by which an accountant's audit must be judged. The court, essentially agreeing with *BarChris*, held that accountants generally "are required to meet only the standard of care expected of persons holding themselves out as skilled accountants."[38] The Seventh Circuit, however, relying on Judge Learned Hand's opinion in *The T.J. Hooper*,[39] went on to assert that compliance with GAAS (Generally Accepting Auditing Standards) does not provide automatic insulation from liability. As the court pointed out, a determination must be made whether the prevailing professional practice constitutes reasonable prudence. Hence, while compliance with GAAS may strongly suggest that the requisite standard of care has been met, "[c]ourts must in the end say what is required; there are precautions so imperative that even their universal disregard will not excuse their omission."[40]

Generally, with respect to accountants' liability under Section 11 (as well as under other provisions of the federal securities law), the lead of *BarChris* concerning the proper standard of care has been followed. Accordingly, it appears that compliance with GAAS normally will provide a shield to charges of carelessness. Note, however, that:

> It is vitally important to point out that this shield only relates to an accountant's care in obtaining essential underlying facts. Compliance with GAAS will not be a shield to liability where an unreasonable judgment is made on the basis of adequate information properly obtained. The decisions scrutinizing accountants' audit procedures have at the same time considered the reasonableness of the judgments made on the basis of the information unearthed during the audit.

> In addition, compliance with GAAS will not act as a shield from liability for misleading presentation of information obtained during the course of a properly conducted audit. In other words, the "investigative" portion of the audit, in which the accountant obtains evidential matter to support the information ultimately presented in financial statements, is only the first step in the evaluation of liability. The next step is to scrutinize the judgments made by the accountant on the basis of the information obtained, and the final step is to scrutinize the fairness of the financial statements taken as a whole. When financial statements are alleged to be false or misleading, carelessness at any of the three levels can lead to liability.[41]

---

[36] 283 F. Supp. at 703.

[37] 503 F.2d 1100 (7th Cir. 1974), *rev'd on other grounds*, 425 U.S. 185 (1976).

[38] *Id.* at 1108; *accord SEC v. Arthur Young & Co.*, 590 F.2d 785 (9th Cir. 1979).

[39] 60 F.2d 737 (2d Cir. 1932).

[40] 503 F.2d at 1114 n.16 (quoting *The T.J. Hooper*, 60 F.2d at 740).

[41] Gruenbaum & Steinberg, *Accountants' Liability and Responsibility: Securities, Criminal*

§ 7.05   IMPACT OF THE INTEGRATED DISCLOSURE SYSTEM

At this point, you may wish to review the discussion on the SEC's integrated disclosure system in § 5.01. Perhaps the most significant liability concern raised by the integrated disclosure system is that certain issuers can incorporate by reference Exchange Act periodic reports into their Securities Act registration statements. Such incorporation of 1934 Act reports may make it substantially more onerous for subject parties to satisfy Section 11's "due diligence" obligation (as well as Section 12(a)(2)'s "reasonable care" standard), thus resulting in greater liability exposure for, among others, directors, and underwriters.

The issue of *underwriter due diligence* in the integrated disclosure process has raised the most serious liability concerns. It has been argued that, given the practical realities, incorporation by reference severely hampers an underwriter's ability to perform the type of due diligence that *BarChris* sets forth. The reasons underlying this assertion include: (1) underwriters will not generally participate in the drafting of the disclosures incorporated by reference from the 1934 Act periodic reports into the 1933 Act registration statement; (2) underwriters, due to management's reluctance to modify previously filed SEC documents that it had approved (irrespective of SEC Rule 412),[42] will be unable to persuade management to improve the disclosures previously made; (3) a registration statement that incorporates by reference normally limits to a significant degree the time period during which such due diligence can be performed; and (4) adoption of the integrated disclosure system comes at a time of intense competition among underwriters.

Taking the above considerations into account, one may argue that it is inevitable that the underwriter's role as a key participant in the registration process significantly recedes in importance. In short, according to many in the securities industry, the SEC's integrated disclosure system has "rendered untenable the underwriter's traditional role and responsibilities in securities distributions."[43]

---

and Common Law, 13 Loyola U.L.A. L. Rev. 247, 260–261 (1980); *see also In re Software Toolworks Inc. Securities Litigation*, 38 F.3d 1078 (9th Cir. 1994); Ebke, *In Search of Alternatives: Comparative Reflections on Corporate Governance and the Independent Auditor's Responsibilities*, 79 Nw. U. L. Rev. 663 (1984); Fiflis, *Current Problems of Accountant's Responsibilities to Third Parties*, 28 Vand. L. Rev. 31 (1975).

[42] Rule 412 is designed to alleviate concerns regarding the modification of disclosures made in previously filed SEC documents. Among other things, the rule sets forth that a modifying or superseding statement made in an SEC filed document is not deemed an admission that the statement that undergoes such change violates the federal securities laws. *See* Fortenbaugh, *Underwriters' Due Diligence*, 14 Rev. Sec. Reg. 799, 805 (1983).

[43] Greene, *supra* note 32, at 797; *see* Coffee, *Brave New World? The Impact(s) of the Internet on Modern Securities Regulation*, 52 Bus. Law. 1195 (1997); Hovdesven & Wolfram, *Underwriter Liability in the Integrated Disclosure System*, Nat'l L.J., July 5, 1982, at 14; Langevoort, *Deconstructuring Section 11: Public Offering Liability in a Continuous Disclosure Environment*, 63 Law & Cont. Prob. 45 (2000); Partnoy, *Barbarians at the Gatekeepers?: A Proposal for a Modified Strict Liability Regime*, 79 Wash. U.L.Q. 491 (2001).

Due to these concerns, the Corporation Finance Committee of the Securities Industry Association (SIA) proposed that an underwriter should be deemed to satisfy its due diligence obligations if it "(1) had read the registration statement and all exhibits and incorporated documents; (2) had discussed the registration statement with the registrant's representatives; and (3) after such review and discussion, did not know of any material misstatement or omission."[44]

The SIA proposal has not been adopted because it neglects established case law and SEC policy that the element of independent verification by the underwriter is essential for establishing due diligence. Instead, the Commission has opted for Rule 176 which basically codifies Section 1704(g) of the American Law Institute's Federal Securities Code. According to the SEC, the rule's basic focus is to permit each person who has potential Section 11 liability to "evaluate the surrounding facts, including the extent of his prior relationship with the issuer, and utilize techniques of investigation appropriate to the circumstances of the offering."[45] Rule 176 provides:

> In determining whether or not the conduct of a person constitutes a reasonable investigation or a reasonable ground for belief meeting the standard set forth in Section 11(c), relevant circumstances include, with respect to a person other than the issuer,
>
> (a)   the type of issuer;
>
> (b)   The type of security;
>
> (c)   The type of person;
>
> (d)   The office held when the person is an officer;
>
> (e)   The presence or absence of another relationship to the issuer when the person is a director or proposed director;
>
> (f)   Reasonable reliance on officers, employees, and others whose duties should have given them knowledge of the particular facts (in light of the functions and responsibilities of the particular person with respect to the issuer and the filing);
>
> (g)   When the person is an underwriter, the type of underwriter, the type of underwriting arrangement, the role of the particular person as an underwriter and the availability of information with respect to the registrant; and
>
> (h)   Whether, with respect to a fact or document incorporated by reference, the particular person had any responsibility for the fact or document at the time of the filing from which it was incorporated.[46]

---

[44] SIA Proposal, as described by Hovdesven & Wolfram, *supra* note 43, at 18.

[45] Securities Act Release No. 6383 (1982).

[46] 17 C.F.R. § 230.176. In 1998, the SEC proposed to amend Rule 176 to provide further guidance for underwriters in the integrated disclosure system. In the proposal, the Commission set forth six practices that evidence the performance of underwriter due diligence under Section 11. The SEC stated that these six factors are not exclusive and that an underwriter's failure to satisfy all six factors should not be deemed determinative of such underwriter's lack of due diligence. These six factors are:

—   Whether the underwriter reviewed the registration statement and conducted a reasonable inquiry into any fact or circumstance that would cause a reasonable person to question whether the

As a general proposition, Rule 176 correctly recognizes the concepts of delegation and specialization for all potentially liable persons (except the issuer) under Section 11. Moreover, subsections (g) and (h) recognize, at least somewhat, the concerns of underwriters in the integrated disclosure system. Nonetheless, the SEC has been criticized for failing to recognize, in view of market realities, the difficult task that underwriters have to independently verify the information contained in the registration statement. This criticism becomes accentuated when applied to the shelf registration process (discussed *infra* § 7.07).

In 1998, the SEC proposed amendments to Rule 176 that, if adopted, will provide further guidance for underwriters in the integrated disclosure framework with respect to their performance of due diligence (*see supra* note 46). One practice set forth in the SEC proposals that to some extent has become a part of underwriter due diligence in the shelf registration context is the issuer's designation of counsel for the (prospective) underwriter. Because counsel normally is selected by the issuer, conflicts of interest dilemmas arise. Nonetheless, the designation of counsel for the underwriter by the issuer is an accepted technique. Pursuant to this designation, counsel selected by the issuer acts on behalf of the prospective underwriter in fulfilling such underwriter's continuous due diligence functions.[47] Perhaps surprisingly, this approach has not been as extensively utilized as the SEC had envisioned. As observed by the New York City Bar Association's Task Force Report on the "Lawyer's Role in Corporate Governance": When the Commission adopted the integrated disclosure framework, "it expected that many eligible issuers, in collaboration with their chosen underwriters and their lawyers, would adopt 'continuous' due diligence programs. However, the number of companies today using such

---

 registration statement contains an untrue statement or material omission;

— Whether the underwriter discussed the information contained in the registration statement with the relevant executive officer(s) of the registrant (including, a minimum, the chief financial officer (CFO) or the chief accounting officer (CAO) (or designee) and the CFO or CAO (or designee) certified that he or she has examined the registration statement and that to the best of his or her knowledge, it does not contain an untrue statement or material omission;

— Whether the underwriter received a Statement on Auditing Standards No. 72 comfort letter from the issuer's auditors;

— Whether the underwriter received a favorable opinion from issuer's counsel opining that nothing has come to its attention that has caused it to believe that the registration statement contains an untrue statement or omits to state a material fact;

— Whether the underwriter employed counsel that, after reviewing the issuer's registration statement, Exchange Act filings and other information, opined that nothing came to its attention that would lead it to believe that the registration statement contains an untrue statement or omits to state a material fact; and

— Whether the underwriter employed and consulted a research analyst that:

  — has followed the issuer or the issuer's industry on an ongoing basis for at least the six months immediately before the commencement of the offering; and

  — has issued a report on the issuer or its industry within the 12 months immediately before commencement of the offering.

Securities Act Release No. 7606A (1998), discussed in Jones & Baez, *New SEC Proposals for the Regulation of Securities Offerings*, 27 Sec. Reg. L.J. 25, 42–43 (1999). To date, the proposed amendments to Rule 176 have not been adopted.

[47] *See In re WorldCom Securities Litigation*, 346 F. Supp. 2d 628, 662 (S.D.N.Y. 2004); Securities Act Release No. 6499 (1983).

continuous due diligence programs appears not to be extensive, and opinions vary on their effectiveness."[48]

It may be argued that the traditional role and responsibilities of the underwriter in the distribution process remain necessary for investor protection, at least until an adequate alternative approach has been adopted. Although underwriters, for good reason, fear increased liability, investor protection should not be lessened. As stated by the Second Circuit:

> No greater reliance in our self-regulatory system is placed on any single participant in the issuance of securities than upon the underwriter. . . . Prospective investors look to the underwriter — a fact well known to all concerned and especially to the underwriter — to pass on the soundness of the security and the correctness of the registration statement and prospectus.[49]

As more recently stated in *WorldCom*, "Rule 176 [does] not alter the fundamental nature of underwriters' due diligence obligations."[50] Hence, at least according to a number of courts, as well as the SEC, a high standard of underwriter due diligence continues to prevail in the integrated disclosure framework.[51]

§ 7.06   DIRECTOR SIGNING OF FORM 10-K

As part of its integrated disclosure framework, the SEC has mandated that a majority of a registrant's directors sign the Form 10-K. In adopting this requirement, the Commission reasoned:

> [A] requirement for the signatures [on the Form 10-K] of a majority of a registrant's directors — in addition to those of its principal executive officer, its principal financial officer, and its controller or principal accounting officer — is an appropriate one under the circumstances. The Commission believes that just as its rules and the administrative focus of the Division of Corporation Finance are being realigned to reflect the shift in emphasis toward relying on periodic disclosure under the Exchange Act, so too the attention of the private sector, including management, directors, accountants, and attorneys, must also be refocused towards Exchange Act filings if a sufficient degree of discipline is to be instilled in the system to make it work. With an expanded signature requirement, the Commission anticipates that directors will be encouraged to devote the needed attention to reviewing the Form 10-K and to seek the involvement of other professionals to the degree necessary to give themselves sufficient

---

[48] New York City Bar Association's Task Force on the "Lawyer's Role in Corporate Governance," Executive Summary, 14 (2007).

[49] *Chris-Craft Industries, Inc. v. Piper Aircraft Corp.*, 480 F.2d 341, 380 (2d Cir. 1973).

[50] *In re WorldCom, Inc. Securities Litigation*, 346 F. Supp. 2d at 670.

[51] *Id.* at 670 (referring to the SEC's focus on high standards with respect to underwriter due diligence in this setting).

comfort. In the Commission's view, this added measure of discipline is vital to the disclosure objectives of the federal securities laws, and outweighs the potential impact, if any, of the signature on legal liability.[52]

Concerns have been expressed that the director signature requirement for the Form 10-K may result in greater liability exposure. For example, the signing of the Form 10-K by a subject director arguably may signify that the director "caused" the filing, failed to act in "good faith," and/or acted with "scienter," thereby giving rise to a host of both SEC and private liability concerns. At this point, it appears that the signature requirement, at least to some extent, has induced directors to scrutinize the Form 10-K and to seek the advice of corporate counsel in this exercise to a much greater degree than previously was the practice. Enactment of the Sarbanes-Oxley Act (SOX) should further encourage such greater scrutiny by directors. Moreover, pursuant to SOX (discussed *supra* § 5.08[B]), the registrant's chief executive officer and chief financial officer must make "certifications" concerning the accuracy of the disclosures made and the efficacy of internal controls with respect to such registrant's Exchange Act periodic SEC filings.[53]

§ 7.07   SHELF REGISTRATION

At this point, you may wish to review the discussion on shelf registration contained in Chapter 5. Generally, Rule 415 governs the registration of securities to be offered and sold on a continuous or delayed basis in the future. Significantly, the rule permits eligible issuers (namely, those offering securities which may be registered on Form S-3 or F-3) to engage in primary at-the-market offerings of equity securities which the issuer expects to offer during the next three years.

The Commission's decision to include equity offerings within Rule 415's scope drew a sharp dissent from then Commissioner Thomas who asserted that the rule should be limited to debt offerings. She argued that Rule 415, when applied to equity offerings,

> (1) jeopardizes the liquidity and stability of our primary and secondary markets by encouraging greater concentration of underwriters, market-makers, and other financial intermediaries and by discouraging individual investor participation in the capital markets thereby furthering the trend toward institutionalization of securities holders, and (2) reduces the quality and timeliness of disclosure available to investors when making their investment decisions. Incurring these risks is antithetical to the statutory duty of the Commission to protect investors and to maintain the integrity of our capital

---

[52] Securities Act Release No. 6231 (1980).

[53] For a discussion of the director signature requirement on the Form 10-K and its potential liability ramifications, see M. Steinberg, Securities Regulation: Liabilities and Remedies § 5.04[3] (2008).

markets.[54]

There is little question that underwriter due diligence concerns are accentuated in the shelf registration setting. In this setting, underwriters assert that they have little, if any, time to perform any meaningful due diligence.[55] Indeed, automatic shelf registration statements for well known seasoned issuers become effective immediately upon filing with the SEC.[56]

The SEC has responded to these concerns by promulgating Rule 176 and by advising potential underwriters to acquire "in advance a reservoir of knowledge" about the issuer. It is arguable, however, that the SEC's position overlooks the manner in which the shelf rule has affected the role of underwriters. First, due to the competitive nature of the shelf registration process, the bargaining position of the underwriter to induce disclosure on the issuer's part has been greatly diminished. Second, potential underwriters have little incentive to develop "in advance a reservoir of knowledge," with its attendant costs, if there is only a possibility that they will be selected.[57]

To date, it appears that underwriters generally have determined how their due diligence functions will be performed in the shelf registration context in a seemingly adequate and cost effective manner. As discussed above, and although not used to the degree once anticipated, one practice is for the subject issuer to designate underwriter's counsel. Pursuant to this designation, counsel, acting on behalf of the prospective underwriter, conducts ongoing due diligence. Although having its shortcomings, this practice provides a means by which continuous due diligence can be conducted by the underwriter's designee. And, of course, it should be kept in mind that the due diligence responsibility remains with the underwriter(s).[58]

---

[54] *See* Securities Act Release No. 6499 (1983).

[55] *See* Ketels, *SEC Rule 415 — The New Experimental Procedures for Shelf Registration*, 10 Sec. Reg. L.J. 318, 335–336 (1982).

[56] *See* Rules 415, 430B; Securities Act Release No. 8591 (2005); *supra* § 5.02[B].

[57] *See generally* Banoff, *Regulatory Subsidies, Efficient Markets, and Shelf Registration: An Analysis of Rule 415*, 70 Va. L. Rev. 135 (1984); Fox, *Shelf Registration, Integrated Disclosure, and Underwriter Due Diligence: An Economic Analysis*, 70 Va. L. Rev. 1005 (1984); Maynard, *Blue Sky Regulation of Rule 415 Shelf-Registered Primary Offerings: The Need for a Limited Form of Federal Preemption*, 22 Ariz. St. L.J. 89 (1990); *supra* note 43 (sources cited therein).

[58] *See supra* notes 47–50 (and accompanying text); *In re WorldCom, Inc. Securities Litigation*, 346 F. Supp. 2d 628 (S.D.N.Y. 2004); Securities Act Release No. 6499 (1983) ("The trend toward appointment of a single law firm to act as underwriters' counsel is a particularly significant development. . . . Registrants appoint the law firm to act as underwriters' counsel either with or without consulting the prospective participating underwriters."); 22 Sec. Reg. & L. Rep. (BNA) 1634 (1990); Frerichs, *Underwriter Due Diligence Within the Integrated Disclosure System — If It Isn't Broken, Don't Fix It*, 16 Sec. Reg. L.J. 386 (1989); Nicholas, *The Integrated Disclosure System and Its Impact Upon Underwriters' Due Diligence: Will Investors Be Protected?*, 11 Sec. Reg. L.J. 3 (1983); Note, *The Impact of the SEC's Shelf Registration Rule on Underwriter's Due Diligence Investigations*; 51 Geo. Wash. L. Rev. 767 (1983); *supra* note 45 (sources cited therein).

§ 7.08   SECTION 12(1) (AS NOW AMENDED SECTION 12(a)(1))

Section 12(1) (as now amended Section 12(a)(1)) of the Securities Act gives teeth to Section 5 by providing the purchaser of securities with an express private right of action against his/her seller if such seller offers or sells a security in violation of Section 5.[59] In an action brought under Section 12, the purchaser may seek rescission or, if he/she no longer owns the securities, damages. Section 12(a)(1) (as well as Section 12(a)(2) discussed in § 7.09) does not provide a plaintiff with a choice of remedies. As stated by the Second Circuit: "If [the] plaintiff owns the stock, he is entitled to rescission but not damages. If [the] plaintiff no longer owns the stock, he is entitled to damages but not rescission."[60]

If a violation of Section 5 has been committed by the seller, the purchaser ordinarily is entitled to recover. In other words, strict liability is imposed against the seller. The exercise of reasonable care or bona fide but unsuccessful efforts to perfect an exemption from registration are irrelevant. Hence, upon the purchaser establishing a prima facie case that the seller violated Section 5, a seller may avoid liability only, for example, by showing that the offering qualifies for an exemption from registration or that the plaintiff is in pari delicto (*see infra* § 8.09). The statute of limitations for Section 12(a)(1) claims is one year.[61]

A key issue under Section 12 is the meaning of the term "seller." Supreme Court and other case law focusing on this question are addressed in § 7.09[B].

§ 7.09   SECTION 12(2) (AS NOW AMENDED SECTION 12(a)(2))

[A]   Overview

Aggrieved purchasers of securities acquired in a public offering by an issuer or its controlling shareholder(s) may seek to invoke Section 12(a)(2) of the Securities Act.[62] Generally, Section 12(2) (as now amended Section 12(a)(2)) affords an express right of action to a purchaser against his/her seller for rescission, or damages if the securities have been disposed of, where the purchaser acquired the securities by means of a prospectus or oral communication (that relates to a prospectus) which contained a material misstatement or half-truth. Proof of reliance is not required. Indeed, to recover under Section 12(a)(2), "a plaintiff need not prove that he ever received the misleading prospectus."[63] Accordingly, Section 12(a)(2)'s terms "do not require that the particular sale to an individual plaintiff directly be by means

---

[59] The definition of "seller" for Section 12 purposes is addressed in § 7.09[B].

[60] *Wigand v. Flo-Tek, Inc.*, 609 F.2d 1028, 1035 (2d Cir. 1979).

[61] *See* Securities Act § 13.

[62] *See Gustafson v. Alloyd Company*, 513 U.S. 561 (1995).

[63] *Sanders v. John Nuveen & Co., Inc.*, 619 F.2d 1222, 1226 (7th Cir. 1980).

of the prospectus alleged to be misleading." Rather, it is sufficient that "the seller sold by means of a misleading prospectus securities of which those purchased by the plaintiff were a part." With respect to oral communications that relate to a prospectus, however, a different result might follow.[64]

Section 12(a)(2) provides the seller with a "quasi due diligence" defense. Once the purchaser has established a prima facie case, the onus is shifted to the seller to establish that he/she did not know, and in the exercise of reasonable care could not have known, of the untruth or omission.

In general terms, a comparison between the Section 12(a)(2) right of action with that provided under Section 11 reveals the following: First, whereas Section 11 only applies to registered offerings, due to the Supreme Court's restrictive decision in *Gustafson v. Alloyd Company*,[65] the Section 12(a)(2) remedy similarly is limited to purchasers of securities in a public offering by an issuer or its controlling shareholder(s). Clearly the remedy is available in registered offerings. Although unclear at the time, *Gustafson* suggests that Section 12(a)(2) also may apply in offerings that take on a public nature but are exempt from Securities Act registration pursuant to Section 3 of that Act. Such offerings may include those public offerings that are state registered but exempt from federal registration pursuant to Regulation A, Rule 144A, Rule 504, Section 3(a)(11) or Rule 147.[66] Prior to the *Gustafson* decision, lower courts uniformly held that Section 12(a)(2) was available in issuer private offerings exempt from registration (such as pursuant to Section 4(2) or Rule 506 of Regulation D);[67] and there existed a split of authority whether the remedy was available in private secondary transactions.[68]

Second, Section 12(a)(2) extends liability only to those who "sold" the securities to the allegedly aggrieved purchasers. On the other hand, Section 11 specifically enumerates those parties who are subject to liability under that provision. In this regard, note that a dealer, although not subject to Section 11 liability, may be liable under Section 12 as a "seller" in a registered offering.[69]

Moreover, in contrast to the specific categories of possible defendants listed in Section 11, Section 12(a)(2) by its terms subjects only "sellers" to potential liability. In this respect, note that underwriters are not necessarily within the reach of Section 12(a)(2). As the Eleventh Circuit has observed: "Since § 12

---

[64] *Id.* at 1226–1227, 1227 n.8.

[65] 513 U.S. 561 (1995).

[66] *See supra* §§ 3.09[B], 3.13 (discussion of exemptions).

[67] *See, e.g., Abell v. Potomac Insurance Company*, 858 F.2d 1104 (5th Cir. 1988).

[68] *Compare Ballay v. Legg Mason Wood Walker, Inc.*, 925 F.2d 682 (3d Cir. 1991) (limiting § 12(2) to initial offerings), *with Pacific Dunlop Holdings, Inc. v. Allen & Co., Inc.*, 993 F.2d 578 (7th Cir. 1993) (holding that § 12(2) extends to secondary transactions). *See generally* Loss, *The Assault on Section 12(2)*, 105 Harv. L. Rev. 908 (1992); Maynard, *Liability Under Section 12(2) of the Securities Act of 1933 for Fraudulent Trading in Post-Distribution Markets*, 32 Wm. & Mary L. Rev. 847 (1991); Weiss, *The Courts Have It Right: Securities Act Section 12(2) Applies Only to Public Offerings*, 48 Bus. Law. 1 (1992).

[69] *See supra* §§ 7.02, 7.04.

does not provide for underwriter liability per se, an underwriter must also be a seller of the security in question to be liable under the section."[70]

Another distinction between Section 11 and Section 12(a)(2) lies in the standard of care defense. Whereas Section 11 establishes an affirmative defense of "reasonable investigation," Section 12(a)(2) provides that the seller exercise "reasonable care." This apparently lower standard of care is consistent with the general notion that sellers of securities may not be intimately involved with the offering and may not have the same access to information as do potential Section 11 defendants. However, as the Seventh Circuit's decision in *Sanders v. John Nuveen & Co., Inc.*[71] indicates, the degree of care to be exercised by sellers who are within the Section 12(a)(2) inner circle may converge with the reasonable investigation standard of Section 11. Nonetheless, the SEC more recently has asserted that "the standard of care under Section 12(a)(2) is less demanding than that prescribed by Section 11, or put another way, that Section 11 requires a more diligent investigation than Section 12(a)(2)."[72]

[B]   The Meaning of "Seller"

Prior to the Supreme Court's decision in *Pinter v. Dahl*,[73] the lower federal courts differed widely as to which parties were regarded as "sellers" under Section 12(a)(2) (as well as under Section 12(a)(1)). While some courts imposed a strict privity requirement,[74] most courts relaxed the privity requirement to some extent. Liability was imposed by a number of courts upon persons as "sellers" for being integrally connected with, or substantially involved in, the transaction.[75]

The Supreme Court in *Pinter* rejected both of the above approaches. While the decision expressly dealt with the definition of "seller" under Section 12(a)(1), lower federal courts overwhelmingly have applied the holding to cases arising under Section 12(a)(2).[76]

In *Pinter*, the Supreme Court construed the term "sell" to encompass those persons who engage in "solicitation" of the buyer. Upon examining the language and purpose of Section 12(a)(1), the Court thereupon defined "seller" under that provision as extending to one "who successfully solicits the

---

[70] *Foster v. Jessup and Lamont Securities Co., Inc.*, 759 F.2d 838, 845 (11th Cir. 1985).

[71] 619 F.2d 1222 (7th Cir. 1980).

[72] Securities Act Release No. 8591 (2005).

[73] 486 U.S. 622 (1988).

[74] *See, e.g., Collins v. Signetics Corp.*, 605 F.2d 110 (3d Cir. 1979); *McFarland v. Memorex Corp.*, 493 F. Supp. 631 (N.D. Cal. 1980). *See generally* Abrams, *The Scope of Liability Under Section 12 of the Securities Act of 1933: "Participation" and the Pertinent Legislative Materials*, 15 Fordham Urban L.J. 877 (1987).

[75] *See, e.g., Davis v. Avco Financial Services, Inc.*, 739 F.2d 1057 (6th Cir. 1984); *Croy v. Campbell*, 624 F.2d 709 (5th Cir. 1980). *See generally* O'Hara, *Erosion of the Privity Requirement in Section 12(2) of the Securities Act of 1933: The Expanded Meaning of Seller*, 31 UCLA L. Rev. 921 (1984).

[76] *See, e.g., Moore v. Kayport Package Express, Inc.*, 885 F.2d 531, 536 (9th Cir. 1989).

purchase, motivated at least in part by a desire to serve his own financial interests or those of the securities owner."[77] Therefore, under Section 12, one may not recover against his/her seller's seller. As the Court stated, "liability under Section 12 is imposed "on only the buyer's immediate seller; remote purchasers are precluded from bringing actions against remote sellers. Thus, a buyer cannot recover against his seller's seller. . . . "[78] Accordingly, for purposes of Section 12, a "seller" includes: (1) one who owned the security sold to the purchaser, (2) an agent for a vendor (such as a broker) who successfully solicited the purchase, (3) one who solicited the purchase with the intent to personally benefit thereby, and (4) one who, without financial benefit to oneself, solicited the purchase with the motivation to serve the owner's financial interests.[79]

The *Pinter* Court's construction of "seller" permits at least two groups of "participants" to avoid Section 12 liability. First, those persons who gratuitously provide advice on investment matters to friends, family members, and acquaintances are not "sellers" so long as they are not motivated by a desire to benefit the securities owner or themselves. Second, professionals, such as accountants and lawyers, whose involvement is solely the performance of their professional services (*e.g.*, counsel drafting the offering document for the issuer-client), are not "sellers."[80]

Significantly, in its 2005 offering rule amendments, the SEC enunciated that an issuer in a registered primary offering as well as an issuer that provides a statutory or a free writing prospectus is deemed a seller for purposes of Section 12.[81] The SEC's position is contrary to some case law.[82] In the 2005 Release, the Commission stated:

> When an issuer registers securities to be sold in a primary offering, the registration covers the offer and sale of its securities to the public. The issuer is selling its securities to the public, although the form of underwriting of such offering, such as a firm commitment underwriting, may involve the sale first by the issuer to the underwriter and then

---

[77] 486 U.S. at 622.

[78] *Id.* at 644 n.21.

[79] Note, moreover, pursuant to SEC rule, an issuer in a registered primary offering is deemed a "seller" under Section 12 as is an issuer that provides a free writing prospectus. *See* Rule 159A; Securities Act Release No. 8591 (2005); discussion *supra* § 4.02[C][2]. The SEC's position is contrary to some case law. *See, e.g., Lone Star Ladies Investment Club v. Schlotzky's, Inc.* 238 F.3d 363, 370 (5th Cir. 2001).

[80] 486 U.S. at 651; *see Wilson v. Saintine Exploration and Drilling Corporation*, 872 F.2d 1124 (2d Cir. 1989); *see also Junker v. Crory*, 650 F.2d 1349 (5th Cir. 1981) (attorney, whose participation was a substantial factor in causing the transaction to take place, deemed a seller for § 12(2) purposes). *See generally* Klock, *Promoter Liability and In Pari Delicto Under Section 12(1): Pinter v. Dahl*, 17 Sec. Reg. L.J. 53 (1989); Prentice, *Section 12 of the 1933 Act: Establishing the Statutory Seller*, 40 Alabama L. Rev. 417 (1989).

[81] Securities Act Release No. 8591 (2005).

[82] *See, e.g., Lone Star Ladies Investment Club v. Schlotsky's Inc.*, 238 F.3d 363, 370 (5th Cir. 2001) (holding that "in a firm commitment underwriting, such as this one, the public cannot ordinarily hold the issuer liable under section 12, because the public does not purchase from the issuer").

the sale by the underwriter to the public. We believe that an issuer offering or selling its securities in a registered offering pursuant to a registration statement containing a prospectus that it has prepared and filed, or by means of other communications that are offers made by or on behalf of or used or referred to by the issuer can be viewed as soliciting purchases of the issuer's registered securities. Therefore, we are adopting a rule providing that under Section 12(a)(2) an issuer in a primary offering of securities [who uses a statutory or a free writing prospectus], regardless of the form of the underwriting arrangement, will be a seller and will be considered to offer or sell the securities to a purchaser in the initial distribution of the securities. . . .[83]

[C]   Secondary Liability

Prior to the Supreme Court's decision in *Central Bank of Denver v. First Interstate Bank of Denver*,[84] a few lower courts recognized secondary liability under Section 12(a)(2) based upon an aiding and abetting rationale.[85] The majority of courts, however, rejected such secondary liability as inappropriate.[86] As discussed in § 9.01, due to the Supreme Court's 1994 decision in *Central Bank of Denver*, it is clear today that liability under Section 12(2) is precluded when premised on such theories as aiding and abetting and conspiracy.[87]

[D]   Limited to Public Offerings

As discussed in § 7.09[A], prior to the Supreme Court's decision in *Gustafson v. Alloyd Company*,[88] a split of authority existed in the lower courts as to whether Section 12(a)(2) could be used by purchasers in the secondary trading context.[89] Confining Section 12(a)(2)'s scope, the *Gustafson* Court limited the provision's application to public offerings by issuers or their controlling shareholders.[90] The consequence is that Section 12(a)(2) may be invoked only by purchasers in registered offerings under the 1933 Act and perhaps by purchasers in Section 3 exempt offerings provided that such

---

[83] Securities Act Release No. 8591 (2005) (also stating that "the Rule, as adopted, will not cover purchasers of the issuer's securities in the aftermarket"); *see* Rule 159A; Gail, *Uncertain Future: Liability Concerns Surrounding the Application of Section 12(a)(2) of the Securities Act of 1933 to Free-Writing Prospectuses After the Enactment of the SEC's Recently Reformed Offering Rules*, 60 SMU L. Rev. 609 (2007).

[84] 511 U.S. 164 (1994).

[85] *See, e.g., In re Caesars Palace Securities Litigation*, 360 F. Supp. 366 (S.D.N.Y. 1973).

[86] *See, e.g., Davis v. Avco Financial Services*, 739 F.2d 1067 (6th Cir. 1984).

[87] *See infra* §§ 10.01–10.02. *See generally* Steinberg, *The Ramifications of Recent U.S. Supreme Court Decisions on Federal and State Securities Regulation*, 70 Notre Dame L. Rev. 489 (1995).

[88] 513 U.S. 561 (1995).

[89] *See supra* note 68 (and accompanying text).

[90] *See* 513 U.S. at 584.

exempt offerings take on a public nature (such as certain offerings conducted pursuant to Rule 144A, Rule 504, Regulation A, or Section 3(a)(11)/Rule 147).[91]

In light of *Gustafson*, Section 12(a)(2) does not extend to secondary transactions (other than public offerings by controlling shareholders). Moreover, the decision makes clear that materially misleading offering documents used in private placements (such as pursuant to the Section 4(2) or Rule 506 exemption) are not within the reach of Section 12(a)(2). Although this latter position may be viewed as dicta, the Court's language and analysis poignantly reflect this result.[92]

The key to the Court's decision was its interpretation of the term "prospectus" as contained in Section 12(a)(2). Although Section 12(a)(2) also provides a remedy based on an actionable "oral communication," such oral communication must relate to a prospectus.[93] Construing the term "prospectus," the Court examined three sections of the Securities Act — Sections 2(a)(10), 10, and 12(a)(2)—in an effort to give the term a consistent meaning throughout the 1933 Act. Focusing on Section 10 which confines the definition of "prospectus" to "public offerings by an issuer or its controlling shareholders," the Court concluded that this definition also applies to Section 12(a)(2). Turning to the definition of "prospectus" contained in Section 2(a)(10), the Court likewise found that "the definitional part of [that] statute must be read in its entirety, a reading which yields the interpretation that the term prospectus refers to a document soliciting the public to acquire securities."[94]

To sum up this important decision, the *Gustafson* Court held that, in defining the term "prospectus," Section 12(a)(2) applies only to public offerings. The Court's language leaves some question whether Section 12(a)(2) is confined to registered offerings or whether its reach also extends to offerings that otherwise would require registration but for the presence of an exemption under Section 3 of the Securities Act (such as a state registered offering where the Rule 147 exemption applies). Under this latter approach, an offering document conveyed to prospective purchasers pursuant to an exempt

---

[91] As stated by one court:

> The line between public offerings and private placements is neither well-defined nor easily decipherable. Even after *Gustafson*, this distinction remains hotly debated by the plaintiffs' and defendants' bars, and has not been entirely resolved by the courts. Ultimately the question is one of fact and demands an inquiry into factors such as the marketing strategies employed, the scope of the Offering and the 'sophistication' of the offerees. . . .

AAL High Yield Bond Fund v. Ruttenberg, C.A. No. 00-C-1404-S at 15–16 (S.D.N.Y. 2001), *quoted in*, Bodner & Welsh, *Institutional Buyer Beware: Recent Decisions Reinforce Narrow Range of Remedies Available to QIBs in Rule 144A Offerings*, 36 Sec. Reg. & L. Rep. (BNA) 1728, 1730 (2004); *see In re Enron Corp. Securities, Derivative & ERISA Litigation*, 310 F. Supp. 2d 819, 861–866, (S.D.N.Y. 2004), *rev'd on other grounds*, 482 F.3d 372 (5th Cir. 2007); *supra* notes 65–68 (and accompanying text).

[92] *See* 513 U.S. at 579–588.

[93] *Id.* at 567–569.

[94] *Id.* at 581–586. Note that the SEC defines a "free writing prospectus" as coming within the term "prospectus" under Section 12(a)(2). *See* Rules 164, 433; Securities Act Release No. 8591; *supra* § 4.02[C][2].

offering that takes on a public nature would be defined as a "prospectus," thereby triggering Section 12(a)(2) availability. In any event, *Gustafson* evidently precludes application of the Section 12(a)(2) right of action for private initial (*e.g.*, Rule 506) offerings as well as secondary (*e.g.*, § 4(1)) transactions.[95]

[E]   The Reasonable Care Defense

Under Section 12(a)(2), the defendant can avoid liability by showing that he/she did not know, and in the exercise of reasonable care could not have known, of the material misstatement or omission. Whether this standard imposes Section 11-type due diligence obligations has been met with mixed reaction.

In defining the meaning of "reasonable care" under Section 12(a)(2), it is important to distinguish the responsibilities of a so-called traditional underwriter from those of a "mere" seller. For example, to require a "seller" in a Rule 504 offering for $700,000 to comply with Section 11 due diligence would arguably impose too harsh a standard. Moreover, in many such offerings, the subject person neither may have the bargaining position to carry out a Section 11-type due diligence investigation nor be intimately involved in the preparation of the prospectus.

On the other hand, where an unregistered offering has many of the characteristics frequently associated with an offering that must be registered (and hence triggers Section 12(a)(2) application even after *Gustafson*), "the standard of 'reasonable care' under Section 12(a)(2) may converge with the standard of 'reasonable investigation' prescribed under Section 11."[96] For example, in *Sanders v. John Nuveen & Co.*,[97] the Seventh Circuit held an underwriter liable under Section 12(a)(2) for failing to make a reasonable investigation. Although stating that it is far from clear that Congress intended to impose a more rigorous standard of care under Section 11 than under Section 12(a)(2), the court also opined: "Since what constitutes reasonable care under § 12(2) depends upon the circumstances, we, of course, do not intimate that the duty of a seller under § 12(2) is always the same as that of an

---

[95] *See Vannest v. Sage Rutty & Co.*, Inc., 960 F. Supp. 651 (W.D.N.Y. 1997) (holding that § 12(2) per *Gustafson* does not extend to Rule 506 private offering); *supra* note 91 (sources cited therein). For further analysis, see Bainbridge, *Securities Act Section 12(2) After the* Gustafson *Debacle*, 50 Bus. Law. 1231 (1995); Fiflis, Gustafson v. Alloyd Co., Inc.: *Judicial vs. Legislative Power*, 23 Sec. Reg. L.J. 423 (1996); Kerr, Ralston *Redux: Determining Which Section 3 Offerings Are Public Under Section 12(2) After* Gustafson, 50 SMU L. Rev. 175 (1996); Maynard, *The Impact of* Gustafson *and Its Methodology*, 24 Sec. Reg. L.J. 61 (1996); Thel, *Section 12(2) of the Securities Act: Does Old Legislation Matter?*, 63 Fordham L. Rev. 1183 (1995); Weiss, *Securities Act Section 12(2) After* Gustafson v. Alloyd Co.: *What Questions Remain?*, 50 Bus. Law. 1209 (1995); *supra* notes 88–94 (and accompanying text).

[96] Brief of the Solicitor General, pp. 7–8, *in Sanders v. John Nuveen & Co.*, 619 F.2d 1229 (7th Cir. 1980), *cert. denied* 450 U.S. 1005 (1981) (urging the Supreme Court to deny the petition for a writ of certiorari); *see In re Software Toolworks Inc. Securities Litigation*, 38 F.3d 1078 (9th Cir. 1994).

[97] 619 F.2d 1222 (7th Cir. 1980).

underwriter in a registration offering under § 11."[98] In sum, under the circumstances at bar, the Seventh Circuit held that Section 12(a)(2)'s reasonable care standard required a reasonable investigation. More recently, on the other hand, the SEC expressed its belief "that the standard of care under Section 12(a)(2) is less demanding than that prescribed by Section 11 or, put another way, that Section 11 requires a more diligent investigation than Section 12(a)(2)."[99]

In a dissent from the denial of certiorari in *Sanders*, two Supreme Court Justices expressed concern that the Seventh Circuit's decision would "be read as recognizing no distinction between the standards of care applicable under §§ 11 and (12)(2), and particularly as casting doubt upon the reasonableness of relying upon the expertise of certified public accountants."[100] Indeed, perhaps the most troubling aspect of the Seventh Circuit's analysis is that, by stating that the underwriter should have examined the company's audited financial statements, the lower court evidently required a higher investigative standard under Section 12(a)(2) than under Section 11. As stated in the dissent:

> Even under § 11 of the Act, an underwriter is explicitly absolved of the duty to investigate with respect to "any part of the registration statement purporting to be made on the authority of an expert" such as a certified accountant if "he had no reasonable ground to believe and did not believe" that the information therein was misleading. This provision is in the Act because, almost by definition, it is reasonable to rely on financial statements certified by public accountants. Yet, in this case, the Court of Appeals nevertheless seems to have imposed the higher duty prescribed by § 11 to investigate, but denied petitioner the right to rely on "the authority of an expert" that also is provided by § 11.[101]

Sanders, although an important case, should not be read, particularly in view of the Supreme Court's dissenters and the SEC's 2005 pronouncement,[102] as requiring underwriters to undertake independent financial investigations. Rather, as in Section 11, such persons should be entitled to rely, absent reason otherwise, on the accuracy of the issuer's audited financial statements. Nonetheless, the decision is significant because it conveys that underwriters of unregistered offerings (that are public in nature and thereby trigger Section 12(a)(2) application even after *Gustafson*) have substantial responsibilities in complying with the "reasonable care" obligation contained in Section 12(a)(2).[103]

---

[98] *Id.* at 1228.

[99] Securities Act Release No. 8591 (2005).

[100] 450 U.S. 1005 (Powell, J., dissenting).

[101] *Id.* at 1009–1010.

[102] *See* Securities Act Release No. 8591 (2005); *supra* note 99 (and accompanying text).

[103] *See generally* Comment, *"Reasonable Care" in Section 12(a)(2) of the Securities Act of 1933*, 48 U. Chi. L. Rev. 372 (1981).

In another case, the Sixth Circuit set forth the following factors in assessing the seller's "reasonable care" defense:

> We believe that the following considerations are pertinent to an analysis of whether a § 12(2) seller has established this affirmative defense [of reasonable care]: (1) the quantum of decisional (planning) and facilitative (promotional) participation, such as designing the deal and contacting and attempting to persuade potential purchasers, (2) access to source data against which the truth or falsity of representations can be tested, (3) relative skill in ferreting out the truth (for example, in this case [the seller's] manager had comparatively greater skill in evaluating judgments based on subsidiary facts, since he performed a similar function in the process of investigating the creditworthiness of borrowers), (4) pecuniary interest in the completion of the transaction, and (5) the existence of a relationship of trust and confidence between the plaintiff and the alleged "seller." These are the circumstances that determine whether a person has exercised due care in this context.[104]

[F]   Indemnification and Contribution

As a general statement, the vast majority of courts refuse to imply a right of action for either contribution or indemnification under Section 12(a)(2) of the Securities Act.[105] The Supreme Court thus far has not resolved this issue but its decision in *Musick, Peeler & Garrett v. Employers Insurance of Wausau*[106] (discussed in § 8.11) strongly points to the denial of this right of action as do other Supreme Court decisions to a lesser degree.[107]

The leading federal appellate court decision is *Baker Watts & Co. v. Miles & Stockbridge*.[108] There, the court reasoned:

---

[104] *Davis v. Avco Financial Services, Inc.*, 739 F.2d 1057, 1068 (6th Cir. 1984); *see Ambrosino v. Rodman & Renshaw, Inc.*, [1992 Transfer Binder] Fed. Sec. L. Rep. (CCH) ¶ 96,969 (7th Cir. 1992) (although not conclusive, court found relevant that the defendant's "exercise of due diligence had been higher than the custom and practice of the industry at that time"); *Dennis v. General Imaging, Inc.*, 918 F.2d 496, 505 (5th Cir. 1990) (citations omitted) ("While the exact requirements of this duty depend on the nature of the relationship of the seller at issue to his buyer, federal courts agree that a showing by the seller that he made reasonable inquiries into the possibility of fraud of the issuer and discovered nothing wrong or that no fraud could be discovered by the exercise of reasonable care, warrants a denial of liability."). *See generally* Maynard, *The Affirmative Defense of Reasonable Care Under Section 12(2) of the Securities Act of 1933*, 64 Notre Dame L. Rev. 57 (1993).

[105] These decisions, for example, include: *Baker, Watts & Company v. Miles & Stockbridge*, 876 F.2d 1101 (4th Cir. 1989); *In re Professional Financial Management*, 683 F. Supp. 1283 (D. Minn. 1988); *In re Olympia Brewing Company Securities Litigation*, 674 F. Supp. 597 (N.D. Ill. 1987).

[106] 508 U.S. 286 (1993).

[107] *See, e.g., Stoneridge Investment Partners LLC v. Scientific-Atlanta, Inc.*, 128 S. Ct. 761 (2008); *Gustafson v. Alloyd Company*, 513 U.S. 561 (1995); *Central Bank of Denver v. First Interstate Bank of Denver*, 511 U.S. 164 (1994).

[108] 876 F.2d 1101 (4th Cir. 1989).

First, [Section 12(2)] itself does not create such remedies [of contribution and indemnification]. Indeed, the statute's protection extends to investors who purchase securities based on misleading statements of material fact; it is not solicitous of unsuccessful defendants in a federal securities action. . . .

Second, the 1933 Act's legislative history and the structure of the federal securities laws do not suggest the recognition of implied rights of contribution and indemnification. There is no indication in the 1933 Act's legislative history, for example, of any congressional intent to create these remedies in § 12(2). This fact, combined with the plain language of the statute, "reinforces our decision not to find such . . . right[s] of action implicit within the section." . . . Moreover, § 11(f) of the 1933 Act and §§ 9(e) and 18(b) of the Securities Exchange Act of 1934 expressly provide rights to contribution in specific circumstances. Congress knows how to define such a right of action in the federal securities laws, and we infer a lack of congressional intent to do so when the particular provision at issue is silent as to the existence of such a remedy. . . .

Third, the underlying purpose of the 1933 Act is "regulatory rather than compensatory." . . . Negligence in the preparation of a securities prospectus was made actionable under § 12(2) of the 1933 Act in order to promote careful adherence to the requirements of the statute. . . . In particular, a right of action for indemnification would frustrate the statute's goal of encouraging diligence and discouraging negligence in securities transactions. An unsuccessful defendant in a federal securities action therefore cannot "escape loss by shifting his entire responsibility to another party." . . .

In sum, we agree with the district court that Congress clearly did not provide private rights of action for contribution or indemnification in § 12(2). . . .[109]

[G]   Affirmative Defense of Section 12(b)

The Private Securities Litigation Reform Act of 1995 amended Section 12 of the Securities Act by adding a new subsection (Section 12(b)). Section 12(b) provides that in actions brought under Section 12(a)(2) a defendant may avoid all or part of the damages that otherwise would be incurred by proving that all or part of the depreciation in the value of the securities in question resulted from factors unrelated to the material misstatement(s) or half-truth(s) that were contained in the prospectus or related oral communications.

---

[109] *Id.* at 1105–1106.

Ch. 7   APPENDIX

DUE DILIGENCE CHECKLIST
(PUBLIC OFFERING)

		PROVIDED	NONE	NOT APPLICABLE (SET FORTH REASON)
1.	Articles of Incorporation for the Company and its subsidiaries, as amended	_____	_____	_____
2.	Bylaws of the Company and its subsidiaries, as amended	_____	_____	_____
3.	Minutes of all Board of Directors and Committee Meetings for the Company and its subsidiaries	_____	_____	_____
4.	Minutes of all Stockholders' Meetings for the Company and its subsidiaries	_____	_____	_____
5.	Copies of reports, proxy statements, registration statements and similar documents filed with the Securities and Exchange Commission and state securities commissions, together with related correspondence	_____	_____	_____
6.	Registration rights agreements with respect to any shares of capital stock or warrants to purchase such shares	_____	_____	_____
7.	All other agreements relating to securities of the Company or any of its subsidiaries, including agreements and investment agreements, stock transfer restriction agreements, voting trusts, or any other such agreements	_____	_____	_____

		PROVIDED	NONE	NOT APPLICABLE (SET FORTH REASON)
8.	Any agreements with regulatory authorities, including any state securities commissions or commissioners, regarding issuance of shares of capital stock of the Company	_____	_____	_____
9.	Any statements of the Board of Directors designating preferences, rights, etc., of any class or series of preferred stock	_____	_____	_____
10.	Schedule of all entities in which the Company owns any outstanding voting securities	_____	_____	_____
11.	List of all offices of the Company and its subsidiaries where the Company and its subsidiaries carry on a material amount of business	_____	_____	_____
12.	List of all offices of the Company and its subsidiaries and the states or other jurisdictions where the Company and its subsidiaries carry on a material amount of business	_____	_____	_____
13.	List and brief description of all material domestic and foreign governmental permits, licenses and approvals held by the Company and its subsidiaries, including those issued by customs authorities	_____	_____	_____

	PROVIDED	NONE	NOT APPLICABLE (SET FORTH REASON)

14. Any employee benefit plans or agreements, stock bonus, profit sharing, stock option, stock purchase, savings or retirement plans or agreements, and all collective bargaining, labor, employment or consulting contracts to which the Company or any of its subsidiaries is a party other than those otherwise called for herein _____ _____ _____

15. Employment Agreements between the company and key employees, together with amendments thereto _____ _____ _____

16. Any partnership or joint venture agreements to which the Company or any of its subsidiaries is a party _____ _____ _____

17. All debentures, notes, loans, lines of credit or revolving credit agreements, both secured and unsecured, mortgages, deeds of trust, security agreements, and other documents relating to indebtedness of the Company not otherwise called for herein _____ _____ _____

18. All guarantees by the Company or any of its subsidiaries of the indebtedness of others _____ _____ _____

19. A brief description of the Company's insurance programs and policies (including keyman life insurance), together with any legal documents pertaining thereto and a list of claims against such insurance program currently pending _____ _____ _____

20. Form of any standard contracts used with Company employees _____ _____ _____

	PROVIDED	NONE	NOT APPLICABLE (SET FORTH REASON)
21. Schedule of all loans and advances outstanding in the last three years (other than routine travel and business expense advances) by the Company or any subsidiary to any officer or director of the Company or any subsidiaries	_____	_____	_____
22. All leases, options to lease or purchase, or purchase contracts relating to real property	_____	_____	_____
23. All material contracts, agreements, notes, or leases not otherwise called for herein to which the Company, its subsidiaries or any of their respective businesses, including any tax sharing agreements with any party	_____	_____	_____
24. List of major vendors/suppliers	_____	_____	_____
25. A schedule of all pending or threatened legal, administrative, arbitrative or other proceedings or governmental investigations pending or threatened against the Company or any other party which might result in (a) damages payable by the Company or any of its subsidiaries, (b) a permanent injunction against the Company or any of its subsidiaries, (c) a material deterioration of the business prospects of the Company and its subsidiaries, taken as a whole, or (d) a change in zoning or building ordinances materially affecting the property or leasehold interests of the Company or any of its subsidiaries:			
(i) parties;	_____	_____	_____
(ii) nature of the proceedings;	_____	_____	_____
(iii) date commenced; and	_____	_____	_____

		PROVIDED	NONE	NOT APPLICABLE (SET FORTH REASON)
(iv)	amount of damages or other relief sought	_____	____	_____
26.	Reports of independent certified public accountants relating to management and accounting procedures of the Company ("management letters")	_____	____	_____
27.	Attorneys' responses to auditor's letters of inquiry relating to the Company	_____	____	_____
28.	All news or press releases of the Company or any of its subsidiaries for the past year	_____	____	_____
29.	A schedule describing any ongoing tax disputes, and copies of revenue agents' reports and correspondence respecting federal or state tax proceedings involving open years or items	_____	____	_____
30.	Copies of any speeches delivered by any officer or director of the Company to securities or financial organizations	_____	____	_____
31.	Copies of any articles published in any financial periodical or newsletter concerning the Company or any of its subsidiaries	_____	____	_____
32.	List and brief description of all trademarks, trade names, copyrights, patents and other similar proprietary rights owned by, or used in the business of, the Company or any of its subsidiaries and all registrations relating thereto	_____	____	_____

	PROVIDED	NONE	NOT APPLICABLE (SET FORTH REASON)
33. Agreements, letters of intent and other documents relating to any pending sales or dispositions of any material portions of the Company's assets			

Chapter 8

SECTION 10(b) AND RELATED ISSUES

§ 8.01 OVERVIEW

This chapter explores developments under Section 10(b) of the Securities Exchange Act and Rule 10b-5 promulgated thereunder by the SEC (as well as certain related issues). Generally, the antifraud provisions of the securities acts were designed to protect investors, to help ensure fair dealing in the securities markets, and to promote ethical business practices. Consistent with these objectives, Section 10(b) makes it unlawful to employ deceptive or manipulative devices "in connection with the purchase or sale of any security." As enacted by Congress, Section 10(b) was designed to be a "catch-all" provision and, as such, it encompasses a broad range of practices in connection with the purchase or sale of any security, irrespective of whether such security is publicly traded.[1]

The language of Section 10(b) does not create an express private remedy for its violation. Neither does the legislative history reveal that Congress intended to create a private right of action under the statute at the time of its passage. Nonetheless, the federal courts have routinely recognized the existence of a private remedy under Section 10(b). As the Supreme Court has recognized, "[t]he existence of this implied remedy is simply beyond peradventure."[2]

In order to establish a successful claim under Section 10(b), a plaintiff must prove certain elements. Many of these elements are explored in depth in this Chapter. These elements include that the plaintiff must (by proof of the preponderance of the evidence):

(1) Establish the *requisite jurisdictional means*. This requirement is normally met without difficulty. For example, as one appellate court has pointed out, "proof of intrastate telephonic messages in connection with the employment of deceptive devices or contrivances is sufficient to confer jurisdiction in a Section 10(b) and Rule 10b-5 action."[3]

(2) Have the status as a *purchaser or seller* of the securities. Note that the defendant need not be a purchaser or seller.[4]

---

[1] *See* A. Bromberg & L. Lowenfels, Securities Fraud & Commodities Fraud (2d ed. 2008).

[2] *Herman & MacLean v. Huddleston*, 459 U.S. 375, 380 (1983).

[3] *Loveridge v. Dreagoux*, 678 F.2d 870, 874 (10th Cir. 1982).

[4] *See Blue Chip Stamps v. Manor Drug Stores*, 421 U.S. 462 (1977); *accord The Wharf (Holdings) Limited v. United International Holdings, Inc.* 532 U.S. 588 (2001); *infra* § 8.02.

(3) Prove *"manipulation" or "deception"* and not "merely" breach of fiduciary duty.[5]

(4) Show that a misstatement or nondisclosure of fact is *material*, signifying that a reasonable investor would consider such information important in making an investment decision. The investor need not show that the misstatement or nondisclosure, if accurately disclosed, would have changed the investment decision. Hence, to satisfy the materiality requirement, "there must be a substantial likelihood that the disclosure of the omitted fact would have been viewed by the reasonable investor as having significantly altered the 'total mix' of information made available."[6] Moreover, in the merger context as well as other situations involving uncertain events, the probability/ magnitude standard has been applied. Under this standard, the existence of materiality depends "at any given time upon a balancing of both the indicated probability that the event will occur and the anticipated magnitude of the event in light of the totality of the company activity."[7]

(5) Establish that the defendant acted with *"scienter,"* signifying knowing or intentional misconduct.[8]

(6) Where called for, show that the plaintiff *relied* on the alleged misrepresentation and exercised *due diligence*.[9]

(7) Establish *causation* between the defendant's wrongful conduct and the plaintiff's loss.[10]

---

[5] *See Santa Fe Industries, Inc. v. Green*, 430 U.S. 462 (1977); *infra* § 8.05.

[6] *Basic, Inc. v. Levinson*, 485 U.S. 224, 232 (1988) (quoting *TSC Industries, Inc. v. Northway, Inc.*, 426 U.S. 438, 449 (1976)).

[7] *SEC v. Texas Gulf Sulphur Co.*, 402 F.2d 833, 849 (2d Cir.) (en banc), *quoted in Basic, Inc. v. Levinson*, 485 U.S. 224, 238 (1988); *see also* SEC Staff Accounting Bulletin No. 99, 64 Fed. Reg. 45150 (1999) (opining that "exclusive reliance on certain quantitative benchmarks to assess materiality in preparing financial statements and performing audits of those financial statements is inappropriate"); *supra* § 5.07.

[8] *See Aaron v. SEC*, 446 U.S. 680 (1980); *Ernst & Ernst v. Hochfelder*, 425 U.S. 185 (1976); *infra* § 8.03.

[9] *See Basic, Inc. v. Levinson*, 485 U.S. 224 (1988); *Affiliated Ute Citizens v. United States*, 406 U.S. 128 (1972); *Brown v. E.F. Hutton Group, Inc.*, 991 F.2d 1020 (2d Cir. 1993); § 8.06 *infra*.

[10] *See Dura Pharmaceuticals, Inc. v. Broudo*, 544 U.S. 336 (2005). Section 21D(b)(4) of the Exchange Act expressly provides that the plaintiff must prove loss causation in any private action arising under the Exchange Act. *See generally* Fox, *Understanding* Dura, 60 Bus. Law. 1547 (2005); Kaufman, *Loss Causation Revisited*, 32 Sec. Reg. L.J. 357 (2004). In *Dura*, the Supreme Court held that plaintiffs in an action seeking damages under Section 10(b) must "allege and prove the traditional elements of causation and loss." 544 U.S. at 346. The Court reasoned:

[A]s a matter of pure logic, at the moment the transaction takes place, the plaintiff has suffered no loss; the inflated purchase payment is offset by ownership of a share that *at that instant* possesses equivalent value. Moreover, the logical link between the inflated share purchase price and any later economic loss is not invariably strong. Shares are normally purchased with an eye toward a later sale. But if, say, the purchaser sells the shares quickly before the relevant truth begins to leak out, the misrepresentation will not have led to any loss. If the purchaser sells later after the truth makes its way into the

(8) Related to the causation requirement, prove that the manipulative or deceptive practice was *"in connection with"* the purchase or sale of a security. Generally, in order to meet this requirement, the proscribed conduct must touch upon and be integral to the purchase or sale of the security.[11]

(9) Where liability is based upon *silence*, establish that the alleged primary violator had a *duty to disclose*.[12]

(10) Prove the extent of *damages* suffered.[13]

In addition, the plaintiff must bring its action within the applicable *statute of limitations* which is two years after the violation was (or, pursuant to the prevailing view, should have been) discovered by the plaintiff and in no event more than five years after the violation.[14]

Note moreover that the plaintiff also *must plead fraud with particularity* in its Section 10(b) cause of action. Rule 9(b) of the Federal Rules of Civil Procedure provides: "In all averments of fraud or mistake, the circumstances constituting fraud or mistake shall be stated with particularity. Malice, intent, knowledge, and other condition of mind of a person may be averred gener-

---

marketplace, an initially inflated purchase price *might* mean a later loss. But that is far from inevitably so. When the purchaser subsequently resells such shares, even at a lower price, that lower price may reflect, not the earlier misrepresentation, but changed economic circumstances, changed investor expectations, new industry-specific or firm-specific facts, conditions, or other events, which taken separately or together, account for some or all of that lower price. . . .

Given the tangle of factors affecting price, . . . logic alone permits us to say that the higher purchase price will *sometimes* play a role in bringing about a future loss. . . . [I]n that sense, one might say that the inflated purchase price suggests that the misrepresentation . . . "touches upon" a later economic loss. But, even if that is so, it is insufficient. To "touch upon" a loss is not to *cause* a loss, and it is the latter that the law requires.

Id. at 342–343 (emphasis in original). For decisions after *Dura*, see, for example, *In re Gilead Sciences Securities Litigation*, 536 F.3d 1049 (9th Cir. 2008); *McCabe v. Ernst & Young, LLP*, 494 F.3d 418 (3d Cir. 2007); *Oscar Private Equity Investments v. Allegiance Telecom, Inc.*, 487 F.3d 261 (5th Cir. 2007); *Teachers Retirement System of Louisiana v. Hunter*, 477 F.3d 162 (4th Cir. 2007). *See generally* Fry, *Pleading and Proving Loss Causation in Fraud-On-The-Market-Based Securities Suits Post-Dura Pharmaceuticals*, 36 Sec. Reg. L.J. 31 (2008).

[11] *See SEC v. Zandford*, 535 U.S. 813 (2002) (holding that because "the SEC complaint describes a fraudulent scheme in which the securities transactions and breaches of fiduciary duty coincide . . . those breaches were therefore 'in connection with' securities sales within the meaning of § 10(b)"); *Superintendent of Life Insurance v. Bankers Life and Casualty Co.*, 404 U.S. 6 (1971); *In re Carter-Wallace, Inc. Securities Litigation*, 150 F.3d 153 (2d Cir. 1998); Black, *The Second Circuit's Approach to the "In Connection With" Requirement of Rule 10b-5*, 53 Brooklyn L. Rev. 539 (1987); Fletcher, *The "In Connection With" Requirement of Rule 10b-5*, 16 Pepperdine L. Rev. 913 (1989).

[12] *See Chiarella v. United States*, 445 U.S. 222 (1980) (discussed in Chapter 12).

[13] *See* M. Kaufman, Securities Litigation: Damages (1989 & Supp.); Thompson, *The Measure of Recovery Under Rule 10b-5: A Restitution Alternative to Tort Damages*, 37 Vand. L. Rev. 349 (1984); *infra* § 8.09.

[14] *See* 28 U.S.C. § 1658(b) (as enacted pursuant to § 804 of the Sarbanes-Oxley Act); *infra* § 8.08.

ally."[15] As applied in the Section 10(b) securities law context, Section 21D(b) of the Securities Exchange Act generally requires that a plaintiff must specifically plead each alleged misrepresentation or nondisclosure and why such is misleading, and must allege specific facts as to each such disclosure deficiency supporting a "strong inference" that the subject defendant knew that the misstatement or omission was false.[16]

Also, as will be discussed in Chapter 10, only primary violators are liable in private actions under Section 10(b). In *Central Bank of Denver v. First Interstate Bank of Denver*, the Supreme Court held that in private actions Section 10(b) liability may not be imposed against aiders and abettors. Nonetheless, the SEC may institute enforcement actions against aiders and abettors for alleged violations of Section 10(b).[17]

The *defendant* may assert a number of *defenses*, including *in pari delicto*, *laches*, and *waiver*. The *in pari delicto* defense is addressed later in the chapter.[18]

With respect to a subject defendant's claim for *indemnification*, because the Supreme Court has ruled that scienter (*e.g.*, deliberate or perhaps reckless misconduct) is required to state a successful Section 10(b) (and Rule 10b-5) claim under the Exchange Act,[19] it appears that indemnification would frustrate the public policy as well as the statutory underpinnings of the Act and therefore is prohibited in the Section 10(b) context.[20]

The right to *contribution* under Section 10(b) likewise has been resolved. In the *Musick Peller* decision, the Supreme Court recognized such a right to contribution under Section 10(b). In the 1995 legislation, Congress codified this right to contribution.[21]

---

[15] Rule 9(b) of the Federal Rules of Civil Procedure; *see Wexner v. First Manhattan Co.*, 902 F.2d 164 (3d Cir. 1996).

[16] *See Tellabs, Inc. v. Makor Issues & Rights, Ltd.*, 551 U.S. 308 (2007). For further discussion, see *infra* § 8.04.

[17] *See* Exchange Act § 20(e) (granting to the SEC authority to pursue aiders and abettors under the 1934 Act); *Central Bank of Denver v. First Interstate Bank of Denver*, 511 U.S. 164 (1994) (holding that aiders and abettors not subject to liability in § 10(b) private actions); *infra* §§ 10.02, 15.04; *cf. Stoneridge Investment Partners, LLC v. Scientific-Atlanta, Inc.*, 128 S. Ct. 761 (2008) (interpreting scope of primary liability under § 10(b)).

[18] *See Bateman Eichler, Hill Richards, Inc. v. Berner*, 472 U.S. 299 (1985); *Hecht v. Harris, Upham & Co.*, 430 F.2d 1202 (9th Cir. 1970); *infra* § 8.10.

[19] *See supra* note 8 (cases cited therein); *infra* § 8.03.

[20] *See, e.g., Globus v. Law Research Serv., Inc.*, 418 F.2d 1276 (2d Cir. 1969); *supra* § 7.09[F].

[21] *See Musick, Peeler & Garrett v. Employers Insurance of Wausau*, 508 U.S. 286 (1993); *infra* § 8.11. *See generally* Fallone, *Section 10(b) and the Vagaries of Federal Common Law: The Merits of Codifying the Private Cause of Action Under a Structuralist Approach*, 1997 U. Ill. L. Rev. 71; Gerla, *Issuers Raising Capital Directly from Investors: What Disclosure Does Rule 10b-5 Require?*, 28 J. Corp. L. 111 (2002); Langevoort & Gulati, *The Muddled Duty to Disclose Under Rule 10b-5*, 57 Vand. L. Rev. 1639 (2004); Myers, *An Issuer's Duty to Disclose: Assessing the Liability Standards for Material Omissions*, 30 Sec. Reg. L. J. 153 (2002); Rose, *Reforming Securities Litigation Reform: Restructuring the Relationship Between Public and Private Enforcement of Rule 10b-5*, 108 Colum. L. Rev. 1301 (2008); Sachs, *Freedom of Contract: The*

§ 8.02   STANDING: THE PURCHASER-SELLER REQUIREMENT

In *Blue Chip Stamps v. Manor Drug Stores*,[22] allegedly defrauded offerees asserted that had the defendant not deceived them, they would have purchased the securities offered. The Supreme Court ruled that the plaintiffs did not have standing to bring a Section 10(b) right of action because they were neither purchasers nor sellers of the subject securities. The Court premised its decision on a number of factors:

> (1) The statutory language of Section 10(b) proscribes manipulation or deception "in connection with the purchase or sale" of securities. This language, along with the pertinent legislative history, indicated that Congress did not intend to grant standing to defrauded (but non-purchasing) offerees.

> (2) Granting standing to offerees under the implied remedy of Section 10(b) would make the Section 10(b) remedy more expansive than the comparable express causes of action that Congress chose to delineate. Hence, granting offerees standing under Section 10(b) evidently would contravene Congress' intent.

> (3) Looking to policy matters, the Court asserted that Section 10(b) litigation poses a greater danger of vexatiousness than litigation in general. According to the Court, this is due to the presence of "strike" suits, potential abuse of the liberal discovery provisions of the Federal Rules of Civil Procedure, and that "hazy issues of historical fact" will be adjudicated on the basis of "oral testimony."[23]

Hence, under the *Blue Chip* standing requirement, three principal types of potential plaintiffs are barred from instituting Section 10(b) litigation:

> First are potential purchasers of shares, either in a new offering or on the Nation's post-distribution trading markets, who allege that they decided not to purchase because of an unduly gloomy representation or the omission of favorable material which made the issuer appear to be a less favorable investment vehicle than it actually was. Second are actual shareholders in the issuer who allege that they decided not to sell their shares because of an unduly rosy representation or a failure to disclose unfavorable material. Third are shareholders, creditors, and perhaps others related to an issuer who suffered loss in the value of their investment due to corporate or insider activities in connection with the purchase or sale of securities which violate Rule 10b-5.[24]

In this regard, shareholders of the second and third categories above, although

---

Trojan Horse of Rule 10b-5, 51 Wash. & Lee L. Rev. 879 (1994); Stern, *The Constitutionalization of Rule 10b-5*, 27 Rutgers L.J. 1 (1995).

[22] 421 U.S. 723 (1975), upholding the *Birnbaum* standing rule, *Birnbaum v. Newport Steel Corp.*, 193 F.2d 461 (2d Cir. 1952).

[23] 421 U.S. at 733–761.

[24] *Id.* at 737–738.

unable to bring a direct action, should be able to institute a derivative action on the issuer's behalf if such issuer is a purchaser or seller of its securities.

The *Blue Chip* standing requirement has been extended by some courts to plaintiffs seeking solely injunctive relief. Hence, when seeking injunctive relief under Section 10(b), the plaintiff must be a purchaser or seller of securities. The policy rationale is that *Blue Chip* applies to injunctive actions due to the need to deter strike suits and the rendering of hazy oral testimony.[25]

It is important to emphasize that, in order to bring a Section 10(b) private cause of action, *only the plaintiff* (not the defendant) must be a "purchaser" or "seller" of the subject securities. Moreover, applying the purchaser-seller requirement, the Supreme Court post-*Blue Chips* has granted standing under Section 10(b) where there was the conveyance of an option to acquire stock that was transacted by means of an oral agreement.[26]

Likewise, the lower federal courts have recognized standing under Section 10(b) in a variety of circumstances, including: in a shareholder derivative action brought on behalf of an allegedly defrauded corporation where the corporation was a purchaser or seller of its securities; in a "forced" sale transaction, such as a "freeze-out" merger; where the plaintiff has "pledged" the securities; and where the plaintiff has entered into a contract to buy or sell the securities.[27]

§ 8.03   REQUISITE CULPABILITY LEVEL

[A]   Private Damages Actions

The Supreme Court in *Ernst & Ernst v. Hochfelder* held that in private actions for damages pursuant to Section 10(b) *scienter* must be proven. The decision was largely predicated on a strict linguistic interpretation of Section

---

[25] *See, e.g., Cowin v Bresler*, 741 F.2d 410 (D.C. Cir. 1984). *But see Simon DeBartolo Group, LP v. Richard F. Jacobs Group, Inc.*, 186 F.3d 157 (2d Cir. 1999) (holding that purchaser-seller standing rule not applicable to actions seeking injunctive relief under § 10(b)).

[26] *The Wharf (Holdings) Limited v. United International Holdings, Inc.*, 532 U.S. 588 (2001). In *Wharf Holdings*, the Supreme Court stated:

> [W]e must assume that the "security" at issue is . . . the [stock] option. . . . [Defendant] Wharf argues that its conduct falls outside Rule [10b-5's] scope. . . . Wharf points out that its agreement to grant [Plaintiff] United an option to purchase shares in the cable system was an oral agreement. And it says that § 10(b) does not cover oral contracts of sale. Wharf points to *Blue Chip Stamps*, in which this Court construed the Act's "purchase or sale" language to mean that only "actual purchasers or sellers of securities" have standing to bring a private action for damages. . . .
>
> *Blue Chip Stamps* involved the question whether the Act protects a person who did not actually buy securities, but who might have done so had the seller told the truth. The Court held that the Act does not cover such a potential buyer, in part for the reason that Wharf states. But United is not a potential buyer; by providing Wharf with its services, it actually bought the option that Wharf sold. And *Blue Chip Stamps* said nothing to suggest that oral purchases or sales fall outside the scope of the Act.

Id. at 593–595. *See* Loewenstein, The Wharf (Holdings) Ltd. v. United Holdings Inc.: *The Supreme Court Breaks Old Ground*, 29 Sec. Reg. L.J. 255 (2001).

[27] For further discussion, see T. Hazen, The Law of Securities Regulation 474–481 (5th ed. 2005); L. Loss & J. Seligman, Securities Regulation 3703–3717 (3d ed. 1991).

10(b). Notably, the Supreme Court's construction of Rule 10b-5 was confined to that given the statutory source upon which the administrative rule (Rule 10b-5) is based, namely, Section 10(b). The *Hochfelder* Court, moreover, pointed out that (1) the 1933 Act's statutory provisions granting private redress for negligent conduct are "subject to significant procedural restrictions not applicable under § 10(b)" and (2) except for the "short-swing" trading prohibition of Exchange Act Section 16(b),[28] "[e]ach of the provisions of the 1934 Act that expressly create civil liability. . . . contains a state of mind condition requiring something more than negligence."[29] Hence, extending Section 10(b) to include negligent conduct in private damages actions, the Court held, would "nullify the effectiveness of the carefully drawn procedural restrictions on these express actions."[30]

While the *Hochfelder* Court stated that the term "scienter" encompasses "a mental state embracing intent to deceive, manipulate, or defraud" and may be shown by "knowing or intentional misconduct,"[31] the Court declined to resolve whether "recklessness" constitutes scienter.[32] This issue is discussed later in this section. Moreover, as discussed in §§ 8.01 and 8.04 of this chapter, pursuant to Rule 9(b) of the Federal Rules of Civil Procedure and Section 21D(b) of the Securities Exchange Act, a plaintiff must plead fraud with particularity when bringing a Section 10(b) right of action.

[B]　　SEC Actions for Injunctive Relief

After the Supreme Court's decision in *Hochfelder*, the question remained whether the SEC was required to establish scienter in an action for injunctive relief brought for alleged violation of Section 10(b). Because the principal focus of an SEC injunctive proceeding ostensibly "is to protect the public against harm, not to punish the offender,"[33] it was argued by some authorities that an SEC action under Section 10(b) could be premised on negligent conduct. Others, relying upon a statutory linguistic analysis, asserted that scienter had to be proven under Section 10(b), irrespective of the plaintiff's identity.[34]

The Supreme Court resolved this issue in *Aaron v. SEC*.[35] Largely relying on the literal language of Section 10(b) as well as pertinent legislative history, the Court concluded that "scienter is an element of § 10(b) and Rule 10b-5,

---

[28] 425 U.S. 185, 208–209 (1976); *see* Securities Act §§ 11, 12(a)(2). For discussion on Section 16(b), see *infra* § 12.08.

[29] 425 U.S. at 209 n.28; *see, e.g.*, Exchange Act §§ 9(e), 18, 20.

[30] 425 U.S. at 210.

[31] *Id.* at 193 n.12, 197.

[32] *Id.* at 193 n.12.

[33] *SEC v. Coven*, 581 F.2d 1020, 1027–1028 (2d Cir. 1978).

[34] *See generally* M. Steinberg & R. Ferrara, Securities Practice: Federal and State Enforcement § 5.01 et. seq. (2d ed. 2005 & Supp.).

[35] 446 U.S. 680 (1980). With respect to the portion of the decision addressing Section 17(a) of the Securities Act, that provision is discussed in Chapters 9 and 15.

regardless of the identity of the plaintiff or the nature of the relief sought."[36] From an SEC enforcement view, *Aaron* is an important case, further aspects of which are discussed in Chapters 9 and 15.

[C] "Recklessness"

A question left open by both *Hochfelder* and *Aaron* is whether reckless conduct constitutes scienter for Section 10(b) purposes. Overwhelmingly, the lower federal courts have concluded that recklessness satisfies the scienter requirement. This position is reinforced by the enactment of the Private Securities Litigation Reform Act of 1995 (PSLRA). That legislation strongly suggests that reckless conduct satisfies Section 10(b)'s scienter requirement except for forward-looking statements by publicly-held enterprises where the defendant's actual knowledge must be proven (as discussed in Chapter 11 herein).

The vast majority of courts have construed reckless conduct within the Section 10(b) context to mean conduct which is "highly unreasonable" and which represents "an extreme departure from the standards of ordinary care" to the extent that the danger was either known to the defendant or [was] so obvious that the defendant must have been aware of it."[37] In the past, some courts adopted a somewhat more relaxed standard. For example, one such view posits that reckless conduct exists if the defendant had reasonable grounds to believe material facts existed that were misstated or omitted, but nonetheless failed to obtain and disclose such facts although he/she could have done so without extraordinary effort.[38] Another approach (which evidently has been abandoned), termed the "barely reckless" standard, deems actionable an allegation that the defendant "should have known," with the proviso that such conduct surpasses that of negligence.[39]

[D] State Court Reaction

Due to the Supreme Court's decisions in the federal securities law area which have had the effect of making a plaintiff's task in establishing a successful cause of action under Section 10(b) more difficult, counsel may deem it wise to consider bringing state common law and/or state securities law claims. In this regard, in construing their respective Blue Sky statutes, a number of state courts have declined to follow the Supreme Court's lead in *Hochfelder* and *Aaron*, thereby holding that scienter is not required to be shown. State court decisions holding that negligence is sufficient culpability to

---

[36] 446 U.S. at 691.

[37] *See, e.g., In re Ikon Office Solutions, Inc. Securities Litigation,* 277 F.3d 658, 667 (3d Cir. 2002); *Hollinger v. Titan Capital Corporation,* 914 F.2d 1564, 1569 (9th Cir. 1990) (en banc); *Sanders v. John Nuveen & Co., Inc.,* 554 F.2d 790, 793 (7th Cir. 1977).

[38] *See Lanza v. Drexel & Co.,* 479 F.2d 1277, 1306 n.98 (2d Cir. 1973) (en banc).

[39] *See Stern v. American Bankshares Corp.,* 429 F. Supp. 818 (E.D. Wis. 1977). *See generally* Johnson, *Liability for Reckless Misrepresentations and Omissions Under Section 10(b) of the Securities Exchange Act of 1934,* 59 U. Cin. L. Rev. 667 (1991); Steinberg & Gruenbaum, *Variations of Recklessness After* Hochfelder *and* Aaron, 8 Sec. Reg. L.J. 179 (1980).

impose liability have distinguished Section 10(b)'s language from that contained in the respective state statute and have found no legislative history in the state statute comparable to that underlying Section 10(b).[40] The subject of state law remedies is discussed in greater detail in Chapter 9.

§ 8.04 PLEADING REQUIREMENTS

As discussed in § 8.01, in addition to pleading fraud with particularity pursuant to Rule 9(b) of the Federal Rules of Civil Procedure, a plaintiff bringing suit under Section 10(b) also must adhere to Section 21D(b) of the Securities Exchange Act. Section 21D(b), enacted pursuant to the Private Securities Litigation Reform Act of 1995 (PSLRA), sets forth:

(1) A requirement that a plaintiff in any private securities fraud action alleging material misstatements and/or omissions "specify [in the complaint] each statement alleged to have been misleading; the reason or reasons why the statement is misleading; and if an allegation regarding the statement or omission is made on information and belief, the complaint shall state with particularity all facts on which that belief is formed."

(2) A requirement that in any private action under the 1934 Act in which the plaintiff "may recover money damages only on proof that the defendant acted with a particular state of mind, the complaint shall, with respect to each such act or omission alleged to violate [the 1934 Act], state with particularity facts giving rise to a strong inference that the defendant acted with the required state of mind."

As the Joint Explanatory Statement of the Conference Committee for this legislation recognized, the foregoing language derives "in part" from the Second Circuit's pleading requirement which is "[r]egarded as the most stringent pleading standard." Nonetheless, the Conference Committee apparently believed that this "stringent pleading standard" was too lax, stating "[b]ecause the Conference Committee intends to strengthen existing pleading requirements, it does not intend to codify the Second Circuit's case law interpreting this pleading standard."[41] In view of this statute and its accompanying legislative history, the pleading requirement in private securities fraud actions undoubtedly poses a difficult barrier for plaintiffs to hurdle.

In cases decided after the PSLRA, the lower federal courts were divided regarding the requisite pleading requirements in securities actions alleging fraud. Some courts continued to embrace the Second Circuit's standard,[42] while

---

[40] *See Kittleson v. Ford*, 93 Wash. 2d 223, 608 P.2d 264 (1980); *Merrill Lynch, Pierce, Fenner & Smith v. Byrne*, 320 So. 2d 436 (Dist. Ct. App. Fla. 1975), *writ discharged*, 341 So. 2d 498 (Fla. 1977). *But see Ohio v. American Equitel Corp.*, 60 Ohio Misc. 7, 395 N.E.2d 1355 (Ct. C.P. Ohio 1979) (requiring scienter to be shown). *See generally* J. Long, Blue Sky Law § 7.01 (2008); M. Steinberg & R. Ferrara, *supra* note 34, at § 13:18.

[41] Private Securities Litigation Reform Act, Joint Explanation of Statement of the Committee of Conference (1995).

[42] Under the Second Circuit's standard that then existed, a plaintiff was required to allege

others more strictly construed the PSLRA's pleading requirements.[43] Due to the sharply differing approaches embraced by the appellate courts,[44] the Supreme Court sought to resolve this issue.

The Court took on this task in *Tellabs, Inc. v. Makor Issues & Rights, Ltd.*[45] In *Tellabs*, plaintiff shareholders alleged that the company and its executives had engaged in a deceptive scheme to falsely inflate the value of the company's stock through a series of materially misleading statements about the company's revenues and demand for some of its products. The district court dismissed the complaint for failure to plead scienter sufficiently, but the Seventh Circuit reversed, holding that the "strong inference" standard was satisfied if the complaint "allege[d] facts from which, if true, a reasonable person could infer that the defendant acted with the required intent."[46]

The Supreme Court ultimately rejected the Seventh Circuit's relatively mild approach as well as stricter standards adhered to by a number of other appellate courts,[47] charting what may be viewed as a "middle" course. Under the Supreme Court's decision in *Tellabs*, to constitute a "strong inference" under the PSLRA, a complaint must plead facts that create an inference of scienter that a reasonable person would deem "cogent and at least as compelling as any opposing inference one could draw from the facts alleged."[48] Thus, under *Tellabs*, when faced with a motion to dismiss, a court must consider favorable as well as opposing plausible explanations to determine whether the inference of scienter is "cogent" and "at least as compelling" as any inference of non-culpable intent.[49] In making this determination, the court must accept all factual allegations in the complaint as true, and must consider the complaint in its entirely, along with documents incorporated by reference and any other matters of which the court may take judicial notice. No allegation should be scrutinized in isolation but rather in the context of the entire complaint. Hence, in *Tellabs*, the Supreme Court mandated a holistic approach in this regard —

---

either (a) "motive" and "opportunity" by the defendant to commit fraud or (b) "facts that constitute strong circumstantial evidence of conscious misbehavior or recklessness." *Press v. Chemical Investment Serv. Corp.*, 166 F.3d 529, 537–538 (2d Cir. 1999).

[43] *See, e.g., In re Silicon Graphics Inc. Securities Litigation*, 183 F.3d 970, 974 (9th Cir. 1999) (rejecting the motive and opportunity test and "requir[ing] plaintiffs to plead, at a minimum, particular facts demonstrating deliberate or conscious recklessness").

[44] In addition to the contrasting positions adopted by the Second and Ninth Circuits cited *supra* notes 42–43, see, *e.g., In re Comshare Inc. Securities Litigation*, 183 F.3d 542, 549 (6th Cir. 1999) (holding that allegations of a defendant's motive and opportunity are not by themselves adequate for pleading scienter but that such allegations constitute a factor, among others, that a court may consider in ascertaining whether a plaintiff has set forth "a strong inference of fraudulent scienter"); *In re Advanta Corp. Securities Litigation*, 180 F 3d 525, 533–34 (3d Cir. 1999) (mandating the pleading of facts with particularity that show the defendant's motive and opportunity to perpetrate fraud or circumstantial evidence of either reckless or intentional misconduct).

[45] 551 U.S. 308, 127 S. Ct. 2499 (2007).

[46] 127 S. Ct. at 2506 (quoting 437 F.3d 588, 502 (7th Cir. 2006)).

[47] *Id.* at 2506.

[48] *Id.* at 2510.

[49] *Id.*

an inquiry into whether all of the facts taken together collectively give rise to the requisite inference of scienter.[50]

The *Tellabs* Court expressly designed this standard to meet the twin goals of the PSLRA: to shield corporations from frivolous, "lawyer-driven" suits on one hand while preserving recompense for investors with meritorious claims on the other.[51] The holding attempts to strike this balance by imposing a heightened threshold pleading requirement on plaintiffs, while still reserving wide judicial latitude in ruling on Rule 12(b)(6) motions. For example, while a complaint must allege facts that give rise to the requisite inference of scienter, *i.e.*, one that is cogent and at least as compelling as other inferences of non-culpable intent, no one allegation or lack thereof normally is dispositive.[52] Because *Tellabs* explicitly rejects any bright-line markers, the trial court retains significant gate-keeping discretion in determining whether a complaint alleges requisite facts to satisfy the "strong inference" of scienter standard.

A plaintiff can establish an inference of scienter by alleging facts that: (1) demonstrate motive and opportunity to commit fraud; or (2) establish a mental state either of actual intent or recklessness.[53] In doing so, plaintiffs may support their complaint by relying on information obtained from confidential sources, but such information cannot compensate for pleading deficiencies under the PSLRA.[54]

Notably, in *Tellabs*, the Supreme Court declined to address whether the PSLRA abolished the "group pleading" doctrine.[55] The group pleading doctrine posits that statements in group-published documents, such as SEC corporate filings and press releases made by a subject issuer, are attributable to directors and officers who exercise day-to-day involvement in normal company operations.[56] Since the passage of the PSLRA, courts overwhelmingly have rejected the "group pleading" doctrine, reasoning that recognition of the doctrine is inconsistent with "the PSLRA's requirements that allegations be set forth with particularity concerning 'the defendant' and scienter be pleaded for 'each act or

---

[50] *Id.* at 2509–11.

[51] *Id.* at 2509.

[52] For example, in *Tellabs*, the Supreme Court noted that the plaintiffs' failure to plead any pecuniary benefit or other allegation of motive on the part of the company's CEO did not negate an inference of scienter standing alone. Absence of motive, while a relevant consideration, was not fatal to the claim since the complaint was to be judged in its entirety. *Id.* at 2511.

[53] *See, e.g., Elam v. Neidorff*, 2008 U.S. App. LEXIS 21579 (8th Cir. 2008); *N.J. Carpenters Pension & Annuity Funds v. Brogan IDEC, Inc.*, 537 F.3d 35 (1st Cir. 2008); *Teamsters Local 445 Freight Division Pension Fund v. Dynex Capital Corp.*, 531 F.3d 190 (2d Cir. 2008); *In re Advanta Corp. Securities Litigation*, 180 F.3d 525 (3d Cir. 1999).

[54] *See, e.g., Mizzaro v. Home Depot, Inc.*, 2008 U.S. App. LEXIS 21091 (11th Cir. 2008); *Novak v. Kasaks*, 216 F.3d 300 (2d Cir. 2000); *In re Intelligroup Securities Litigation*, 527 F. Supp. 2d 262 (D.N.J. 2007). *See generally* Kaufman & Wunderlich, *Congress, the Supreme Court and the Proper Role of Confidential Informants in Securities Fraud Litigation*, 36 Sec. Reg. L.J. 2 (2008).

[55] 127 S. Ct. at 2511 n.6.

[56] *See Wool v. Tandem Computers, Inc.*, 818 F.2d 1433, 1440 (9th Cir. 1987) (adopting "group published" doctrine).

omission' sufficient to give 'rise to a strong inference that the defendant acted with the required state of mind.' "[57]

Since *Tellabs* was decided by the Supreme Court in 2007, scores of lower federal courts have applied its standards. These decisions make clear that the lower federal courts retain considerable gate-keeping discretion in ascertaining whether a subject complaint alleges sufficient facts to meet the "strong inference" of scienter standard.[58]

§ 8.05 THE "MANIPULATION" OR "DECEPTION" REQUIREMENT

[A] Breach of Fiduciary Duty Not Sufficient

Santa Fe Industries, Inc. v. Green[59] involved the merger of the Kirby Lumber Corporation into its parent, Santa Fe Industries, Inc., which owned ninety-five percent of Kirby's stock. Santa Fe availed itself of a simplified Delaware procedure known as a "short-form" merger, under which a parent that owns at least ninety percent of a subsidiary's outstanding stock can absorb the subsidiary without being required to obtain approval by the shareholders of either corporation. The day after the merger became effective, Kirby's minority shareholders were informed that they would receive $150 in cash for each of their shares, and that, if dissatisfied, they could seek appraisal in the Delaware courts.[60]

Santa Fe also provided the Kirby shareholders with an information statement containing facts and figures that convinced one of the recipients that Kirby stock was actually worth at least $772 a share. Rather than alleging that these materials contained misrepresentations and nondisclosures, the plaintiff claimed that the gross undervaluation of his shares was itself a "fraud" within the meaning of Section 10(b) and Rule 10b-5.[61]

The Supreme Court rejected this argument, holding that the transaction "was neither deceptive nor manipulative and therefore did not violate either § 10(b) of the [Exchange] Act or Rule 10b-5."[62] The Court largely premised its decision on Section 10(b)'s language and the statute's legislative history, finding "no indication that Congress meant to prohibit any conduct not involving manipulation or deception."[63] Further support was found by

---

[57] *Winer Family Trust v. Queen*, 503 F.3d 319, 337 (3d Cir. 2007) (citing cases and quoting *Southland Securities Corp. v. INSpire Invoice Solutions, Inc.*, 365 F.3d 353, 364 (5th Cir. 2004)); *see infra* § 10.03[C].

[58] *See, e.g., supra* notes 54, 57 (cases cited therein); 63 Bus. Law. 981–91 (cases discussed therein).

[59] 430 U.S. 462 (1977).

[60] *Id.* at 466–467; *see* 8 Del. Code Ann. § 253 ("short-form" merger statute).

[61] 430 U.S. at 474.

[62] *Id.*

[63] *Id.* at 473.

examining the Exchange Act's fundamental purpose of implementing a philosophy of full and fair disclosure. Once adequate disclosure has taken place, the fairness of the transaction is at most a tangential concern of the federal Securities Acts. Therefore, according to the Supreme Court, claims challenging solely the fairness of transactions or internal corporate mismanagement are best relegated to state law.[64]

Santa Fe was scarcely a surprise after the Court's previous decisions in *Ernst & Ernst v. Hochfelder*[65] and *Cort v. Ash.*[66] *Hochfelder* held that there can be no implied private right of action for damages under Section 10(b) and Rule 10b-5, absent an allegation of scienter. The decision was largely predicated on a strict construction of Section 10(b). This approach to the language of the statute was expressly affirmed and adopted by the *Santa Fe* Court. In *Cort*, the Court demonstrated its reluctance to imply federal causes of action in areas traditionally left to state law. There, the court observed that "corporations are creatures of state law, and investors commit their funds to corporate directors on the understanding that, except where federal law *expressly* requires certain responsibilities of directors with respect to stockholders, state law will govern the internal affairs of the corporation."[67] Both cases evidence the Court's contraction of the scope of the federal securities laws. *Santa Fe* combined the approaches of *Hochfelder* and *Cort*, employing a narrow approach to construction and stressing that the regulation of the internal management of corporations is within the ambit of state corporation law.

Santa Fe is one of the more important decisions that the Supreme Court has handed down in the federal securities law area. Had the decision gone the other way, garden variety suits for breach of fiduciary duty that occurred in connection with the purchase or sale of a security (irrespective of whether there had been adequate disclosure) would have been actionable under Section 10(b). *Santa Fe* thus signifies that a federal claim under Section 10(b) must allege manipulation or deception.

[B]   Federal Claims Premised on Breach of Fiduciary Duty

The *Santa Fe* decision had a second aspect, arising from the Court's comment in footnote 14 of the opinion. In that footnote, the Court stated that the failure to provide the minority with advance notice of the merger was not a material nondisclosure because, as the plaintiffs conceded, "under Delaware law [the plaintiffs] could not have enjoined the merger because an appraisal proceeding [was] their sole remedy in the Delaware courts for any alleged

---

[64] *Id.* at 477–80. *But see* Thel, *The Original Conception of Section 10(b) of the Securities Exchange Act*, 42 Stan. L. Rev. 385 (1990).

[65] 425 U.S. 185 (1976); *see supra* § 8.03[A].

[66] 422 U.S. 66 (1975) (declining to imply private right of action under federal statute, discussed *infra* § 9.02[B]).

[67] *Id.* at 80 (emphasis in original).

unfairness in the terms of the merger."[68] Today, in long-form mergers, plaintiffs would not make this concession.

[1]   Post-*Santa Fe* State Court Decisions

Subsequent to *Santa Fe*, Delaware[69] and a number of other state courts[70] held that appraisal is not a shareholder's sole remedy when a merger is unfair. Based on these decisions, under certain circumstances, aggrieved shareholders may bring suit in state court to enjoin a merger that has not been consummated. For example, in Delaware, with respect to long-form mergers, a shareholder is not relegated to the appraisal remedy and may seek to enjoin a merger where "fraud, misrepresentation, self-dealing, deliberate waste of corporate assets, or gross and palpable overreaching are involved."[71]

[2]   Post-*Santa Fe* Federal Court Decisions

In view of these post-*Santa Fe* state court decisions, aggrieved shareholders in a number of jurisdictions not only may seek redress under state law, they also can institute a Section 10(b) right of action in certain circumstances. Where the material misrepresentation(s) or omission(s), if there had been adequate disclosure, would have enabled shareholders to take corrective steps to avoid financial loss, such as procuring a state court injunction against the contemplated action, a federal Section 10(b) right of action may be invoked.[72] Hence, to a certain extent, federal claims under Section 10(b) based partially on breach of fiduciary duty under state law still survive. This rationale has been called the "*Goldberg* line of cases" or the "lost state remedy theory." The Supreme Court has raised but declined to resolve the validity of this theory.[73]

Stated differently, subject to certain caveats, minority shareholders are entitled to the disclosure of information needed to determine whether the

---

[68] 430 U.S. at 474 n.14.

[69] *See Weinberger v. UOP, Inc.*, 457 A.2d 701 (Del. 1983); *Singer v. Magnovox Co.*, 380 A.2d 969 (Del. 1977). *But see Glassman v. Unocal Exploration Corp.*, 777 A.2d 242 (Del. 2001) (holding that, absent fraud or illegality, appraisal is sole remedy of a minority shareholder in short-form merger).

[70] *See, e.g., Alpert v. 28 Williams St. Corp.*, 63 N.Y. 2d 557, 483 N.Y.S. 2d 667, 473 N.E. 2d 19 (1984); *Perl v. IU International Corp.*, 607 P.2d 1036 (Hawaii 1980). *But see Steinberg v. Amplica, Inc.*, 42 Cal. 3d 1198, 233 Cal. Rptr. 249, 729 P.2d 683 (1986) (appraisal sole remedy).

[71] *Weinberger v. UOP, Inc.*, 457 A.2d 701, 714 (Del. 1983). Note, however, that where the parent corporation owns at least ninety percent of the subsidiary, a short-form merger may be effected. *See* 8 Del. Code § 253. In such a short-term merger, absent fraud or illegality, a minority shareholder is relegated solely to the appraisal remedy. *See Glassman v. Unocal Exploration Corp.*, 777 A.2d 242 (Del. 2001). *See generally* Steinberg, *Short-Form Mergers in Delaware*, 27 Del. J. Corp. L. 489 (2002).

[72] *See, e.g., Howing Co. v. Nationwide Corp.*, 972 F.2d 700 (6th Cir. 1992); *Healey v. Catalyst Recovery, Inc.*, 616 F.2d 641 (3d Cir. 1980); *Alabama Farm Bureau Mutual Casualty Co. v. American Fidelity Life Insurance Co.*, 606 F.2d 602 (5th Cir. 1979); *Goldberg v. Meridor*, 567 F.2d 209 (2d Cir. 1977). *But see Isquith v. Caremark International, Inc.*, 136 F.3d 531 (7th Cir. 1998) (rejecting *Goldberg* line of cases).

[73] *Virginia Bankshares, Inc. v. Sandberg*, 501 U.S. 1083, 1106–08 (1991).

board of directors has breached its fiduciary duty under state law. Failure to provide this information, according to a number of courts,[74] may be a material deception actionable under Section 10(b). This federal right to information extends well beyond the freeze-out merger situation. Indeed, subject to certain caveats, it encompasses every corporate transaction in securities that shareholders could have attacked under state law, had disclosure of the requisite facts been provided.

[3]   Caveats

There are a number of caveats to the foregoing. First, assuming that disclosure to shareholders is required, the board of directors need only disclose objective facts. There is no requirement for the board to engage in subjective revelation or characterize its actions with pejorative nouns or adjectives. As stated by one court, "[t]he unclean heart of a director is not actionable, whether or not it is 'disclosed' unless the impurities are translated into actionable deeds or omissions both objective and external."[75] Or, as more recently enunciated by the Supreme Court in *Virginia Bankshares, Inc. v. Sandberg*: "We hold disbelief or undisclosed motivation, standing alone, insufficient to satisfy [an actionable claim]."[76]

Moreover, the courts consistently have required Rule 10b-5 claims to allege more than the bare availability of state court injunctive relief. For example, when shareholder approval of a transaction is not required, the courts have reasoned in the derivative suit context that disclosure to a disinterested board of directors is equivalent to disclosure to the shareholders. Stated differently, the knowledge of the disinterested board of directors is attributed to the corporation, thereby precluding a finding of deception.[77] Of course, in nonderivative actions, where an individual shareholder is the purchaser or seller of securities, a Section 10(b) claim need only allege that such shareholder was deceived. In these direct (as compared to derivative) actions, the deception requirement is satisfied by alleging that there was a material misrepresentation or nondisclosure in the flow of information between the majority and the individual shareholder that deprived the plaintiff of enjoining the transaction under state law.[78]

A troublesome issue in determining whether a corporation has been deceived is the proper definition of a "disinterested" director. A director's "financial stake" in the subject transaction would clearly render such person "interested."[79] The presence of certain other conduct, such as improper influence upon a director by a controlling person or the failure to apprise a

---

[74] *See supra* note 72 (cases cited therein).

[75] *Stedman v. Storer*, 308 F. Supp. 881, 887 (S.D.N.Y. 1969) (*quoted in Biesenbach v. Guenther*, 588 F.2d 400, 402 (3d Cir. 1978)); *see Goldberg v. Meridor*, 567 F.2d 209, 218 n.8 (2d Cir. 1977).

[76] 501 U.S. 1083, 1096 (1991).

[77] *See, e.g., Maldonado v. Flynn*, 597 F.2d 789 (2d Cir. 1979).

[78] *See e.g., Healey v. Catalyst Recovery Co.*, 626 F.2d 641 (3d Cir. 1980).

[79] *See, e.g., Tyco Labs., Inc. v. Kimball*, 444 F. Supp. 292 (E.D. Pa. 1977).

director of material facts, should likewise disqualify the director.[80] The crucial criterion should be whether a director can exercise *independent judgment* on behalf of the corporation and its shareholders.

Based on the above, only if corporate action requires shareholder approval or if the directors are interested or not informed, will nondisclosure provide the basis for a claim of deception of a corporation in a derivative action under Section 10(b). Even in such cases, however, the bare allegation of nondisclosure will not suffice to state a federal claim. Another limitation imposed by *Santa Fe* is that the aggrieved shareholder must also allege that, had the corporate malfeasance been disclosed, state court remedies would have been available. In this vein, a question left unanswered after *Santa Fe* is whether the complainant must show not only that a suit in state court could been brought, but also that such a suit would have been won. The courts are split on this issue. While some courts appear to require that the complainant show that he/she would have been awarded relief in the state court action,[81] others require the plaintiff to show a reasonable basis or probability of success.[82] In *Virginia Bankshares*, the Supreme Court raised yet declined to resolve the validity of this rationale, coined the "lost state remedy theory."[83]

[4]   Summation

Based on *Santa Fe* and its progeny, although unfairness alone is an insufficient basis for a federal claim, there are circumstances, subject to certain limitations, in which unfairness coupled with either a failure to disclose or an affirmative misrepresentation remains a firm foundation for a federal claim. Interestingly, the viability of any such Section 10(b) claim will present local law questions akin to those with which the federal judiciary grapples in diversity cases governed by the rule of *Erie Railroad Co. v. Tompkins*.[84] Significantly, however, unlike the *Erie* doctrine, under which federal courts apply state substantive law in order to recognize state created remedies and liabilities, *Santa Fe*'s footnote fourteen, as construed by the lower federal courts, conditions the existence of a *federal* right upon the applicable *state*

---

[80] *See generally Maldonado v. Flynn*, 597 F.2d 789 (2d Cir. 1979).

[81] *See, e.g., Madison Consultants v. Federal Deposit Insurance Corp.*, 710 F.2d 57 (2d Cir. 1983); *Kidwell ex rel. Penfold v. Meikle*, 597 F.2d 1273 (9th Cir. 1979).

[82] *See e.g., Healey v. Catalyst Recovery, Inc.*, 616 F.2d 641 (3d Cir. 1980); *Alabama Farm Bureau Mutual Casualty Co. v. American Fidelity Life Insurance Co.*, 606 F.2d 602 (5th Cir. 1979).

[83] 501 U.S. at 1106–08. Cases decided after *Virginia Bankshares* support the continued validity of the "lost state remedy" theory. *See, e.g., Wilson v. Great American Enterprises, Inc.*, 979 F.2d 924 (2d Cir. 1992); *Howing Company v. Nationwide Corporation*, 972 F.2d 700 (6th Cir. 1992). *But see Isquith v. Caremark International, Inc.*, 136 F.3d 531 (7th Cir. 1998) (expressing disapproval of theory). *See generally* Loewenstein, *The Supreme Court, Rule 10b-5 and the Federalization of Corporate Law*, 39 Ind. L. Rev. 17 (2005); Steinberg & Reece, *The Supreme Court, Implied Rights of Action, and Proxy Regulation*, 54 Ohio St. L.J. 67, 101–13 (1993). For further discussion of *Virginia Bankshares*, see *infra* § 9.05[B].

[84] 304 U.S. 64 (1938).

law.[85]

[C]   Manipulation

Manipulative acts or practices are prohibited under the federal securities laws.[86] As stated by the Supreme Court, manipulation implicates "intentional or willful conduct designed to deceive or defraud investors by controlling or artificially affecting the price of securities."[87] As set forth by the Supreme Court in a subsequent decision, manipulation encompasses "practices, such as wash sales, matched orders or rigged prices, that are intended to mislead investors by artificially affecting market activity."[88] Nonetheless, such fictitious devices (*e.g.*, wash sales or matched orders) are not essential to a finding of manipulation. As the SEC and a number of courts have stated, the alleged manipulator's intentional creation of a false impression of market activity is sufficient.[89] To identify conduct that is "unrelated to the natural forces of supply and demand,"[90] courts assess whether the subject transactions convey "a false pricing signal to the market."[91] In this context, manipulative

---

[85] The *Goldberg*-line of cases has been subject to criticism. *See, e.g., Isquith v. Caremark International, Inc.*, 136 F.3d 531 (7th Cir. 1998); *Healey v. Catalyst Recovery Co.*, 616 F.2d 641, 651 (Aldisert, J., dissenting). *See generally* Ferrara & Steinberg, *A Reappraisal of* Santa Fe: *Rule 10b-5 and the New Federalism*, 129 U. Pa. L. Rev. 263 (1980).

[86] *See, e.g.*, Securities Act § 17(a); Securities Exchange Act §§ 9(a), 10(b), 15(c); SEC Regulation M. Note that a private plaintiff in a Section 9 or 10(b) claim must allege the illegal manipulative activity with particularity pursuant to the pleading requirements of the Private Securities Litigation Reform Act (PSLRA). *See ATSI Communications, Inc. v. The Shaar Fund, Ltd.*, 493 F.3d 87, 102 (2d Cir. 2007).

Generally, Section 15(c) of the Exchange Act addresses deceptive and manipulative conduct by broker-dealers in the over-the-counter market. *See SEC v. Resch-Cassin & Co.*, 362 F. Supp. 964 (S.D.N.Y. 1973); Securities Exchange Act Release No. 3505 (1943). Regulation M relaxes certain restrictions on offering participants when the SEC deems the risk of manipulation to be small. *See* Adoption of Regulation M, Securities Exchange Act Release No. 38067 (1996) (stating that "Regulation M significantly eases regulatory burdens on offering participants by (i) eliminating the trading restrictions for underwriters of actively-traded securities, (ii) reducing the scope of coverage for other securities, (iii) reducing restrictions on issuer plans, (iv) providing a more flexible framework for stabilizing transactions, and (v) deregulating rights offerings").

[87] *Ernst & Ernst v. Hochfelder*, 425 U.S. 185, 199 (1976).

[88] *Santa Fe Industries, Inc. v. Green*, 430 U.S. 462, 476 (1977). Wash sales are transactions that involve no change in beneficial ownership, while matched orders are orders for the purchase or sale of a security with the knowledge that corresponding orders for substantially the same size and price have been or will be entered at substantially the same time, either by the same person or by different parties. Such transactions can be used to create a false appearance of active trading in the subject security. *See Ernst & Ernst*, 425 U.S. at 205 n.25; *see also* Securities Exchange Act § 9(a)(1) (describing prohibited practices).

[89] *See, e.g., ATSI Communications, Inc. v. The Shaar Fund, Ltd.*, 493 F.3d 87 (2d Cir. 2007); *Pagel, Inc., v. SEC*, 803 F.2d 942 (8th Cir. 1986); *In re Halsey, Stuart & Co.*, 30 SEC 106 (SEC 1949); *see also Markowski v. SEC*, 274 F.3d 525 (D.C. Cir. 2001).

[90] *Mobil Corp. v. Marathon Oil, Corp.*, 669 F.2d 366, 374 (6th Cir. 1981); *see Gurary v. Winehouse*, 190 F.3d 37, 45 (2d Cir. 1999).

[91] *ATSI Communications, Inc. v. The Shaar Fund, Ltd.*, 493 F.3d 87, 100 (2d Cir. 2007); *see Regents of the University of California v. Credit Suisse First Boston*, 482 F.3d 372, 390 (5th Cir. 2007); *SEC v. First Jersey Securities, Inc.*, 101 F.3d 1450, 1466 (2d Cir. 1996); *Sullivan & Long, Inc.*

conduct may be distinguished from lawful activity by inquiring whether the alleged violator "inject[ed] inaccurate information into the marketplace or creat[ed] a false impression of supply and demand for the security . . . for the purpose of artificially depressing or inflating the price of the security."[92]

Note that in private and SEC actions manipulation is actionable under both Section 9 of the Exchange Act and Section 10(b) of that Act. For example, to prove manipulation under Section 9(a)(2) of the Exchange Act, the following must be shown: "(1) that the defendant [acting with scienter] effected a series of transactions in a security registered on a national securities exchange, (2) creating actual or apparent active trading in such security, or raising or depressing the price of such security, (3) for the purpose of inducing the purchase or sale of such security by others."[93] As a generalization, manipulation under Section 10(b) is easier to prove than under Section 9(a). Importantly, Section 10(b) covers stock manipulation that is perpetrated in the over-the-counter (OTC) market as well as on a stock exchange. Moreover, unlike Section 9(a), a plaintiff seeking relief under Section 10(b) need not prove that the allegedly illegal actions "had an effect on the price of the stock."[94]

§ 8.06 THE RELIANCE REQUIREMENT

[A]   Generally

Proof of reliance normally is required to help prove the causal connection between the defendant's wrongdoing and the complainant's loss. Positive proof of reliance has not been demanded of the plaintiff where unnecessary to show causation. In such instances, upon demonstrating materiality (*e.g.*, of the nondisclosure), the complainant enjoys a presumption of reliance which the defendant can rebut (*e.g.*, by showing that the plaintiff would not have acted

---

v. Scattered Corp., 47 F.3d 857, 861 (7th Cir. 1995).

[92] *GFL Advantage Fund, Ltd. v. Colkitt*, 272 F.3d 189, 207 (3d Cir. 2001) (*quoted in ATSI Communications*, 493 F.3d at 101).

[93] McLucas & Angotti, *Market Manipulation*, 22 Rev. Sec. & Comm. Reg. 103, 105 (1989); *see Chemetron Corp v. Business Foods, Inc.*, 682 F.2d 1149, 1163–1164 (5th Cir. 1982), *vacated and remanded on other grounds*, 460 U.S. 1007 (1983) (stating that "[t]o make out a violation of subsection 9(a)(1) in a private action under subsection 9(e), a plaintiff must prove the existence of (1) a wash sale or matched orders in a security (2) done with scienter (3) for the purpose of creating a false or misleading appearance of active trading in that security (4) on which the plaintiff relied (5) that affected plaintiff's purchase or selling price").

[94] *GFL Advantage Fund, Ltd. v. Colkitt*, 272 F.3d 189, 206 (3d Cir. 2001). For commentary on manipulation, see A. Bromberg & L. Lowenfels, *supra* note 1, at §§ 6:55-6:88; T. Hazen, *supra* note 27, at §§ 6.1, 12.1, 14.3[6]; Fischel & Ross, *Should the SEC Prohibit "Manipulation" in Financial Markets?*, 105 Harv. L. Rev. 503 (1991); Howard, *Frontrunning in the Marketplace: A Regulatory Dilemma*, 19 Sec. Reg. L.J. 263 (1989); Lowenfels & Bromberg, *Securities Market Manipulations: An Examination and Analysis of Domination and Control, Frontrunning and Parking*, 55 Albany L. Rev. 293 (1991); Poser, *Stock Market Manipulation and Corporate Control Transactions*, 40 U. Miami L. Rev. 671 (1986); Thel, *Regulation of Manipulation Under Section 10(b): Securities Prices and the Text of the Securities Exchange Act of 1934*, 1988 Colum. Bus. L. Rev. 359.

differently had he/she known of the nondisclosure). As the Supreme Court stated in *Affiliated Ute Citizens v. United States*:[95]

> Under the circumstances of this case involving primarily a failure to disclose, positive proof of reliance is not a prerequisite to recovery. All that is necessary is that the facts withheld be material in the sense that a reasonable investor [would] have considered them important in the making of this decision. . . . This obligation to disclose and this withholding of a material fact establish the requisite element of causation in fact.[96]

Hence, in cases involving primarily a failure to disclose, the plaintiff's reliance is presumed. Although a number of courts have recognized this presumption also in "half-truth" cases,[97] others hold to the contrary. The Fifth Circuit, for example, has opined that the presumption of reliance extends only to situations involving "primarily a failure to disclose, implicating the first or third subparagraph of . . . Rule [10b-5] [and not to cases involving] primarily a misstatement or failure to state a fact necessary to make those statements not misleading [*i.e.*, "half-truth" cases], classified under the second subparagraph of the Rule."[98]

[B]   The "Fraud on the Market" Theory

Plaintiffs also may enjoy a presumption of reliance by invoking the "fraud on the market" theory. This theory postulates that investors assume that the market price of a security is determined by the available material information and that no unsuspected fraudulent conduct has affected the price. The use of this theory to apply a rebuttable presumption of reliance received Supreme Court approbation in *Basic, Inc. v. Levinson*.[99]

In *Basic*, the Court quoted from a lower court decision which explained the rationale of the fraud on the market theory in the following terms:

> In face-to-face transactions, the inquiry into an investor's reliance upon information is into the subjective pricing of that information by that investor. With the presence of a market, the market is interposed between seller and buyer and, ideally, transmits information to the investor in the processed form of a market price. Thus the market is performing a substantial part of the valuation process performed by the investor in a face-to-face transaction. The market is acting as the unpaid agent of the investor, informing him that given all the informa-

---

[95] 406 U.S. 128 (1972).

[96] *Id.* at 153–154.

[97] *See, e.g., Holmes v. Bateson*, 583 F.2d 545, 558 (1st Cir. 1978). *See generally* Langevoort, *Half-Truths: Protecting Mistaken Inferences By Investors and Others*, 52 Stan. L. Rev. 87 (1999).

[98] *Huddleston v. Herman & MacLean*, 640 F.2d 534, 548 (5th Cir. 1981), *aff'd on other grounds*, 459 U.S. 375 (1983); *accord Binder v. Gillespie*, 172 F.3d 649 (9th Cir. 1999).

[99] 485 U.S. 224 (1988). Other aspects of the *Basic* decision are addressed *infra* § 11.04.

tion available to it, the value of the stock is worth the market price.[100]

The Supreme Court's decision in *Basic* recognized the reality of the modern securities markets involving the trading of hundreds of millions of shares on a daily basis and that most ordinary investors do not read corporate reports or press releases. Acknowledging the presence of impersonal trading markets, the Court relied in part on economic theory and empirical studies to support its holding. In so ruling, the Court promoted the use of the class action to redress Section 10(b) violations. If the Court had required positive proof of individualized reliance from each plaintiff, individual issues may have predominated over the common ones, thereby impeding certification of class actions in this context.[101] Hence, the Court's decision looked to policy grounds as well to help ensure that ordinary investors have a viable recourse when they are defrauded in the impersonal trading markets.[102] Accordingly, the Court concluded:

> An investor who buys or sells stock at the price set by the market does so in reliance on the integrity of that price. Because most publicly available information is reflected in market price, an investor's reliance on any public material misrepresentations, therefore, may be presumed for purposes of a Rule 10b-5 action.[103]

It should be observed that only six Justices took part in the Court's decision, with Chief Justice Rehnquist, Justice Scalia, and Justice Kennedy not participating. In a sharp dissent, Justice White, joined by Justice O'Connor, disagreed with the Court's embracement of the fraud on the market theory, asserting:

> [I]n adopting a "presumption of reliance," the Court *also* assumes that buyers and sellers rely — not just on the market price — but on the *"integrity"* of that price. It is this aspect of the fraud-on-the-market hypothesis which most mystifies me. . . .

> Even if securities had some "value"—knowable and distinct from the market price of a stock — investors do not always share the Court's presumption that a stock's price is a "reflection of [this] value." Indeed, "many investors purchase or sell stock because they believe the price *inaccurately* reflects the corporation's worth." If investors really

---

[100] 485 U.S. at 244 (quoting *In re LTV Securities Litigation*, 88 F.R.D. 134, 143 (N.D. Tex. 1980)).

[101] As subsequently stated by the Fifth Circuit in *Unger v. Amedisys, Inc.*, 401 F.3d 316, 322 (5th Cir. 2005):

> Without an initial demonstration of market efficiency, there is no assurance that the available material information concerning the stock translates into an effect on the market price and supports a classwide presumption of reliance. Absent an effective market, individual reliance by each plaintiff must be proven, and the proposed class will fail the predominance requirement. Because this inquiry can prove decisive for class certification, and because, given the realities of litigation costs, certification can compel settlements without trial, courts have frequently applied rigorous, though preliminary, standards of proof to the market efficiency determination. . . . Although the court's determination for class certification purposes may be revised (or wholly rejected) by the ultimate factfinder, the court may not simply presume the facts of an efficient market.

[102] 485 U.S. at 245–46.

[103] *Id.* at 247.

believed that stock prices reflected a stock's "value," many sellers would never sell, and many buyers never buy. . . . "[104]

[1] Characteristics of an "Efficient" Market

In order for the presumption of the efficient market theory to apply, the subject security must be traded in an *efficient* market. In making this determination, the principal focus is on the market for that particular security and not on the location (such as the New York Stock Exchange or the Nasdaq Stock Market) where such security trades. Hence, for fraud on the market purposes, the market for each security is distinct, leading to the conclusion that a stock exchange (or over-the-counter market) can be efficient for some securities listed on such exchange but not for others.[105]

Therefore, what factors generally comprise an efficient market to support the *Basic* presumption of reliance? In *Unger v. Amedisys, Inc.*, the Fifth Circuit looked to the following factors:

> Courts have relied on several factors to determine whether a stock traded in an "efficient market": (1) the average weekly trading volume expressed as a percentage of total outstanding shares; (2) the number of securities analysts following and reporting on the stock; (3) the extent to which market makers and arbitrageurs trade in the stock; (4) the company's eligibility to file SEC registration Form S-3 (as opposed to Form S-1. . . .); (5) the existence of empirical facts "showing a cause and effect relationship between unexpected corporate events or financial releases and an immediate response in the stock price"; (6) the company's market capitalization; (7) the bid-ask spread for stock sales; and (8) float, the stock's trading volume without counting insider owned stock. . . .

> Although this does not represent an exhaustive list, and in some cases one of the above factors may be unnecessary, once a court endeavors to apply these factors, they must be weighed analytically, not merely counted, as each of them represents a distinct facet of market efficiency. . . .[106]

The foregoing factors have been applied by courts with regularity when determining whether a subject security trades in an efficient market.[107] One

---

[104] *Id.* at 256 (White, J., concurring in part and dissenting in part) (emphasis in original, citations omitted). *See generally* Symposium, *Revisiting the Mechanisms of Market Efficiency*, 28 J. Corp. L. No. 4 (2003); Black, *The Strange Case of Fraud on the Market: A Label in Search of a Theory*, 52 Albany L. Rev. 923 (1988); Langevoort, *Theories, Assumptions, and Securities Regulation: Market Efficiency Revisited*, 140 U. Pa. L. Rev. 851 (1992); Stout, *The Unimportance of Being Efficient: An Economic Analysis of Stock Market Pricing and Securities Regulation*, 87 Mich. L. Rev. 613 (1988); Wang, *Some Arguments That the Stock Market is Not Efficient*, 19 U.C. Davis L. Rev. 341 (1986).

[105] *See Harman v. Lyphomed, Inc.*, 122 F.R.D. 522, 525–526 (N.D. Ill. 1988).

[106] 401 F.3d 316, 323 (5th Cir. 2005).

[107] *See, e.g., Teamsters Local 445 Freight Division Pension Fund v. Bombardier, Inc.*, 546 F.3d 196 (2d Cir. 2008) (focusing on three of the above criteria, namely, the number of financial analysts

factor — namely, whether SEC Form S-3 is available — should be deemed far less significant today due to the Commission's expansion of eligibility of the Form S-3 to issuers whose securities are traded on a national securities exchange (as contrasted to the former $75 million float requirement).[108]

In a decision that may be viewed as novel and antithetical to investor interests, the Fifth Circuit in *Oscar Private Equity Investments v. Allegiance Telecom, Inc.*, held that plaintiffs must "demonstrate loss causation before triggering the presumption of reliance" and that "loss causation must be established at the class certification stage by a preponderance of the evidence."[109] Stated somewhat differently, the court held that plaintiffs may invoke *Basic's* fraud-on-the-market presumption of reliance only if they also show loss causation. Dissenting, Judge Dennis observed that the majority's approach "takes the novel step of making proof of loss causation a prerequisite to the establishment of reliance through the fraud-on-the-market presumption for purposes of [class] certification." The majority's holding, accordingly, "inexplicably requires plaintiffs to prove the separate element of loss causation at the class certification stage."[110] Thus far, the Fifth Circuit's approach has been rejected elsewhere. As the Second Circuit has held, to invoke the fraud-on-the-market theory, actual price impact is not required to be shown. Rather, under the Supreme Court's decision in *Basic*, "if plaintiffs can show that the alleged misrepresentation was material and publicly transmitted into a well-developed market, then reliance will be presumed. . . . "[111]

---

reporting on the security, the presence of market makers who were making a market in the security, and whether the market price of the security reacted promptly to unexpected material events or financial releases); *In re Polymedica Corp. Securities Litigation*, 432 F.3d 1 (1st Cir. 2005); *In re Xcelera.Com Securities Litigation*, 430 F.3d 503 (1st Cir. 2005); *No. 84 Employer-Teamster Joint Council Pension Trust Fund v. America West Holding Corp.*, 320 F.3d 920 (9th Cir. 2003); *Freeman v. Laventhol & Horwath*, 915 F.2d 193 (6th Cir. 1990); *Cammer v. Bloom*, 711 F. Supp. 1264 (D.N.J. 1989).

[108] Today, the Form S-3 can be used in primary offerings of common stock by an issuer which has timely filed Exchange Act reports for the prior twelve months, has a class of equity security traded on a national securities exchange, and is not (and has not been for at least twelve months) a shell company. *See* Securities Act Release No. 8878 (2007). This expansion of Form S-3 to encompass issuers' securities that may not be traded in an efficient market is a significant departure from prior SEC policy. *See supra* § 5.02.

[109] *Oscar Private Equity Investment v. Allegiance Telecom, Inc.*, 487 F.3d 261, 269–70 (5th Cir. 2007).

[110] *Id.* at 278 (Dennis, J., dissenting).

[111] *In re Salomon Analyst Metromedia Litigation*, 2008 U.S. App. LEXIS 20570 (2d Cir. 2008) (also stating that "plaintiffs do not bear the burden of showing an impact on price" and that "[u]nder *Basic* . . . the burden of showing that there was no price impact is properly placed on defendants at the rebuttal stage"); *see In re Nature's Sunshine Products, Inc. Securities Litigation*, 251 F.R.D. 656 (D. Utah 2008); *In re Micron Technologies, Inc. Securities Litigation*, 247 F.R.D. 627 (D. Idaho 2007).

[2]   Rebutting the Fraud on the Market Presumption of Reliance

In *Basic*, both the majority and the dissent observed that application of the fraud on the market theory creates a *rebuttable* presumption of reliance. In practice, this presumption generally has been rebutted when the disclosure deficiencies were corrected in the market by extensive media coverage. In such cases, because the press coverage credibly made available to the market the accurate information, the otherwise actionable misstatement (or omission) was rendered immaterial. The defendants' task in making this showing is difficult. To rebut the *Basic* presumption of reliance in this context, therefore, it must be shown that "any material information which [the defendants misstated or] fail[ed] to disclose must [have been] transmitted to the public with a degree of intensity and credibility sufficient to effectively counterbalance any misleading impression created by the [defendants] . . . "[112]

[C]   The "Fraud to Enter the Market" Theory

A more expansive version of the fraud-on-the-market theory, also called the "fraud to enter the market" theory, applies this doctrine to the offering context where no active trading market exists for the issuer's stock. The leading case is *Shores v. Sklar*[113] in which the Fifth Circuit sitting en banc adopted the theory, with ten judges dissenting. The Supreme Court has yet to rule on the theory's validity in this context.

In *Shores*, the plaintiff purchased bonds without reading the offering circular. He alleged in a Section 10(b) cause of action that the defendants had perpetrated a fraudulent scheme on the investment community by bringing unmarketable securities into the open market. Invoking the fraud to enter the market theory, the court held that an investor is entitled to rely on the integrity of the market to the extent that the securities offered for sale are entitled to be in the marketplace. To recover under this theory, the plaintiff must establish that the bonds would never have been issued or marketed. Proof that the bonds would have been offered at a lower price is not sufficient.[114] Thus, "the fraudulent scheme [must be] so pervasive that without it the issuer would not have issued, the dealer could not have dealt in, and the buyer could not have bought [the securities], because they would not have been offered at any price."[115] As subsequently construed by the Fifth Circuit, securities are deemed not entitled to be marketed, "only where the promoters knew the enterprise itself was patently worthless."[116]

---

[112] *In re Apple Computer Securities Litigation*, 886 F.2d 1109, 1116 (9th Cir. 1988); *see Raab v. General Physics Corporation*, 4 F.3d 286, 289 (4th Cir. 1993); *Wielgos v. Commonwealth Edison Co.*, 892 F.2d 509, 516 (7th Cir. 1989).

[113] 647 F.2d 462 (5th Cir. 1981) (en banc).

[114] *Id.* at 469–471.

[115] *Id.* at 464 n.2.

[116] *Abell v. Potomac Insurance Company*, 858 F.2d 1104, 1121–1122 (5th Cir. 1988), *vacated on other grounds*, 492 U.S. 914 (1988).

While the Fifth Circuit in *Shores* and its progeny examined how the market would have likely responded to the securities being offered absent the fraud, other courts have focused on the integrity of the regulatory process. For example, the Ninth Circuit held that reliance may be presumed if the investor "relie[d], at least indirectly, on the integrity of the regulatory process and the truth of any representations made to the appropriate agencies and the investors at the time of the original issue."[117]

The Seventh Circuit in *Eckstein v. Balcor Film Investors*[118] rejected the *Shores* "fraud to enter the market" theory. The court reasoned:

> *Shores* held that an investor may maintain an action under Section 10(b) by establishing that the fraud permitted the securities to exist in the market — that but for the fraud the securities would have been "unmarketable" — and that the investor relied on their existence. [We reject the *Shores* rationale.] . . . The existence of a security does not depend on, or warrant, the adequacy of disclosure. Many a security is on the market even though the issuer or some third party made incomplete disclosures. Federal securities law does not include "merit regulation." Full disclosure of adverse information may lower the price, but it does not exclude the security from the market. Securities of bankrupt corporations trade freely; some markets specialize in penny stocks. Thus the linchpin of *Shores* — that disclosing bad information keeps securities off the market, entitling investors to rely on the presence of the securities just as they would rely on statements in a prospectus — is simply false.[119]

After rejecting the *Shores* rationale, the Seventh Circuit opted for a different approach. In *Eckstein*, the limited partnership offering was subject to a minimum sale requirement. To prevail on the issue of reliance, the Seventh Circuit required that plaintiffs prove that, absent the fraud, the limited partnership would not have met the minimum sale requirement.[120]

[D]   Plaintiff Due Diligence

The plaintiff "due diligence" requirement has been equated by a number of courts with the element of justifiable reliance. Generally, the following factors are deemed relevant in determining whether the plaintiff's reliance was justifiable:

> (1) the sophistication and expertise of the plaintiff in financial and securities matters; (2) the existence of long standing business or personal relationships; (3) access to the relevant information; (4) the

---

[117] *Arthur Young & Co. v. United States District Court*, 549 F.2d 686, 695 (9th Cir. 1977). The Tenth Circuit has adopted a similar approach. *See T.J. Raney & Sons, Inc., v. Fort Cobb, Okla. Irrigation Fuel Authority*, 717 F.2d 1330, 1332 (10th Cir. 1983).

[118] 8 F.3d 1121 (7th Cir. 1993).

[119] *Id.* at 1130–31.

[120] *Id.* at 1131. *See generally* Herzog, *Fraud Created the Market: An Unwise and Unwarranted Extension of Section 10(b) and Rule 10b-5*, 63 Geo. Wash. L. Rev. 359 (1995).

existence of a fiduciary relationship; (5) concealment of the fraud; (6) the opportunity to detect the fraud; (7) whether the plaintiff initiated the stock transaction or sought to expedite the transaction; and (8) the generality or specificity of the misrepresentations.[121]

Two policy rationales for the plaintiff due diligence requirement are: "First, general principles of equity suggest that only those who have pursued their own interests with care and good faith should qualify for the judicially created private [Rule] 10b-5 remedies. Second, by requiring plaintiffs to invest carefully, the court promotes the anti-fraud policies of the Acts and engenders stability in the markets."[122]

In light of the Supreme Court's decision in *Hochfelder* requiring a plaintiff to prove the defendant's scienter in order to recover under Section 10(b),[123] courts have altered the plaintiff's due diligence burden. Rather than mandating that the plaintiff establish due care, these courts now require that such plaintiff's burden simply is to negate that he/she acted recklessly when engaging in the subject securities transaction.[124]

Two interesting issues have surfaced in the plaintiff due diligence setting. The first issue, called the "bespeaks caution" doctrine (which has been codified by Congress), concerns whether disclosure of the pertinent risk factors (and other cautionary statements) in the written offering documents will render the plaintiff's reliance on certain forward-looking or "soft" statements contained in other portions of such offering materials unjustified. The second issue is whether a plaintiff may justifiably rely on allegedly false oral statements when the written offering documents are accurate.

[1]   The "Bespeaks Caution" Doctrine

The "bespeaks caution" doctrine may be viewed from both "materiality" and "reliance" perspectives. The doctrine, which does not extend to statements of historical fact, provides that "where an offering statement, such as a prospectus, [contains] statements of future forecasts, projections and expectations with adequate cautionary language, those statements are not actionable as securities fraud."[125] Hence, under the "bespeaks caution" doctrine, adequate cautionary statements make reliance on the projections or

---

[121] *Zobrist v. Coal-X, Inc.*, 708 F.2d 1511, 1516 (10th Cir. 1983). This standard has been applied by many courts. *See, e.g., Brown v. E.F. Hutton Group, Inc.*, 991 F. 2d 1020 (2d Cir. 1993); *Myers v. Finkle*, 950 F.2d 165 (4th Cir. 1991).

[122] *Dupuy v. Dupuy*, 551 F.2d 1005, 1014 (5th Cir. 1977).

[123] *See supra* § 8.03[A].

[124] *Mallis v. Bankers Trust Co.*, 615 F.2d 68, 79 (2d Cir. 1980). *See Landry v. All American Assurance Co.*, 688 F.2d 381, 392–93 (5th Cir. 1982); Gabaldon, *Unclean Hands and Self-Inflicted Wounds: The Significance of Plaintiff Conduct in Actions for Misrepresentation Under Rule 10b-5*, 71 Minn. L. Rev. 317 (1986); Sachs, *The Relevance of Tort Law Doctrines to Rule 10b-5: Should Careless Plaintiffs Be Denied Recovery?*, 71 Cornell L. Rev. 96 (1985).

[125] *In re Donald J. Trump Casinos Securities Litigation*, 793 F. Supp. 543, 544 (D.N.J. 1992), *aff'd*, 7 F.3d 357 (3d Cir. 1993); *see Livid Holdings Ltd. v. Salomon Smith Barney Inc.*, 416 F.3d 940, 948 (9th Cir. 2005) (holding that "extension of the bespeaks caution doctrine to statements of

other soft information unreasonable and renders the statements, when read in conjunction with the cautionary language, immaterial.[126] The Private Securities Litigation Reform Act of 1995 (PSLRA) codifies the "bespeaks caution" doctrine. This doctrine is addressed more fully in Chapter 11.

[2] Reliance on Oral Statements Inconsistent with Written Offering Materials

Another interesting issue that surfaces in securities litigation is whether a plaintiff justifiably relies on allegedly false or misleading oral statements when the written offering documents (such as a prospectus or private placement memorandum) are accurate. In most jurisdictions, the fact that the written offering documents are accurate is not dispositive. When analyzing this issue, courts have focused on the reliance and materiality components.[127]

With respect to the issue of reliance (also referred to in this setting as plaintiff due diligence or justifiable reliance), many courts embrace the eight-factor test set forth above.[128] In adhering to this standard, "no single factor is determinative; all relevant factors must be considered and balanced to determine whether reliance was justified."[129] Nonetheless, as applied by a number of courts, a key determinant is whether there exists a fiduciary relationship between the defendant and plaintiff.[130] Some courts also give great weight to the level of the plaintiff's financial sophistication.[131]

That the plaintiff failed to read the offering document, allegedly because of the document's complexity, is irrelevant. In other words, provided that the offering document is timely transmitted and contains sufficient disclosure, the contents of such offering document are imputed to the investor even if not read by the investor.[132] Nonetheless, if key disclosures (such as risk factors) are

---

historical fact is inappropriate"); *see also Asher v. Baxter International, Inc.*, 377 F.3d 727 (7th Cir. 2004).

[126] *See, e.g., Rubinstein v. Collins*, 20 F.3d 160, 167 (5th Cir. 1994). For legal commentary on the "bespeaks caution" doctrine as well as the federal legislation providing a safe harbor for certain forward-looking statements, see, for example, Barondes, *The Bespeaks Caution Doctrine: Revisiting the Application of Federal Securities Law to Opinions and Estimates*, 19 J. Corp. L. 243 (1994); Langevoort, *Disclosures That "Bespeak Caution,"* 49 Bus. Law. 481 (1994); O'Hare, *Good Faith and The Bespeaks Caution Doctrine: It's Not Just a State of Mind*, 58 U. Pitt. L. Rev. 619 (1997); Symposium, 51 Bus. Law. No. 4 (1996); Symposium, 33 San Diego L. Rev. No. 3 (1996); Symposium, 24 Sec. Reg. L.J. No. 2 (1996); Note, *Who Is Bespeaking to Whom? Plaintiff Sophistication, Market Information, and Forward-Looking Statements*, 45 Duke L.J. 579 (1995); *see also* Ahdieh, *The Strategy of Boilerplate*, 104 Mich. L. Rev. 1033 (2006).

[127] *See, e.g., Myers v. Finkle*, 950 F.2d 165 (4th Cir. 1991).

[128] *See supra* note 121 (and accompanying text).

[129] *Zobrist v. Coal-X, Inc.*, 709 F.2d 1511, 1516–1517 (10th Cir. 1983).

[130] *See, e.g., Brown v. E.F. Hutton Group, Inc.*, 991 F.2d 1020, 1031–33 (2d Cir. 1993).

[131] *See, e.g., Myers v. Finkle*, 950 F.2d 165, 165–167 (4th Cir. 1991). *See generally Layman v. Combs*, 981 F.2d 1093, 1103–08 (9th Cir. 1993) (Kozinski, J., dissenting); Fletcher, *Sophisticated Investors Under the Federal Securities Laws*, 1988 Duke L.J. 1081.

[132] 950 F.2d at 167 (stating that "[i]nvestors are charged with constructive knowledge of the

buried in the offering document or indigestible, a different result may follow.[133]

Some courts, particularly the Seventh Circuit, adhere to a more restrictive approach based on a "materiality" analysis. Stated generally, under this interpretation, the written word trumps the oral.[134] Hence, so long as the written words are clear and complete, "written words govern oral ones in order to reward truthful disclosures and facilitate accurate assessment of risk."[135] Under this analysis, an oral statement that contradicts disclosures in the written offering is deemed immaterial (because such oral statement does not significantly alter the mix of information on which the investor acts).[136]

§ 8.07 CUMULATIVE REMEDIES

Under a cumulative interpretation of the securities laws, a party may invoke a remedy even though another statute may provide another remedy for the same conduct. In *Herman & MacLean v. Huddleston*,[137] the Supreme Court adopted a cumulative construction to Section 10(b), thereby recognizing an implied right of action for damages under Section 10(b) despite the apparent availability of an express cause of action under Section 11 of the 1933 Act. The Court reasoned that, unlike Section 11, Section 10(b) imposes a heavier burden on the plaintiff by mandating that the defendant's scienter be proven in order to recover. Moreover, while Section 11 applies solely in the registered offering context, Section 10(b) is a "catch-all" antifraud provision designed to reach manipulative or deceptive practices in connection with the purchase or sale of any security, whether traded in the primary or secondary markets.[138]

Although the Court in *Huddleston* did not directly hold, its language strongly suggests that a cumulative approach between Section 10(b) and other express rights of action, such as Section 12(a)(2) of the Securities Act and Section 18(a) of the Exchange Act, is appropriate where the express remedy does not require the plaintiff to prove scienter.[139] In other words, the various procedural restrictions that apply in actions invoking the express remedies (which restrictions are somewhat absent in suits brought under Section 10(b)) are counterbalanced by Section 10(b)'s scienter requirement. Based in large part on this rationale, the lower courts adhere to a cumulative approach where

---

risks and warnings contained in the private placement memoranda"); *see also Sylverson v. Firepond, Inc.*, 383 F.3d 745 (8th Cir. 2004).

[133] *See, e.g., Kennedy v. Tallant*, 710 F.2d 711, 720 (11th Cir. 1983).

[134] *See, e.g., Eckstein v. Balcor Film Investors*, 8 F.3d 1121, 1131–32 (7th Cir. 1993); *Acme Propane, Inc. v. Tenexco, Inc.*, 844 F.2d 1317, 1325 (7th Cir. 1988). In *Eckstein*, the Seventh Circuit also stated that "in the event statements in sales brochures and the prospectus do not agree, the prospectus wins." 8 F.3d at 1131.

[135] 844 F.2d at 1325.

[136] *See, e.g., Teamsters Local 282 Pension Trust Fund v. Angelos*, 762 F.2d 522, 530 (7th Cir. 1985); *Flamm v. Eberstadt*, 814 F.2d 1169, 1173 (7th Cir. 1983).

[137] 459 U.S. 375 (1983).

[138] *Id.* at 380–84; *see SEC v. J.W. Barclay & Co., Inc.*, 442 F.3d 834, 841 (3d Cir. 2006).

[139] *Id.* at 382–387.

the express remedy invoked is Section 11 or 12(a)(2) of the Securities Act or Section 18(a) of the Exchange Act.[140]

Huddleston retains particular significance with respect to 1934 Act Section 18(a) claims.[141] Section 18(a) provides an express right of action for damages (subject to a good faith defense) when an investor purchases or sells a security in reliance upon a materially false or misleading statement that is contained in a document filed with the SEC pursuant to the Exchange Act, where such statement affects the price of the security. Because of Section 18(a)'s strict reliance and causation requirements, a suit based solely on Section 18(a) may pose challenging hurdles. Moreover, because of Section 18(a)'s focus on individualized proof of reliance, class action certification may well be problematic.[142] Accordingly, the Section 10(b) action is normally the preferred route.[143] Whether the increasingly intensive focus by institutional and other sophisticated investors on 1934 Act reports will result in more Section 18(a) actions being brought remains to be seen.[144]

A more difficult issue is presented when a cumulative approach is sought to be invoked between Section 10(b) and Section 9 of the Exchange Act. Under Section 9 (which provides a private remedy for purchasers and sellers who have been victimized by stock manipulation), the plaintiff in order to recover must prove scienter, reliance, causation, and damages. Moreover, plaintiffs suing under Section 9 are subject to rigorous procedural limitations. As one court has observed, Section 9 "permits the court to require security for costs, limits damages to losses sustained by reason of the unlawful price manipulation, provides for contribution by persons not joined as defendants in the original action, and permits the court to assess attorneys' fees against either party."[145] Hence, due to the breadth of the Section 9 requirements, plaintiffs bringing suit under Section 10(b) are subject to no additional burdens. Indeed, when contrasted with the Section 9 express remedy, the Section 10(b) right of action is more attractive in a number of respects and is not less attractive in any respect.[146]

---

[140] *See, e.g., Berger v. Bishop Investment Corp.*, 695 F.2d 302 (8th Cir. 1982); *Wachovia Bank & Trust Co. v. National Student Marketing Corp.* 650 F.2d 342 (D.C. Cir. 1980); *Ross v. A.H. Robins, Co.*, 607 F.2d 545 (2d Cir. 1979).

[141] *See* Steinberg, *The Propriety and Scope of Cumulative Remedies Under the Federal Securities Laws*, 67 Cornell L. Rev. 557, 579–84 (1982).

[142] *Compare Beebe v. Pacific Realty Trust*, 99 F.R.D. 60 (D. Ore. 1983) (denying class certification due to § 18's reliance requirement), *with Simpson v. Specialty Retail Concepts*, 149 F.R.D. 94 (M.D.N.C. 1993) (holding § 18 common issues prevailed over issue of reliance, thereby granting class certification). *See generally* Grant & McIntyre, *Class Certification and Section 18 of the Exchange Act*, 35 Rev. Sec. & Comm. Reg. 255 (2002).

[143] *See generally* L. Loss & J. Seligman, *supra* note 27, at 4296–4300; Siegel, *Interplay Between the Implied Remedy Under Section 10(b) and the Express Causes of Action of the Federal Securities Laws*, 62 Bos. U. L. Rev. 385 (1982).

[144] *See* discussion *infra* § 9.07.

[145] *Wolgin v. Magic Marker Corp.*, 82 F.R.D. 168, 180 (E.D. Pa. 1979). *See* discussion *supra* § 8.05[C].

[146] *See generally Chemetron Corp. v. Business Funds, Inc.*, 718 F.2d 725 (5th Cir. 1983), 682 F.2d 1149 (5th Cir. 1982).

Nonetheless, cogent reasons exist for recognizing a cumulative remedy in this context. Perhaps the most persuasive is that an exclusive approach precluding a Section 10(b) right of action where a Section 9 express remedy is available would afford less protection to investors who trade on a national securities exchange than to those who trade in the over-the-counter market. It is beyond dispute that Section 9 applies by its terms only to transactions on a national securities exchange. To fill this vacuum, courts have uniformly held that such manipulative practices that occur in the over-the-counter market may be redressed by private claimants under Section 10(b).[147] Because these claimants are not saddled with the limitations of Section 9, they may successfully seek redress under Section 10(b) in situations in which injured investors who trade on a national securities exchange under an exclusive construction of remedies would be denied recovery.[148]

Such a result is not only misplaced but is contrary to congressional intent. The Securities Acts Amendments of 1964 were the ultimate result of a congressionally-mandated special study conducted by the Securities and Exchange Commission.[149] The study recommended, inter alia, that Congress strengthen over-the-counter regulation. Congress followed this recommendation in order to provide, as much as practicable, equality of regulation between the national securities exchange and over-the-counter markets. At no time, however, did Congress intend to create greater rights on behalf of over-the-counter investors as compared to those given to investors who trade in stock exchange listed securities.

Thus, Congress' approach is sound and firmly rooted in the reality of the operations of the securities markets. In contrast, an exclusive construction of remedies fragmentizes the operational components of the securities markets and ignores that the markets operate as a unified whole where those desiring to buy or sell may do so with confidence. Denying private parties the use of Section 10(b) with respect to manipulative schemes in listed securities would insulate from monetary liability practices repugnant to the notions of honesty and fairness. Such a construction goes far toward undermining the very interests the securities laws were designed to promote.[150]

§ 8.08 STATUTE OF LIMITATIONS

Today, the statute of limitations for Section 10(b) claims is two years after discovery of the violation by the plaintiff and in no event more than five years after the violation. This statute was enacted as part of the Sarbanes-Oxley Act of 2002 (SOX).

---

[147] *See, e.g., Wachovia Bank & Trust Co. v. National Student Marketing Co.*, 650 F.2d 342 (D.C. Cir. 1980).

[148] *See* discussion *supra* § 8.05[C].

[149] Report of Special Study of Securities Markets of the Securities and Exchange Commission, H.R. Doc. No. 95, 88th Cong., 1st Sess. (1963).

[150] *See supra* notes 138–43 (sources cited therein).

Perhaps surprisingly, increasing the length of the applicable statute of limitations is the one express change that the Sarbanes-Oxley Act effected with respect to private rights of action. Instead of amending Section 10(b) to set forth a statute of limitations, Congress elected to amend 28 U.S.C. § 1658 (which contains a general statute of limitations).[151] As enacted, Section 1658(b) provides that:

> [A] private right of action that involves a claim of fraud, deceit, manipulation, or contrivance in contravention of a regulatory require- ment concerning the securities laws, as defined in section 3(a)(47) of the Securities Exchange Act of 1934, may be brought not later than the earlier of —
>
> (1) 2 years after the discovery of the facts constituting the violation; or
> (2) 5 years after such violation.[152]

Prior to the enactment of SOX, being an implied private right of action, Section 10(b) did not provide by its terms for a statute of limitations. In *Lampf*, the Supreme Court chose a Section 10(b) statute of limitations of one-year after discovery within a three-year period of repose framework (one-year/three-year limitations period) and held that the doctrine of equitable tolling was unavail- able under Section 10(b).[153] Today, the SOX two-year/five-year statute of limitations applies to actions based on violation of Section 10(b) (as well as SEC rules and regulations prescribed thereunder that provide for a private remedy). Other federal securities law rights of action that require proof of fraud, deceit or manipulation likewise are subject to the two-year/five-year statute of limitations.[154] Although the language of 28 U.S.C. § 1658 suggests that the plaintiff must have actual knowledge of the facts constituting the violation, lower federal courts continue, as they did prior to SOX, to impose an inquiry notice standard. Under this approach, the two-year period in the statute begins to run when the plaintiff knew or should have known of the facts constituting the violation.[155]

---

[151] 28 U.S.C. § 1658(a) sets forth a four-year statute of limitations unless otherwise provided by law.

[152] 28 U.S.C. § 1658. Section 3(a)(47) of the Exchange Act states: "The term 'securities laws' means the Securities Act of 1933, the Securities Exchange Act of 1934, the Sarbanes-Oxley Act of 2002, the Public Utility Holding Company Act of 1935, the Trust Indenture Act of 1939, the Investment Company Act of 1940, the Investment Advisers Act of 1940, and the Securities Investor Protection Act of 1970."

[153] *Lampf, Pleva, Lipkind, Prupis & Petigrow v. Gilbertson*, 501 U.S. 350 (1991). Under the doctrine of equitable tolling, generally the statute of limitations is tolled during the time in which the victim of the fraud remains in ignorance of it through no lack of diligence on his/her part. *See id.* at 363.

[154] Nonetheless, lower courts thus far have declined to extend 28 U.S.C. § 1658 to claims (such as Section 11 of the Securities Act or Section 14(a) of the Exchange Act) that do not require proof of fraud, where the complainant elects to plead fraud or deception. *See, e.g., In re Alstom SA Securities Litigation*, 406 F. Supp. 2d 402 (S.D.N.Y. 2005) (and cases cited therein).

[155] *See e.g., Shah v. Meeker*, 435 F.3d 244 (2d Cir. 2006). For case law prior to SOX, see, for example, *Dodds v. Cigna Securities, Inc.*, 12 F.3d 346 (2d Cir. 1993). Note that the courts have applied Section 1658 on a prospective, not retroactive, basis. *See, e.g., Margolies v. Deason*, 464

§ 8.09   MEASURE OF DAMAGES

Much of the discussion that follows applies to damages under the securities laws in general. Because the proper measure of damages most often arises in Section 10(b) litigation, the subject will be treated here. For damages in insider trading cases, Chapter 12 should be consulted.

The federal securities laws limit recovery to "actual damages." Although this measure does not preclude a recovery of damages that exceed mere compensation, punitive damages may not be awarded.[156] Moreover, in SEC enforcement actions, disgorgement and monetary penalties may be levied for violations of Section 10(b) as well as for violations of other provisions of the securities laws.[157]

Section 28(a) of the Exchange Act thus has been construed by the courts to prohibit recovery of punitive, as opposed to compensatory damages, and to prevent double recovery by those who assert both state and federal claims which arise out of the same conduct.[158] The measures of compensatory damages adopted by the courts primarily include the out-of-pocket measure[159] and, in some circumstances, the rescissionary[160] and benefit-of-the-bargain measures.[161] In certain contexts, other measures of damages have been applied.[162] As a general proposition, however, "[t]he customary measure of damages in a Rule 10b-5 case is the out-of-pocket loss."[163]

Nonetheless, where the amount of damages can be determined with reasonable certainty, courts may apply the benefit-of-the-bargain measure, particularly if such application is necessary to prevent unjust enrichment.[164] A number of courts, however, have refused to apply this measure due to the asserted speculative nature of the damages which would otherwise be

---

F.3d 547 (5th Cir. 2006). For discussion of the statute of limitations in SEC enforcement actions, see *infra* § 15.08.

[156] *See Randall v. Loftsgaarden*, 478 U.S. 647 (1986).

[157] *See* discussion *infra* §§ 15.04[B], 15.05[D], 15.07.

[158] *See, e.g., Affiliated Ute Citizens v. United States*, 406 U.S. 128, 155 (1972); *Osofsky v. Zipf*, 645 F.2d 107, 111 (2d Cir. 1981); *Gould v. American-Hawaiian Steamship Co.*, 535 F.2d 761, 781 (3d Cir. 1976).

[159] *See, e.g., Estate Counselling Service, Inc. v. Merrill Lynch, Pierce, Fenner & Smith, Inc.*, 303 F.2d 527, 533 (10th Cir. 1962) (defining the out-of-pocket measure as "the difference between the contract price, or the price paid, and the real or actual value at the date of the sale, together with such outlays as are attributable to the defendant's conduct").

[160] *See, e.g., Blackie v. Barrack*, 524 F.2d 891, 909 (9th Cir. 1975); *see also Randall v. Loftsgaarden*, 478 U.S. 647 (1986).

[161] *See, e.g., Osofsky v. Zipf*, 645 F.2d 107, 111–15 (3d Cir. 1981).

[162] *See, e.g., Chasins v. Smith Barney & Co.*, 428 F.2d 1167, 1173 (2d Cir. 1970) (awarding a defrauded buyer the value of the consideration paid for the security less the sale price of the security prior to plaintiff's awareness of the misconduct). For the disgorgement measure, see *infra* note 166 and accompanying text.

[163] *Hackbart v. Holmes*, 675 F.2d 1114, 1121 (10th Cir. 1982).

[164] *Id.* at 1122; *see Madigan, Inc. v. Goodman*, 498 F.2d 233, 239 (7th Cir. 1974).

awarded.[165]

In addition, the Private Securities Litigation Reform Act of 1995 (PSLRA) added a new Section 21D(e) to the Securities Exchange Act. In general, this provision places a limitation on damages in 1934 Act actions where the plaintiff attempts to establish such damages by reference to the market price of a security. In this context, the award of damages is the difference between the purchase or sale price paid or received by the plaintiff, as applicable, and the mean trading price of the security during the 90-day period beginning on the date on which the information correcting the misstatement or omission that is the basis for the action is disseminated to the market. For these purposes, the "mean trading price" of such security is the average of the daily trading price of such security, determined as of the close of the market each day during the 90-day period referred to above.

In sum, as set forth by Professor Kaufman, the key measures of damages are as follows:

> The benefit-of-the-bargain measure is generally understood as the difference between the represented value of the security purchased or sold and the fair value of the security on the date of the trade. Out-of-pocket relief . . . represents "the difference between the fair value of all that the [plaintiff] received and the fair value of what he would have received had there been no fraudulent conduct." . . . Disgorgement. . . . returns to the plaintiff the amount of the defendant's unjust enrichment. Under the disgorgement theory, the plaintiff recovers the defendant's profit resulting from the fraud, rather than the plaintiff's losses. Finally, rescission, by contrast, is the judicial act of undoing a transaction, restor[ing] each party to its pre-transaction condition.[166]

---

[165] *See, e.g., Barrows v. Forest Laboratories, Inc.,* 742 F.2d 54 (2d Cir. 1984). *See generally* Alexander, *Rethinking Damages in Securities Class Actions,* 48 Stan. L. Rev. 1487 (1996); Dickey & Mays, *Effect on Rule 10b-5 Damages of the 1995 Private Securities Litigation Reform Act: A Forward-Looking Assessment,* 51 Bus. Law. 1203 (1996); Easterbrook & Fischel, *Optimal Damages in Securities Cases,* 52 U. Chicago L. Rev. 611 (1985); Lowenfels & Bromberg, *Compensatory Damages in Rule 10b-5 Actions: Pragmatic Justice or Chaos?,* 30 Seton Hall L. Rev. 1083 (2000); Thompson, *Simplicity and Certainty in the Measure of Recovery Under Rule 10b-5,* 51 Bus. Law. 1177 (1996); Thompson, *The Measure of Recovery Under Rule 10b-5: A Restitution Alternative to Tort Damages,* 37 Vand. L. Rev. 349 (1984); Comment, *The Measure of Damages Under Section 10(b) and Rule 10b-5,* 46 Md. L. Rev. 1266 (1987).

[166] Kaufman, *No Foul, No Harm: The Real Measure of Damages Under Rule 10b-5,* 39 Cath. U. L. Rev. 29, 31 (1989); *see* M. Kaufman, Securities Litigation: Damages (1989 & Supp.); *supra* note 165 (authorities cited therein).

§ 8.10 *IN PARI DELICTO* DEFENSE

In the past, considerable debate was generated regarding the propriety of the *in pari delicto* defense in securities litigation.[167] In the *Bateman Eichler* case,[168] the Supreme Court limited the availability of the defense in a Section 10(b) civil damages action where corporate insiders and a broker allegedly conveyed false "inside" information. In so doing, the Court applied a two-part test to ascertain whether the *in pari delicto* defense should be permitted. First, it looked to the relative culpability of the parties to the action. Second, the Court examined public policy considerations. Hence, a Section 10(b) action for damages may be barred on the grounds of the plaintiff's own culpability only where: (1) as a direct result of his/her own actions, the plaintiff bears at least substantially equal responsibility for the violations he/she seeks to redress; and (2) preclusion of suit would not significantly interfere with the effective enforcement of the federal securities laws and protection of the investing public.[169]

Turning to the first prong, the *Bateman Eichler* Court found that the plaintiff "tippees" were less blameworthy than the defendant "tippers." As the Court stated, "[i]n the context of insider trading, we do not believe that a person whose liability is solely derivative can be said to be as culpable as one whose breach of duty gave rise to that liability in the first place."[170]

Regarding the second prong, the Court asserted that permitting private suits for damages in this context would enhance the enforcement of the securities laws and would serve as a deterrent to the perpetration of insider trading. Moreover, by bringing such an action and exposing oneself to civil and criminal penalties, a tippee would not enjoy a "heads-I-win, tails-you-lose" scenario. Accordingly, public policy would be promoted by allowing such actions.[171]

After *Bateman Eichler*, it was uncertain whether the Court's analysis therein applied to the federal securities laws in general. The Court answered this question affirmatively in an action involving Section 12(1) [now 12(a)(1)] of the Securities Act, *Pinter v. Dahl*.[172] In *Pinter*, the Court held that the *Bateman Eichler* standard "provides the appropriate test for allowance of the *in pari delicto* defense in a private action under any of the federal securities laws."[173] The Court reasoned that, irrespective of whether the substantive statute imposes liability for willful or negligent misconduct or even is one of strict liability (such as Section 12(a)(1)), there may be occasions where the

---

[167] *See, e.g.,* Comment, *Rule 10b-5: The In Pari Delicto and Unclean Hands Defenses,* 58 Cal. L. Rev. 1149 (1970).

[168] *Bateman Eichler, Hill Richards, Inc. v. Berner,* 472 U.S. 299 (1985).

[169] *Id.* at 310–11.

[170] *Id.* at 313 (citing *Dirks v. SEC,* 463 U.S. 646 (1983)).

[171] 472 U.S. at 315–16.

[172] 486 U.S. 622 (1988). For discussion on Section 12(a)(1), see *supra* § 7.08.

[173] 486 U.S. at 622.

objective of deterring unlawful conduct is served better by precluding suit rather than by allowing recovery.[174]

Applying the *Bateman Eichler* standard to the Section 12(1) [now 12(a)(1)] litigation at bar, the *Pinter* Court's analysis indicates that the *in pari delicto* defense will rarely be successful in this context. According to the Court, the defense can be used only when the plaintiff's role in the offer or sale of the securities is more that of a promoter than an investor. Whether a plaintiff primarily is an investor or a promoter depends on several factors, such as "the extent of the plaintiff's financial involvement compared to that of third parties solicited by the plaintiff, the incidental nature of the plaintiff's promotional activities, the benefits received by the plaintiff from his promotional activities, and the extent of the plaintiff's involvement in the planning stages of the offering."[175]

In the Section 12(a)(1) setting, in situations where the plaintiff is deemed to be primarily an investor, the *in pari delicto* defense is unavailable. This is true even if the plaintiff-investor actively participates in the distribution of the unregistered securities. The *Pinter* Court reasoned that a contrary holding would pose a significant obstacle to the effective enforcement of the Securities Act's registration provisions and to the goal of investor protection.[176]

§ 8.11 CONTRIBUTION, PROPORTIONATE LIABILITY, AND RELATED ISSUES

In *Musick, Peeler & Garrett v. Employers Insurance of Wausau*,[177] the Supreme Court recognized an implied right of action for contribution under Section 10(b). The Court focused its inquiry on "how the 1934 Congress would have addressed the issue had the [Section 10(b)] action been included as an express provision in the 1934 Act."[178] Of the eight liability provisions contained in the 1933 and 1934 Acts, the Court found that 1934 Act Sections 9 and 18 impose liability upon defendants who occupy a position most similar to Section 10(b) defendants for ascertaining entitlement to contribution. Since both Sections 9 and 18 expressly provide for contribution, the Court reasoned that "consistency requires us to adopt a like contribution rule for the right of action existing under Rule 10b-5."[179]

The Court rejected the argument that two of its relatively recent decisions outside of the securities law arena that declined to recognize an action for

---

[174] *Id.* at 634.

[175] *Id.* at 639 (citations omitted).

[176] *Id.* at 638. For lower court case law, see, *e.g.*, *Brandaid Marketing Corp. v. Biss*, 462 F.3d 216 (2d Cir. 2006); *Ross v. Bolton*, 904 F.2d 819 (2d Cir. 1990). *See generally* Klock, *Promoter Liability and In Pari Delicto Under Section 12(1):* Pinter v. Dahl, 17 Sec. Reg. L.J. 53 (1989).

[177] 508 U.S. 286 (1993).

[178] *Id.* at 294.

[179] *Id.* at 297.

contribution[180] signified that contribution likewise was inappropriate under Section 10(b). The Court reasoned that these cases construed statutory provisions that provided for express rights of action but did not by their terms recognize a right to contribution. While the ramifications of these cases may foreclose recognizing a right to contribution under express securities law remedial provisions that do not by their terms provide for this right of action (such as with respect to Securities Act Section 12(a)(2)),[181] a different analysis applies to implied rights. Here, because the judiciary has implied the Section 10(b) private right of action, it is the Court's role to elaborate, define, and shape the contours of this remedy.[182] Applying this analysis, the Court concluded that "[t]hose charged with liability in a [Section 10(b)] action have a right to contribution against other parties who have joint responsibility for the violation."[183]

The Supreme Court in *Musick* declined to focus on how contribution should be apportioned among the (alleged) tortfeasors. Historically, three methods emerged: pro rata, proportionate fault, and pro tanto.

The first measure, *the pro rata method*, was the least favored and has been rejected by Congress in its enactment of the Private Securities Litigation Reform Act of 1995 (PLSRA). Under this approach, "the judgment amount is simply divided by the number of defendants, settling and non-settling, that are found liable."[184] Although this method of allocating contribution lends itself to ease of administration, its major disadvantage is that the parties' relative culpability is not a consideration.[185] Due to this drawback, the pro rata method is "rarely invoked."[186]

Under *the proportionate fault method*, the "jury assesses the relative culpability of both settling and non-settling defendants, and the *non*-settling defendant pays a commensurate percentage of the judgment."[187] The Supreme Court has adopted this approach in the maritime context, holding that under the proportionate fault method "no suits for contribution from settling defendants are permitted, nor are they necessary, because the non-settling defendants pay no more than their share of the judgment."[188] Several courts have applied the proportionate fault method.[189] Under this method, the plaintiff assumes the risk of a "bad" settlement, and therefore has an incentive to

---

[180] *See Texas Industries, Inc. v. Radcliff Materials, Inc.*, 481 U.S. 630 (1981) (no right to contribution based on violation of § 1 of the Sherman Act); *Northwest Airlines, Inc. v. Transport Workers*, 451 U.S. 77 (1981) (no right to contribution pursuant to Equal Pay Act and Title VII of the Civil Rights Act of 1964).

[181] The issue of contribution under Section 12(a)(2) is addressed *supra* § 7.09[F].

[182] 508 U.S. at 291.

[183] *Id.* at 298.

[184] *In re Jiffy Lube Securities Litigation*, 927 F.2d 151, 161 (4th Cir. 1991).

[185] *See Smith v. Mulvaney*, 827 F.2d 558, 561 (9th Cir. 1987).

[186] *Cortec Industries, Inc. v. Sun Holding L.P.*, 839 F. Supp. 1021, 1026 (S.D.N.Y. 1993).

[187] *In re Jiffy Lube*, 927 F.2d at 160 n.3 (emphasis supplied).

[188] *McDermott, Inc. v. Amclyde*, 511 U.S. 202, 209 (1994).

[189] *See, e.g., Bragger v. Trinity Enterprise Corp.*, 30 F.3d 14, 17 (2d Cir. 1994) (dicta); *Franklin*

procure from each settling defendant a share of damages that is proportionate to each such defendant's culpability. A key disadvantage to this method is that the factfinder must ascertain not only the degree of culpability of each nonsettling defendant but also of each of the settling parties who no longer are parties to the action.[190]

Turning to the third approach, *the pro tanto method* "reduces a nonsettling defendant's liability for a judgment against him/her in the amount paid by a settling defendant."[191] Or, phrased differently, under this approach, "when a plaintiff receives a settlement from one defendant, a nonsettling defendant is entitled to a credit of the settlement amount against any judgment obtained by the plaintiff against the nonsettling defendant so long as both the settlement and judgment represented common damages."[192] The pro tanto method is favorable for plaintiffs as the risk of a "bad" settlement is borne by the nonsettling defendants who must pay the balance of the plaintiff's damages. This prospect gives rise to concerns of collusion between the plaintiff and a "favored" defendant as well as the imposition of damages against a non-settling defendant out of proportion to such party's relative fault. Nonetheless, this method encourages settlement and eliminates the need for any further consideration of the culpability of settling defendants even if the remaining defendants proceed to trial. Moreover, a "fairness" hearing to approve a pretrial settlement may be conducted by the court, thereby helping to ensure that the settlement amounts resemble each settling party's relative culpability.[193]

Issues relating to contribution and proportionate fault were addressed by Congress' enactment of the Private Securities Litigation Reform Act. Pursuant to the PSLRA, Congress amended the Securities Exchange Act to add new Section 21D(g) thereto. This new section (1) circumscribes the scope of the current joint and several liability scheme; (2) creates a proportionate liability framework for actions brought against multiple defendants under the Exchange Act or against "outside directors" of the issuer whose securities are the subject of an action under Section 11 of the Securities Act; and (3) clarifies several issues relating to partial settlements in federal securities actions.

First, the statute limits the application of joint and several liability for damages to apply only if the trier of fact specifically determines that the defendant in question "knowingly committed" a violation of the Securities Exchange Act (or, if an outside director, of Section 11 of the Securities Act). The section provides that the term "knowingly committed" requires actual

---

v. Kaypro Corporation, 884 F.2d 1222 (9th Cir. 1989); *In re Del-Val Corporation Securities Litigation*, 868 F. Supp. 547 (S.D.N.Y. 1994).

[190] *See Alvarado Partners L.P. v. Mehta*, 723 F. Supp. 540, 552–553 (D. Colo. 1989).

[191] *In re Masters Mates & Pilots Pension Plan*, 957 F.2d 1020, 1029 (2d Cir. 1992).

[192] *Singer v. Olympia Brewing Co.*, 878 F.2d 596, 600 (2d Cir. 1989).

[193] *See In re Masters Mates & Pilots Pension Plan*, 957 F.2d at 1029; *Cortec Industries*, 839 F. Supp. at 1027; *MFS Municipal Income Trust v. American Medical Int'l, Inc.*, 751 F. Supp. 279, 287 (D. Mass. 1990). *See generally* Friedman, *Contribution and Partial Settlements in Securities Fraud Actions in Light of* McDermott, Inc. v. AmClyde, 23 Sec. Reg. L.J. 143 (1995); Moses & Sutton, *Contribution Under Rule 10b-5*, 26 Rev. Sec. & Comm. Reg. 159 (1993).

knowledge as the scienter standard and specifically provides that recklessness cannot constitute a knowing violation. Further, the PSLRA codifies the right to contribution among such joint tortfeasors recognized by the Supreme Court in *Musick, Peeler.* Under this framework of contribution, the legislation provides that the liability of such defendants is to be premised upon findings of percentage of responsibility as to each jointly and severally liable defendant.

Second, by implication, in all actions wherein the "knowingly committed" scienter standard cannot be proven by the plaintiff but the lesser standard of recklessness may be shown, the PSLRA creates a proportionate liability scheme and (with certain exceptions) restricts liability for damages solely to that portion of the judgment that corresponds to the percentage of each individual defendant's responsibility for plaintiffs' losses. In addition, if certain individually liable defendants' shares of liability are uncollectible due to insolvency or some other reason, the statute requires additional proportionate contributions either from the jointly and severally liable defendants or, if still uncollectible, from other proportionately liable defendants for those uncollectible shares in certain specified circumstances.

The PSLRA further provides specific guidelines for determining the percentage of each individual defendant's responsibility for damages in the form of directing the court (1) to instruct the trier of fact to answer special interrogatories; or (2) to itself make special findings with respect to multiple defendants on specific issues. Such issues are to include, among other things, the percentage of responsibility of each defendant and whether the defendant "knowingly committed" violations so as to properly place that defendant within the joint and several liability scheme.

Third, the PSLRA, in addressing the subject of partial settlements in federal securities actions, provides for the discharge of all claims for contribution brought by any other persons, whether or not such persons have themselves settled with the plaintiff, against any defendant that has settled any private action at any time prior to judgment. Moreover, the section requires that a settlement bar order be entered by the court constituting the discharge of all obligations to the plaintiff of the settling defendant "arising out of the action." The legislation makes clear that such bar orders apply to contribution actions brought by and against the settling defendant.

In addition, the PSLRA provides for a new judgment reduction method applicable in multidefendant partial settlement cases. This method serves to reduce the plaintiff's subsequent judgment against any nonsettling defendant by the *greater* amount of either (1) the proportionate responsibility of the settling defendant(s) as determined by the court or jury, or (2) the amount that such settling defendant(s) already paid to the plaintiff pursuant to the respective settlement agreement.[194]

---

[194] *See* Langevoort, *The Reform of Joint and Several Liability Under the Private Securities Litigation Reform Act of 1995: Proportionate Liability, Contribution Rights and Settlement Effects*, 51 Bus. Law. 1157 (1996); Steinberg & Olive, *Contribution and Proportionate Liability Under the Federal Securities Laws*, 50 SMU L. Rev. 337 (1996).

§ 8.12 THE PRIVATE SECURITIES LITIGATION REFORM ACT (PSLRA): CLASS ACTION REFORM AND RELATED ISSUES

[A] Class Action Reform

The PSLRA amends both the Securities Act and the Exchange Act to add new Sections 27(a) and 21D(a), respectively. These sections are intended to address the problem of "professional plaintiffs" and other abusive practices in private securities class actions. The content of these sections includes the following:

(1) A requirement that each plaintiff seeking to serve as a representative party on behalf of a class file with the complaint a sworn certification that: (i) the plaintiff reviewed the complaint and authorized its filing; (ii) the plaintiff did not purchase the securities in question at the direction of counsel or in order to participate in a private action; (iii) the plaintiff is willing to both serve as a representative party on behalf of the class and provide both deposition and trial testimony; (iv) sets forth all of such plaintiff's particular securities transactions that are the subject of the class action; (v) identifies any other action filed during the preceding three-year period in which the plaintiff sought to serve as a representative party on behalf of a class; and (vi) the plaintiff will not accept payment for serving as a representative party on behalf of a class beyond the plaintiff's pro rata share of any recovery, except as approved by the court. The plaintiff's filed certification will not be deemed a waiver of the attorney-client privilege.

(2) Guidelines for early notice (not later than twenty days after the filing of the complaint) to class members pertaining to the appointment of the lead plaintiff. Such notice must appear "in a widely circulated national business-oriented publication or wire service." Within sixty days of such publication, any member of the purported class may seek to serve as lead plaintiff.

(3) Provisions requiring the court to consider any motion by a purported class member in response to the class notice to be appointed as the lead plaintiff. These provisions require the court to adopt a rebuttable presumption that the "most adequate plaintiff" is the person with the largest financial interest in the relief sought by the class, but allows for discovery on such motions in limited circumstances. However, these provisions also mandate restrictions on "professional plaintiffs" in declaring that, except as the court may otherwise permit (such as with respect to institutional investors), a person may be a lead plaintiff (or an officer, director, or fiduciary of a lead plaintiff) in no more than five securities class actions brought as plaintiff class actions during any three-year period.

(4) Provisions limiting the lead plaintiff's recovery to its proportionate share of any judgment or settlement, as well as reasonable costs and expenses, including lost wages.

(5) The prohibition of settlements under seal except in limited circumstances.

(6) Provisions limiting the award of attorneys' fees and expenses to a "reasonable percentage" of the amount of any damages and prejudgment interest "actually paid" to the class. These provisions do not address how attorneys' fees should be calculated in cases where the relief awarded or settlement does not include monetary damages.

(7) Specific and mandatory procedures for the disclosure of settlement terms to class members (including disclosure of the amount of plaintiff recovery, statement of attorneys' fees and costs sought, identification of lawyers' representatives to answer questions, and statement of the reasons for settlement).

(8) Provisions requiring the court to determine whether an interest on the part of plaintiff's counsel in the securities in question constitutes a conflict of interest sufficient to disqualify the attorney from representing the party.

In addition, the 1934 Act is amended to authorize the court to require security for payment of class action fees and expenses.

These sections taken together likely have reduced the abusive practices of plaintiffs' counsel in securities class actions. However, it is evident that the efficacy of these sections depend on the extent to which institutional investors choose to "come forward" and utilize the PSLRA framework.[195]

[B] Sanctions for Abusive Litigation

The PSLRA amends the 1933 and 1934 Acts to mandate court review, upon final adjudication of private securities actions thereunder, of the parties' or their attorneys' compliance with Rule 11(b) of the Federal Rules of Civil Procedure requirements for a good faith factual and legal basis as to any pleading or dispositive motion. If the court finds that there is a "substantial failure" of the parties or attorneys to comply with its provisions, the court is directed to impose mandatory sanctions in accordance with Rule 11.

The provisions set forth a rebuttable presumption that sanctions for violation of Rule 11(b) are the reasonable attorneys' fees and costs incurred as a direct result of such violation. This presumption may be rebutted by the

---

[195] Securities Act § 27; Securities Exchange Act § 21D; Private Securities Litigation Reform Act, Joint Explanatory Statement of the Committee of Conference (1995); *see* T. Hazen, *supra* note 27, at 316–18, 512–17; *Symposium*, 51 Bus. Law. No. 4 (1996); *Symposium*, 33 San Diego L. Rev. No. 3 (1996); *Symposium*, 24 Sec. Reg. L.J. No. 2 (1996); Symposium, 76 Wash. U.L.Q. No. 2 (1998).

sanctioned party or attorney only upon proof that (i) the award will present an unreasonable burden or (ii) the violation was "de minimis."[196]

[C]   Stay of Discovery and Preservation of Evidence

The PSLRA amends the 1933 and 1934 Acts to provide for (i) a stay of discovery during the pendency of any motion to dismiss unless the court finds that particularized discovery is necessary to preserve evidence or to prevent undue prejudice to a party; and (ii) the preservation of evidence relevant to the allegations of the complaint during the pendency of any stay of discovery. A party aggrieved by the willful failure of an opposing party to comply with the provisions requiring preservation of evidence may seek appropriate sanctions. These provisions therefore enable defendants who succeed in their motions to dismiss to avoid the discovery and related expenses associated with securities litigation.[197]

[D]   Auditor Disclosure of Corporate Fraud

The PSLRA amends the 1934 Act by adding a Section 10A thereto. Section 10A sets forth requirements for audits conducted by an independent public accountant of an issuer's financial statements to include certain procedures to (1) detect illegal acts that would have a direct and material effect on the determination of financial statement amounts; (2) identify related party transactions material to financial statements; and (3) evaluate an issuer's ability to continue as a going concern. The statutory language makes clear that the above procedures are to be carried out in accordance with current generally accepted accounting principles (GAAP) "as may be modified from time to time by the [SEC]." The existing auditing standards provide for all three types of procedures prescribed in Section 10A.

Section 10A further specifies notification and reporting guidelines for a public accountant who becomes aware of information indicating possible illegal activities during the course of an audit. The provisions also appear to codify current generally accepted accounting principles. If, in the course of an audit the public accountant detects or otherwise becomes aware of information indicating that an illegal act has or may have occurred, the accountant must (1) determine the likelihood that an illegal act has occurred; (2) determine the possible effect of the illegal act on the issuer's financial statements, including contingent effects such as fines, penalties, or damages; and (3) inform appropriate management and assure that the issuer's audit committee (or, if none, its board of directors) is adequately informed (unless such illegal act clearly is inconsequential).

A further requirement is imposed by Section 10A when the subject accountant concludes that: (1) the illegal act has a material effect on the issuer's financial statements; (2) senior management has not taken "timely and appropriate remedial actions" in regard to the illegal act; and (3) the failure to

---

[196] *See supra* note 195 (sources cited therein).

[197] *Id.*

take "remedial action" is likely to cause the accountant to depart from a standard report or to resign from its capacity as auditor. Under these conditions the accountant must, "as soon as is practicable," report such conclusions to the board of directors. A board of directors receiving a report from such an accountant must inform the SEC within one business day of receipt of the report and must give the accountant a copy of the notice sent to the SEC. If, however, the accountant does not receive a copy of the notice within this time, such accountant must provide the SEC with a copy of such accountant's report (or documentation of such accountant's oral report) to the board of directors within one business day after the issuer fails to provide to the accountant the notice copy. Even if the accountant elects to resign, it must still furnish the SEC with a copy of its report within the same time period.

As a last point, Section 10A stipulates that an accountant who furnishes a report to the SEC under this statute will not be held liable in any private action for any findings, conclusions, or statements in the report. However, the willful failure to file a required report will subject the accountant "and any other person that the [SEC] finds was a cause of such violation" to cease-and-desist proceedings as well as the imposition of civil penalties.[198]

§ 8.13　EXTRATERRITORIAL JURISDICTION

Extraterritorial jurisdiction implicating the federal securities laws comes into play in a number of different contexts, including in civil litigation involving Section 10(b). For purposes of organization, this subject will be treated here.

[A]　Transnational Fraud

The principal extraterritorial application of the federal securities laws has involved the area of transnational fraud. In an effort to protect American investors and to prevent this country from being employed as a base for deceptive conduct in transactions abroad affecting American or foreign investors, the U.S. courts have given broad extraterritorial application to the antifraud provisions of the federal securities laws. To determine whether subject matter jurisdiction exists, two tests have developed: (1) the "conduct" test and (2) the "effects" test.

Under the *conduct* test, courts generally have applied Section 10(b) of the Exchange Act to foreign transactions occurring abroad when fraudulent conduct of material importance (*e.g.*, a misstatement causing an investor's acquisition of a security) or conduct integrally associated with a fraud (*e.g.*, the drafting of an inaccurate offering document used to sell stock) that directly caused the plaintiff's alleged damages took place within the United States.[199] Hence, in situations in which conduct transpiring in the United States was

---

[198] *See* discussion *infra* §§ 10.03, 15.04[A], [B], 15.07; *supra* note 195 (sources cited therein).

[199] *See, e.g., Kautbar SDN BHD v. Steinberg*, 149 F.3d 659 (7th Cir. 1998); *Robinson v. TCI/US West Cable Communications*, 117 F.3d 900 (5th Cir. 1997); *Butte Mining PLC v. Smith*, 76 F.3d 287 (9th Cir. 1996) (setting forth a somewhat more relaxed standard); *Leasco v. Data Processing Equipment Corp.*, 468 F.2d 1326 (2d Cir. 1972).

merely preparatory to the fraud, courts frequently have declined to find subject matter jurisdiction where the complainant was a foreign, rather than a United States, citizen.[200] Nonetheless, subject matter jurisdiction would be appropriate in the case of a foreign plaintiff where "culpable acts or omissions occurring [in the United States] directly caused losses to investors abroad."[201]

Applying the *effects* test, courts have found subject matter jurisdiction when securities transactions outside of the United States had substantial and foreseeable injurious effects in this country. For example, fraudulent conduct undertaken abroad, which caused a decrease in the value of stock listed on a U.S. exchange, was viewed as coming within the ambit of the federal securities laws, irrespective that no conduct, preparatory or otherwise, took place in the United States in regard to the transaction abroad.[202] The number of defrauded U.S. residents compared to foreign residents also has been considered by U.S. courts under the effects test.[203]

[B] Securities Act Registration

In 1990, the SEC adopted Regulation S in an attempt to clarify the extraterritorial application of Section 5 of the Securities Act. The ramifications of Regulation S and its impact on extraterritorial application are addressed in § 3.17. As a general matter, note that in this context antifraud issues are not implicated.

---

[200] *See, e.g., Morrison v. National Australia Bank,* 547 F.3d 167 (2d Cir. 2008); *Zoelsch v. Arthur Andersen & Co.,* 824 F.2d 27 (D.C. Cir. 1987); *Bersch v. Drexel Firestore, Inc.,* 519 F.2d 974 (2d Cir. 1978).

[201] *Morrison v. National Australia Bank,* 547 F.3d 167 (2d Cir. 2008); *see SEC v. Berger,* 322 F.3d 187 (2d Cir. 2003); *Alfadda v. Fenn,* 935 F.2d 475 (2d Cir. 1991); *Psimenos v. E.F. Hutton & Co.,* 722 F.2d 1041 (2d Cir. 1983); *ITT v. Cornfeld,* 619 F.2d 909 (2d Cir. 1980); *see also Europe & Overseas Commodity Traders, S.A. v. Banque Paribas London,* 147 F.3d 118 (2d Cir. 1998) (declining to exercise jurisdiction even though key misstatements were made in the United States where none of the parties or companies were U.S. citizens or entities); *supra* note 199 (cases cited therein).

The Second Circuit recently interpreted the parameters of subject matter jurisdiction in a "foreign-cubed" securities action. *Morrison v. National Australia Bank,* 547 F.3d 167 (2d Cir. 2008). In a "foreign-cubed" suit, "a set of (1) *foreign* plaintiffs is suing (2) a *foreign* issuer in an American court for violations of American securities laws based on securities transactions in (3) *foreign* countries." *Id.* As stated by the Second Circuit in *Morrison*:

> Under the "conduct" component, subject matter jurisdiction exists if activities in this country were more than merely preparatory to a fraud and culpable acts or omissions occurring here directly caused losses to investors abroad. Our determination of whether American activities "directly" caused losses to foreigners depends on what and how much was done in the United States and on what and how much was done abroad.

[202] *See, e.g., Schoenbaum v. Firstbrook,* 405 F.2d 200, *modified en banc,* 405 F.2d 215 (2d Cir. 1969); *see also Itoba Ltd. v. Lep Group PLC,* 54 F.3d 118 (2d Cir. 1995).

[203] *See, e.g., IIT v. Vencap, Ltd.,* 519 F.2d 1001 (2d Cir. 1975).

[C] Tender Offers

Another area involving the extraterritorial application of the securities laws is tender offer regulation. Foreign issuers seeking to purchase the securities of other foreign issuers which have U.S. shareholders have been careful to restrict their public communications concerning the bid in order to avoid triggering the Williams Act as well as the SEC's tender offer rules. This approach may be successful in certain situations. In one such instance, for example, General Electric Company plc made an offer to acquire a number of shares of the Plessey Company plc. Both companies were doing business pursuant to Great Britain law. Plessey, however, had American Depository Receipts (ADRs) trading in the U.S. securities markets and had certain other Dollar Shares registered in this country. To avoid implicating the United States tender offer regimen, General Electric refrained from issuing any press releases to the American press concerning the bid, made it clear in its communications to the press that the bid was neither being made in the United States nor was such bid for the Plessey ADRs or Dollar Shares, and took additional precautions to help guarantee that shares would not be accepted from stockholders in the United States.[204]

A United States district court ruled that the federal tender offer regimen did not extend to the General Electric offer. The court opined that, as contrasted with the antifraud provisions, it was more appropriate under the tender offer provisions to assess considerations of comity and policy in this area. As such, the court, after evaluating relevant factors, declined to invoke extraterritorial jurisdiction.[205] However, as the Second Circuit more recently held, if allegations of fraud are present in the tender offer setting, then the "conduct" and "effects" tests discussed above[206] are the proper standards.[207]

---

[204] *The Plessey Company PLC v. The General Electric Company PLC*, 628 F. Supp. 477, 479–86 (D. Del. 1986).

[205] *Id.* at 494–97.

[206] *See supra* notes 199–203 (and accompanying text).

[207] *See Consolidated Gold Fields PLC v. Minorco, S.A.*, 871 F.2d 252 (2d Cir. 1989). *See generally* Buxbaum, *Multinational Class Actions Under Federal Securities Law: Managing Jurisdictional Conflict*, 46 Colum. J. Tran'l L. 14 (2007); Choi & Guzman, *Portable Reciprocity: Rethinking the International Reach of Securities Regulation*, 71 S. Cal. L. Rev. 903 (1998); Lowenfels & Bromberg, *U.S. Securities Fraud Across the Border: Unpredictable Jurisdiction*, 55 Bus. Law. 975 (2000); Mann & Barry, *Developments in the Internationalization of Securities Enforcement*, 39 Int'l Law. 667, 937 (2005); Sachs, *The International Reach of Rule 10b-5: The Myth of Congressional Silence*, 28 Colum. J. Tran. L. 677 (1990); Thomas, *Extraterritorial Application of the United States Securities Laws: The Need for a Balanced Policy*, 7 J. Corp. L. 189 (1982).

Chapter 9

ALTERNATIVE REMEDIES

§ 9.01 INTRODUCTION

As Chapters 7 and 8 have discussed, Section 11 of the Securities Act and Section 10(b) of the Exchange Act play important roles in securities litigation. These provisions, however, may be unavailable to a complainant for a number of reasons. For example, the securities may have been purchased in the aftermarket, hence making the Section 11 right of action unavailable (unless the plaintiff meets the onerous "tracing" requirement). Or, alternatively, the complainant may be unable to invoke the Section 10(b) remedy because he/she is not a "purchaser" or "seller" or cannot establish that the defendant acted with scienter. Or, as a last example, the alleged violation may have occurred in connection with a proxy solicitation or tender offer. Under such circumstances, counsel should focus on the availability of alternative remedies, including the invocation of implied remedies.

Moreover, even where a right of action may be successfully established (such as under Section 10(b)), counsel, where appropriate, still should assess the viability of remedies afforded by other provisions. For example, recovery may be afforded under Section 14(a) based on the defendant's negligence whereas Section 10(b) mandates proof of scienter. As another example, Section 29(b) of the Exchange Act may provide an aggrieved party with the right to rescind the subject transaction. As an additional point, counsel always should assess the advisability of seeking relief under the applicable state common and statutory (including "Blue Sky") laws.

§ 9.02 IMPLIED RIGHTS OF ACTION — IN GENERAL

[A] Pre-1975 Approach

Prior to 1975, the federal courts liberally recognized implied private rights of action, generally looking to whether the granting of an implied remedy would benefit the class sought to be protected by the statute. For example, in *J.I. Case Co. v. Borak*,[1] the Supreme Court recognized an implied right of action under Section 14(a) of the Exchange Act (the "proxy" provision), reasoning that such an implied right would promote investor protection and serve as a necessary supplement to SEC enforcement action.

---

[1] 377 U.S. 426 (1964).

[B] The *Cort* Formulation and Its Apparent Demise

The liberal construction to implied rights of action halted with the Supreme Court's decision in *Cort v. Ash*.[2] There, the Court formulated a four-prong standard:

> First, is the plaintiff "one of the class for whose especial benefit the statute was enacted," — that is, does the statute create a federal right in favor of the plaintiff? Second, is there any indication of legislative intent, explicit or implicit, either to create such a remedy or to deny one? Third, is it consistent with the underlying purpose of the legislative scheme to imply such a remedy for the plaintiff? And finally, is the cause of action one traditionally relegated to state law, in an area basically the concern of the States, so that it would be inappropriate to infer a cause of action based solely on federal law?[3]

In subsequent decisions, the Supreme Court embraced the *Cort* formulation with varying levels of enthusiasm.[4] Perhaps somewhat ironically (given the pre-1975 broad construction to implied rights), certain members of the Court criticized the *Cort* standard as being "an open invitation to federal courts to legislate causes of action not authorized by Congress."[5]

The evident demise of the *Cort* formulation was evidenced by *Transamerica Mortgage Advisors, Inc. v. Lewis*,[6] where the Supreme Court refused to imply a private right of action under the antifraud provision of the Investment Advisers Act, Section 206. There, the Court, relying on its prior decision in *Redington*,[7] stated that the central inquiry is to examine Congress' intent. Hence, the Court reasoned:

> The question whether a statute creates a cause of action, either expressly or by implication, is basically a matter of statutory construction. While some opinions of the Court have placed considerable emphasis upon the desirability of implying private rights of action in order to provide remedies thought to effectuate the purposes of a given statute, what must ultimately be determined is whether Congress intended to create the private remedy asserted. . . . We accept this as the appropriate inquiry to be made in resolving the issue presented by the case before us.[8]

---

[2] 422 U.S. 66 (1975).

[3] *Id.* at 78.

[4] *Compare Cannon v. University of Chicago*, 441 U.S. 677 (1979), *with Touche Ross & Co. v. Redington*, 422 U.S. 560 (1979) (*discussed in* Steinberg, *Implied Rights of Action Under Federal Law*, 55 Notre Dame Law. 33 (1979)).

[5] *See Cannon v. University of Chicago*, 441 U.S. 677, 731 (1979) (Powell, J., dissenting).

[6] 444 U.S. 11 (1979).

[7] *Touche Ross & Co. v. Redington*, 442 U.S. 560 (1979) (holding that no implied private right of action exists under Exchange Act § 17(a)).

[8] 444 U.S. at 15–16.

Thus, in *Lewis* the Court adhered to what has been viewed as a restrictive approach. Some other cases, however, indicated that the *Cort* formulation possibly survived. *California v. Sierra Club*,[9] a non-securities law case, highlighted the disagreement on the Court concerning the continued viability of *Cort*. There, in declining to imply a right of action under the pertinent statute, the five-member majority adhered to the *Cort* formulation and asserted:

> Combined, these four factors present the relevant inquiries to pursue in answering the recurring question of implied causes of action. Cases subsequent to *Cort* have explained that the ultimate issue is whether Congress intended to create a private right of action, but the four factors specified in *Cort* remain the "criteria through which this intent could be discerned."[10]

Concurring in the judgment, Justice Rehnquist (joined by three other Justices) in a separate opinion believed that "the Court's opinion places somewhat more emphasis on *Cort v. Ash* than is warranted in light of several more recent 'implied right of action' decisions which limit it."[11]

Nonetheless, more recent U.S. Supreme Court decisions such as *Virginia Bankshares*[12] and *Central Bank of Denver*[13] reflect a return to a more restrictive approach. In *Virginia Bankshares*, for example, the Court approvingly quoted from *Touche Ross v. Redington* that the "central inquiry remains whether Congress intended to create, either expressly or by implication, a private cause of action." Hence, the Court in *Virginia Bankshares* made clear that congressional intent is "accorded primacy among the considerations that might be thought to bear on any decision to recognize a private remedy."[14] Similarly, in *Central Bank of Denver*, the Court focused on the language of the statute as the controlling factor.[15]

---

[9] 451 U.S. 287 (1981).

[10] *Id.* at 293.

[11] *Id.* at 302 (Rehnquist, J., concurring in the judgment).

[12] *Virginia Bankshares, Inc. v. Sandberg*, 501 U.S. 1083 (1991).

[13] *Central Bank of Denver v. First Interstate Bank of Denver*, 511 U.S. 164 (1994). *See Stoneridge Investment Partners, LLC v. Scientific-Atlanta, Inc.*, 128 S. Ct. 761, 772 (2008) (stating that "it is settled that there is an implied cause of action only if the underlying statute can be interpreted to disclose the intent to create one"); *Alexander v. Sandoval*, 532 U.S. 275, 290 (2001) (stating that "[t]he express provision of one method of enforcing a substantive rule suggests that Congress intended to preclude others").

[14] 501 U.S. at 1103. Reflecting on the viability of the four-prong *Cort* test, the Seventh Circuit has opined that the test survives "only nominally." Hence, "courts may not recognize an implied remedy absent persuasive evidence that Congress intended to create one." *Spicer v. Chicago Board of Options Exchange, Inc.*, 977 F.2d 255, 258 (7th Cir. 1992).

[15] 511 U.S. at 173; *see Alexander v. Sandoval*, 532 U.S. 275, 286–287 (2001) (in finding no private right of action under disparate-impact regulations adopted pursuant to the Civil Rights Act of 1964, stating that "the judicial task is to interpret the statute Congress has passed to determine whether it displays an intent to create not just a private right but also a private remedy [and that] statutory intent . . . is determinative"). *See generally* Grundfest, *Disimplying Private Rights of Action Under the Federal Securities Laws: The Commission's Authority*, 107 Harv. L. Rev. 961 (1994).

§ 9.03 AVAILABILITY OF IMPLIED RIGHTS OF ACTION UNDER SELECT STATUTES

The lower federal courts have issued scores of decisions focusing on whether a private right of action should be implied under certain provisions of the federal securities laws. A number of these provisions are discussed later in this Chapter.

The federal courts, for example, have:

— Refused to recognize an implied right of action under Section 6 of the Exchange Act (i) against a national securities exchange based on the exchange's failure to enforce its own rules;[16] or (ii) against a broker-dealer, listed corporation, or other subject party based on a violation of exchange rules.[17]

— Declined to imply a private damages action under Section 7 of the Exchange Act on behalf of investors against financial institutions and brokers for violation of the margin requirements. In this regard, Section 7 authorizes the Federal Reserve Board to regulate margin transactions and prohibits violation of the Board's regulations. Generally, the regulations promulgated by the Board under the authority of Section 7 set the margin rate for securities purchased at 50 percent, meaning that the purchaser must advance the other 50 percent of the purchase price of the securities bought "on margin."[18] Declining to imply a Section 7 right of action, the Second Circuit reasoned:

> We . . . hold that no private right of action exists under Section 7. First, . . . there is simply no evidence that in passing Section 7 Congress intended to create a private action. . . . Second, Section 7 was clearly not passed for the "especial benefit" of individual investors. The major reason for enacting Section 7 was to control the excessive use of credit in securities transactions. . . . Finally, it is doubtful that allowing a private cause of action would be consistent with the underlying purposes of the legislative scheme. As stated above, the underlying purpose of Section 7 is to regulate the use of credit in securities transactions. As the addition of Section 7(f) makes clear, this regulation is aimed at both lenders and investors. While allowing a private cause of action could conceivably deter violations by lenders, it seems just as conceivable that it could encourage violations by investors seeking to shift the risk of loss.[19]

— In the tender offer setting, implied a private right of action for damages under the tender offer antifraud statute, Section 14(e) of the Exchange Act, on behalf of target corporation shareholders but not a damages remedy on behalf of the offeror.[20] With respect to the availability of *injunctive* (rather than

---

[16] *See, e.g., Walck v. American Stock Exchange, Inc.*, 687 F.2d 778 (3d Cir. 1982).

[17] *See, e.g., Jablon v. Dean Witter & Co.*, 613 F.2d 677 (9th Cir. 1980). *But see Buttrey v. Merrill Lynch, Pierce, Fenner & Smith, Inc.*, 410 F.2d 135 (7th Cir. 1979), for a more liberal construction.

[18] *See Walck v. American Stock Exchange, Inc.*, 687 F.2d 778 (3d Cir. 1982).

[19] *Bennett v. United States Trust Company of New York*, 770 F.2d 308, 312 (2d Cir. 1985).

[20] *See Piper v. Chris-Craft Industries, Inc.*, 430 U.S. 1 (1977) (applying *Cort*, defeated tender

monetary) relief under Sections 13(d), 14(d), and 14(e) of the 1934 Act,[21] courts generally have implied such a right of action on behalf of an issuer (namely the "target") corporation based on the rationale that the target company is the "only party with both the capability and incentive to pursue [a prospective bidder's] violations."[22]

— Implied private rights of action under certain provisions of the Investment Company Act[23] and the Trust Indenture Act.[24]

§ 9.04　SECTION 17(a) OF THE SECURITIES ACT

[A]　Generally

Section 17(a) of the Securities Act provides:

> It shall be unlawful for any person in the offer or sale of any securities by the use of any means or instruments of transportation or communication in interstate commerce or by the use of the mails, directly or indirectly —
>
> (1) to employ any device, scheme, or artifice to defraud, or
>
> (2) to obtain money or property by means of any untrue statement of a material fact or any omission to state a material fact necessary in order to make the statements made, in the light of the circumstances under which they were made, not misleading, or

---

offeror does not have standing to bring an implied action for damages under § 14(e)); *Panter v. Marshall Field & Co.*, 646 F.2d 271 (7th Cir. 1981) (target shareholders sought relief under § 14(e)).

[21] *See, e.g., Motient Corp. v. Dondero*, 529 F.3d 532 (5th Cir. 2008) (holding no private right of action for damages exists under § 13(d)). Sections 13(d), 14(d) and 14(e) were passed by Congress in 1968 as part of the Williams Act which, in effect, amended the Exchange Act. They are discussed in Chapter 14.

[22] *Indiana National Corp. v. Rich*, 712 F.2d 1180, 1184 (7th Cir. 1983). ("In this respect and for this limited purpose, therefore, the issuer corporation acts on the shareholders' behalf in bringing a suit for injunctive relief until an accurate Schedule 13D is filed."); *see Mobil Corp. v. Marathon Oil Co.*, 669 F.2d 366 (6th Cir. 1981); *Dan River, Inc. v. Unitex, Ltd*, 624 F.2d 1216 (4th Cir. 1980). *But see Edelson v. Chi'en*, 405 F.3d 620 (7th Cir. 2005) (opining that § 13(d) may be invoked by a plaintiff only in the setting of a tender offer or other share acquisition relating to control); *In re Dow Chemical Securities Bhopal Litigation*, [2000–2001 Transfer Binder] Fed. Sec. L. Rep. (CCH) ¶ 91,282 (S.D.N.Y. 2000) (holding bidder corporation's shareholders lacked standing to bring § 13(d) action); *Mates v. North American Vaccine, Inc.*, 53 F. Supp. 2d 814 (D. Md. 1999) (former member of issuer's board of directors lacked standing to bring § 13(d) action in her individual capacity). *See also* discussion *infra* § 14.07.

[23] *See, e.g., Bancroft Convertible Fund, Inc. v. Zico Investment Holdings, Inc.*, 825 F.2d 731 (3d Cir. 1987); *Fogel v. Chestnut*, 668 F.2d 100 (2d Cir. 1981). *But see Olmsted v. Pruco Life Insurance Co.*, 283 F.3d 429 (2d Cir. 2002) (no private right of action under the Investment Company Act for violation of statutory provisions concerning the levying of charges, fees and expenses upon variable annuity contracts); *Jacobs v. Bremner*, 378 F. Supp. 2d 861 (N.D. Ill. 2005) (no private right of action under § 36(a) of the Investment Company Act).

[24] *See, e.g., Ziffiro v. First Pennsylvania Banking and Trust Co.*, 623 F.2d 290 (3d Cir. 1980). *See generally* Johnson, *The "Forgotten" Securities Statute: Problems in the Trust Indenture Act*, 13 Toledo L. Rev. 92 (1981).

(3) to engage in any transaction, practice, or course of business which operates or would operate as a fraud or deceit upon the purchaser.

Section 17(a), the 1933 Act's antifraud provision, applies only to the offer or sale of securities. Hence, the prohibitions of Section 17(a) do not reach fraud in the purchase of securities. Based upon the Supreme Court's decisions in *United States v. Naftalin*[25] and *Aaron v. SEC*,[26] Section 17(a) has emerged as an attractive enforcement weapon for the SEC.

[B]   Supreme Court Decisions

The Supreme Court in *Naftalin* handed down three significant principles regarding Section 17(a). First, the protection afforded by Section 17(a)(1) extends beyond investors to encompass financial intermediaries such as broker-dealers. Second, the language of Section 17(a) relating to the prohibition of fraud "in" an offer or sale of securities (as contrasted with Section 10(b)'s "in connection with" language) was sufficiently inclusive to cover the defendant Naftalin's misconduct. And third, Section 17(a) not only applies in the initial offering context but also extends to the secondary trading markets.[27] This last holding is particularly important. Prior to *Naftalin*, some authorities believed that, as part of the Securities Act which is directed at the regulation of initial offerings, Section 17(a) was likewise limited to the initial offering context. Hence, with respect to misconduct occurring in the aftermarket context involving the offer or sale of securities, *Naftalin's* effect is to subject such misconduct to the prohibitions of both Section 17(a) and Section 10(b).[28]

The importance of *Naftalin* to the SEC became evident when the Supreme Court handed down its decision in *Aaron*. In *Aaron*, the Court, applying a linguistic analysis, held that in SEC actions seeking injunctive relief, scienter must be proven to establish a violation of Section 10(b) of the Exchange Act and Section 17(a)(1) of the Securities Act.[29] To show violations of Section 17(a)(2) and 17(a)(3), on the other hand, the SEC need only establish the defendant's negligence.[30]

Note the effect of *Aaron*, when considered in light of *Naftalin*. Upon the making of a proper showing (*i.e.*, a reasonable likelihood that, absent the ordering of an injunction, future violations will occur), the SEC can invoke Section 17(a)(2) or 17(a)(3) to obtain injunctive relief based on a defendant's negligent misconduct which occurred in the offer or sale of securities in the

---

[25] 441 U.S. 768 (1979).

[26] 446 U.S. 680 (1980).

[27] 441 U.S. at 773–78.

[28] For further discussion, see Steinberg, *Section 17(a) of the Securities Act After* Naftalin *and* Redington, 68 Georgetown L.J. 163 (1979).

[29] 446 U.S. at 696.

[30] *Id.* at 696–697. The *Aaron* decision also is discussed *supra* § 8.03[B], *infra* § 15.05[A].

secondary trading markets. In view of this consequence, Section 17(a) becomes an appealing enforcement weapon to the SEC in the "offer or sale" context.

Moreover, based upon legislation enacted in 1990, the SEC has cease and desist authority.[31] This remedy, coupled with the effects of *Naftalin* and *Aaron*, provides the Commission with the authority to issue a cease and desist authority based upon a party's negligent conduct. Hence, Section 17(a) is a powerful weapon in the SEC's arsenal.

[C] Availability of Implied Right of Action

Based upon a linguistic analysis (as the Supreme Court applied in *Aaron*), the assertion has been made that, if a private damages action were implied under Section 17(a), the requisite culpability standard would be that of negligence.[32] On the other hand, the Supreme Court has stressed that it is inappropriate to imply a private right of action that is significantly more expansive than the provisions that Congress expressly chose to provide. Because Sections 11 and 12(a)(2) of the Securities Act subject plaintiffs to certain procedural limitations and have a culpability standard resembling that of negligence, an argument can be made that liability should be imposed pursuant to Section 17(a) only for actions that are more blameworthy, namely, for intentional or reckless misconduct.[33]

Perhaps the most important issue that has not been resolved by the Supreme Court in regard to Section 17(a) is whether an implied private right of action exists. Although a number of older cases implied such a remedy,[34] the more recent decisions with near unanimity have declined to do so.[35] Applying the *Cort* and more restrictive formulations, these courts have concluded that Congress did not intend to create a Section 17(a) private right of action. As stated by the Fifth Circuit:

> [I]t would appear that the *Cort* test as applied to § 17(a) of the Securities Act of 1933 points away from the implication of a private cause of action. This, together with the Supreme Court's conservative interpretation of the test in recent years, leads us to the conclusion that the district court correctly dismissed this theory of relief [thereby denying the existence of a § 17(a) private right of action].[36]

---

[31] The SEC's cease and desist authority is discussed *infra* § 15.04[A].

[32] *See Landry v. All American Assurance Co.*, 688 F.2d 381, 387 (5th Cir. 1982).

[33] *See Ernst & Ernst v. Hochfelder*, 425 U.S. 185 (1976), discussed *supra* § 8.03[A].

[34] *See, e.g., Newman v. Prior*, 518 F.2d 97 (4th Cir. 1975).

[35] *See, e.g., Finkel v. Stratton Corp.*, 962 F.2d 169 (2d Cir. 1992); *Bath v. Bushkin, Gaims, Gaines and Jones*, 913 F.2d 817 (10th Cir. 1990); *Sears v. Likens*, 912 F.2d 889 (7th Cir. 1990); *Newcome v. Esrey*, 862 F.2d 1099 (4th Cir. 1988); *Currie v. Cayman Resources Corporation*, 835 F.2d 780 (11th Cir. 1988); *Krause v. Prettyman*, 827 F.2d 346 (8th Cir. 1987); *In re Washington Public Power Supply Securities Litigation*, 823 F.2d 1349 (9th Cir. 1987) (en banc).

[36] *Landry v. All American Assurance Co.*, 688 F.2d 381, 391 (5th Cir. 1982).

§ 9.05　SECTION 14(a) OF THE EXCHANGE ACT

Section 14(a) of the Exchange Act and the SEC rules and regulations promulgated thereunder regulate the solicitation of proxies with respect to securities registered under Section 12 of that Act. Section 14(a) "was intended to promote the free exercise of the voting rights of stockholders by ensuring that proxies would be solicited with explanation to the stockholder of the real nature of the questions for which authority to cast his vote is sought."[37]

[A]　Elements of Private Right of Action

Generally, Rule 14a-9 prohibits the solicitation of proxies which contain any materially false or misleading statement. Due to the Supreme Court's decision in *J.I. Case v. Borak*,[38] it is clear that an implied private right of action exists under Section 14(a) and Rule 14a-9. Also, although not definitively resolved, it appears that an implied right of action exists under Rule 14a-8, the SEC shareholder proposal rule.[39]

---

[37] *Mills v. Electric Auto-Lite Co.*, 396 U.S. 375, 381 (1970).

[38] 377 U.S. 426 (1964).

[39] *See American Federation of State, County & Municipal Employees v. American International Group, Inc.*, 462 F.3d 121 (2d Cir. 2006); *Roosevelt v. E.I. Du Pont De Nemours & Co.*, 958 F.2d 416 (D.C. Cir. 1992); *see also Rauchman v. Mobil Corporation*, 739 F.2d 205 (6th Cir. 1984) (leaving issue unresolved). For material on Rule 14a-8 as well as the SEC's rules relating to communications among shareholders, see Securities Exchange Act Release No. 56914 (2007); Securities Exchange Act Release No. 40018 (1998); Securities Exchange Act Release No. 31326 (1992); Brown, *The Shareholder Communication Rules and the Securities and Exchange Commission: An Exercise in Regulatory Utility or Futility?*, 13 J. Corp. L. 683 (1988); Cane, *The Revised SEC Shareholder Proxy Proposal System: Attitudes, Results and Perspectives*, 11 J. Corp. L. 57 (1985); Dent, *Toward Unifying Ownership and Control in the Public Corporation*, 1989 Wisc. L. Rev. 881; Fisch, *From Legitimacy to Logic: Reconsidering Proxy Regulation*, 46 Vand. L. Rev. 1129 (1993); Ryan, *Rule 14a-8, Institutional Shareholder Proposals, and Corporate Democracy*, 23 Ga. L. Rev. 97 (1988); Symposium on Proxy Reform, 17 J. Corp. L. No. 1 (1991); Thomas & Martin, *The Effect of Shareholder Proposals on Executive Compensation*, 67 U. Cin. L. Rev. 1021 (1999).

In a decision impacting the ability of shareholders to nominate candidates for director, the Second Circuit, in *American Federation of State, County & Municipal Employees, Employees Pension Plan v. American International Group, Inc.*, 462 F.3d 121, 123 (2d Cir. 2006), stated:

This case raises the question of whether a shareholder proposal requiring a company to include certain shareholder-nominated candidates for the board of directors on the corporate ballot can be excluded from the corporate proxy materials on the basis that the proposal "relates to an election" under Securities Exchange Act Rule 14a-8(i)(8) ("election exclusion" or "Rule 14a-8(i)(8)"). Complicating this question is not only the ambiguity of Rule 14a-8(i)(8) itself but also the fact that the Securities and Exchange Commission (the "SEC" or "Commission") has ascribed two different interpretations to the Rule's language. The SEC's first interpretation was published in 1976, the same year that it last revised the election exclusion. The Division of Corporation Finance (the "Division"), the group within the SEC that handles investor disclosure matters and issues no-action letters, continued to apply this interpretation consistently for fifteen years until 1990, when it began applying a different interpretation, although at first in an ad hoc and inconsistent manner. The result of this gradual interpretive shift is the SEC's second interpretation, as set forth in its amicus brief to this Court. We believe that an agency's interpretation of an ambiguous regulation made at the time the regulation was implemented or revised should control unless that agency has offered sufficient reasons for its changed interpretation. Accordingly, we hold that a shareholder proposal that seeks to amend the corporate bylaws to establish a procedure by which shareholder-

The standard of materiality, as the Supreme Court held in *TSC Industries, Inc. v. Northway, Inc.*,[40] is that "there is a substantial likelihood that a reasonable shareholder would consider [such information] important in deciding how to vote."[41] Note that this standard does not require proof that accurate disclosure of the misrepresented or omitted fact would have caused a reasonable shareholder to change his/her vote but only that a substantial likelihood existed that accurate disclosure "would have been viewed by the reasonable investor as having altered the 'total mix' of information made available."[42]

The Supreme Court has addressed the issue of a plaintiff's task in establishing reliance and causation in a Section 14(a) action. In *Mills v. Electric Auto-Lite Co.*,[43] the Court held that, provided that the misstatement or omission is material and thus had "a significant propensity to affect the voting process," a plaintiff in a derivative or class action under Section 14(a) and Rule 14a-9 is ordinarily neither required to show reliance nor loss causation. Hence, according to the Supreme Court in *Mills*, upon a finding of materiality, "a shareholder has made a sufficient showing of causal relationship between the violation and the injury for which he seeks redress if . . . he proves that the proxy solicitation itself . . . was an essential link in the accomplishment of the transaction."[44] In the *Virginia Bankshares*[45] case, discussed in § 9.05[B], the Court elaborated upon Section 14(a)'s causation requirement.

Regarding the requisite state of mind for liability purposes, Section 14(a) and Rule 14a-9, unlike Section 10(b), do not by their terms require that

---

nominated candidates may be included on the corporate ballot does not relate to an election within the meaning of the Rule and therefore cannot be excluded from corporate proxy materials under that regulation.

In response to the Second Circuit's decision, the SEC proposed diametrically opposed alternatives relating to shareholders' access to nominate directors on the subject company's proxy ballot. The first alternative would allow a shareholder (or group of shareholders) owning five percent of the corporation's stock to include in such company's proxy materials shareholder-proposed bylaws setting forth procedures for shareholders to nominate directors. If approved by the shareholders, such amendments to the bylaws would be binding. The second alternative proposed by the SEC, which may be coined the "non-access" approach, authorizes the subject company to exclude from its proxy materials all shareholder proposals that seek to amend the company's bylaws in order to implement procedures concerning director nominations. *See* Securities Exchange Act Releases Nos. 56160, 56161 (2007).

Subsequently, the SEC adhered to the "non-access" approach, thereby permitting companies to exclude from their proxy statements such shareholder proposals. Hence, shareholder proposals relating to the adoption of bylaw amendments that would create procedures for shareholders to nominate directors are excludable. Securities Exchange Act Release No. 56914 (2007); *see* Scannell, Cox, *in Denying Access, Puts His SEC Legacy on Line*, Wall St. J., Nov. 29, 2007, at C1 (stating that the SEC's action "set off a storm of criticism from shareholder activists and Democrats").

[40] 426 U.S. 438 (1976).

[41] *Id.* at 449.

[42] *Id.*

[43] 396 U.S. 375 (1970).

[44] *Id.* at 384–85.

[45] 501 U.S. 1083 (1991).

deceptive or manipulative conduct be shown. As a consequence, where injunctive relief rather than damages is sought, some courts will order relief based upon the objective sufficiency of the disclosure (hence, ordering corrective disclosure without inquiry as to mental culpability).[46] Where damages are sought, most courts apply a negligence standard. For example, according to the Third Circuit:

> The language of Section 14(a) and Rule 14a-9(a) contains no suggestion of a scienter requirement, merely establishing a quality standard for proxy material. The importance of the proxy provision to informed voting by shareholders has been stressed by the Supreme Court, which has emphasized the broad remedial purpose of the section, implying a need to impose a high standard of care on the individuals involved. And, unlike Sections 10(b) and 18 of the Act, which encompass activity in numerous and diverse areas of securities markets and corporate management, Section 14(a) is specially limited to materials used in soliciting proxies. Given all of these factors the imposition of a standard of due diligence as opposed to actual knowledge or gross negligence is quite appropriate.[47]

On the other hand, in *Adams v. Standard Knitting Mills*[48] the Sixth Circuit took the position that scienter is required in private damage actions against accountants for false and misleading audited financial statements contained in proxy materials. In taking this position, the Sixth Circuit noted, however, that other circuits had prescribed a negligence standard under Section 14(a) when the defendant was a corporation issuing the proxy statement. The Sixth Circuit distinguished these cases, stating that scienter was required in the case at bar because accountants, among other things, are removed from the issuing corporation and do not stand to benefit from a misleading proxy statement.[49] A number of courts have disagreed with the Sixth Circuit's rationale, imposing liability against collateral participants based on negligence.[50]

[B]   A Look at *Virginia Bankshares*

In a 1991 decision having significant ramifications, the Supreme Court examined Section 14(a) and Rule 14a-9. In *Virginia Bankshares, Inc. v. Sandberg*,[51] the Court addressed two outstanding issues in this area:

> [W]hether a statement couched in conclusory or qualitative terms purporting to explain directors' reasons for recommending certain corporate action can be materially misleading within the meaning of Rule 14a-9, and whether causation of damages compensable under

---

[46] *See, e.g., Ash v. LFE Corp.*, 525 F.2d 215 (3d Cir. 1975). *But see Plant Industries, Inc. v. Bregman*, 490 F. Supp. 265 (S.D.N.Y. 1980).

[47] *Gould v. American Hawaiian S.S. Co.*, 535 F.2d 761, 797–98 (3d Cir. 1976).

[48] 623 F.2d 422 (6th Cir. 1980).

[49] *Id.* at 428.

[50] *See, e.g., Herskowitz v. Nutri/System, Inc.*, 857 F.2d 179 (3d Cir. 1988).

[51] 501 U.S. 1083 (1991).

§ 14(a) can be shown by . . . member[s] of a class of minority shareholders whose votes are not required by law or corporate bylaw to authorize the corporate action subject to the proxy solicitation.[52]

As to the first issue, Justice Souter, writing for the Court, opined that statements of reason, opinion, or belief are not actionable without some misstatement of the facts underpinning the reason, opinion, or belief. Specifically, he noted that such statements contain two components: the opinion itself and the factual basis for the opinion. Assuming that the undergirding facts are neither false nor misleading, a statement of belief might be objectionable in one regard—"solely as a misstatement of the psychological fact of the speaker's belief in what he says."[53] However, to base Section 14(a) and Rule 14a-9 liability on mere disbelief or undisclosed belief would be to authorize litigation founded solely on the " 'impurities' of a director's 'unclean heart.' "This the Court refused to do. Rather, to impose liability, a plaintiff carries the burden of demonstrating "something false or misleading in what the statement expressly or impliedly declare[s] about its subject."[54]

Hence, nondisclosure of "true purpose"[55] is not actionable. However, when there is a material misstatement of reason, opinion or belief as well as the factual basis therefor, a Section 14(a) right of action exists under the reasoning of *Virginia Bankshares.* Note, moreover, that the rendering of such opinion or belief and the factual basis therefor by an eligible registrant may be phrased as "forward-looking" information, thereby invoking the safe harbor provisions of the Private Securities Litigation Reform Act (discussed *supra* § 8.06[D], *infra* § 11.05[D]).

Regarding the second issue, causation, the Court refused to extend the "essential link" test which it enunciated in *Mills v. Electric Auto-Lite Co.* to the situation at bar. The *Mills* Court held that once "there has been a finding of materiality, a shareholder has made a sufficient showing of causal relationship between the violation and the injury for which he seeks redress if . . . he proves that the proxy solicitation itself, rather than the particular defect in the solicitation materials, was an essential link in the accomplishment of the transaction."[56]

The Court in *Mills* left open the question of whether it was possible for minority shareholders to satisfy the causation requirement when their votes were not necessary to approve the transaction.[57] The Second Circuit in *Schlick v. Penn-Dixie Cement Corp.* addressed this issue, adverting to *Borak* and embracing the "broad remedial purposes" of the Securities Acts.[58] There, the court considered the defendant's argument that the "minority stockholders'

---

[52] *Id.* at 1087.

[53] *Id.* at 1095.

[54] *Id.* at 1095–96.

[55] *See* discussion *supra* § 8.06[B].

[56] 396 U.S. 375, 385 (1970).

[57] *Id.* at 385 n.7.

[58] 507 F.2d 374, 383 (2d Cir. 1974).

votes [were] meaningless since the insiders . . . had enough votes to approve the transaction in any event."[59] Asserting that minority shareholder approval is not meaningless, but rather has value "whether or not it is strictly essential to the power to act," the court answered the question left open in *Mills* in the affirmative.[60]

The Supreme Court rejected this purportedly expansive construction of *Mills* in *Virginia Bankshares*, holding that under the facts presented, shareholders whose votes were not necessary to consummate the transaction did not show the requisite causation for Section 14(a) purposes.[61] Structuring its inquiry around the policies of its seminal decision in *Blue Chip Stamps v. Manor Drug Stores*,[62] the Court reasoned that to recognize causation under the plaintiff minority shareholder's theory would produce hazy issues. Such recognition would give rise to protracted litigation, the resolution of which would be unreliable: "Given a choice, we would reject any theory of causation that raised such prospects, and we reject this one."[63]

Even though rejecting the plaintiffs' arguments relating to causation in the case at hand, the Court nonetheless left a crucial issue unresolved: Whether the requisite showing of causation may be made if, due to a materially false or misleading statement or other deceptive conduct, the shareholder is lulled into bypassing a state remedy that otherwise would have been available to protect such shareholder from financial loss (called the "lost state remedy" theory).[64]

After *Virginia Bankshares*, a number of lower federal courts have given their approval to the "lost state remedy" theory in this context. In one such case, the Second Circuit ruled for the plaintiffs, reasoning that the defendants' deficient proxy statement may have induced the plaintiffs to forfeit their state-based appraisal rights.[65] Similarly, the Third Circuit has stated that causation may be shown when "the [defendant's] misstatement or omission has caused the minority shareholders to forego an opportunity under state law to enjoin a merger."[66]

In conclusion, although *Virginia Bankshares* on its face is a proxy case, its implications reach far beyond the Section 14(a) region of securities law. Instead, the decision's ramifications flow into other areas of securities jurisprudence as well as into the unevenly treated context of actions implied under federal law.

---

[59] *Id.* at 382.

[60] *Id.* at 382–84.

[61] 501 U.S. at 1106–07.

[62] 421 U.S. 723 (1975) (discussed *supra* § 8.02).

[63] 501 U.S. at 1106.

[64] *Id.* at 1107–08. The subject of lost state remedies also is discussed *supra* § 8.05[B].

[65] *Wilson v. Great American Industries, Inc.*, 979 F.2d 924 (2d Cir. 1992).

[66] *Scattergood v. Perelman*, 945 F.2d 618, 626 n.4 (3d Cir. 1991); *see Howing Co. v. Nationwide Corp.*, 927 F.2d 700 (6th Cir. 1992); Steinberg & Reece, *The Supreme Court, Implied Rights of Action, and Proxy Regulation*, 54 Ohio St. L.J 67 (1993). *But see Isquith v. Caremark International, Inc.*, 136 F.3d 531 (7th Cir. 1998).

[C]   Contexts Where Proxy Provisions Apply

Although the areas covered by the proxy provisions are limited, the Section 14(a) right of action may be available in a variety of factual contexts. For example, material misrepresentations contained in a proxy statement of information relating to shareholders' assessment of management's integrity and competence (including disclosure of executive compensation) implicates Section 14(a).[67] Moreover, certain breach of fiduciary duty claims, patterned after the *Goldberg* Section 10(b) line of cases (*see* § 8.05[B]), are actionable under Section 14(a), provided that there is a proxy solicitation coupled with inadequacy of disclosure.[68] The Section 14(a) remedy also comes into play in proxy fights for corporate control.[69] And, as a final example, Section 14(a) may be invoked in connection with merger transactions.[70] Interestingly, because Section 14(a) does not have a purchaser-seller standing requirement and because the requisite culpability standard may be that of negligence, plaintiffs may be successful in a Section 14(a) right of action where such relief would be denied under Section 10(b).[71]

§ 9.06   SECTION 29(b) OF THE EXCHANGE ACT

Although not invoked with great frequency, Section 29(b) can serve as a powerful weapon for aggrieved litigants. Under the provision's language, every contract formed or performed in contravention of the 1934 Act or any rule or regulation prescribed thereunder "shall be void" as regards the rights of the violating party or his/her successor who takes with knowledge. This is the case even though the provision violated itself provides no private right of action. As the Supreme Court has stated, Section 29(b) impliedly "confers a 'right to rescind' a contract void under the criteria of the statute."[72]

Taken literally, Section 29(b)'s language, to quote Judge Friendly, is "[d]raconian."[73] Due to the "devastating meaning" of the provision's language,

---

[67] *See, e.g., Gaines v. Haughton*, 645 F.2d 761 (9th Cir. 1981); Securities Exchange Act Release No. 54302 (2006) (adoption of amendments to rules requiring disclosure concerning, inter alia, executive compensation and related-party transactions).

[68] *See, e.g., Weisberg v. Coastal States Gas Corp.*, 609 F.2d 650 (2d Cir. 1979).

[69] *See, e.g., GAF Corporation v. Heyman*, 724 F.2d 727 (2d Cir. 1983); discussion *infra* § 14.03.

[70] *See, e.g., Tracinda Corp. v. DaimlerChrysler AG*, 502 F.3d 212 (3d Cir. 2007); *Pavlidis v. New England Patriots Football Club, Inc.*, 737 F.2d 1227 (1st Cir. 1984).

[71] *See generally* R. Thomas & C. Dixon, Aranow & Einhorn on Proxy Contests for Corporate Control (3d ed. 1998); Bainbridge, *Redirecting State Takeover Laws at Proxy Contests*, 1992 Wisc. L. Rev. 1071; Bradford, *The Possible Future of Private Rights of Action for Proxy Fraud: The Parallel Between* Borak *and* Wilko, 70 Neb. L. Rev. 306 (1991); Gelb, *Implied Private Actions Under SEC Rules 14a-9 and 10b-5: The Impact of* Virginia Bankshares, Inc. v. Sandberg, 76 Marquette L. Rev. 363 (1993); Steinberg, *Fiduciary Duties and Disclosure Obligations in Proxy and Tender Contests for Corporate Control*, 30 Emory L.J. 169 (1981); Symposium on Proxy Reform, 17 J. Corp. L. No. 1 (1991).

[72] *Transamerica Mortgage Advisors, Inc. v. Lewis*, 444 U.S. 11, 17 (1979); *see Mills v. Electric Auto-Lite Co.*, 396 U.S. 375, 387–388 (1970).

[73] *Pearlstein v. Scudder & German*, 429 F.2d 1136, 1149 (2d Cir. 1970) (Friendly, J., dissenting).

a number of courts have held that Section 29(b) merely codifies common law principles of illegal bargain in the application of the Exchange Act.[74]

Some courts, however, have construed Section 29(b) according to its language. In these decisions, the provision has been interpreted to provide plaintiffs with the relief sought, namely, the rescission of the subject transaction. For example, a number of courts hold that, pursuant to Section 29(b), a plaintiff can avoid a contract if it can be shown that: (1) the contract involved a "prohibited transaction", namely, that in the making or performance of the contract, there was perpetrated a violation of an Exchange Act provision or any rule or regulation prescribed thereunder; (2) there exists contractual privity between the plaintiff and the defendant; and (3) the plaintiff is in the class of persons the Exchange Act was designed to protect.[75] Once the plaintiff proves the above, the defendant may raise available equitable defenses, such as laches, estoppel, and "unclean hands."[76]

If the elements of the Section 29(b) right of action are satisfied, a plaintiff may rescind a contract, even after performance has been rendered. Given a remedial construction, Section 29(b) may subject every transaction, from an ordinary purchase of securities, to a complex merger, reorganization, proxy contest, or tender offer to which the Exchange Act applies, to its voidability provisions. However, in view of current judicial interpretation, such an expansive interpretation of Section 29(b) is unlikely.[77]

§ 9.07   SECTION 18 OF THE EXCHANGE ACT

Section 18 provides an express right of action for damages on behalf of an allegedly aggrieved purchaser or seller against any person who makes or causes to be made a materially false or misleading statement in any document filed with the SEC pursuant to the Exchange Act. The statute requires the complainant to prove that, in reliance on such materially false or misleading statement, that he/she purchased or sold the subject security at a price which was affected by the disclosure deficiency. Hence, both reliance and loss

---

[74] *See, e.g., Occidental Life Insurance Co. v. Pat Ryan & Associates*, 496 F.2d 1255 (4th Cir. 1974).

[75] *See, e.g., Berckeley Investment Group, Ltd. v. Colkitt*, 455 F.3d 195, 205 (3d Cir. 2006); *Regional Properties, Inc. v. Financial and Real Estate Consulting Company*, 678 F.2d 552, 559 (5th Cir. 1982); *Pompano-Windy City Parners, Ltd. v. Bear Stearns & Co., Inc.*, 794 F. Supp. 1265, 1288 (S.D.N.Y. 1992). According to the Third Circuit, the applicable test "is whether the securities violations are inseparable from the underlying agreement between the parties. If an agreement cannot be performed without violating the securities laws, that agreement is subject to rescission under Section 29(b)." *Berckeley Investment Group*, 455 F.3d at 206, *relying on GFL Advantage Fund, Ltd. v. Colkitt*, 272 F.3d 189, 201–202 (3d Cir. 2001).

[76] *Regional Properties*, 678 F.2d at 562–563.

[77] *See supra* notes 74–75 (cases cited therein); Gruenbaum & Steinberg, *Section 29(b) of the Securities Exchange Act of 1934: A Viable Remedy Awakened*, 48 Geo. Wash. L. Rev. 1 (1979); *see also* Scott, *A Broker-Dealer's Civil Liability to Investors for Fraud: An Implied Private Right of Action Under Section 15(c)(1) of the Securities Exchange Act of 1934*, 63 Indiana L.J 687 (1988) (discussing the availability of an implied right of action under § 15(c)(1) as well as the application of the § 29(b) remedy).

causation must be proven.[78] Significantly, to establish the element of reliance, the plaintiff must show that he/she (or his/her designee) actually read the relevant parts of the document in question (either by reading the filed document itself or as the pertinent document was described in another source).[79] The statute allows for contribution[80] and sets forth a one-year/three-year statute of limitations (namely, that suit must be instituted within one year after discovery of the facts constituting the violation and in no event more than three years after the violation's occurrence).[81] Under Section 18, the defendant has an affirmative defense of showing good faith and lack of knowledge that the subject statement was materially false or misleading.[82]

Because of Section 18's strict reliance requirement, the statute in the past was not invoked with frequent success. This result may be changing to some extent because of increasing resort to the statute by institutional investors. Due to that institutional investors read and analyze Exchange Act reports filed by a subject registrant, the reliance requirement does not pose a significant hurdle for such investors.[83] At least according to some courts, however, the individualized proof of reliance mandated by Section 18 may preclude class certification, thereby relegating complainants to pursue solely individual actions.[84]

§ 9.08 THE RACKETEER INFLUENCED AND CORRUPT ORGANIZATIONS ACT (RICO)

In 1995, Congress severely limited civil RICO actions in securities-related litigation.[85] Even prior to that legislation, the courts already had constricted civil RICO by setting forth various requirements.[86] Generally, prior to the 1995

---

[78] Exchange Act § 18(a). Note that under Section 18(a), "the court may, in its discretion, require an undertaking for the payment of the costs of such suit, and assess reasonable costs, including reasonable attorneys' fees, against either party litigant." *Id.*

[79] *See, e.g., In re Digi International,* 6 F. Supp. 2d 1089 (D. Minn. 1998); *In re American Continental Corp. Securities Litigation,* 794 F. Supp. 1424 (D. Ariz. 1992); *Walsh v. Butcher & Sherrerd,* 452 F. Supp. 80 (E.D. Pa. 1978); *Jacobson v. Peat, Marwick, Mitchell & Co.,* 445 F. Supp. 518 (S.D.N.Y. 1977). Note that the SEC has exempted from Section 18 coverage financial statements contained in a registrant's quarterly filings on Form 10-Q. *See* Exchange Act Rule 15(d)-13(e).

[80] Exchange Act § 18(b).

[81] Exchange Act § 18(c).

[82] Exchange Act § 18(a). *See generally* L. Loss & J. Seligman, Securities Regulation 4296–4300 (3d ed. 1992).

[83] *See* Eisenhofer & Grant, *Institutional Investors and Section 18 of the Exchange Act,* 33 Rev. Sec. & Comm. Reg. 54 (2000).

[84] *Compare Beebe v. Pacific Realty Trust,* 99 F.R.D. 60 (D. Ore. 1983) (denying class certification due to § 18's reliance requirement), *with Simpson v. Specialty Retail Concepts,* 149 F.R.D. 94 (M.D.N.C. 1993) (certifying class and finding that § 18 common issues prevailed over issue of reliance). *See* Grant & McIntyre, *Class Certification and Section 18 of the Exchange Act,* 35 Rev. Sec. & Comm. Reg. 255 (2002); discussion *supra* § 8.07.

[85] In enacting the Private Securities Litigation Reform Act of 1995, Congress amended Section 1964(c) of RICO.

[86] *See, e.g., International Data Bank v. Zepkin,* 812 F.2d 149 (4th Cir. 1987) (applying

legislation, civil RICO provided an express right of action to redress fraud in the sale of securities (as well as for mail and wire fraud).[87]

To state a claim for damages under RICO, the complainant first must allege a violation of the substantive RICO statute,[88] commonly referred to as "criminal RICO." The constituent elements of criminal RICO, as set forth by the Second Circuit, are "(1) that the defendant (2) through the commission of two or more acts (3) constituting a 'pattern' (4) of 'racketeering activity' (5) directly or indirectly invests in, or maintains an interest in, or participates in (6) an 'enterprise' (7) the activities of which affect interstate or foreign commerce."[89] After adequately alleging the foregoing, a private plaintiff, in order to invoke RICO's civil provisions for treble damages, attorneys' fees and costs, must satisfy a second burden, namely that he was "injured in his business or property *by reason* of a violation of Section 1962 [criminal RICO]."[90]

Pursuant to the Private Securities Litigation Reform Act of 1995 (PSLRA), Congress amended Section 1964(c) of RICO to eliminate securities fraud as a predicate act in a civil RICO action. According to the Joint Explanatory Statement of the Conference Committee for the legislation, the Committee also "intend[ed] that a plaintiff may not plead other specified offenses, such as mail or wire fraud, as predicate acts under civil RICO if such offenses are based on conduct that would have been actionable as securities fraud." An exception is made, thereby permitting a civil RICO action to be initiated in this context, when any person has been criminally convicted in connection with the fraud, in which case the statute of limitations commences to run on the date the conviction becomes final.

---

purchaser-seller standing requirement to civil RICO actions premised on securities fraud).

[87] 18 U.S.C. § 1964(c). *See generally* D. Abrams, The Law of Civil RICO (1991); Blakey & Gettings, *Racketeer Influenced and Corrupt Organizations (RICO): Basic Concepts — Criminal and Civil Remedies*, 53 Temple L.Q. 1009 (1980); Bridges, *Private RICO Litigation Based Upon "Fraud in the Sale of Securities"*, 18 Ga. L. Rev. 43 (1983); MacIntosh, *Racketeer Influenced and Corrupt Organizations Act: Powerful New Tool of the Defrauded Securities Plaintiff*, 31 Kansas L. Rev. 7 (1982); Mathews, *Shifting the Burden of Losses in the Securities Markets: The Role of Civil RICO in Securities Litigation*, 65 Notre Dame L. Rev. 896 (1990); Tyson & August, *The Williams Act After RICO: Has the Balance Tipped in Favor of Incumbent Management?*, 35 Hastings L.J. 53 (1983); Comment, *RICO and Securities Fraud: A Workable Limitation*, 83 Colum. L. Rev. 1513 (1983).

[88] 18 U.S.C. § 1962.

[89] *Moss v. Morgan Stanley, Inc.*, 719 F.2d 5, 17 (2d Cir. 1983). Criminal RICO, therefore, makes unlawful:

    (1) using income derived from a pattern of racketeering activity to acquire an interest in an enterprise;

    (2) acquiring or maintaining an interest in an enterprise through a pattern of racketeering activity or collection of an unlawful debt;

    (3) conducting the affairs of an enterprise through a pattern of racketeering activity; and

    (4) conspiring to commit any of these offenses.

18 U.S.C. § 1962(a)-(d).

[90] 18 U.S.C. § 1964(c) (emphasis added).

§ 9.09   STATE SECURITIES AND COMMON LAW REMEDIES

In the last two decades, the U.S. Supreme Court has handed down a number of restrictive decisions under the federal securities laws. Due to this development, the question arises whether investors should consider pursuing their state law actions with greater vigor.

[A]   Obstacles to State Law Relief

[1]   Overview

In some situations, plaintiffs should pursue their grievances under the federal securities acts. For example, a state such as New York declines to recognize a private right of action under its securities laws.[91] In addition, certain other states in their respective securities statutes provide private redress for purchasers only,[92] and afford a shorter statute of limitations than that prescribed by federal law.[93] Moreover, by premising liability upon the status of the primary violator as a seller, many of these statutes evidently cannot be invoked against a corporate defendant and its fiduciaries in secondary market frauds, such as when a company allegedly issues a deliberately false press release or earnings statement.[94] Adoption of a sufficiently broad definition of "seller" in this context would expand the statute's scope to encompass such situations.[95]

Another significant downside to state law is with respect to class action litigation. Unlike federal law which recognizes the fraud on the market theory to create a presumption of reliance,[96] thereby facilitating use of the class action

---

[91] *See CPC Int'l v. McKesson Corp.*, 70 N.Y.2d 268, 519 N.Y.S. 2d 804, 514 N.E.2d 116 (1987). Note, however, that depending on the circumstances, a complainant may be entitled to relief under common law based on, for example, negligent misrepresentation or fraud. *See, e.g., Vereins-Und Westbank, A.G. v. Carter*, 691 F. Supp. 704 (S.D.N.Y. 1988) (applying New York law); *Veras Investment Partners LLC v. Akin, Gump, Strauss, Hauer & Feld LLP*, 851 N.Y.S. 2d 61 (N.Y. Sup. 2007).

[92] *See, e.g.,* North Dakota Comm. Code § 10-04-17 *(construed in Weidner v. Engelhart*, 176 N.W.2d 509, 513 (N.D. 1970)); Ohio Rev. Code § 1707.43; *see also* Uniform Securities Act § 410(a), *reprinted in,* 1 Blue Sky L. Rep. (CCH) ¶ 5500, at 1566 (Adopted 1956).

[93] *See, e.g.,* Ga. Code § 97-114(d); Mo. Code § 409.411(e); N.C. Securities Act § 78A-56(f); Va. Code § 13.1-522(D); *Clouser v. Temporaries, Inc.*, [1990–1991 Transfer Binder] Fed. Sec. L. Rep. (CCH) ¶ 95,846 (D.D.C. 1989) (holding claim was barred by the two-year District of Columbia blue sky statute of limitations, D.C. Code § 2-2613(e)).

[94] Hence, many states have adopted the Section 12(a)(2) counterpart but have declined to provide a private remedy for the Rule 10b-5 counterpart. *Compare* Texas Securities Act Art. 581-33A(2) (Section 12(a)(2) counterpart), *with* Washington Securities Act, RCW 21.20.010 (Rule 10b-5 counterpart).

[95] For example, holding that a company issuing a materially misleading press release aided the sale, played an integral role in the sale, or solicited the transaction for its financial benefit would, depending upon the standard adopted, confer "seller" status upon the entity, thereby subjecting it to liability exposure in secondary open market transactions.

[96] *Basic, Inc. v. Levinson*, 485 U.S. 224 (1988) (discussed *supra* § 8.06[B]).

mechanism, a number of state courts have declined to adopt this doctrine with respect to actions alleging common law fraud.[97] The consequence is that individualized proof of reliance is required, hence impeding class certification. For example, in rejecting the fraud on the market in cases alleging common law fraud, the California Supreme Court opined that recognition of the theory would eliminate the reliance requirement.[98] Similarly, the Delaware Supreme Court has held that "[a] class action may not be maintained in a purely common law or equitable fraud case since individual questions of law or fact, particularly as to the element of justifiable reliance, will inevitably predominate over common questions of law or fact."[99]

[2] The Securities Litigation Uniform Standards Act (SLUSA)

Enactment of the Securities Litigation Uniform Standards Act of 1998 (SLUSA or the Uniform Standards Act) severely limits the availability of state law redress. Indeed, regarding securities class actions[100] involving nationally traded securities,[101] SLUSA[102] generally preempts state law.[103] Certain

---

[97] Because many blue sky remedial statutes do not have a reliance requirement, this issue most frequently arises with respect to common law fraud claims. *See, e.g., Peil v. Speiser,* 806 F.2d 1154, 1163 n.17 (3d Cir. 1986) ("While the fraud on the market theory is good law with respect to the Securities Acts, no state courts have adopted the theory, and thus direct reliance remains a requirement of a common law securities fraud claim."); *Mirkin v. Wasserman,* 5 Cal. 4th 1082, 23 Cal. Rptr. 2d 101, 858 P.2d 568 (1993); *Gaffin v. Teledyne, Inc.,* 611 A.2d 467, 474 (Del. 1991); *Antonson v. Robertson,* 141 F.R.D. 501, 508 (E.D. Kan. 1991). *But see* Ohio Rev. Code § 1707.43 (no reliance requirement); *Hurley v. Federal Deposit Insurance Corp.,* 719 F. Supp. 27, 34 n.4 (D. Mass. 1989); *Allyn v. Wortman,* 725 So. 2d 94, 101 (Miss. 1998); *Arnold v. Dirrim,* 398 N.E.2d 426 (Ind. App. 1979).

[98] *Mirkin v. Wasserman,* 5 Cal. 4th 1082, 23 Cal. Rptr. 2d 101, 858 P.2d 568 (1993). Importantly, the court recognized that the state securities law provisions discussed at bar contained no reliance requirement.

[99] *Gaffin v. Teledyne, Inc.,* 611 A.2d 467, 474 (Del. 1992).

[100] Pursuant to the Securities Litigation Uniform Standards Act of 1998, a "covered class action" means:

(i) any single lawsuit in which —

(I) damages are sought on behalf of more than 50 persons or prospective class members, and questions of law or fact common to those persons or members of the prospective class, without reference to issues of individualized reliance on an alleged misstatement or omission, predominate over any questions affecting only individual persons or members; or

(II) one or more named parties seek to recover damages on a representative basis on behalf of themselves and other unnamed parties similarly situated, and questions of law or fact common to those persons or members of the prospective class predominate over any questions affecting only individual persons or members; or

(ii) any group of lawsuits filed in or pending in the same court and involving common questions of law or fact, in which —

(I) damages are sought on behalf of more than 50 persons; and

(II) the lawsuits are joined, consolidated, or otherwise proceed as a single action for any purpose.

Uniform Standards Act § 101, *amending* Securities Act § 16(f)(2)(A) and Exchange Act § 28(f)(5)(B).

[101] The term nationally traded security or "covered security" means a security that meets the

important exceptions exist, however, thereby preserving state securities and common law in those situations. For example, individual as well as derivative actions may be pursued under state law.[104] State law also may be invoked in suits challenging the conduct of a subject issuer, any of its affiliates, or affected corporate fiduciaries with respect to specified actions — namely, going-private transactions, tender offers, mergers, and the exercise of appraisal rights.[105] Importantly, SLUSA declines to preempt in any way the authority of the state securities commissions, thereby empowering the states to continue their investigatory and enforcement functions.[106]

The impact of SLUSA is significant. Prior to its enactment, proponents asserted that publicly-held companies were reluctant to disclose forward-looking information,[107] irrespective of the safe harbor provided by the Private Securities Litigation Reform Act of 1995. The concern remained that such disclosure of forward-looking information would subject the applicable company to state court class actions.[108] SLUSA's enactment, generally preempting state law in securities class actions involving nationally traded

---

standards set forth in Section 18(b) of the Securities Act. These securities include those that are listed for trading on the New York Stock Exchange, American Stock Exchange, and the Nasdaq Stock Market (NMS). Securities issued by registered investment companies also are defined as nationally traded securities.

[102] Pub. L. No. 105-353, 112 Stat. 3227 (1998); *see* H. R. Rep. No. 105-803, 105th Cong., 2d Sess. (1998).

[103] *See* Uniform Standards Act § 101, *amending*, Securities Act § 16 and Exchange Act § 28.

[104] *See* Uniform Standards Act § 101, *amending*, Securities Act § 16(f)(2)(B) and Exchange Act § 28(f)(5)(C) (stating that "the term 'covered class action' does not include an exclusively derivative action brought by one or more shareholders on behalf of a corporation"). For the definition of "covered class action," see *supra* note 100.

[105] *See* Uniform Standards Act § 101, *amending*, Securities Act § 16(d)(1) and Exchange Act § 28(f)(3)(A). In addition, the Uniform Standards Act excludes from federal preemption suits instituted by a state, a political subdivision thereof, or a state pension plan provided that such state, political subdivision thereof, or state pension plan is named as a plaintiff in such action and has authorized its participation in such action. *See* Uniform Standards Act § 101, *amending*, Securities Act § 16(d)(2) and Exchange Act § 28(f)(3)(B). As another exception, "a covered class action that seeks to enforce a contractual agreement between an issuer and an indenture trustee may be maintained in a State or Federal court by a party to the agreement or a successor to such party." Uniform Standards Act § 101, *amending*, Securities Act § 16(d)(3) and Exchange Act § 28(f)(3)(C).

[106] *See* Uniform Standards Act § 101, *amending*, Securities Act § 16(e) and Exchange Act § 28(f)(4) (stating that "[t]he securities commission (or any agency or office performing like functions) of any State shall retain jurisdiction under the laws of such State to investigate and bring enforcement actions").

[107] *See* Levine & Pritchard, *The Securities Litigation Uniform Standards Act of 1998: The Sun Sets on California's Blue Sky Laws*, 54 Bus. Law. 1, 12 (1998) (sources cited therein).

[108] *See* Grundfest, et al., *Securities Class Action Litigation in 1998: A Report to NASDAQ From the Stanford Law School Securities Class Action Clearinghouse*, 1070 PLI/Corp 69 (1998) ("Since passage of the Reform Act, a substantial portion of class action litigation has shifted from federal to state court in an apparent attempt to evade the Act's provisions."); Grundfest & Perino, *Securities Litigation Reform: The First Year's Experience — A Statistical Analysis of Class Action Securities Fraud Litigation Under the Private Securities Litigation Reform Act of 1995*, Stan. L. Sch. (Feb. 27, 1997); *Securities Class Actions Seem to be Moving to State Courts, According to New Study*, 29 Sec. Reg. & L. Rep. (BNA) 311 (1997).

securities,[109] generally has provided sufficient comfort to induce many subject registrants to disclose forward-looking information.[110]

In *Merrill Lynch, Pierce, Fenner & Smith, Inc. v. Dabit*,[111] the Supreme Court construed the "in connection with the purchase or sale" language of SLUSA in the context of a securities class action brought in state court on behalf of those shareholders who held (but did not purchase or sell) the subject securities. In the decision below, the Second Circuit incorporated the *Blue Chip* purchaser-seller standing limitation for Section 10(b) private actions[112] into SLUSA. Based on this analysis, fraud is deemed "in connection with the purchase or sale" of securities under SLUSA if such misconduct is alleged by a purchaser or seller. Accordingly, the Second Circuit concluded that holders of the subject securities, who allegedly were fraudulently induced not to sell, fell outside of SLUSA's parameters and were therefore able to pursue their class action claims in state court.[113]

The Supreme Court reversed and held that the holders were precluded from bringing their state class action under SLUSA. Construing SLUSA's "in connection with the purchase or sale" language broadly, the Court opined that "it is enough that the fraud alleged 'coincide' with a securities transaction — whether by the plaintiff or by someone else."[114] Hence, the requisite showing under SLUSA to show preemption is that the alleged deception occur in connection with the purchase or sale of the security, not that the deception be perpetrated against an identifiable purchaser or seller.[115] The Supreme Court's decision in *Dabit* thus signifies that state class actions brought by holders involving a nationally traded security are preempted under SLUSA. The Court concluded: "For purposes of SLUSA preemption . . . the identity of the plaintiffs does not determine whether the complaint alleges fraud 'in connection with the purchaser or sale' of securities. The misconduct of which [the plaintiffs] complain here — fraudulent manipulation of stock prices — unquestionably qualifies [under SLUSA] as fraud 'in connection with the purchase or sale' of securities. . . ."[116]

---

[109] Note, however, that the preservation of state derivative actions along with the Delaware Supreme Court's interpretations relating to a corporate fiduciary's duty of candor may not foreclose state litigation in the general disclosure context. *See, e.g., Malone v. Brincat*, 722 A.2d 5 (Del. 1998).

[110] *See generally* J. Hamilton & T. Trautmann, Securities Litigation Uniform Standards Act of 1998: Law and Explanation (1998); Casey, *Shutting the Doors to State Court: The Securities Litigation Uniform Standards Act of 1998*, 27 Sec. Reg. L.J. 141 (1999); Levine & Pritchard, *supra* note 107; Painter, *Responding to a False Alarm: Federal Preemption of State Securities Fraud Causes of Action*, 84 Cornell L. Rev. 1 (1998).

[111] 547 U.S. 71 (2006).

[112] *See Blue Chip Stamps v. Manor Drug Stores*, 421 U.S. 723 (1975) (discussed *supra* § 8.02).

[113] *Dabit v. Merrill Lynch, Pierce, Fenner & Smith, Inc.*, 395 F.3d 25 (2d Cir. 2005), *rev'd*, 547 U.S. 71 (2006).

[114] 547 U.S. at 85.

[115] *Id.*

[116] *Id.* at 88; *see* Loewenstein, Merrill Lynch v. Dabit: *Federal Preemption of Holders' Class Actions*, 34 Sec. Reg. L.J. 209 (2006).

[B]   Advantages of State Claims

On the other hand, there may be several distinct advantages for plaintiffs to bring state blue sky and common law claims.[117] Importantly, many state securities acts provide that, if appropriate, successful plaintiffs may recover reasonable attorneys' fees and punitive damages.[118] Another significant advantage relates to the statute of limitations issue. Although the Sarbanes-Oxley Act extended the statute of limitations for rights of action based on fraud to two years after discovery of the facts constituting the violation and in no event more than five years after the violation,[119] a number of other federal securities remedies have a one-year/three-year limitations period (namely one year from the date that the plaintiff discovered (or should have discovered) the facts constituting the violation and in no event more than three years after the violation).[120]

By contrast, many of the state blue sky statutes contain a longer statute of limitations under "Section 12(a)(2)" types of statutes. For example, Texas has a three year/five year limitations period. In other words, the Texas statute provides a statute of limitations barring such an action "more than three years after discovery of the untruth or omission, or after discovery should have been made by the exercise of reasonable diligence; or more than five years after the sale [or purchase]."[121] Other more flexible statutes of limitations include those of Florida (two year/five year),[122] Michigan (two year/four year),[123] Ohio (two year/four year),[124] California (one year/four year),[125] and Pennsylvania (one

---

In a subsequent decision, the Supreme Court held that when a securities class action is remanded to state court by a federal district court under SLUSA, that order is not appealable. *Kircher v. Putnam Funds Trust*, 547 U.S. 633 (2006). The Court's decision is significant because "[s]ecurities defendants will no longer be able to tie up a case on appeal for years litigating the propriety of a remand when the district court finds that the plaintiff's case does not implicate SLUSA." Coyle, *High Court Makes a Call in "Removal Wars,"* Nat. L. J., June 19, 2006, at p. 4.

[117] *See* Branson, *Collateral Participant Liability Under State Securities Laws*, 19 Pepp. L. Rev. 1027 (1992); Steinberg, *The Emergence of State Securities Laws: Partly Sunny Skies for Investors*, 62 U. Cin. L. Rev. 395 (1993).

[118] *See, e.g.*, Uniform Securities Act § 410(a), *supra* note 85, at 1566 (**I don't think this is the right cross-ref**); Ariz. Rev. Stat. § 44-2001; Wash. Rev. Code § 21.20.430(1), (2). Punitive damages also may be awarded in appropriate situations, such as where malice or egregious fraud is shown. *See* Ohio Rev. Code § 2315.21(B); *Price v. Griffin*, 359 A.2d 582, 589–90 (D.C. Ct. App. 1976).

[119] 28 U.S.C. § 1658 (discussed *supra* § 8.08).

[120] *See, e.g.*, Securities Act § 13 (for § 11 and § 12(a)(2) claims); Exchange Act §§ 9, 18.

[121] Tex. Civ. Stat. Ann. Art. 581-33H(2), (3). In addition, the Texas statute provides a limitations period of three years for registration violations. *Id.* Art. 581-33H(1). By contrast, the Securities Act generally provides a one-year statute of limitations for actions brought under Section 12(a)(1) for registration violations. *See* Securities Act § 13; discussion *supra* § 7.08.

[122] Fla. Stat. Ann. § 95.11(4)(e); *accord* New Mexico Securities Act, N.M. Art. 58-13B-41 (two year/five year).

[123] Mich. Comp. Laws Ann. § 451.810(e).

[124] Ohio Rev. Code Ann. § 1707.43. For the two-year period in the statute, at least under some circumstances, that period "begins to run upon the actual discovery of the defect." *Eastman v. Benchmark Minerals, Inc.*, 34 Ohio App. 3d 255, 258, 518 N.E.2d 23, 25 (1986).

[125] Cal. Corp. Code § 25506.

year/four year).[126] As to the outside limit, there appears to be no equitable tolling allowed.[127] Nonetheless, for those statutes that contain a flat period (for example, that suit must be brought within two years after the transaction), there is some authority that the statute may be tolled due to the defendant's fraudulent concealment.[128] Moreover, in cases of common law fraud, it is well established that the statute of limitations may be equitably tolled.[129]

Another example is that many state securities statutes provide for monetary damages based on negligent material misrepresentations or omissions made in the initial offering context as well as in the secondary trading markets.[130] Under federal law, if Section 10(b) is invoked, scienter must be shown.[131] In addition, these state securities statutory counterparts are more expansive than Section 12(a)(2). Accordingly, under a number of these statutes, plaintiffs may have a four or five-year limitations period to bring an action based on negligently made statements in the secondary markets.

Moreover, although some state courts have followed the Supreme Court's decision in *Pinter v. Dahl*[132] for defining who is a "seller" under the applicable state securities statute,[133] a number of states adhere to more expansive standards.[134] For example, the "substantial factor" test was used by several

---

[126] Pa. Stat. Ann. tit. 70, § 1-504(a).

[127] *See, e.g., SEC v. Seaboard Corp.*, 677 F.2d 1301, 1308 (9th Cir. 1982) (interpreting California statute); *Gilbert Family Partnership v. NIDO Corporation*, 679 F. Supp. 679, 685 (E.D. Mich. 1988) (interpreting Michigan statute); *Bull v. American Bank & Trust Co.*, 641 F. Supp. 62, 67 (E.D. Pa. 1986) (interpreting Pennsylvania statute).

[128] *See, e.g., Barton v. Peterson*, 733 F. Supp. 1482, 1492–1493 (N.D. Ga. 1990) (interpreting Georgia law); *Platsis v. E.F. Hutton & Company, Inc.*, 642 F. Supp. 1277, 1304–05 (W.D. Mich. 1986), *aff'd*, 829 F.2d 13 (6th Cir. 1987) (construing Michigan Uniform Securities Act § 410(e)).

[129] *See Willis v. Maverick*, 760 S.W.2d 642, 644–645 (Tex. 1988); *Lampf, Pleva, Lipkind, Prupis & Pettigrow v. Gilbertson*, 501 U.S. 350, 377–378 (1991) (Kennedy, J., dissenting) ("Only a small number of States constrain fraud actions with absolute periods of repose. . . . ").

[130] For example, the Washington Supreme Court, in *Kittilson v. Ford*, 93 Wash. 2d 223, 608 P.2d 264 (1980) (a civil action for damages), rejected the *Hochfelder* scienter standard. In distinguishing *Hochfelder* and holding that negligence is sufficient to impose liability, the *Kittilson* court reasoned:

> We believe the holding in *Ernst & Ernst v. Hochfelder* [425 U.S. 185 (1976)] [is] inapplicable to our Securities Act. First, the "manipulative or deceptive" language of Section 10(b) of the 1934 Act is not included in the Washington Act. Secondly, in contrast to the federal scheme, the language of Rule 10b-5 is not derivative but is the statute in Washington. Finally, no legislative history similar or analogous to Congressional legislative history exists in Washington.

[131] *Aaron v. SEC*, 446 U.S. 680 (1980); *Ernst & Ernst v. Hochfelder*, 425 U.S. 185 (1976).

[132] 486 U.S. 622 (1988) (defining seller under Securities Act § 12(1) as extending to one "who successfully solicits the purchase, motivated at least in part by a desire to serve his own financial interests or those of the securities owner") (discussed *supra* § 7.09[B]). Lower federal courts overwhelmingly have applied *Pinter* to Section 12(2) (now 12(a)(2)) actions. *Id.*

[133] *See, e.g., Baker, Watts & Co., v. Miles & Stockbridge*, 95 Md. App. 145, 620 A.2d 356 (1993); *State v. Williams*, 98 N.C. App. 274, 279, 390 S.E.2d 746, 749 (1990); *Biales v. Young*, 432 S.E.2d 482 (S.C. 1993).

[134] *See, e.g., State ex. rel. Mays v. Ridenhour*, 811 P.2d 1220 (Kan. 1991); *Anders v. Dakota Land & Development Co.*, 380 N.W.2d 862, 867–868 (Minn. App. 1980); *Price v. Brydon*, 307 Or. 146, 764 P.2d 1370 (1988); *Hines v. Data Line Systems, Inc.*, 114 Wash. 2d 127, 787 P.2d 8, 20 (1990).

lower federal courts prior to *Pinter* for defining the term "seller" under Section 12 of the Securities Act.[135] Under this test, one is deemed a "seller" if his/her actions played an integral role or were a substantial contributing factor in the transaction.[136] Certainly, the liability net extends farther under this definition of "seller."

Also, a number of the state statutes extend liability exposure to those who materially aid in consummating the transaction.[137] This concept of secondary liability is particularly important in view of the U.S. Supreme Court's decision in *Central Bank of Denver* foreclosing aiding and abetting liability in private actions under Section 10(b).[138] Depending on the applicable state statute, aider liability may encompass only specified persons (such as employees of the seller, broker-dealers, and agents) or may reach any person irrespective of such person's relationship with the seller.[139] Hence, the provision of aider liability under state securities statutes enables a plaintiff successfully to reach certain parties who would avoid liability under the federal securities laws, either because they were not "sellers" under the *Pinter* test or were aiders and abettors rather than primary violators.[140]

There are other key advantages for plaintiffs under certain of the state securities provisions. For example, many states hold that reliance is not

---

An even more expansive definition of "seller" may have been recognized in *Lutheran Brotherhood v. Kidder Peabody & Co.*, 829 S.W.2d 300, 306 (Tex. App.), *set aside on other grounds*, 840 S.W.2d 384 (Tex. 1992) (stating that Texas' § 12(a)(2) counterpart, Art. 581-33(A)(2), "applies if the defendant was any link in the chain of the selling process").

[135] *See, e.g.*, *Davis v. Avco Financial Services, Inc.*, 739 F.2d 1057, 1067–68 (6th Cir. 1984) (defining a seller as one who is integrally connected with or substantially involved in the transaction).

[136] *Id.*

[137] *See, e.g.*, Ariz. Rev. Stat. Ann. § 44-2003; Or. Rev. Stat. § 59.115(3); Ohio Rev. Code § 1707.43; *Sterling Trust Company v. Adderley*, 168 S.W. 3d 835 (Tex. 2005). *See generally* J. Long, Blue Sky Law § 7.08 (2008).

[138] *Central Bank of Denver v. First Interstate Bank of Denver*, 511 U.S. 164 (1994) (discussed *infra* §§ 10.01–10.03).

[139] *Compare* Uniform Securities Act § 410(b) (1956) (providing for aider liability upon any employee of the seller, broker-dealer or agent unless such person meets the reasonable care defense), *with* Tex. Rev. Stat. Ann. art. 581-33F(2) (1977) (providing for liability against material aiders upon proof of intentional or reckless misconduct). For application of the reasonable care standard as an affirmative defense, see, *e.g.*, *Arnold v. Dirrim*, 398 N.E.2d 426, 434–35 (Ind. App. 1979); *McGarrity v. Craighill*, 83 N.C. App. 106, 111–12, 349 S.E.2d 311, 314–15 (1986). For discussion of the reckless disregard standard and comparison to the provisions of the Uniform Securities Act, see *Sterling Trust Company v. Adderley*, 168 S.W.3d 835 (Tex. 2005).

[140] *See, e.g.*, *Price v. Brydon*, 307 Or. 146, 764 P.2d 1370 (1988) (holding that attorney's actions in an offering could be viewed as materially aiding the sale). *But see Riedel v. Acutate of Colorado*, 773 F. Supp. 1055, 1066 (S.D. Ohio), *aff'd*, 947 F.2d 955 (6th Cir. 1991) (interpreting Ohio law, court stated that "an attorney providing professional services is not liable under Section 1707.43"). *See generally* Long, *Developments and Issues in Civil Liability Under Blue Sky Law*, 62 U. Cin. L. Rev. 439 (1993); Morrison, *Participant Liability Under Blue Sky Rescission Statutes*, 33 Sec. Reg. L.J. 102 (2005); Steinberg & Claassen, *Attorney Liability Under State Securities Laws: Landscapes and Minefields*, 3 U. Cal. Berkeley Bus. L.J. 1 (2005).

required to be shown under the applicable blue sky statute,[141] hence facilitating class action certification. Proving loss causation also may be dispensed with by plaintiffs in a number of states.[142] This more relaxed liability framework prompted Professor Cane to poignantly observe:

> It would seem that a plaintiff bringing a suit under [the Florida statute] could rescind [the transaction] without a showing of proximate cause, or any damage, or any scienter on the part of the defendant. . . . Was the intent of the Florida legislature to create a system of investor insurance?[143]

In addition to their state blue sky claims, investors also may emerge victorious when seeking relief on common law fraud, negligent misrepresentation, and breach of fiduciary duty grounds. In the *Virginia Bankshares* case, for example, although defeated on their federal and state securities law claims, the plaintiffs were awarded hefty damages on their breach of fiduciary duty claims.[144] In some states, even though not a purchaser or seller of stock, a shareholder who held the subject securities may be entitled to bring a common law action for fraud.[145] And, as another example, the Eleventh Circuit held that, although unsuccessful on their federal and state securities law claims, the plaintiffs established a meritorious breach of fiduciary duty claim against their broker.[146] In so holding, the court asserted that "the [federal and state] securities fraud statutes do not co-opt the existence of separate claims under state fiduciary principles."[147]

In conclusion, provided that SLUSA does not preclude the action, the state securities laws are being invoked by plaintiffs with greater frequency. Due to their more flexible construction, many of the state statutes provide the plaintiff with a right of action where such right may be lacking under federal law.

---

[141] *See, e.g.,* Cal. Corp. Code §§ 25400, 25500; *Mirkin v. Wasserman,* 5 Cal. 4th 1082, 23 Cal. Rptr. 2d 101, 858 P.2d 568 (1993); Ohio Rev. Code § 1707.43; *Roger v. Lehman Bros. Kuhn Loeb, Inc.,* 621 F. Supp. 114, 118 (S.D. Ohio 1985) (interpreting Ohio Rev. Code Ann. § 1707.43); Texas Securities Act, Art. 581-33A(2); *Anderson v. Vinson Exploration, Inc.,* 832 S.W.2d 657 (Tex. App. 1992).

[142] *See E.F. Hutton & Company, Inc. v. Rousseff,* 537 So. 2d 978, 981 (Fla. 1989).

[143] Cane, *Proximate Causation in Securities Fraud Actions for Rescission,* Fla. Bar Bus. Quart. Rep., Vol. 2, No. 2, at p. 14 (Spring 1989).

[144] *See Sandberg v. Virginia Bankshares, Inc.,* 979 F.2d 332, 342–48 (4th Cir. 1992).

[145] *See Small v. Fritz Companies,* 65 P.3d 1255 (Cal. 2003) (allowing persons who allegedly were wrongfully induced to hold their stock rather than selling such securities to bring suit based on common law fraud and negligent misrepresentation); *Gutman v. Howard Savings Bank,* 748 F. Supp. 254, 266 (D.N.J. 1990) (interpreting New Jersey law, standing to bring common law fraud claim granted and reliance may be shown in regard thereto where alleged misstatements were made directly to the complainant). *But see Moxley v. Citigroup Global Markets, Inc.,* 2006 U.S. Dist. LEXIS 11679 (S.D.N.Y. 2006) (holding that Georgia would not recognize common law "holder" claims).

[146] *Gochnauer v. A.G. Edwards & Sons, Inc.,* 810 F.2d 1042 (11th Cir. 1987); *see Malone v. Brincat,* 722 A.2d 5 (Del. 1998); *EBC I Inc. v. Goldman Sachs & Co.,* 799 N.Y.S 2d 170 (Ct. App. 2005) (recognizing breach of fiduciary duty action based on failure to disclose profit-sharing arrangement).

[147] 810 F.2d at 1050 (interpreting Florida law).

Hence, one consequence of the federal courts' restrictive approach to the remedial provisions of the Securities Acts has been to induce plaintiffs more frequently to file their actions in the state courts. Given the broad relief awarded in some of these state court proceedings, this result in the end may be more detrimental to defendants. Hence, it indeed is ironic that many plaintiffs, by electing to bring suit in state court, may well be better off than they were prior to the time that the federal courts embarked on their restrictive approach.

Although plaintiffs may elect to bring their state claims along with their federal securities law claims in federal district court,[148] an increasing number of complainants are declining this option.[149] Perhaps this result is due to perceptions that state judges may be more inclined to permit issues to reach the jury and the relatively large number of significant damage verdicts awarded in the state courts.[150] Moreover, as evidenced by a number of decisions, there may be the concern that federal courts may construe the state securities laws at bar consistently with and no broader than federal law.[151] Such holdings, of course, provide an additional incentive for plaintiffs to institute their actions in state court and seek more remedial interpretations.

Nonetheless, as discussed earlier,[152] it must be emphasized that pursuant to the Securities Litigation Uniform Standards Act (SLUSA), state law (with certain exceptions) is preempted in class actions involving nationally traded securities. In such circumstances, federal law serves as the sole source for plaintiff redress.

---

[148] Of course, there are situations where only state law claims are available, hence mandating that suit be brought in state court (unless the requirements of diversity of citizenship jurisdiction are met). See 28 U.S.C. § 1332. One such example is where the applicable statute of limitations has expired for the federal securities law claims but not for the state law claims.

[149] By bringing the action in state court, a plaintiff therefore bypasses remedies afforded by the Exchange Act, such as Section 10(b), due to that Act's provision for exclusive federal jurisdiction. See Exchange Act § 27, 15 U.S.C. § 78aa. Electing to forego Exchange Act remedies and opt for the state court forum calls for counsel and client to address significant substantive and tactical questions. See M. Steinberg, Lawyering and Ethics for the Business Attorney (2d ed. 2007).

[150] See, e.g., Moffett & Petzinger, Pennzoil Wins $10.53 Billion in Suit Against Texaco; Verdict Is Called Highest Civil Judgment in History, Wall St. J., Nov. 20, 1985, at 3.

[151] See, e.g., Abell v. Potomac Insurance Company, 858 F.2d 1104, 1130–31 (5th Cir. 1988), vacated on other grounds, Fryer v. Abell, 492 U.S. 914 (1989) (interpreting Louisiana law); Capri v. Murphy, 856 F.2d 473, 479 (2d Cir. 1988) (interpreting Connecticut law). See generally Branson, Securities Litigation in State Courts — Something Old, Something New, Something Borrowed, 76 Wash. U.L.Q. 509 (1998); Geyer, Miglets & Rowley, Civil Liability and Remedies in Ohio Securities Transactions, 70 U. Cin. L. Rev. 939 (2002); Klock, Litigating Securities Fraud As a Breach of Fiduciary Duty in Delaware, 28 Sec. Reg. L.J. 296 (2001); Steinberg, The Ramifications of Recent U.S. Supreme Court Decisions on Federal and State Securities Regulation, 70 Notre Dame L. Rev. 489 (1995); supra notes 137, 140 (sources cited therein).

[152] See discussion supra notes 100–116 (and accompanying text).

Chapter 10

SECONDARY LIABILITY

This chapter considers secondary liability under the federal securities laws. Three different theories of liability are highlighted: aiding and abetting, controlling person, and *respondeat superior*. Importantly, these theories also are applicable under many of the state securities statutes.[1] In addition, the ensuing discussion addresses distinctions between primary and secondary conduct.

§ 10.01 AIDING AND ABETTING LIABILITY

Prior to the Supreme Court's decision in *Central Bank of Denver*,[2] virtually every lower federal court considering the issue recognized the propriety of aiding and abetting liability under Section 10(b) of the Exchange Act as well as certain other provisions.[3] However, in *Central Bank of Denver*, the Supreme Court held that Section 10(b) of the Exchange Act does not provide for the imposition of aiding and abetting liability in private litigation. The Court made crystal clear that its construction was based on "a strict statutory construction" and that the issue before it was one involving "the scope of conduct prohibited by § 10(b)."[4] Importantly, the Court's rationale extends to preclude aiding and abetting liability from being imposed by private plaintiffs for alleged violations of other federal securities law provisions.[5] Likewise, private liability premised

---

[1] *See* J. Long, *Blue Sky Law* § 7.08 (2008). Steinberg, *The Ramifications of Recent U.S. Supreme Court Decisions on Federal and State Securities Regulation*, 70 Notre Dame L. Rev. 489 (1995); discussion § 9.09 *supra*. Note that the subject of liability in the SEC enforcement context for failure to supervise is addressed in § 13.05 *infra*.

[2] 511 U.S. 164 (1994).

[3] *See, e.g.*, *IIT v. Cornfeld*, 619 F.2d 909 (2d Cir. 1980); Olson, *The End of the Section 10(b) Aiding and Abetting Liability Fiction*, 8 Insights No. 6, at 3 (1994) ("The Court's decision overruled decisions from 11 federal courts of appeals which had recognized Section 10(b) aiding and abetting liability.").

[4] 511 U.S. at 173–175.

[5] After examining Sections 11 and 12 of the Securities Act and Sections 9, 16, 18, and 20A of the Exchange Act, the Court concluded that none of these express causes of action provided for aider and abettor liability. *Id.* at 178–180. Hence, the Court's analysis in *Central Bank of Denver* certainly should extend to other implied causes of action, such as Section 14(a) of the Exchange Act. Indeed, the statutory language of Section 14(a), like that of Section 10(b), "controls" and "bodes ill" for litigants who seek to hold collateral parties liable as aiders and abettors. *Id.* at 175. For treatment of secondary liability based on aiding and abetting in different contexts, such as in cases of commercial fraud, see Mason, *Civil Liability for Aiding and Abetting*, 61 Bus. Law. 1135 (2006).

on the doctrine of "conspiracy" is unavailable.[6] Moreover, prior to the enactment of the Private Securities Litigation Reform Act of 1995, the Court's restrictive approach was interpreted by many authorities to extend to the SEC, thereby precluding the Commission from bringing enforcement actions premised on aider and abettor liability (except where a statute provides for such liability).[7]

Nonetheless, discussion of aider and abettor liability principles should be undertaken for a number of reasons. For example, in view of Section 20(e) of the Securities Exchange Act enacted as part of the Private Securities Litigation Reform Act, the SEC may pursue aiders and abettors for violations of the Exchange Act and rules prescribed thereunder.[8] Injunctions also may be procured by the Commission against those who aid and abet violations of the Investment Advisers Act.[9] Moreover, although the Commission's cease and desist power against those who are a "cause" of an alleged violation evidently is more expansive than aider and abettor liability principles,[10] the Commission still may draw on some of these principles to ascertain the parameters of the liability net. And, as a last example, a number of state securities statutes provide for aiding and abetting liability.[11]

Prior to the Supreme Court's decision in *Central Bank of Denver*, the lower federal courts overwhelmingly held that aiding and abetting liability was appropriate under Section 10(b) of the Exchange Act as well as certain other provisions.[12] Although courts differed on the precise content of the various elements giving rise to aiding and abetting liability,[13] three basic prerequisites emerged: (1) a primary securities law violation by another, (2) substantial assistance by the alleged aider and abettor in the commission of the primary violation, and (3) requisite "knowledge" on the part of such alleged aider and abettor that his/her conduct was improper.[14]

---

[6] *See* 511 U.S. at 200 n.12 (Stevens, J., dissenting). Applying the analysis contained in *Central Bank of Denver*, lower courts overwhelmingly have rejected application of conspiracy doctrine under the federal securities laws. *See, e.g., Dinsmore v. Squadron, Ellenoff, Plesant, Sheinfield & Sorkin*, 135 F.3d 837 (2d Cir. 1998).

[7] *See* Gorman, *Who's Afraid of 10b-5? The Scope of a Section 10(b) Cause of Action After Central Bank of Denver*, 22 Sec. Reg. L.J. 247 (1994).

[8] *See* Sections 15(b)(4)(E), 15(b)(6)(A)(i), 20(e) of the Exchange Act.

[9] *See* Section 209(d) of the Investment Advisers Act.

[10] *See* Martin, Mirvis & Herlihy, *SEC Enforcement Powers and Remedies Are Greatly Expanded*, 19 Sec. Reg. L.J. 19, 23 (1991) (stating that the concept of a "cause" of a violation in relation to the SEC's cease and desist authority "would appear to go far beyond traditional concepts of aiding and abetting violations"). *See* Chapter 15 *infra.*

[11] *See, e.g.*, Texas Securities Act Art. 581–33(F)(2); J. Long, *supra* note 1, at § 7.08. A number of state statutes are more expansive, imposing liabilities on those who "materially aid" the sale. *See* § 9.09 *supra.*

[12] *See* note 3 *supra.*

[13] Compare *Rolf v. Blyth, Eastman Dillon & Co., Inc.*, 570 F.2d 38 (2d Cir. 1978), with *Schatz v. Rosenberg*, 943 F.2d 485 (4th Cir. 1991).

[14] *See, e.g.*, cases cited 511 U.S. at 192 n.1 (Stevens, J., dissenting); note 3 *supra.*

In determining whether the requisite knowledge had been shown,[15] reckless conduct[16] sufficed if a fiduciary relationship existed between the complainant and the alleged aider and abettor.[17] Absent a fiduciary relationship, a number of courts required conscious intent,[18] particularly if the alleged violator was performing ordinary tasks constituting "the daily grist of the mill."[19] Disagreeing, other courts found recklessness to suffice where the alleged aider and abettor had reason to foresee that third parties would be relying on his/her conduct[20] or where he/she derived financial benefit from the wrongdoing.[21] Still other courts as a general principle deemed reckless conduct to satisfy the "knowledge" requirement.[22]

In view of the Supreme Court's decision in *Central Bank of Denver*, private parties increasingly will assert theories of liability based on primary violations. This subject is addressed in § 10.03.

§ 10.02   APPLICATION OF *CENTRAL BANK OF DENVER* TO THE SEC

As a general proposition, prior to the enactment of Section 20(e) of the Exchange Act as part of the Private Securities Litigation Reform Act of 1995 (PSLRA), a persuasive argument existed that the SEC could not bring an enforcement action premised on aider and abettor liability under Section 10(b). Although the Supreme Court's holding in *Central Bank of Denver* was confined to private parties, its rationale arguably extended to SEC actions. The Court made crystal clear that its interpretation was based on "a strict statutory construction" and that the issue before it was one involving "the scope of conduct prohibited by § 10(b)."[23] The situation present in *Central Bank of Denver* thus is akin to that of *Ernst & Ernst v. Hochfelder*.[24] There, the Court,

---

[15] Questions also arose as to whether the defendant's conduct constituted "substantial assistance." For a narrow view, see *Schatz v. Rosenberg*, 943 F.2d 485 (4th Cir. 1991) (lawyer drafting of key documents not substantial assistance). This view largely was rejected, even by those courts which otherwise adhered to a restrictive approach. *See, e.g., Abell v. Potomac Insurance Co.*, 858 F.2d 1104 (5th Cir. 1988), *vacated on other grounds*, 492 U.S. 914 (1989).

[16] Courts generally have adopted the "highly" reckless standard, defined as conduct that represents "an extreme departure from the standards of ordinary care . . . to the extent that the danger was either known to the defendant or so obvious that the defendant must have been aware of it." *Hollinger v. Titan Capital Corp.*, 914 F.2d 1564, 1569–1570 (9th Cir. 1990) (en banc) (and cases cited therein). *See* § 8.03[C] *supra.*

[17] *See, e.g., Abell v. Potomac Insurance Co.*, 858 F.2d 1104 (5th Cir. 1988), *vacated on other grounds*, 492 U.S. 914 (1989).

[18] *See, e.g., Schatz v. Rosenberg*, 943 F.2d 485 (4th Cir. 1991).

[19] *See, e.g., Farlow v. Peat, Marwick, Mitchell & Co.*, 956 F.2d 982 (10th Cir. 1992).

[20] *See, e.g., Breard v. Sachnoff*, 941 F.2d 142 (2d Cir. 1991); *SEC v. Electronics Warehouse, Inc.*, 689 F. Supp. 53 (D. Conn.), *aff'd*, 891 F.2d 457 (2d Cir. 1989).

[21] *See, e.g., Walck v. American Stock Exchange, Inc.*, 687 F.2d 778, 791 n.18 (3d Cir. 1992); *Gould v. American-Hawaiian S.S. Co.*, 535 F.2d 761, 780 (3d Cir. 1976).

[22] *See, e.g., Stern v. American Bankshares, Inc.*, 429 F. Supp. 818 (E.D. Wis. 1977).

[23] 511 U.S. at 173–175. *See* discussion § 8.03 *supra.*

[24] 425 U.S. 185 (1976).

applying a strict statutory construction to ascertain the scope of conduct proscribed by Section 10(b), held that scienter must be shown in private actions for damages under that statute.[25] Thereafter, applying *Hochfelder's* rationale, the Court in *Aaron v. SEC*[26] held that scienter must be proven in SEC enforcement actions for violation of Section 10(b).[27] Following this logic, it appeared as a general proposition that the SEC no longer could institute an enforcement action under Section 10(b) based on aider and abettor liability. Note that this argument still may be asserted with respect to the viability of aider and abettor principles under the Securities Act.

Nonetheless, unlike the *Hochfelder-Aaron* scienter scenario, aiding and abetting a federal securities law violation gives rise by statute to criminal liability exposure. Accordingly, under this rationale, the criminal aid-abet statute provides ample authority for the SEC to pursue aiders and abettors.[28]

With respect to the Exchange Act, Congress resolved this issue in favor of the SEC by adding pursuant to the PSLRA a new subsection (e) to Section 20, thereby authorizing the SEC to seek injunctive relief and/or certain money penalties against aiders and abettors for violations of the 1934 Act (or any rule or regulation thereunder). Specifically, the section provides that any person who "knowingly provides substantial assistance" to another person in violation of the Exchange Act (or any rule or regulation thereunder) shall be liable "to the same extent as the person to whom such assistance is provided." Hence, this section preserves aiding and abetting liability in SEC enforcement actions brought for violations of the 1934 Act.[29] Nonetheless, the mental culpability standard (although seemingly requiring actual knowledge) awaits clarification by the federal courts. Moreover, perhaps surprisingly, Congress has declined to provide the SEC with express authority to pursue aiders and abettors for 1933 Act violations. Accordingly, whether the Commission has aiding and abetting authority for Securities Act registration (Section 5) and antifraud (Section 17(a)) violations is uncertain. Hence, the applicability of *Central Bank of Denver* to SEC enforcement actions under the Securities Act remains unresolved.

---

[25] *Id.* at 201.

[26] 446 U.S. 680 (1980).

[27] *Id.* at 689–695. *See* discussion § 8.03[B] *supra*, § 15.05[B] *infra.*

[28] *See* 18 U.S.C. § 2(a) ("Whoever commits an offense against the United States or aids, abets, counsels, commands, induces or procures its commission, is punishable as a principal."); Bromberg, *Aiding and Abetting: Sudden Death and Possible Resurrection*, 24 Rev. Sec. & Comm. Reg. 133, 138 (1994) (pointing to criminal aid-abet statute as grounds for recognizing SEC authority to pursue aiders and abettors).

[29] For SEC enforcement actions brought against alleged aiders and abettors, see, *e.g.*, *SEC v. Fisher*, [2008 Transfer Binder] Fed. Sec. L. Rep. (CCH) ¶ 94,794 (E.D. Mich. 2008); *SEC v. Orr*, [2006 Transfer Binder] Fed. Sec. L. Rep. (CCH) ¶ 93,838 (E.D. Mich 2006); *SEC v. DiBella*, [2005–2006 Transfer Binder] Fed. Sec. L. Rep. (CCH) ¶ 93,625 (D. Conn. 2005).

§ 10.03   DISTINGUISHING PRIMARY FROM SECONDARY CONDUCT

In *Central Bank of Denver*, the Supreme Court invalidated one of the principal methods of recovery for private litigants under Section 10(b) of the Securities Exchange Act of 1934. The Court held that private litigants could no longer bring Section 10(b) claims against those who aid and abet a primary Section 10(b) violation. Focusing primarily on a textual analysis of Section 10(b), the Court stated that "the statute prohibits only the making of a material misstatement (or omission) or the commission of a manipulative act. . . . The proscription does not include giving aid to a person who commits a manipulative or deceptive act."[30] On first impression, this holding seemingly released from liability so-called "secondary" actors (such as accountants, lawyers and underwriters) whose assistance was a substantial factor in the issuance of a materially misleading disclosure document or other statement that was used in the securities marketplace. However, the Court held further that:

> The absence of § 10(b) aiding and abetting liability does not mean that secondary actors in the securities market are always free from liability under the Securities Acts. Any person or entity, including a lawyer, accountant, or bank, who employs a manipulative device or makes a material misstatement (or omission) on which a purchaser or seller of securities relies may be liable as a primary violator under 10b-5, assuming all of the requirements for primary liability under Rule 10b-5 are met.[31]

This language opens the door to pursue liability against secondary actors for primary violations of Section 10(b). Yet, while the Supreme Court recognizes that primary liability may be imposed upon secondary actors in certain situations under Section 10(b), the Court's language leaves numerous questions unresolved.

The Supreme Court sought to clarify the scope of Section 10(b) liability in *Stoneridge Investment Partners, LLC v. Scientific-Atlanta, Inc.*[32] In *Stoneridge*, investors in Charter Communications, Inc., a cable operator, alleged that the defendants, Scientific-Atlanta, Inc., and Motorola, Inc., acted with Charter executives to engage in a deceptive scheme to inflate Charter's financial results to meet analyst expectations. As part of this scheme, Charter arranged to overpay Scientific-Atlanta and Motorola on purchases of digital cable equipment, with the understanding that the defendants would then return these overpayments to the company by buying advertising from Charter. Based on these transactions, Charter fraudulently overstated its revenue and operating cash flow by $17 million in financial statements filed with the SEC. Plaintiffs, purchasers of Charter stock, alleged that by participating in these transactions, Scientific-Atlanta and Motorola had primarily violated Section

---

[30] 511 U.S. at 177.

[31] *Id.* at 191.

[32] 128 S. Ct. 761 (2008).

10(b) by engaging in a deceptive scheme.[33]

The Supreme Court upheld dismissal of the case, concluding that, as alleged, Scientific-Atlanta and Motorola were not primary violators. Notably, the Court rejected the assertion that only public misstatements and failures to disclose fall within the deceptive acts prohibited by Section 10(b) with an explicit statement that conduct may itself be deceptive within the meaning of the statute.[34] Ultimately, however, the Court's holding turned on the element of reliance.

Because the investing public had no knowledge of the transactions between Charter and the defendants, the Court held that the plaintiffs could not establish the requisite reliance.[35] The Court emphasized that Charter had ultimate control over recording the transactions, conferring with its auditor, and issuing its financial statements.[36] Accordingly, because the plaintiffs did not rely on the subject defendants' alleged misconduct, private primary liability under Section 10(b) was not appropriate. As stated by the Supreme Court: "[N]o member of the investing public had knowledge, either actual or presumed, of respondents' deceptive acts during the relevant times [and that] as a result, [plaintiffs] cannot show a claim upon any of the respondents' actions except in an indirect claim that we find too remote for liability."[37]

Stoneridge thus dealt a severe, if not fatal, blow to the "scheme" theory of liability that had been embraced by a number of lower federal courts.[38] Under the "scheme" theory, "where . . . [a defendant such as] a financial institution enters into deceptive transactions as part of a scheme . . . that institution is subject to private liability under Section 10(b). . . . "[39] Persons who direct or "orchestrate" a fraudulent scheme are thereby subject to Section 10(b) primary liability under this theory even if their actions are not communicated to the investing public.[40] Clearly, after *Stoneridge*, such primary liability under Section 10(b) is viable only if investors knew ("actual or presumed") of the subject defendant's allegedly deceptive acts.[41] Lower court decisions after

---

[33] *Id.* at 766–767.

[34] *Id.* at 769 (stating that "[c]onduct itself can be deceptive").

[35] *Id.* at 769–770.

[36] *Id.* at 770, 774.

[37] *Id.* at 769.

[38] *See, e.g., In re Enron Securities Derivative & ERISA Litigation*, 235 F. Supp. 2d 549 (S.D. Tex. 2002), 439 F. Supp. 2d 692 (S.D. Tex. 2006), *rev'd*, 482 F.3d 372 (5th Cir. 2007).

[39] *In re Parmalat Securities Litigation*, 376 F. Supp. 2d 472, 509 (S.D.N.Y. 2005).

[40] *See* Beattie, *The New Minefield: The Scheme Theory of Primary Liability Comes of Age in the Post-Enron Era*, 33 Sec. Reg. L.J. 92 (2006); McLaughlin, *Liability Under Rules 10b-5(a) & (c)*, 31 Del. J. Corp. L. 631 (2006). A number of federal lower courts rejected "scheme" liability under Section 10(b) prior to *Stoneridge*. *See, e.g., Regents of University of California v. Credit Suisse First Boston*, 482 F.3d 372 (5th Cir. 2007). *See also, Ziemba v. Cascade International, Inc.*, 256 F.3d 1194 (11th Cir. 2001).

[41] 128 S. Ct. at 769 (stating that "[n]o member of the investing public had knowledge, either actual or presumed, of respondents' deceptive acts during the relevant times"). *See* Black, *Stoneridge Investment Partners v. Scientific-Atlanta, Inc.: Reliance on Deceptive Conduct and the Future of Securities Fraud Class Actions*, 36 Sec. Reg. L.J. 330 (2008).

Stoneridge have applied that decision's rationale to foreclose Section 10(b) primary liability based on the "scheme" theory.[42]

Thus, although the Supreme Court's decision in *Stoneridge* confines the scope of Section 10(b) primary liability, a number of issues merit discussion.

[A]   Primary Liability Where the Secondary Actor Speaks

One type of misconduct with respect to which courts nearly universally agree gives rise to primary Section 10(b) liability exposure is when a secondary actor makes a material misstatement in the form of a signed document or a direct oral misrepresentation to a third party. Where a secondary actor makes such a materially misleading statement, primary liability principles under Section 10(b) apply.[43]

Courts have little trouble agreeing that primary liability exposure is appropriate when a secondary actor makes direct *oral* misrepresentations to investors.[44] As stated by the Sixth Circuit, "while an attorney representing the seller in a securities transaction may not always be under an independent duty to volunteer information about the financial condition of his client, he assumes a duty to provide complete and non-misleading information with respect to subjects on which he undertakes to speak."[45] And, as the Ninth Circuit has opined in a decision handed down after *Stoneridge*: "An attorney who undertakes to make representations to prospective purchasers of securities is under an obligation to tell the truth about those securities."[46]

Courts also have imposed primary liability on secondary actors with respect to direct *written* misrepresentations. For accountants, primary liability has been imposed on outside auditors when they have issued formal audit opinions or certifications of an issuer's financial statements that contain materially false representations.[47] Similarly, where a lawyer issues an opinion letter containing material misrepresentations, courts will apply primary liability principles. In

---

[42] *See, e.g., Pugh v. Tribune Company*, 521 F.3d 686 (7th Cir. 2008); *In re Nature's Sunshine Products Securities Litigation*, 2008 U.S. Dist. LEXIS 73031 (D. Utah 2008).

[43] *See, e.g., Anixter v. Home Stake Production Co.*, 77 F.3d 1215, 1225 (10th Cir. 1996) (concluding that "in order for accountants to 'use or employ' a 'deception' actionable under the antifraud law, they must themselves make a false or misleading statement (or omission) that they know or should know will reach potential investors").

[44] *See Rubin v. Schottenstein, Zox & Dunn*, 143 F.3d 263, 266–268 (6th Cir. 1998) (holding that primary liability under § 10(b) appropriate where attorney for issuer falsely represented to third party investor about the financial condition of his client and when attorney knew that the investor would reasonably rely on his statements).

[45] *Id.* at 268. *See also, Kline v. First Western Government Securities, Inc.*, 24 F.3d 480, 491 (3rd Cir. 1994) (stating that "when a professional 'undertakes the affirmative act of communicating or disseminating information,' there is a general obligation or 'duty' to speak truthfully").

[46] *Thompson v. Paul*, 547 F.3d 1055 (9th Cir. 2008).

[47] *See, e.g., Cooper v. Pickett*, 137 F.3d 616, 621 (9th Cir. 1997) (holding that plaintiff's § 10(b) claim against accountant erroneously dismissed where complaint alleged that accountant knowingly certified false and misleading financial statements and also deliberately or recklessly did not comply with Generally Accepted Auditing Standards).

fact, an attorney's use of cautionary language in the opinion seeking to dissuade third party reliance on the conclusions reached therein may not preclude the imposition of primary liability.[48] Further, even where counsel's opinion letter containing material disclosure deficiencies is intended only for the client, the lawyer nonetheless can be held primarily liable under Section 10(b) to the extent that the lawyer subsequently acquiesces in the circulation of the letter to potential investors.[49]

Although frequently sued, accountants and lawyers are not the only professionals who risk primary liability for making affirmative statements. For example, investment bankers and underwriters may incur primary liability for rendering materially misleading valuations or forecasts regarding subject companies.[50]

[B]   Primary Liability Where the Secondary Actor Drafts a Misstatement

One area in which the *Central Bank* decision has had a profound effect relates to situations in which the secondary actor has drafted a materially misleading document for her client that is transmitted to shareholders or prospective investors. In order for primary liability exposure to arise, lower courts after *Central Bank* have assessed whether the secondary actor must actually sign, certify, or be named in a document containing material disclosure deficiencies.

[1]   Pre-*Central Bank* Case Law

Prior to the Supreme Court's rejection of aiding and abetting liability in *Central Bank*, Section 10(b) claimants frequently sought recovery through the imposition of *primary* liability upon secondary actors.[51] A number of courts held that a claim alleging this type of misconduct was insufficient to sustain primary liability. Indeed, courts adhering to this approach concluded that by

---

[48] See, e.g., *Kline v. First Western Government Securities, Inc.*, 24 F.3d at 483–490 (where law firm was put on notice that investors were relying on firm's tax opinion letters, law firm could be held primarily liable under § 10(b) for misstatements and omissions contained in those letters even though firm stated in the letters that the opinions were based on assumed facts represented to the firm by the client and that the firm conducted no independent investigation into whether those represented facts accurately reflected reality). *See generally* D. Glaser, S. FitzGibbon, & S. Weise, Legal Opinions (2d ed. 2004).

[49] *See, e.g.*, *Ackerman v. Schwartz*, 947 F.2d at 848 (Although the attorney had no duty to the investors to blow the whistle on his client and he had no duty to correct a letter he had not authorized to be circulated in the first place, the attorney cannot evade primary § 10(b) liability to the extent he permitted the promoters to release his opinion letter to the investors when he knew such letter contained material misrepresentations.). *See generally* M. Steinberg, Attorney Liability After Sarbanes-Oxley § 2.05 (2008).

[50] *See, e.g.*, *Cooper v. Pickett*, 137 F.3d at 629 (primary liability appropriate where underwriters' analysts allegedly were aware of undisclosed facts showing that there was no reasonable basis for their optimistic forecasts, and therefore, that they did not genuinely believe such forecasts).

[51] *See e.g.*, *Abell v. Potomac Insurance Co.*, 858 F.2d 1104 (5th Cir. 1988); *vacated on other grounds*, 492 U.S. 914 (1989).

drafting documents to its client's specifications, counsel's services merely constituted "the daily grist of the mill."[52] The Fourth Circuit, rejecting primary liability principles in this context, perceived the defendant law firm as merely a "scrivener" of its client's disclosure materials.[53]

Courts often disagreed as to what conduct would suffice for the imposition of Section 10(b) liability. In *Abell v. Potomac Insurance Co.*,[54] for example, the underwriter's counsel included several misstatements in the bond offering documents at its client's request.[55] Although the law firm allowed its firm name to be included in the document as underwriter's counsel, the law firm did not sign the document or opine as to the completeness or accuracy of the statements contained therein.[56] Reversing the district court's findings of primary liability against underwriter's counsel, the Fifth Circuit found that counsel had not made any affirmative misstatements upon which plaintiffs had relied.[57]

In *Schatz v. Rosenberg*,[58] the Fourth Circuit reviewed the allegations presented in plaintiffs' pleadings to determine whether the allegations could sustain a finding of primary or secondary liability under Section 10(b). Plaintiffs alleged that the defendant law firm supplied a misstated letter from its client to such plaintiffs regarding its client's financial position[59] and drafted closing documents containing misrepresentations made by its client.[60] The court held that by simply forwarding a letter from the law firm's client to plaintiffs, the law firm had not made any affirmative misstatement.[61] Further, by drafting closing documents containing representations by the law firm's client, the law firm did not warrant its client's probity.[62] The court concluded

---

[52] *Id.* at 1128.

[53] *Schatz v. Rosenberg*, 943 F.2d at 497 (4th Cir. 1991) (stating that the law firm "did no more than 'paper the deal' or act as scrivener for [its client]").

[54] 858 F.2d 1104 (5th 1988), *vacated on other grounds*, 492 U.S. 914 (1989).

[55] *See* 858 F.2d at 1111–12. As underwriter's counsel, defendant undertook the responsibilities of preparing and revising the bond offering documents and performing due diligence to ensure the accuracy and completeness of those documents. However, the documents did not disclose that the issuer had received a negative viability report with regard to the project. Also undisclosed was the fact that the issuer had obtained the land for the project through a less than arm's length transaction. And finally, the offering documents misrepresented the nature of the principal's pledge of collateral towards the success of the project.

[56] *Id.* at 1126.

[57] *Id.* at 1123. The court noted that the defendant limited its role in the bond offering to the legal work it did for the bond underwriters. *See* note 55 *supra*. "Consequently, [defendant] *never made any statements* on its own behalf directly to the bondholders, but only checked and revised statements *made* in the offering statement." *Id.* (emphasis added).

[58] 943 F.2d 485 (4th Cir. 1991).

[59] *Id.* at 494.

[60] *Id.* Despite the fact that the client was actually insolvent at the time, the closing documents drafted by the defendant law firm represented that the client's net worth exceeded $7 million. *Id.* at 488.

[61] *Id.* at 494. Note that the plaintiffs did not allege that the law firm had made any representations other than those made by the law firm's client.

[62] *Id.* (asserting that the lawyers did not make any affirmative representations about their client

that the law firm could not be held liable under Section 10(b) for the misrepresentations made by the client, even though the lawyers incorporated the client's misrepresentations into legal documents necessary for closing the transaction.[63]

In *Molecular Technology v. Valentine*,[64] on the other hand, the Sixth Circuit took a broader approach to pre-*Central Bank* Section 10(b) liability. The defendant in *Molecular Technology* was a lawyer who drafted and edited various documents in connection with a merger between his client and a third party.[65] The attorney also played a similar role in several of the new company's subsequent securities offerings.[66] The court applied the "direct contacts" test for determining whether the defendant was liable as a primary violator.[67]

Under the Sixth Circuit's application of the direct contacts test, attorneys who draft disclosure materials with the expectation that such materials will be furnished to investors are deemed primary participants.[68] The court held there was sufficient evidence to support a finding that the lawyer knew the information in the document was materially false and that such information was to be furnished to, and relied upon by, the third party. Further, the court found that there was adequate evidence that the attorney took a sufficiently active role in editing the information such that the subject misrepresentations could be deemed his own. Applying the "direct contacts" test, the court found that counsel had a duty to provide materially correct information to the third party. For breaching that duty, the attorney was subject to primary liability under Section 10(b).[69] In a decision after *Stoneridge*, a federal district court in the Sixth Circuit upheld the continued validity of the direct contacts test.[70]

[2]   Post-*Central Bank* and *Stoneridge* Case Law

In a number of jurisdictions, a secondary actor who drafts a misstatement communicated to investors may be subject to Section 10(b) primary liability exposure. In *In re Software Toolworks Incorporated Securities Litigation*,[71]

---

to plaintiffs; rather they only put their client's representations to paper).

[63] *Id.* at 495.

[64] 925 F.2d 910 (6th Cir. 1991).

[65] *Id.* at 913–18.

[66] *Id.* at 913–14.

[67] *Id.* at 917. The court stated the test as follows:

> [O]nly those individuals who had an affirmative obligation to reveal what was allegedly omitted can be held as a primary participant in the alleged deception. A person undertaking to furnish information, which is misleading because of a failure to disclose a material fact, is a primary participant. Conversely, a person who does not undertake to furnish any information, and who is not aware of what information has been furnished, is under no duty to disclose material information in his possession.

[68] 925 F.2d at 917–18.

[69] *Id.* at 918.

[70] *See Burket v. Hyman Lippitt, P.C.*, [2008 Transfer Binder] Fed. Sec. L. Rep. (CCH).
¶ 94,704 (E.D. Mich. 2008).

[71] 50 F.3d 615 (9th Cir. 1994).

for example, the Ninth Circuit addressed Section 10(b) claims brought against accountants and underwriters for drafting alleged misstatements that appeared in documents transmitted to the SEC. The Section 10(b) claims in *Software Toolworks* focused on a letter that was sent to the SEC by the company regarding its quarterly financial results.[72] Allegedly, the letter falsely stated that Software Toolworks did not have preliminary financial data available for the quarter and misleadingly described the nature of Software Toolworks' original equipment manufacturing contracts in its quarterly financial statements.[73]

In reversing the district court's grant of summary judgment for the underwriters and the accountants, the Ninth Circuit found that a jury could properly hold these secondary actors primarily liable under Section 10(b). According to the court, such liability would appropriately be based on findings that (1) the secondary actors were members of the drafting group; (2) that they had access to all information that was available; and (3) that those actors deliberately chose to conceal the truth about the figures in the SEC letter.[74]

In *Klein v. Boyd*,[75] the Third Circuit addressed primary securities fraud charges against attorneys who allegedly compiled and drafted their client's private offering disclosure package. Specifically, in *Klein*, the defendant law firm drafted a disclosure package regarding its client, a limited partnership, to prospective investors. Plaintiffs alleged that the disclosure package omitted that the majority owner of the general partner had a record of securities fraud, regulatory sanctions, and claims of fraudulent conduct. The investors brought a Section 10(b) claim against the law firm for failing to disclose this information.[76]

The Third Circuit endorsed the Ninth Circuit's reasoning in *Software Toolworks* that primary liability is appropriate where the "secondary actor's participation in the creation of the fraudulent statement is so significant that the secondary actor can fairly be said to have made the statement."[77] Accordingly, the Third Circuit promulgated a four-factor test to determine when a lawyer in similar circumstances may be held primarily liable. Under the court's test, such an attorney may be held primarily liable under Section 10(b) when: (1) the lawyer knows (or is reckless in not knowing) that the statement will be relied upon by investors; (2) the lawyer is aware (or is reckless in not being aware) of the material misstatement or omission; (3) the lawyer played such a substantial role in the creation of the statement that the lawyer can fairly be said to be the "author" or "co-author" of the statement; and (4) the other requirements of primary liability are satisfied.[78] According to

---

[72] *Id.* at 625–29.

[73] *Id.* at 628.

[74] *Id.* at 627, 629.

[75] [1998 Transfer Binder] Fed. Sec. L. Rep. (CCH) ¶ 90,136 (3d Cir. 1998), *vacated for rehearing en banc,* [1998 Transfer Binder] Fed. Sec. L. Rep. (CCH) ¶ 90,165 (3d Cir. 1998).

[76] [1998 Transfer Binder] Fed. Sec. L. Rep. (CCH) ¶ 90,136, at pp. 90,318–90,320.

[77] *Id.* at p. 90,326 n.7.

[78] *Id.* at p. 90,318 n.1.

the court, such a lawyer may be a primary violator regardless of whether investors knew of the lawyer's involvement at the time the document was distributed to such investors.[79]

Subsequently, the Third Circuit granted a motion for reconsideration in which it vacated the judgment in *Klein*. The court then set the case for rehearing *en banc*.[80] After the judgment was vacated, however, the parties settled the matter before rehearing took place.

In an attempt to clarify the appropriate standard of primary liability for this type of misconduct, the SEC submitted a brief as *amicus curiae* in *Klein*. In its analysis, the Commission interpreted the Supreme Court's language in *Central Bank*. Specifically, the SEC reviewed the language from *Central Bank* establishing primary liability for secondary actors who "make a misstatement."[81]

The Commission argued that primary liability for a secondary actor who makes a false statement is not contingent upon public attribution of the statement to the secondary actor. To so limit *Central Bank* would be inconsistent with the language of Section 10(b). Section 10(b) makes it unlawful "for any person, directly or indirectly . . . [t]o use or employ any manipulative or deceptive device or contrivance." To that end, a person who creates a misrepresentation, but takes care not to be identified publicly with it, "indirectly" uses or employs a deceptive device or contrivance and should be liable. The Commission argued further that it is the misrepresentation — not the person who made such misrepresentation — upon which a plaintiff must rely. By stating that liability exposure exists "where any person makes a material misstatement on which a purchaser or seller relies," the focus is on the misrepresentation, not on the particular actor. Therefore, the Commission proposed the following standard:

> "[A] person who has the requisite *scienter* can be liable as a primary violator of Section 10(b) of the Securities Exchange Act of 1934 and Rule 10b-5 thereunder when he or she, acting alone or with others, *creates a misrepresentation*, whether or not the person is identified with the misrepresentation by name."[82]

Subsequently, even after *Stoneridge*, a number of courts have adopted the SEC's reasoning, concluding that lawyers and others who draft their clients' disclosure materials incur Section 10(b) liability exposure.[83]

---

[79] *Id.* at p. 90,324.

[80] *See* [1998 Transfer Binder] Fed. Sec. L. Rep. (CCH) ¶ 90,165 (3d Cir. 1998).

[81] Brief of the SEC, *Amicus Curiae* in *Klein v. Boyd*, at 12, Nos. 97-1143, 97-1261 (3d Cir. 1998).

[82] *Id.* at 15-20. Surprisingly, the SEC gratuitously conceded that "[u]nder the Commission's test, however, a person who prepares a truthful and complete portion of a document would not be liable as a primary violator for misrepresentations in other portions of the document. Even assuming such a person knew of misrepresentations elsewhere in the document and thus had the requisite scienter, he or she would not have created those misrepresentations." *Id.* at 18.

[83] *See, e.g., SEC v. Wolfson*, 539 F.3d 1249 (10th Cir. 2008) (stating that "when a non-employee

This rationale has been rejected by other courts, opining that drafting a client's disclosure documents is not sufficient to invoke Section 10(b) primary liability. Under this rationale, liability under Section 10(b) may be limited to the issuance of legal opinions and other statements that the subject attorney makes and upon which complainants rely having knowledge of the maker's identity (e.g., the identity of legal counsel who makes the statement).[84]

[C]   Duty to "Blow the Whistle"

The focus of the preceding discussion has been on primary liability under Section 10(b) based on a secondary actor's own conduct. The following analysis examines a different issue, namely, a secondary actor's duty under the federal securities laws to disclose his/her client's misstatements to third parties (such as the SEC or the subject corporation's shareholders).

To establish Section 10(b) liability exposure on this basis, it is initially incumbent upon plaintiffs to prove that the secondary actor has a duty to disclose.[85] Several federal appellate courts have concluded that the federal securities laws are not the source of such a duty.[86] Rather, the secondary actor's duty to disclose may arise where a fiduciary or other confidential relationship is found to exist.[87] Where such a relationship can be established, courts have held that primary section 10(b) liability may be imposed for a breach of the duty to disclose that arises from that relationship.[88]

For lawyers, the duty to disclose or "blow the whistle" on their clients does not seem likely to arise. Rather, as stated by the Seventh Circuit in *Barker*,

---

consultant causes misstatements or omissions within periodic financial reports submitted to the Commission, knowing that those misstatements or omissions will reach investors, he can be held primarily liable under the anti-fraud provisions of the federal securities laws").

[84] *See, e.g., Ziemba v. Cascade International, Inc.*, 256 F.3d 1194 (11th Cir. 2001). With respect to the primary liability exposure of secondary actors who participate in disclosure deficiencies made to investors, see, *e.g., Wright v. Ernst & Young, L.L.P.*, 152 F.3d 169 (2d Cir. 1998); *Shapiro v. Cantor*, 123 F.3d 717 (2d Cir. 1997); *Carley Capital Group v. Deloitte & Touche, L.L.P.*, 27 F. Supp. 2d 1324 (N.D. Ga. 1998). *See also, In re Bristol Myers Squibb Co. Securities Litigation*, 586 F. Supp. 2d 148 (S.D.N.Y. 2008) (stating that an officer's allegedly deceptive conduct in negotiating a settlement on an issuer's behalf could constitute a primary violation of § 10(b) as the officer's role as lead negotiator placed him "at the heart of [the issuer's] false and misleading conduct").

[85] *See, e.g., Fortson v. Winstead, McGuire, Sechrest & Minick*, 961 F.2d 469, 472 (4th Cir. 1992), *citing, Chiarella v. United States*, 445 U.S. 222, 228 (1980) (*quoting* Restatement (Second) of Torts § 551(2)(a) (1976)).

[86] *See, e.g., Fortson v. Winstead, McGuire, Sechrest & Minick*, 961 F.2d at 472; *Schatz v. Rosenberg*, 943 F.2d at 490–92; *Abell v. Potomac Ins. Co.*, 858 F.2d at 1124; *Barker v. Henderson, Franklin, Starnes & Holt*, 797 F.2d at 496.

[87] *Fortson*, 961 F.2d at 272 (*citing Windon Third Oil & Gas Drilling Partnership v. FDIC*, 805 F.2d 342, 347 (10th Cir. 1986)). *See Chiarella v. United States*, 445 U.S. 222, 228 (1980) (holding in § 10(b) insider trading context duty to disclose arises from a fiduciary or similar relationship of trust and confidence); *Barker*, 797 F.2d at 496 (finding that because neither § 10(b) nor Rule 10b-5 imposes such a duty to disclose, any such duty "must come from a fiduciary relation outside the securities law").

[88] Before *Central Bank* the overwhelming majority of courts held that the duty to blow the whistle did not exist. *See e.g., Schatz v. Rosenberg*, 943 F.2d at 490–94.

"[t]o the contrary, attorneys have privileges not to disclose."[89] Further, the Model Rules of Professional Conduct confine the acceptable actions of a lawyer such that only rarely should circumstances occur in which the lawyer's relationship with a third party would give rise to a duty higher than that owed to his/her clients.[90] As a result, courts overwhelmingly hold that a lawyer does not have a duty to disclose his/her client's fraudulent activities to third parties.[91]

For accountants, the question of whether a duty to disclose exists becomes more difficult. Accountants' duties differ from those of attorneys. Addressing this distinction in *United States v. Arthur Young & Co.*,[92] the Supreme Court stated:

> An independent certified public accountant performs a different role [than counsel whose role is to serve the client]. By certifying the public reports that collectively depict a corporation's financial status, the independent auditor assumes a public responsibility transcending any employment relationship with the client. The independent public accountant performing this special function owes ultimate allegiance to the corporation's creditors and stockholders, as well as to the investing public. This "public watchdog" function demands that the accountant maintain total independence from the client at all times and requires complete fidelity to the public trust.[93]

This generalized duty is heightened by Section 10A of the Exchange Act which was enacted pursuant to the Private Securities Litigation Reform Act of 1995. Depending on the circumstances, an accountant's duty to blow the whistle may arise statutorily under Section 10A. This provision requires accountants in certain situations to report their clients' illegal acts directly to the SEC.[94]

---

[89] 797 F.2d at 497.

[90] *See* Model Rules of Professional Conduct, Rule 1.6(b)(2) (stating that in this context an attorney may disclose only when necessary "to prevent the client from committing a crime or fraud that is reasonably certain to result in substantial injury to the financial interests or property of another and in furtherance of which the client has used or is using the lawyer's services"); Model Rules of Professional Conduct Rule 1.7(a)(2) (absent informed consent and satisfaction of other specified conditions, proscribing a lawyer's representation of a client if that representation "will be materially limited by the lawyer's responsibilities to another client, a former client or a third person or by a personal interest of the lawyer").

[91] *See, e.g., Fortson*, 961 F.2d at 474–75 (holding that duty to investigate and disclose client's misstatements did not arise under state common law, ABA Ethics Opinions or Federal Treasury Regulations); *Schatz*, 943 F.2d at 490–95 (concluding that duty to disclose client's misrepresentations did not arise under state ethics rules or state common law, and reasoning that "[t]he better rule — that attorneys have no duty to 'blow the whistle' on their clients — allows clients to repose complete trust in their lawyers." *Id.* at 493.).

[92] 465 U.S. 805 (1984).

[93] *Id.* at 817. Compare *Shapiro v. Cantor*, 123 F.3d 717 (2d Cir. 1997) (where an issuer's fraudulent omission from the offering statement relates to an area wholly distinct from the expertised portion of the offering statement certified by the accountants, the accountants have no duty to disclose the fraudulent misrepresentation to the third party purchaser).

[94] *See* discussion §§ 5.08, 8.12 *supra.*

§ 10.04 CONTROLLING PERSON LIABILITY

Section 15 of the Securities Act imposes joint and several liability on any person who controls a person liable under Section 11 or 12 "unless the controlling person had no knowledge of or reasonable grounds to believe in the existence of the facts by reason of which the liability of the controlled person is alleged to exist." Section 20(a) of the Exchange Act provides that "every person who . . . controls any person liable under any provision of this title . . . shall also be liable jointly and severally with and to the same extent as such controlled person to any person to whom such controlled person is liable, unless the controlling person acted in good faith and did not directly or indirectly induce the act or acts constituting the violation or cause of action." As has been pointed out, "[t]he reason for this difference in language is hard to fathom, especially since Section 15 of the 1933 Act was amended in the bill which enacted the 1934 Act, and harder still to interpret."[95]

The term "control" is not defined in the Securities Acts. Pursuant to Rule 405, however, the Commission has defined the term to encompass "the possession, direct or indirect, of the power to direct or cause the direction of the management and policies of a person."[96] The courts generally are in accord with this standard. For example, as stated by one appellate court, control was established when the defendant "had the requisite power to directly or indirectly control or influence corporate policy."[97] Or, as stated by the Seventh Circuit: "We have looked to whether the alleged control person actually participated in, that is, exercised control over, the operations of the person in general and, then to whether the alleged control person possessed the power or ability to control the specific transaction or activity upon which the primary violation was predicated, whether or not that power was exercised."[98]

As set forth above, Section 20(a) absolves the controlling person of liability if he/she acted in good faith and did not directly or indirectly induce the violation. The statutory language places the burden of proof on the controlling person to establish the good faith defense. This view has been widely adopted,[99] although some courts require the complainant to plead "culpable conduct."[100] With respect to the state of mind required to establish liability, the Supreme Court in *Hochfelder* stated that the controlling person provision "contains a state-of-mind condition requiring something more than negligence."[101]

---

[95] *See* R. Jennings, H. Marsh, & J. Coffee, *Securities Regulation* 1131 (7th ed. 1992).

[96] 17 C.F.R. § 230.405.

[97] *G. A. Thompson & Co., Inc. Partridge*, 636 F.2d 945, 958 (5th Cir. 1981).

[98] *Harrison v. Dean Witter Reynolds, Inc.*, 974 F.2d 945, 958 (7th Cir. 1981).

[99] *See, e.g., In re Stone & Webster, Inc. Securities Litigation*, 424 F.3d 24, 26 (1st Cir. 2005).

[100] *See, e.g., Mishkin v. Ageloff*, 1998 WL 651065, at *23 (S.D.N.Y. 1998) (requiring "a plaintiff, at the pleading stage, to allege particular facts that give rise to a 'strong inference' of the requisite state of mind").

[101] 425 U.S. at 209. As recently held by the Eleventh Circuit, damages incurred by a control person are determined based on the standards set forth in the Private Securities Litigation Reform Act. *See LaPerriere v. Vesta Insurance Group*, 526 F.3d 715 (11th Cir. 2008); discussion § 8.11 *supra*.

Applying the above standards, a number of courts have adopted the "culpable participant" test, signifying that the defendant's inaction, such as lack of supervision, "was deliberate and done intentionally to further the fraud."[102] On the other hand, the apparent majority of courts have adopted a more remedial interpretation.[103] For example, over twenty-five years ago, the Second Circuit opined that, in the brokerage house setting, the controlling person must show that "it has maintained and enforced a reasonable and proper system of supervision and internal control over sales personnel."[104] In *Hollinger v. Titan Capital Corp.*,[105] the Ninth Circuit, sitting en banc, stated:

> Section 20(a) provides that the "controlling person" can avoid liability if she acted in good faith and did not directly or indirectly induce the violations. By making the good faith defense available to controlling persons, Congress was able to avoid what it deemed to be an undesirable result, namely that of insurer's liability, and instead it made vicarious liability under § 20(a) dependent upon the broker-dealer's good faith.

> Contrary to the district court's ruling, the broker-dealer cannot satisfy its burden of proving good faith merely by saying that it has supervisory procedures in place, and therefore, it has fulfilled its duty to supervise. A broker-dealer can establish the good faith defense only by proving that it "maintained and enforced a reasonable and proper system of supervision and internal control."[106]

What constitutes "good faith" and "noninducement" under Section 20(a) should depend on the particular facts and circumstances. Although negligence theoretically is not sufficient to impose liability, a more relaxed form of reckless conduct should suffice. In determining whether the controlling person acted "recklessly," one should look to customary industry practice and the realistic practicalities of the trade. For example, the failure of a broker-dealer to institute adequate (not necessarily sure-proof) supervisory and internal control procedures should be viewed as reckless conduct. Under such circumstances, by ignoring an obvious danger, the controlling person's failure to institute such

---

[102] *Sharp v. Coopers & Lybrand*, 649 F.2d 175, 185 (3d Cir. 1981). In a more recent case, the Third Circuit may have relaxed this test, opining that "[t]he complaint contains no factual support for the conclusion that the [brokerage] firms knew *or should have known* of the [the broker's] misconduct or that any failure to adequately supervise him was to further the fraud." *Ash v. Ameritreat, Inc.*, [1999–2000 Transfer Binder] Fed. Sec. L. Rep. (CCH) ¶ 90,616, at 92,801, summarily reported at, 189 F.3d 463 (3d Cir. 1999) (emphasis supplied). *See also, SEC v. J.W. Barclay & Co., Inc.*, 442 F.3d 834, 841 n. 8 (3d Cir. 2006).

[103] *See* cases cited *infra* notes 104–106 and accompanying text.

[104] *Marbury Management, Inc. v. Kohn*, 629 F.2d 705, 716 (2d Cir. 1980). More recent Second Circuit case law may be read as requiring that the controlling person's culpability be part of the complainant's prima facie case, thereby implicitly overruling *Marbury Management. See Ganino v. Citizens Utilities Co.*, 228 F.3d 154 (2d Cir. 2000); *Boguslavsky v. Kaplan*, 159 F.3d 715 (2d Cir. 1998); *SEC v. First Jersey Securities, Inc.*, 101 F.3d 1450 (2d Cir. 1996).

[105] 914 F.2d 1564 (9th Cir. 1990) (en banc).

[106] *Id.* at 1575–76. *See Harrison v. Dean Witter Reynolds, Inc.*, 974 F.2d 873 (7th Cir. 1992).

mechanisms constitutes an extreme departure from the standards of ordinary care.[107]

§ 10.05   RESPONDEAT SUPERIOR LIABILITY

A controversial issue involves whether the common law principle of respondeat superior is compatible with the federal securities laws. Under this theory, a principal (e.g., a broker-dealer firm) is held liable for the securities law violations committed by its agent (e.g., a broker) when such agent acts within the scope of his/her employment having actual or apparent authority.[108]

A number of courts have rejected in all cases the application of respondeat superior liability under the federal securities laws. To hold otherwise, these courts reason, in effect would negate the controlling person provisions. For example, one court has reasoned:

> Noteworthy in each [controlling person] provision is the inclusion of a defense from liability based on "good faith" or lack of knowledge or reasonable belief. When originally passed by Congress, § 15 of the 1933 Act held controlling persons absolutely liable for § 11 and § 12 violations by controlled persons. Congress, in passing the 1934 Act, amended § 15 of the earlier Act, adding the language beginning at "unless the controlling person had no knowledge of or reasonable ground to believe in the existence of facts by reason of which the liability of the controlled person is alleged to exist."

Hence, the controlling person provision in the 1934 Act, Section 20(a), contains the "good faith" defense to liability. According to these courts, Congress had rejected an insurer's liability standard for controlling persons in favor of a specified standard — a duty to take due care or act in good faith.[109]

On the other hand, prior to the Supreme Court's decision in *Central Bank of Denver*,[110] a majority of courts held that respondeat superior liability may be imposed under the federal securities laws. Those courts favoring imposition of respondeat superior liability reasoned that the controlling person provisions were enacted by Congress to supplement common law agency principles in

---

[107] *See Dellastatious v. Williams*, 242 F.3d 191, 194 (4th Cir. 2001) ("To determine whether the good-faith affirmative defense has been satisfied under Section 20(a), defendants must show that they did not act recklessly."). *See* generally Carson, *The Liability of Controlling Persons Under the Federal Securities Acts*, 72 Notre Dame L. Rev. 263 (1997); Lowenfels & Bromberg, *Controlling Person Liability Under Section 20(a) of the Securities Exchange Act and Section 15 of the Securities Act*, 53 Bus. Law. 1 (1998).

A split of authority exists whether the SEC is a "person" within the framework of Section 20(a). The Sixth Circuit holds that Section 20(a) may be invoked only by private litigants. *See SEC v. Coffey*, 493 F.2d 1304 (6th Cir. 1974). A number of other courts, however, hold that the SEC as well as private parties may invoke Section 20(a). *See, e.g., SEC v. J.W. Barclay & Co.*, 442 F.3d 834 (3d Cir. 2006).

[108] *See, e.g., Paul F. Newton & Co. v. Texas Commerce Bank*, 630 F.2d 1111 (5th Cir. 1980).

[109] *Carpenter v. Harris, Upham & Co., Inc.*, 594 F.2d 388, 393 (4th Cir. 1979).

[110] 511 U.S. 164 (1994), *discussed in*, §§ 10.01–10.03 *supra*.

order to reach individuals (such as intermediate and upper-level supervisors) who have no agency or employment relationship with the primary violator. As to the entity, the imposition of respondeat superior liability is appropriate.[111]

Thus, as a general principle, the common law doctrine of respondeat superior has been accepted in the federal securities law context by the overwhelming majority of federal appellate courts.[112] Nonetheless, in view of the Supreme Court's *Central Bank of Denver* decision, the continued vitality of respondeat superior liability is open to debate. There, the Court, applying a strict statutory construction, held that private actions based on aiding and abetting are not permitted under Section 10(b). The Court's language and tenor arguably signify that other common law theories of liability, unless provided for by statute, likewise will be rejected.[113]

This assertion is evidenced further by the Supreme Court's focus in *Central Bank* on the statutorily provided controlling person provision of the Exchange Act. In this regard, the Court stated:

> Congress did not overlook secondary liability when it created the private rights of action in the 1934 Act. Section 20 of the 1934 Act imposes liability on "controlling persons". . . . This suggests that "when Congress wished to create such [secondary] liability, it had little trouble doing so."[114]

As Justice Stevens observed in his dissent, the majority's rationale suggests that lower court decisions recognizing respondeat superior liability "appear unlikely to survive."[115]

Nonetheless, even after *Central Bank of Denver*, lower courts have held that the doctrine of respondeat superior survives under the federal securities laws.[116] In a case not arising under the federal securities laws, the Third Circuit in a post-*Central Bank* decision reasoned:

---

[111] *See, e.g., Henricksen v. Henricksen*, 640 F.2d 880 (7th Cir. 1981). There are certain exceptions to this general proposition. *See, e.g.*, Section 20A of the Exchange Act (Congress manifesting its intent that the doctrine of respondeat superior liability not apply in private rights of action brought by contemporaneous traders for alleged insider trading violations).

[112] *See, e.g., Hollinger v. Titan Capital Corp.*, 914 F.2d 1564 (9th Cir. 1990) (en banc) (and cases cited therein).

[113] *See* Booth, *Vicarious Liability and Securities Fraud*, 22 Sec. Reg. L.J. 347 (1995); Mathews *The Supreme Court's Central Bank Decision*, Nat. L.J., May 23, 1994, at B4, B6.

[114] 511 U.S. at 184.

[115] *Id.* at 200 n.12 (Stevens, J., dissenting). The same holds true for the common law theory of conspiracy. *Id. See supra* note 6 and accompanying text.

[116] *See, e.g., Seolas v. Bilzerian*, 951 F. Supp. 978 (D. Utah 1997) (holding that *Central Bank* "does not abolish respondeat superior as a theory of liability under § 10(b)"); *In re Stat-Tech Securities Litigation*, 905 F. Supp. 1416 (D. Colo. 1995) (same). *But see ESI Montgomery County, Inc. v. Montenay International Corporation*, [1996–1997 Transfer Binder] Fed. Sec. L. Rep. (CCH) ¶ 99,345 (S.D.N.Y. 1996) (holding theory of respondeat superior eliminated in light of *Central Bank*). *See also*, Langevoort, *Words From On High About Rule 10b-5: Chiarella's History, Central Bank's Future*, 20 Del. J. Corp. L. 865, 893–896 (1995) (observing "a substantial difference between the aiding and abetting and respondeat superior issues").

The language of *Central Bank* is undeniably broad, and the dissent warned that other mechanisms of common law secondary liability — such as "respondeat superior and other common-law agency principles" – may not survive the majority's construction of Section 10(b) of the Exchange Act. . . . Nonetheless, we do not believe that the Court's restrictive reading of the Exchange Act impacts on the determination of the scope of liability [in this case].

In *Central Bank*, the Supreme Court primarily was concerned with broadening the range of unlawful conduct beyond that specifically proscribed by the Act. As the Court framed this issue, aiding and abetting constituted a separate cause of action, and in order to find such liability, the Court would have to imply a private right of action under the statute beyond that which already had been implied. . . .

By contrast, courts imposing liability on agency theories are not expanding the category of affirmative conduct proscribed by the relevant statute; rather, they are deciding on whose shoulders to place responsibility for conduct indisputably proscribed by the relevant statute. The principal is held liable not because it committed some wrongdoing outside the purview of the statute which assisted the wrongdoing prohibited by the statute, but because its status merits responsibility for the tortious actions of its agent.[117]

Note, however, that unlike many other federal statutes, the 1933 and 1934 Acts expressly allow for the imposition of secondary liability against principals by means of the controlling person provisions. This distinction may "bode ill" for those seeking to invoke the doctrine of respondeat superior liability under the federal securities laws.[118] Note that even if the doctrine of respondeat superior liability ultimately is rejected by the federal courts in the federal securities law context, the doctrine may still be invoked under state securities law.[119]

As a final comment, when executive officers of a corporation or persons of similar status of any like enterprise improperly act with actual or apparent authority within the course and scope of their employment, it may be asserted that such enterprise should be held primarily liable. As stated by the Third Circuit, because executive officers make policy and generally have the authority to bind the corporation, "[t]heir action in behalf of the corporation is therefore primary, and holding a corporation liable for their action does not require respondeat superior."[120]

---

[117] *American Telephone and Telegraph Company v. Winback and Conserve Program, Inc.*, 42 F.3d 1421, 1430–31 (3d Cir. 1994) (interpreting liability under the Lanham Act).

[118] *See* 511 U.S. at 175; *id.* at 200 n.12 (Stevens, J., dissenting).

[119] *See, e.g.*, Texas Securities Act Art. 581-33M ("The rights and remedies provided by this Act are in addition to any other rights (including exemplary or punitive damages) or remedies that may exist at law or in equity.").

[120] *Sharp v. Coopers & Lybrand*, 649 F.2d 175, 182 n.8 (3d Cir. 1981), *citing, Holmes v. Bateson*, 583 F.2d 542, 561 (1st Cir. 1978). *See also In re Atlantic Financial Management*, 784 F.2d 29, 32 (1st Cir. 1986) (stating that "[t]here are strong reasons for believing that the 'direct or indirect' language of the Securities Act encompasses . . . common law agency liability").

Chapter 11

ISSUER AFFIRMATIVE DISCLOSURE OBLIGATIONS

§ 11.01 OVERVIEW

With certain exceptions, there is no affirmative duty for an issuer to disclose material nonpublic information. Despite the unwillingness of the courts and the SEC to recognize such a general mandate, there exist issuer affirmative disclosure requirements in a number of specific circumstances. As discussed in this Chapter, these circumstances include:

(1) when SEC rules and regulations require disclosure of specified information;

(2) when mandatory disclosure of forward-looking information is called for by Item 303 of Regulation S-K which pertains to "Management's Discussion and Analysis of Financial Condition and Results of Operation" (MD&A) (*see* § 5.05[C] *supra*);

(3) when selective dissemination of material information has been inadvertently made to investors or analysts, disclosure to the investing marketplace must be promptly made (*see* Regulation FD, § 11.08 *infra.*);

(4) when the issuer is purchasing or selling its securities in the markets;

(5) when the information revealed by the issuer contains a material disclosure deficiency at the time that the statement was made; under such circumstances, there exists a "duty to correct";

(6) when the issuer previously has made a public statement that, although accurate when made, continues to be "alive" in the marketplace and has become materially false or misleading as a result of subsequent events; under such circumstances, a "duty to update" may exist; and

(7) when material nonpublic information has been leaked by, or rumors in the marketplace are attributable to, the issuer.

In this regard, the impact of Section 409 of the Sarbanes-Oxley Act of 2002 (contained in Section 13(l) of the Securities Exchange Act) is significant. That statute amended the Exchange Act to require "real time" disclosure by reporting issuers. Such reporting companies must, as the SEC determines by rule, disclose to the public "on a rapid and current basis" any additional information regarding material changes in the financial operations or condition of the subject enterprise. Implementing this directive in 2004, the SEC has developed a more comprehensive framework with respect to "real time" disclosure by Exchange Act reporting companies (*see* § 11.07 *infra*).

In other situations, the law is less clear as to the existence and scope of an issuer's affirmative duty to disclose, such as in the case of "soft" information, merger negotiations, and bad financial news. Moreover, the impact of "safe harbor" provisions with respect to an issuer's disclosure of certain forward-looking information (such as those "safe harbors" contained in the Private Securities Litigation Reform Act (PSLRA) as well as in SEC rules) should be addressed in this context (*see* § 5.05[A]-[B] *supra*, § 11.05 *infra*).

In analyzing an issuer's obligations in this setting, the Supreme Court's decision in *Chiarella v. United States*[1] should be kept in focus. There, the Court held that, absent a duty to disclose, silence by a subject party will not incur Section 10(b) liability.

Consistent with *Chiarella*, it may be posited that an issuer of securities has a duty to disclose all material information when it is selling its securities. In other words, because a fiduciary relationship exists between shareholders and corporate directors (as well as executive officers), there arises an affirmative obligation to disclose all material information in the purchase-sale context even if such information is not specifically called for by SEC regulation. The First Circuit, however, has rejected this rationale in the Securities Act registration context, opining: "Although in the context of a public offering there is a strong affirmative duty of disclosure, it is clear that an issuer of securities owes no absolute duty to disclose all material information. The issue, rather, is whether the securities law imposes on defendants a 'specific obligation' to disclose information of the type that plaintiffs claim was omitted."[2]

According to a number of authorities, the theoretical underpinnings for recognizing a broad affirmative duty for a publicly-held company to disclose promptly (absent justifiable reason otherwise) all material information may be premised on two sources. First, by circulating a regular flow of information to the securities markets, a publicly-held company implicitly represents that information previously disclosed remains accurate. By failing to disclose, thereby inducing marketplace reliance that the previously disclosed information represents present conditions, the company has engaged in "deception" under Section 10(b).[3] Second, the "shingle" theory, currently applied to broker-dealers, could be extended to encompass publicly-held companies. Such companies, the argument generally posits, have a duty to deal fairly with their

---

[1] 445 U.S. 222 (1980). For discussion of *Chiarella*, see Chapter 12.

[2] *Cooperman v. Individual, Inc.*, 171 F.3d 43, 49–50 (1st Cir. 1999).

[3] *See, e.g.*, Bauman, *Rule 10b-5 and the Corporation's Affirmative Duty to Disclose*, 67 Geo. L.J. 935 (1979). *But see* Sheffey, *Securities Law Responsibilities of Issuers to Respond to Rumors and Other Publicity: Reexamination of a Continuing Problem*, 57 Notre Dame Law. 755 (1982); Note, *Disclosure of Material Inside Information: An Affirmative Corporate Duty?*, 1980 Ariz. St. L.J. 795, 801. *See generally* Myers, *An Issuer's Duty to Disclose: Assessing the Liability Standards for Material Omissions*, 30 Sec. Reg. L.J. 153 (2002); Williams, *The Securities and Exchange Commission and Corporate Social Transparency*, 112 Harv. L. Rev. 1197 (1999).

shareholders and the securities markets, the breach thereof constituting "deception" under Section 10(b).[4]

Despite the above arguments, neither the courts nor the SEC are willing to recognize such a general mandate. Hence, although the foregoing rationales arguably make good policy, they have not been accepted. Nonetheless, remember that in certain situations SEC rules may require that the issuer affirmatively disclose material events or transactions that are reasonably certain to occur in the future. At this time, you may wish to review the ramifications of Regulation S-K Item 303, Management Discussion and Analysis (MD&A), in § 5.05[C] *supra*. In addition, provided that the company is acting in good faith and with a reasonable basis, forward looking information that is not required to be disclosed in the MD&A may be voluntarily disclosed pursuant to Securities Act Rule 175 and Exchange Act Rule 3b-6. The parameters of this safe harbor have been expanded for Exchange Act reporting companies pursuant to legislation enacted by Congress in 1995 (*see* § 5.05[B] *supra*, § 11.05[D] *infra*).

§ 11.02 IMPACT OF THE "MD&A" REQUIREMENTS

With respect to the mandatory disclosure of forward-looking information, Item 303 of Regulation S-K plays an important role in requiring such disclosure in certain situations. Indeed, as stated by one source, "the MD&A has become a major, if not the major, item of narrative disclosure that is studied, together with the financial statements, for investment decision and analysis purposes."[5] On a number of occasions, the Commission has addressed a registrant's disclosure obligations under the "MD&A" — namely, under Item 303 pertaining to "Management's Discussion and Analysis of Financial Condition and Results of Operation."[6] The SEC has stated:

> As to prospective information, the MD&A Release sets forth the following test for determining when disclosure is required:
>
> > Where a trend, demand, commitment, event or uncertainty is known, management must make two assessments:
> >
> > (1) Is the known trend, demand, commitment, event or uncertainty likely to come to fruition? If management determines that it is not reasonably likely to occur, no disclosure is required.
> >
> > (2) If management cannot make that determination, it must evaluate objectively the consequences of the known trend, demand, commitment, event or uncertainty, on the assumption that it will come to fruition. Disclosure is then required unless management determines that a material effect on the registrant's

---

[4] *See* Bauman, *supra* note 3, at 944–45. With respect to the "shingle theory," see, *e.g.*, *Hanly v. SEC*, 415 F.2d 589 (2d Cir. 1969); discussion in § 13.03 *infra*.

[5] Schneider, *MD&A Disclosure*, 22 Rev. Sec. & Comm. Reg. 149, 150 (1989).

[6] *See, e.g.*, SEC Financial Reporting Release No. 36, 6 Fed. Sec. L. Rep. (CCH) ¶¶ 73,192–73,193 (1989) (MD&A Release).

financial condition or results of operations is not reasonably likely to occur.

Where the test for disclosure is met, MD&A disclosure of the effects [of such uncertainty,] quantified to the extent reasonably practicable, [is] required.[7]

In view of SEC enforcement activity and the likelihood that private litigation in this area will ensue with some frequency, it has been contended that rigorous interpretations of the MD&A requirements will present a "gold mine" for the plaintiffs' bar. However, due to that the PSLRA provides for an expansive "safe harbor" for MD&A disclosures relating to forward looking information and the imposition of rigorous pleading requirements, this consequence thus far has not eventuated.[8] Nonetheless, SEC enforcement developments may suggest that, even if the likelihood of a contingent event's actual occurrence is relatively remote, it may be prudent for the registrant to disclose in the MD&A any such contingency of substantial magnitude.[9]

§ 11.03   RUMORS AND THIRD PARTY STATEMENTS

The circulation of rumors in the marketplace concerning a material development affecting a particular issuer (e.g., being awarded a major contract or being the subject of a tender offer) is common. Also commonplace are forecasts by financial analysts regarding a company's forthcoming earnings. The question arises whether an issuer has a duty to respond to rumors or to third party (mis)statements under Section 10(b) when such communications are not attributable to the corporation. In the *Fluor* case, the Second Circuit construed this disclosure duty narrowly, asserting that "[a] company has no duty to correct or verify rumors in the marketplace unless those rumors can be attributed to the company."[10] Or, as more recently phrased by the Fourth Circuit, "[t]he securities laws require [the company] to speak truthfully to investors; they do not require the company to police statements made by third

---

[7] *In the Matter of Caterpillar, Inc.*, SEC Administrative No. 3–7692 (1992), *quoting*, MD&A Release, note 6 *supra. See* Securities Act Release No. 8350, [2003–2004 Transfer Binder] Fed. Sec. L. Rep. (CCH) ¶ 87,127 (2003) (setting forth guidelines to assist registrants and issuers in "preparing MD&A disclosure that is easier to follow and understand; and in providing information that more completely satisfies our previously enumerated principal objectives of MD&A").

[8] *See In re Sofamor Danek Group, Inc.*, 123 F.3d 394 (6th Cir. 1997) (rejecting that MD&A Item 303 creates a private right of action, stating that a § 10(b) action based on deficient MD&A disclosure is not precluded, and holding that under circumstances presented no § 10(b) recovery allowed).

[9] *See* Herlihy & Katz, *Recent Developments Concerning Disclosure*, 1991 M & A and Corp. Gov. L. Rep. 395, 411; Seamons, *Requirements and Pitfalls of MD&A Disclosure*, 25 Sec. Reg. L.J. 239 (1997); Note, *Environmental Disclosures and SEC Reporting Requirements*, 17 Del. J. Corp. L. 483 (1992); discussion in § 5.05[C] *supra*, § 11.05[D] *infra*.

[10] *State Teachers Retirement Board v. Fluor Corp.*, 654 F.2d 843, 850 (2d Cir. 1981). *See State Teachers Retirement Board v. Fluor Corp.*, 500 F. Supp. 278, 292–93 (S.D.N.Y. 1980), *aff'd in part*, *rev'd in part*, 654 F.2d 843 (2d Cir. 1981), where the district court stated that a company may have a duty to respond under Section 10(b) where there are present widespread rumors, a substantial and rapid movement in the price of the subject corporation's stock, and the possession of a high degree of scienter.

parties for inaccuracies. . . . "[11] Nonetheless, if the company adopts or becomes entangled with rumors or third party statements (such as analysts' forecasts), so as to render such statements attributable to the company, Section 10(b) liability may ensue. In the context of analysts' forecasts, a company may be deemed to be sufficiently entangled when, after reviewing such forecasts, it makes an express (or implied) representation that the information contained therein is accurate or is consistent with the company's own views. On the other hand, no entanglement should exist if the company merely provides to analysts historical data or corrects solely factual inaccuracies contained in draft analyst documents.[12]

Note, moreover, that both the district court and the Second Circuit in *Fluor* stated that (under the circumstances at issue) the subject corporation had a justifiable business reason for delaying disclosure of the information. In this regard, *Fluor* represents the accepted view that practical justifications for delaying disclosure by an issuer of material nonpublic information generally fall into three categories: "delay while corporate officials ascertain and verify information [until] it is 'ripe for disclosure'; delay while a corporation pursues a business opportunity that would be jeopardized by immediate disclosure; and delay because disclosure would expose the corporation to undue and avoidable risk of loss."[13]

In certain circumstances, it is possible that an issuer may have a duty to seek a halt in the trading of its stock.[14] Moreover, the rules and other pronouncements of the self-regulatory organizations (SROs), including the New York and American Stock Exchanges, impose affirmative and timely disclosure requirements that are more rigorous than current Section 10(b) case law.[15] Violation of these rules, however, although perhaps resulting in SRO disciplinary action, do not provide investors with an implied right of action for damages under the federal securities laws (*see* § 9.03 *supra*). This position may stem from the belief that, where there are no prior inadequate disclosures, no mandated SEC disclosure requirements, nor the presence of "insider" trading, disclosure determinations and the timing of such disclosure generally are left best to the discretion of management. Moreover, if regulation is to have a role in this setting, such regulation should be conducted and enforced by the self-regulatory organizations without the threat of private monetary liability.

---

[11] *Raab v. General Physics Corp.*, 4 F.3d 286, 288 (4th Cir. 1993).

[12] *See, e.g., Elkind v. Liggett & Myers, Inc.*, 635 F.2d 156, 163 (2d Cir. 1980); *In re Caere Corporate Securities Litigation*, 837 F. Supp. 1054, 1059 (N.D. Cal. 1999). *See generally* Note, *Securities Issuer Liability for Third Party Misstatements: Refining the Entanglement Standard*, 53 Vand. L. Rev. 947 (2000).

[13] Vaughn, *Timing of Disclosure*, 13 Rev. Sec. Reg. 911, 913 (1980).

[14] *See* 654 F.2d at 851 n.7.

[15] *See, e.g.*, New York Stock Exchange, Listed Company Manual §§ 202.01–.06.

§ 11.04   DISCLOSURE OF MERGER NEGOTIATIONS

With respect to disclosure of merger negotiations, the Supreme Court's decision in *Basic, Inc. v. Levinson* provides guidance. There, the issuer on three separate occasions falsely denied that it was engaged in merger negotiations.[16] In assessing whether these misstatements were "material," the Supreme Court adopted the fact-specific inquiry of *Texas Gulf Sulphur*.[17] Under this standard, the materiality of merger negotiations "depend[s] at any given time upon a balancing of both the indicated probability that the event will occur and the anticipated magnitude of the event in light of the totality of the company activity."[18]

In applying this fact-specific inquiry in a given situation, the Court opined:

> Whether merger discussions in any particular case are material therefore depends on the facts. Generally, in order to assess the *probability* that the event will occur, a factfinder will need to look to indicia of interest in the transaction at the highest corporate levels. Without attempting to catalog all such possible factors, we note by way of example that board resolutions, instructions to investment bankers, and actual negotiations between principals or their intermediaries may serve as indicia of interest. To assess the *magnitude* of the transaction to the issuer, . . . a factfinder will need to consider such facts as the size of the two corporate entities and of the potential premiums over market value. No particular event or factor short of closing the transaction need be either necessary or sufficient by itself to render merger discussions material.[19]

It should be emphasized that the Supreme Court's decision in *Basic* interpreted the issue of "materiality" for Section 10(b) purposes in the merger/acquisition setting. As the Court stated, the case did not address when, if ever, a company must affirmatively disclose the existence of such negotiations: "[T]his case does not concern the *timing* of a disclosure; it concerns only its accuracy and completeness."[20]

---

[16] 485 U.S. 224, 227–228 (1988). *See generally* Bagby & Ruhnka, *The Predictability of Materiality in Merger Negotiations Following Basic*, 16 Sec. Reg. L.J. 245 (1988); Brown, *Corporate Secrecy, the Federal Securities Laws, and the Disclosure of Ongoing Negotiations*, 36 Cath. U.L. Rev. 93 (1986); Gabaldon, *The Disclosure of Preliminary Merger Negotiations as an Imperfect Paradigm of Rule 10b-5 Analysis*, 62 N.Y.U. L. Rev. 1218 (1987).

[17] *SEC v. Texas Gulf Sulphur Co.*, 401 F.2d 833 (2d Cir. 1968) (en banc).

[18] 485 U.S. at 238, *quoting*, 401 F.2d at 849.

[19] 485 U.S. at 239 (italics supplied). For a more recent decision interpreting *Basic* restrictively, see *Phillips v. LCI International, Inc.*, 190 F.3d 609 (4th Cir. 1999). *But see In re MCI Worldcom. Inc. Securities Litigation*, [2000 Transfer Binder] Fed. Sec. L. Rep. (CCH) ¶ 90,950 (E.D.N.Y. 2000) (alleged statements falsely denying existence of merger discussions held actionable under § 10(b)). With respect to the concept of qualitative materiality, see discussion §§ 5.06–5.07 *supra*.

Note that the test of materiality set forth by the U.S. Supreme Court in *Basic* may be the law of Delaware. *See Alessi v. Beracha*, 849 A.2d 939 (Del. Ch. 2004), *distinguishing, Bershad v. Curtiss-Wright Corp.*, 535 A. 2d 840 (Del. 1987) (containing language that merger negotiations not material until agreement is reached as to price and structure of the transaction).

[20] 485 U.S. at 235.

Hence, it is important to emphasize that the issuer in *Basic* elected to speak. Thus, the case neither involved the timing of disclosure nor an issuer's obligation to speak.[21] As a result, the decision may seem more expansive than, in actuality, it is. In this regard, absent the existence of certain triggering events, such as the presence of a competing tender offer where SEC Schedule 14D-9 requires disclosure of merger negotiations,[22] present law may not require the issuer affirmatively to disclose the existence of such negotiations, even if they are material. The SEC has taken this position:

> In urging that merger negotiations may become material before there is certainty of an agreement, we are not suggesting that material merger negotiations therefore have to be disclosed to the public as a matter of course. We agree with the court below that corporations ordinarily have no duty to disclose even material merger negotiations.[23]

One may inquire whether Item 303 MD&A disclosure impacts upon this analysis. As set forth by the SEC:

> While Item 303 could be read to impose a duty to disclose otherwise nondisclosed preliminary merger negotiations, as known events or uncertainties reasonably likely to have material effects on future financial condition or results of operations, the Commission did not intend to apply and has not applied, Item 303 in this manner. . . .

> [W]here disclosure is not otherwise required, and has not otherwise been made, the MD&A need not contain a discussion of the impact of such negotiations where, in the registrant's view, inclusion of such information would jeopardize completion of the transaction. Where disclosure is otherwise required or has otherwise been made by or on behalf of the registrant, the interests in avoiding premature disclosure no longer exist. In such case, the negotiations would be subject to the same disclosure standards under Item 303 as any other known trend, demand, commitment, event or uncertainty.[24]

In view of the *Basic* decision, issuers may well be inclined to remain silent until an agreement relating to price and structure of the transaction is reached. Moreover, a "no comment" statement, according to language in *Basic*, is "generally the functional equivalent of silence."[25] Unfortunately, issuer silence, absent justifiable business reasons for maintaining secrecy, conflicts with the

---

[21] *Id.*

[22] 17 C.F.R. § 240.14d-101, item 7 (calling for a subject company's management to disclose merger negotiations even though the terms of the prospective transaction and the potential offeror's identity need not be revealed if such disclosure would jeopardize the ongoing negotiations). *See generally* Branson, *SEC Nonacquiescence in Judicial Decisionmaking: Target Company Disclosure of Acquisition Negotiations*, 46 Md. L. Rev. 1001 (1987).

[23] *See* Brief for the SEC as Amicus Curiae in *Levinson v. Basic, Inc.*, 786 F.2d 741 (6th Cir. 1986), *vacated and remanded*, 485 U.S. 224 (1988).

[24] SEC Financial Reporting Release No. 36, 6 Fed. Sec. L. Rep. (CCH) ¶ 73,197 (1989).

[25] 485 U.S. at 239 n.17.

disclosure policies of the federal securities acts. Nonetheless, given the enormous liability potential, issuer silence (or "no comment") may be a practical policy to implement.

§ 11.05   DISCLOSURE OF "SOFT" INFORMATION

[A]   Generally

Traditionally, the securities laws have required disclosure of "hard" information, that is, factual, objectively verifiable data.[26] "Soft" information, on the other hand, predominantly focuses on forward-looking statements, such as projections, forecasts, and predictions.[27] Moreover, soft information need not necessarily relate to expectations regarding the future, but may include any statement that cannot be factually supported, whether due to a lack of substantiating data or because the information consists primarily of subjective evaluations or opinions. Accordingly, soft information may be defined as "statements of subjective analysis or extrapolation, such as opinions, motives, and intentions, or forward-looking statements, such as projections, estimates and forecasts."[28] Note, however, that under certain circumstances, such information is required to be disclosed today pursuant to the Item 303 MD&A disclosure mandates.[29]

Until the mid-1970s the SEC and the courts discouraged and even prohibited the disclosure of soft information.[30] The major concern was that investors, particularly the unsophisticated, might attach too much significance to information that is of questionable reliability.[31] On the other hand, the flow of soft information to the marketplace may enable sophisticated investors more intelligently to evaluate the total mix of information influencing their decisionmaking.[32]

Merger mania in the late 1970s and the 1980s brought the issue of disclosing soft information into sharper focus. For example, in a departure from its

---

[26] *See generally* Securities Act Release No. 6084 (1979).

[27] *Id.*

[28] *In re Craftmatic Securities Litigation,* 890 F.2d 628, 642 (3d Cir. 1989); *see Garcia v. Cordova,* 930 F.2d 826, 830 (10th Cir. 1990); Karjala, *A Coherent Approach to Misleading Corporate Announcements, Fraud, and Rule 10b-5,* 52 Albany L. Rev. 957 (1988); Kerr, *A Walk Through the Circuits: The Duty to Disclose Soft Information,* 46 Md. L. Rev. 1071 (1987); Poole, *Improving the Reliability of Management Forecasts,* 14 J. Corp. L. 547 (1989); Rowe, *Projections, Appraisals, and Other Soft Information,* 23 Rev. Sec. & Comm. Reg. 37 (1990); Schneider, *Nits, Grits and Soft Information in SEC Filings,* 121 U. Pa. L. Rev. 254, 255 (1972).

[29] *See* §§ 5.05[C], 11.02 *supra.*

[30] *See, e.g., Gerstle v. Gamble-Skogmo, Inc.,* 478 F.2d 1281, 1294 (2d Cir. 1973); Securities Act Release No. 5180 (1971).

[31] *See, e.g., South Coast Services Corp. v. Santa Ana Valley Irrigation Co.,* 699 F.2d 1265, 1271 (9th Cir. 1982).

[32] *See generally,* Hiler, *The SEC and the Courts' Approach to Disclosure of Earnings Projections, Asset Appraisals, and Other Soft Information: Old Problems, Changing Views,* 46 Md. L. Rev. 1114 (1987).

traditional view that forward-looking information is untrustworthy and, hence, discouraged, the SEC adopted Securities Act Rule 175 (as well as Exchange Act Rule 3b-6),[33] which encourages issuer use of financial projections and establishes a "safe harbor" for parties who invoke the rule (see § 5.05[A]).[34] Embracing the utility of soft information to a greater degree, the PSLRA enacted by Congress in 1995 generally broadens the safe harbor provisions to encompass oral and written statements, even if not filed with the SEC, by publicly-held companies and those acting on their behalf.[35]

As a general proposition, even if not coming within the safe harbor provisions of Rule 175 and Rule 3b-6, "[f]orward-looking statements need not be correct; it is enough that they have a reasonable basis."[36] Isolated and general remarks about future results, not worded as guarantees, normally are not actionable as they are viewed as soft, "puffing" statements.[37] Recognizing that the securities laws do not serve as investment insurance,[38] courts have rejected conclusory allegations of fraud based on hindsight.[39] This "fraud-by-hindsight" defense has been applied by a number of courts, frequently by such courts granting motions to dismiss due to the plaintiff's failure to plead fraud with particularity as required by Rule 9(b) of the Federal Rules of Civil Procedure and the PSLRA.[40] From a general perspective, the Private Securities Litigation Reform Act, enacted in 1995, codifies this judicial reluctance to impose monetary liability with respect to forward-looking statements.[41]

[B]   Application to "Merger" Context

In the context of "mergers" and related transactions, a small number of courts have required companies to disclose forward-looking information in certain circumstances.[42] However, most courts continue to adhere to the

---

[33] 17 C.F.R. § 230.175. *See* Securities Act Release No. 6084 (1979). The safe harbor rule under the Exchange Act in this setting is Rule 3b-6, 17 C.F.R. § 240.3b-6.

[34] Rule 175 is discussed in greater detail in § 5.05[A] *supra. See generally* Dennis, *Mandatory Disclosure Theory and Management Projections: A Law and Economics Perspective* 46 Md. L. Rev. 1197 (1987); authorities cited note 28 *supra.*

[35] *See* § 11.05[D] *infra.*

[36] *Wielgos v. Commonwealth Edison Co.*, 892 F.2d 509, 513 (7th Cir. 1989).

[37] *See, e.g., City of Monroe Employees Retirement System v. Bridgestone Corp.*, 399 F.3d 651 (6th Cir. 2005); *Raab v. General Physics Corp.*, 4 F.3d 286, 290 (4th Cir. 1993). For commentary critical of broad application of the "puffery" defense, see Lee, *The Puffery Defense: From Used Car Salesman to CEO*, 30 Sec. Reg. L.J. 401 (2002); O'Hare, *The Resurrection of the Dodo: The Unfortunate Re-Emergence of the Puffery Defense in Private Securities Fraud Actions*, 59 Ohio St. L.J. 1697 (1998); Padfield, *Is Puffery Material to Investors? Maybe We Should Ask Them*, 10 U. Pa. J. Bus. & Emp. L. 339 (2008).

[38] *See, e.g., DiLeo v. Ernst & Young*, 901 F.2d 624, 627 (7th Cir. 1990).

[39] *See, e.g., Krim v. BancTexas Group, Inc.*, 989 F.2d 1435, 1448–50 (5th Cir. 1993).

[40] For further discussion, see discussion in §§ 8.01, 8.03[A] *supra.*

[41] *See* § 11.05[D] *infra.*

[42] *See, e.g., Flynn v. Bass Brothers Enterprises, Inc.*, 744 F.2d 978 (3d Cir. 1984).

traditional philosophical concerns as a basis for not imposing liability upon issuers who decline to disclose soft information.[43]

Hence, while soft information in the "merger" context historically has been treated as immaterial as a matter of law, a minority view suggests that this is no longer so. The leading case for the proposition that there is an affirmative duty to disclose soft information when certain indicia of reliability are present is *Flynn v. Bass Brothers Enterprises*.[44] In that case the Third Circuit canvassed the events marking what it considered to be the emergence of a new public policy favoring the disclosure of soft information, spawned "in response to developing corporate trends, such as the increase in mergers,"[45] and held:

> In order to give full effect to the evolution of the law of disclosure, . . . today we set forth the law for disclosure of soft information as it is to be applied from this date on. Henceforth, the law is not that asset appraisals are, as a matter of law, immaterial. Rather, in appropriate cases, such information must be disclosed. Courts should ascertain the duty to disclose asset valuations and other soft information on a case by case basis, by weighing the potential aid such information will give a shareholder against the potential harm, such as undue reliance, if the information is released with a proper cautionary note.
>
> The factors a court must consider in making such a determination are: the facts upon which the information is based; the qualifications of those who prepared or compiled it; the purpose for which the information was originally intended; its relevance to the stockholders' impending decision; the degree of subjectivity or bias reflected in its preparation; the degree to which the information is unique; and the availability to the investor of other more reliable sources of information.[46]

Sharply contrasting *Flynn* is the Sixth Circuit's approach in *Starkman v. Marathon Oil Co.*,[47] in which the court declined to recognize a mandatory obligation to disclose asset appraisals or financial projections, unless "the predictions underlying the appraisal or projection are substantially certain to hold."[48] Criticizing the Third Circuit's approach in *Flynn*, the Sixth Circuit reasoned:

> By its very nature . . . this sort of judicial cost-benefit analysis [referring to *Flynn*] is uncertain and unpredictable, and it moreover neglects the role of the market in providing shareholders with information regarding the target's value through competing tender offers.

---

[43] *See, e.g., Starkman v. Marathon Oil Co.*, 772 F.2d 231 (6th Cir. 1985). Note, however, that disclosure may be required in certain circumstances pursuant to the Item 303 MD&A disclosure mandates. *See* §§ 5.05[C], 11.02 *supra.*

[44] 744 F.2d 978 (3d Cir. 1984).

[45] *Id.* at 986.

[46] *Id.* at 988.

[47] 772 F.2d 231 (6th Cir. 1985).

[48] *Id.* at 241.

Our approach, which focuses on the certainty of the data underlying the appraisal or projection, ensures that the target company's shareholders will receive all essentially factual information, while preserving the target's discretion to disclose more uncertain information without the threat of liability, provided appropriate qualifications and explanations are made.[49]

Flynn represents an approach aimed at addressing investor concerns, whereas *Starkman* illustrates the disclosure concerns from an issuer's perspective. Both views have merit, but each is too one-sided. The cost-benefit analysis advocated by the Third Circuit does not promote certainty, because the approach calls for a court to determine the qualitative value of the enumerated factors with the benefit of hindsight and on an ad hoc basis. Under this approach, judicial guidelines may well have little stability, because the subjective nature of the inquiry is likely to result in the factors being applied differently under an ad hoc analysis. In addition, the Third Circuit's desire "to give full effect to the evolution in the law of disclosure"[50] overlooks the fact that, while the securities laws are designed to protect investors, they are not intended to impose undue hardship upon issuers. The issuer's duty to disclose should be based on what is fair and reasonable from both an investor's and an issuer's perspective.

On the other hand, the Sixth Circuit's approach in *Starkman* is too rigid. Disclosure, a key concept underlying the securities laws, is subordinated to the perceived need to avoid imposing liability in circumstances in which certainty cannot be assured. The *Starkman* court's concern is misplaced, because an important policy underlying the disclosure doctrine is issuer fair dealing through the sharing of information that is material to investor decisionmaking. Congress, the SEC, and the courts generally require issuers to make accurate and complete disclosure of specified information in order to enhance the level of investor decisionmaking and to ensure that the information disclosed is not materially misleading. All that should be required in the context of soft information is that the available material data be accurately disclosed; it need not be certain.

---

[49] *Id.* at 242. The Sixth Circuit in *Starkman* observed that in a going private transaction implicating SEC Rule 13e-3 asset appraisals rendered by outside sources, such as an investment banker, must be disclosed in the Schedule 13E-3. The Sixth Circuit subsequently construed the disclosure parameters of outside appraisals rendered in going private transactions in *Howing Company v. Nationwide Corp.*, 972 F.2d 700 (6th Cir. 1992), 927 F.2d 263 (6th Cir. 1991), 826 F.2d 1470 (6th Cir. 1987). The Sixth Circuit opined:

> The issuer in this case . . . choose to rely on the expertise of the [investment bank] First Boston. The problem with defendants adopting the First Boston opinion letter as their disclosure to shareholders is that this one-page letter is itself woefully inadequate when measured against the specific disclosure requirements of the Rule. An issuer cannot insulate itself from 13e-3 liability by relying on an investment banker's opinion letter which itself does not comply with the specific disclosure requirements of the Rule.

826 F.2d at 1479. *See* Kofele-Kale, *The SEC's Going-Private Rules — Analysis and Developments*, 19 Sec. Reg. L.J. 139 (1991).

[50] 744 F.2d at 988.

Clearly, there is a need for an approach that embraces both investor and issuer concerns. While an affirmative duty to disclose has been held to exist only in certain situations,[51] consistent application of the disclosure principle underlying the securities laws should require that, to ensure investor decision-making based on a flow of accurate information between the issuer and the financial markets, soft information must be affirmatively disclosed in certain circumstances.[52]

[C]   The "Bespeaks Caution" Doctrine

The "bespeaks caution" doctrine serves as an inducement for issuers to include cautionary warnings, qualifications, and disclaimers in regard to projections and other forward-looking information disseminated to the marketplace.[53] The bespeaks caution doctrine states that "where an offering statement [or other disclosure document], such as a prospectus, accompanies statements of future forecasts, projections and expectations with adequate cautionary language, those statements are not actionable as securities fraud."[54] According to the doctrine, cautionary statements make reliance on the projections or other soft information unreasonable and that the statements, when read in conjunction with the cautionary language, are immaterial.[55] Moreover, the Private Securities Litigation Reform Act of 1995 (PSLRA) codifies the "bespeaks caution" doctrine (*see* § 11.05[D] *infra*).

The Third Circuit's decision in *In re Donald J. Trump Casinos Securities Litigation*[56] provides an illustrative application of the bespeaks caution doctrine. There, a partnership offered $675 million in bonds to finance the completion of the Taj Mahal hotel/casino. Although the prospectus for the bonds stated the Partnership believed that the operation of the business would generate funds sufficient to cover its debt service, the prospectus identified several risk factors and indicated that there could be no assurance that actual operating results would meet the disclosed expectations. When the partnership defaulted on the interest payments, the bondholders filed suit alleging securities fraud.[57]

In *Trump* the Third Circuit held that the prospectus included "warnings and cautionary language . . . tailored to the specific future projections,

---

[51] *See* §§ 5.05[C], 11.01–11.02 *supra.*

[52] For further discussion, see, *e.g.*, Steinberg & Goldman, *Issuer Affirmative Disclosure Obligations — An Analytical Framework for Merger Negotiations, Soft Information and Bad News*, 46 Md. L. Rev. 923, 934–946 (1987).

[53] *See* Langevoort, *Disclosures That "Bespeak Caution,"* 49 Bus. Law. 481 (1994). O'Hare, *Good Faith and The Bespeaks Caution Doctrine: It's Not Just a State of Mind*, 58 U. Pitt. L. Rev. 619 (1997).

[54] *In re Donald J. Trump Casinos Securities Litigation*, 793 F. Supp. 543, 544 (D.N.J. 1992), *aff'd*, 7 F.3d 357 (3d Cir. 1993).

[55] *See, e.g., In re Worlds of Wonder Securities Litigation*, 35 F.3d 1407, 1414 (9th Cir. 1994); *I. Meyer Pincus & Assoc., P.C. v. Oppenheimer & Co.*, 936 F.2d 759, 761 (2d Cir. 1992).

[56] 7 F.3d 357 (3d Cir. 1993).

[57] *Id.* at 365–71.

estimates or opinions in the prospectus."[58] The court held that the risk disclosures defeated the materiality of the forward-looking statements:

> [W]hen an offering document's forecasts, opinions or projections are accompanied by meaningful cautionary statements, the forward-looking statements will not form the basis for a securities fraud claim if those statements did not affect the "total mix" of information the document provided investors. In other words, cautionary language, if sufficient, renders the alleged omissions or misrepresentations immaterial as a matter of law.[59]

Importantly, the bespeaks caution doctrine is subject to limitations.[60] For example, not just any cautionary language will render accompanying forward-looking statements immaterial; the language must be "tailored to the specific future projections, estimates or opinions" at issue.[61] A blanket warning that an investment is risky is likely to be insufficient to ward off a securities fraud claim.[62] Another limitation stands for the proposition that the bespeaks caution doctrine does not apply to historical information (e.g., facts). As one court has stated, "[f]raud is still fraud, and all the cautionary language in the world will not replace a true material omission or misstatement of a fact which would matter to a reasonable investor."[63] Additionally, the bespeaks caution doctrine only applies to situations in which there was an affirmative disclosure of soft information, and therefore does not extend to allegations that there was a failure to disclose such information.[64]

In sum, when reviewing disclosure documents, issuers and their counsel should assess whether the soft information conveyed is adequately counterbalanced by specific cautionary language.[65] The nature of the cautionary language will depend on the circumstances and context in which the underlying soft information is being conveyed. For example, soft information relating to internal rates of return ordinarily will require more specific risk disclosures than will vague statements of optimism. Additionally, a more detailed disclosure of risks generally should be contained in a prospectus as compared to a press release.[66]

---

[58] *Id.* at 371–72.

[59] *Id.* at 371.

[60] As a general proposition, the "bespeaks caution doctrine applies only to cases where the disclosure of information was made in good faith and on a reasonable basis, unless . . . the forward-looking statement in controversy is so generalized and so significantly qualified by cautionary language that [it] is immaterial as a matter of law." Rosen, *Liability for 'Soft Information': New Developments and Emerging Trends*, 23 Sec. Reg. L.J. 3, 36 (1995).

[61] *Id. See Kline v. First Western Gov't Sec., Inc.*, 24 F.3d 480, 489 (3d Cir. 1994).

[62] *See, e.g., Rubinstein v. Collins*, 20 F.3d 160, 168 (5th Cir. 1994).

[63] *In re Integrated Resources Real Estate Ltd. Partnership Securities Litigation*, 815 F. Supp. 620, 674 (S.D.N.Y. 1993).

[64] *See In re Worlds of Wonder Securities Litigation*, 814 F. Supp. 850, 858 (N.D. Cal. 1993), *aff'd in part, rev'd in part*, 35 F.3d 1407 (9th Cir. 1994).

[65] *See* sources cited note 53 *supra.*

[66] *See* Rosen, *supra* note 60, at 34; *see also* Langevoort, note 53 *supra.*

Thus, carefully crafted risk disclosure statements that bespeak caution can deter the bringing of securities fraud claims and can enhance the likelihood of successfully fending off such claims if litigation is initiated.

[D]   The Private Securities Litigation Reform Act — Safe Harbor for Certain Forward-Looking Statements

The Private Securities Litigation Reform Act of 1995 amended the Securities Act by adding a new Section 27A and further amended the Securities Exchange Act by adding a new Section 21E. The new sections generally provide 1934 Act reporting companies (as well as those acting on their behalf and underwriters with respect to information furnished by or derived from information provided by such companies) with a safe harbor from liability in private actions for certain forward-looking statements (e.g., projections). The safe harbor is applicable to both forward-looking written and oral statements, so long as (1) the statement is identified as a forward-looking statement and is accompanied by meaningful cautionary statements, thus codifying the "bespeaks caution" doctrine;[67] (2) the statement lacks materiality; *or* (3) the plaintiff fails to prove that the statement was made with actual knowledge of its falsity (irrespective of whether cautionary language is included).

---

[67] An example of a subject issuer's statements that are identified as forward-looking and that seek to accompany such forward-looking statements with meaningful cautionary disclosure is as follows:

Some of the statements under "Summary," "Risk Factors," "Dividend Policy and Restrictions," "Management's Discussion and Analysis of Financial Condition and Results of Operations," "Business," "Regulation" and elsewhere in this prospectus may include forward-looking statements which reflect our current views with respect to future events and financial performance. Statements which include the words "may," "will," "should," "could," "would," "predicts," "potential," "continue," "future," "estimates," "expect," "intend," "plan," "believe," "project," "anticipate" and similar statements of a future or forward-looking nature identify forward-looking statements for purposes of the federal securities laws or otherwise.

All forward-looking statements address matters that involve risks and uncertainties. Accordingly, there are or will be important factors that could cause actual results to differ materially from those indicated in these statements. We believe that these factors include the following:

- our high degree of leverage and significant debt service obligations;

- our ability to amend our new credit facility in ways that restrict our right to pay dividends on our common stock;

- any adverse changes in government regulation;

- the risk that we may not be able to retain existing customers or obtain new customers;

- the risk of technological innovations outpacing our ability to adapt or replace our equipment to offer comparable services;

- the risk of increased competition in the markets we serve;

- the risk of weaker economic conditions within the United States;

- changes in accounting policies or practices adopted voluntarily or as required by accounting principles generally accepted in the United States; and

- the matters described under "Risk Factors" herein.

The safe harbor also contains specific provisions for oral forward-looking statements made by an issuer or those acting on its behalf under (1) above. Such oral forward-looking statements are protected if such statements are accompanied by cautionary language and identify "readily available" documentation from which an investor can obtain additional information regarding the substance of such oral statements. The legislation provides that such documentation is to be deemed "readily available" if it is either filed with the SEC or otherwise generally disseminated.

The applicability of the safe harbor provisions is subject to enumerated exclusions, such as with respect to certain excluded issuers (e.g., penny stock issuers) and to statements made in specific contexts (e.g., tender offers).

In addition, the safe harbor section specifies that its provisions do not impose a duty to update a forward-looking statement. It is unclear whether this language is meant to eliminate the "duty to update" any forward-looking statement or merely to clarify that no implied "duty to update" may be gleaned from this section. Hence, the breadth of this language will be developed by the courts.

In regard to this legislatively enacted safe harbor for forward-looking information, the Joint Explanatory Statement of the Conference Committee is useful:

> The Conference Committee has adopted a statutory "safe harbor" to enhance market efficiency by encouraging companies to disclose forward-looking information. This provision adds a new Section 27A to the 1933 Act and a new Section 21E of the 1934 Act which protects from liability in private lawsuits certain "forward-looking" statements made by persons specified in the legislation.

> The first prong of the safe harbor protects a written or oral forward-looking statement that is: (i) identified as forward-looking, and (ii) accompanied by meaningful cautionary statements identifying important factors that could cause actual results to differ materially from those projected in the statement.

> Under this first prong of the safe harbor, boilerplate warnings will not suffice as meaningful cautionary statements identifying important factors that could cause actual results to differ materially from those projected in the statement. The cautionary statements must convey substantive information about factors that realistically could cause results to differ materially from those projected in the forward-looking statement, such as, for example, information about the issuer's business.

> Courts may continue to find a forward-looking statement immaterial — and thus not actionable under the 1933 Act and the 1934 Act — on other grounds. To clarify this point, the Conference Committee includes language in the safe harbor provision that no liability attaches to forward-looking statements that are "immaterial."

The second prong of the safe harbor provides an alternative analysis. This safe harbor also applies to both written and oral forward-looking statements. Instead of examining the forward-looking and cautionary statements, this prong of the safe harbor focuses on the state of mind of the person making the forward-looking statement. A person or business entity will not be liable in a private lawsuit for a forward-looking statement unless a plaintiff proves that person or business entity made a false or misleading forward-looking statement with actual knowledge that it was false or misleading. The Conference Committee intends for this alternative prong of the safe harbor to apply if the plaintiff fails to prove the forward-looking statement (1) if made by a natural person, was made with the actual knowledge by that person that the statement was false or misleading; or (2) if made by a business entity, was made by or with the approval of an executive officer of the entity with actual knowledge by that officer that the statement was false or misleading.

The Conference Committee recognizes that, under certain circumstances, it may be unwieldy to make oral forward-looking statements relying on the first prong of the safe harbor. Companies who want to make a brief announcement of earnings or a new product would first have to identify the statement as forward-looking and then provide cautionary statements identifying important factors that could cause results to differ materially from those projected in the statement. As a result, the Conference Committee has provided for an optional, more flexible rule for oral forward-looking statements that will facilitate these types of oral communications by an issuer while still providing to the public information it would have received if the forward-looking statement was written. The Conference Committee intends to limit this oral safe harbor to issuers or the officers, directors, or employees of the issuer acting on the issuer's behalf.

This legislation permits covered issuers, or persons acting on the issuer's behalf, to make oral forward-looking statements within the safe harbor. The person making the forward-looking statement must identify the statement as a forward-looking statement and state that results may differ materially from those projected in the statement. The person must also identify a "readily available" written document that contains factors that could cause results to differ materially. The written information identified by the person making the forward-looking statement must qualify as a "cautionary statement" under the first prong of the safe harbor (i.e., it must be a meaningful cautionary statement or statements that identify important factors that could cause actual results to differ materially from those projected in the forward-looking statement.) For purposes of this provision, "readily available" information refers to SEC filed documents, annual reports and other widely disseminated materials, such as press releases.

The safe harbor provision protects written and oral forward-looking statements made by issuers and certain persons retained or acting on behalf of the issuer. The Conference Committee intends the statutory safe harbor protection to make more information about a company's future plans available to investors and the public. The safe harbor covers underwriters, but only insofar as the underwriters provide forward-looking information that is based on or "derived from" information provided by the issuer. Because underwriters have what is effectively an adversarial relationship with issuers in performing due diligence, the use of the term "derived from" affords underwriters some latitude so that they may disclose adverse information that the issuer did not necessarily "provide." The Conference Committee does not intend the safe harbor to cover forward-looking information made in connection with a broker's sales practices.

The Conference Committee has determined that the statutory safe harbor should not apply to certain forward-looking statements. Thus, the statutory safe harbor does not protect forward-looking statements: (1) included in financial statements prepared in accordance with generally accepted accounting principles; (2) contained in an initial public offering registration statement; (3) made in connection with a tender offer; (4) made in connection with a partnership, limited liability company or direct participation program offering; or (5) made in beneficial ownership disclosure statements filed with the SEC under Section 13(d) of the 1934 Act.

This legislation also makes clear that nothing in the safe harbor provision imposes any duty to update forward-looking statements.

The Conference Committee does not intend for the safe harbor provisions to replace the judicial "bespeaks caution" doctrine or to foreclose further development of that doctrine by the courts.

From judicial decisions construing the safe harbor provisions of the PSLRA, it seems clear that, consistent with the Act's legislative history, adequate cautionary language may be held to accompany the forward-looking statements even if the registrant fails to identify the particular factor that causes such forward-looking statements not to come to fruition. As stated by Judge Easterbrook: "First, . . . cautions must be tailored to the risks that accompany the particular projections. Second, the cautions need not identify what actually goes wrong and caused the projections to be inaccurate; prevision is not required."[68] In any event, even if not accompanied by meaningful cautionary

---

[68] *Asher v. Baxter International Inc.*, 377 F.3d 727, 732 (7th Cir. 2004); *see Baron v. Smith*, 380 F.3d 49 (1st Cir. 2004); *Rombach v. Chang*, 355 F.3d 164 (2d Cir. 2004); *Halperin v. eBanker USA.com, Inc.*, 295 F.3d 352, 359 (2d Cir. 2002); *Helwig v. Vencor, Inc.*, 251 F.3d 540, 558–559 (6th Cir. 2001) (en banc); *Harris v. Ivax Corporation*, 182 F.3d 799, 805–806 (11th Cir. 1999). *See generally* Bloomenthal, *The Private Securities Litigation Reform Act — How Safe Is The Safe Harbor?*, *18 Sec. & Fed. Corp.* L. Rep. 97 (1996); O'Hare, *Good Faith and The Bespeaks Caution Doctrine: It's Not Just a State of Mind*, 58 U. Pitt. L. Rev. 619 (1997); Symposium, 51 Bus. Law. No. 4 (1996); Symposium, 33 San Diego L. Rev. No. 3 (1996); Symposium, 24 Sec. Reg. L.J. No. 2 (1996).

language, a forward-looking statement is actionable in private litigation only if the complainant proves materiality as well as the defendant's actual knowledge of the falsity.

§ 11.06 DUTY TO UPDATE

The duty to update may arise in a number of different circumstances. Generally, such a duty may be present when the issuer previously has made a statement that, although accurate when made, continues to be "alive" in the marketplace and has become materially false or misleading as a result of subsequent events. This duty may be implicated, for example, in the context of merger negotiations, disclosure of "soft" information, and responding to rumors.

Perhaps significantly the PSLRA specifies that its safe harbor provisions do not impose a duty to update forward-looking statements. It is unclear whether this language is intended to eliminate the "duty to update" in this context or merely to clarify that no implied duty to update may be derived from the Act. Accordingly, the significance of this language will be construed by the courts. In this regard, it has become customary for subject issuers to seek to eliminate a duty to update forward-looking statements made. A representative illustration provides: "We undertake no obligation to publicly update or review any forward-looking statements, whether as a result of new information, future developments or otherwise."

In certain settings, SEC rules specifically mandate a duty to update. In the tender offer context, for instance, SEC Rule 14e-2 calls for the subject company to disclose to its security holders its position toward the takeover bid and inform such security holders of any material change relating to the position previously taken.

Judicial decisions addressing the duty to update from a general perspective are relatively sparse. For example, the First Circuit in *Backman v. Polaroid Corp.* opined that, "in special circumstances, a statement, correct at the time, may have a forward intent and connotation upon which parties may be expected to rely." If that is the situation and if "there is a change, correction, more exactly, further disclosure, may be called for."[69]

Construing the First Circuit's decision in the foregoing case, one securities practitioner opined:

> For the first time, a court's careful analysis in a specific factual context makes completely clear that the duty to update is not nearly as

---

[69] 910 F.2d 10, 17 (1st Cir. 1990) (en banc); *see Weiner v. The Quaker Oats Company*, 129 F.3d 310 (3d Cir. 1997) (holding duty to update existed); *Rubinstein v. Collins*, 20 F.3d 160, 170 n. 41 (5th Cir. 1994) (stating that "it appears that defendants have a duty under Rule 10b-5 to correct statements if those statements have become materially misleading in light of subsequent events"). *But see Phillips v. LCI International, Inc.*, 190 F.3d 609 (4th Cir. 1999) (suggesting issuers have no duty to update forward-looking statements); *Grassi v. Informational Resources, Inc.*, 63 F.3d 596, 599 (7th Cir. 1995) (stating that "a company has no duty to update forward-looking statements merely because changing circumstances have proven them wrong").

broad as some of the authorities seem to suggest. The duty is not triggered simply because a prior statement would no longer be true if repeated at a later date in the light of intervening facts. [The court] did not articulate in detail precisely when an updating duty would exist, but the brief discussion suggests that the duty would arise primarily in special circumstances.[70]

§ 11.07 REAL-TIME DISCLOSURE

Implementing the directive set forth by the Sarbanes-Oxley Act for the SEC to adopt "a rapid and current" reporting regime with respect to material changes in a subject registrant's financial condition or operations,[71] the Commission in 2004 promulgated amendments to the Form 8-K.[72] By reorganizing and expanding reportable event requirements within the Form 8-K, registrants have greater responsibility with respect to disclosing particular material events in a timely manner. Prior to the amendments, Form 8-K disclosure requirements for reportable events were rather limited.[73] Public companies were able to delay the disclosure of many material events until the next periodic report.[74] Since a number of significant disclosures were delayed, certain material events were not timely disclosed. To help correct this problem, the SEC's amendments to the Form 8-K expand the disclosure requirements and shorten the time frame for specified reportable events.[75]

Section 409 of the Sarbanes-Oxley Act requires that "[e]ach issuer reporting under Section 13(a) and 15(d) shall disclose to the public on a rapid and current basis such additional information concerning material changes in the financial condition or operations of the issuer, in plain English, which may include trend and qualitative information and graphic presentations, as the Commission determines, by rule, is necessary or useful for the protection of investors and in the public interest."[76] In accord with Section 409, the Form 8-K amendments shorten the filing deadline for companies mandated to disclose a broad array of material events listed within Form 8-K to four business days after the event has

---

[70] Schneider, *The Uncertain Duty to Update* — Polaroid II *Brings a Welcome Limitation*, 4 Insights No. 10, at 2, 10 (1992); *see* Block, Radin & Carlinsky, *A Post-*Polaroid *Snapshot of the Duty to Correct Disclosure*, 1991 Colum. Bus. L. Rev. 139, 140; Rosenblum, *An Issuer's Duty Under Rule 10b-5 to Correct and Update Materially Misleading Statements*, 40 Cath. U. L. Rev. 289, 291 (1991); Note, *Rule 10b-5 and Voluntary Corporate Disclosures to Security Analysts*, 92 Colum. L. Rev. 1517, 1543–1544 (1992).

[71] *See* Sarbanes-Oxley Act § 409, *amending*, § 13(l) of the Exchange Act; discussion § 5.08[M] *supra.*

[72] *See* Securities Act Release No. 8591 (2005); Securities Exchange Act Release Nos. 49424 (2004), 54302 (2006). Note that more recently the SEC staff has posted updated Form 8-K guidance. *See* www.sec/gov/divisions/corpfin/guidance/8-Kinterp.htm. *See generally* Horwich, *New Form 8-K and Real-Time Disclosure*, 37 Rev. Sec. & Comm. Reg. 109 (2004).

[73] *See* 17 C.F.R. § 249.308 (2003) (Form 8-K prior to the 2004 SEC amendments).

[74] *See Gallagher v. Abbott Laboratories*, 269 F.3d 806 (7th Cir. 2001); *Greenfield v. Heublein, Inc.*, 740 F.2d 751 (3d. Cir. 1984).

[75] *See* Securities Exchange Act Release No. 49424 (2004).

[76] Section 409 of Sarbanes-Oxley Act, *amending*, § 13(l) of the Exchange Act.

occurred. In addition, the Commission adopted a safe harbor to insulate companies from liability under Section 10(b) of the Exchange Act if they fail to file particular items within the Form 8-K.[77] The specific Form 8-K items covered by the safe harbor are discussed below.

In the Form 8-K amendments, the Commission has categorized the listed items into nine sections. Summarized succinctly, the nine sections are as follows:

Section 1 — Registrant's Business and Operations

Item 1.01 Entry into a Material Definitive Agreement — A company entering into or amending a material definitive agreement, not within the normal course of business, must disclose the date of the agreement, parties involved and their relationship to the company, and a brief description of the agreement's terms and conditions.

Item 1.02 Termination of a Material Definitive Agreement — A company terminating such an agreement must disclose the specifics of the transaction, including, but not limited to, the date of the termination, a brief description of the material circumstances, and any penalty fees.

Item 1.03 Bankruptcy or Receivership — Disclosure is mandated when a receiver or similar authority has been appointed for the subject registrant or its parent enterprise during bankruptcy proceedings or when the government takes control over the company's assets.

Section 2 — Financial Information

Item 2.01 Completion of Acquisition or Disposition of Assets — A subject company or any of its majority-owned subsidiaries must disclose any significant amount of assets that have been acquired or disposed of when not within the normal course of business.

Item 2.02 Results of Operations and Financial Condition — If a subject registrant or any person acting on its behalf makes a public announcement or issues a press release disclosing material non-public information regarding its financial status for a completed quarterly or annual period, generally such registrant must disclose the date of the announcement or release, briefly identify the announcement or release, and provide the text of such announcement or release as an exhibit to the Form 8-K.[78]

Item 2.03 Creation of a Direct Financial Obligation or an Obligation Under an Off-Balance Sheet Arrangement of a Registrant — A company that becomes subject to a material direct financial obligation must disclose the date the obligation began, briefly describe the subject agreement, disclose the amount of the obligation as well as the payment terms and any other material terms of the agreement. If the obligation results from an off-balance sheet arrangement that

---

[77] *See* Securities Exchange Act Release No. 49424 (2004); *infra* note 87 and accompanying text.

[78] Under certain circumstances, Item 2.02 does not require the registrant to furnish a Form 8-K. See Item 2.02(b) of Form 8-K.

makes the company directly or contingently liable, the company must also disclose the additional financial liability that may be incurred.

Item 2.04 Trigger Events That Accelerate or Increase a Direct Financial Obligation or an Obligation Under an Off-Balance Sheet Arrangement — A company under a direct financial obligation or an off-balance sheet arrangement that has such obligation accelerated or increased as a result of a triggering event must disclose the specifics of the triggering event, as well as any additional material obligations.

Item 2.05 Costs Associated with Exit or Disposal Activities — When a company commits to an exit or disposal plan, disposes of long-term assets or terminates employees, with respect to which material charges will be incurred pursuant to generally accepted accounting principles, the registrant must disclose the date of the commitment, reasons for the action, and amounts associated with the action that the registrant estimates will be incurred.

Item 2.06 Material Impairments — When a board of directors (or its designees) determines that an asset is materially impaired, the company must disclose the date of the material charge, a description of the impaired assets, reasons for the material charge, and an estimate of the impairment charge.

Section 3 — Securities and Trading Markets

Item 3.01 Notice of Delisting or Failure to Satisfy a Continued Listing Rule or Standard; Transfer of Listing — When a company receives notice regarding material non-compliance with any listing rule or possible delisting, it must disclose the date the notice was received, the rule or standard that the registrant fails to satisfy, and any actions taken by the registrant with respect to the notice. If a company's securities are delisted, it must disclose the date its securities were delisted.

Item 3.02 Unregistered Sales of Equity Securities — A company selling unregistered equity securities must disclose called for information regarding the issuance if such issuance accounts for more than a specified percent (for most companies, one percent) of the securities outstanding of the same class.

Item 3.03 Material Modifications to Rights of Security Holders — When a company materially modifies any rights of registered securities, it must disclose a description of the modifications.

Section 4 — Matters Related to Accountants and Financial Statements

Item 4.01 Changes in Registrant's Certifying Accountant — A company must disclose when its independent accountant has resigned or been dismissed or when a new independent accountant has been engaged.

Item 4.02 Non-Reliance on Previously Issued Financial Statements or a Related Audit Report or Completed Interim Review — When a board of directors (or its designees) conclude that any previously issued financial statement cannot be relied upon due to error, the registrant must identify the financial statement, the surrounding facts in regard thereto, any discussions with the independent accountant (including the advice given by the accountant), and the circumstances that gave rise to the discovery. Under certain circumstances, the registrant must file the accountant's letter as an exhibit to such registrant's amended Form 8-K.

Section 5 — Corporate Governance and Management

Item 5.01 Changes in Control of Registrant — When a change in control of a registrant occurs, a company must disclose the person(s) currently in control, the date and description of the circumstances surrounding the change, and the amount of control that was acquired.

Item 5.02 Departure of Directors or Certain Officers; Election of Directors; Appointment of Certain Officers; Compensatory Arrangements of Certain Officers — When an officer is appointed or a director is elected, the company must disclose his/her name and background, the date of the appointment or election, the committees on which such director will serve and other specified information. When a director resigns, chooses not to be reelected, or is removed due to disagreements with the company, the company must disclose the date the director left, any positions the director held, a brief description of any disagreement that occurred, and any statements made by the director regarding the disagreement.[79] On the other hand, when a specified executive officer resigns, retires or is removed, the registrant need only disclose such event and the date thereof. Disclosure is not required concerning the circumstances surrounding the officer's departure. In addition, disclosure is required when the registrant enters into or amends employment and compensation arrangements that are deemed material with specified executive officers.[80]

Item 5.03 Amendments to Articles of Incorporation or Bylaws; Change In Fiscal Year — When a company amends its articles of incorporation, bylaws, or fiscal year-end date, it must disclose the effective date of the amendments and the description of the new provision if the company did not provide such information in its SEC filed proxy or information statement.

Item 5.04 Temporary Suspension of Trading under Registrant's Employee Benefit Plans — No later than four business days after receiving notification that trading of securities in its employee benefit plans has been temporarily suspended, the registrant must provide the specified information called for by Item 504 of Form 8-K.

Item 5.05 Amendments to the Registrant's Code of Ethics, or Waiver of a Provision of the Code of Ethics — A registrant must disclose any amendments

---

[79] Recently, the SEC brought an enforcement action against Hewlett-Packard Co. for declining to reveal the reasons for a director's resignation. The director had resigned due to issues raised by the company's investigation of boardroom leaks. *See* CCH Fed. Sec. L. Rep. No. 2278, at 7 (2007). *See generally* Lawton, *H-P Settles Civil Charges in "Pretexting" Scandal*, Wall St. J., Dec. 8, 2006, at A3; Waldman, Clark & Stecklow, *H-P's Hurd Admits "Disturbing" Tactics Were Used in Probe*, Wall St. J., Sept. 23, 2006, at A1. With respect to five directors resigning due to disagreement at Affiliated Computer Services, see Karnitschnig & Bandler, *A Failed Deal at ACS Sets Off a Board Brawl*, Wall St. J., Nov. 2, 2007, at C1.

[80] These Item 502 disclosures relating to employment and compensation arrangements were adopted by the SEC in Securities Exchange Act Release No. 54302 (2006).

to its Code of Ethics and any waivers thereto granted by the registrant.

Section 6 Asset-Backed Securities — The items set forth in Item 6 of Form 8-K apply only to asset-backed securities.

Section 7 — Regulation FD

Item 7.01 Regulation FD Disclosure — If an issuer or any person acting on behalf of an issuer selectively discloses any material nonpublic information, Regulation FD (Fair Disclosure) requires the issuer to disclose this information to the public in a timely manner.[81] One way an issuer may publicly disclose this material information is under this Section of Form 8-K.

Section 8 — Other Events

Item 8.01 Other Events — A company may, at its option, disclose any other information or event not called for by Form 8-K.

Section 9 — Financial Statements and Exhibits

Item 9.01 Financial Statements and Exhibits — A registrant must list any financial statement as well as any financial information and exhibits that are filed (or furnished) as part of the subject Form 8-K.

Although the Form 8-K provides a rather detailed list, there is material information within particular items that the SEC does not require a company to disclose pursuant to Form 8-K. For example, under Item 1.02, "Termination of a Material Definitive Agreement," registrants do not have to disclose in the Form 8-K the loss, in the ordinary course of business, of a material contract or a material decline in business relationships with the company's customers. Even though Form 8-K disclosure is not required of this material development, a company must disclose this information in its next Form 10-Q, for example, pursuant to the Management Discussion and Analysis (MD&A) as required under Item 303 of Regulation S-K. Within the MD&A, a company must assess if the loss of a major contract is likely to occur and if so, disclosure will be required due to its material effect on the company.[82]

In not mandating disclosure in Form 8-K of a registrant's loss of a material contract, the Commission believed that such disclosure would create difficulty in determining when the contract terminated and could be used by customers as a negotiation ploy.[83] Nonetheless, the irretrievable loss of a major contract presumptively is material to investors. Arguably, shareholders ought to be promptly provided with this information in order to decide whether to terminate their investment.[84]

---

[81] Securities Exchange Act Release No. 43154 (2004), *discussion in*, § 11.08 *infra*.

[82] 17 C.F.R. § 229.303 (2006); *see In re Cambrex Corp. Securities Litigation*, [2005–2006 Transfer Binder] Fed. Sec. L. Rep. (CCH) ¶ 93,561 (D.N.J. 2005); discussion §§ 5.05[C], 11.02 *supra*.

[83] *See* Securities Exchange Act Release No. 49424 (2004).

[84] *See* Steinberg & Goldman, *supra* note 52, at 948–951.

In addition, the Commission declined to require that a subject company disclose in the Form 8-K the reasons for the resignation or removal of an executive officer. The SEC's rationale was that the revelation of the purported reasons may embarrass the officer or result in a potential defamation suit against the company brought by the officer.[85] Given the importance of an executive officer's resignation and the leverage that institutional investors have to induce issuer disclosure of the reasons underlying the termination, it is surprising that the SEC elected not to mandate a more comprehensive disclosure.

Along with the Form 8-K listed Items, the Commission adopted a safe harbor for selective Items within the Form 8-K to protect against liability under Section 10(b) if a company fails to file those particular Items in a timely manner.[86] Note that although failure to timely file the Form 8-K with respect to these Items will not subject a company to liability under Section 10(b), fraud liability may be incurred if the Form 8-K contains any materially false or misleading statement. Moreover, if a company fails to disclose the selective Items within Form 8-K, the company still may incur liability under Section 13(a) of the Exchange Act (a reporting violation based on negligence) and, in any event, must disclose the information in its next Form 10-Q. Failure to accurately disclose the called for information in the next Form 10-Q will subject the company to liability exposure under Section 10(b).[87]

§ 11.08   REGULATION FD

The SEC adopted Regulation FD (Fair Disclosure) in response to the perceived unfairness when companies selectively disclose material nonpublic information to analysts, institutional investors, and other securities market insiders. The Regulation's basic premise provides that "when an issuer, or

---

[85] *See* Securities Exchange Act Release No. 49424 (2004).

[86] *Id.* The Form 8-K safe harbor includes:

Item 1.01	Entry into a Material Definitive Agreement
Item 1.02	Termination of a Material Definitive Agreement
Item 2.03	Creation of a Direct Financial Obligation or an Obligation under an Off-Balance Sheet Arrangement of a Registrant
Item 2.04	Trigger Events that Accelerate or Increase a Direct Financial Obligation or an Obligation under an Off-Balance Sheet Arrangement
Item 2.05	Costs Associated with Exit or Disposal Activities
Item 2.06	Material Impairments
Item 4.02(a)	Non-Reliance on Previously Issued Financial Statements or a Related Audit Report or Completed Interim Review (in the case where a company makes the determination and does not receive a notice described in Item 4.02(b) from its independent accountant)
Item 502(e)	Executive Officer Employment and Compensation Arrangements

[87] *Id.*; *see* Securities Exchange Act Release No. 49424 (2004).

person acting on its behalf, discloses material nonpublic information to [selective] persons . . . , it must make public disclosure of that information."[88] The timing of when the issuer must make such a public disclosure depends on whether the selective disclosure was intentional or non-intentional. As summarized by the SEC:

> *Regulation FD (Fair Disclosure)* is a new issuer disclosure rule that addresses selective disclosure. The Regulation provides that when an issuer, or person acting on its behalf, discloses material nonpublic information to certain enumerated persons (in general, securities market professionals and holders of the issuer's securities who may well trade on the basis of the information), it must make public disclosure of that information. The timing of the required public disclosure depends on whether the selective disclosure was intentional or non-intentional; for an intentional selective disclosure, the issuer must make public disclosure simultaneously; for a non-intentional disclosure, the issuer must make public disclosure promptly. Under the Regulation, the required public disclosure may be made by filing or furnishing a Form 8-K, or by another method or combination of methods that is reasonably designed to effect broad, non-exclusionary distribution of the information to the public.[89]

[A]   Purposes of Regulation FD

The SEC sought to address several concerns by promulgating Regulation FD. First, it believed that issuers often disclose important nonpublic information, such as advance warnings of earnings results, to securities analysts and/or institutional investors before making such information available to the general investing public. The Commission warned that as a result of this practice, the investing public might not believe that they are on an equal playing field with market insiders and may thereby lose confidence in the integrity of the securities markets. Second, the SEC stated that selective disclosure closely resembles the "tipping" of inside information, but noted that the current state of insider trading law may not create liability for an issuer's

---

[88] Selective Disclosure and Insider Trading, Securities Exchange Act Release No. 43154 (2000), 2000 SEC LEXIS 1672 (hereinafter the "Regulation FD Release"). The discussion in this Section is derived from the SEC Release. The discussion that follows also appears to a large extent in Steinberg, Securities Regulation: Liabilities and Remedies (2008).

[89] *Id.* As set forth in the Glossary to this text:

> Regulation FD prohibits issuers or individuals acting on their behalf from selectively disclosing material nonpublic information to certain enumerated persons (generally securities market professionals and holders of the issuer's securities who may well trade on the basis of the information) without disclosing the information publicly. If the selective disclosure is intentional, then the issuer must publicly disclose the information simultaneously by filing or furnishing a Form 8-K to the SEC or in a manner reasonably designed to provide broad distribution of the information. If the selective disclosure is unintentional, then the issuer must disclose the information to the public promptly, but in no event after the later of 24 hours or the opening of the next day's trading on the New York Stock Exchange. Violating Regulation FD exposes the issuer to SEC administrative and civil enforcement action, but does not by itself impose any Rule 10b-5 antifraud liability on the issuer or establish a private right of action.

selective disclosure.[90] Third, the Commission perceived that the integrity of the securities markets was threatened by issuers selectively disclosing information as a means to secure favorable reviews by analysts. Specifically, analysts may feel pressured to report about a company in a positive light or risk losing their access to company personnel. Finally, the SEC opined that recent technological advances, particularly in the communications area, no longer pose undue impediments to timely public disclosure.

[B]   Scope of Regulation FD

Regulation FD's scope focuses on those who are prohibited from selectively disclosing material nonpublic information and those to whom such selective disclosure is directed. The Regulation prohibits a company, or persons acting on such company's behalf, from selectively disclosing material inside information regarding such company or its securities.[91] For the purpose of the Regulation, an issuer includes a company that has a class of securities registered under Section 12 of the Exchange Act or is required to file reports under Section 15 of that Act.[92]

Regulation FD defines a "person acting on behalf of the issuer" as "any senior official of the issuer . . . or any other officer, employee, or agent of an issuer who regularly communicates with any [enumerated recipient of information discussed below] . . . , or with holders of the issuer's securities."[93] This definition focuses on those whose job function regularly entails the disclosure of company-related information to the enumerated recipients. Selective disclosure by personnel who may occasionally interact with analysts or investors, for example, would not give rise to liability under Regulation FD. Thus, material nonpublic information disclosed in the due course of business to customers and suppliers would be outside the scope of the Regulation. The Commission, however, has noted that a senior official cannot escape liability by directing non-covered personnel to make a selective disclosure of information to someone within the classes of enumerated recipients. In such a case, the senior official would be held responsible for making the selective disclosure under Section 20(b) of the Exchange Act. Finally, the definition of a "person acting on behalf of the issuer" specifically excludes an "officer, director, employee, or agent of an issuer who discloses material nonpublic information

---

[90] "[I]n light of the 'personal benefit' test set forth in the Supreme Court's decision in *Dirks v. SEC*, 463 U.S. 646 (1983), many have viewed issuer selective disclosures to analysts as protected from insider trading liability." Regulation FD Release, *supra* note 88, at n.7. Nevertheless, the Commission reiterated that it would institute enforcement actions based on violations of Section 10(b) where selective disclosures violated the insider trading prohibitions. *See* § 12.02 *infra*.

[91] 17 C.F.R. § 243.100(a).

[92] 17 C.F.R. § 243.101(b). Among other entities, the Regulation expressly excludes from the definition of "issuer" any foreign government or foreign private issuer.

[93] 17 C.F.R. § 243.101(c). The Regulation defines "senior official" as "any director, executive officer, investor relations or public relations officer, or other person with similar functions." 17 C.F.R. § 243.101(f).

in breach of a duty of trust or confidence to the issuer."[94] Such conduct would violate the insider trading prohibitions.[95]

Regulation FD applies when material nonpublic information is selectively disclosed to one of four enumerated classes of recipients outside the issuer:

- a broker or a dealer, or a person associated with a broker or dealer;
- an investment adviser, an institutional investment manager, or a person associated with either;
- an investment company or affiliated person thereof; or
- a holder of the issuer's securities, where it is reasonably foreseeable that the holder will purchase or sell the issuer's securities based on the information.[96]

The Regulation expressly excludes, and thus does not apply to, the following: a "person who owes a duty of trust or confidence to the issuer" (e.g., temporary insiders); a "person who expressly agrees to maintain the disclosed information in confidence"; a credit rating agency, "provided the information is disclosed solely for the purpose of developing a credit rating and the entity's ratings are publicly available"; and, with certain exceptions, in connection with "a securities offering registered under the Securities Act."[97] Furthermore, although not specifically referenced, disclosures to the media or communications to government agencies are outside the Regulation's scope.

[C]　Meaning of "Material" and "Nonpublic"

Although the Regulation refers to "material" and "nonpublic" information, it does not define those terms. Instead, the SEC relies on case law to define these terms. Thus, information is material if "there is a substantial likelihood that a reasonable shareholder would consider it important in making an investment decision . . . [and that] would have been viewed by the reasonable investor as having significantly altered the total mix of information made available."[98] Information is nonpublic "if it has not been disseminated in a manner making [such information] available to investors generally."[99]

Although the Commission declined to establish a bright-line test for materiality, it offered several examples of information that likely would require issuers to make a materiality determination: (1) earnings information; (2) mergers, acquisitions, tender offers, joint ventures, or changes in assets; (3) new products or discoveries, or developments regarding customers or

---

[94]　17 C.F.R. § 243.101(c).

[95]　*See* discussion §§ 12.02–12.03 *infra.*

[96]　*See* 17 C.F.R. § 243.100(b)(1)(i)-(iv).

[97]　17 C.F.R. § 243.100(b)(2)-(3). The Regulation lists attorneys, investment bankers, and accountants as examples of those who may owe a duty of trust or confidence to the issuer.

[98]　Regulation FD, *supra* note 88, quoting *TSC Industries, Inc. v. Northway, Inc.*, 426 U.S. 438, 449 (1976). The Regulation FD Release also cites SEC Staff Accounting Bulletin 99 (1999) (*see* § 5.07 *supra*) as authority supporting its definition of "materiality."

[99]　Regulation FD Release, *supra* note 88, citing *SEC v. Texas Gulf Sulphur*, 401 F.2d 833, 854 (2d Cir. 1968).

suppliers; (4) changes in control or in management; (5) change in auditors; (6) events regarding the issuer's securities; and (7) bankruptcies or receiverships. With this or any other information, the key for any materiality determination is on what significance a reasonable investor would place on the information.[100]

[D]   Intentional or Non-Intentional Selective Disclosure

Another important issue under Regulation FD involves whether the issuer selectively disclosed the information intentionally or non-intentionally. This assessment determines when the issuer must make the information publicly available. If the issuer intentionally and selectively discloses material nonpublic information, then it must disclose the same information simultaneously to the public. But if the selective disclosure is non-intentional, the issuer must disclose the information promptly, which is defined "as soon as reasonably practicable (but in no event after the later of 24 hours or the commencement of the next day's trading on the New York Stock Exchange) after a senior official of the issuer . . . learns that there has been a non-intentional disclosure by the issuer or person acting on behalf of the issuer of information that the senior official knows, or is reckless in not knowing, is both material and non-public."[101]

The standard for determining whether a selective disclosure was "intentional" meshes with the Regulation's definitions of materiality and nonpublic. The Regulation defines "intentional" to be that "the person making the disclosure either knows, or is reckless in not knowing, that the information he or she is communicating is *both* material and nonpublic."[102] Thus, if an issuer were merely negligent in erroneously judging whether a certain piece of selectively disclosed information is either material or nonpublic, Regulation FD would not impose liability. By using this standard, the Commission seeks to provide "additional protection that issuers need not fear being second-guessed by the Commission in enforcement actions for mistaken judgments regarding materiality in close cases."[103] Nonetheless, the SEC warned that the determination of materiality should take into account all facts and circumstances. Thus, for example, a materiality judgment that might not be reckless in the context of an impromptu answer to an unexpected question at a press conference may be reckless in the context of a prepared written statement where the issuer has more time to evaluate the information it is about to disclose. Furthermore, if an issuer displays a pattern of "mistaken" judgments regarding materiality, that company's credibility would be harmed when it comes to future claims that any particular disclosure was not intentional.

---

[100] *See* Regulation FD Release, note 88 *supra.* The Commission acknowledges that this information is not material per se.

[101] 17 C.F.R. § 243.101(d).

[102] 17 C.F.R. § 243.101(a) (emphasis added).

[103] *See* Regulation FD Release, note 88 *supra* (stating that "in the case of a selective disclosure attributable to a mistaken determination of materiality, liability will arise only if no reasonable person under the circumstances would have made the same determination").

[E]   Methods For Making Public Disclosure

Regulation FD provides issuers with flexibility in determining how to publicly disclose material nonpublic information when they have engaged in selective disclosure of such information. Whatever method the issuer chooses must be "reasonably designed to provide broad, non-exclusionary distribution of the information to the public."[104] One clear method that an issuer can use is either to file or furnish a Form 8-K with the SEC.[105]

The Regulation also provides that other methods of public disclosure may be acceptable, such as press releases, press conferences, or conferences that the public can attend or listen to by telephone or teleconference. In using these alternatives, however, the issuer must select a method or combination of methods that are reasonably calculated to provide a broad and effective public disclosure given that issuer's particular circumstances. Thus, for example, an issuer cannot rely solely on issuing a press release if it knows that its press releases are not routinely reported by the wire services. Furthermore, even though the Internet can be an effective method of disclosing information in conjunction with other methods, issuers cannot simply post information on their own Internet website as a sole means to satisfy Regulation FD's public disclosure requirements. In addition, the Commission will take into account whether a company deviated from its usual practices for making a public disclosure in determining whether the method of disclosure in any particular case complies with the Regulation.

The SEC, recognizing that a single method of disclosure may not be possible or desirable, offered a model for making a planned disclosure of material information. First, the issuer should issue a press release distributed through regular channels. Second, it should provide adequate notice through a press release and/or website posting of a scheduled conference call to discuss the particular information, giving investors information on the time and date of the call as well as how to access it. Third, the issuer should hold the conference call in an open manner, such that investors can listen to (but not necessarily ask questions during) the conference call either over the telephone or the Internet. The Commission also suggested that companies make taped replays of the conference call available for some time after they take place so as to allow other investors to listen to it.

---

[104] 17 C.F.R. § 243.101(e)(2).

[105] 17 C.F.R. § 243.101(e)(1). With respect to "filing" versus "furnishing" the information on Form 8-K, the SEC stated:

> [I]ssuers may choose either to "file" a report under Item 5 of Form 8-K or to "furnish" a report under Item 9 of Form 8-K that will not be deemed "filed." If an issuer chooses to file the information on Form 8-K, the information will be subject to liability under Section 18 of the Exchange Act. The information also will be subject to automatic incorporation by reference into the issuer's Securities Act registration statements, which are subject to liability under Sections 11 and 12(a)(2) of the Securities Act. If an issuer chooses instead to furnish the information, it will not be subject to liability under Section 11 of the Securities Act or Section 18 of the Exchange Act for the disclosure, unless it takes steps to include that disclosure in a filed report, proxy statement, or registration statement. All disclosures on Form 8-K, whether filed or furnished, will remain subject to the antifraud provisions of the federal securities laws.

[F]   Exclusions for Registered Offerings

Generally, Regulation FD "does not apply to disclosures made in connection with a securities offering registered under the Securities Act."[106] Nevertheless, a reporting company's unregistered offerings are subject to Regulation FD. The Commission noted that in the context of such offerings, the company should either make selectively disclosed information public or secure a confidentiality agreement from the recipient. It also warned public companies undertaking unregistered offerings that if they fail to adhere to Regulation FD, they may risk losing their exemption from registration. A company's failure to adhere to Regulation FD, however, will not cause it to lose the availability of using short-form Securities Act registration form S-3 or cause its shareholders to lose their ability to sell their securities under Securities Act Rule 144(c).[107]

[G]   SEC Enforcement, No Private Remedy

An issuer that allegedly violates Regulation FD will be subject to SEC enforcement action. The Commission, for example, has procured cease-and-desist orders, injunctions, and, in connection therewith, money penalties. The SEC also has brought enforcement actions against individuals affiliated with issuers that allegedly have violated Regulation FD.[108]

---

[106] Regulation FD Release, note 88 *supra*. With respect to communications made in connection with a registered offering that is excluded from Regulation FD coverage, the SEC in Securities Act Release No. 8591 (2005) stated:

> [A]s amended, Regulation FD will not apply to disclosures made in the following communications in connection with a registered securities offering that is of the type excluded from the Regulation:
>
> • a registration statement filed under the Securities Act, including a prospectus contained therein;
>
> • a free writing prospectus used after filing of the registration statement for the offering or a communication falling within the exception to the definition of prospectus contained in a clause (a) of Securities Act Section 2(a)(10);
>
> • any other Section 10(b) prospectus;
>
> • a notice permitted by Securities Act Rule 135;
>
> • a communication permitted by Securities Act Rule 134; or
>
> • an oral communication made in connection with the registered securities offering after filing of the registration statement for the offering under the Securities Act.
>
> • . . .
>
> In view of our new rules to expand permissible communications, we believe it is appropriate to clarify that the communications excluded from the operation of Regulation FD are, in fact, those communications that are directly related to a registered securities offering. Communications not contained in our enumerated list of exceptions from Regulation FD — for example, the publication of regularly released factual business information or regularly released forward-looking information or pre-filing communications — are subject to Regulation FD.

Id.

[107] *See* 17 C.F.R. § 243.103.

[108] *See, e.g., SEC v. Flowserve Corp.*, SEC Litigation Release No. 19154 (D.D.C. 2005); *In the Matter of Secure Computing Corp.*, Securities Exchange Act Release No. 46895 (2002). The SEC,

The Regulation, however, does not create any private right of action. Furthermore, it expressly does not establish any Rule 10b-5 antifraud liability for cases based "solely" on an issuer's failure to comply with Regulation FD.[109] Nevertheless, Rule 10b-5 liability may still arise if, for example, the company's public disclosure, designed to satisfy Regulation FD, contains a material misstatement or omits material information.

§ 11.09　RESPONDING TO AUDITOR REQUESTS

A customary practice of auditors is to transmit audit inquiry letters to client corporations, which thereupon forward such requests to their counsel for assessment and response. Such a letter normally asks counsel to provide the auditor with certain information regarding the client's affairs. The information provided is employed by the auditor in opining on the corporation's annual financial reports.[110] Among other items, the audit inquiry letter will seek information relating to contingent liabilities.[111]

Such "loss contingency" requests may cause tension. On the one hand, there is counsel's desire to preserve the client's confidences and secrets, as well as the client's desire to avoid disclosure of unfavorable information. For example, disclosure of a contingent unasserted liability may amount to advertising a client's possibly illegal conduct — a particularly undesirable event for the corporation where potential plaintiffs are ignorant of the possible claim. In addition, disclosure of a client's confidences incurs risk of waiving both the attorney-client and work product privileges. On the other hand, the auditor has a legitimate need to obtain adequate information in order to fulfill its duties consistent with the policy supporting public confidence in published financial statements.[112]

---

however, lost an enforcement proceeding alleging Regulation FD violations in *SEC v. Siebel Systems, Inc.*, 384 F. Supp. 2d 694 (S.D.N.Y. 2005). Critical of the SEC, the court commented:

> The SEC . . . scrutinized, at an extremely heightened level, every particular word used in the statement, including the tense of verbs and the general syntax of each sentence. No support for such an approach can be found in Regulation FD. . . . Such an approach places an unreasonable burden on a company's management and spokespersons to become linguistic experts, or otherwise live in fear of violating Regulation FD should the words they use later be interpreted by the SEC as connoting even the slightest variance from the company's public statements.

Id. at 704. *See* Brown, *First Reg FD Decision Finds SEC's "Excessive Scrutiny" Chills Disclosure*, 37 Sec. Reg. & L. Rep (BNA) 2102 (2005).

[109] *See* 17 C.F.R. § 243.102 ("No failure to make a public disclosure required solely by [Regulation FD] shall be deemed to be a violation of Rule 10b-5 . . . under the Securities Exchange Act."). Furthermore, the safe harbor for forward-looking statements provided by the Private Securities Litigation Reform Act may be invoked in this context. *See* § 11.05(D) *supra.*

[110] *See* Hooker, *Lawyer's Responses to Audit Inquiries and the Attorney-Client Privilege*, 35 Bus. Law. 1021 (1980).

[111] *See* American Bar Association, *Statement of Policy Regarding Lawyers' Responses to Auditors' Requests for Information*, 31 Bus. Law. 1709, 1712 (1976).

[112] *Id.* at 1710; Hooker, *supra* note 110, at 1021–1034; Subcommittee on Audit Inquiry Responses, *Inquiry of a Client's Lawyer Concerning Litigation, Claims, and Assessments*, 45 Bus. Law. 2245, 2251 (1990).

Competing against these considerations is the ever-present threat that an attorney's failure to disclose material facts may subject the attorney and client to liability exposure under federal and state securities laws as well as under common law. In addition to potential liability under the securities acts' antifraud provisions, SEC rules impose Section 13(b)(2) liability on an officer or director of a registrant who, with the requisite intent, makes a materially false or misleading statement to an auditor. Such liability also extends to others, including attorneys, who, with the requisite culpability, "provid[e] an auditor with an inaccurate or misleading legal analysis."[113]

In an effort to resolve these competing interests, the Financial Accounting Standards Board promulgated its Statement of Financial Accounting Standards No. 5 ("SFAS 5") and the ABA adopted its Statement of Policy Regarding Lawyers' Responses To Auditors' Requests for Information. Pursuant to the truce arrived at through these pronouncements, the following applies with respect to "loss contingencies":

> When properly requested by the client, it is appropriate for the lawyer to furnish to the auditor information concerning the following matters if the lawyer has been engaged by the client to represent or advise the client professionally with respect thereto and he has devoted substantive attention to them in the form of legal representation or consultation:
>
> (a) overly threatened or pending litigation, whether or not specified by the client;
>
> (b) a contractually assumed obligation which the client has specifically identified and upon which the client has specifically requested, in the inquiry letter or a supplement thereto, [for] comment to the auditor;
>
> (c) an unasserted possible claim or assessment which the client has specifically identified and upon which the client has specifically requested, in the inquiry letter or a supplement thereto, [for] comment to the auditor.[114]

According to the ABA Policy Statement, counsel normally should not express judgment as to the outcome of claims delineated unless it appears to counsel that an unfavorable outcome is either "probable" or "remote." With respect to *unasserted possible claims or assessments*, where a potential claimant has not manifested an awareness of the potential claim, disclosure is required only if the *client* concludes that "(i) it is probable that a claim will be asserted, (ii) there is a reasonable possibility, if the claim is in fact asserted, that the outcome will be unfavorable, and (iii) the liability resulting from such

---

[113] *See* Sarbanes-Oxley Act § 303(a); SEC Rule 13b2–2; discussion in § 5.08[D] *supra*.

[114] ABA Statement of Policy, *supra* note 111, at 1712; *see Tew v. Arky, Freed, Stearns, Watson, Greer, Weaver & Harris*, 655 F. Supp. 1573 (S.D. Fla. 1987) (holding that a law firm had no disclosure obligation to the auditor of its client because the subject client did not identify its financial troubles in the auditor's inquiry letter and did not ask the law firm to comment with respect thereto).

unfavorable outcome would be material to [the company's] financial condition."[115] Hence, by leaving the decision to reveal contingent liability for unasserted claims to the client, nondisclosure will be the likely consequence. Unless directed by the client, counsel has no duty under this framework to comment on such unasserted claims.[116]

---

[115] ABA Statement of Policy, *supra* note 111, at 1713–14.

[116] Steinberg, *Attorney Liability for Client Fraud,* 1991 Colum. Bus. L. Rev. 1, 22–25; *see* Fuld, *Lawyers' Responses to Auditors — Some Practical Aspects,* 44 Bus. Law. 159 (1988); Hinsey, *Communications Among Attorneys, Management and Auditors,* 36 Bus. Law. 727 (1981); Hooker, *Lawyers' Responses to Audit Inquiries and the Attorney-Client Privilege,* 35 Bus. Law. 1021 (1980); Lorne, *The Corporate and Securities Adviser: The Public Interest, and Professional Ethics,* 76 Mich. L. Rev. 425, 448 (1978); Rigby, *The Attorney-Auditor Relationship: Responding to Audit Inquiries, the Disclosure of Loss Contingencies and the Work Product Privilege,* 35 Sec. Reg. L.J. 3 (2007); Winer & Seabolt, *Responding to Audit Inquiries in a Time of Heightened Peril,* 36 Sec. Reg. & L. Rep. (BNA) 1902 (2004).

Chapter 12

INSIDER TRADING

§ 12.01 OVERVIEW

The subject of "insider" trading has been the focus of increased judicial scrutiny, vigorous SEC enforcement, and congressional attention. The Supreme Court has decided three major cases in this area. In *Chiarella v. United States*, the Court asserted that the imposition of liability under Section 10(b) and Rule 10b-5 for trading on material nonpublic information must be premised upon a duty to disclose.[1] In *Dirks v. SEC*, the Court held that the duty of tippers-tippees to disclose or abstain from trading under Section 10(b) and Rule 10b-5 depends on "whether the insider [tipper] personally will benefit [e.g., by receipt of pecuniary gain or reputational enhancement that will translate into future earnings], directly, or indirectly, from his disclosure. Absent some personal gain, there has been no breach of duty to stockholders. And absent a breach by the insider, there is no derivative breach [by the tippee]."[2] And, in *United States v. O'Hagan*, the Court upheld the validity of the misappropriation theory as well as SEC Rule 14e-3.[3]

Decided in the early 1980s, *Chiarella* and *Dirks*, although embracing certain traditional principles that had been adopted by the lower courts and the SEC,[4] posed difficulties for the SEC and private claimants. Generally, the SEC has met this challenge. In both *Chiarella* and *Dirks*, for example, the Court left unresolved the viability of the misappropriation theory. After *Chiarella*, the SEC and the Department of Justice successfully invoked this rationale. For example, in *United States v. Newman*,[5] the Second Circuit upheld an indictment on the grounds that the defendants had allegedly misappropriated valuable nonpublic information entrusted to them in the utmost secrecy. The court found that the defendants had "sullied the reputations" of their employers, investment banks, "as safe repositories of client confidences" and had deceived the clients of these investment banks "whose takeover plans were

---

[1] 445 U.S. 222 (1980).

[2] 463 U.S. 646, 663 (1983).

[3] 521 U.S. 642 (1997). Although it did not address the "misappropriation" theory in depth, another Supreme Court case in the insider trading area is *Carpenter v. United States*, 484 U.S. 19 (1987).

[4] *See, e.g., SEC v. Texas Gulf Sulphur Co.*, 401 F.2d 833 (2d Cir. 1968) (en banc), *cert. denied*, 394 U.S. 976 (1969) (imposing a duty on corporate officers and directors premised on the equal access theory to disclose or refrain from trading on material nonpublic information); *In re Cady, Roberts & Co.*, 40 S.E.C. 907 (1961) (same).

[5] 664 F.2d 12 (2d Cir. 1981).

keyed to target company stock prices fixed by market forces, not artificially inflated through purchases by purloiners of confidential information."[6] Ultimately, as discussed in § 12.03, the Supreme Court upheld the misappropriation theory's validity in *United States v. O'Hagan.*[7]

After *Chiarella*, investors trading contemporaneously in the securities markets in misappropriation cases initially were left without a remedy. In *Moss v. Morgan Stanley*,[8] for example, the Second Circuit, in affirming the dismissal of an action seeking monetary damages for violations of Section 10(b), held that the plaintiffs failed to prove that the defendants breached a duty owed to them. In response, Congress enacted Section 20A of the Exchange Act to provide contemporaneous traders with an express right of action against those on the opposite side of the transaction who allegedly engaged in illegal insider trading of the same class of securities.[9]

Another example of the SEC's reaction to *Chiarella* was its promulgation, pursuant to Section 14(e) of the Williams Act, of Rule 14e-3 which seeks to deter insider and tippee trading in the tender offer setting. Generally, the Rule, with certain exceptions, contains broad "disclose or abstain from trading" as well as "anti-tipping" provisions. With certain exemptions, Rule 14e-3 applies the disclose-or-abstain provision where an individual is in possession of material information relating to a tender offer and knows or has reason to know that such information is nonpublic and was obtained directly or indirectly from the offeror, the subject corporation, any of their affiliated persons, or any person acting on behalf of either company.[10]

In the release adopting Rule 14e-3, the Commission asserted that *Chiarella* did not limit its authority under Section 14(e) to prescribe such a mandate regulating insider trading in the tender offer context.[11] In *O'Hagan*, the Supreme Court upheld Rule 14e-3's validity at least as applied to the facts at bar.[12]

Congress also has been active in this area by enacting legislation in 1984 and 1988. Due to the difficulty in comprehensively defining "insider trading," Congress elected to leave the further development of this concept to judicial interpretation. Among other provisions, the legislation amended the Exchange Act to authorize the SEC to seek the imposition of a civil monetary penalty amounting to three times the profit received or loss avoided due to the violative transaction(s). As provided by the 1988 legislation, under certain conditions, broker-dealers, investment advisers, and others are subject to the treble

---

[6] *Id.* at 17–18.

[7] 521 U.S. 642 (1997).

[8] 719 F.2d 5 (2d Cir. 1983).

[9] For more discussion on *Chiarella, Dirks,* and their implications, see W. Wang & M. Steinberg, Insider Trading (2d ed. 2005 & Supp.).

[10] *See* 17 C.F.R. § 240.14e-3.

[11] *See* Securities Exchange Act Release No. 17120 (1980).

[12] 521 U.S. 642 (1997). For commentary, see Loewenstein, *Section 14(e) of the Williams Act and the Rule 10b-5 Comparisons*, 71 Geo. L.J. 1311 (1983). For further discussion, see § 12.07 *infra.*

monetary penalty for illegal inside trades effected by those persons who are under their control.[13]

§ 12.02   SUPREME COURT DECISIONS OF THE EARLY 1980s — *CHIARELLA* AND *DIRKS*

A fundamental tenet underlying the federal securities laws, at least since the SEC's decision nearly five decades ago in *Cady Roberts*,[14] is that "insiders" and, in certain circumstances, their tippees must either disclose material nonpublic information in their possession prior to trading or refrain from such trading. Unfortunately, although seemingly straightforward, the theoretical underpinnings for a duty to "disclose or abstain" from trading as well as its application to concrete factual situations and the persons to whom the duty should run have not always been clear.

In *Chiarella v. United States*,[15] the Supreme Court held that under Section 10(b) of the Exchange Act and Rule 10b-5 promulgated thereunder a financial printer, who purchased stock after deciphering information gleaned from confidential documents entrusted to his employer that certain companies were to be the targets of mergers or tender offers, did not breach a duty to the investing public.[16] In so doing, the Court rejected the parity of information[17] and parity of access to information[18] principles that a number of lower courts had embraced. Hence, the Court held that silence, absent a duty to disclose, will not give rise to Section 10(b) liability. Such liability based on silence, the Court asserted, "is premised upon a duty to disclose arising from a relationship of trust and confidence between parties to a transaction."[19]

With respect to insiders, the *Chiarella* Court reinforced the principle, expanded upon in *Dirks v. SEC*,[20] that a duty to disclose or abstain from trading arises where such persons possess material nonpublic information.[21] Quoting from the SEC's decision in *Cady Roberts*, the *Chiarella* Court stated that the obligation to disclose or abstain from trading derives from

---

[13] For further discussion, see §§ 12.06[B], 12.07 *infra.* For commentary on the 1984 and 1988 legislation, see Aldave, *The Insider Trading and Securities Fraud Enforcement Act of 1988: An Analysis and Appraisal*, 52 Albany L. Rev. 893 (1988); Friedman, *The Insider Trading and Securities Fraud Enforcement Act of 1988*, 68 N. Car. L. Rev. 465 (1990); Kaswell, *An Insider's View of the Insider Trading and Securities Fraud Enforcement Act of 1988*, 45 Bus. Law. 145 (1989); Langevoort, *The Insider Trading Sanctions Act of 1984 and Its Effect on Existing Law*, 37 Vand. L. Rev. 1273 (1984); Silver, *Penalizing Insider Trading: A Critical Assessment of the Insider Trading Sanctions Act of 1984*, 1985 Duke L.J. 960.

[14] *In re Cady, Roberts & Co.*, 40 S.E.C. 907 (1961).

[15] 445 U.S. 222 (1980).

[16] *Id.* at 226–35.

[17] *See, e.g.*, *SEC v. Texas Gulf Sulphur Co.*, 401 F.2d 833 (2d Cir. 1968) (en banc), *cert. denied*, 394 U.S. 976 (1969).

[18] *See, e.g.*, *United States v. Chiarella*, 588 F.2d 1358 (2d Cir. 1978), *rev'd*, 455 U.S. 222 (1980).

[19] 445 U.S. at 230.

[20] 463 U.S. 646 (1983).

[21] 445 U.S. at 226–27.

an affirmative duty to disclose material information [which] has been traditionally imposed on corporate "insiders," particularly officers, directors, or controlling stockholders. We . . . have consistently held that insiders disclose material facts which are known to them by virtue of their position but which are not known to persons with whom they deal and which, if known, would affect investment judgment.[22]

Significantly, the *Chiarella* Court did not address the issue of whether the financial printer could have been held liable pursuant to the misappropriation theory under Section 10(b) and Rule 10b-5. Had this theory been applied, as it ultimately was embraced by the Court nearly two decades later in *O'Hagan*,[23] *Chiarella* would have breached a duty to the acquiring corporation and to his employer when he traded on the basis of information he procured by virtue of his strategic position.

Turning to the Supreme Court's decision in *Dirks*, the Court held that the duty of tippees to disclose or abstain from trading depends on whether the tipper has him/herself breached a fiduciary duty to the corporation's shareholders by divulging the information to the tippee. "Thus, the test is whether the insider personally will benefit, directly or indirectly, from his disclosure. Absent some personal gain, there has been no breach of duty to stockholders. And absent a breach by the insider, there is no derivative breach [by the tippee]."[24] Such personal benefit may be shown by the insider's receipt of pecuniary gain or reputational enhancement that will translate into future earnings.[25] Also, the requisite showing of benefit may be made by the insider making a gift of confidential information to the tippee. In such circumstances, "[t]he tip and trade resemble trading by the insider himself followed by a gift of the profits to the recipient."[26] In order to hold the tippee liable under Section 10(b) for trading on the information conveyed by the insider, the tippee must or should have known that the insider breached his/her fiduciary duty by disclosing such confidential information to the tippee.[27]

By holding that (1) there must be a breach of the insider's fiduciary duty to the corporation's shareholders before the tippee inherits the duty to disclose or abstain and (2) by premising the existence of a breach on whether the insider will personally benefit from disclosing the information to the tippee, the Court

---

[22] *Id.*, , quoting *In re Cady Roberts & Co.*, 40 S.E.C. 907, 911 (1961). *See generally* Heminway, *Materiality Guidance in the Context of Insider Trading: A Call for Action*, 52 Am. U.L. Rev. 1131 (2005); Langevoort, *Insider Trading and the Fiduciary Principle: A Post-*Chiarella *Restatement*, 70 Cal. L. Rev. 1 (1982); Wang, *Trading on Material Nonpublic Information on Impersonal Stock Markets: Who Is Harmed and Who Can Sue Whom Under SEC Rule 10b-5?*, 54 So. Cal. L. Rev. 1217 (1981).

[23] 521 U.S. 642 (1997); *see* § 12.03 *infra*.

[24] 463 U.S. at 662.

[25] *Id.* at 664.

[26] *Id.*

[27] *Id.* at 660. For decisions after *Dirks*, see, *e.g.*, *United States v. Blackwell*, 459 F.3d 739 (6th Cir. 2006); *United States v. McDermott*, 277 F.3d 240 (2d Cir. 2002); *SEC v. Maio*, 51 F.3d 623 (7th Cir. 1995); cases cited in note 29 *infra*. *See also*, *United States v. Evans*, 486 F.3d 315 (7th Cir. 2007) (affirming conviction of tippee irrespective that tipper was acquitted).

in *Dirks* made it more difficult for the SEC and private claimants to prove liability. In imposing a motivational requirement, the Court arguably "excuses a knowing and intentional violation of an insider's duty to shareholders if the insider does not act from a motive of personal gain."[28] The task of proving such a motive in many cases must rest on circumstantial evidence and may be troublesome.[29] Moreover, the benefit apparently must be a personal one which, at least in most instances, must enrich the insider monetarily. Other types of benefits, such as an enhanced reputation which does not translate into future earnings, may be insufficient to find a breach. Liability also may not be imposed against the "loose-lipped" director or officer who divulges confidential corporate information to such persons as financial analysts, broker-dealers and golfing cronies without any intention to make a gift or personally benefit therefrom. This result constitutes a departure from prior lower court case law.[30]

In contrast to the generally restrictive nature of the holding, the *Dirks* Court recognized the "quasi-insider" principle, stating:

> Under certain circumstances, such as where corporate information is revealed legitimately to an underwriter, accountant, lawyer, or consultant working for the corporation, these outsiders may become fiduciaries of the shareholders. The basis for recognizing this fiduciary duty is not simply that such persons acquired nonpublic corporate information, but rather that they have entered into a special confidential relationship in the conduct of the business of the enterprise and are given access to information solely for corporate purposes. . . . [W]hen such a person breaches his fiduciary relationship, he may be treated more properly as a tipper than as a tippee. . . . For such a duty to be imposed, however, the corporation must expect the outsider to keep the disclosed nonpublic information confidential, and the relationship at least must imply such a duty.[31]

Hence, under this rationale, individuals enjoying a special relationship with the corporation, such as accountants, attorneys, consultants, and underwriters, may be viewed as insiders when they trade on material nonpublic information that they legitimately received during the course of that relationship.

---

[28] 463 U.S. at 671–74 (Blackmun, J., dissenting).

[29] *See, e.g., SEC v. Switzer*, 590 F. Supp. 756 (W.D. Okla. 1984); *Cf. SEC v. Ginsburg*, 362 F.3d 1292 (11th Cir. 2004), *rev'g*, 242 F. Supp. 2d 1310 (S.D. Fla. 2002) (reversing district court and holding that sufficient evidence existed to conclude that insider improperly tipped family members). *See generally* Hiler, Dirks v. SEC — *A Study in Cause and Effect*, 43 Md. L. Rev. 292 (1984).

[30] *See, e.g., Elkind v. Liggett & Myers, Inc.*, 635 F.2d 156, 165 (2d Cir. 1980). Note that the SEC's Regulation Fair Disclosure (FD) regulates issuer selective disclosure practices. Interestingly, the Commission opted to adopt the rule pursuant to its asserted authority under Section 13(a) of the Exchange Act. *See* Securities Exchange Act Release No. 43154 (2000); § 11.08 *supra*.

[31] 463 U.S. at 677 n.14.

§ 12.03   THE MISAPPROPRIATION THEORY

[A]   *United States v. O'Hagan*

The misappropriation theory posits that a person perpetrates fraud "in connection with" a securities transaction, and hence violates Section 10(b) of the Exchange Act and Rule 10b-5 promulgated thereunder, when he/she misappropriates material nonpublic information for securities trading purposes, breaching a fiduciary-like duty owed to the source of such information. This theory targets "outsiders" of an enterprise who become privy to confidential information but who owe no fiduciary duty to that enterprise's shareholders. Accordingly, the theory fills the gap left open by traditional insider trading liability in that the breach of a duty owed is not to a trader on the other side of the transaction but rather is owed to the source of the information.[32]

In *United States v. O'Hagan*,[33] the Supreme Court held that to establish liability under the misappropriation theory a fiduciary-like duty must exist between the misappropriator of the information and the source of such information. Under this theory, the misappropriator is using his position to deceive those who entrusted him with the confidential information.[34] In other words, an enterprise's confidential information constitutes property with respect to which such enterprise has a right of exclusive use. And because the disclosure obligation is owed to the source of the information, the undisclosed misappropriation of such confidential information is viewed as fraud akin to embezzlement.[35]

Hence, deception by means of nondisclosure is fundamental to liability under the misappropriation theory.[36] Accordingly, "full disclosure [to the source of the information] forecloses liability under the misappropriation theory."[37] The deception underlying the misappropriation theory thus focuses on feigning fidelity to the information's source to whom a fiduciary-like duty is owed. Consequently, if the fiduciary timely reveals to such source that she plans to trade (or tip), there is no deception perpetrated and accordingly no

---

[32] *See United States v. O'Hagan*, 521 U.S. 642, 652 (1997). An example of a breach to the source of the information is an attorney who in the course of her employment learns of a client's contemplated merger for a target corporation and then purchases stock in the target corporation before the merger is publicly announced. *See, e.g.*, *United States v. Grossman*, 843 F.2d 78, 86 (2d Cir. 1988). Another example is where an employee of an investment advisor learns of a prospective recommendation of a particular stock by his employer and purchases that stock in advance of the recommendation. *Cf. United States v. Carpenter*, 484 U.S. 19 (1987).

[33] 521 U.S. 642 (1997).

[34] *Id.* at 652.

[35] *Id.* at 654.

[36] Misappropriation is a "deceptive device or contrivance" within the meaning of Section 10(b). *United States v. O'Hagan*, 521 U.S. at 653–54 (holding that a misappropriator engages in deception and stating "[a] fiduciary who pretends loyalty to the principal while secretly converting the principal's information for personal gain dupes or defrauds the principal").

[37] *Id.* at 655.

Section 10(b) violation.[38] Nonetheless, even if the fiduciary makes such disclosure, she still may remain liable under state law, such as for breach of the duty of loyalty and under certain federal statutes, including mail and wire fraud.[39]

Section 10(b) mandates that "the misappropriator's deceptive use of information be 'in connection with the purchase or sale of [a] security.' "[40] Such deception occurs "in connection with" the purchase or sale of a security when the fiduciary's fraud is consummated. And the fraud under Section 10(b) is consummated, not when the fiduciary procures the confidential information, but when without adequate revelation to his source(s), he utilizes the information to engage in securities trading (or to engage in "tipping").[41] Thus, the "in connection with" requirement limits liability under the misappropriation theory to using material confidential information in order to profit (or avoid loss) when engaging in securities transactions.[42]

[B]   Family and Other Personal Relationships

After *O'Hagan*, the applicability of the misappropriation theory in the business setting — such as where an employee purloins material nonpublic information from his/her employer — is well established. In the context of family and other personal relationships, however, the misappropriation theory's impact is less certain.

For example, in *United States v. Chestman*,[43] the Second Circuit rejected the government's reliance on the misappropriation rationale under the facts presented when the wife entrusted inside information to her husband. The court asserted that "a fiduciary duty cannot be imposed unilaterally by entrusting a person with confidential information" and that "marriage does not, without more, create a fiduciary relationship."[44] No such duty arose in the

---

[38] *Id.* at 654–55.

[39] *Id.* at 655; *see United States v. Carpenter*, 484 U.S. 19 (1987); *Diamond v. Oreamuno*, 24 N.Y.2d 494, 248 N.E.2d 910 (1969); *Brophy v. Cities Service Co.*, 31 Del. Ch. 241, 70 A.2d 5 (1949); W. Wang & M. Steinberg, Insider Trading, *supra* note 9, at § 15.2; Hazen, *Corporate Insider Trading: Reawakening the Common Law*, 39 Wash. & Lee L. Rev. 845 (1982).

[40] *United States v. O'Hagan*, 521 U.S. at 655–56. For recent Supreme Court decisions interpreting the "in connection with" requirement, see *SEC v. Zandford*, 535 U.S. 813 (2002); *Wharf (Holdings) Ltd. v. United International Holdings, Inc.*, 532 U.S. 588 (2001).

[41] 521 U.S. at 656.

[42] *Id.* For decisions after *O'Hagan* invoking the misappropriation theory, see, *e.g.*, *SEC v. Talbot*, 530 F.3d 1085 (9th Cir. 2008); *SEC v. Rocklage*, 470 F.3d 1 (1st Cir. 2006); *United States v. Bhagat*, 436 F.3d 1140 (9th Cir. 2006); *United States v. Falcone*, 257 F.3d 226 (2d Cir. 2001); *See generally* Symposium, 20 Cardozo L. Rev. No. 1 (1998); Nagy, *Reframing the Misappropriation Theory of Insider Trading: A Post-*O'Hagan *Suggestion*, 59 Ohio St. L.J. 1223 (1998); Painter, Krawiec & Williams, *Don't Ask, Just Tell: Insider Trading After* United States v. O'Hagan, 84 Va. L. Rev. 153 (1998); Ramirez & Christopher, *The Misappropriation Theory of Insider Trading Under* United States v. O'Hagan, 26 Sec. Reg. L.J. 162 (1998); Weiss, United States v. O'Hagan: *Pragmatism Returns to the Law of Insider Trading*, 23 J. Corp. L. 1 (1998).

[43] 947 F.2d 551 (2d Cir. 1991).

[44] *Id.* at 567–68.

case at bar because, according to the Second Circuit, the inside information was gratuitously communicated to the husband by the wife with no promise by the husband to keep the information confidential. Further, the court concluded that the husband was not part of the family's "inner circle" (that included the wife's parents), signifying that a fiduciary or comparable duty was not present.[45]

So much for "family values." One can understandably be upset by the law giving greater sanctity to a shareholder's relationship with a director of a publicly-held company (with whom such shareholder has never spoken or met) than to one's spouse, parent, child, or sibling. Evidently by adopting Rule 10b5-2, the SEC agrees with the asserted absurdity of this approach. The Rule provides a non-exclusive list of three situations in which a person is deemed to have a relationship of trust and confidence for purposes of invoking the misappropriation theory. Rule 10b5-2 thus triggers application of the misappropriation theory when the person receiving the material nonpublic information trades or tips in the following situations: (1) when such recipient explicitly agreed to maintain the confidentiality of the information; (2) when a reasonable expectation of confidentiality existed due to that the persons who had the communication(s) (including the misappropriator) enjoyed a history, practice, or pattern of sharing confidences; and (3) when the source of the information (i.e., the person providing such information) was a spouse, child, parent, or sibling of the person receiving the information, unless it can be established as an affirmative defense that on the facts and circumstances of the particular family relationship that no reasonable expectation of confidentiality existed.[46]

§ 12.04　"POSSESSION" VS. "USE"

When charged with insider trading, a defendant may contend that he/she had planned to purchase or sell the subject securities prior to coming into possession of the inside information. In response, the SEC's position generally has been that mere possession, rather than use, of the material nonpublic information is sufficient to trigger liability under Section 10(b).[47] Likewise, the Second Circuit, endorsing the "possession" standard, opined that "material

---

[45] *Id.* at 570–71; *accord SEC v. Reed*, 601 F. Supp. 685 (S.D.N.Y.), *rev'd on other grounds*, 773 F.2d 447 (2d Cir. 1985). *But see SEC v. Yun*, 327 F.3d 1263, 1272–1273 (11th Cir. 2003) (stating that "a spouse who traded in breach of a reasonable and legitimate expectation of confidentiality held by the other spouse sufficiently subjects the former to insider trading liability [and that such can be shown if] the husband and wife had a history or practice of sharing business confidences, and those confidences generally were maintained by the spouse receiving the information"); *SEC v. Falbo*, 14 F. Supp. 2d 508 (S.D.N.Y. 1998) (under facts at bar, invoking the misappropriation theory and finding breach of spouse's duty of confidentiality).

[46] Securities Exchange Act Release No. 43154 (2000).

[47] *See, e.g., Report of the Investigation in the Matter of Sterling Drug, Inc.*, Securities Exchange Act Release No. 14675 (1978) (asserting that "[i]f an insider sells his securities while in possession of material nonpublic information, such an insider is taking advantage of his position to the detriment of the public").

information cannot lie idle in the human brain."[48]

Disagreeing, the Ninth and Eleventh Circuits,[49] have held that proof of use rather than mere possession is consistent with Section 10(b)'s scienter requirement.[50] Language in the Supreme Court's decision in *O'Hagan* also supports the "use" approach.[51] In *SEC v. Adler*, the Eleventh Circuit held that Section 10(b)'s scienter requirement mandates that the Commission must establish that the defendant when he/she traded actually "used" the material nonpublic information. Phrased somewhat differently, the SEC must show that the defendant's knowledge of such information constituted a substantial factor in his/her decision to purchase or sell the subject securities at the particular price or at the particular time.[52] Importantly, however, the court held that a defendant's knowing possession of material nonpublic information when trading raises a strong inference of use. Such inference may be rebutted by the defendant establishing that he/she had independent, justifiable reasons for engaging in the particular transactions at that time and in the amount traded.[53] Similarly, the Ninth Circuit in *United States v. Smith* adopted the "use" rather than "possession" standard.[54] The court, however, declined to adhere to the Eleventh Circuit's inference of use (upon a showing of knowing possession) due to constitutional reasons arising from a criminal prosecution.[55]

Reacting to the Ninth and Eleventh Circuit decisions, the SEC adopted Rule 10b5-1.[56] The Rule triggers liability exposure when a person purchases or sells securities while "aware" of material nonpublic information. Hence, a trade is deemed to be "on the basis" of material nonpublic information under Rule 10b5-1 if the trader was "aware" of such information at the time of the purchase or sale. The Rule reflects the position that one who is aware of inside information at the time of trading will have inevitably made use of such information. While the awareness standard expands the scope of insider trading liability (as compared to the Ninth and Eleventh Circuits' approaches), the SEC posits that Rule 10b5-1 enhances investor confidence and the integrity of the securities markets.

Under Rule 10b5-1, an affirmative defense generally is available if the trader engages in the specified transaction(s) pursuant to a pre-existing plan, contract, or instruction that is binding and specific. Under such circumstances, the inside

---

[48] *United States v. Teicher*, 987 F.2d 112, 120 (2d Cir. 1993).

[49] *See United States v. Smith*, 155 F.3d 1051 (9th Cir. 1998); *SEC v. Adler*, 137 F.3d 1325 (11th Cir. 1998).

[50] *See* § 8.03 *supra.*

[51] *See United States v. O'Hagan*, 521 U.S. at 656 (stating that, under the misappropriation theory, "the fiduciary's fraud is consummated . . . when without disclosure to his principal, he *uses* the information to purchase or sell securities") (emphasis added).

[52] 137 F.3d at 1337.

[53] *Id.*

[54] 155 F.3d at 1066.

[55] *Id.* at 1067–69 (stating that "a knowing possession standard would . . . go a long way toward making insider trading a strict liability crime").

[56] Securities Exchange Act Release No. 43154 (2000).

information was not a factor in the trading decision. More specifically, to establish the affirmative defense, a person must satisfy the following criteria. First a person must demonstrate that prior to becoming aware of the inside information, he/she had entered into a binding contract to purchase or sell the security, had provided instructions to another person to execute the trade for the instructing person's account, or had adopted a written plan for trading securities. Second, the person must demonstrate that, with respect to the purchase or sale, the contract, instructions, or plan: expressly specified the amount(s), price(s) and date(s); provided a written formula, algorithm, or computer program for determining the amount(s), price(s), and date(s); or did not permit the person to exercise any influence over how, when, or whether to execute the trade(s) (and in the event that any other person exercised such influence that person was not aware of the material, nonpublic information). Third, the person must demonstrate that the trade(s) that occurred were pursuant to the previously established contract, instructions, or plan. This means that the person neither may alter or deviate from the contract, instruction or plan nor enter into a corresponding or opposite, hedging transaction with respect to those securities. Furthermore, the defense is governed by a good-faith requirement that the person did not enter into the contract, instruction, or plan as part of a scheme to avoid liability under Rule 10b5-1.[57]

Rule 10b5-1 provides another affirmative defense for trading parties that are entities. This defense is available as an alternative to the defense discussed above. Under the provisions of this defense, an entity will not be liable if it demonstrates that the individual responsible for the investment decision on behalf of the entity was not aware of the material inside information, and that the entity had implemented reasonable policies and procedures to prevent insider trading.[58]

§ 12.05 RIGHT OF ACTION FOR CONTEMPORANEOUS TRADERS

After the Second Circuit's decision adopting the misappropriation theory in *United States v. Newman*,[59] the question remained whether purchasers and sellers of securities had a cause of action for monetary damages under Section 10(b) even though the defrauding parties who misappropriated the inside

---

[57] Rule 10b5-1(c); SEC Release, note 56 *supra.*

[58] Rule 10b5-1(c); SEC Release, note 56 *supra; see* Securities Act Release No. 8869 (2007). *See generally,* Horwich, *The Origin, Application, Validity, and Potential Misuse of Rule 10b5-1,* 62 Bus. Law. 913 (2007); Karmel, *The Controversy of Possession Versus Use,* N.Y.L.J., Dec. 17, 1998, at 3; McLucas & Walker, *Insider Trading Developments: Do the* Adler *and* Smith *Cases Portend Tougher Times for SEC Enforcement?,* 32 Rev. Sec. & Comm. Reg. 93 (1999); Nagy, *The "Possession Vs. "Use" Debate In The Context of Securities Trading By Traditional Insiders: Why Silence Can Never Be Golden,* 67 U. Cin. L. Rev. 1129 (1999); Sinai, *A Challenge to the Validity of Rule 10b5-1,* 30 Sec. Reg. L.J. 261 (2002).

[59] 664 F.2d 12 (2d Cir. 1981), *discussed in,* § 12.01 *supra.*

information owed them no fiduciary duty. In *Moss v. Morgan Stanley, Inc.*,[60] the Second Circuit held that in order to recover under Section 10(b) for monetary damages it must be shown that the defendant breached a duty owed to the plaintiff. Relying on *Chiarella*, the court asserted that the relationship giving rise to a duty to disclose must be between the parties to the transaction. Hence, because the misappropriators in *Moss* owed no fiduciary duty to the plaintiff, no Section 10(b) right of action was available.[61]

In subsequently enacted legislation, Congress nullified the *Moss* decision in this respect. In the Insider Trading and Securities Fraud Enforcement Act of 1988, Congress enacted Section 20A of the Exchange Act to provide an express right of action on behalf of "contemporaneous traders" who were trading the same class of securities on the opposite side of the transaction during the time that the allegedly illegal inside trade(s) occurred. Thus, to recover under this express right of action, the plaintiff must be trading contemporaneously with and on the opposite side of the transaction from the inside trader. Moreover, the damages available in an action instituted under Section 20A on behalf of contemporaneous traders are limited to the profit gained or loss avoided by the defendant's illegal trades.[62]

Importantly, Section 20A does not limit a complainant's entitlement to private rights of action under other provisions of the Exchange Act, such as Section 10(b). In this regard, a private right of action under Section 10(b) may be available against inside traders (as well as their tippers) on behalf of certain noncontemporaneous traders. Such a situation may arise when, due to insider trading which has increased the price of the target company's stock, a bidder must pay more to acquire such stock. In the House Report accompanying the 1988 legislation, the Committee took the position that a Section 10(b) right of action exists in the above situation and that a plaintiff should be able to recover the full extent of any actual damages incurred.[63]

Moreover, as part of the Insider Trading Sanctions Act of 1984, Congress added Section 20(d) to the Exchange Act. That provision states:

> Wherever communicating, or purchasing or selling a security while in possession of, material nonpublic information would violate, or result in liability to any purchaser or seller of the security under any provision of this Act, or any rule or regulation thereunder, such conduct in connection with a purchase or sale of a put, call, straddle, option, or privilege with respect to such security or with respect to a

---

[60] 719 F.2d 5 (2d Cir. 1983).

[61] *Id.* at 15–16. *But see O'Connor & Associates v. Dean Witter Reynolds, Inc.*, 529 F. Supp. 1179 (S.D.N.Y. 1981) (right of action extended to options trader even though insiders owed such person no fiduciary duty).

[62] *See* H.R. Rep. No. 100–910 to accompany H.R. 5133, 100 Cong., 2d Sess. (1988); Fed. Sec. L. Rep. (CCH) No. 1309 (Oct. 26, 1988); 20 Sec. Reg. & L. Rep. (BNA) 1623 (1988); authorities cited note 13 *supra*. With respect to the contemporaneous trading requirement, see *Brody v. Transitional Hospitals Corp.*, 280 F.3d 997 (9th Cir. 2002).

[63] H.R. Rep. No. 100–910, *supra* note 62, at 28; *see Litton Industries, Inc. v. Lehman Brothers Kuhn Loeb, Inc.*, 967 F.2d 742 (2d Cir. 1992).

group or index of securities including such security, shall also violate and result in comparable liability *to any purchaser or seller of that security* under such provision, rule or regulation.[64]

Section 20(d)'s effect is to provide, within the confines of *Chiarella* and *Dirks*, an option-trading plaintiff with a private right of action against an inside trader of options.[65] Note, however, that a distinct issue is presented as to whether an *option* trader has a private cause of action against an inside *stock* trader. Section 20(d) does not resolve this issue. The lower federal courts are divided.[66]

§ 12.06 DAMAGES AND PENALTIES

[A]   Damages — Section 10(b) Actions

The measure of damages for insider trading in open market transactions under Section 10(b) has received diverse treatment from the relatively few courts that have considered the issue. *Shapiro v. Merrill Lynch, Pierce, Fenner & Smith, Inc.*[67] represents an expansive approach. There, the Second Circuit, relying on *Affiliated Ute Citizens v. United States*,[68] stated that "[t]he proper test to determine whether causation in fact has been established in a nondisclosure case is 'whether the plaintiff would have been influenced to act differently than he did if the defendant had disclosed to him the undisclosed fact.'"[69] After finding that causation in fact had been established (notwithstanding that all transactions occurred on a national securities exchange), the court formulated a potentially broad measure of damages:

> [W]e hold that defendants are liable in this private action for damages to plaintiffs who, during the same period that defendants traded in or recommended trading in Douglas common stock, purchased Douglas stock in the open market without knowledge of the material inside information which was in the possession of defendants.[70]

Having so held, the Second Circuit, however, left to the district court's discretion the proper measure of damages, noting its concern with the potential for draconian liability.[71]

---

[64] 15 U.S.C. § 78t(d) (emphasis supplied).

[65] *See* Thel, *Section 20(d) of the Securities Exchange Act: Congress, The Supreme Court, the SEC and the Process of Defining Insider Trading*, 69 N.C. L. Rev. 1261 (1991); Wang, *A Cause of Action for Option Traders Against Insider Option Traders*, 101 Harv. L. Rev. 1056 (1988).

[66] *Compare Deutschman v. Beneficial Corp.*, 841 F.2d 502 (3d Cir. 1988) (providing a right of action), *with Laventhall v. General Dynamics Corp.*, 704 F.2d 407 (8th Cir. 1983) (not permitting suit). *See generally* Joo, *Legislation and Legitimation — Congress and Insider Trading in the 1980s*, 82 Ind. L.J. 575 (2007).

[67] 495 F.2d 228 (2d Cir. 1974).

[68] 406 U.S. 128 (1972).

[69] 495 F.2d at 239.

[70] *Id.* at 241.

[71] *Id.*

In *Fridrich v. Bradford,*[72] the Sixth Circuit rejected the *Shapiro* analysis. Disagreeing with the Second Circuit, the *Fridrich* court found that the plaintiffs had failed to show that their loss was caused by the defendants' inside trading. The Sixth Circuit supported its holding by pointing out that an award of damages to contemporaneous traders in the open market would create a windfall for fortuitous investors while being essentially punitive. Although the court recognized that it could limit the amount of recovery to the defendants' profits, it declined to do so.[73]

Subsequently, in *Elkind v. Liggett & Myers, Inc.*[74] the Second Circuit, although not expressly rejecting the *Shapiro* rationale, greatly limited the potential damages recovery. There, the court considered three alternative measures of damages: (1) out-of-pocket, (2) market-repercussion, and (3) disgorgement. Rejecting the out-of-pocket measure, the court pointed out that this measure is normally directed toward compensating a trader for damages which are directly traceable to the defendant's perpetration of a fraud upon the trader. In an impersonal open market, however, "uninformed traders . . . are not induced by representations on the part of the tipper or tippee to buy or sell."[75] Secondly, the Second Circuit observed that the out-of-pocket measure posed serious proof problems as the "value" of the stock traded during the period of nondisclosure can often be hypothetical. Lastly, the court concluded that the out-of-pocket measure had the potential for the imposition of "draconian, exorbitant damages, out of all proportion to the wrong committed."[76]

The *Elkind* court also rejected the market-repercussion theory of damages. This measure would allow recovery of damages caused by erosion of the stock's market price that is traceable to the defendant's wrongful trading. The rationale underlying the theory is that "if the market price is not affected by the [defendant's] trading, the uninformed investor is in the same position as he would have been had the insider abstained from trading." Upon analysis, the Second Circuit rejected this theory due to the difficult problems of proof it would impose on plaintiffs and that adoption of the theory would frequently preclude recovery for an insider's breach of his/her duty to disclose the confidential information prior to trading.[77]

The *Elkind* court thereupon adopted a third alternative, the disgorgement measure of damages. This measure also is the proper measure of damages under Section 20A for contemporaneous traders who trade on the opposite side of the transaction from the defendant.[78] Under the *Elkind* formulation, the measure of damages is as follows:

---

[72] 542 F.2d 307 (6th Cir. 1976).

[73] *Id.* at 318–22.

[74] 635 F.2d 156 (2d Cir. 1980).

[75] *Id.* at 169.

[76] *Id.* at 170.

[77] *Id.* at 171.

[78] *See* H.R. Rep. No. 100–910, note 63 *supra*; discussion § 12.05 *supra.*

(1) [T]o allow any uninformed investor, where a reasonable investor would either have delayed his purchase or not purchased at all if he had the benefit of the tipped information, to recover any post-purchase decline in market value of his shares up to a reasonable time after he learns of the tipped information or after there is a public disclosure of it but (2) limit his recovery to the amount gained by the [subject violator] as a result of his selling at the earlier date rather than delaying his sale until the parties could trade on an equal informational basis. . . . Should the intervening buyers, because of the volume and price of their purchases, claim more than the [subject violator's] gain, their recovery (limited to that gain) would be shared *pro rata*.[79]

[B]   Penalties

A number of different parties may be subject to a variety of monetary penalties under the federal securities laws for engaging in illegal insider trading. These parties may include actual traders, their tippers, as well as broker-dealers and investment advisers (when they fail to take appropriate steps to prevent the insider trading violation(s) or fail to maintain and enforce policies and procedures reasonably designed to prevent the occurrence of such trading). Penalties that may be levied in this context are (1) requiring the subject party to "disgorge" the ill-gotten profits (or loss avoided) in an SEC enforcement action,[80] (2) subjecting individuals to a criminal fine and imprisonment,[81] and (3) in an SEC enforcement action, within a court's discretion, ordering the subject party to pay into the United States Treasury a treble damages penalty amounting to three times the profit gained or loss avoided.[82] These penalties, together with the imposition of jail terms and the availability of civil damages, are intended to strongly deter insider trading. As an additional measure to combat insider trading, the SEC may award "bounties" (up to ten percent of the amount disgorged or monetary penalty imposed) to persons who provide information concerning insider trading violations.[83]

---

[79] 635 F.2d at 172. *See generally* Dougherty, *A [Dis]semblance of Privity: Criticizing the Contemporaneous Trader Requirement in Insider Trading*, 24 Del. J. Corp. L. 83 (1999).

[80] *See, e.g.*, *SEC v. Commonwealth Chemical Securities, Inc.*, 574 F.2d 90, 102–03 (2d Cir. 1978); *see* § 15.05[D] *infra.*

[81] *See* Section 32(a) of the Exchange Act, 15 U.S.C. § 78ff(a) (as amended by the Insider Trading and Securities Fraud Enforcement Act of 1988); 18 U.S.C. § 1348 (as enacted pursuant to the Sarbanes-Oxley Act of 2002).

[82] *See* Section 21A of the Exchange Act, 15 U.S.C. § 78u-1.

[83] *See* Section 21A(e) of the Exchange Act, 15 U.S.C. § 78u-1(e); authorities cited note 13 *supra*. For discussion on liability of controlling persons in this context, see Steinberg & Fletcher, *Compliance Programs for Insider Trading*, 47 SMU L. Rev. 1783, 1788–89 (1994):

> To recover these penalties [under the 1988 legislation], the Commission must prove that the controlling person "knew or recklessly disregarded the fact that such controlled person was likely to engage in the act or acts constituting the violation and failed to take appropriate steps to prevent such act or acts before they occurred." . . .
>
> If the controlling person is a broker-dealer or investment advisor, [the 1988 legislation] provides the Commission with more potent ammunition for imposing the new

§ 12.07   RULE 14e-3

Subsequent to the Supreme Court's decision in *Chiarella*, the SEC, in an effort to regulate insider and tippee trading in the tender offer context, adopted Rule 14e-3 which establishes a "disclose or abstain from trading" rule under Section 14(e) of the Exchange Act. As adopted, with certain exceptions, Rule 14e-3 applies this disclose-or-abstain provision to the possession of material information relating to a tender offer where the person knows or has reason to know that the information is nonpublic and was received directly or indirectly from the offeror, the subject corporation, any of their affiliated persons, or any person acting on behalf of either company. Moreover, the rule contains a broad anti-tipping provision and provides for certain exceptions pertaining to sales to the offeror and to certain activities by multiservice financial institutions.[84]

In this regard, the rule exempts purchases and sales by multiservice financial institutions, such as broker-dealers, if it can be shown that "the individuals making the investment decision did not know the nonpublic information and that the [broker-dealer] had established policies and procedures, reasonable under the circumstances, to ensure that its [employees] would not violate [the] rule." Such procedures may "include Chinese Walls and restricted-list procedures designed to prevent individual decisionmakers from learning or using such information."[85]

In the release adopting Rule 14e-3, the Commission asserted that *Chiarella* did not limit its authority under Section 14(e) to prescribe such a mandate regulating insider trading in the tender offer context.[86] As applied to the facts presented in the cases thus far decided, Rule 14e-3 has been upheld, including by the Supreme Court in *O'Hagan*.[87] Limiting its holding to the charges brought against O'Hagan, the Supreme Court upheld Rule 14e-3's validity

---

monetary penalties. [It] sets forth an affirmative duty on broker-dealers and investment advisors to maintain adequate procedures to protect against insider trading and it defines a separate standard for controlling person liability in reference to that duty. First, [the legislation] added Section 15(f) of the Exchange Act and Section 204A of the Investment Advisors Act of 1940 which impose an affirmative duty on broker-dealers and investment advisors to maintain "written policies and procedures reasonably designed" to prevent insider trading violations. Second, Section 21A(b)(1)(B) subjects broker-dealers and investment advisors to controlling person liability if they "knowingly or recklessly failed to establish, maintain, or enforce" those procedures and "such failure substantially contributed to or permitted the occurrence" of the insider trading violation.

For further discussion, see *infra* note 85 and accompanying text.

[84] Securities Exchange Act Release No. 17120 (1980). Note that Rule 14e-3 becomes applicable when "a substantial step" has been taken "in connection with" a tender offer, even if in fact a tender offer is not ultimately made. *See SEC v. Mayhew*, 121 F.3d 44 (2d Cir. 1997).

[85] W. Wang & M. Steinberg, Insider Trading, *supra* note 9, at § 9.2; *see Koppers Co., Inc. v. American Express Co.*, 689 F. Supp. 1371, 1413 (W.D. Pa. 1988); SEC Division of Market Regulation, *Broker-Dealer Policies and Procedures Designed to Segment the Flow and Prevent the Misuse of Material Nonpublic Information*, [1989–1990 Transfer Binder] Fed. Sec. L. Rep. (CCH) ¶ 84,520 (1990); Poser, *Conflicts of Interest Within Securities Firms*, 16 Brook. J. Int'l L. 111 (1990).

[86] *See* Securities Exchange Act Release No. 17120 (1980).

[87] *See United States v. O'Hagan*, 521 U.S. 642, 672–73 (1997); *United States v. Chestman*, 947 F.2d 551, 559, 563 (2d Cir. 1991) (en banc).

without requiring proof that a fiduciary duty was breached. The Court stated:

> [I]t is a fair assumption that trading on the basis of material, nonpublic information will often involve a breach of a duty of confidentiality to the bidder or target company or their representatives. The SEC, cognizant of the proof problem that could enable sophisticated traders to escape responsibility, placed in Rule 14e-3(a) a "disclose or abstain from trading" command that does not require specific proof of a breach of fiduciary duty. That prescription, we are satisfied, applied to this case, is a "means reasonably designed to prevent" fraudulent trading on material, nonpublic information in the tender offer context.[88]

§ 12.08 THE MAIL AND WIRE FRAUD STATUTES

Although not available to the SEC, the mail and wire fraud statutes, as seen from the Supreme Court's decision in *Carpenter v. United States*,[89] are potent weapons in the U.S. Attorney's arsenal to combat alleged criminal offenses involving insider trading. These statutes prohibit the use of the mails or the use of "wire communication" in furtherance of a scheme to defraud.[90] Moreover, these statutes constitute predicate offenses under RICO,[91] thereby providing the U.S. Attorney with enhanced prosecutorial powers in this setting.[92]

§ 12.09 BLACKOUT PERIODS — INSIDER TRADING PROHIBITIONS

As set forth in the Sarbanes-Oxley Act, directors and executive officers of a publicly-held enterprise may not trade any equity security of the subject enterprise, acquired through the scope of employment, during a "blackout" period. Violation of this directive gives rise to both private and government (e.g., SEC) redress. The SEC has adopted Regulation BTR to govern this prohibition against insider trading during blackout periods. This subject is addressed at greater length in Chapter 5 of the text (*see* § 5.08[G], [R][3] *supra*).

---

[88] 521 U.S. at 676.

[89] 484 U.S. 19 (1987); *see United States v. Bryan*, 58 F.3d 933 (4th Cir. 1995) (rejecting application of misappropriation theory under § 10(b) but affirming convictions based on mail and wire fraud).

[90] 18 U.S.C. §§ 1341, 1343; *see Schmuck v. United States*, 489 U.S. 705 (1989); *Carpenter v. United States*, 484 U.S. 19 (1987); *Pereira v. United States*, 347 U.S. 1 (1954).

[91] *See* 18 U.S.C. § 1961. RICO is discussed in § 9.08 *supra*.

[92] *See* W. Wang & M. Steinberg, *supra* note 9, at § 11.1 et seq.

§ 12.10   SECTION 16 — "SHORT-SWING" TRADING

[A]   Overview

Section 16 of the Exchange Act applies to directors, officers, and beneficial owners of more than ten percent of any class of equity security of an issuer (other than an exempted security),[93] with such class of equity security having been registered pursuant to Section 12(b) or 12(g) of the Exchange Act.[94] The statute seeks to deter insider trading based on the use of material nonpublic information by such persons. Section 16 contains three key provisions in attempting to meet this objective.

1. Section 16(a) of the Exchange Act requires that, upon becoming an officer, director, or ten percent equity shareholder of a Section 12(b) or 12(g) issuer, such individual must file with the SEC (and with the self-regulatory organization (SRO) with which the stock is listed or traded) a report disclosing the number of the corporation's shares beneficially owned. Subsequent reports must be filed on a timely basis to reflect changes in the number of shares beneficially owned (note that the Sarbanes-Oxley Act requires that such reports now must be filed with the SEC by the end of the second business day following the execution of the transaction — *see* discussion § 5.08[J] *supra*).

2. Section 16(c) prohibits such insiders to transact short sales in their issuers' equity securities.

3. Generally, "Section 16(b) is designed to permit the corporation or a security holder bringing an action upon behalf of the corporation to recover for the benefit of the corporation short-swing profits arising from the purchase [and sale or sale and purchase] by insiders within any six-month period of equity securities of the company."[95]

Under Section 16(b), an irrebuttable presumption is created when "insiders" engage in such short-swing transactions. The profits that the insider gained from the transaction(s) are recoverable by the issuer in a suit initiated by it, or if it declines to do so, in a properly instituted shareholder's suit expressly authorized by the statute. In view of the broad remedial nature of the statute, a strict formula for computing "profit realized" has been established. Such a formula is designed "to squeeze all possible profits out of stock transactions, and thus to establish a standard so high as to prevent any conflict between the selfish interest of a fiduciary officer, director, or stockholder and the faithful performance of his duty."[96] The formula established matches the lowest price "in" with the highest price "out," thus

---

[93] Exempt securities for purposes of Section 16 include, for example, municipal bonds, obligations of the United States, and securities issued in connection with certain employee benefit plans. *See* Securities Exchange Act Release No. 18114 (1981).

[94] Hence, these equity securities are either listed on a national securities exchange (§ 12(b)) or are securities of an issuer having at least 500 shareholders of record and $10 million in total assets (§ 12(g) and Rule 12g-1).

[95] H. Bloomenthal, Securities Law 365 (1966).

[96] *Smolowe v. Delendo Corp.*, 136 F.2d 231 (2d Cir. 1943).

ensuring recovery of all possible profits. In fact, this formula can yield a profit when in actuality a loss has been suffered.[97]

Moreover, an insider's intent to profit under a transaction that falls within Section 16(b)'s scope need not be shown in order for there to be recovery. As the Seventh Circuit (as well as other courts) pointed out, an insider is "deemed capable of structuring his dealings to avoid any possibility of taint and therefore must bear the risks of any inadvertent miscalculation."[98] In some situations, however, the courts, by finding that certain unorthodox transactions do not constitute the predicate purchase or sale, have displayed a judicial reluctance to impose liability under Section 16(b) where no congressional purpose would be served.[99]

[B]   Relevant Issues

The issues dealing with the construction of Section 16(b), at times, are complex. The following discussion seeks to highlight the key concepts. For more extensive treatment, other sources should be consulted.[100]

[1]   Beneficial Ownership and the Concept of Attribution

A significant problem that arises with respect to the concepts of attribution and beneficial ownership in the context of Section 16(b) is in attempting to determine whether, and the extent to which, a corporate insider will be liable for short-swing trading profits when the securities are held by another person, group, or organization. This issue may arise, for example, within the context of family-related transactions, of a related trust, of a partnership in which the insider is a partner, or of a corporation in which the insider is an officer, director or shareholder. The question becomes one of the responsibility of the corporate insider for the acts of such parties and his/her relationship with these other parties.

The definition of "beneficial owner" for purposes of Section 16(b) focuses on whether the insider has a pecuniary interest. Subject to certain exceptions, Rule 16a-1(a)(2) defines "beneficial owner" as "any person who, directly or indirectly, through any contract, arrangement, understanding, relationship or otherwise, has or shares direct or indirect pecuniary interest in the equity securities." Under the SEC rules, a person has such a pecuniary interest when he/she has an opportunity to share in any profit generated from the subject securities transactions. On a non-exclusive basis, the rules provide a number of situations where an individual is deemed to have such an indirect interest. As

---

[97] *See Morales v. Consolidated Oil & Gas, Inc.*, [1982 Transfer Binder] Fed. Sec. L. Rep. (CCH) ¶ 98,796 (S.D.N.Y. 1982).

[98] *Bershad v. McDonough*, 428 F.2d 693, 696 (7th Cir. 1970); *see Whiting v. Dow Chemical Co.*, 523 F.2d 680, 687 (2d Cir. 1975) ("[T]he unwary who fall within [§ 16(b's)] terms have no one but themselves to blame.").

[99] *See, e.g., Kern County Land Co. v. Occidental Petroleum Corp.*, 411 U.S. 582 (1973).

[100] *See, e.g.,* P. Romeo & A. Dye, Section 16 Treatise and Reporting Guide (2008).

one example, securities held by a member of an insider's "immediate family," who shares the same household as such insider, creates a presumption (that is rebuttable) that the insider beneficially owns the securities.[101]

Although the SEC's rules define the term "beneficial ownership" for purposes of Section 16, they leave a number of issues unresolved. Moreover, the Commission's approach is not binding on the courts. Therefore, case law remains important.

The cases involving beneficial ownership and the concept of attribution have failed to provide clear standards. Nonetheless, two important factors are (1) whether the insider exercised control over the securities and (2) the insider's ability to benefit, directly or indirectly, from the profits generated from the short-swing transactions.[102] On the other hand, the Seventh Circuit has applied a more restrictive analysis. Rather than focusing on control over the securities, the court looked to whether the insider stood to receive a direct monetary benefit from the subject transactions. The court held that

> profit realized by a corporate insider [for purposes of Section 16(b)] means direct pecuniary benefit to the insider. . . . [I]t is not enough that ties of affinity and consanguinity between the . . . recipient and the insider make it likely that the insider will experience an enhanced sense of well-being as a result of the receipt, or will be led to reduce his gift-giving to the recipient.[103]

[2]   Directors

Directors and any person performing similar functions (irrespective of whether the business organization is incorporated) are subject to Section 16(b). A key issue in this setting is whether a business organization can be viewed as a director of another entity by virtue of that organization having a representative on the latter entity's board of directors.

Generally, the courts have answered the above question affirmatively, holding that a corporation may "deputize" one of its directors or other person to serve on a second corporation's board. For example, the Second Circuit in *Feder v. Martin Marietta Corp.*[104] imposed liability based on the deputization theory. There, the court found that the president and chief executive officer of Martin Marietta had been "deputized by or represented" Martin Marietta during the time he served as a director of Sperry Rand. Therefore, the court concluded that Martin Marietta was in effect a director of Sperry Rand and

---

[101] *See* Securities Exchange Act Release No. 28869, [1990–1991 Transfer Binder] Fed. Sec. L. Rep. (CCH) ¶ 84,709 (1991).

[102] *See, e.g., Whittaker v. Whittaker Corp.*, 639 F.2d 516 (9th Cir. 1981); *Whiting v. Dow Chemical Co.*, 523 F.2d 680, 688 (2d Cir. 1975); *Atamil Corp. v. Pryor*, 405 F. Supp. 1222 (S.D. Ind. 1975).

[103] *CBI Industries, Inc. v. Horton*, 682 F.2d 643, 646 (7th Cir. 1982).

[104] 406 F.2d 260 (2d Cir. 1969). For more recent cases that address the deputization theory, see *Roth v. Perseus LLC*, 522 F.3d 242 (2d Cir. 2008); *Dreiling v. American Express Co.*, 458 F.3d 942 (9th Cir. 2006).

was forced to disgorge the profits it acquired in the short-swing trading of Sperry Rand stock.

[3] Officers

In determining whether an individual is an officer for Section 16 purposes, Rule 16a-1(f) focuses on whether such person performs significant policy-making functions. Consistent with this perspective, the rule specifically includes those individuals who clearly hold policy-making duties, such as the company's president, principal financial officer, and any vice-president in charge of a key business division.[105]

The SEC's position on this issue basically follows case law. The focus of the inquiry in ascertaining who is an officer for purposes of Section 16 is upon an individual's functions and responsibilities within the organizational structure. This matter can arise in several different settings. Primarily, however, the issue is whether one, lacking in a title representing him/her as an officer, nevertheless in fact had that status, or, conversely, whether one having the title of officer, for example as vice president, had a role so devoid of decision-making functions that he/she could not in reality be called an officer within the meaning of Section 16. For example, the Ninth Circuit has opined:

> [T]he title "Vice President" does no more than raise an inference that the person who holds the title has the executive duties and the opportunities for confidential information that the title implies. The inference can be overcome by proof that the title was merely honorary and did not carry with it any of the executive responsibilities that otherwise might be assumed.[106]

[4] Ten Percent Beneficial Owners

Unlike the situation for directors and officers, Section 16(b) imposes liability on a ten percent beneficial owner if that person had that status both when the securities were acquired and when they were sold. Hence, in *Foremost-McKesson, Inc. v. Provident Securities Co.*,[107] the Supreme Court held that "in a purchase-sale sequence, a beneficial owner must account for profits only if he was a beneficial owner before the purchase."[108] And, in *Reliance Electric Co. v. Emerson Electric Co.*,[109] the high Court ruled that liability pursuant to Section 16(b) normally cannot be based on a beneficial owner's sale of securities which takes place after his/her ownership was reduced to less than ten percent. This is so, even if at the time when the seller owned more than ten percent of the stock, he/she deliberately structured two separate transactions so as to reduce the extent of liability. For example, the first such sale transaction could be arranged so as to result in the beneficial owner holding

---

[105] 17 C.F.R. § 240.16a1(f).

[106] *Merrill Lynch, Pierce Fenner and Smith v. Livingston*, 566 F.2d 1119, 1122 (9th Cir. 1978).

[107] 423 U.S. 232 (1976).

[108] *Id.* at 250.

[109] 404 U.S. 418 (1972).

9.9% of the company's stock. In the second transaction, the beneficial owner could sell the remaining shares. Provided that in such a two-stage transaction the sales are not "legally tied" to one another,[110] the beneficial owner under *Reliance* is liable under Section 16(b) only as to the first transaction.[111]

[5]   Objective Approach vs. Pragmatic Approach

Persons are subject to Section 16(b) liability only if they engage in a "purchase" and "sale" or "sale" and "purchase" of a subject security within a six-month period. As such, an insider's liability may turn upon whether there indeed has been a "purchase" and "sale" within Section 16(b)'s scope.

The traditional and still commonly used approach is objective. The "objective" approach works in a mechanical fashion. Courts applying it neither will inquire into an insider's reasons for engaging in the transaction nor will they ascertain his/her access to or use of inside information. Consequently, any transaction that can be viewed as a "purchase" or "sale" and brought within the ambit of the statute will result in liability.[112]

Due to its unfair consequences in certain situations, the objective approach is subject to criticism. As a result, the "pragmatic" approach has been employed in certain "unorthodox" transactions, such as stock reclassifications, dealings in options, warrants, and rights, stock conversions, and exchanges pursuant to mergers. As stated by one commentator:

> The pragmatic approach involves a number of elements. First, and most important, it applies only in certain unusual circumstances. If these circumstances exist, then the transaction is characterized as "unorthodox." Unorthodox transactions are ill-defined, but they usually have peculiar features that either make it unfair to apply Section 16(b) or make it difficult to determine whether or when a purchase or sale has taken place.[113]

The pragmatic approach received Supreme Court approbation in *Kern County Land Co. v. Occidental Petroleum Corp.*[114] The Court reasoned:

> In deciding whether borderline transactions are within the reach of the statute, the courts have come to inquire whether the transaction may serve as a vehicle for the veil which Congress sought to prevent — the realization of short-swing profits based upon access to inside information — thereby endeavoring to implement Congressional objectives without extending the reach of the statute beyond its intended limits. . . . [T]he prevailing view is to apply the statute only when its

---

[110] *Id.* at 421; *see Reece Corp. v. Walco National Corp.*, [1981–1982 Transfer Binder] Fed. Sec. L. Rep. (CCH) ¶ 98,289 (S.D.N.Y. 1981).

[111] 404 U.S. at 422–25.

[112] *See, e.g., Park and Tilford, Inc. v. Shulte*, 160 F.2d 984 (2d Cir. 1947).

[113] Tomlinson, *Section 16(b): A Single Analysis of Purchases and Sales — Merging the Objective and Pragmatic Analyses*, 1981 Duke L.J. 941, 947.

[114] 411 U.S. 582 (1973).

application would serve its goals. . . . [I]n interpreting the terms "purchase" and "sale," courts have properly asked whether the particular type of transaction is one that gives rise to speculative abuse.[115]

Several courts have employed the pragmatic approach in a variety of contexts. Using this approach, Section 16(b) liability has been imposed in some cases[116] but not in others.[117] From these cases as well as from the scholarly commentary, the key inquiries in applying the pragmatic approach include:

(1) Is the transaction in question of a type that may be characterized as unorthodox?

(2) Did the insider have control over the timing of the decision involved in the transaction?

(3) Did the insider have access to inside information, irrespective of whether that information was in fact used?[118]

Importantly, "the law is clear that the pragmatic approach is used to determine the boundaries of Section 16(b)'s definitional scope only in borderline situations, particularly those involving unorthodox transactions."[119] When a subject transaction is deemed as clearly coming within Section 16(b)'s language, the objective approach is to be applied.[120]

---

[115] *Id.* at 594–95 (citations omitted).

[116] *See, e.g., Colan v. Mesa Petroleum Co.*, 951 F.2d 1512 (9th Cir. 1991); *Texas International Airlines v. National Airlines, Inc.*, 714 F.2d 533 (5th Cir. 1983).

[117] *See, e.g., At Home Corp. v. Cox Communications, Inc.*, 446 F.3d 403 (2d Cir. 2006); *Heublein, Inc. v. General Cinema Corp.*, 722 F.2d 29 (2d Cir. 1983).

[118] W. Wang & M. Steinberg, *supra* note 9, at § 14.1 et seq. (and authorities cited therein); Tomlinson, *supra* note 113, at 949. *See generally* A. Jacobs, Section 16 of the Securities Exchange Act (2008); P. Romeo & A. Dye, Section 16 Treatise and Reporting Guide (2008); Ferber, *Short-Swing Transactions Under the Securities Exchange Act*, 16 Rev. Sec. Reg. 801 (1983); Hazen, *The New Pragmatism of Section 16(b) of the Securities Exchange Act of 1934*, 54 N.C. L. Rev. 1 (1975); O'Conner, *Toward a More Efficient Deterrence of Insider Trading: The Repeal of Section 16(b)*, 58 Fordham L. Rev. 309 (1989); Steinberg & Lansdale, *The Judicial and Regulatory Constriction of Section 16(b) of the Securities Exchange Act of 1934*, 68 Notre Dame L. Rev. 33 (1992); Taylor, *Teaching an Old Law New Tricks: Rethinking Section 16*, 39 Ariz. L. Rev. 1315 (1997); Thel, *The Genius of Section 16: Regulating the Management of Publicly Held Companies*, 42 Hastings L.J. 391 (1991); Tomlinson, *Section 16(b): A Single Analysis of Purchases and Sales — Merging the Objective and Pragmatic Analyses*, 1981 Duke L.J. 941; Wentz, *Refining a Crude Thumb: The Pragmatic Approach to Section 16(b) of the Securities Exchange Act of 1934*, 70 Nw. U. L. Rev. 221 (1975).

[119] *Gund v. First Florida Banks, Inc.*, 726 F.2d 682, 686 (11th Cir. 1984) (citations omitted).

[120] *See* sources cited in W. Wang & M. Steinberg, *supra* note 9, at § 14.10.

Chapter 13

BROKER-DEALER REGULATION

§ 13.01 OVERVIEW

Preceding chapters have discussed the availability of private rights of action under various provisions of the Securities Acts. Broker-dealers, of course, may be subject to primary liability if their misconduct falls within the parameters of these provisions. Under Section 11(a)(5) of the Securities Act, for example, if a broker-dealer acts as an underwriter with respect to a registered offering, such broker-dealer would be subject to liability for material misstatements or omissions contained in the registration statement.[1] In response, the broker-dealer may assert the Section 11(b)(3) due diligence defense. As an underwriter, however, the broker-dealer would be subject to the strengthened due diligence requirement outlined in *Escott v. BarChris Construction Corporation*.[2]

Under Section 12 of the Securities Act, a broker-dealer would be liable for making an offer or sale of securities either in violation of the Section 5 registration requirements or the making of a material misrepresentation or half-truth contained in a prospectus (or oral communication relating to such prospectus). Earlier material discussed the construction that the Supreme Court has given the terms "seller" and "prospectus" under Section 12.[3] A dealer, by definition, would fall within Section 12's definition of "seller" if it acts as principal. A broker becomes a "seller" under Section 12 when, acting as an agent, it successfully solicits the transaction. As with Section 11, the broker-dealer has a diligence-based defense against Section 12(a)(2) liability. The broker-dealer may defend by showing that it exercised "reasonable care," a standard that, as applied by some courts, may require a stringent showing.[4] Note, moreover, the issue whether Section 12(a)(2) may be invoked in the secondary trading markets against such parties as broker-dealers has been resolved by the Supreme Court in *Gustafson* (where the Court held that Section 12(a)(2) applies only to public offerings by an issuer or its controlling shareholders).[5]

---

[1] *See, e.g., Feit v. Leasco Data Processing Equipment Corp.*, 332 F. Supp. 544 (E.D.N.Y. 1971).

[2] 283 F. Supp. 643 (S.D.N.Y. 1968); *see* discussion §§ 7.02, 7.04 *supra*.

[3] *Gustafson v. Alloyd Company*, 513 U.S. 561 (1995), *discussed in*, § 7.09[A], [D] *supra; Pinter v. Dahl*, 486 U.S. 622 (1988), *discussed in*, § 7.09[B] *supra*.

[4] *See Sanders v. John Nuveen & Co.*, 619 F.2d 1222 (7th Cir. 1982); discussion § 7.09[E] *supra*.

[5] *Gustafson v. Alloyd Company*, 513 U.S. 561 (1995), *discussed in*, § 7.09[A], [D] *supra*.

Broker-dealers are subject to a number of other provisions. For example, Section 17(a) of the Securities Act and Section 15(c) of the Exchange Act are potent enforcement weapons against broker-dealers who engage in fraud in the offer or sale of securities.[6] Additionally, the insider trading provisions similarly affect the activities of broker-dealers.[7]

Moreover, a broker-dealer may be subject to liability under the Section 10(b) antifraud provision[8] as well as secondary liability principles.[9] As discussed in Chapter 9, broker-dealers also may incur liability under state securities and common law. The material in this chapter addresses special concepts and theories of liability with regard to broker-dealers.

Also, it should be pointed out that brokers and dealers must register under both federal and state law.[10] In addition, depending on the amount of assets under management, investment advisers must register under federal law or state law.[11] The failure to register may result in government enforcement action, including criminal prosecution. Also, plaintiffs may seek relief in private litigation based on a broker-dealer's failure to register. The Fifth Circuit's decision in *Regional Properties* (*see* § 9.06) serves as an example of relief being afforded to the plaintiffs even where the broker-dealer's failure to register caused the plaintiffs no harm.

Note also that broker-dealer regulation is subject to self-regulatory organization (SRO) oversight. The key SRO regulator is the Financial Industry Regulatory Authority (FINRA).

Sections 5, 6, 15A, 17A, and 19 of the Exchange Act contain the general federal regulatory framework for SROs. For example, Sections 6 and 15A require adoption of rules governing the admission and conduct of an SRO's members; and Section 19(b) and (g) addresses the SEC oversight and the SRO enforcement of these rules. If a broker-dealer runs afoul of an SRO rule, such broker-dealer is subject to sanctions. However, private litigants may not sue for damages under the federal securities laws for broker-dealer violations of SRO

---

[6] *See United States v. Naftalin*, 441 U.S. 768 (1979), *discussed in*, § 9.04 *supra*.

[7] *See* §§ 12.01-12.08 *supra*.

[8] *See* Chapter 8 *supra*; *see also* SEC Regulation NMS, Securities Exchange Act Release No. 51808, [2005 Transfer Binder] Fed. Sec. L. Rep. (CCH) ¶ 87,414 (2005) ("Regulations NMS includes new substantive rules that are designed to modernize and strengthen the regulatory structure of the U.S. equity markets.").

[9] *See* Chapter 10 *supra*.

[10] *See* R. Janvey, Regulation of the Securities and Commodities Markets ¶¶ 4.01-4.02 (1992); D. Lipton, Broker-Dealer Regulation (1990); Lipton, *A Primer on Broker-Dealer Regulation*, 36 Cath. U. L. Rev. 899 (1987).

[11] *See* Bagnall & Cannon, *The National Securities Markets Improvement Act of 1996: Summary and Analysis*, 25 Sec. Reg. L.J. 3, 13–15 (1997) (pointing out that under the 1996 federal legislation "investment advisers with assets under management of $25 million or more and advisers to [SEC] registered investment companies will fall exclusively under [SEC] jurisdiction" but that states still retain their enforcement powers against such advisers or associated persons where fraud has been committed); Friedman, *The Impact of NSMIA on State Regulation of Broker-Dealers and Investment Advisers*, 53 Bus. Law. 511 (1998).

rules.[12]

Also, many aspects of broker-dealer regulation and liability have been discussed in previous chapters. In examining the issues contained in this chapter, the materials in earlier parts of the text should be consulted. As further illustrations:

(1) With respect to the duty of a broker-dealer to register with the SEC and with the states and private liability ramifications for the failure to do so, see the *Regional Properties* case in § 9.06 *supra.*

(2) Broker-dealer liability for insider trading is addressed throughout Chapter 12 as well as the imposition upon a broker-dealer or investment adviser of a treble monetary penalty based upon the illegal inside trading of a controlled person.

(3) Defenses that a broker-dealer may raise, such as *in pari delicto*, are discussed in §§ 8.10, 9.06 *supra.*

(4) Secondary liability of broker-dealers for aiding and abetting, as control persons, and under *respondeat superior* is addressed in Chapter 10. Note that the SEC has express statutory authority to proceed in the broker-dealer and investment adviser contexts on the basis of aider and abettor liability principles.

Broker-dealers thus are subject to vigorous SEC oversight, including the bringing of enforcement actions. This subject is addressed in Chapter 15.

§ 13.02   ARBITRATION

[A]   Key Supreme Court Decisions

In *Shearson/American Express, Inc. v. McMahon,*[13] the Supreme Court held that pre-dispute arbitration agreements between brokerage firms and their customers did not contravene the Securities Exchange Act and the Racketeer Influenced and Corrupt Organizations Act (RICO). Hence, such claims ordinarily are arbitrable consistent with the terms of the applicable arbitration agreement. The following discussion focuses on the validity of such pre-dispute arbitration agreements under the securities laws.

---

[12] Early authority on the issue was mixed. *Compare Buttrey v. Merrill Lynch, Pierce, Fenner & Smith, Inc.,* 410 F.2d 135 (7th Cir. 1969) (allowing implied right), *with Plunkett v. Dominick & Dominick, Inc.,* 414 F. Supp. 885 (D. Conn. 1976) (rejecting implied right). Over the last three decades, as the Supreme Court has restricted the recognition of implied private rights of action, courts have uniformly rejected an implied private right of action for violations of SRO rules. *See, e.g., Carrott v. Shearson Hayden Stone, Inc.,* 724 F.2d 821 (9th Cir. 1984); *Thompson v. Smith Barney, Harris Upham & Co.,* 709 F.2d 1413 (11th Cir. 1983); *Jablon v. Dean Witter & Co.,* 614 F.2d 677 (9th Cir. 1980). For further discussion, see §§ 9.02–9.03, *supra.*

[13] 482 U.S. 220 (1987).

In *McMahon*, the Supreme Court relied in large part on the Federal Arbitration Act (FAA)[14] which establishes a "federal policy favoring arbitration."[15] This policy is prevalent even when a claim is based on a federal statutory right. As a consequence, the burden is on the party opposing the validity of the arbitration agreement to show that Congress intended to preserve the availability of a judicial forum, irrespective of the terms of an arbitration agreement.[16] Accordingly, in order to preclude application of the FAA, according to the Court, the party seeking to avoid arbitration "must demonstrate that Congress intended to make an exception to the Arbitration Act for claims arising under . . . the Exchange Act, an intention discernible from the text, history, or purposes of the statute."[17]

Upon examining Section 29(a) of the Exchange Act which renders void any stipulation whereby a person waives compliance with any 1934 Act provision, the Court opined that Section 29(a) only proscribes waiver of the Exchange Act's *substantive* obligations. By contrast, Section 29(a) does not preclude parties from waiving a judicial forum in favor of an arbitral tribunal.[18]

The Court's holding in *McMahon* takes a far different view of arbitration than its 1953 decision in *Wilko v. Swan*.[19] In holding that pre-dispute arbitration agreements were not enforceable in actions brought pursuant to Section 12(2) [now 12(a)(2)] of the Securities Act, the *Wilko* Court invoked the anti-waiver provision of the Securities Act, Section 14, which is Section 29(a)'s counterpart. Underlying the *Wilko* Court's holding was its hostility to the arbitration process. Succinctly put, the Court believed that arbitration would fail to protect the investor's substantive rights. As a consequence, a judicial forum was necessary to ensure that the statutory rights created by Section 12(2) would be adequately protected.[20]

Although declining to overrule *Wilko* at that time,[21] the Supreme Court in *McMahon* asserted that, in view of the increased regulatory oversight of arbitration since *Wilko* was handed down, a party's 1934 Act substantive rights are not waived by enforcing a predispute arbitration agreement. Pursuant to the 1975 Amendments to the 1934 Act, the SEC now "has broad authority to oversee and to regulate the rules adopted by the [self-regulatory

---

[14] 9 U.S.C. § 1 et seq.

[15] *Moses H. Cone Memorial Hospital v. Mercury Construction Corp.*, 460 U.S. 1, 24 (1983).

[16] 482 U.S. at 227, *relying on, Mitsubishi Motors Corp. v. Soler Chrysler-Plymouth, Inc.*, 473 U.S. 614 (1985); *Dean Witter Reynolds, Inc. v. Byrd*, 470 U.S. 213 (1985); *Scherk v. Alberto-Culber Co.*, 417 U.S. 506 (1974).

[17] 482 U.S. at 227.

[18] *Id.* at 228–38.

[19] 346 U.S. 427 (1953).

[20] *Id.* at 432–437. *See generally* Brown, Shell & Tyson, *Arbitration of Customer-Broker Disputes Arising Under the Federal Securities Laws and RICO*, 15 Sec. Reg. L.J. 3 (1987); Comment, *Predispute Arbitration Agreements Between Brokers and Investors: The Extension of Wilko to Section 10(b) Claims*, 46 Md. L. Rev. 339 (1987).

[21] 482 U.S. at 234 ("*[S]tare decisis* concerns may counsel against upsetting *Wilko's* contrary conclusion under the Securities Act").

organizations] relating to customer disputes, including the power to mandate the adoption of any rules it deems necessary to ensure that arbitration procedures adequately protect statutory rights."[22] Accordingly, the *McMahon* Court held:

> We conclude, therefore, that Congress did not intend for § 29(a) to bar enforcement of all predispute arbitration agreements. In this case, where the SEC has sufficient statutory authority to ensure that arbitration is adequate to vindicate Exchange Act rights, enforcement does not effect a waiver of "compliance with any provision" of the Exchange Act under § 29(a).[23]

Subsequently, in *Rodriguez De Quijas v. Shearson/American Express, Inc.*,[24] the Supreme Court overruled *Wilko*. Holding that predispute agreements to arbitrate claims under the Securities Act are enforceable, the Court stated:

> [I]n *McMahon* the Court declined to read § 29(a) of the Securities Exchange Act of 1934, the language of which is in every respect the same as that in § 14 of the 1933 Act, to prohibit enforcement of predispute agreements to arbitrate. The only conceivable distinction in this regard between the Securities Act and the Securities Exchange Act is that the former statute allows concurrent federal-state jurisdiction over causes of action and the latter statute provides for exclusive federal jurisdiction. But even if this distinction were thought to make any difference at all, it would suggest that arbitration agreements, which are "in effect, a specialized kind of forum-selection clause," . . . should not be prohibited under the Securities Act, since they, like the provision for concurrent jurisdiction, serve to advance the objective of allowing buyers of securities a broader right to select the forum for resolving disputes, whether it be judicial or otherwise. And in *McMahon* we explained at length why we rejected the *Wilko* Court's aversion to arbitration as a forum for resolving disputes over securities transactions, especially in light of the relatively recent expansion of the Securities and Exchange Commission's authority to oversee and to regulate those arbitration procedures. . . .[25]

---

[22] *Id.* at 233–34.

[23] *Id.* at 238. *But see id.* at 252–68 (Blackmun, J., concurring in part and dissenting in part).

[24] 490 U.S. 477 (1989).

[25] *Id.* at 482–83. Also, the Court in *Rodriguez* relied on the "strong language of the Arbitration Act" under which "the party opposing arbitration carries the burden of showing that Congress intended in a separate statute to preclude a waiver of judicial remedies, or that such a waiver of judicial remedies inherently conflicts with the underlying purposes of that other statute." *Id.* at 483. For other Supreme Court decisions in the securities arbitration area, see, *e.g.*, *Hall Street Associates, LLC v. Mattel, Inc.*, 128 S. Ct. 1396 (2008) (holding that in arbitrations conducted pursuant to the Federal Arbitration Act, parties not allowed to expand by contract grounds for judicial review); *Buckeye Check Cashing, Inc. v. Cardegna*, 546 U.S. 440 (2006) (holding that "regardless of whether the challenge is brought in federal or state court, a challenge to the validity of the contract as a whole, and not specifically to the arbitration clause, must go to the arbitrator"); *First Options of Chicago, Inc. v. Kaplan*, 514 U.S. 938 (1995) (holding that (1) issue whether parties

[B]   Aftermath of *McMahon* and *Rodriguez*

In the aftermath of *McMahon* and *Rodriguez*, many believe that securities arbitration favors the industry. As stated in a *New York Times* article: "The [brokerage] houses basically like the current system because they own the stacked deck."[26] A 1992 U.S. General Accounting Office Report on Securities Arbitration, however, does not agree: "GAO's analysis of statistical results of decisions in arbitration cases at both industry-sponsored and independent forums showed no indication of a pro-industry bias in decisions at industry-sponsored forums." Nonetheless, as Professor Wallace points out: "Given the prominence that securities arbitration enjoy[s], probing questions must be asked regarding the effectiveness [and] basic fairness of the procedures that effectuate it."[27]

Even though not finding a pro-industry bias, the GAO report nonetheless was critical, stating that "GAO's review of arbitration procedures showed that arbitration forums lacked internal controls to provide a reasonable level of assurance regarding either the independence of the arbitrators or their competence in arbitrating disputes." Needless to say, such lack of internal controls, as found by the GAO, bring into question the integrity of the arbitration process. A more recent study conducted by Professors Black and Gross similarly found that "broker-dealer clients involved in arbitration largely believe that arbitrators were competent and understood the issues, but they were less sure that the arbitrators were open-minded, impartial, and properly applying the law."[28]

Fortunately, certain improvements have been made. For example, in cases involving public customers, an arbitration panel consists of a majority of public arbitrators. The rules define those who qualify as public arbitrators to exclude, for instance, securities industry retirees. Such individuals may serve only as industry arbitrators comprising a minority of the panel. The rules also call for: preservation of a record of the proceeding; disclosure to the parties of certain

---

agreed to arbitrate a certain matter is question for the court to decide and (2) standard that court of appeals should apply when reviewing district court decision confirming an arbitration award "should proceed like review of any other district court decision . . . , i.e., accepting findings of fact that are not 'clearly erroneous' but deciding questions of law de novo"); *Mastrobuono v. Shearson Lehman Hutton, Inc.*, 515 U.S. 52 (1995) (holding that award of punitive damages in arbitration proceeding not precluded by terms of brokerage firm-client agreement where agreement did not expressly refer to punitive damages and was ambiguous in this regard, resulting in such ambiguity being construed against the drafter of the agreement — the brokerage firm). *See also Nielson v. Piper, Jaffray & Hopwood, Inc.*, 66 F.3d 145 (7th Cir. 1995) (applying NASD rule placing class actions outside the purview of otherwise enforceable arbitration agreements).

[26] Galberson, *When the Investor Has a Gripe*, N.Y. Times, March 29, 1987, at 1, 8; *see* Black, *Is Securities Arbitration Fair to Investors?*, 25 Pace L. Rev. 1 (2004); Johnson, *Wall Street Meets the Wild West: Bringing Law and Order to Securities Arbitration*, 84 N.C. L. Rev. 123 (2005).

[27] Wallace, *Securities Arbitration After* McMahon, Rodriguez, *and the New Rules: Can Investors' Rights Really Be Protected?*, 43 Vand. L. Rev. 1199, 1202 (1990).

[28] *Survey Shows Some Clients See Process as Tilted Against Them*, 40 Sec. Reg. & L. Rep. (BNA) 198 (2008) (survey was conducted for the Securities Industry Conference on Arbitration). *But see* Kaplinsky & Levin, *Consumer Arbitration: If the FAA "Ain't Broke," Don't Fix It*, 63 Bus. Law. 907 (2008).

past or existing affiliations of the arbitrators that are likely to affect their impartiality; adoption of procedures to facilitate the resolution of discovery disputes; and providing in the statement of award the arbitrators' and parties' names, a summary of the relevant issues in controversy, the damages and/or other relief sought and awarded, a statement of any other issues resolved, and the signatures of the arbitrators who concurred in the award.[29] In addition, as currently proposed but not at this time adopted, an arbitration panel under specified circumstances would be required to provide an "explained" award, namely, the setting forth of "a fact-based award stating the reason(s) each alleged cause of action was granted or denied."[30]

[C] Arbitration Today

Arbitration today, although more complex than in yesteryear,[31] remains a relatively informal process. Rather than burdensome pleading requirements as frequently mandated by federal law, a complainant in arbitration need only specify the relevant facts and the remedies sought.[32] Although discovery is permitted to an increasing extent,[33] including written requests for information and document requests,[34] a number of the more costly and time-consuming aspects of discovery found in federal and state court litigation often are not present. Hence, depositions are rarely permitted. Granting of a dispositive motion (such as a motion for summary judgment) prior to the formal hearing remains relatively infrequent.[35]

At the formal hearing, the panel is comprised of a majority of public arbitrators. Unlike a judicial proceeding, formal rules of evidence do not apply, thereby allowing the introduction of hearsay.[36] Relevance and materiality are

---

[29] *See* Securities Exchange Act Release No. 26805 (1989); NASD Discovery Guide, available at www.nasd.com/web/groups/med arb/documents/mediation arbitration/nasdw 009420.pdf.

[30] NASD Proposed Rule 10330(j)(2), 70 Fed. Reg. 41065 (July 15, 2005), *discussed in,* Black & Gross, *The Explained Award of Damocles: Protection or Peril in Securities Arbitration,* 34 Sec. Reg. L.J. 17 (2006); *see* Symposium, 76 U. Cin. L. Rev. No. 2 (2008); Symposium, 62 Brooklyn L. Rev. No. 4 (1996); Katsoris, *Roadmap to Securities ADR,* 11 Fordham J. Corp. & Fin. L. 413 (2006); Nichols, *Arbitrator Selection at the NASD: Investor Perception of a Pro-Securities Industry Bias,* 15 Ohio St. J. Disp. Res. 63 (1999); Poser, *Making Securities Arbitration Work,* 50 SMU L. Rev. 277 (1996); Ramirez, *Arbitration and Reform in Private Securities Litigation: Dealing with the Meritorious as Well as the Frivolous,* 40 Wm. & Mary L. Rev. 1055 (1999); Shell, *Arbitration and Corporate Governance,* 67 N.C. L. Rev. 517 (1989).

[31] *See* Report of the Arbitration Policy Task Force to the Board of Governors, National Association of Securities Dealers, Inc., [1995–1996 Transfer Binder] Fed. Sec. L. Rep. (CCH) ¶ 85,735, at 87,463–87,468 (1996) (hereinafter Ruder Report).

[32] Securities Industry Conference of Arbitration (SICA), Uniform Code of Arbitration (UCA) § 13.

[33] *See* Ruder Report, *supra* note 31, at 87,463.

[34] *See supra* note 32, UCA § 20(a)–(c).

[35] *See* Ruder Report, *supra* note 31, at 87,468; M. Cane & P. Shub, Securities Arbitration: Law and Procedure 114 (1991).

[36] M. Cane & P. Shub, *supra* note 35, at 37; S. Jaffee, Broker-Dealers and Securities Markets: A Guide to the Regulatory Process 19 (1977).

key criteria in the arbitrators' determination relating to the weight given to evidence proffered.[37]

Arbitrators, not being bound by precise legal standards in their decisions, may render awards premised on the standards of applicable self-regulatory organizations' (SROs') standards, industry custom, or even concepts of equity and fairness. Indeed, damages may be awarded to claimants for violations of SRO rules where no monetary remedy is provided for such misconduct under federal or state securities law.[38] Moreover, many arbitrators are not attorneys and, even for those who are lawyers, they may not have expertise in securities law.[39]

No written decision generally is required by the arbitration rules; only the names of the parties, a summary of the issues presented, the relief sought and awarded, statement of other issues resolved (e.g., jurisdictional rulings), the names of the arbitrators, and the signatures of the arbitrators who concur in the award are necessary.[40] The rationale frequently provided for not requiring written opinions is that mandating such opinions would contravene the policies underlying arbitration which are to provide an expeditious, efficient and informal forum of alternative dispute resolution.[41] Another argument advanced is that requiring written opinions would be time consuming and burdensome, thereby deterring many qualified individuals from agreeing to serve as arbitrators.[42] Nonetheless, as currently proposed but not at this time adopted, an arbitration panel under specified circumstances would have to provide an "explained" award, namely, the setting forth of "a fact-based award stating the general reason(s) for the arbitrators' decision."[43]

There may be another key reason why arbitrators avoid writing opinions: Because the panel's decision can be overturned by a federal court only on narrow grounds, such as bias, misconduct, or manifest disregard of the law,[44]

---

[37] *See supra* note 32, UCA § 21; A Bromberg & L. Lowenfels, Securities Fraud and Commodities Fraud § 14:6 (2008).

[38] *See* A. Bromberg & L. Lowenfels, *supra*, at § 14:7; Sullivan, *The Scope of Modern Arbitral Awards*, 62 Tulane L. Rev. 1113 (1988).

[39] *See* Ruder Report, *supra* note 31, at 87,468–87,469; Johnson *supra* note 26, at 159–70.

[40] *See, e.g.*, NASD Arbitration Code, Rule 41.

[41] *See, e.g., Raiford v. Merrill Lynch, Pierce, Fenner & Smith Inc.* 903 F.2d 1410, 1413 (11th Cir. 1990); *Sargent v. Paine Webber Jackson & Curtis Inc.*, 882 F.2d 529, 532 (D.C. Cir. 1989); *Sobel v. Hertz, Warner & Co.*, 469 F.2d 1211, 1214 (2d Cir. 1972).

[42] *See* Katzler, *Should Mandatory Written Opinions Be Required in All Securities Arbitrations? The Practical and Legal Implications to the Securities Industry*, 45 Am. U. L. Rev. 151, 164 (1995).

[43] FINRA, Proposed Rule Change Relating to Arbitrators Providing an Explained Decision, 73 Fed. Reg. 64995 (Oct. 27, 2008).

[44] Section 10 of the Federal Arbitration Act (FAA), 9 U.S.C. § 10. Although error of law is not provided as a basis for vacating an award pursuant to § 10, federal courts have embraced a standard focusing on manifest disregard of the law by the arbitrators as a ground for vacating an award. *See Kashner Davidson Securities Corp. v. Mscisz*, 531 F.3d 68 (1st Cir. 2008); Cane & Greenspon, *Securities Arbitration: Bankrupt, Bothered & Bewildered*, 7 Stan. J. L. Bus. & Fin. 131, 148 n. 100 (2002) (citing cases). Nonetheless, the burden to show "manifest disregard" is a high one for

the writing of an opinion draws a road map by which a disgruntled party will have greater likelihood of upsetting the arbitral award. Moreover, being pressed for time, inadequately paid, and not accomplished in authoring written opinions (particularly in a complex area like securities law), any written decision incurs the risk of being viewed with disfavor by a learned federal court. Because arbitrators perceive that they act in good faith, follow the spirit if not the letter of the applicable law, and seek to do justice, they thus are reluctant to explain their rationale in a written opinion. The end product is one that reaches a defined result with no reasoning provided to support such result and with the losing party having little likelihood of overturning such result.[45]

§ 13.03   SPECIAL CONCEPTS OF FRAUD FOR BROKER-DEALERS

Under Section 10(b) as well as under certain other provisions (such as Section 17(a) of the Securities Act), a number of principles have been developed to hold broker-dealers to a fairly strict standard of conduct. One such theory is the shingle theory which posits that by hanging out its "shingle," a broker-dealer impliedly represents that its conduct and the behavior of its employees will be fair and will comport with professional norms. As the Second Circuit stated in *Hanly v. SEC*: "A securities dealer occupies a special relationship to the buyer of securities in that by his position he impliedly represents he has an adequate basis for the opinions he renders."[46] One aspect of this duty, labeled the "suitability" theory, recognizes an implied representation by the broker that it will recommend only those securities suitable for each customer's investment objectives and economic status.[47]

A number of other implied representations have been recognized as coming within the shingle theory, including:

---

aggrieved parties. *See, e.g., Merrill Lynch, Pierce, Fenner & Smith Inc. v. Jaros*, 70 F.3d 418, 421 (6th Cir. 1995); *Advest Inc. v. McCarthy*, 914 F.2d 6, 10 (1st Cir. 1990); *Merrill, Lynch, Pierce, Fenner & Smith Inc. v. Bobker*, 808 F.2d 930, 934 (2d Cir. 1986). A number of courts have held that the U.S. Supreme Court's decision in *Hall Street Associates, L.L.C. v. Mattel, Inc.*, 128 S. Ct. 1396 (2008), signifies that manifest disregard of the law no longer is a basis for vacating an arbitration award. *See, e.g., Citigroup Global Markets, Inc. v. Bacon*, 2009 U.S. App. LEXIS 4543 (5th Cir. 2009). Other courts disagree, holding that the manifest disregard standard remains valid. *See, e.g., Stolt-Nielson SA v. Animal Feeds Int'l Corp.*, 548 F.3d 85 (2d Cir. 2008).

[45] *See* S. Jaffee, *supra* note 36, at 339; Steinberg, *Securities Arbitration: Better for Investors than the Courts?*, 62 Brooklyn L. Rev. 1503 (1996).

[46] *Hanly v. SEC*, 415 F.2d 589, 596–597 (2d Cir. 1969). *See generally* Karmel, *Is the Shingle Theory Dead?*, 52 Wash. & Lee L. Rev. 1271 (1995).

[47] *See* M. Cane & P. Shub, *supra* note 35, at 132–74; N. Poser, Broker-Dealer Law and Regulation: Private Rights of Action (1995); Booth, *The Suitability Rule, Investor Diversification, and Using Spread to Measure Risk*, 54 Bus. Law. 1599 (1999); Kerr, *Suitability Standards: A New Look at Economic Theory and Current SEC Disclosure Policy*, 16 Pac. L.J. 805 (1985); Lowenfels & Bromberg, *Suitability in Securities Transactions*, 54 Bus. Law. 1557 (1999); O'Hare, *Retail Investor Remedies Under Rule 10b-5*, 76 U. Cin. L. Rev. 521 (2008); Poser, *Liability of Broker-Dealers for Unsuitable Recommendations to Institutional Investors*, 2001 BYU L. Rev. 1493 (2001); Smith, *Rethinking a Broker's Obligations to Its Customers — The Dramshop Cases*, 30 Sec. Reg. L.J. 51 (2002).

(1) An implied representation of fair pricing, including any markup or markdown;

(2) An implied representation that the broker-dealer will execute only authorized transactions for its customers;

(3) An implied representation to disclose any special consideration that influences the broker-dealer's recommendation;

(4) An implied representation to execute promptly customers' orders; and

(5) An implied representation that any recommendation made by a broker-dealer to a customer has a reasonable basis.[48]

One may inquire, however, whether aspects of the shingle theory still provide the basis for a Section 10(b) right of action in light of the Supreme Court's holding in *Santa Fe* that deception or manipulation must be shown (*see* § 8.05). Although not definitively resolved, a number of courts have taken the position that certain components of the shingle theory no longer are viable. For example, in *Pross v. Baird, Patrick & Co., Inc.*,[49] a Section 10(b) claim based on unauthorized trading by a broker was dismissed. The court reasoned that the claim was in actuality one for breach of fiduciary duty not involving the element of deception necessary to invoke Section 10(b).[50]

Nonetheless, the shingle theory basically remains good law. Arguably, it should remain so in view of the investing public's reliance (which may be called a "relational reliance" interest) on broker-dealers, investment advisers, and other financial professionals. The shingle theory is premised on the proposition that these experts make certain implied representations to their customers. Consequently, where a customer relies on a broker-dealer's fair dealing, the failure by such broker-dealer to disclose its noncompliance with the implied representation(s) made constitutes deception for Section 10(b) purposes.[51]

Another basis upon which brokers have been held liable is for churning. Generally, a claim for churning is established by the plaintiff showing "(1) that the trading in his account was excessive in light of his investment objectives; (2) that the broker in question exercised control over the trading in the account; and (3) that the broker acted with the intent to defraud or with the wilful and reckless disregard for the interests of his client."[52]

---

[48] M. Steinberg & R. Ferrara, Securities Practice: Federal and State Enforcement § 2:17 (2d ed. 2001 & ann. supp.) (and authorities cited therein).

[49] 585 F. Supp. 1456 (S.D.N.Y. 1984).

[50] *Id.* at 1460–61; *accord Shamsi v. Dean Witter Reynolds, Inc.*, 743 F. Supp. 87, 91 (D. Mass. 1989). *But see Rivera v. Clark Melvin Securities Corp.*, [1999 Transfer Binder] Fed. Sec. L. Rep. (CCH) ¶ 90,524 (D.P.R. 1999); *Cruse v. Equitable Securities of New York, Inc.*, 678 F. Supp. 1023 (S.D.N.Y. 1987). *See generally* Weiss, *A Review of the Historic Foundations of Broker-Dealer Liability For Breach of Fiduciary Duty*, 23 J. Corp. L. 65 (1997).

[51] *See* Langevoort, *Fraud and Deception by Securities Professionals*, 61 Texas L. Rev. 1247, 1280–83 (1983).

[52] *Mihara v. Dean Witter & Co.*, 619 F.2d 814, 820–21 (9th Cir. 1980). Nonetheless, in a nondiscretionary account, the broker's duties are more limited. As stated by the Second Circuit:

With respect to establishing "excessive trading" for churning purposes, courts often look to the "turnover ratio"[53] and the "commission ratio."[54] Nonetheless, as the Ninth Circuit opined, no single factor identifies excessive trading.[55]

As a final point, courts allow brokers to engage in certain nonactionable puffery. Such statements that "this deal will make you rich" and "I'm the best broker in Kansas City" are not actionable due to lack of materiality and lack of justifiable reliance (*see* § 8.06[D] *supra*). On the other hand, where specific and realistic percentages are communicated to the investor, such as "your return will be eight percent annually," many courts will find such a statement to constitute actionable misrepresentation.[56]

§ 13.04 CONFLICTS AND SCREENING PROCEDURES

Broker-dealers perform various functions including investment banking, brokerage activities, underwriting, research, investment advice, and investment management. Potential conflicts can arise when information gathering and investment decision functions affect the same issuer. The investment banking department could obtain material, nonpublic information on a publicly-held issuer while the brokerage section is recommending trades in the same issuer's securities or while the trading department is executing trades in the issuer's securities for the firm's own proprietary accounts or as a market maker.[57]

It is uncontested that a broker ordinarily has no duty to monitor a nondiscretionary account, or to give advice to such a customer on an ongoing basis. The broker's duties ordinarily end after each transaction is done, and thus do not include a duty to offer unsolicited information, advice, or warnings concerning the customer's investments. A nondiscretionary customer by definition keeps control over the account and has full responsibility for trading decisions. On a transaction-by-transaction basis, the broker owes duties of diligence and competence in executing the client's trade orders, and is obliged to give honest and complete information when recommending a purchase or sale. The client may enjoy the broker's advice and recommendations with respect to a given trade, but has no legal claim on the broker's ongoing attention.

DeKwiatkowski v. Bear, Stearns & Co., 306 F.3d 1293, 1302 (2d Cir. 2002).

[53] The turnover ratio is "the ratio of the total cost of the purchases made for the account during a given period of time to the amount invested." A. Bromberg & L. Lowenfels, *supra* note 37, at § 13:115.

[54] The commission ratio is "the ratio of the broker's commissions generated by the account to the size of the customer's investment in that amount." *Id.* at § 13:119.

[55] *Nesbit v. McNeil*, 896 F.2d 380, 383 (9th Cir. 1990).

[56] *See, e.g., Cohen v. Prudential-Bache Securities, Inc.*, 713 F. Supp. 653 (S.D.N.Y. 1989) (and cases discussed therein).

[57] *See, e.g.,* Levine, et al., *Multiservice Securities Firms: Coping with Conflicts in a Tender Offer Context*, 23 Wake Forest L. Rev. 41 (1988); Lipton & Mazur, *The Chinese Wall Solution to the Conflict Problems of Securities Firms*, 50 N.Y.U. L. Rev. 459 (1975). The propriety of such procedures as Chinese Walls to limit a broker-dealer's liability has been criticized. For example, Professor Poser opines that "[t]he Chinese Wall . . . makes it difficult . . . for a multiservice firm to fulfill its duty of undivided loyalty to clients." Poser, *Conflicts of Interest Within Securities Firms*, 16 Brooklyn J. Int'l L. 111 (1990).

Moreover, the Sarbanes-Oxley Act, SEC Regulation AC, and self-regulatory organization rules address the objectivity and sufficiency of disclosure of analyst research reports. This subject is addressed in Chapter 5 of the text (§ 5.08[Q]).

[A]   In General

Screening (commonly called "Chinese Wall") procedures consist of policies and procedures designed to control the flow of material, nonpublic information within a multiservice financial firm.[58] In the broker-dealer context, a Chinese Wall isolates the investment banking department from the brokerage, research, and other departments and also limits the flow of sensitive information on a need-to-know basis.[59] In the case of banks, the Chinese Wall segregates the trust department from the commercial lending as well as the securities underwriting departments.[60]

Although Chinese Wall policies and procedures differ among firms, institutions employ numerous such practices to control the flow of information between departments.[61] In addition to general written policies and educational programs, consideration should be given to the implementation of procedures such as the following: (i) physical separation of departments in different wings or floors of a building; (ii) maintenance of separate accounting systems, records, and support staff; (iii) clearly identifying sensitive documents, employing secure filing systems, and restricting access by persons in departments where a breach of confidentiality could occur, such as a bank's trust department or a broker-dealer's trading section; (iv) limiting attendance at meetings where sensitive topics will be discussed; (v) restricting the transfer of personnel from one department into another; (vi) restricting directors, officers and employees from serving dual roles in more than one market sensitive area, such as the arbitrage and underwriting sections of a broker-dealer; and (vii) using code names in documents to conceal the identity of issuers.[62]

Generally, these policies and procedures focus on the activities of the sections of a firm that will frequently come into possession of material,

---

[58] *See* Securities Exchange Act Release No. 17120, [1980 Transfer Binder] Fed. Sec. L. Rep. (CCH) ¶ 82,646, at 83,461 (1980) (hereinafter SEC Rule 14e-3 Release).

[59] *See In re Merrill, Lynch, Pierce, Fenner & Smith*, 43 S.E.C. 933, [1967–1969 Transfer Binder] Fed. Sec. L. Rep. (CCH) ¶ 77,629 (1968) (Exhibit A) (providing example of Chinese Wall policy that Merrill Lynch agreed to employ in a settlement of charges of violating the antifraud provisions of the federal securities laws).

[60] *See* Board of Governors of the Federal Reserve System, *Policy Statement Concerning the Use of Inside Information*, 43 Fed. Reg. 12,755, 12,756 (March 17, 1978) (hereinafter Federal Reserve Policy).

[61] *See* SEC Division of Market Regulation, *Broker-Dealer Policies and Procedures Designed to Segment the Flow and Prevent the Misuse of Material Nonpublic Information*, [1989–1990 Transfer Binder] Fed. Sec. L. Rep. (CCH) ¶ 84,520, at 80,620–80,625 (1990) (hereinafter SEC Division Report).

[62] *See* Federal Reserve Policy, *supra* note 60, at 12,756; Doty & Powers, *Chinese Walls: The Transformation of a Good Business Practice*, 26 Am. Crim. L. Rev. 155, 175–77 (1988).

nonpublic information, such as the investment banking section of a broker-dealer. At times, persons in other departments must be consulted on sensitive matters, such as when an opinion must be obtained from an analyst in the research department. In these instances, the research analyst would be "brought over the wall": the analyst would be required to operate under the same procedures that limit the investment banking section.[63]

[B]   The Need for Reinforcement Measures

In addition to the information segregation measures outlined above, the SEC and commentators have focused on the need for financial intermediaries to maintain reinforcement mechanisms. These other procedures, primarily restricted and watch lists, frequently are employed by multiservice financial firms to cope with their conflicting duties and avert the imposition of liability.[64] Internal audits and other enforcement measures are also utilized to ensure compliance and to detect breaches of the wall.[65] When personnel are brought over the wall, they become subject to these reinforcement procedures as well.[66]

To prevent leaks of inside information, the implementation by multiservice financial firms of reinforcement measures are key components of an effective compliance program.[67] Thus, the Commission often describes adequate procedures for financial intermediaries to include Chinese Walls,[68] restricted lists,[69] watch lists,[70] and other procedures[71] designed to prevent violations of the securities laws.

---

[63] *See* Doty & Powers, *supra* note 62, at 175–77.

[64] *See* SEC Rule 14e-3 Release, *supra* note 58, at 83,461; Levine, et al., *supra* note 57, at 58.

[65] *See* Doty & Powers, *supra* note 62, at 175–77.

[66] *See id.* at 177 (including restricted lists, limits on employee securities transactions, and internal audits).

[67] *See* SEC Division Report, *supra* note 61, at 80,623–80,625.

[68] *See supra* notes 57–67 and accompanying text.

[69] *See* Broker-Dealer Internal Control Procedures for High Yield Securities, Report by the SEC Division of Market Regulation, [1993 Transfer Binder] Fed. Sec. L. Rep. (CCH) ¶ 85,251, at 84,680 n. 15 (1993) (hereinafter Commission Division Report):

> When an investment banking transaction becomes "public" (through a filing with the Commission or otherwise), firms will add the issuer's securities to a "restricted" list accessible to personnel throughout the firm. Once this is done, most, if not all, trading by proprietary and employee accounts is prohibited for set time periods. . . . Because the effects of such restrictions are so wide-ranging, securities are not added to the list until deals are made public. Otherwise, adding a security to this list might send a signal both within and outside the firm that a nonpublic transaction is imminent.

[70] *Id.* at 84,680 n. 14:

> At most firms, the compliance or legal staff maintains a "watch" or "grey" list of securities. A security is added to this list whenever an investment banking engagement is entered into between the broker-dealer and the security's issuer — or in any other instance in which one part of the broker-dealer has received material, nonpublic information concerning the issuer. The compliance or legal staff uses this list to monitor the firm's activities. For example, if a firm employee buys or sells a security on this list, the compliance or legal staff needs to determine if this transaction is indicative of a "breach" of Chinese Wall procedures.

[C]   Regulatory Treatment of Chinese Walls

Although no definitive answer has emerged from case law regarding the propriety of screening (or Chinese Wall) procedures to limit a broker-dealer's liability to its investor-clients,[72] the SEC expressed its approval for such procedures in the tender offer setting when it adopted Rule 14e-3. Rule 14e-3 provides a safe harbor to that rule's "disclose or abstain" provision for entities that implement certain policies and procedures. With certain exceptions, Rule 14e-3 generally imposes liability on persons who are in possession of material, nonpublic information relating to a tender offer and who purchase or sell (or tip such information relating to) the subject securities, unless the information and its source are publicly disclosed in a timely manner.[73]

The Rule provides a safe harbor for entities that would otherwise violate its provisions. This safe harbor covers purchases and sales by nonnatural persons, typically multiservice financial institutions, if the entity can show that the individuals making the investment decision did not know the nonpublic information and that the entity had established policies and procedures, reasonable under the circumstances, to ensure that its individuals would not violate Rule 14e-3. In determining the reasonableness of the policies and procedures, the Rule takes into account the nature of the entity's business. Chinese Walls and restricted lists are specifically identified as examples of policies and procedures that may prevent individual decisionmakers from learning or using such inside information.[74]

§ 13.05   SECONDARY LIABILITY — FAILURE TO SUPERVISE

Principles relating to secondary liability, including liability based on aiding and abetting, control person, and respondeat superior, are discussed in Chapter 10. As discussed earlier, the SEC has express statutory authority to bring

---

[71] *Id.* at 84,680 n. 16:

Many firms have implemented a third type of list for use after a securities is added to the watch or grey list but before the security has been added to the restricted list. If compliance or legal personnel determines that the firm's or employees' activities should in some way be limited, the security is placed on this list. For example, just prior to the public announcement of an investment banking transaction, the compliance or legal staff may instruct the firm's market makers to trade the issuer's securities in a "passive" manner, (i.e., by executing only unsolicited customer trades).

[72] *See, e.g., Slade v. Shearson, Hammill & Co.,* [1973–1974 Transfer Binder] Fed. Sec. L. Rep. (CCH) ¶ 94,439 (S.D.N.Y.), *remanded,* 517 F.2d 398 (2d Cir. 1974); *Cotton v. Merrill Lynch, Pierce, Fenner & Smith, Inc.,* 699 F. Supp. 251 (N.D. Okla. 1988); discussion in Steinberg & Fletcher, *Compliance Programs for Insider Trading,* 47 SMU L. Rev. 1783, 1806–1811 (1994).

[73] The person must know or have reason to know that the information has been acquired directly or indirectly from certain parties involved in the tender offer, including the offering person, the issuer of the target securities, and any persons acting on their behalf. *See also* SEC Rule 17j-1 (requiring registered investment companies to adopt and enforce written codes of ethics, including conflict of interest situations where access persons obtain material nonpublic information).

[74] *See* SEC Rule 14e-3 Release, *supra* note 58, at 83,461. *See generally* W. Wang & M. Steinberg, Insider Trading § 13.5 (2d ed. 2005 & ann. supp.).

enforcement actions against broker-dealers and investment advisers as aiders and abettors.

Another basis for liability relating to SEC enforcement practice is premised on "failure to supervise." In this regard, Section 15(b)(4)(E) of the Exchange Act authorizes the SEC to sanction a broker-dealer if such broker-dealer or any of its associated persons fails reasonably to supervise another person who commits certain enumerated securities law violations, if such person is subject to his/her supervision. The statute contains a safe harbor provision, providing a defense if there have been established and implemented adequate procedures which would reasonably be expected to prevent and detect pertinent violations.[75]

---

[75] *See* 15 U.S.C. § 78o(b)(4)(E). For example, in a release entitled "Supervisory Responsibilities of Broker-Dealer Management," Securities Exchange Act Release No. 8404 (1968), the SEC asserted that the following supervisory functions should be fulfilled:

> (1) The review of the firm's methods of obtaining customers' accounts, including provisions for assuring that adequate information is obtained as to the customers' objectives, needs and finances. (2) The review of customer accounts, including a review for churning and switching of securities in customers' accounts as well as unsuitable recommendations and sales of unregistered securities. (3) The review of methods of recruiting and training of employees, including provisions for assuring that salesmen will not be hired unless the firm can adequately service the business created and maintain an appropriate ratio between sales personnel and back office personnel. . . . (4) The review of back office operations, i.e., all systems and procedures, including the currency and accuracy of books and records, the status and causes of "fails to receive" and "fails to deliver," net capital, credit extensions and financial reports. Attention also should be given to operations that can or should be automated. Prompt delivery of securities to customers and prompt disbursement of customers' funds should be emphasized. . . . (5) The review of sales techniques and methods of salesmen. Specifically, procedures should be used for the review of salesmen's telephone recommendations to customers, sales correspondence with customers, new issue sales, suitability of recommendations and discretionary accounts.

Id.; *see In re UBS PaineWebber, Inc.*, [2003 Transfer Binder] Fed Sec. L. Rep. (CCH) ¶ 86,959 (SEC 2003); *In re FSC Securities Corp.*, Securities Exchange Act Release No. 40765 (1998); *SEC v. Prudential Securities*, [1993 Transfer Binder] Fed. Sec. L. Rep. (CCH) ¶ 97,780 (D.D.C. 1993); *In re Gutfreund*, [1992 Transfer Binder] Fed. Sec. L. Rep. (CCH) ¶ 85,067 (SEC 1992); *In re Salomon Brothers, Inc.*, [1991–1992 Transfer Binder] Fed. Sec. L. Rep. (CCH) ¶ 84,948 (SEC 1992). *See generally* N. Poser, Broker-Dealer Law and Regulation (3d ed. 2002); ABA Task Force, *Broker-Dealer Supervision of Registered Representatives and Branch Office Operations*, 44 Bus. Law. 1361 (1989); Ferrara & Sanger, *Derivative Liability in Securities Laws: Controlling Person Liability, Respondeat Superior, and Aiding and Abetting*, 40 Wash. & Lee L. Rev. 1007 (1983); Janvey, *The Feuerstein Report of Investigation: Supervisory Responsibilities of Legal and Compliance Officers of Brokerage Firms*, 21 Sec. Reg. L.J. 166 (1993); Lowenfels & Bromberg, *Broker-Dealer Supervision: A Troublesom Area*, 25 Seton Hall L. Rev. 527 (1994); Uhlenhop, *Critical Elements of an Effective Supervisory Structure*, 30 Rev. Sec. & Comm. Reg. 173 (2005).

Chapter 14

CORPORATE CONTROL ACQUISITIONS AND CONTESTS

§ 14.01 INTRODUCTION

This Chapter addresses three types of corporate control acquisitions or contests: the proxy battle, the going-private transaction, and the hostile tender offer. Although state law is very relevant in these contexts, emphasis is placed (due to the subject matter covered in the course) on securities regulation.

In focusing on this Chapter, one should keep in mind that hostile proxy and tender offer fights, by their nature, are contests for corporate control. In this way, they are quite similar. As Judge Friendly stated in *Electronic Specialty Company v. International Controls Corp.*:[1]

> [T]ender offers [and] proxy contests . . . are alike in the fundamental feature that they generally are contests. This means that the participants on both sides act, not "in the peace of a quiet chamber," but under the stresses of the marketplace. They act quickly, sometimes impulsively, often in angry response to what they consider, whether rightly or wrongly, to be low blows by the other side. Probably there will no more be a perfect tender offer than a perfect trial. Congress intended to assure basic honesty and fair dealing, not to impose an unrealistic requirement of laboratory conditions that might make the new statute a potent tool for incompetent management to protect its own interests against the desires and welfare of the stockholders. These considerations bear on the kind of judgment to be applied in testing conduct — on both sides — and also on the issue of materiality.[2]

§ 14.02 GOING-PRIVATE TRANSACTIONS

Generally, "[a] going-private transaction is a transaction or series of transactions instituted by the controlling shareholders of a publicly-held corporation and designed to eliminate or substantially reduce the corporation's [public] outstanding equity, thereby returning the corporation to private ownership."[3] Generally, these transactions often take the form of a cash-out (or more pejoratively "freeze-out" or "squeeze-out") merger and result in compel-

---

[1] 409 F.2d 937 (2d Cir. 1969).

[2] *Id.* at 948.

[3] Comment, *Regulating Going-Private Transactions: SEC Rule 13e-3*, 80 Colum. L. Rev. 782 (1980).

ling the minority stockholders to exchange their shares for cash.[4]

[A]   State Law

In *Singer v. Magnavox Co.*,[5] the Delaware Supreme Court held that, in order to adhere to a controlling shareholder's fiduciary duties to the subsidiary corporation and its minority shareholders, a cash-out merger must have a proper business purpose and must be entirely fair to the minority. A number of states adhere to the *Singer* standards.[6] The Delaware high court itself, however, in *Weinberger v. UOP, Inc.*,[7] abandoned the business purpose test and confined its inquiry in long-form mergers to the "entire fairness" standard. In so doing, the court formulated a more liberal approach to valuation, permitting such elements as premiums over market price offered in similar transactions and future earnings potential (so long as not speculative) to be considered.

The *Weinberger* court's approach facilitates mergers and normally relegates a minority shareholder to the appraisal remedy. However, as stated by that court, in long-form mergers, "[t]he appraisal remedy we approve may not be adequate in certain cases, particularly where fraud, misrepresentation, self-dealing, deliberate waste of corporate assets, or gross and palpable overreaching are involved."[8] Nonetheless, in short-form mergers, the Delaware Supreme Court has held that, absent fraud or illegality, appraisal is a minority shareholder's exclusive remedy.[9]

It should be pointed out that a number of states do not follow *Singer* or *Weinberger*. For example, in some states, absent fraud or illegality, appraisal is a minority shareholder's sole remedy in a (long-form) cash-out merger.[10] A few states accomplish this result by statute. A Minnesota, statute, for instance, provides that corporations may merger "with or without a business purpose" and that the remedy for lack of "entire fairness" is appraisal.[11]

In leveraged buy-outs where incumbent management takes a substantial equity position in the surviving entity, it appears that the *Revlon* principles[12]

---

[4] *Id.* See generally A. Borden & J. Yunis, Going Private (2008); McGuinness & Rehbock, *Going-Private Transactions: A Practitioner's Guide*, 30 Del. J. Corp. L. 437 (2005).

[5] 380 A.2d 969 (Del. 1977).

[6] *See, e.g.*, *Alpert v. 28 Williams St. Corp.*, 63 N.Y. 2d 557, 483 N.Y.S. 2d 667, 473 N.E. 2d 19 (1984); *Perl v. IU Int'l Corp.*, 61 Hw. 622, 607 P.2d 1036 (1980).

[7] 457 A.2d 701 (Del. 1983).

[8] *Id.* at 714; *see Cede & Co. v. Technicolor, Inc.*, 684 A. 2d 289 (Del. 1996); *Kahn v. Lynch Communication Systems, Inc.*, 669 A. 2d 79 (Del. 1995); *Cinerama, Inc. v. Technicolor, Inc.*, 663 A. 2d 1156 (Del. 1995); Weiss, *Balancing Interests in Cash-Out Mergers: The Promise of Weinberger v. UOP, Inc.*, 8 Del. J. Corp. L. 1 (1983).

[9] *Glassman v. Unoocal Exploration Corporation*, 777 A.2d 242 (Del. 2001). *See generally* Steinberg, *Short-Form Mergers in Delaware*, 27 Del. J. Corp. L. 489 (2002).

[10] *See, e.g.*, *Steinberg v. Amplica, Inc.*, 42 Cal. 3d 1198, 233 Cal. Rptr. 249, 729 P.2d 683 (1986); *Yanow v. Teal Industries, Inc.*, 178 Conn. 262, 422 A.2d 311 (1979).

[11] Minn. Stat. Ann. § 302A.601.

[12] The *Revlon* principles are discussed in § 14.09[B] *infra*.

frequently will apply.[13] Unlike cash-out mergers, leveraged buy-outs enable incumbent managements to put up little cash of their own and, through the use of borrowed funds collateralized by corporate assets (the repayment of such funds to be made by means of future revenues or the sale of certain assets), eliminate the public shareholders and gain for themselves a substantial equity position. Critics view such transactions as implicating inherent conflicts of interest, calling for the application of heightened fiduciary duty standards. Given the conflicts of interest and potential for abuse present, leveraged buy-out proposals benefitting incumbent management should be left open for a substantial period of time in order to enable unaffiliated third parties to make competing bids, thereby effectuating the "auction" process.[14]

[B]　Federal Law

In addition to Section 10(b) of the Exchange Act, Section 13e-3 and 13e-4 of the Exchange Act and the SEC rules promulgated thereunder (Rules 13e-3 and 13e-4) are the principal federal securities law provisions governing going-private transactions. Rule 13e-3 is a comprehensive rule that prohibits fraudulent, deceptive or manipulative practices in connection with going private transactions and sets forth filing, disclosure, and dissemination requirements.[15] Rule 13e-4 is narrower in scope and applies to an issuer's tender offer for its own securities ("self tenders"). It, like Rule 13e-3, is an antifraud provision and mandates extensive disclosure.[16] Moreover, the same procedural requirements that apply in third-party tender offers pursuant to Section 14(d) generally are extended by Rule 13e-4 to issuer self tenders.[17] Note that an issuer self tender which comes under Rule 13e-4 also may be a going-private transaction within Rule 13e-3's reach. Under such circumstances, both Rule 13e-3 and Rule 13e-4 apply.[18]

Rule 13e-3 calls for subject parties to disclose extensive information with respect to a going-private transaction by filing a Schedule 13E-3 with the SEC. The disclosures include: (1) a description of both the benefits and detriments of the transaction to the issuer as well as to affiliated and unaffiliated shareholders; (2) disclosure of any report, opinion, or appraisal received from an outside party concerning the going-private transaction; (3) disclosure of any plans by the issuer to merge, reorganize, sell assets or make any other material change after the transaction; (4) disclosure of the source and total

---

[13] *See, e.g., MacAndrews & Forbes Holdings v. Revlon, Inc.*, 506 A.2d 173 (Del. 1986).

[14] *Id.*; *see* DeMott, *Directors' Duties in Management Buyouts and Leveraged Recapitalizations*, 49 Ohio St. L.J. 517 (1988); Lowenstein, *Management Buyouts*, 85 Colum. L. Rev. 730 (1985); Morrissey, *Law, Ethics and the Leveraged Buyout*, 65 U. Det. L. Rev. 403 (1988); Steinberg & Lindahl, *The New Law of Squeeze-Out Mergers*, 62 Wash. U.L. Q. 351 (1984).

[15] *See* Securities Exchange Act Release No. 16075 (1979).

[16] *See* Securities Exchange Act Release No. 16112 (1979); *see also* Securities Exchange Act Release No. 42055 (1999).

[17] *See* Securities Exchange Act Release No. 54684 (2006); [1985–1986 Transfer Binder] Fed. Sec. L. Rep. (CCH) ¶ 83,954 (SEC 1986).

[18] Securities Exchange Act Release No. 16112 (1979); *see* Manges, *SEC Regulation of Issuer and Third-Party Tender Offers*, 8 Sec. Reg. L.J. 275 (1981).

amount of funds for the transaction, an estimation of anticipated expenses, a summary of any loan agreements, and arrangements to finance and repay loans; and (5) disclosure of whether the subject parties reasonably believe that the transaction is fair to unaffiliated stockholders and the factors upon which they have that belief.[19]

As to the last disclosure listed above, some commentators assert that, by requiring that the subject parties disclose whether they "reasonably believe" that the going-private transaction is fair, the SEC is engaging in impermissible substantive regulation.[20] In this respect, the Supreme Court's decision in *Schreiber* (discussed in § 14.09[A]) is relevant.[21] There, the Supreme Court held that Section 14(e) of the Exchange Act is premised on the truthful disclosure of adequate information rather than on the substantive fairness of the transaction. Because both Sections 13(e) and 14(e) were enacted as part of the Williams Act in 1968 (as an amendment to the Exchange Act) and contain in part similar language, the assertion that Rule 13e-3's disclosure of "fairness" provision is invalid may have an even stronger basis today. Nonetheless, an argument can be made that, in prescribing this requirement, the Commission has focused on its disclosure function rather than engaging principally in substantive regulation.[22] Note, moreover, that minority shareholders, provided they can show a material misrepresentation or nondisclosure along with the loss of an otherwise available state remedy in connection with the going private transaction, may avail themselves of the Section 10(b) or Section 14(a) right of action.[23]

§ 14.03   PROXY CONTESTS

Under federal law, proxy contests principally are governed by Section 14(a) of the Exchange Act and SEC rules prescribed thereunder. In this regard, the legal standards underlying a private right of action under Section 14(a) are addressed in § 9.05. That discussion should be reviewed at this point.

Until relatively recently, it generally was thought that the tender offer had replaced the proxy battle as the means for procuring corporate control or effecting a change in corporate policies. "This situation was attributed to the difficulty of ousting an incumbent management (unless it was demonstrably incompetent and the insurgents had a large stock position), the significant amount of money and time consumed by a proxy fight, and the impossibility of

---

[19] Schedule 13E-3, 17 C.F.R. § 240.13e-100; *see Howing Co. v. Nationwide Corp.*, 826 F.2d 1470 (6th Cir. 1987), 927 F.2d 263 (6th Cir. 1991), 972 F.2d 700 (6th Cir. 1992).

[20] *See, e.g.,* Note, *Rule 13e-3 and the Going-Private Dilemma: The SEC's Quest for a Substantive Fairness Doctrine*, 58 Wash. U.L.W. 883 (1980).

[21] 472 U.S. 1 (1985). *Schreiber* is discussed in § 14.09[A] *infra.*

[22] *See generally* Kofele-Kale, *The SEC's Going-Private Rules: Analysis and Developments*, 19 Sec. Reg. L.J. 139 (1991).

[23] *See Virginia Bankshares, Inc. v. Sandberg*, 501 U.S. 1083 (1991); *Wilson v. Great American Industries, Inc.*, 979 F.2d 924 (2d Cir. 1992); discussion §§ 8.05[B], 9.05[B] *supra.*

recouping proxy fight costs if the insurgents failed to take control."[24] To a degree, however, the proxy fight has seen a partial renaissance. While this renaissance arguably may be more in response to market conditions than to regulatory developments, it also reflects changes in the regulatory context. Indeed, with the proliferation of state takeover statutes, SEC tender offer regulations, and court battles, the costs of pursuing a hostile tender offer can be exorbitant (e.g., costs of acquiring a controlling interest, attorney and investment banker fees, and, depending upon market conditions, high interest rates).[25]

Nonetheless, proxy contests normally are viable today when economic benefits accrue to the shareholders. A number of these battles have had as the insurgents' main objective the sale or liquidation of certain assets of the corporation, particularly where the company's stock was trading at what was viewed as an unreasonably low price. The proceeds from the sale of such assets then may be passed onto the shareholders as a cash distribution. More recently, insurgents have engaged in proxy contests to effectuate their takeover bids — the proxy contest being used as a means to successfully consummate an unsolicited tender offer.

Given the "hurly-burly" of proxy contests, courts generally apply a standard of fair accuracy.[26] "[N]it-picking should not become the name of the game."[27] Nonetheless, as discussed in Chapter 9, an implied private right of action exists to redress violations of Section 14(a), particularly where materially false or misleading statements have been made.[28]

Section 14(a) of the Exchange Act and SEC rules promulgated thereunder regulate the solicitation of proxies in regard to securities registered under Section 12 of the 1934 Act. These rules, contained in Regulation 14A, prescribe certain filing, dissemination, disclosure and substantive requirements with respect to proxy solicitations. Significantly, Rule 14a-12 authorizes the participants to make both oral and written communications to shareholders prior to the filing of a proxy statement, provided that: all such written communications are filed with the SEC on the date of their first use; no form of proxy is provided to shareholders; shareholders are advised of the identity of the participants in the solicitation and provided with a description of such participants' interests or are informed where to locate such information; and shareholders are advised to read the proxy statement prior to voting. Hence, although communications may be made prior to the filing of a proxy statement, no proxies may be sought before a proxy statement required by Rule 14a-3 is furnished. In addition, the

---

[24] Brown, *Changes in Offeror Strategy in Response to New Laws and Regulations*, 25 Case West. Res. L. Rev. 843, 865–866 (1978).

[25] *See generally* Bainbridge, *Redirecting State Takeover Laws at Proxy Contests*, 1992 Wisc. L. Rev. 1071; Bebchuck & Kahan, *A Framework for Analyzing Legal Policy Towards Proxy Contests*, 78 Calif. L. Rev. 1071 (1990).

[26] *See General Time Corporation v. Talley Industries, Inc.*, 403 F.2d 159, 162 (2d Cir. 1968).

[27] *Kennecott Copper Corp. v. Curtiss-Wright Corp.*, 584 F.2d 1195, 1200 (2d Cir. 1978).

[28] *See* § 9.05[A] *supra*.

antifraud provisions of Rule 14a-9 apply in this setting.[29]

§ 14.04   A PRIMER ON THE WILLIAMS ACT

[A]   Introduction

By the mid-1960's the frequency of cash tender offers had risen to levels that made many people uncomfortable. This discomfort was felt from the corridors of the SEC, where secret corporate control transactions that had somehow slipped between the regulatory cracks were viewed with great suspicion, to the boardrooms of many of the nation's corporations, where fear of being swallowed up by corporate raiders was spreading. The rate of tender offers, although small when compared to today's world of merger mania, had increased from 8, involving $200 million in 1960, to 107, involving $1 billion by 1966.[30]

There were many reasons for this takeover boom, not the least of which was a thriving economy that had left many corporations cash-rich and looking for investments. The perfect vehicle for investment in many cases proved to be the cash tender offer; there was little regulation compared to other control transaction devices (such as public exchange offers and proxy contests); and, results could be achieved swiftly and often with little resistance from the surprised incumbent managements.

Some viewed these new developments as a natural consequence of a pent-up economy that was showing signs of growth. Indeed, many saw the movement as a healthy signal of a mature, capitalist economy that promoted competition between managements as well as between products. In this kind of economy, most inefficient managements would gradually give way to those best able to accumulate and distribute earned profits to shareholders. Others were not quite as optimistic and feared that once-proud companies were falling prey to larger corporate raiders that would all too frequently victimize the smaller companies. In the process, shareholders, who had little understanding of these corporate maneuvers, would suffer.

The Williams Act of 1968,[31] which amended the Securities Exchange Act of 1934, was the legislative attempt at accommodating both of these viewpoints. The Act required offerors to disclose information that was material to a shareholder's decision whether to tender his/her shares, while, at the same time, not imposing too stringent regulations that would impede the efficacy of the cash tender offer vehicle.

---

[29] *See* 17 C.F.R. § 240.14a-12; Securities Exchange Act Release No. 42055 (1999). *See generally* R. Thomas & C. Dixon, Aranow & Einhorn on Proxy Contests for Corporate Control (3d ed. 1998); M. Waters, Proxy Regulation (1992); Symposium, 17 J. Corp. L. No. 1 (1991); Fisch, *From Legitimacy to Logic: Reconstructing Proxy Regulation*, 46 Vand. L. Rev. 1129 (1993); Steinberg, *Fiduciary Duties and Disclosure Obligations in Proxy and Tender Contests for Corporate Control*, 30 Emory L.J. 169 (1981); sources cited note 25 *supra.*

[30] 113 Cong. Rec. S. 24,664 (daily ed. Aug. 30, 1967) (statement of Senator Williams).

[31] S. 510, Pub. L. 90–439, 82 Stat. 454 (1968).

The Williams Act, as adopted, was the ultimate product of the dialogue engendered by congressional proposals. The first attempt at legislation in this area came in 1965 when Senator Harrison Williams of New Jersey introduced S. 2731. Stories of giant corporate raiders swallowing or gutting small proud companies upset many members of Congress, particularly since this situation was due, at least in part, to a loophole in the securities laws.

Before the Williams Act's passage, an offeror could avoid federal filing, dissemination, and disclosure obligations by procuring control through a cash tender offer.[32] Corporations and individuals took advantage of another disclosure loophole by buying up shares of an acquisition prospect in the open market until they had gained control or had acquired a substantial percentage of the company's stock. This could be accomplished swiftly and secretly without the attendant regulation that accompanied other merger vehicles such as the public exchange offer or the proxy contest.[33]

Although the philosophy of the proposed 1965 legislation was attractive to some members, hearings were never held and the bill died. One reason for that bill's failure was the feeling that it was too favorable to the incumbents in a tender offer contest, and, hence, would stifle economically beneficial corporate combinations. For example, one provision of the bill would have required a bidder to give incumbent management twenty days notice of its intention to commence a tender offer. Many felt that this kind of notice would have effectively eliminated hostile cash tender offers by allowing incumbent managements more time to implement various defensive tactics, thereby causing the defeat of hostile takeover bids.[34]

By 1967 proponents had refined their proposals. The major advocates for the legislation were the SEC and a coalition of corporate leaders who feared that, without some regulation, a detrimental tender offer fever would sweep the country, causing great harm to the American economy. These strange bedfellows provided a rather broad base of support for S. 510.

[B]   Legislation

The legislation, as enacted in 1968, added Sections 13(d), (e), and 14(d), (e), and (f) to the Exchange Act. Many of the tender offer provisions in the Act are set forth in Section 14(d). That Section principally contains disclosure mandates and provisions designed to give shareholders sufficient time in a noncoercive setting to make informed investment decisions. A number of these provisions have been modified by the SEC pursuant to its rulemaking powers.[35] Section 14(e) is a broad antifraud provision which makes it unlawful

---

[32] *See Piper v. Chris-Craft Industries, Inc.,* 430 U.S. 1, 22 (1977); R. Clark, Corporate Law § 13.3 (1986).

[33] *See* Cohen, *A Note on Takeover Bids and Corporate Purchases of Stock,* 22 Bus. Law. 149 (1966).

[34] See the discussion in Brudney, *A Note on Chilling Tender Solicitations,* 21 Rutgers L. Rev. 609 (1967).

[35] *See* discussion in § 14.08 *infra.*

for any person to make false or misleading statements of material fact, or to engage in fraudulent, deceptive or manipulative acts or practices in connection with a tender offer. In 1970, Congress amended Section 14(e) to give the SEC broad rulemaking authority under that statute.

Some of the procedural provisions evidently did not provoke much debate. For example, Section 14(d)(5) allows a shareholder to withdraw his/her tendered shares within seven days after the offer commences and after sixty days following the commencement of the offer. This provision now has been expanded by SEC Rule 14d-7 to permit a shareholder to withdraw the shares tendered during the entire period that the offer remains open.[36] This withdrawal right changes the pre-Williams Act irrevocability of tendered shares, thereby enabling the shareholder to withdraw his/her shares and not be indefinitely held to a decision to tender that is not in one's best interest. Moreover, Section 14(d)(6) softens the "stampede" effect of coercing shareholders to rapidly tender their stock in first-come first-serve offers by providing for a pro rata purchase of all shares tendered within ten days of the initial offer. As with the withdrawal right, the SEC pursuant to Rule 14d-8 has expanded this right to proration to encompass the entire offering period.[37]

The disclosure provisions of Sections 13(d)(1) and 14(d)(1) are what apparently caused the greatest stir in Congress and among the academics. Section 13(d)(1) requires disclosure within ten days from any person (or group) who becomes the direct, indirect, or beneficial owner of five percent of a company's outstanding stock. This post-transaction filing requirement is principally directed at providing notice to the marketplace where a potential shift in corporate control may take place.[38] Section 14(d)(1) governs the cash tender offer and mandates the filing by an offeror of essentially the same information as required by Section 13(d)(1). These disclosures include:

(1) the background and identity of the offeror;

(2) the source and amount of funds used;

(3) the purpose of the contemplated purchases;

(4) the number of shares owned;

(5) information regarding any special arrangements involving the offer; and

(6) such additional information as the SEC may prescribe.[39]

---

[36] 17 C.F.R. § 240.14d-7. Note, however, that Rule 14d-11 allows a bidder to have a subsequent offering period without withdrawal rights immediately after the offer's termination. *See* discussion § 14.08 *infra.*

[37] 17 C.F.R. § 240.14d-8; *see* Bloomenthal, *The New Tender Offer Regimen, State Regulation and Preemption*, 30 Emory L.J. 35 (1981).

[38] *See Treadway Companies, Inc., v. Care Corp.*, 638 F.2d 357, 380 (2d Cir. 1980).

[39] 17 C.F.R. §§ 240.13(d)(1), 240.14(d)(1); *see Motient Corp. v. Dondero*, 529 F.3d 532 (5th Cir. 2008) (holding no private right of action for money damages under § 13(d)); *Edelson v. Ch'ien*, 405 F.3d 620–634 (7th Cir. 2005) (holding that § 13(d) private right of action may be recognized "only in the context of a tender offer or other contest for control"); cases cited in § 9.03 *supra.*

A fundamental purpose of these disclosures is to protect shareholders from having to make hasty and uninformed decisions on whether or not it would be in their best interests to tender their shares for the offered price. Critics, on the other hand, believe that the information required to be disclosed is largely irrelevant to the shareholder's decision and that by, forcing disclosure, the economic incentive to embark on a takeover bid is needlessly impaired.[40]

Nonetheless, Section 13(d) has a significant loophole. Because the disclosures required by Section 13(d) need not be made until ten days after attaining five percent ownership, additional purchases may be made during this period so long as they do not constitute a "tender offer." This ten-day "window" permits potential acquirors to enhance their ownership level well beyond that contemplated by Congress through means of open market purchases and privately negotiated transactions. In this regard, however, the mandates of the Hart-Scott-Rodino Antitrust Improvements Act of 1976 in many situations will limit such purchases.[41]

Another provision of the Williams Act, Section 14(e), is designed to protect shareholders from fraud, deception and manipulation in connection with tender offers. Prior to enactment of this legislation, shareholders had to rely on the reach of Section 10(b) which is directed at preventing such practices in connection with the purchase or sale of any security. The problem is that Section 10(b) does not reach far enough due to at least two reasons: (1) generally, in cases of nondisclosure (i.e., silence), the statute is deemed not to be applicable unless there is a duty to disclose,[42] and (2) there must be a purchase or sale to trigger the statute's application.[43] In the pre-Williams Act era, therefore, unless a tender offer actually commenced and shares were purchased or sold, there was presumably no effective federal remedy for the SEC and private parties to invoke. Moreover, disclosure was not generally required until the offeror became a controlling shareholder with all the fiduciary duties that came with that status or unless the insurgent was receiving material nonpublic information derived from a corporate source.[44] Thus, Section 14(e) filled the need for legislation in this area and gave further substance to the disclosure requirements under Section 14(d).

As enacted, the legislation was designed to protect the valid interests of the target corporation's stockholders and to enable both the bidder and target managements to present their positions to the stockholders.[45] The neutral

---

[40] *See generally* Brudney, *supra* note 34, at 617–620.

[41] *See* discussion § 14.07 *infra.*

[42] *See Chiarella v. United States*, 445 U.S. 222 (1980); discussion in Chapter 12 *supra; see also* Note, *The Regulation of Corporate Tender Offers Under Federal Securities Law: A New Challenge for Rule 10b-5*, 33 U. Chicago L. Rev. 359, 373 (1966).

[43] *See The Wharf (Holdings) Limited v. United International Holdings, Inc.*, 532 U.S. 588 (2001); *Blue Chip Stamps v. Manor Drug Stores*, 421 U.S. 723 (1975); discussion § 8.02 *supra.*

[44] *See SEC v. Texas Gulf Sulphur Co.*, 401 F.2d 833 (2d Cir. 1968) (en banc); *Diamond v. Oreamuno*, 24 N.Y. 2d 494, 248 N.E. 2d 910 (1969).

[45] *See* House Comm. on Interstate and Foreign Commerce, Disclosure of Corporate Equity Ownership, H.R. Rep. No. 1711, 90th Cong., 2d Sess. 4, *reprinted in*, 1968 U.S. Code Cong. & Ad.

position taken by the Act was emphasized by its primary sponsor, Senator Williams: "We have taken extreme care to avoid tipping the scales either in favor of management or in favor of the person making the takeover bid."[46] Hence, the even-handed disclosure approach of the Act was adopted in an attempt to ensure that target corporation shareholders had sufficient information, and the time necessary, to make informed uncoerced investment decisions.[47]

[C] Debate

The advocates of the legislation insisted that the disclosure provisions of the Williams Act were absolutely essential for protection of shareholders.[48] Critics, on the other hand, were convinced that the disclosure provisions were irrelevant to a shareholder's decision to tender his/her shares. They viewed with cynicism the motives of the proponents seeking legislation, arguing that the primary beneficiaries of the disclosure provisions were the potential target managements, not the shareholders.[49] As for the SEC, its interests were shareholder protection and maintaining the integrity of the securities markets. Irrespective of such warranted SEC concerns, critics felt that the requirement of disclosure was unnecessary in light of the dampening effect it would have on the efficient combinations of businesses.[50] The ultimate issue therefore is whether the disclosure provisions designed to protect shareholders and the securities markets justify the alleged discouragement of business combinations.

Generally, critics took exception to the disclosure provisions for three alleged reasons: First, as mentioned above, the disclosure required was asserted to be irrelevant to a shareholder's decision on whether to tender the shares. Second, the legislation, at least in part, confused a free market philosophy with that of a distribution of wealth philosophy. And third, the practical effects of the legislation would destroy the climate for efficient business combinations.[51]

To the proponents, the disadvantages of the legislation were overwhelmingly outweighed by the advantages that would be gained from it. As one Senator put it, "[d]espite the sneers of a few cynics back in 1934, full disclosure has provided a strong stimulus to the American investor. Now is the

---

News 2811, 2813; Senate Comm. on Banking and Currency, Full Disclosure of Corporate Equity Ownership and in Corporate Takeover Bids, S. Rep. No. 550, 90th Cong., 1st Sess. 3 (1967).

[46] 113 Cong. Rec. 24664 (1967).

[47] *See* Statement by Senator Kuchel, Full Disclosure of Corporate Ownership and in Corporate Takeover Bids: Hearings on S. 510 Before the Senate Subcomm. on Securities of the Comm. on Banking and Currency, 90th Cong., 1st Sess. 46 (1967); sources cited in notes 45–46 *supra*.

[48] *See* Cohen, *supra* note 33, at 156–57.

[49] *See* Manne, *Cash Tender Offers for Shares — A Reply to Chairman Cohen*, 1967 Duke L.J. 231.

[50] *Id.* at 245.

[51] *Id.* at 245–253; *see also* Brudney, *supra* note 34, at 616–41.

time to eliminate the few areas where full disclosure is not available."[52] In other words, the protection of shareholders and the integrity of the market as a whole outweighed any dampening effect on the efficient combinations of businesses.

Despite the controversy stirred, there was in fact relatively little opposition to the bill once it reached the floor of both Houses. In fact, it passed both the House and the Senate on a voice vote.[53] There may be a number of explanations accounting for this development. First, there was a broad consensus between the SEC and the corporate sector, which gave great impetus to the legislation. Second, the legislation was politically feasible to support since it was ostensibly aimed at protecting the securities markets and innocent shareholders of large publicly-held corporations. Also, as contrasted with today's attitudes, tender offers were viewed by many somehow as a sneaky, "ungentlemanly" way to conduct corporate transactions. Hence, the Williams Act's approach based on full disclosure, with no side purportedly having an unfair advantage over the other and the shareholder being the ultimate beneficiary, merited support.

§ 14.05   DEFINITION OF TENDER OFFER

The conventional tender offer generally is easily identified. Its characteristics frequently are a publicized bid to purchase shares of stock at a premium over market price made directly to the target corporation's shareholders with certain conditions attached, frequently including a time limit for the duration of the offer and financing contingencies.[54] Tender offers, however, also may be unconventional. One such unconventional tender offer, for example, involved a bid made to approximately thirty sophisticated investors who owned 34% of the outstanding stock. Solicitors acting on behalf of the bidder followed a prearranged script, offered a premium over market price with no room for negotiation, and left the offer open for a short time period. Applying an eight-factor analysis discussed below, the court held that the solicitations constituted a tender offer under the Williams Act.[55]

The significance of the above holding is that conventional as well as unconventional tender offers trigger application of the Williams Act's regulatory framework. Unconventional tender offers are unlikely to satisfy the requirements of Section 14(d) and SEC rules thereunder, such as the twenty business day time period within which an offer remains open and the right of shareholders during the offer to withdraw their shares tendered. Moreover, an offeror must file a Schedule TO providing detailed disclosures.[56]

---

[52] 111 Cong. Rec. S. 28,260 (daily ed. Oct. 22, 1965) (Statement of Senator Williams).

[53] S. 510, 90th Cong., 2d Sess., 114 Cong. Rec. H. 21,484 (daily ed. July 15, 1968), 114 Cong. Rec. S. 21,954 (daily ed. July 18, 1968).

[54] *See Hanson Trust PLC v. SCM Corporation*, 774 F.2d 47, 54–55 (2d Cir. 1985).

[55] *Wellman v. Dickinson*, 475 F. Supp. 783 (S.D.N.Y. 1979), *aff'd on other grounds*, 682 F.2d 355 (2d Cir. 1982).

[56] See § 14.08 *infra* for further discussion on the SEC's tender offer rules.

The unconventional tender offer today is a rare occurrence. That is because courts hold that (1) open market purchases on a stock exchange or in the over-the-counter market[57] as well as (2) privately negotiated transactions between an acquiror and sophisticated investors[58] normally do not constitute a tender offer. In making this determination, a number of courts apply the following eight-factor test:

(1) active and widespread solicitation of public shareholders for the shares of an issuer;

(2) solicitation made for a substantial percentage of the issuer's stock;

(3) offer to purchase made at a premium over the prevailing market price;

(4) terms of the offer are firm rather than negotiable;

(5) offer contingent on the tender of a fixed number of shares, often subject to a fixed maximum number to be purchased;

(6) offer open only for a limited period of time;

(7) offeree subjected to pressure to sell the stock;

(8) public announcements of a purchasing program concerning the target company precede or accompany rapid accumulation of large amounts of the target company's securities.[59]

The eight-factor test, although flexible, is uncertain in its application. In any given situation, solicitations may constitute a tender offer even though some of the eight factors are not satisfied. Conversely, a tender offer may not exist even though many of the factors are present. Hence, the eight-factor test is akin to an ad hoc balancing test in which the various factors are weighed.[60]

Due to the uncertainty of the above standard, the Second Circuit has adopted a different formulation. In *Hanson Trust PLC v. SCM Corporation*,[61] a corporation withdrew its tender offer after being confronted with a competing offer and with tactics engaged in by target management favoring the "white knight." After terminating its offer, the corporation, engaging in what is called a "market sweep," purchased shares from five arbitrageurs constituting about 25% of the target's stock. In ascertaining whether these solicitations were a tender offer, the court reasoned:

[S]ince the purpose of § 14(d) is to protect the ill-informed solicitee, the question of whether a solicitation constitutes a "tender offer" within the meaning of § 14(d) turns on whether, viewing the transaction in the light of the totality of circumstances, there appears to be a

---

[57] *See, e.g., SEC v. Carter Hawley Hale Stores, Inc.*, 760 F.2d 945 (9th Cir. 1985).

[58] *See, e.g., Brascan Ltd. v. Edper Equities, Ltd.*, 477 F. Supp. 773 (S.D.N.Y. 1979).

[59] *See SEC v. Carter Hawley Hale Stores, Inc.*, 760 F.2d 945, 950 (9th Cir. 1985).

[60] *See id.* at 950–52.

[61] 774 F.2d 47 (2d Cir. 1985).

likelihood that unless the pre-acquisition filing strictures of that statute are followed, there will be a substantial risk that solicitees will lack information needed to make a carefully considered appraisal of the proposal put before them.[62]

Looking at such factors as the small number of solicitees and the solicitees' high level of financial acumen, the Second Circuit held that a tender offer had not been made.[63]

Critics assert that the Second Circuit's decision in *Hanson Trust* provides a means by which an acquiror can "sidestep" the Williams Act and SEC regulations thereunder. The Wall Street Journal evidently believed this to be the case and reacted favorably to this perceived development. In an editorial entitled "A Happy Jig," the Journal applauded the *Hanson Trust* decision as signaling the emergence of a "new deregulated takeover market" in which acquirors would no longer "hav[e] to worry about the costs and delays of securities regulations," hence resulting in "more simplified takeovers — and more profits for shareholders."[64] On the other hand, although full disclosure certainly is the principal objective of the Williams Act, it may be asserted that another purpose is to ensure the evenhanded treatment of all shareholders, including the small unsophisticated shareholder. "Market sweeps" discriminate against the ordinary investor and, arguably, should not be permitted.

In 1983, the SEC established an Advisory Committee on Tender Offers. After conducting a series of meetings, the Advisory Committee issued its Report, consisting of fifty recommendations. Most pertinent for our purposes here, Recommendation 14 provided:

> No person may acquire voting securities of an issuer, if, immediately following such acquisitions, such person would own more than 20% of the voting power of the outstanding voting securities of that issuer unless such purchases were made (i) from the issuer or (ii) pursuant to a tender offer. The Commission should retain broad exemptive power with respect to this provision.[65]

Moreover, in an apparent but not vigorous effort to restrain the use of market sweeps, the Commission in 1987 proposed Rule 14d-11. That proposal, which was not adopted by the SEC, would have imposed a cooling-off period for the purchase of a target's stock upon a party who has withdrawn a tender offer.[66]

---

[62] *Id.* at 57.

[63] *Id.* at 57–58.

[64] Editorial, "A Happy Jig," *Wall St. J.*, Oct. 7, 1985.

[65] *See* Advisory Committee on Tender Offers, U.S. SEC, Report of Recommendations (1983). *See generally* Quinn & Martin, *The SEC Advisory Committee on Tender Offers and Its Aftermath — A New Chapter in Change-of-Control Regulation, in,* Tender Offers: Developments and Commentaries 9 (M. Steinberg ed. 1985).

[66] *See* Securities Exchange Act Release No. 24976 (1987). *See generally* Tyson, *The Williams Act After* Hanson Trust v. SCM Corporation*: Post-Tender Offer Purchases by the Tender Offeror,* 61 Tulane L. Rev. 1 (1986).

§ 14.06 CONSTITUTIONALITY OF STATE TAKEOVER STATUTES

In *Edgar v. MITE*,[67] the Supreme Court, in an opinion written by Justice White, declared the Illinois Business Takeover Act unconstitutional on interstate commerce grounds, reasoning that the burdens imposed on interstate commerce by the Act were excessive in relation to the local interests served. Another portion of Justice White's opinion, not joined in by the majority of the Court, asserted that the Illinois Act was unconstitutional under the Supremacy Clause.[68]

In the aftermath of the Supreme Court's decision in *MITE*, several state statutes, having provisions similar to the Illinois Act, were declared unconstitutional by the lower federal courts. Cognizant of the constitutional infirmities of their takeover statutes, several states responded by enacting "second generation" statutes which sought to pass constitutional scrutiny.[69]

[A] The *CTS* Decision

In *CTS Corp. v. Dynamics Corp. of America*,[70] the Supreme Court upheld one version of the second-generation statutes. There, the Court held that the Control Share Acquisitions Chapter of the Indiana Business Corporation Law[71] does not violate the Constitution on either preemption or interstate commerce grounds. In brief, the Indiana statute, which applies to corporations chartered in Indiana and which have certain other connections with that state, focuses on the acquisition of "control shares" in such a corporation. Under the Act, a control share acquisition is one which, but for the operation of the Act, would raise the purchaser's voting power to or above any of three thresholds: (1) one-fifth and less than one-third, (2) one-third and less than a majority, or (3) above a majority. When a control share transaction occurs, the acquiring entity does not have voting rights with respect to those shares unless a majority of the disinterested shares[72] entitled to vote approves the transaction. Such vote must take place within fifty days if the acquiring entity so requests.[73]

Even though the fifty day period of the Indiana statute exceeds the minimum twenty business day period which a tender offer must remain open under the Williams Act, the Supreme Court stated that this extra delay was

---

[67] 457 U.S. 624 (1982).

[68] *Id.* at 630–40. *See generally* Sargent, *On the Validity of State Takeover Regulation: State Responses to* MITE *and* Kidwell, 42 Ohio St. L.J. 689 (1981).

[69] *See* Romano, *The Political Economy of Takeover Statutes*, 73 Va. L. Rev. 111 (1987).

[70] 481 U.S. 69 (1987).

[71] Ind. Code § 23-1-42-1 to 23-1-42-11.

[72] "Interested shares" are those beneficially controlled by the entity acquiring the corporation, an officer or an inside director of the subject corporation. *Id.* § 23-1-42-3.

[73] *Id.* § 23-1-42-7. Such a request must be made when the acquiror files an "acquiring person statement" with the corporation. The expenses of the meeting are to be paid by the acquiring person. *Id.* For further details of the Indiana Act, see 481 U.S. at 72–75.

permissible. Only unreasonable delays, the Court asserted, are unconstitutional. Moreover, to preempt the Indiana Act, the Court felt, would bring into question the constitutionality of a wide variety of state corporate laws of hitherto unquestioned validity. Such statutes include permitting corporations to have cumulative voting and the staggering of director terms, which, like the Indiana statute, may delay or limit the exercise of control by a successful bidder. Hence, the Court concluded:

> In our view, the possibility that the Indiana Act will delay some tender offers is insufficient to require a conclusion that the Williams Act pre-empts the [Indiana] Act. The longstanding prevalence of state regulation in this area suggests that, if Congress had intended to preempt all State laws that delay the acquisition of voting control following a tender offer, it would have said so explicitly.[74]

Likewise, the *CTS* Court found that the Indiana statute does not offend the Commerce Clause. Upon examination, the Indiana Act neither discriminates against interstate commerce nor does it create an impermissible risk of inconsistent regulation by the various states. As a basis for its holding, the Court relied on the premise that a state's authority to regulate domestic corporations is a fundamental precept of corporate law. In its role as regulator of corporate governance, a state has an interest in facilitating stable relationships among the participants in its domestic corporations. Applying these principles, the Court stated:

> The primary purpose of the [Indiana] Act is to protect the shareholders of Indiana corporations. It does this by affording shareholders, when a takeover offer is made, an opportunity to decide collectively whether the resulting change in voting control of the corporation, as they perceive it, would be desirable. A change of management may have important effects on the shareholders' interest; it is well within the State's role as overseer of corporate governance to offer this opportunity.[75]

[B]   The "Third Generation" Statutes

After *CTS*, a number of different types of state "anti-takeover" statutes exist. These statutes, many of which have been upheld as constitutional,[76] play an integral role in the takeover process. Significantly, unlike the Illinois statute

---

[74] 481 U.S. at 86.

[75] *Id.* at 91; *see AMP, Inc. v. Allied Signal Corp.*, 168 F.3d 649 (3d Cir. 1999) (interpreting Pennsylvania control share acquisitions statute). *See generally* Langevoort, *The Supreme Court and the Politics of Corporate Takeovers: A Comment on* CTS Corp. v. Dynamics Corp. of America, 101 Harv. L. Rev. 96 (1987).

[76] The Delaware statute has been upheld as constitutional. *See, e.g., BNS Inc. v. Koppers Co.*, 683 F. Supp. 458 (D. Del. 1988). The Wisconsin Statute was constitutionally upheld in *Amanda Acquisition Corporation v. Universal Foods Corporation*, 877 F.2d 496 (7th Cir. 1989). *But see Rocket Acquisition Corp. v. Ventana Medical Systems, Inc.*, 2007 U.S. Dist. LEXIS 62361 (D. Ariz. 2007) (holding Arizona Anti-Takeover Act unconstitutional on basis that the statutes "constitute[d] an impermissible risk of inconsistent regulation in violation of the Commerce Clause because of the

declared unconstitutional in *MITE*, these third-generation statutes do not directly impact upon an offeror making a tender offer for all shares outstanding. Nonetheless, aspects of these statutes may deter prospective offerors from engaging in takeover bids.

In addition to the control share acquisition type of statute upheld as constitutional in *CTS*, other types of statutes include:

"Fair Price" Statute — This type of statute reaches fundamental "second step" transactions, such as mergers or sales of substantially all assets, which frequently follow a hostile tender offer for a bare majority of the target's shares. The statute basically provides that such a transaction can be undertaken only if: (1) a majority of the disinterested shares of the subject corporation approve or (2) the same price is paid in the second-step transaction as was paid in the first-step tender offer. There are a number of variations to this type of statute.[77]

"Right of Redemption" Statute — With certain exceptions, this type of statute provides that once a person or group owns twenty percent of a class of voting shares registered under the Exchange Act, that person or group is deemed to be a controlling shareholder. Attainment of that status requires such shareholder "to offer to purchase the remaining shares of all of the other shareholders at a statutorily defined price reflecting the highest premium paid by [such shareholder] in accumulating target stock."[78]

"Classified Board" Statute — This statute requires all publicly-held companies to have classified boards of directors, divided into three classes (being equal or nearly as equal in number as possible). Generally, each class is to serve staggered three-year terms. Removal of directors may be only for cause.[79]

"Other Constituency" or "Stakeholder" Statute — This type of statute, enacted in a majority of the states, authorizes a corporation's board of directors to consider non-shareholder interests, such as those of employees, customers, communities and suppliers, when making business decisions. Whereas most states apply this type of statute to directors' conduct in general, some states limit its application to takeovers.[80]

"Disgorgement" Statute — Enacted in Pennsylvania, a target company or any of its shareholders suing derivatively may bring an action against a

---

statutes' reach and application to foreign corporations").

[77] *See generally* Scriggins & Clarke, *Takeovers and the 1983 Maryland Fair Price Legislation*, 43 Md. L. Rev. 266 (1984).

[78] Bainbridge, *supra* note 25, at 1099, *interpreting*, 15 Pa. Cons. Stat. Ann. §§ 2542–2546. *See generally* Newlin & Gilmer, *The Pennsylvania Shareholder Protection Act: A New State Approach to Deflecting Corporate Takeover Bids*, 40 Bus. Law. 111 (1984).

[79] *See* H.B. 5556, 1990 Mass. Adv. Legis. Serv. 5–6 (Law. Co-op).

[80] Tyler, *Other Constituency Statutes*, 59 Mo. L. Rev. 373, 379–380 (1994) (citing state statutes); *see* Bainbridge, *Interpreting Nonshareholder Constituency Statutes*, 19 Pepp. L. Rev. 971 (1992); Committee on Corporate Laws, *Other Constituencies Statutes: Potential for Confusion*, 45 Bus. Law. 2253 (1990); Symposium, 21 Stetson L. Rev. No. 1 (1991).

controlling person (or group) seeking disgorgement of any profits made upon the sale of such person's shares in the company if the sale is within eighteen months after such person attained control status. Under the statute, control status is achieved when, for example, the person or group has voting power over at least 20% of the corporation's voting stock.[81]

"Business Combination Restriction" Statute — This type of statute, codified in such states as Delaware, New Jersey, New York, and Pennsylvania, generally provides that, with certain exceptions, if a person acquires a certain percentage of stock (e.g., 15% or more under the Delaware statute) without the approval of the board of directors of the subject corporation, that person becomes an interested shareholder and may not consummate a business combination (e.g., a merger) with the subject corporation for a substantial period of time (three years under the Delaware statute and five years under the New York statute). There are certain exceptions where the business combination restriction does not apply. One such exception under the Delaware statute is that the acquisition by a controlling shareholder of at least 85% of the voting stock[82] in a tender offer or other acquisition entitles the interested shareholder to engage in a merger without being subject to the three-year prohibition. Another exception occurs when the target's board of directors approves the contemplated business combination before the time that the prospective acquiror becomes an interested shareholder.[83]

[C]   Need for Federal Preemption

To proponents of takeover activity, the *CTS* decision and the enactment of the state anti-takeover statutes signal a defeat for the American economy, market efficiency, and shareholder protection for at least three reasons. First, because there will be fewer tender offers, shareholders will be denied the opportunity to realize the full value of their stock, hence losing the opportunity for substantial profits. Second, inefficient managements will become more entrenched, thereby making their removal more difficult. This consequence harms not only shareholders but also the proficiency of American industry and

---

[81] *See* Bainbridge, *supra* note 25, at 1090–96.

[82] Shares owned by the target's directors and officers are not counted when determining whether the interested shareholder attains 85% stock ownership. *See* 8 Del. Code Ann. § 203.

[83] *See* 8 Del. Code Ann. § 203; N.Y. Bus. Corp. Law § 912(b). *See generally* Bainbridge, *State Takeover and Tender Offer Regulations Post-*MITE*: The Maryland, Ohio and Pennsylvania Attempts*, 90 Dick. L. Rev. 731 (1986); Booth, *The Promise of State Takeover Statutes*, 86 Mich. L. Rev. 1635 (1988); Bradford, *Protecting Shareholders from Themselves? A Policy and Constitutional Review of a State Takeover Statute*, 67 Neb. L. Rev. 459 (1988); Brown, *Regulatory Intervention in the Market for Corporate Control*, 23 U.C. Davis L. Rev. 1 (1989); Butler & Ribstein, *State Anti-Takeover Statutes and the Commerce Clause*, 57 U. Cin. L. Rev. 611 (1988); Cox, *The Constitutional "Dynamics" of the Internal Affairs Rule — A Comment on* CTS *Corporation*, 13 J. Corp. L. 317 (1988); Hazen, *State Anti-Takeover Legislation: The Second and Third Generations*, 23 Wake Forest L. Rev. 77 (1988); Johnson & Millon, *Misreading the Williams Act*, 87 Mich. L. Rev. 1862 (1989); Palmiter, *The* CTS *Gambit: Stanching the Federalization of Corporate Law*, 69 Wash. U.L.Q. 445 (1991); Pinto, *The Constitution and the Market for Corporate Control: State Takeover Statutes After* CTS Corp., 29 Wm. & Mary L. Rev. 699 (1988); sources cited notes 68–81 *supra*.

our nation's quest to maintain its status as a world economic leader. Third, the efficient deployment of corporate assets to their most productive capacity will be impeded, again resulting in harm to shareholders, market efficiency, and our nation's economic proficiency.[84]

To such proponents, in view of the adverse effect that the state anti-takeover statutes have on our nation's (as well as the international) securities markets, Congress should preempt this area. The consequences of takeover activity present dilemmas of national and worldwide concern. They are not adequately debated and resolved by the respective states enacting legislation to protect their parochial interests.

As former SEC Chairman (and now Professor) David S. Ruder has remarked:

> Limitations on the free transferability of securities of corporations which are owned by shareholders nationwide diminish the efficiency, depth, and liquidity of the nation's securities markets. Accordingly, I believe that federal law should control in that area by preempting state statutes that unduly interfere with the free transferability of securities. I believe that corporations whose activities and ownership are national in scope should not be given protection against takeovers by the states where their primary production facilities are located. Just as I believe it to be imprudent for Congress to regulate internal corporate affairs through tender offer regulation, I believe it is imprudent for states to use their authority over matters of internal governance as a means of regulating the interstate market for corporate control.[85]

§ 14.07   DISCLOSURE OF BENEFICIAL OWNERSHIP INTEREST

As discussed in § 14.04[B], Section 13(d)(1) of the Exchange Act and Rule 13d-1 prescribed thereunder require any person or group of persons agreeing to act together who acquire beneficial ownership of more than five percent of a class of equity security registered under Section 12 of the Act to disclose, within ten days, specific information by filing a Schedule 13D with the SEC and by sending copies to the issuer and to each exchange on which the security is traded. In short, "Schedule 13D requires disclosure of the identity of the issuer and the security, the identity, background, and citizenship of the reporting persons, the source and amount of funds used to acquire the securities, the purpose of the transaction, the reporting person's interest in the securities including trading history for the last 60 days and any contracts, arrangements, understandings or relationships with respect to the securities to which the

---

[84] See Judge Posner's opinion in *CTS*, 794 F.2d 250 (7th Cir. 1986), *rev'd*, 481 U.S. 69 (1987).

[85] "Federal Preemption of State Anti-Takeover Legislation," Remarks of David S. Ruder, Chairman, Securities and Exchange Commission, Before the 26th Annual Corporate Counsel Institute, at 8–9 (Chicago Oct. 7, 1987), *reported in*, Fed. Sec. L. Rep. (CCH) No. 1256, at 8–9 (1987). *See generally* Coffee, *Regulating the Market for Corporate Control: A Critical Assessment of the Tender Offer's Role in Corporate Governance*, 84 Colum. L. Rev. 1145 (1984).

reporting person or group is a party."[86]

Importantly, the requirements of Section 13(d) apply irrespective of whether the person (or group) acquiring five percent beneficial ownership intends to make a tender offer. The objective of the statute is to alert the securities markets of potential shifts in corporate control.[87] Although courts have declined to recognize a damages remedy under Section 13(d),[88] a majority of courts have implied a private right of action for injunctive relief under Sections 13(d) and 14(d)-(e) on behalf of an issuer corporation.[89] The rationale is that, despite the Supreme Court's holding in *Piper v. Chris-Craft Industries*[90] that a defeated tender offeror does not have standing under Section 14(e) to bring an action for damages, the target company frequently may be the only willing party with the resources to maintain an injunctive action against a prospective bidder. In situations where the bidder's potential conduct may harm the company and its shareholders, granting standing to the target corporation to seek injunctive relief is therefore a practical approach to protecting shareholders and the marketplace.[91]

With respect to the type of relief awarded for a Section 13(d) violation, the usual remedy has been to require the violating party to amend its previous disclosures and to prohibit additional purchases until such corrective disclosure has been made. Some courts, however, have deemed such relief insufficient and have ordered disgorgement, disenfranchisement, divestiture, or rescission of shares acquired during the period that the misleading Section 13(d) disclosures were disseminated in the marketplace.[92] While some may applaud these measures, it also should be kept in mind that such actions for equitable relief under Section 13(d) may serve as a delaying tactic, thereby providing target management with sufficient time to develop and implement a successful defensive strategy to fend off the hostile offeror.

A major problem with Section 13(d) that has drawn attention is that a beneficial owner of more than five percent of a subject security need not disclose such ownership status until ten days after attaining that status. As a result, such parties may acquire additional shares through privately negotiated

---

[86] Bialkin, Attora & D'Alimonte, *Why, When and How to Conduct a Proxy Battle for Corporate Control, in,* Proxy Contests and Battles for Corporate Control 87, 117 (1981); *see* Block & Rudoff, *Schedule 13D Problems Associated with Large Accumulations of Stock,* 10 Sec. Reg. L.J. 3 (1982).

Note that certain passive investors are allowed to file an abbreviated Schedule — a Schedule 13G — rather than a Schedule 13D. *See* Securities Exchange Act Release No. 39538 (1998).

[87] *See GAF Corp. v. Milstein,* 453 F.2d 709, 719 (2d Cir. 1971).

[88] *See, e.g., Stromfeld v. Great Atlantic and Pacific Tea Co., Inc.,* 484 F. Supp. 1264 (S.D.N.Y. 1980). *See* cases cited in note 39 *supra;* sources cited in § 9.03 *supra.*

[89] *See, e.g., Indiana National Corp. v. Rich,* 712 F.2d 1180 (7th Cir. 1983); cases cited in § 9.03 *supra.*

[90] 430 U.S. 1 (1977).

[91] *See, e.g., Mobil Corp. v. Marathon Oil Co.,* 669 F.2d 366, 371 (6th Cir. 1981); *see also Edelson v. Ch'ien,* 405 F.3d 620, 634 (7th Cir. 2005) (holding that § 13(d) private right of action may be recognized "only in the context of a tender offer or other contest for control").

[92] *See, e.g., SEC v. First City Financial Corporation, Ltd.,* 688 F. Supp. 705 (D.D.C. 1988), *aff'd,* [1989–1990 Transfer Binder] Fed. Sec. L. Rep. (CCH) ¶ 94,801 (D. C. Cir. 1989).

transactions and open market purchases during that ten-day "window" period so long as the acquisitions do not constitute a "tender offer." This loophole makes possible the accumulation of securities, representing a potential shift in corporate control, without adequate notification and disclosure of pertinent information to the marketplace. It has been proposed that Congress should close this loophole by either: (1) prohibiting additional accumulations above the five percent level unless there has been prior disclosure of the requisite information[93] or (2) deeming acquisition of more than twenty (or some other) percent of an equity security, with certain exceptions, to constitute a tender offer, thereby triggering the disclosure and dissemination requirements of the Williams Act.[94] Nonetheless, in practical effect, application of the Hart-Scott-Rodino Antitrust Improvements Act will limit such purchases in many situations.

Generally, the Hart-Scott-Rodino Antitrust Improvements Act of 1976 (HSR Act) imposes upon certain tender offerors and their targets in specified transactions pre-acquisition notification and disclosure requirements. Pursuant thereto, information relevant to the transaction must be furnished to the Antitrust Division of the Department of Justice and the Federal Trade Commission.[95]

Under the HSR Act, an acquiring entity that is of a certain size generally must file and follow that Act's preacquisition waiting period prior to purchasing more than a specified monetary amount of the target corporation's voting securities. Hence, "notification under the [HSR] Act may be required at a time when the acquiring company owns a much lower percentage of the target's voting securities that it could purchase by the time a Schedule 13D is required to be filed."[96] Stated another way, "an accumulation of stock prior to making a hostile raid may trigger the obligation to file a Form [under the HSR Act], and thereby compel the raider to surface and disclose its intentions, even if it does not meet the five-percent reporting threshold for the filing of a Schedule 13D."[97]

---

[93] *See, e.g.*, Advisory Comm. on Tender Offers, U.S. SEC, Report of Recommendations 21–22 (1983).

[94] *Id.* at 23–23; *see* Tender Offer Reform Act of 1987, H.R. 2172, 100th Cong., 1st Sess. (1987) (if enacted, would have prohibited, with certain exceptions, the acquisition of more than ten percent of a target's stock except by means of a tender offer). *See generally* Steinberg, *Tender Offer Regulation: The Need for Reform*, 23 Wake Forest L. Rev. 1 (1988).

[95] *See generally* S. Axinn, B. Fogg & N. Stoll, *Acquisitions Under the Hart-Scott-Rodino Antitrust Improvements Act* (2005); Easterbrook & Fischel, *Antitrust Suits by Targets of Tender Offers*, 80 Mich. L. Rev. 1155 (1982).

[96] Axinn, Fogg & Stoll, *Contests for Corporate Control Under the New Law of Preacquisition Notification*, 24 N.Y.L.S. L. Rev. 857, 866–67 (1979).

[97] M. Lipton & E. Steinberg, Takeovers and Freezeouts § 7.02[5] (1999).

§ 14.08   SEC TENDER OFFER RULES

As evidenced by its 1999 amendments,[98] the SEC has been active in the tender offer rulemaking setting. The rules are quite extensive, mandating, inter alia, that both the offeror and the subject (i.e., target) corporations file detailed disclosure schedules. For example, a Schedule TO must be filed with the SEC in issuer and third-party tender offers. Moreover, Rule 14d-9 requires the subject company to file with the Commission a Schedule 14D-9 which calls for the disclosure of specified information.[99] The SEC "believes that the disclosure elicited by the Schedule will assist security holders in making their investment decisions and in evaluating the merits of a solicitation/recommendation."[100] Such information includes, if material, a description of any arrangement or other understanding and conflicts of interest between, among others, the offeror, the subject corporation, and their affiliates. Disclosure is also required in the Schedule of certain negotiations and transactions (e.g., merger negotiations) undertaken by the target company in response to the tender offer.[101] Moreover, in order to adhere to the disclosure requirements of Rule 14e-2,[102] the subject company in the Schedule 14D-9 must advise shareholders of its position in regard to the tender offer and the reasons therefor.

The SEC's tender offer rules cover a number of other matters. Rule 14d-6(d), for instance, expressly requires an offeror to disclose promptly any material change in the information provided to shareholders.[103] Rule 14e-8 prohibits a bidder from engaging in fraudulent or manipulative conduct when announcing a tender offer. For example, violation of Rule 14e-8 would occur if the supposed bidder had no intention or financial means to commence and complete the tender offer within a reasonable time period.[104] Also, to reduce the previous regulatory imbalances between cash tender offers and stock exchange offers, the SEC in 1999 elected to allow exchange offers to commence upon the filing of a registration statement. Nonetheless, the bidder cannot purchase any securities tendered in the exchange offer until the effectiveness of the registration statement and the timely disclosure of all material changes.[105]

---

[98] Securities Exchange Act Release No. 42055 (1999).

[99] 17 C.F.R. § 240.14d-9.

[100] *See* Securities Exchange Act Release No. 16384 (1979).

[101] Compare this disclosure requirement with the duty affirmatively to disclose merger and similar negotiations in other contexts, discussed in § 11.04 *supra.* Rule 14d-9 allows target companies to solicit and make recommendations to their security holders to the same degree that offerors are permitted to do so, provided that any such communication is filed with the SEC on the date of first use and contains a legend advising security holders to read the Schedule 14D-9 disclosure document where it is provided. *See* Securities Exchange Act Release No. 42055 (1999).

[102] SEC Rule 14e-2, 17 C.F.R. § 240.14e-2 (Rule 14e-2 generally obligates the target company to transmit to its shareholders within ten business days of the commencement of the tender offer a statement of its position in regard thereto).

[103] 17 C.F.R. § 240.14d-6(d).

[104] 17 C.F.R. § 240.14e-8; *see* Securities Exchange Act Release No. 42055 (1999).

[105] Securities Exchange Act Release No. 42055 (1999).

Another SEC tender offer rule, Rule 14d-8, extends the proration period from the previous ten-calendar-day period to the entire period that the offer remains open (under Rule 14(e)(1) a tender offer must remain open for at least twenty business days).[106] Generally, Rule 14d-8 obligates a bidder in an oversubscribed partial tender offer "to take up and pay for" shares tendered on a pro rata basis "during the period such offer, request, or invitation remains open." The Rule precipitated comment on the extent of the Commission's rulemaking authority and on the broader question of its effect on the balance between the bidder and target in two-tier offers, particularly where the pressure on shareholders to tender is accentuated by a price differential between the tender offer and the proposed subsequent merger.[107]

Rule 14d-11 adopted in 1999, allows bidders in third-party tender offers to have a subsequent offering period, lasting from three to twenty business days, as selected by the bidder, during which no withdrawal rights are permitted. If the bidder elects to have a subsequent offering period, the same consideration must be paid as was paid in the initial period.[108]

Other significant SEC actions in the tender offer context include the adoption of the "all holders" and "best price" mandates under Rules 13e-4 and 14d-10.[109] The effect of these rules, in practical effect, is to nullify the Delaware Supreme Court's decision in *Unocal v. Mesa Petroleum Co.*[110] In *Unocal*, the Delaware high court, applying a modified version of the business judgment rule, upheld the target management's use of a discriminatory issuer tender offer which excluded the hostile shareholder from participation. Under the SEC's rules, by contrast, both issuer and third-party tender offers must be open to all shareholders and the best price paid to any tendering security holder must be paid to any other tendering security holder. Thus, the SEC's rule signifies that exclusionary tender offers for publicly-held companies no longer remain a viable defensive strategy. Moreover, in 2006, the SEC adopted amendments to the best price rule to clarify that the Rule's mandates extend only to the consideration offered and paid by the bidder to tendering shareholders. The amendments make clear that the best price rule does not encompass employment compensation, severance, or other types of employee benefit arrangements.[111]

---

[106] 17 C.F.R. § 240.14d-8.

[107] *See* Brennan, *SEC Rule 14d-8 and Two-Tier Offers*, *in*, Tender Offers: Developments and Commentaries 109 (M. Steinberg ed. 1985).

[108] 17 C.F.R. § 240.14d-11; *see* Securities Exchange Act Release No. 42055 (1999).

[109] 17 C.F.R. §§ 240.13e-4, 240.14d-10; Securities Exchange Act Release No. 23421 (1986).

[110] 493 A.2d 946 (Del. 1985).

[111] *See* Securities Exchange Act Release No. 54684 (2006). In adopting amendments to the best price rule for both issuer and third-party tender offers, the Commission stated:

> We are adopting amendments to the language of the third-party and issuer tender offer best-price rules to clarify that the provisions apply only with respect to the consideration offered and paid for securities tendered in a tender offer. We also are amending the third-party and issuer tender offer best-price rules to provide that any consideration that is offered and paid accordingly to employment compensation, severance or other employee benefit arrangements entered into with security holders of the subject company that meet certain requirements will not be prohibited by the rules.

§ 14.09   SUBSTANTIVE REGULATION OF DEFENSIVE TACTICS

[A]   Federal Law

With respect to the legitimacy of defensive tactics under federal law, the key issue is whether Section 14(e), the antifraud provision of the Williams Act, regulates substantive conduct. In other words, is Section 14(e)'s purpose solely that of ensuring adequate and fair disclosure or does the statute have a broader reach? In adhering to the former approach, the Supreme Court definitively resolved this issue in *Schreiber v. Burlington Northern, Inc.*[112] The statutory analysis and policy implications of that decision merit attention.

Prior to the Supreme Court's decision in *Schreiber*, the Williams Act could have been applied in either of two ways to ensure that target shareholders normally had an opportunity to accept or reject a tender offer. First, conduct by management that deprives shareholders of an opportunity to tender may be held to constitute "constructive fraud" within the meaning of Section 14(e) of the Williams Act. Although the Supreme Court held in *Santa Fe Industries, Inc. v. Green*[113] that "mere" breaches of fiduciary duty not amounting to "manipulation" or "deception" do not violate Section 10(b) of the Exchange Act and Rule 10b-5 promulgated thereunder, Section 14(e) ought to be interpreted differently. Unlike Section 10(b), Section 14(e) by its terms prohibits "fraudulent" acts or practices. This difference in statutory language and the legislative history of Section 14(e) support giving it a broader reach than Section 10(b). Second, defensive tactics, the practical effect of which prevent shareholders from tendering in response to a bid, could have been viewed as "manipulative" under Section 14(e). Under this rationale, target management could be found to have engaged in "manipulative" practices proscribed by Section 14(e) when it artificially impedes the operation of a fair market for the corporation's stock by such tactics as granting options on valuable corporate assets to friendly third parties.[114]

Prior to *Schreiber*, a few courts held that certain defensive tactics engaged in by target management, even though fully disclosed, constituted

---

Finally, we are amending the third-party and issuer tender offer best-price rules to provide a safe harbor provision so that arrangements that are approved by certain independent directors of either the subject company's or the bidder's board of directors, as applicable, will not be prohibited by the rules. These amendments are intended to make it clear that the best-price rule was not intended to capture employment compensation, severance or other employee benefit arrangements.

Id.; *see* Obi, *SEC Rule 14d-10(e)(2) Amendment: Is This the Optimal Solution to the Tender Offer "Best-Price Rule" Dilemma?*, 35 Sec. Reg. L.J. 355 (2007).

[112] 472 U.S. 1 (1985).

[113] 430 U.S. 462 (1977), *discussed in*, § 8.04 *supra.*

[114] Steinberg, *supra* note 94, at 19–20; *see* Junewicz, *The Appropriate Limits of Section 14(e) of the Securities Exchange Act of 1934*, 62 Texas L. Rev. 1171 (1984); Loewenstein, *Section 14(e) of the Williams Act and the Rule 10b-5 Comparisons*, 71 Georgetown L.J. 1311 (1983); Weiss, *Defensive Responses to Tender Offers and the Williams Act's Prohibition Against Manipulation*, 35 Vand. L. Rev. 1087 (1982); *see also* Hannes & Yadlin, *The SEC Regulation of Takeovers: Some Doubts from a Game Theory Perspective and a Proposal for Reform*, 25 Yale J. Reg. 35 (2008).

"manipulation" under Section 14(e).[115] The Supreme Court in *Schreiber* rejected this interpretation, holding that Section 14(e)'s reach is limited to that of disclosure. In assessing Section 14(e)'s scope, the Court stated: "All three species of misconduct listed in Section 14(e), i.e., fraudulent, deceptive or manipulative . . . are directed at failure to disclose."[116] Hence, the *Schreiber* decision clearly limits the availability of federal law remedies in a tender offer situation. In so doing, the Supreme Court echoed the rationale of *Santa Fe* and relegated the policing of the substantive fairness of tender offers to state corporation law. Consequently, after *Schreiber*, to support a Section 14(e) right of action, a plaintiff must allege either misrepresentation or nondisclosure.

The *Schreiber* Court's decision signifies that, with certain exceptions such as the "all holders rule,"[117] the legitimacy of takeover maneuvers employed in multibillion dollar tender offers having both national and international ramifications will be examined solely under state law. To proponents of corporate accountability and shareholder democracy, the states' continual "race for the bottom" signals that meritorious interests will be neglected.[118] The decision also means that the state of Delaware, being the predominant state of incorporation for publicly-held companies, may well have the principal voice in determining the validity of takeover tactics.[119]

[B]   State Law

The following discussion succinctly treats the application of state law with respect to the legitimacy of takeover tactics engaged in by a target corporation's board of directors. Generally, in a number of jurisdictions, so long as the target's board (relying upon outside directors and experts) adopts defensive tactics for the purpose of maintaining the company as an independent viable entity, the business judgment rule will apply to insulate those actions from successful challenge.[120] The business judgment rule basically provides that corporate officers and directors will be shielded from judicial inquiry into the propriety of their decisions and from liability for harm to the corporation resulting from their decisions, so long as (1) the decision was

---

[115] *See, e.g., Mobil Corp. v. Marathon Oil Co.,* 669 F.2d 366 (6th Cir. 1981) (target oil company's grant to competing tender offeror of certain options considered "manipulative" within meaning of § 14(e)); *Data Probe Acquisition Corp. v. Datatab, Inc.,* 568 F. Supp. 1538 (S.D.N.Y.) (self-serving grant of option to purchase shares of target by target's management was "manipulative device"), *rev'd,* 722 F.2d 1 (2d Cir. 1983), *cert. denied,* 465 U.S. 1052 (1984).

[116] 472 U.S. at 8.

[117] *See* Rules 13e-4, 14d-10, *discussed in,* § 14.08 *supra.*

[118] *See generally* Cary, *Federalism and Corporate Law: Reflections Upon Delaware,* 83 Yale L.J. 663 (1974).

[119] *See* Fiflis, *Of Lollipops and Law — A Proposal for a National Policy Concerning Tender Offer Defenses,* 19 U.C. Davis L. Rev. 303, 306 (1986) ("One may properly ask whether it is appropriate for Delaware, which conceivably may not be the abode of a single Unocal shareholder, to fix national policy in an international securities market, while Congress and the federal courts, Nero-like, abdicate a policymaking role.").

[120] *Unitrin, Inc. v. American General Corp.,* 651 A.2d 1361 (Del. 1995); *Paramount Communications, Inc. v. Time, Inc.,* 571 A.2d 1140 (Del. 1990); *Moran v. Household International, Inc.,* 500 A.2d 1346 (Del. 1985); *Unocal Corp. v. Mesa Petroleum Co.,* 493 A.2d 946 (Del. 1985).

within management's authority to make, and (2) such corporate fiduciaries (a) made adequate inquiry and were sufficiently informed with respect to the determination, (b) acted in good faith and had no disabling conflict of interest, and (c) had a rational basis for believing that the business judgment was in the corporation's best interests.[121] As the Supreme Court of Delaware has pointed out, the doctrine is an acknowledgment of the managerial prerogatives of corporate directors under state law: "It is a [rebuttable] presumption that in making a business decision the directors of a corporation acted on an informed basis, in good faith and in the honest belief that the action taken was in the best interests of the company."[122]

In ascertaining whether the business judgment rule will be applied in a given situation involving defensive tactics undertaken by the target's board of directors, a distinction has been made between defensive maneuvers employed to maintain the corporation as an independent, viable entity and those measures implemented to favor one bidder over another in a "sale" or "auction" setting. In the "sale" context, courts have refused to apply the business judgment rule to target management's actions.[123] Where "lock-up" and "no-shop" clauses are extended to management's favored suitor in such an active bidding situation, thereby precluding the auction process from ultimately resulting, the directors must demonstrate "some rationally related benefit accruing to the stockholders."[124]

Significantly, however, the business judgment rule continues to be the prevalent standard when assessing target management's actions taken for the purpose of maintaining the company as an on-going independent entity.[125] This standard has been applied to show-stop tactics, such as the taking on of $10 billion of debt,[126] unilateral adoption by a board of directors of an anti-takeover "poison pill" amendment to the corporation's by-laws which, if triggered, would result in the entity's liquidation,[127] invocation of the "Just Say No" defense,[128]

---

[121] *See* American Law Institute, Principles of Corporate Governance and Structure: Analysis and Recommendations § 4.01 (1994).

[122] *Aronson v. Lewis*, 473 A.2d 805, 812 (Del. 1984). Generally, to overcome the presumption of the business judgment rule, the plaintiff must show "gross negligence." *Id.*

[123] *See, e.g., Edelman v. Fruehauf Corp.*, 798 F.2d 882 (6th Cir. 1986) (applying Michigan law); *Hanson Trust v. ML SCM Acquisition, Inc.*, 781 F.2d 264 (2d Cir. 1986) (applying New York law); *MacAndrews & Forbes Holdings v. Revlon, Inc.*, 506 A.2d 173 (Del. 1986).

[124] Revlon, 506 A.2d at 182; *see Paramount Communications, Inc. v. QVC Network, Inc.*, 637 A.2d 34 (Del. 1994).

[125] *See, e.g., Gearhart Indus. v. Smith Int'l*, 741 F.2d 707 (5th Cir. 1984) (applying Texas law); *Turner Broadcasting Sys. v. CBS*, 627 F. Supp. 901 (N.D. Ga. 1985) (applying New York law); *Moran v. Household Int'l*, 500 A.2d 1346 (Del. 1985). *But see Dynamics Corp. of Am. v. CTS Corp.*, 794 F.2d 250 (7th Cir. 1986) (applying Indiana law), *rev'd* on other grounds, 481 U.S. 69 (1987); *Norlin Corp. v. Rooney, Pace, Inc.*, 744 F.2d 255 (2d Cir. 1984) (applying New York law).

[126] *See, e.g., Paramount Communications, Inc. v. Time, Inc.*, 571 A.2d 1140 (Del. 1990).

[127] E.g., *Revlon*, 506 A.2d at 180. For other decisions focusing on poison pill provisions, including "dead hand" provisions (provisions that have the effect of maintaining incumbent directors in place even after an insurgent victory), compare *Quickturn Design Systems, Inc. v. Shapiro*, 721 A. 2d 1281 (Del. 1998) (holding delayed redemption provision invalid under Delaware Corporation Code § 141(a)) and *Bank of New York v. Irving Bank Corp.*, 528 N.Y.S.2d 482 (N.Y.

and to corporate recapitalizations and restructurings, such as issuer self-tenders, dividend pay-outs, and related techniques.[129] Moreover, a number of courts have held that the grant of a lock-up to a potential acquiring entity, when no other bidder is on the scene, is also protected by the business judgment rule.[130]

As commentators have pointed out,[131] the Delaware Supreme Court in the takeover setting has not applied the business judgment rule in its traditional form. In *Unocal Corp. v. Mesa Petroleum Co.*,[132] the Delaware high court acknowledged that "[b]ecause of the omnipresent specter that a board may be acting primarily in its own interests . . . there is an enhanced duty which calls for judicial examination at the threshold before the protections of the business judgment rule may be conferred."[133] Hence, before the business judgment rule may be invoked, target management must show that there were "reasonable grounds for believing that a danger to corporate policy and effectiveness existed" and that the action taken was "reasonable in relation to the threat posed."[134] Nonetheless, as more recently held by the Delaware Supreme Court, "if the board of directors' response is not draconian (preclusive or coercive) and is within a 'range of reasonableness,' a court must not substitute its judgment for the board's."[135]

Thus far, opinions differ whether this modified application of the business judgment rule has had a major substantive impact.[136] An interesting point is

---

Supr. Ct. 1988) (holding that dead hand provision contravened New York corporation law), with *Invacare Corp. v. Healthdyne Technologies, Inc.*, 968 F. Supp. 1578 (N.D. Ga. 1977) (interpreting Georgia law, upholding dead hand provision and stating that "the concept of continuing directors is an integral part of a takeover defense and is not contrary to public policy in Georgia").

[128] *Moore Corp. v. Wallace Computer Services, Inc.*, 907 F. Supp. 1545 (Del 1995) (interpreting Delaware law, upholding target board's refusal to redeem the subject corporation's poison pill when faced with an all-cash, all-share offer at a substantial premium).

[129] E.g., *Unocal*, 493 A.2d at 954.

[130] *See, e.g.*, *Revlon*, 506 A.2d at 181.

[131] *See, e.g.*, Bainbridge, *Exclusive Merger Agreements and Lock-Ups in Negotiated Corporate Acquisitions*, 75 Minn. L. Rev. 239 (1990); Bradford, *Stampeding Shareholders and Other Myths: Target Shareholders and Hostile Tender Offers*, 15 J. Corp. L. 417 (1990); Chiapinelli; *The Life and Adventures of Unocal — Part I: Moore the Marrier*, 23 Del. J. Corp. L. 85 (1998); Johnson, *Corporate Takeovers and Corporations: Who Are They For?*, 43 Wash. & Lee L. Rev. 781 (1986); Taylor, *New and Unjustified Restrictions on Delaware Directors' Authority*, 21 Del. J. Corp. 837 (1996).

[132] 493 A.2d 946 (Del. 1985).

[133] *Id.* at 954.

[134] *Id.* at 955; *see* Bainbridge, Unocal *at 20 : Director Primacy in Corporate Takeovers*, 31 Del. J. Corp. L. 769 (2006).

[135] *Unitrin, Inc. v. American General Corp.*, 651 A. 2d 1361, 1388 (Del. 1995).

[136] *See Omnicare, Inc. v. NCS Healthcare, Inc.*, 818 A. 2d 914 (Del. 2003) (in a three to two decision holding that the defensive measures at issue were coercive and were not within *Unocal's* range of reasonableness); *see also* Gilson & Kraakman, *Delaware's Intermediate Standard for Defensive Tactics: Is There Substance to Proportionality Review?*, 44 Bus. Law. 247 (1989); Griffin, *The Costs and Benefits of Precommitment: An Appraisal of* Omnicare v. NCS Healthcare, 29 J. Corp. L. 569 (2004); Steinberg, *Nightmare on Main Street: The* Paramount *Picture Horror Show*, 16 Del. J. Corp. L. 1, 18–26 (1990).

that, at least under Delaware law, by retaining outside advisers (such as investment bankers and lawyers) and relying extensively on outside directors, the board, in all probability, will be able to rebut assertions that the defensive maneuvers implemented were primarily motivated by entrenchment purposes, i.e., a desire to retain control.[137] As a result, under Delaware law, if a breach were shown, it would be of the duty of care rather than of loyalty. Consequently, pursuant to the 1986 statutory amendments to Delaware law, the directors would be absolved from monetary liability unless their actions constituted bad faith or intentional misconduct.[138]

A minority of courts, on the other hand, have declined to invoke the business judgment rule to management's tactics that evidence an intention to retain control.[139] Instead, in these situations, the burden is placed upon the board to "prove that the transaction was fair and reasonable to the corporation."[140] This standard is more protective of shareholder interests but its strict implementation has certain deficiencies. From a practical standpoint, it is undeniable that incumbent corporate management in nearly all hostile takeover bid situations wishes to retain control.[141] This attitude may be based on financial self-interest, prestige, or a sincere (but perhaps misguided) belief that the incumbent's continued stewardship is in the corporation's best interests. Hence, attention should focus on both the motive and effect of the directors' actions upon shareholder decisionmaking.

Unfortunately, vigorous application of a fairness standard may subject directors to astronomical monetary damages, totaling hundreds of millions, if not billions, of dollars.[142] The current director and officer insurance procurement and price dilemmas would be exacerbated, resulting in outside directors becoming even less inclined to serve on corporate boards. The consequence may be that courts would respond by making overly lenient factual determinations to whatever legal standard is applied in assessing alleged director misconduct, except perhaps in cases seeking exclusively injunctive relief. A better approach may be to: (1) recognize that takeovers deeply affect corporate constituencies in addition to shareholders, (2) permit

---

[137] *Revlon*, 506 A.2d at 181.

[138] *See* Delaware S. Bill 533, L. 1986, *amending*, Del. Code Ann. tit. 8, § 102. This comment presumes that the limitation on liability provision has been added to the corporation's articles of incorporation. *See generally* Balotti & Gentile, *Elimination or Limitation of Director Liability for Delaware Corporations*, 12 Del. J. Corp. L. 5 (1987).

[139] *E.g., Dynamics Corp. of America v. CTS Corp.*, 794 F.2d 250 (7th Cir. 1986) (applying Indiana law), *rev'd on other grounds*, 481 U.S. 69 (1987); *Norlin Corp. v. Rooney, Pace, Inc.*, 744 F.2d 255 (2d Cir. 1984) (applying New York law); *Heckmann v. Ahmanson*, 168 Cal. App. 3d 119, 214 Cal. Rptr. 177 (1986).

[140] *Norlin*, 744 F.2d at 265.

[141] *See Johnson v. Trueblood*, 629 F.2d 287, 292–293 (3d Cir. 1980) (construing Delaware law); Winter, *Paying Lawyers, Empowering Prosecutors, and Protecting Managers: Raising the Cost of Capital in America*, 1993 Duke L.J. 945, 973 (asserting that "[t]here is virtually no way for a court to distinguish between defensive measures generated by a desire to retain office and defensive measures generated to preserve a corporate policy without regard to who retains office").

[142] *See Panter v. Marshall Field & Co.*, 646 F.2d 271 (7th Cir. 1981) (applying Delaware law) (over $200 million in damages sought).

management to take these non-investor interests into account in certain circumstances, (3) scrutinize defensive tactics by their effect on shareholder decisionmaking, (4) apply a fairly strict standard when assessing the legitimacy of "show-stopper" and similar maneuvers, and (5) implement a functional ceiling on damages that promotes the competing policies at stake.[143]

§ 14.10   VIEWS OF COMMENTATORS

Several commentators have expressed their opinions regarding the need for tender offer reform. The following summarizes a number of these divergent views.

1. *Application of the Business Judgment Rule* — These commentators believe that the business judgment rule, if the requirements of the rule are met, should govern the legitimacy of defensive takeover tactics.[144]

2. *Reliance on Outside Directors* — This view posits that deference to defensive tactics undertaken by a target's board of directors should be given by courts only if the outside directors have a significant role in determining the target's response to the takeover bid.[145]

3. *"Fairness" Standard* — Under this standard, the business judgment rule would not apply in the takeover setting. Rather, target management would have the burden of establishing that the defensive actions taken were fair to the corporation and its shareholders.[146]

4. *"Freeze" Period* — This proposal would establish a "freeze" period during which a hostile tender offer would remain open for a substantial period of time, such as six months, in order to enable shareholders to make informed decisions. During this "freeze" period, any "structural" change in the company (for example, an option to sell the target's "crown jewel") would require shareholder approval.[147]

---

[143] For further discussion, see Steinberg, note 94 *supra. See generally* Bainbridge, *Precommitment Strategies in Corporate Law: The Case of Dead Hand and No Hand Pills*, 29 J. Corp. L. 1 (2003); Bedchuck & Ferrell, *A New Approach to Takeover Law and Regulatory Competition*, 87 Va. L. Rev. 111 (2001); Johnson & Millon, *Misreading the Williams Act*, 87 Mich. L. Rev. 1862 (1989); Johnson & Siegel, *Corporate Mergers: Redefining the Role of Target Directors*, 136 U. Pa. L. Rev. 315 (1987); Lipton, *Corporate Governance in the Age of Finance Corporatism*, 136 U. Pa. L. Rev. 1 (1987); Loewenstein, *Toward An Auction Market for Corporate Control and the Demise of the Business Judgment Rule*, 63 So. Cal. L. Rev. 65 (1989); McGinty, *Replacing Hostile Takeovers*, 144 U. Pa. L. Rev. 983 (1996).

[144] *See, e.g.,* Lipton, *Takeover Bids in the Target's Boardroom*, 35 Bus. Law 101 (1979); Steinbrink, *Management's Response to the Takeover Attempt*, 28 Case W. Res. L. Rev. 882 (1978).

[145] *See, e.g.,* Gelfond & Sebastian, *Reevaluating the Duties of Target Management in a Hostile Tender Offer*, 60 B.U.L. Rev. 403 (1980); Williams, *Role of Directors in Takeover Offers*, 13 Rev. Sec. Reg. 963 (1980).

[146] *See generally* Prentice, *Target Board Abuse of Defensive Tactics: Can Federal Law Be Mobilized to Overcome the Business Judgment Rule?*, 8 J. Corp. L. 337 (1983).

[147] *See, e.g.,* Goldberg, *Regulation of Hostile Tender Offers: A Dissenting View and Recommended Reforms*, 43 Md. L. Rev. 225 (1984) (authored by former U.S. Supreme Court Justice

5. *"Modified Shareholder Choice"* — Pursuant to this proposal, target shareholders would have an unimpeded right to tender their shares to the hostile bidder, subject to the exception that target management may take appropriate steps to fend off a hostile bid if it affirmatively shows that the offeror constituted a clear threat to the target's business, including the equity interests of the shareholders.[148]

6. *"The Passivity Approach"* — Tender offers are viewed as beneficial to shareholders and the economy under this approach. They encourage managerial efficiency, competition, proficient use of corporate assets, and shareholder gain. As a result, when a tender offer is made, target management under this approach must remain totally passive. Under this approach, no defensive tactics are permitted.[149]

7. *"The Auction Model"* — This approach takes on a number of variations. Basically, this proposal entitles target management to communicate to shareholders regarding its position on the takeover bid but does not permit the use of significant defensive maneuvers. Moreover, target management may (or "should" or "must" depending on the particular approach) put the corporation up for "auction," seeking out more favorable bids from other prospective offerors.[150]

Arthur Goldberg); Lowenstein, *Pruning Deadwood in Hostile Takeovers: A Proposal for Legislation*, 83 Colum. L. Rev. 249 (1983).

[148] *See, e.g.*, Steinberg, note 94 *supra.*

[149] *See, e.g.*, Easterbrook & Fischel, *The Proper Role of Target Management in Responding to a Tender Offer*, 94 Harv. L. Rev. 1161 (1981).

[150] *See e.g.*, Bebchuck, *The Case for Facilitating Competing Tender Offers*, 95 Harv. L. Rev. 1028 (1982); Gilson, *A Structural Approach to Corporations: The Case Against Defensive Tactics in Tender Offers*, 33 Stan. L. Rev. 819 (1981); Oesterle, *Target Managers as Negotiating Agents for Shareholders in Tender Offers: A Reply to the Passivity Thesis*, 71 Cornell L. Rev. 53 (1985); *see also* Bebchuck & Ferrell, *Federalism and Corporate Law: The Race to Protect Managers from Takeovers*, 99 Colum. L. Rev. 1168 (1999).

Chapter 15

SEC ENFORCEMENT

§ 15.01 INTRODUCTION

Congress enacted the federal securities laws in light of a perceived need to protect investors and the integrity of the marketplace. To help ensure that the purposes of the federal securities laws are fulfilled, Congress vested the SEC with broad investigatory and enforcement powers. As part of its investigatory authority, the Commission may subpoena witnesses and records. Once the Commission obtains sufficient information to believe that a violation of the federal securities laws has occurred, it may bring an enforcement action either administratively or in a federal district court.

The overwhelming percentage of SEC enforcement actions are settled pursuant to the consent negotiation process where the defendant neither admits nor denies the Commission's allegations. Parties generally consent rather than litigate due to a number of factors. These include that the SEC may have a strong case, the financial costs involved in litigating with the Commission, avoidance of adverse publicity that would be generated by prolonged litigation, disruption of normal operations that would otherwise result due to management's attention being diverted, and fear of offensive collateral estoppel should the SEC emerge victorious. With respect to this last factor, there is the concern that an adverse decision in an SEC contested matter may result in the initiation of private damages actions in which the claimants seek to estop the defendants from relitigating issues resolved against them in the prior SEC action.[1]

SEC enforcement (as well as state "blue sky" enforcement) raises a multitude of issues. A number of the key topics are discussed in this Chapter. For more extensive treatment, other sources should be consulted.[2]

---

[1] *See Parklane Hosiery Co., Inc. v. Shore,* 439 U.S. 322 (1979); authorities cited note 2 *infra.*

[2] *See* Enforcement Manual Issued by the Securities and Exchange Commission Division of Enforcement (2008) (hereinafter SEC Enforcement Manual), *available at* www.sec/divisions/enforce/enforcementmanual.pdf. For other sources, see, *e.g.*, American Bar Association, The Securities Enforcement Manual: Tactics and Strategies (Kirkpatrick & Lockhart, LLP 2d ed. 2007); H. Friedman, Securities and Commodities Enforcement (2006); J. Long, Blue Sky Law (2008); M. Steinberg & R. Ferrara, Securities Practice: Federal and State Enforcement (2d ed. 2001 & 2009 Supp.).

State securities law enforcement mechanisms are fairly similar to those employed under federal law and comprise an important part of securities law enforcement. As stated by Dean Sargent:

> Blue sky enforcement actions are not only large in number, but varied in purpose and form. They may be used to combat both fraud and registration violations. They also may be used to discipline securities professionals carrying on business within the state. The

§ 15.02   SEC SUBPOENA POWER

[A]   Overview

SEC investigations normally are nonpublic and may take the form of a preliminary inquiry or a formal investigation. Frequently, a substantial portion of the materials in the Commission's files is obtained in the informal stage through cooperation. However, if the SEC is unable to elicit the needed information informally, it must initiate a formal investigation and seek authorization from the courts to compel uncooperative sources to supply the desired information. An informal inquiry or investigation can be commenced by the SEC's enforcement division and does not involve the use of subpoenas. The formal investigation, on the other hand, requires Commission authorization and, when necessary, court enforcement as well.[3]

Pursuant to a formal order of investigation, which outlines the general scope of the Commission's inquiry, the SEC can issue subpoenas if it determines that the documents and witnesses ordered produced may be relevant. If the party to whom the subpoena is issued refuses to voluntarily produce the requested information, the Commission must petition a federal district court for an order that compels compliance with the subpoena.[4] Because the Commission's subpoena enforcement power is expansive and constitutes a necessary element of its investigations, the courts frequently order enforcement.[5]

An SEC investigation serves to uncover facts that may reveal whether a violation of the securities laws has occurred.[6] Because such an investigation by

---

action may take the shape of an informal investigation, a formal administrative proceeding, a civil suit by the administrator or a criminal prosecution. These actions frequently end in settlement, but they also may conclude with application of one or more of a variety of possible remedies, including denial, suspension, or revocation of a securities exemption or of a broker-dealer, agent, or investment adviser registration, an injunction, an appointment of a receiver, or a criminal conviction.

Sargent, *Blue Sky Enforcement Actions — Some Practical Considerations*, 14 Sec. Reg. L.J. 343, 344 (1987). Note also that broker-dealer regulation is subject to self-regulatory organization (SRO) oversight. The key SRO regulator is the Financial Industry Regulatory Authority (FINRA). *See generally* Crimmins & Robertson, *What's Important in the SEC's Enforcement Manual*, 40 Sec. Reg. & L. Rep. (BNA) 1697 (2008); Eisenberg, *Beyond the Basics: Seventy-Five Defenses Securities Litigators Need to Know*, 62 Bus. Law. 1281 (2007); Karmel, *Creating Law at the Securities and Exchange Commission: The Lawyer as Prosecutor*, 61 Law & Contem. Prob. 33 (1998); Long, *A Guide to the Investigative and Enforcement Provisions of the Uniform Securities Act*, 37 Wash. & Lee L. Rev. 739 (1980); Mann & Barry, *Developments in the Internationalization of Securities Enforcement*, 39 Int'l Law. 667, 937 (2005); McLucas, Taylor & Matthews, *A Practitioners Guide to the SEC's Investigative and Enforcement Process*, 70 Temple L. Rev. 53 (1997); Prentice, *The Inevitability of a Strong SEC*, 91 Cornell L. Rev. 775 (2006); Razzano, *To Cooperate With the Securities and Exchange Commission or Not to Cooperate — That Is the Question*, 31 Sec. Reg. L.J. 410 (2003); Williams, *The Securities and Exchange Commission and Corporate Social Transparency*, 112 Harv. L. Rev. 1197 (1999).

[3] *See* SEC Rules of Practice, 17 C.F.R. § 202.5; Securities Act Release No. 6345 (1981); SEC Enforcement Manual, *supra* note 2, at § 2.3.3.

[4] *See, e.g.*, § 21(b) of the Exchange Act.

[5] *See, e.g.*, *SEC v. Brigadoon Scotch Distributing Co.*, 480 F.2d 1047 (2d Cir. 1973).

[6] *See, e.g.*, *United States v. Morton Salt Co.*, 338 U.S. 632 (1950).

itself carries no formal sanctions, judicial intervention may be necessary to enforce compliance with an SEC subpoena. Accordingly, the courts possess the power to hold a party in contempt for noncompliance with subpoenas they have ordered enforced.[7] A party commits civil contempt by disobeying a court order after knowledge that the order has been issued.[8]

[B]   Supreme Court Standards

The Supreme Court has established standards that must be met by an administrative agency before a subpoena will be enforced by the lower courts. In *United States v. Powell*,[9] the Court determined that an agency seeking enforcement of a subpoena does not have the burden of establishing probable cause. Rather, the agency must show "that the investigation will be conducted pursuant to a legitimate purpose, that the inquiry may be relevant to the purpose, that the information sought is not already within the [agency's] possession, and that the administrative steps required by the [federal statutes] have been followed."[10] If the Commission can establish these four elements, it will be deemed to have affirmatively established agency good faith, and the burden thereupon will shift to the opposing party to challenge on an appropriate ground.[11]

To procure enforcement under the *Powell* standards, the SEC is not required to provide evidence of probability of coverage under the securities statutes or the likelihood of a violation of these statutes.[12] Rather, the agency must demonstrate that the investigation falls within the mandate Congress granted to the SEC and that the documents sought are reasonably relevant to the inquiry.[13] The subpoena cannot be issued in bad faith,[14] its scope cannot be too indefinite,[15] and compliance with the subpoena cannot be too burdensome.[16]

Although demonstrating agency bad faith is difficult for those opposing enforcement of an SEC subpoena, this sometimes can be shown.[17] However, the other appropriate grounds for fending off enforcement of such a subpoena, including the assertion of first,[18] fourth,[19] and fifth[20] amendment constitutional

---

[7] *See, e.g.,* § 21(c) of the Exchange Act.

[8] *See Penfield Co. v. SEC,* 330 U.S. 585 (1947).

[9] 379 U.S. 48 (1964).

[10] *Id.* at 57–58.

[11] *Id.* at 58.

[12] *Id.* at 51–58.

[13] *See Oklahoma Press Publishing v. Walling,* 327 U.S. 186 (1946).

[14] 379 U.S. at 58.

[15] *See SEC v. Blackfoot Bituminous, Inc.,* 622 F.2d 512 (10th Cir. 1080).

[16] *See SEC v. Savage,* 513 F.2d 188 (7th Cir. 1975) (per curiam).

[17] *See SEC v. Wheeling-Pittsburgh Steel Corp.,* 648 F.2d 118 (3d Cir. 1981) (en banc). *See generally* Comment, *SEC v. Wheeling-Pittsburgh Steel Corp. — Informant Bad Faith Defense to Enforcement of an Administrative Subpoena,* 7 J. Corp. L. 121 (1984).

[18] *See, e.g., SEC v. McGoff,* 647 F.2d 185 (D.C. Cir. 1981). With respect to subpoenas issued to

challenges, rarely succeed. Hence, although judicial enforcement of an SEC subpoena may not be automatic, such enforcement generally is likely if the purpose of the SEC's request is legitimate and if the information sought is relevant to that purpose.

[C]   Notice to Third Parties

The formal order of investigation, to which the Commission's subpoena power attaches, ordinarily names the initial subject(s) of the SEC's inquiry. In practice, the Commission may not include the identification of all or even a substantial number of the parties who may be implicated in the investigation. Also, the formal order does not indicate the third parties to whom the Commission may issue subpoenas. A target of an investigation, unless informed by a third party who receives a subpoena, thus may remain ignorant of the parties from whom the Commission seeks information.

In *SEC v. Jerry T. O'Brien, Inc.*,[21] the Supreme Court refused to require the Commission to provide notice to the targets of subpoenas issued to third parties in nonpublic investigations. In reaching its decision, the Court explored three sources from which such a requirement had to be derived if it were to be imposed upon the Commission: "a constitutional provision; an understanding on the part of Congress, inferable from the structure of the securities laws, regarding how the SEC should conduct its inquiries; or the general standards governing judicial enforcement of administrative subpoenas enunciated in . . . *Powell.*"[22]

The Court found that neither the fourth, fifth nor sixth amendment mandated that notice of third party subpoenas be given in order to protect the target's constitutional rights. The fourth amendment affords no support because a third party provides information to the Commission. Even though the target may have communicated the subpoenaed information to the third party in confidence, the target may not rely on the third party's fourth amendment protection to claim an unreasonable search or seizure when the third party relinquishes the information. Neither the due process clause nor the self-incrimination clause of the fifth amendment apply to the third party notice situation. The due process clause under such circumstances does not apply because no adjudication of legal rights occurs in an administrative investigation. The self-incrimination clause does not apply because a third party answers the subpoena; the target is not compelled to act as a witness

---

journalists, such subpoenas are appropriate pursuant to SEC rule only if the information sought is essential, cannot be procured otherwise, and if negotiation attempts with the subject media organization fail. *See* 17 C.F.R. § 202.10; Securities Exchange Act Release No. 53638 (2006); SEC Enforcement Manual, *supra* note 2, at § 3.2.5; Scannell, *SEC Adopts Subpoena Policy for Media in Wake of Dispute*, Wall St. J., April 13, 2006, at p. A2.

[19] *See, e.g., See v. City of Seattle*, 387 U.S. 541 (1967).

[20] *See, e.g., Couch v. United States*, 409 U.S. 322 (1973).

[21] 467 U.S. 735 (1984).

[22] *Id.* at 741, citing *United States v. Powell*, 379 U.S. 48 (1964).

against him/herself. Finally, the protection of the sixth amendment's confrontation clause arises only upon the initiation of criminal proceedings.[23]

The Court rejected the structural statutory argument for requiring notice because, rather than supporting the purpose of the securities laws, notice to targets of third party subpoenas undermines Congress' intent to provide the Commission with expansive power to issue and enforce subpoenas. The federal securities laws contain no specific provision relating to notice of third party subpoenas, and the Court found no evidence that Congress desired the Commission to adopt any procedures to implement the practice. Instead, the Court determined that "Congress intended to vest the SEC with considerable discretion in determining when and how to investigate possible violations of the statutes administered by the Commission."[24]

Finally, the Court considered the argument that the right to notice of third party subpoenas issued in an SEC investigation stems from the standards governing judicial enforcement of administrative subpoenas embraced in *Powell*. The Court rejected the argument on two bases: "[f]irst, administration of the notice requirement . . . would be highly burdensome for both the Commission and the courts"; and, "[s]econd, the imposition of a notice requirement on the SEC would substantially increase the ability of persons who have something to hide to impede legitimate investigations by the Commission."[25] In its holding, the Court recognized that, when the Commission initiates an investigation, it frequently does not know which parties will be "targets" of the investigation. To police the SEC's process of identifying targets, the district court would have to intervene by conducting a hearing "to determine the scope and thrust of the ongoing investigation." Moreover, if a target had notice of third party subpoenas, the target could delay the investigation by discouraging third parties from complying with the subpoenas.[26]

Also, a target, following the progress of the Commission's inquiry by knowing to whom subpoenas were issued, could destroy crucial evidence before the SEC could gain possession. The Court concluded that the SEC was not prohibited from notifying a target of any subpoena it issues, but refused to impose a judicial mandate which would "curtail the Commission's discretion to determine when such notice would be appropriate and when it would not."[27]

---

[23] 467 U.S. at 742–43.

[24] *Id.* at 745.

[25] *Id.* at 748, citing *United States v. Powell*, 379 U.S. 48 (1964).

[26] 467 U.S. at 749–750. As recently stated by the SEC Enforcement Division, "the SEC is not required to provide any type of target notification when it issues subpoenas to third parties. . . ." SEC Enforcement Manual, *supra* note 2, at § 3.3.2.

[27] 467 U.S. at 750–51. For further discussion, see Steinberg, *SEC Subpoena Enforcement Practice*, 11 J. Corp. L. 1 (1985). *See also* Cole, *Revoking Our Privileges: Federal Law Enforcement's Multi-Front Assault on the Attorney-Client Privilege*, 48 Vill. L. Rev. 469 (2003).

§ 15.03   PARALLEL PROCEEDINGS

Parallel proceedings, that is, concurrent or successive civil proceedings by the SEC (or another administrative agency) and criminal investigation by the U.S. Attorney (or another prosecutorial entity) generally are constitutional. As stated by the Fifth Circuit: "There is no generally federal constitutional, statutory, or common law rule barring the simultaneous prosecution of separate civil and criminal actions by different agencies against the same defendants involving the same transactions."[28]

Hence, absent government abuse, parallel proceedings are restricted only in limited circumstances.[29] A key issue that has arisen but is not yet resolved is whether SEC subpoenas issued pursuant to a Commission investigation may be enforced after a criminal indictment has been returned. One federal appellate court has framed this issue as follows:

> Other than where there is specific evidence of agency bad faith or malicious governmental tactics, the strongest case for deferring civil proceedings until after completion of criminal proceedings is where a party under indictment for a serious offense is required to defend a civil or administrative action involving the same matter. The noncriminal proceeding, if not deferred, might undermine the party's Fifth Amendment privilege against self-incrimination, expand rights of criminal discovery beyond the limits of Federal Rule of Criminal Procedure 16(b), expose the basis of the defense to the prosecution in advance of criminal trial, or otherwise prejudice the case. If delay of the noncriminal proceeding would not seriously injure the public interest, a court may be justified in deferring it. In some such cases, however, the courts may adequately protect the government and the private party by merely deferring civil discovery or entering an appropriate protective order.[30]

In many such instances, the most feasible alternative may well be to place protective conditions on the exercise of the SEC's power to transmit information after return of an indictment. This approach would permit the Commission to pursue its civil enforcement functions, yet prevent undue expansion of discovery by prohibiting disclosure (of the information uncovered) between the SEC and the pertinent prosecuting entity.[31]

---

[28] *SEC v. First Financial Group of Texas, Inc.*, 659 F.2d 660, 666 (5th Cir. 1980); *see United States v. Stringer*, 521 F.3d 1189 (9th Cir. 2008).

[29] *See United States v. Kordel*, 397 U.S. 1 (1970).

[30] *SEC v. Dresser Industries, Inc.*, 628 F.2d 1368, 1375–76 (D.C. Cir. 1980) (en banc). Note that, depending on the circumstances, a criminal defendant may prefer the SEC case to continue in order to gain access to evidence and other relevant information that may prove helpful in the defense of the criminal proceeding. *See SEC v. Doody*, 186 F. Supp. 2d 379 (S.D.N.Y 2002).

[31] 628 F.2d at 1376, 1391. *See United States v. Stringer*, 521 F.3d 1189, 1131 (9th Cir. 2008) (stating that "nothing in the government's actual conduct of those investigations amounted to deceit or an affirmative misrepresentation justifying the rare sanction of dismissal of criminal charges or suppression of evidence received in the course of the investigation").

Today, the potential adverse ramifications incurred from parallel proceedings no longer are confined to SEC-Department of Justice referrals. As a number of episodes illustrate,[32] there is the distinct possibility that information transmitted to the SEC will be referred to other federal and state regulatory agencies. Moreover, pursuant to requests under the Freedom of Information Act,[33] the Commission may release documents and other information to private litigants involving matters that previously were subject to SEC scrutiny. Hence, in today's expanding world of parallel proceedings, the adverse consequences that may flow from providing information to the SEC can be massive.[34]

§ 15.04   SEC ADMINISTRATIVE ENFORCEMENT REMEDIES

The SEC has a number of administrative enforcement remedies it may invoke when alleged violations of the federal securities laws have been perpetrated by persons and entities subject to the Commission's administrative jurisdiction. The following discussion highlights key SEC administrative enforcement remedies.

[A]   Cease and Desist Orders

In legislation enacted in 1990, Congress granted the SEC authority to seek an administrative cease and desist order against *any* person based on *any* violation of the federal securities laws. A cease and desist order also may be imposed against any person who is deemed a "cause" of the subject violation, signifying that such person knew or should have known that his/her conduct would contribute to the violation. Moreover, the order entered may require not only that the party cease and desist from the proscribed acts but that he/she effect compliance within prescribed time periods and pursuant to specified conditions.[35] Under this authority, the SEC has ordered subject parties to effect "undertakings" in a variety of factual settings.[36] Importantly, in regard to "regulated" persons (such as broker-dealers, investment advisers and their "associated" persons), the Commission in a cease and desist action can procure an order for an accounting as well as disgorgement.[37]

---

[32] *See, e.g., Permian Corp. v. United States*, 665 F.2d 1214 (D.C. Cir. 1981).

[33] 5 U.S.C. § 552.

[34] For more extensive treatment of parallel proceedings, see Pickholz, *The Expanding World of Parallel Proceedings*, 53 Temple L.Q. 1100 (1982); Steinberg & Brennan, *Parallel Proceedings*, 8 Corp. L. Rev. 335 (1985); Note, *Using Equitable Powers to Coordinate Parallel Civil and Criminal Actions*, 98 Harv. L. Rev. 1023 (1985).

[35] *See* § 8A of the Securities Act, § 21C of the Exchange Act, § 9(f) of the Investment Company Act, § 203(k) of the Investment Advisors Act.

[36] *See* Mathews, Citera & Greenfield, *1991–1992 Securities Enforcement Review*, 7 Insights Nos. 1, 2 (Jan./Feb. 1993) (discussing proceedings).

[37] *See* § 21B(e) of the Exchange Act. Regulated persons include brokers, dealers, investment advisers, investment companies, and their associated persons. The SEC also can seek a temporary cease and desist order against regulated persons on an emergency basis.

Note that in order to obtain a cease and desist order, the SEC must prove a violation of the securities laws and provide a justifiable explanation why such sanction is appropriate.[38] A single isolated violation may not be sufficient.[39] With respect to the requisite culpability, negligence is sufficient for the entry of a cease and desist order if the underlying violation does not require scienter.[40] Where, however, the underlying violation requires proof of reckless or intentional misconduct, a showing of scienter may have to be made.[41]

[B]   Money Penalties

The SEC in administrative actions may levy money penalties against "regulated" persons, provided that the Commission concludes that the penalty imposed is in the "public interest" and that the defendant engaged in the prohibited conduct (such as willfully violating the federal securities laws; aiding and abetting, or failing reasonably to supervise another person under such party's control). In determining whether a money penalty and the extent to which such penalty is in the "public interest", Congress enumerated several factors that the Commission may consider.[42] Moreover, generally, the more severe the violation committed, the greater the money penalty that may be levied. Since 1990 (when this provision was enacted), the SEC frequently has ordered money penalties in its administrative proceedings.[43]

---

[38] *See Geiger v. SEC*, 363 F.3d 481 (D.C. Cir. 2004) (also stating that the SEC may procure a cease and desist order on a lesser showing than that required for an injunction).

[39] *See WHX Corp. v. SEC*, 362 F.3d 854 (D.C. Cir. 2004).

[40] *See KPMG, LLP v. SEC*, 289 F.3d 109 (D.C. Cir. 2002).

[41] *See Howard v. SEC*, 376 F.3d 1136 (D.C. Cir. 2004). *See generally* discussion in M. Steinberg & R. Ferrara, *supra* note 2, at § 6:15 (and authorities cited therein); Hansen, *The Securities and Exchange Commission's Use of Cease and Desist Powers*, 20 Sec. Reg. L.J. 339, 347–48 (1993) (asserting that SEC should be held to same showing in cease and desist proceeding as that required for an injunction). *See also Precious Metals Assoc., Inc. v. CFTC*, 620 F.2d 900, 912 (1st Cir. 1980) (requiring Commodity Futures Trading Commission (CFTC) to show defendant's "proclivity to violate the law" to obtain cease and desist order).

[42] Three tiers of money penalties exist with more severe penalties associated with each tier: tier (1) — technical violations; tier (2) — violations that encompass fraud, manipulation, or deliberate disregard of a regulatory mandate; and tier (3) — violations that come within tier (2) above and that result (or pose the risk of resulting) in substantial losses. Moreover, in determining whether the penalty is in the "public interest," relevant factors include the severity of the defendant's conduct, the harm resulting from such conduct, the extent of unjust enrichment, whether the defendant is a repeat offender, the need to deter such conduct, and "such other matters as justice may require." *See* § 21B of the Exchange Act, § 203(i) of the Investment Advisors Act, § 9(d) of the Investment Company Act.

[43] *See, e.g., In re Nasdaq Fraud Investigation*, [1999 Transfer Binder] Fed. Sec. L. Rep. (CCH) ¶ 86,105 (SEC 1999); *In re Invesco, MIM, PLC*, Securities Exchange Act Release No. 30878, 51 SEC Docket 1333 (1992); *see also Rockies Fund v. SEC*, 428 F 3d 1088 (D.C. Cir. 2005) (holding that ordering of third-tier money penalty by SEC without adequate explanation was arbitrary and capricious). When the Commission seeks a money penalty, a five-year statute of limitations evidently applies. *See 3M Corporation v. Browner*, 17 F.3d 1453 (D.C. Cir. 1994) (construing 28 U.S.C. § 2462); § 15.08 *infra*. Note that the SEC can establish a "Fair Fund" for the benefit of aggrieved investors when disgorgement and a money penalty are ordered in an administrative enforcement action. *See* § 5.08[R][6] *supra*.

[C]   Refusal and Stop Orders

Section 8 of the Securities Act generally governs the time in which SEC filed registration statements of securities offerings and amendments thereto become effective. Section 8(b) and Section 8(d) respectively authorize the Commission to issue refusal orders and stop orders in connection with materially incomplete, inaccurate, or false and misleading registration statements. Furthermore, Section 8(e) empowers the SEC to make an examination in any case in order to determine whether a stop order should be issued under Section 8(d).[44]

[D]   Summarily Suspending Trading in a Security

Summary suspensions of over-the-counter or exchange trading of a security are imposed by the SEC under Section 12(k) of the Exchange Act. This sanction is not to exceed ten days. The Supreme Court in *SEC v. Sloan*[45] held that the Commission was not authorized to summarily suspend trading in a security for successive ten-day periods, unless such successive suspension was based on new circumstances. The Court thus required the SEC to provide notice and right to a hearing with regard to suspensions for extended periods of time.

[E]   Broker-Dealer Disciplinary Sanctions

Broker-dealer (and associated persons) disciplinary sanctions may be imposed pursuant to several provisions contained in the Exchange Act. Persons or entities registered as broker-dealers, as well as any person "associated" with a broker-dealer, are vulnerable to SEC discipline under these provisions. After providing notice and opportunity for a hearing, broker-dealer sanctions may include outright revocation of registration (or denial of registration), suspension of registration, censure, or barring an associated person from associating with a broker-dealer (*see* Section 15(b)(4) and (6) of the 1934 Act). Moreover, pursuant to Section 15A, a broker-dealer or associated person, inter alia, can be barred from becoming a member (or becoming associated with a member) of a registered securities association (i.e., the NASD). Also, pursuant to Section 19(h) of the Exchange Act, the SEC can suspend or revoke the registration or take other disciplinary action against a registered securities association as well as suspend or expel a member or person associated with a member of such association.[46] As a final example, under the 1990 legislation, the Commission may levy money penalties against broker-dealers and their associated persons who engage in violative conduct.[47]

---

[44] *See* McLucas, *Stop Order Proceedings Under the Securities Act of 1933: A Current Assessment*, 40 Bus. Law. 515 (1985).

[45] 436 U.S. 103 (1978).

[46] *See* Mathews, *Litigation and Settlement of SEC Administrative Enforcement Proceedings*, 29 Cath. U.L. Rev. 215, 222–23 (1980). For SEC disciplinary proceedings against investment advisers, see § 203(e), (f) of the Investment Advisers Act, 15 U.S.C. § 80b-3(e), (f).

[47] *See* discussion § 15.04[B] *supra*.

[F]   Section 15(c)(4) Disciplinary Proceedings

Administrative proceedings involving certain defective Exchange Act reports filed with the SEC may be adjudicated pursuant to Section 15(c)(4) of the 1934 Act. Section 15(c)(4) authorizes the Commission to order compliance with the provisions of Section 12, 13, 14 or 15(d) of the Exchange Act and the rules or regulations thereunder. For example, if a Section 12 or 15(d) registrant fails to comply with, in any material way, the continuous reporting requirements of Section 13, such as the timely and accurate filing of annual and other periodic reports, the Commission may, after notice and opportunity for hearing, publish its findings and issue an order requiring compliance. The order may be directed not only to the registrant but also to any person who "caused" such registrant's failure to comply.[48]

In 1984 Congress enacted the Insider Trading Sanctions Act (ITSA). The ITSA, inter alia, expanded Section 15(c)(4) so as to enable the SEC to bring administrative actions to remedy violations of the proxy and tender offer provisions contained in Section 14 of the Exchange Act. The Act also clarified that the Commission may proceed administratively against persons (such as officers, directors, and perhaps attorneys) who are a "cause" of a failure to comply with Section 12, 13, 14 or 15(d).[49] Nonetheless, in view of legislation enacted in 1990 granting the SEC cease and desist power,[50] Section 15(c)(4) today is invoked on a far less frequent basis.[51]

[G]   Section 21(a) Reports of Investigation

Section 21(a) of the Exchange Act allows the Commission, in its discretion, to "make such investigations as it deems necessary to determine whether any person has violated, is violating, or is about to violate any provision of this title," and "to publish information concerning any such violations." Moreover, pursuant to Section 21(a), the SEC "may require or permit any person to file with it a statement in writing . . . as to all the facts and circumstances concerning the matter . . . investigated." Although a Section 21(a) report is not actually an adjudicatory type of proceeding, it is used by the SEC as a substitute for administrative disciplinary or civil injunctive suits in marginal, nonegregious cases, at times having the effect of inducing subject parties to settle.

These settlements frequently enable the Commission to present its position regarding the conduct in question, thereby providing notice of the SEC's future enforcement posture on the issue. Moreover, through the Section 21(a)

---

[48] *See* McLucas & Romanowich, *SEC Enforcement Proceedings Under Section 15(c)(4) of the Securities Exchange Act of 1934*, 41 Bus. Law. 145 (1985).

[49] *Id.*

[50] *See* § 15.04[A] *supra.*

[51] *See In re Kern*, [1988–1989 Transfer Binder] Fed. Sec. L. Rep. (CCH) ¶ 84,342 (ALJ 1988), *aff'd solely as to discontinuation of proceedings*, [1991 Transfer Binder] Fed. Sec. L. Rep. (CCH) ¶ 84,815 (SEC 1991). *See generally Report of the ABA's Section of Business Law Task Force on SEC Section 15(c)(4) Proceedings*, 46 Bus. Law. 255 (1990).

report procedure, the Commission can avoid the usual requirement of having to find an actual violation while persuading subject parties to modify their conduct or take, what the SEC views as, corrective steps. Hence, in these Section 21(a) reports, the Commission criticizes policies and decisions made by subject parties, thus directing to all concerned the areas in which the Commission desires reform.[52]

§ 15.05   SEC INJUNCTIONS

[A]   Standards for Injunctive Relief

As in any other type of case where permanent injunctive relief is sought, a defendant's violation of the federal securities laws is not by itself sufficient for the SEC to obtain an injunction. Rather, the test generally applied is whether there is a reasonable likelihood that the defendant, if not enjoined, will again engage in the violative conduct.[53] In identifying the relevant factors that demonstrate a reasonable likelihood of future violations, one appellate court pointed to "the degree of scienter involved, the sincerity of defendant's assurances against future violations, the isolated or recurrent nature of the infraction, defendant's recognition of the wrongful nature of his conduct, and the likelihood, because of defendant's professional occupation, that future violations might occur."[54] Other factors deemed relevant include the gravity of the offense committed,[55] the time elapsed between the violation and the court's decision,[56] whether the defendant, in good faith, relied on advice of counsel,[57] and the adverse effect an injunction would have on the defendant.[58]

The Supreme Court's decision in *Aaron v. SEC*[59] casts light on this issue. There, the Court held that the SEC must prove scienter in civil enforcement actions to enjoin violations of Section 10(b) of the Exchange Act, Rule 10b-5 promulgated thereunder, and Section 17(a)(1) of the Securities Act,[60] but need not prove scienter under Section 17(a)(2) or 17(a)(3).[61] The Court noted that under Section 17(a)(2) and 17(a)(3), "the degree of intentional wrongdoing evident in a defendant's past conduct" is an important factor in determining

---

[52] For further discussion, see M. Steinberg & R. Ferrara, *supra* note 2, at § 4:16; American Bar Association, *Report of the Task Force on Exchange Act Section 21(a) Written Statements*, 59 Bus. Law. 531 (2004).

[53] *See, e.g.*, *SEC v. Advance Growth Capital Corp.*, 470 F.2d 40, 53 (7th Cir. 1972). *See generally* Morrissey, *SEC Injunctions*, 68 Tenn. L. Rev. 427 (2001).

[54] *See, e.g.*, *SEC v. Universal Major Indus. Corp.*, 546 F.2d 1044, 1048 (2d Cir. 1976); *see also* *SEC v. Calvo*, 378 F.3d 1211 (11th Cir. 2004); *SEC v. Cavanagh*, 155 F.3d 129 (2d Cir. 1998).

[55] *See, e.g.*, *SEC v. Manor Nursing Centers, Inc.*, 458 F.2d 1082, 1102 (2d Cir. 1972).

[56] *See, e.g.*, *SEC v. Monarch Fund*, 608 F.2d 938, 943 (2d Cir. 1979).

[57] *See, e.g.*, *Howard v. SEC*, 376 F.3d 1136, 1147 (D.C. Cir. 2004).

[58] *See, e.g.*, *SEC v. Manor Nursing Centers, Inc.*, 458 F.2d 1082, 1102 (2d Cir. 1972).

[59] 446 U.S. 680 (1980).

[60] *Id.* at 687–96.

[61] *Id.* at 696–700.

whether the Commission has "establish[ed] a sufficient evidentiary predicate to show that such future violation may occur."[62] The presence or lack of scienter is "one of the aggravating or mitigating factors to be taken into account" in a court's exercise of its equitable jurisdiction.[63] In a concurring opinion, former Chief Justice Burger asserted that the SEC "will almost always" be required to show that the defendant's past conduct was more culpable than negligence. The Chief Justice concluded that "[a]n injunction is a drastic remedy, not a mild prophylactic, and should not be obtained against one acting in good faith."[64]

It has been contended that the *Aaron* Court's language, even apart from the former Chief Justice's concurring opinion, could require the SEC to prove scienter in order to make a "proper showing" for obtaining injunctive relief under *any* section of the securities acts.[65] Indeed, more recently, the SEC has experienced greater difficulty in procuring injunctions.[66] Nonetheless, the absence of scienter may not preclude the granting of such relief where the applicable statutory provision requires only negligent culpability. For example, where a defendant has committed prior violations, where his/her carelessness has been egregious, where public investors have been severely injured, or where the defendant's occupation increases the probability of future violations, a court (considering the totality of the circumstances) may order injunctive relief.[67]

Importantly, under certain state securities law provisions, injunctions and even criminal convictions may be obtained without proof of scienter. As Dean Sargent comments: "The current trend among the intermediate state appellate courts . . . seem[s] to be moving away from proof of guilty knowledge, mens rea, evil purpose, or even recklessness in criminal cases for securities fraud."[68]

[B]   Implications of *Central Bank of Denver* and the PSLRA

As discussed earlier,[69] the Supreme Court's decision in *Central Bank of Denver* was believed by many authorities to preclude the SEC in certain situations from bringing an enforcement action premised on aider and abettor

---

[62] *Id.* at 701.

[63] *Id.*

[64] *Id.* at 703 (Burger, C.J., concurring).

[65] *See* Huffman, *Aaron Restricts SEC Enforcement*, Legal Times, June 9, 1980, at 2.

[66] *E.g., SEC v. Steadman*, 967 F.2d 1636 (D.C. Cir. 1992) (denying SEC's request for injunctive relief, court stated that "injunctive relief is reserved for willful lawbreakers or those whose operations are so persistently sloppy as to pose a continuing danger to the investing public"). *See SEC v. Happ*, 392 F.3d 12 (1st Cir. 2004). *See generally* Eisenberg, *Litigating with the SEC — A Reasonable Alternative to Settlement*, 21 Sec. Reg. L.J. 421 (1994).

[67] *See SEC v. Washington County Utility District*, 676 F.2d 218 (6th Cir. 1982); *SEC v. Murphy*, 626 F.2d 633 (9th Cir. 1980). For further discussion on *Aaron*, see §§ 8.03[B], 9.04[B] *supra.*

[68] Sargent, *A Blue Sky State of Mind: The Meaning of "Willfully" in Blue Sky Criminal Cases*, 20 Sec. Reg. L.J. 96, 98 (1992); *See* Long, *supra* note 2, at § 8.04[3].

[69] *See* §§ 8.03[B], 10.02 *supra.*

liability. However, unlike the *Hochfelder/Aaron* analogy addressed earlier,[70] aiding and abetting a federal securities law violation statutorily gives rise to criminal liability exposure.[71] Under this rationale, the criminal aid-abet statute provided ample authority for the SEC to pursue aiders and abettors.

With respect to violations of the Exchange Act, it is now clear that the SEC has such aiding and abetting authority. In 1995, the Private Securities Litigation Reform Act (PSLRA) was enacted, amending Section 20 of the Securities Exchange Act by adding a new subsection (e). Section 20(e) authorizes the SEC to seek injunctive relief and/or certain money penalties against aiders and abettors for violations of the 1934 Act (or any rule or regulation thereunder). Specifically, the section provides that any person who "knowingly provides substantial assistance to another person in violation of" the Exchange Act (or any rule or regulation thereunder) shall be liable "to the same extent as the person to whom such assistance is provided." Hence, this section preserves aiding and abetting liability in certain SEC enforcement actions. Nonetheless, the mental culpability standard (namely, whether actual knowledge must be shown or recklessness suffices) requires clarification.[72] Moreover, the PSLRA declines to grant the SEC express aiding and abetting authority with respect to Securities Act violations.

Besides its aiding and abetting authority, the SEC has powerful enforcement weapons. For example, the Commission may bring an administrative cease and desist proceeding against persons who are a "cause" of the alleged violation, thus encompassing those persons who "should have known" that their conduct "would contribute" to such violation.[73] Hence, even though the SEC must proceed administratively, the Commission should be able to spread the liability net as far. After all, establishing one as a "cause" of a violation should prove easier than proving aiding and abettor liability.[74]

Moreover, in view of Section 15(b)(4)(E) and Section 15(b)(6)(A) of the Exchange Act,[75] the Commission has express statutory authority to proceed against brokers and dealers (and associated persons) who aid and abet securities law violations.[76] Similarly, those who aid and abet violations of the Investment Advisers Act are subject to SEC enforcement action.[77] Hence, *Central Bank of Denver* thus far has not been problematic for the SEC's enforcement program. With respect to financial intermediaries, this is

---

[70] *See* §§ 8.02[A]-[B], 10.01–10.02 *supra.*

[71] 18 U.S.C. § 2(a). *See* Bromberg, *Aiding and Abetting: Sudden Death and Possible Resurrection,* 24 Rev. Sec. & Comm. Reg. 133, 136 (1994).

[72] *Compare Howard v. SEC,* 376 F.3d 1136 (D.C. Cir. 2004) (extreme recklessness standard applied), *with SEC v. KPMG LLP,* 412 F. Supp. 2d 349 (S.D.N.Y. 2006) (under circumstances at bar, requiring proof of actual knowledge).

[73] *See* § 15.04[A] *supra.*

[74] *See* Martin, Mirvis & Herlihy, *SEC Enforcement Powers and Remedies Are Greatly Expanded,* 19 Sec. Reg. L.J. 19, 23 (1993).

[75] 15 U.S.C. § 78o(b)(4)(E), 78o(b)(6)(A)(i).

[76] *Id.*

[77] 15 U.S.C. § 80b-9(d).

especially true given the Commission's rigorous use of the controlling person and failure to supervise provisions to hold broker-dealer executives, supervisors, and branch managers accountable.[78] As a last point, whereas prior to *Central Bank of Denver* the Commission was content to allege aider and abettor liability, the SEC now seeks an expansion of conduct that constitutes primary liability (*see* § 10.03 *supra*).

[C]   Collateral Consequences

The primary purpose of injunctive relief under the federal securities laws is to deter future violative conduct, not to punish the violator.[79] As Judge Friendly noted, however, an injunction can have severe collateral consequences.[80] For example, an injunction not only harms one's reputation but it also serves as the basis for contempt sanctions if the injunctive order subsequently is violated.[81] Issuance of an SEC injunction can cause the suspension or revocation of a broker-dealer's registration, or constitute grounds for prohibiting any person from associating with a broker-dealer.[82] Similarly, an injunction disqualifies the subject party from serving as a director, officer, or employee of a registered investment company.[83] It can constitute a basis for barring an attorney, accountant, or other professional from practicing before the SEC.[84] Additionally, a Regulation A exemption from Securities Act registration may be unavailable to an enjoined issuer of securities.[85] As a final example, the Commission frequently requires that an injunction be disclosed in certain filings, reports, statements, or other information sent to shareholders and investors.[86]

Largely because of these consequences, the courts have required the SEC "to go beyond the mere facts of past violations and demonstrate a realistic likelihood of recurrence."[87] Employing this standard, courts have concluded in

---

[78] *See, e.g., In re Prudential Securities, Inc.*, [1993 Transfer Binder] Fed. Sec. L. Rep. (CCH) ¶ 85,238 (SEC 1993); discussion § 13.05 *supra*.

[79] *See Aaron v. SEC*, 446 U.S. 680 (1980); *Hecht Co. v. Bowles*, 321 U.S. 321 (1944). Note that when the SEC seeks injunctive and other equitable relief (such as disgorgement), no applicable statute of limitations evidently applies. *See, e.g., SEC v. Rind*, 991 F.2d 1486 (9th Cir. 1993); § 15.08 *infra*.

[80] *See SEC v. Commonwealth Chemical Securities, Inc.*, 574 F.2d 90, 99 (2d Cir. 1978).

[81] *See, e.g., United States v. Custer Channel Wing Corp.*, 327 F.2d 675 (4th Cir. 1967).

[82] *See* § 15(b)(4)(C) of the Exchange Act, 15 U.S.C. § 78o(b)(4)(C); *SEC v. Geon Indus., Inc.*, 531 F.2d 39, 55 (2d Cir. 1976).

[83] *See* § 9(a)(2) of the Investment Company Act, 15 U.S.C. § 80a-9(a)(2). The SEC can lift or waive this disqualification pursuant to Section 9(c) of the Act.

[84] *See* SEC Rule 102(e)(3)(i), 17 C.F.R. § 201.2(e)(3)(i). Rule 102(e) is discussed in § 15.09[A] *infra*.

[85] *See* Rule 262 of Regulation A, 17 C.F.R. § 230.262.

[86] *See* Item 401(d) of Regulation S-K, 17 C.F.R. § 229.401(d). *See generally* Andre, *The Collateral Consequences of SEC Injunctive Relief: Mild Prophylactic or Perpetual Hazard?*, 1981 U. Ill. L. Rev. 625.

[87] *SEC v. Commonwealth Chemical Securities, Inc.*, 574 F.2d 90, 100 (2d Cir. 1978).

a number of cases that the SEC has not made a sufficient showing and have denied the Commission's request for injunctive relief.[88]

[D]   Ancillary or Other Equitable Relief

Over the years, the SEC has sought, and successfully obtained, ancillary or other equitable relief against an enjoined party. Examples of such relief include disgorgement, appointment of a receiver, appointment of independent members to the board of directors, and appointment of a special counsel.[89] The basis for ordering such relief derives from the inherent equitable authority of the federal courts.[90] Indeed, even if a court refuses to grant the SEC's request for an injunction, it may nevertheless grant other equitable relief.[91] Any doubt as to the propriety of such relief has been resolved by the Sarbanes-Oxley Act. Section 21(d)(5) of the Securities Exchange Act, as amended by SOX, provides: "In any action proceeding brought or instituted by the Commission under any provision of the securities laws, the Commission may seek, and any Federal court may grant, any equitable relief that may be appropriate or necessary for the benefit of investors."[92]

[E]   Modification or Dissolution of SEC Injunctions

In view of the collateral consequences imposed by SEC injunctions, subject parties may seek to have the particular injunction modified or dissolved. The traditional view, derived from the Supreme Court's decision in *United States v. Swift & Co.*,[93] places a heavy burden upon the party seeking modification or dissolution. Writing at the time he was a federal appellate judge, former Justice Blackmun construed *Swift* as follows:

---

[88] *See, e.g.*, *SEC v. Happ*, 392 F.3d 12 (1st Cir. 2004); *SEC v. Caterinicchia*, 613 F.2d 102 (5th Cir. 1980); discussion § 15.05[A] *supra*.

[89] *See, e.g.*, *SEC v. Colello*, 139 F.3d 674 (9th Cir. 1998) (recouping proceeds from illegal conduct); *SEC v. Mayhew*, 121 F.3d 44 (2d Cir. 1997) (disgorgement); *SEC v. Rind*, 991 F.2d 1486 (9th Cir. 1993) (holding no right to jury trial when SEC seeks disgorgement of alleged illicit profits); *CFTC v. American Metals Exchange Corp.*, 991 F.2d 71 (3d Cir. 1993) (stating that proper measure of disgorgement is amount of defendant's ill-gotten gains, not amount of investors' losses); *SEC v. Manor Nursing Centers, Inc.*, 458 F.2d 1082 (2d Cir. 1972) (disgorgement); *SEC v. Fifth Ave. Coach Lines, Inc.*, 280 F. Supp. 3 (S.D.N.Y. 1968), *aff'd*, 435 F.2d 510 (2d Cir. 1971) (receiver); *SEC v. Coastal States Gas Corp.*, SEC Lit. Rel. No. 6054 (S.D. Tex. Sept. 12, 1973) (independent members of board of directors). *See generally* Farrand, *Ancillary Remedies in SEC Civil Enforcement Suits*, 89 Harv. L. Rev. 1779 (1976).

[90] *See SEC v. Wencke*, 622 F.2d 1363, 1369 (9th Cir. 1980). *See generally* Hazen, *Administrative Enforcement: An Evaluation of the Securities and Exchange Commission's Use of Injunctions and Other Enforcement Methods*, 31 Hastings L.J. 444 (1979).

[91] *See, e.g.*, *SEC v. Commonwealth Chemical Securities, Inc.*, 574 F.2d 90, 102–103 (2d Cir. 1978).

[92] Sarbanes-Oxley Act § 305(b), *amending*, § 21(d)(5) of the Exchange Act. *See* discussion in § 5.08[R][7] *supra*. For critical analysis concerning a number of the more far reaching forms of equitable relief ordered prior to the 2002 SOX amendment, see discussion in Dent, *Ancillary Relief in Federal Securities Law: A Study in Federal Remedies*, 67 Minn. L. Rev. 865 (1983).

[93] 286 U.S. 106 (1932).

(1) [T]hat, where modification and amendment of an existing decree is under consideration, there are "limits of inquiry" for the decree court and for the reviewing court; (2) that the inquiry is "whether the changes are so important that dangers, once substantial have become attenuated to a shadow"; (3) that the movants must be "suffering hardship so extreme and unexpected" as to be regarded as "victims of oppression"; and (4) that there must be "[n]othing less than a clear showing of grievous wrong evoked by new and unforeseen conditions." Phrased in other words, this means for us that modification is only cautiously to be granted; that some change is not enough; that the dangers which the decree was meant to foreclose must almost have disappeared; that hardship and oppression, extreme and unexpected, are significant; and that the movants' task is to provide close to an unanswerable case. To repeat: caution, substantial change, unforeseenness, oppressive hardship, and a clear showing are the requirements.[94]

Swift's stringent guidelines have been applied by numerous courts in a variety of contexts, including where modification or dissolution of an SEC injunction is sought.[95] A number of courts, however, have declined to follow *Swift's* rigorous requirements. These courts reason that subsequent Supreme Court decisions have departed from *Swift's* restrictive standards.[96] Hence, the Second Circuit, while noting that changes in fact or law provide the strongest reasons for modifying an injunction,[97] held that modification or dissolution also is appropriate "where a better appreciation of the facts in light of experience indicate that the decree is not properly adapted to accomplishing its purposes."[98]

A significant decision departing from the *Swift* standards in the securities law area is *SEC v. Warren*.[99] Distinguishing *Swift*, the district court in *Warren* exercised its "inherent equitable power to weigh the severity of the alleged danger which the injunction was designed to eliminate against the continuing necessity for the injunction and the hardship brought by its prospective application."[100] Weighing these factors, the court granted the motion to dissolve the injunction.[101] On appeal, the Third Circuit affirmed on substantially the same reasoning.[102]

---

[94] *Humble Oil & Refining Co. v. American Oil Co.*, 405 F.2d 803, 813 (8th Cir. 1969).

[95] *See, e.g., SEC v. Advance Growth Capital Corp.*, 539 F.2d 649 (7th Cir. 1976).

[96] *See Rufo v. Inmates of Suffolk County Jail*, 502 U.S. 367 (1992); *United States v. United Shoe Machinery Corp.*, 391 U.S. 244 (1968); *System Federation v. Wright*, 364 U.S. 642 (1961).

[97] *King-Seeley Thermos Co. v. Aladdin Industries, Inc.*, 418 F.2d 31, 35 (2d Cir. 1979).

[98] *Id.*

[99] 76 F.R.D. 405 (W.D. Pa. 1977), *aff'd*, 583 F.2d 115 (3d Cir. 1978).

[100] 76 F.R.D. at 408.

[101] *Id.* at 407–08.

[102] 583 F.2d at 120–22; *see SEC v. Coldicutt*, 258 F.3d 939, 945 (9th Cir. 2002) (refusing to dissolve the subject injunction based on the movant's failure to demonstrate that "compliance with the injunction has become substantially more onerous, unworkable because of unforeseen obstacles, detrimental to the public interest, or legally impermissible").

Another development in this area has been that, even where the SEC makes the necessary showing, some courts have hesitated to order an unconditional permanent injunction. The conditions that courts have attached to the imposition of an injunction include automatic dissolution after a fixed number of years, suspension after the defendant fulfills certain requirements, and permitting a petition for dissolution after a fixed period of time on a lesser showing than that required by *Swift*.[103] Although the SEC, at times, has agreed to certain of these limitations pursuant to the consent process, the Commission's position appears to be that upon making a proper showing, it is entitled as a matter of statutory right to the ordering of a permanent injunction.[104]

Hence, the continued viability of the stringent *Swift* standard is open to debate. Perhaps a better approach would be for courts faced with a motion to modify or dissolve an injunction to apply an ad hoc balancing test. This standard would consider such factors as (1) subsequent change of fact or law, (2) the extent of adverse, unforeseen collateral consequences, (3) whether the injunction has fulfilled its objectives, (4) whether the individual deterrent effect of the injunction has ceased, (5) the decree's effect on societal deterrence, (6) whether a government entity is a party to the litigation and the adverse effect that granting of the motion would have on such entity's resources, and (7) the extent and nature of the public or other countervailing interest involved.[105]

§ 15.06   OFFICER AND DIRECTOR BARS

The SEC may seek in federal court an order prohibiting a person from serving as an officer or director of a publicly-held enterprise. Such an order may be conditional or unconditional; it may be of permanent duration or for a specified time period as directed by the court. The conditions for an officer or director bar are that the individual violated the antifraud provisions of Section 17(a)(1) of the 1933 Act or Section 10(b) of the 1934 Act (or any rule thereunder) and that such conduct demonstrates unfitness to serve in this fiduciary capacity.[106]

Even prior to Congress' enactment of an officer/director bar provision in 1990, the SEC occasionally procured such orders as a type of equitable relief.[107] In one such case, the Second Circuit focused on proscribed conduct that occurred prior to the 1990 legislation. Granting broad equitable relief, the court

---

[103] See, for example, the district court's order as set forth in *SEC v. Blazon Corp.*, 608 F.2d 960 (9th Cir. 1979), the validity of which the Ninth Circuit did not resolve.

[104] *See* Brief of the SEC at 10, *SEC v. Associated Minerals, Inc.*, Nos. 79–1449, 79–1450 (6th Cir. 1980).

[105] For further discussion, see Steinberg, *SEC and Other Permanent Injunctions — Standards for Their Imposition, Modification, and Dissolution*, 66 Cornell L. Rev. 27, 71–73 (1980).

[106] *See* § 20(e) of the Securities Act, 15 U.S.C. § 77t(e); § 21(d)(2) of the Exchange Act, 15 U.S.C. § 78u(d)(2). Note that prior to the Sarbanes-Oxley Act, the standard was "substantial unfitness." Sarbanes-Oxley Act § 305, *amending,* § 20(e) of the Securities Act & 21(d)(2) of the Exchange Act. *See* discussion in § 5.08[F] *supra.*

[107] *See, e.g., SEC v. Florafax Int'l, Inc.*, SEC Litig. Release No. 10617, 31 SEC Docket 1038 (N.D. Okla. 1984).

ordered disgorgement of illicit profits, an officer/director bar, and a voting trust to sterilize the violators' controlling interests in publicly-held entities.[108] Not surprisingly, the Commission has been inclined to invoke this remedy with greater vigor in view of the express statutory authority now provided by federal law.[109]

§ 15.07 COURT ORDERED MONEY PENALTIES

The SEC also may seek court ordered money penalties against *any* person for *any* violation of the securities laws or of an SEC cease and desist order. If such money penalty is accompanied by an order of disgorgement, the Commission may seek to establish a "Fair Fund" for the benefit of aggrieved investors (*see* § 5.08[R][6] *supra*).

The penalty amount levied by the court is determined in view of the facts and circumstances and increases in amount according to the severity of the violation committed. As set forth by one source:

> The penalties are subject to three-tier maximums for each "violation." First, [with respect to so-called technical violations,] the maximum is the greater of $5,000 for a natural person or $50,000 for a corporation or other entity, or the "gross amount of pecuniary gain to such defendant" resulting from the violation. Second, if the violation included "fraud, deceit, manipulation, or deliberate disregard of a regulatory requirement," the maximums are $50,000 and $250,000, respectively, or the gross pecuniary gain. Third, if the violation in addition resulted in or created, directly or indirectly, "substantial losses" or "a significant risk of substantial losses to others," the maximums are $100,000 [for a natural person] and $500,000 [for a corporation or other entity], or the gross pecuniary gain.[110]

In 2006, the Commission sought to clarify its policy with respect to the levying of money penalties against publicly-held companies. As identified by the SEC, two key considerations are: the receipt (or absence) of a direct benefit to the corporation as a consequence of the illegality; and (2) whether the company's shareholders will be unfairly injured by the levying of a money penalty. Other factors, as enunciated by the Commission, include: "the need to deter the particular type of offense; the extent of the injury to innocent parties;

---

[108] *SEC v. Posner*, 16 F.3d 520 (2d Cir. 1994).

[109] *See, e.g., SEC v. Softpoint, Inc.*, 958 F. Supp. 846 (S.D.N.Y. 1997); Callcott, *Patterns of SEC Enforcement Under the 1990 Remedies Act: Officer-And-Director Bars*, 21 Sec. Reg. L.J. 347, 360 (1994) (citing cases); *see also SEC v. Patel*, 61 F.3d 137 (2d Cir. 1995) (order of permanent bar of corporate officer vacated and remanded for justifiable factual basis for such bar order). *See generally* Barnard, *Rule 10b-5 and the "Unfitness" Question*, 47 Ariz. L. Rev. 9 (2005); Barnard, *SEC Debarment of Officers and Directors After Sarbanes-Oxley*, 59 Bus. Law. 391 (2004).

[110] Martin, Mirvis & Herlihy, *supra* note 74, at 21, interpreting § 21(b)(3) of the Exchange Act; *see* Laby & Callcott, *Patterns of SEC Enforcement Under the 1990 Remedies Act: Civil Money Penalties*, 58 Albany L. Rev. 5 (1994). *See generally* Black, *Should the SEC Be a Collection Agency for Defrauded Investors?*, 63 Bus. Law. 317 (2008); Ferrara, Ferrigno & Darland, *Hardball! The SEC's New Arsenal of Enforcement Weapons*, 47 Bus. Law. 33 (1991).

whether complicity in the violation is widespread throughout the corporation; the level of intent on the part of the perpetrators; the degree of difficulty in detecting the particular type of offense; presence or lack of remedial steps by the corporation; and extent of cooperation with the Commission and other law enforcement."[111] Whether the SEC's pronouncement will result in greater predictability in this context awaits determination.

§ 15.08 STATUTES OF LIMITATIONS

As a general principle, the courts have held that there exists no applicable statute of limitations when the SEC seeks equitable relief.[112] Although some sources disagree,[113] this principle extends not only to Commission requests seeking injunctive relief but also to other equitable remedies, such as disgorgement.[114] Nonetheless, the SEC's pursuit of stale claims certainly is relevant in a court's determination whether to grant the relief requested. Moreover, when the SEC institutes an action for monetary penalties, a five-year statute of limitations applies. This five-year limitations period also extends to non-monetary disciplinary sanctions that are viewed as punitive rather than remedial.[115]

§ 15.09 PROFESSIONAL RESPONSIBILITY

This Section will address select issues with respect to a securities lawyer's professional responsibilities. The focus of the following discussion is on Rule 102(e) and the SEC's Standards of Conduct.

[A]   Rule 102(e) [formerly Rule 2(e)]

SEC Rule of Practice 102(e), now codified in Section 4C of the Securities Exchange Act, provides that the Commission may suspend, limit, or bar "any person" from practicing before it "in any way" if the SEC finds, after notice and opportunity for hearing, that such person is deemed:

(1)   not to possess the requisite qualifications to represent others;

(2)   to be lacking in character or integrity, or to have engaged in unethical or improper professional conduct; or

---

[111] Statement of the Securities and Exchange Commission Concerning Financial Penalties, SEC Release No. 2006–4 (2006). *See* M. Steinberg & R. Ferrara *supra* note 2, at § 6:8 (2009 Supp.).

[112] *See, e.g., SEC v. Rind,* 991 F.2d 1486 (9th Cir. 1993).

[113] *See, e.g.,* Riesenberg, *Application of Statutes of Limitations to SEC Disgorgement Actions,* 8 Insights No. 2, at p. 17 (Feb. 1994).

[114] *See, e.g., SEC v. Williams,* 886 F. Supp. 28 (D. Mass. 1995).

[115] *See, e.g.,* 28 U.S.C. § 2462; *Johnson v. SEC,* 87 F.3d 484 (D.C. Cir. 1996) (under facts of case, SEC imposition of censure and six-month suspension deemed a "penalty," thereby invoking § 2462's five-year limitations period); *SEC v. Rind,* 991 F.2d 1492 (staleness of claims relevant factor in determining whether to award relief sought). *See generally* Brodsky & Eggers, *The Statute of Limitations in SEC Civil Enforcement Actions,* 23 Sec. Reg. L.J. 123 (1995); Gordon, *SEC Administrative Proceedings: Five-Year Statute of Limitations Period Held Applicable,* 24 Sec. Reg. L.J. 420 (1997).

(3)   to have willfully violated, or willfully aided and abetted the violation of, any provision of the securities laws or the rules and regulations issued thereunder.

Despite the broad language of Rule 102(e), its application to date has been limited to disciplining attorneys, accountants, engineers, and other similar professionals. Traditionally, this Rule has been viewed as a necessary adjunct "to the Commission's power to protect the integrity of its administrative procedures and the general public."[116]

It has been argued without success that the SEC is abusing its Rule 102(e) authority by administratively litigating matters involving conduct which arguably does not come within the ambit of "practicing before the Commission."[117] This assertion stems from the fact that the SEC defines "practicing before the Commission" in a broad manner. Thus, the disciplinary authority of Rule 102(e) may come into play in connection with the registration provisions, as well as the periodic and other reporting requirements, to the extent that any or all of these filings and registration applications can be defined as "practicing" before the SEC. For example, attorneys who, under Rule 102(e), engage in improper counseling of their clients with respect to required reports filed with the SEC, can be suspended from practicing before the Commission.[118]

With respect to attorneys, the SEC's most prominent decision was the *Carter and Johnson* proceeding.[119] Although the Commission held that the

---

[116] *Touche Ross & Co. v. SEC*, 608 F.2d 570, 582 (2d Cir. 1979). *See In re Carter & Johnson*, [1981 Transfer Binder] Fed. Sec. L. Rep. (CCH) ¶ 82,847 (SEC 1981). Rule 102(e), as codified in Section 4C(b) of the Exchange Act, defines "improper professional conduct" for accountants to include:

(1)   intentional or knowing conduct, including reckless conduct, that results in a violation of applicable professional standards; and

(2)   negligent conduct in the form of:

(A)   a single instance of highly unreasonable conduct that results in a violation of applicable professional standards in circumstances in which the registered public accounting firm knows, or should know, that heightened scrutiny is warranted; or

(B)   repeated instances of unreasonable conduct, each resulting in a violation of applicable professional standards, that indicate a lack of competence to practice before the Commission.

For more recent Rule 102(e) proceedings against accountants, see, *e.g.*, *McCurdy v. SEC*, 396 F.3d 1258 (D.C. Cir. 2005) (accountant's one-year suspension from practicing before the Commission upheld); *Checkowsky v. SEC*, 139 F.3d 221 (D. C. Cir. 1998) (ordering Rule 102(e) proceeding against two auditors dismissed due to SEC's failure to articulate applicable legal standard); *In re Grant Thornton*, 2004 WL 1750732 (SEC 2004) (pursuant to settlement, accounting firm was censured, disgorged allegedly wrongfully obtained profits, paid a $1.5 million civil penalty, and agreed to expend at least $1 million for staff fraud-detection training).

[117] *See In re Keating, Muething & Klekamp*, [1979 Transfer Binder] Fed. Sec. L. Rep. (CCH) ¶ 82,124 (SEC 1979) (Karmel, Comm'r, dissenting); Kelleher, *Scourging the Moneylenders from the Temple: The SEC, Rule 2(e), and the Lawyers*, 17 San Diego L. Rev. 501 (1980).

[118] *See, e.g., In re Fields*, [1972–1973 Transfer Binder] Fed. Sec. L. Rep. (CCH) ¶ 79,407 (SEC 1973), *aff'd without opinion*, 495 F.2d 1075 (D.C. Cir. 1974).

[119] *In re Carter and Johnson*, [1981 Transfer Binder] Fed. Sec. L. Rep. (CCH) ¶ 82,847 (SEC 1981).

respondents did not violate Rule 2(e) (now Rule 102(e)), it set forth standards that apply today:

> The Commission is of the view that a lawyer engages in "unethical or improper professional conduct" under the following circumstances: When a lawyer with significant responsibilities in the effectuation of a company's compliance with the disclosure requirements of the federal securities laws becomes aware that his client is engaged in a substantial and continuing failure to satisfy those disclosure requirements, his continued participation violates professional standards unless he takes prompt steps to end the client's non-compliance. . . .

> We do not imply that a lawyer is obliged, at the risk of being held to have violated Rule 2(e), to seek to correct every isolated disclosure action or inaction which he believes to be at variance with applicable disclosure standards, although there may be isolated disclosure failures that are so serious that their correction becomes a matter of primary professional concern. It is also clear, however, that a lawyer is not privileged to unthinkingly permit himself to be co-opted into an ongoing fraud and cast as a dupe or a shield for a wrongdoing client.

> Initially, counselling accurate disclosure is sufficient, even if his advice is not accepted. But there comes a point at which a reasonable lawyer must conclude that his advice is not being followed, or even sought in good faith, and that his client is involved in a continuing course of violating the securities laws. At this critical juncture, the lawyer must take further, more affirmative steps in order to avoid the inference that he has been co-opted willingly or unwillingly, into the scheme of non-disclosure.

> The lawyer is in the best position to choose his next step. Resignation is one option, although we recognize that other considerations, including the protection of the client against foreseeable prejudice, must be taken into account in the case of withdrawal. A direct approach to the board of directors or one or more individual directors or officers may be appropriate; or he may choose to try to enlist the aid of other members of the firm's management. What is required, in short, is some prompt action that leads to the conclusion that the lawyer is engaged in efforts to correct the underlying problem, rather than having capitulated to the desires of a strong-willed, but misguided client.

> Some have argued that resignation is the only permissible course when a client chooses not to comply with disclosure advice. We do not agree. Premature resignation serves neither the end of an effective lawyer-client relationship nor, in most cases, the effective administration of the securities laws. The lawyer's continued interaction with his client will ordinarily hold the greatest promise of corrective action. So long as a lawyer is acting in good faith and exerting reasonable efforts to prevent violations of the law by his client, his professional obligations have been met. In general, the best result is that which promotes

the continued, strong-minded and independent participation by the lawyer.

We recognize, however, that the "best result" is not always obtainable, and that there may occur situations where the lawyer must conclude that the misconduct is so extreme or irretrievable, or the involvement of his client's management and board of directors in the misconduct is so thorough-going and pervasive that any action short of resignation would be futile. We would anticipate that cases where a lawyer has no choice but to resign would be rare and of an egregious nature.[120]

It should be emphasized that the Commission in the *Carter and Johnson* proceeding focused on counsel's obligations to seek the undertaking of corrective action *within* the corporate structure when fraud is afoot. The Commission did not address counsel's duty to disclose to the SEC, to the public, or to affected third parties.[121]

[B]   SEC Standards of Conduct

As discussed earlier in this text,[122] the Sarbanes-Oxley Act directed the SEC to adopt a rule:

(1)   requiring [a subject] attorney to report evidence of a material violation of securities law or breach of fiduciary duty or similar violation by the company or any agent thereof, to the chief legal counsel or the chief executive officer of the company (or the equivalent thereof); and

(2)   if the counsel or officer does not appropriately respond to the evidence (adopting, as necessary, appropriate remedial measures or sanctions with respect to the violation), requiring [such] attorney to report the evidence to the audit committee of the board of directors of the issuer or to another committee of the board of directors comprised solely of directors not employed directly or indirectly by the issuer, or to the board of directors.[123]

---

[120] *Id.* at 84,172–84,173.

[121] *Id.* at 84,173 n.78. *See generally* M. Steinberg, Attorney Liability After Sarbanes-Oxley § 2.04 (2008); Gruenbaum, *Clients' Frauds and Their Lawyer's Obligations*, 68 Georgetown L.J. 191 (1979); Kramer, *Clients' Frauds and Their Lawyer's Obligations: A Study in Professional Irresponsibility*, 67 Georgetown L.J. 991 (1978); Lorne, *The Corporate and Securities Adviser, The Public Interest, and Professional Ethics*, 76 Mich. L. Rev. 425 (1978); Maxey, *SEC Enforcement Actions Against Securities Lawyers: New Remedies vs. Old Policies*, 22 Del. J. Corp. L. 539 (1997); Painter, *The Moral Interdependence of Corporate Lawyers and Their Clients*, 67 So. Cal. L. Rev. 507 (1994); Painter & Duggan, *Lawyer Disclosure of Client Fraud: Establishing a Firm Foundation*, 50 SMU L. Rev. 225 (1996); Seamons, *Inside the Labyrinth of the Elusive Standard Under the SEC's Rule 2(e)*, 23 Sec. Reg. L.J. 57 (1995); Sonde, *The Responsibility of Professionals Under the Federal Securities Laws — Some Observations*, 68 Nw. U.L. Rev. 1 (1973).

[122] *See* discussion in § 5.08[P] *supra*.

[123] Sarbanes-Oxley Act § 307.

Responding to this directive, the SEC promulgated its "Standards of Professional Conduct" for attorneys who practice before the Commission.[124] These Standards implement "up the ladder" reporting and recognize the propriety of a Qualified Legal Compliance Committee (QLCC) as an alternative.[125] Nonetheless, the Standards do not require (but do allow) counsel to make a "noisy withdrawal" (whereby the attorney must notify the SEC that he/she disaffirms documents that he/she had prepared during the course of the representation) in situations where the corporate client refuses to take corrective action after such counsel went "up-the-ladder."[126] Stated succinctly, the SEC's Standards of Conduct:

- require an attorney to report evidence of a material violation, determined according to an objective standard, "up-the-ladder" within the issuer to the chief legal counsel or the chief executive officer of the company or the equivalent;

- require an attorney, if the chief legal counsel or the chief executive officer of the company does not respond appropriately to the evidence, to report the evidence to the audit committee, another committee of independent directors, or the full board of directors;

- clarify that the rules cover attorneys providing legal services to an issuer who have an attorney-client relationship with the issuer, and who have notice that documents they are preparing or assisting in preparing will be filed with or submitted to the Commission;

- provide that foreign attorneys who are not admitted in the United States, and who do not advise clients regarding U.S. law, would not be covered by the rule, while foreign attorneys who provide legal advice regarding U.S. law would be covered to the extent they are appearing and practicing before the Commission, unless they provide such advice in consultation with U.S. counsel;

- allow an issuer to establish a "qualified legal compliance committee" (QLCC) as an alternative procedure for reporting evidence of a material violation. Such a QLCC would consist of at least one member of the issuer's audit committee, or an equivalent committee of independent directors, and two or more independent board members, and would have the responsibility, among other things, to recommend that an issuer implement an appropriate response to evidence of a material violation. One way in which an attorney could satisfy the rule's reporting obligation is by reporting evidence of a material violation to a QLCC;

- allow an attorney, without the consent of an issuer client, to reveal confidential information related to his or her representation to the extent the attorney reasonably believes necessary (1) to prevent the issuer from committing a material violation likely to cause substantial financial injury to the financial interests or property of the issuer or investors; (2) to prevent the issuer from committing an illegal act; or

---

[124] *See* 17 C.F.R. § 205; Securities Exchange Act Release No. 47276 (2003).

[125] *See* discussion in § 5.08[P] *supra*.

[126] *See* Securities Exchange Act Release Nos. 46868 (2002), 47276 (2003).

(3) to rectify the consequences of a material violation or illegal act in which the attorney's services have been used;

- state that the rules govern in the event the rules conflict with state law, but will not preempt the ability of a state to impose more rigorous obligations on attorneys that are not inconsistent with the rules; and
- affirmatively state that the rules do not create a private cause of action and that authority to enforce compliance with the rules is vested exclusively with the Commission.[127]

§ 15.10 SARBANES-OXLEY ACT ENHANCED ENFORCEMENT

As discussed in Chapter 5, the Sarbanes-Oxley Act (SOX) provides the SEC with enhanced enforcement remedies. These remedies include the SEC obtaining:

- a court order freezing certain extraordinary payments made by a subject corporation to a corporate director, officer, employee, or other agent during a Commission investigation;[128]
- forfeiture of bonuses and disgorgement of profits by a chief executive officer and/or chief financial officer where a publicly-held company must prepare an accounting restatement "as a result of misconduct";[129]
- an officer or director bar based on the subject fiduciary's being found liable for securities fraud and deemed "unfit" to serve in such capacity;[130]
- upon an order of disgorgement and the levying of a civil money penalty, a "Fair Fund" for the benefit of aggrieved investors to help offset their losses incurred as a result of the illegalities committed;[131] and
- the award by a federal court of "any equitable relief that may be appropriate or necessary for the benefit of investors."[132]

---

[127] SEC Press Release No. 2003–13 (2003). To a large extent, particularly with respect to up-the-ladder reporting and permissive disclosure of client illegality to third parties, the SEC Standards resemble existing ethical rules set forth by the American Bar Association. *See* Model Rules of Professional Conduct, Rules 1.6, 1.13. For further discussion, see M. Steinberg, *supra* note 121, at §§ 3.02-3.05; Symposium, 52 Am. U. L. Rev. No. 3 (2003); Symposium, 74 Fordham L. Rev. No. 3 (2005); Symposium, 8 Stan. J. Law Bus. & Fin. No. 1 (2002); Symposium, 70 Tenn. L. Rev. No. 1 (2002); Symposium, 46 Washburn L.J. No. 1 (2006); Symposium, 3 Wyo. L. Rev. No. 2 (2003); Cramton, Cohen & Koniak, *Legal and Ethical Duties of Lawyers After Sarbanes-Oxley*, 48 Vill. L. Rev. 725 (2004); Groskaufmanis, *Climbing "Up the Ladder": Corporate Counsel and the SEC's Reporting Requirement for Lawyers*, 89 Cornell L. Rev. 511 (2004); Karmel, *The Securities and Exchange Commission Goes Abroad to Regulate Corporate Governance*, 33 Stetson L. Rev. 849 (2004); Warren, *Revenue Recognition and Corporate Counsel*, 56 SMU L. Rev. 885 (2003).

[128] *See* discussion § 5.08[R][5] *supra.*

[129] *See* discussion § 5.08[E] *supra.*

[130] *See* discussion §§ 5.08[F], 15.06 *supra.*

[131] *See* discussion § 5.08[R][6] *supra.*

[132] Sarbanes-Oxley Act § 305(b), amending § 21(d)(5) of the Exchange Act; *see* discussion §§ 5.08[R][7], 15.05[D] *supra.*

Ch. 15 APPENDIX

SEC Order Directing a Private Investigation

UNITED STATES OF AMERICA
BEFORE THE
SECURITIES AND EXCHANGE COMMISSION

In the Matter of XYZ Corporation	:	**ORDER DIRECTING A PRIVATE**
	:	**INVESTIGATION AND**
File No. _____	:	**DESIGNATING OFFICERS**
		TO TAKE TESTIMONY

I

The Commission's public files disclose that XYZ Corporation is a corporation with its principal executive offices in Sandusky, Ohio. Its common stock is registered with the Commission pursuant to Section 12(g) of the Securities Exchange Act of 1934 (the "Exchange Act") and is quoted on the NASD Stock Market ("NASDAQ"). XYZ Corporation has filed with the Commission registration statements and annual, quarterly and other periodic reports pursuant to Section 13 of the Exchange Act.

II

Members of the staff have reported information to the Commission tending to show that, during the period from on or about April 15, 2007, through August 31, 2008:

A. XYZ Corporation, its present and former officers, directors, employees, affiliates and other persons or entities, directly and indirectly, in connection with the purchase or sale of securities, may have employed, or may be employing, devices, schemes or artifices to defraud, may have made, or may be making, untrue statements of material facts and may have omitted, or may be omitting, to state material facts necessary in order to make the statements made, in the light of the circumstances under which they were made, not misleading, and may have engaged, or may be engaging in transactions, acts, practices or courses of business which operate or have operated as a fraud and deceit upon other persons, including purchasers and sellers of such securities, concerning, among other things, the inventory, sales, payroll taxes, cash flow and the financial condition and performance of XYZ Corporation.

B. XYZ Corporation, its present and former officers, directors, employees, affiliates and other persons or entities, directly or indirectly, may have filed or caused to be filed with the Commission certain annual, quarterly and other reports pursuant to the Exchange Act which may have contained untrue statements of material facts or may have omitted information or material facts necessary in order to make the statements made, not misleading, and which may have failed to contain information required to be set forth therein concerning, among other things, the matters referred to in Paragraph II.A. above.

C. XYZ Corporation, its present and former officers, directors, employees, affiliates and other persons or entities, directly and indirectly, may have failed to or caused the failure to:

1. make and keep books, records, and accounts which, in reasonable detail, accurately and fairly reflect transactions and dispositions of the corporate funds of XYZ Corporation, and

2. devise and maintain a system of internal accounting controls sufficient to provide reasonable assurances that:
   a. transactions are executed in accordance with management's general or specific authorization;
   b. transactions are recorded as necessary to permit preparation of financial statements in conformity with generally accepted accounting principles or any other criteria applicable to such statements and to maintain accountability for assets;
   c. access to assets is permitted only in accordance with management's general or specific authorization; and
   d. the recorded accountability for assets is compared with the existing assets at reasonable intervals and appropriate action is taken with respect to any differences.

D. XYZ Corporation, its present and former officers, directors, employees, affiliates and other persons or entities, directly or indirectly, may have falsified, or caused the falsification of, books, records and accounts referred to in Subparagraphs II.C.1 and 2 above.

III

The Commission, having considered the foregoing, and deeming such acts and practices, if true, to be in possible violation of Section 17(a) of the Securities Act of 1933 and Sections 10(b), 13(a) and 13(b)(2)(A) and (B) of the Exchange Act of 1934 ("Exchange Act") and Rules 10b-5, 12b-20, 13a-1, 13a-13, 13b2-1, and 13b2-2 thereunder, finds it necessary and appropriate and hereby:

ORDERS, pursuant to Section 20(a) of the Securities Act and Section 21(a) of the Securities Exchange Act that a private investigation be conducted to determine whether any person, persons or entities have engaged, are engaging, or are about to engage in any of the aforesaid acts or practices, or in acts or practices of similar purport or object; and

FURTHER ORDERS, pursuant to Section 19(b) of the Securities Act and Section 21(b) of the Securities Exchange Act, that, for the purpose of such investigation, [names of SEC attorneys and investigators inserted here], and each of them, are hereby designated as officers of this Commission and each of them are empowered to administer oaths and affirmations, subpoena witnesses, compel their attendance, take evidence, and require the production of any books, papers, correspondence, memoranda or other records and materials deemed relevant or material to the investigation, and to perform all other duties in connection therewith as prescribed by law.

By the Commission

_____
Secretary

SEC Subpoena Order

SUBPOENA DUCES TECUM
UNITED STATES OF AMERICA
SECURITIES AND EXCHANGE COMMISSION

To: T.J. Maloney
     P.O. Box 934
     Dallas, Texas 75225

At the instance of the Securities and Exchange Commission you are hereby required to appear before [names of SEC attorneys and investigators inserted here], Officers of the Securities and Exchange Commission, at 801 Cherry Street, 19th Floor in the City of Fort Worth, TX 76102 on the 14th day of July 2008, at 9:00 o'clock a.m. of that day, to testify in the matter of XYZ Enterprises, Inc. involving a private investigation by the Commission pursuant to Section 20(a) of the Securities Act of 1933 and Section 21(a) of the Securities Exchange Act of 1934.

And you are hereby required to bring with you and produce at said time and place the following books, papers, and documents:

All monthly and quarterly brokerage account statements for your own account and for any account under your direction or control from March 15, 2007 through December 31, 2007; all calendars, logs, day timers or other documents reflecting meetings held or to be held from March 15, 2007 through December 31, 2007; all business, personal, mobil, and cellular telephone records for the period March 15, 2007 through December 31, 2007; all expense reports and supporting documentation from March 15, 2007 through December 31, 2007; all bank records for all accounts under your control or in which you have a direct or indirect or beneficial interest from March 15, 2007 through December 31, 2007.

Fail not at your peril,

In testimony whereof, the seal of the Securities and Exchange Commission is affixed hereto, and the undersigned, a member of said Securities and Exchange Commission, or an officer designated by it, has hereunto set his hand at Fort Worth, Texas, this 30th day of June 2008.

_____
[name of SEC attorney or investigator]

GLOSSARY

This Glossary is designed to familiarize the reader with key securities law terms, statutes, rules, and other regulations. Although not intended to be comprehensive or exhaustive, the Glossary should prove useful.

GENERAL TERMS

Acceleration: Process by which the SEC can expedite a registration statement's effective date, thereby avoiding § 8(a)'s twenty day waiting requirement. *See § 8(a) of the Securities Act; Rule 460.*

Accredited Investor: Class of investor defined in such provisions as § 2(a)(15) of the Securities Act and Rule 501(a), for purposes of the exempt offering provisions of Regulation D and § 4(6) of the Securities Act, to include certain institutional investors as well as financially sophisticated and/or wealthy investors. *See Uniform Limited Offering Exemption (ULOE); § 4(6) of the Securities Act; Rules 505 and 506; Regulation D.*

Affiliate: Generally, an affiliate of an issuer is one who controls, is controlled by, or is under common control with, either directly or indirectly through one or more intermediaries, such issuer. *See Control Person; Rule 405.*

"All-or-None" Offering: Type of offering whereby all the securities offered must be sold at a specified price within a specified time with the amount due to the seller at a specified date and where the purchase price will be refunded if the offering is not fully subscribed. Pursuant to Rule 10b-9, such offerings are prohibited unless such conditions are met.

American Stock Exchange (AMEX): Exchange where the securities of smaller and perhaps newer companies are traded, as compared to the New York Stock Exchange with its larger companies and more stringent listing requirements. *See Securities Exchanges.*

Annual Report to Security Holders: Pursuant to Rule 14a-3 and Rule 14c-3, an annual report is to be furnished to an issuer's security holders. The annual report is not deemed a filed document for Exchange Act § 18(a) liability purposes. *See § 14(a) of the Exchange Act; Rule 14a-9.*

Auditor Disclosure of Corporate Fraud: Section 10A of the Exchange Act sets forth requirements for audits conducted by an independent public accountant of an issuer's financial statements to include certain procedures to (1) detect illegal acts that would have a direct and material effect on the determination of financial statement amounts; (2) identify related party transactions material to financial statements; and (3) evaluate an issuer's ability to continue as a going concern. The statutory language makes clear that the above procedures are to be carried out in accordance with current generally accepted accounting principles, "as may be modified from time to time by the [SEC]." *See § 10A of the Exchange Act.*

Automatic Shelf Registration: A more flexible version of shelf registration for offerings by well-known seasoned issuers whereby such issuers may register unspecified amounts of securities on Form S-3 (or Form F-3) registration statements, which become effective immediately upon filing. *See Shelf Registration; Well-Known Seasoned Issuers; Rule 415.*

"Bad Boy" Disqualifications: Refers to provisions contained in certain SEC rules (such as Rule 262 of Regulation A) disqualifying an issuer from using certain exemptions from registration if the issuer or its affiliated persons, executive officers, directors, or other like persons have been subject to disciplinary action during the previous five years (or ten years for Rule 262(b)(1)), including a criminal conviction relating to the sale of securities and the imposition of an SEC injunction.

"Bespeaks Caution" Doctrine: Provides that forward-looking statements included in a disclosure document (such as a registration statement or a Form 10-K) are not actionable as securities fraud, provided that such statements are accompanied by specific and meaningful cautionary language. *See Forward-Looking Statement; Safe Harbor for Certain Forward-Looking Statements; "Soft" Information.*

"Best Efforts" Underwriting: Type of underwriting arrangement where the underwriters agree to act as agents for the issuer and use their "best efforts" in finding purchasers for the securities being offered. To the extent that the underwriters are unsuccessful in finding purchasers, the securities are not sold. *See Underwriting; "Firm Commitment" Underwriting.*

"Blank Check" Company: A developmental stage company that has (1) no specific business plan or purpose, or (2) the business plan of which is to merge with an unidentified company or companies. *See "Blank Check" Offering; Penny Stock; § 7 of the Securities Act.*

"Blank Check" Offering: The offering of securities of a "blank check" company. *See "Blank Check" Company; Penny Stock; § 7 of the Securities Act.*

"Blue Sky" Laws: Term used to refer to the body of state securities laws. Some states have statutes that only require disclosure of material information, while other states have merit regulation which requires, in addition to full disclosure, that the securities offered meet a test of substantive fairness. *See Merit Regulation; Regulation by Qualification.*

Bond: Type of security which evidences a debt on which the issuing governmental body or corporation promises to pay the holder of the bond a specified amount of interest for a predetermined length of time, with repayment of the principal amount at a specified expiration date. A bond (as distinguished from a debenture or other debt security) is secured by the corporation's assets. *See Debentures; Debt Securities.*

Broker: Generally, a "person" engaged in the business of purchasing or selling securities for the account of others.

Cease and Desist Order: Pursuant to the 1990 Enforcement Remedies Act, an order issued by the SEC prohibiting a subject "person" from carrying on its proscribed conduct. *See Enforcement Remedies Act; § 8A of the Securities Act; § 21C of the Exchange Act.*

Certifications: Pursuant to the Sarbanes-Oxley Act (SOX), a subject registrant's chief executive officer and chief financial officer each must certify in the subject company's periodic reports as to the accuracy of the disclosures made and the integrity of such company's disclosure controls and practices. *See Sarbanes-Oxley Act; §§ 302, 906 of SOX.*

"Change in Circumstances" Doctrine: Doctrine which holds that the concept of underwriter status can be avoided if a party can establish that he/she purchased the subject securities with investment intent but that subsequent unforeseen changes compelled the earlier than planned sale of the securities. Although the SEC has evidently rejected this defense to underwriter status, courts nonetheless may accept its validity.

Churning: Refers to the practice of a broker-dealer engaging in excessive trading in a customer account over which it has control for the purpose of generating commissions.

Comfort Opinion: A statement furnished by an attorney, acting either as counsel for the issuer or for the underwriter, providing that, based on counsel's participation in the preparation of the registration statement and conferences with representatives of the issuer, underwriters and public accountants, he/she has no reason to believe that the registration statement violates § 11. In order to avoid § 11 liability, counsel should ensure that neither the opinion nor its contents appear in the registration statement.

Conditioning the Market: See *"Gun-Jumping."*

Control Person: Pursuant to Rule 405, a control person is any person who directly or indirectly possesses the power to direct the management or policies of an entity. *See Affiliate; Rule 405.*

Covered Security: Pursuant to the National Securities Markets Improvement Act of 1996 (NSMIA), the SEC is granted exclusive authority over the registration of specified "covered" securities, thereby preempting state regulation of such offerings. *See National Securities Markets Improvement Act of 1996; § 18 of the Securities Act.*

Crown Jewel: Antitakeover device whereby the target company sells (or grants an option to purchase) its most valuable asset — its "crown jewel" — to a third party, the effect of which is to make the company less attractive to an unfriendly bidder.

Dealer: Generally, a "person" engaged in the business of purchasing or selling securities for its own account.

Debentures: Type of debt security that is not secured by a mortgage on the issuing corporation's assets, but is only backed by the company's general credit. Issuances of debentures are subject to the Trust Indenture Act of 1939 as well as the Securities Act of 1933. The antifraud provisions of § 10(b) of the Exchange Act also apply. *See Bonds; Debt Securities.*

Debt Securities: Refers to bonds, notes, debentures, and other evidences of indebtedness in which investors furnish capital to a corporation in return for a promise by the corporation to repay the principal in full at a future specified date and to pay the investor a fixed rate of interest thereon for the term of the loan. The issuance of debt securities is subject to the Trust Indenture Act of 1939 and to the Securities Act. The antifraud provisions of § 10(b) of the Exchange Act apply as well. *See Bonds; Debentures.*

Deficiency Letter: Letter sent by the SEC's Division of Corporation Finance to an issuer notifying it of deficiencies in its Securities Act registration statement. Amendments to the registration statement are subsequently filed in response thereto. This letter also is known as a "letter of comments."

Derivatives: Instruments, the value of which are limited to, or derived from, the worth of an underlying asset (*e.g.*, stock, currencies, or commodities), indices (*e.g.*, a stock market index), or interest rates.

Director/Officer Bar: A court order prohibiting a person from serving as an officer or director of a publicly-held entity who has violated certain securities acts' antifraud provisions and whose conduct demonstrates "unfitness." *See § 20(e) of the Securities Act; § 21(d) of the Exchange Act.*

"Disclose or Abstain" Rule: Doctrine promulgated by the courts in the insider trading context which provides that under certain circumstances (see *Chiarella*, 445 U.S. 222 (1980), *Dirks*, 463 U.S. 646 (1983) and *O'Hagan*, 521 U.S. 642 (1997)), one with material nonpublic information concerning a company's securities, the affairs of a company, or the market for the company's stock must either refrain from trading (or tipping) based on such information or must disclose such information to the investing public before trading (or tipping) on it.

Due Diligence (As a Defense): In the securities offering context, refers to the functions performed by various parties, including underwriters, to help ensure that the prospectus contains no material misstatement or omission. The standard of conduct required of parties to successfully invoke the due diligence defense varies depending on such factors as the statute implicated (*e.g.*, § 11 as compared to § 12(a)(2) of the Securities Act), the party's relationship with the issuer, whether the defendant is an expert or non-expert, and whether the portion of the offering document in question is an expertised or non-expertised portion.

Due Diligence (Plaintiff): In the securities litigation context, particularly with respect to the issue of justifiable reliance under § 10(b) of the Exchange Act and the period of constructive notice under applicable statutes of limitations, refers to the plaintiff's obligation to protect his/her investment interests. *See Justifiable Reliance; Statute of Limitations.*

"Economic Reality": Looking at the prefatory language, "unless the context otherwise requires," contained in § 2 of the Securities Act and § 3(a) of the Exchange Act, courts, in ascertaining whether a security exists, decipher the economic reality of a transaction rather than applying a literal construction.

"Economic Risk" Test: Under Rule 146 (which has been superseded by Rule 506), test used to determine whether offerees or purchasers of securities are able to bear the economic risks of the investment and, hence, help qualify the offering for exemption from registration pursuant to § 4(2). Rule 506 has eliminated this test. The test, however, still remains applicable under certain states' Blue Sky laws.

Efficient Market Theory: *See "Fraud on the Market" theory.*

Electronic Data Gathering, Analysis, and Retrieval System (EDGAR): Registrants subject to EDGAR must file with the SEC virtually all documents by means of electronic submission.

Enforcement Remedies Act: This Act, enacted in 1990, authorizes the SEC, *inter alia,* to issue cease and desist orders, obtain monetary penalties, order disgorgement in specified situations, and procure director and officer bar orders from the federal courts.

Exempt Securities: Specific securities or categories of securities which are never required to be registered under § 5 of the 1933 Act. The exemption is predominantly due to the intrinsic character or nature of the issuer itself. Examples of exempt securities include certain short-term promissory notes or bills of exchange, securities issued or guaranteed by municipalities, state or federal governments, and securities issued by nonprofit, religious, educational or charitable organizations. *See Transactional Exemptions; § 3(a) of the Securities Act.*

Express Causation Requirement: Enacted as part of the PSLRA, Section 21D(b)(4) of the Exchange Act expressly requires that a plaintiff prove loss causation in any private action under the Exchange Act. *See Private Securities Litigation Reform Act (PSLRA).*

Fair Fund: Enacted by Congress pursuant to the Sarbanes-Oxley Act, upon an order of disgorgement accompanied with the levying of a money penalty, allowing the SEC to set up a "Fair Fund" from these proceeds for the benefit of aggrieved investors.

"Family Resemblance" Test: Test adopted by the U.S. Supreme Court (*see: Reves,* 494 U.S. 56 (1990)) to determine whether a note is a security. Beginning with the presumption that a note of greater than a nine-month duration is a security, the family resemblance test analyzes each note by examining four factors: (1) the motivations that would prompt a reasonable buyer and seller to enter into the transaction; (2) the plan of distribution; (3) the reasonable expectations of the investing public concerning the note in question; and (4) any relevant risk reducing factors, such as the presence of a regulatory scheme or collateralization.

FINRA: With respect to broker-dealer self-regulatory (SRO) oversight (including examination and enforcement functions), the key SRO regulator is the Financial Industry Regulatory Authority. *See NASD; New York Stock Exchange.*

"Firm Commitment" Underwriting: Type of underwriting arrangement whereby the underwriters agree to purchase from the issuer the securities being offered for the purpose of reselling them to participating dealers and the public. To the extent that the underwriters are not successful in finding purchasers, they must pay for and hold the securities for their own account. *See Underwriting; "Best Efforts" Underwriting.*

Float: The aggregate market value of an entity's voting securities held by nonaffiliates.

Foreign Corrupt Practices Act (FCPA): A 1977 amendment to the Exchange Act, this legislation requires an Exchange Act reporting company to maintain reasonably accurate and detailed books and records (in addition to its normal Exchange Act reporting requirements) and to devise and maintain an internal accounting system that will reasonably insure proper accountability of assets and internal control of accounting practices and procedures. Foreign bribery also is prohibited. *See §§ 13(b)(2) and 30A of the Exchange Act.*

Forward-Looking Statement: Generally refers to "soft" future-oriented information rather than historical "hard" information, encompassing projections of future performance and appraisals of specified assets. *See "Bespeaks Caution" Doctrine; "Soft" Information; Private Securities Litigation Reform Act.*

"Fraud on the Market" Theory: Theory used by courts (and acquiesced in by the Supreme Court) to apply the presumption of reliance in securities litigation (*e.g.*, § 10(b) litigation). This theory posits that the market price of an issuer's stock traded in an efficient market reflects all available public information regarding that issuer.

Free Writing Prospectus: A written communication that is deemed a § 10 prospectus and constitutes an offer to sell the securities that are (or in the case of a well known seasoned issuer will be) the subject of a registration statement. A free writing prospectus is not a statutory prospectus. *See Prospectus; Well Known Seasoned Issuer; § 10(b) of the Securities Act.*

General Solicitation: Lack of general solicitation is a necessary condition to perfect certain exemptions from Securities Act registration, such as Rules 505 and 506 of Regulation D and the Section 4(2) and 4(6) exemptions. According to the SEC, the presence of a preexisting relationship with the offeree is an important factor in determining the lack of general solicitation. The substantial compliance standard of Rule 508 provides no defense if there is general solicitation. *See Private Offering Exemption; §§ 4(2), 4(6); Rules 505, 506, 508.*

Glass-Steagall Act: Popular name for the Banking Act of 1933. In essence, this legislation required that investment banking be separated from commercial banking. It has been repealed. *See Gramm-Leach-Bliley Act; Investment Banking.*

Going-Private: Refers to a transaction or series of transactions in a publicly-held company whereby the controlling (or other) group substantially reduces or eliminates entirely the number of shares held by the public by inducing shareholders to exchange their stock for cash, thereby causing the company to attain privately-held status. Such transactions are regulated by Rules 13e-3 and 13e-4 and, of course, state law. *See Leveraged Buyout (LBO); § 13(e) of the Exchange Act; Rules 13e-3, 13e-4; Schedule 13E-3.*

Going-Public: Process whereby an issuer embarks upon a plan of financing in which securities are sold to the investing public. The issuer thereby becomes subject to the reporting requirements of the Exchange Act. *See Initial Public Offering (IPO).*

Golden Parachute: A generous severance package that compensates certain key executives if control of a target company changes in the event of a corporate takeover.

Graphic Communication: All electronic communications other than telephone and other live, in real-time communications to a live audience, including any form of electronic media, such as audiotapes, videotapes, facsimiles, CD-ROM, electronic mail, Internet websites, and computers, computer networks, and other forms of computer data compilation.

Gramm-Leach-Bliley Act: Act repealing the Glass-Steagall Act of 1933, this legislation (enacted in 1999), among other things, creates a regulatory framework premised on "functional regulation," authorizes the formation of "financial holding companies" that can provide a full array of financial products, and permits subsidiaries of banks (rather than banks themselves) to take part in an expansive range of financial activities.

"Greenmail":   The purchase of a substantial block of the subject company's securities by a (potentially) unfriendly suitor with the primary purpose of inducing the subject company to repurchase the block at a premium over the amount paid by the potential suitor.

"Gun-Jumping":   The publication of information of an offering or other conduct prior to the filing of a Securities Act registration statement (the pre-filing period) resulting in a conditioning of the public market or a stimulation of interest in the securities to be registered. Such conduct for certain issuers and under certain circumstances constitutes a violation of the § 5(c) proscription against offers to sell in the pre-filing period. *See § 5(c) of the Securities Act; Securities Act Rules 163, 163A, 168, 169.*

Horizontal Commonality: One of the two types of "common enterprise" for purposes of the *Howey* investment contract test. Generally, horizontal commonality looks to the relationships which exist between an individual investor and the pool of other investors. A pooling of the interests of the investors is essential to finding the presence of horizontal commonality; all courts have held that horizontal commonality is sufficient to meet the common enterprise requirement of the *Howey* test. *See Vertical Commonality; Howey Test.*

"Hot Issue":   Occurs where the price of an offering of securities quickly rises to a substantial premium above the initial offering price. The demand for the securities offered may be accompanied by an investor stampede to purchase the coveted "hot" stock.

Howey Test: Test promulgated by the Supreme Court in the *Howey* case, 328 U.S. 293 (1946), to determine when an investment contract exists for purposes of § 2(a)(1) of the Securities Act and § 3(a)(10) of the Exchange Act. "The test is whether the scheme involves an investment of money in a common enterprise with profits to come solely from the efforts of others." The test subsequently has been elaborated upon by the lower courts. *See Investment Contract.*

In Registration: Refers to the entire registration process, generally from the pre-filing period until the prospectus delivery requirements have been satisfied.

Initial Public Offering (IPO):   The first public offering of securities that an issuer makes. By so doing, the issuer "goes public" and becomes subject to the Exchange Act's reporting obligations. *See "Going-Public".*

Insider Trading Sanctions Act (ITSA):   Enacted in 1984, and amended in 1988, this legislation authorizes the SEC, *inter alia*, to seek the imposition of a civil monetary penalty amounting to three times the profit received or loss avoided against any person unlawfully purchasing or selling securities while in possession of material nonpublic information, unlawfully tipping material nonpublic information, or substantially contributing to the violation's occurrence by a brokerage firm's (or investment adviser's) failure to maintain and enforce an adequate law compliance monitoring system. Under certain circumstances, other "entities" (such as corporations, accounting and law firms) also may be subject to a treble money penalty. *See Insider Trading and Securities Fraud Enforcement Act (ITSFEA).*

Insider Trading and Securities Fraud Enforcement Act (ITSFEA): Enacted in 1988, this Act increases the SEC's enforcement powers with respect to insider trading through, *inter alia*, enhanced money penalties, more rigorous provisions with respect to control person liability, and authorization for awarding bounties to informants. *See Insider Trading Sanctions Act (ITSA).*

Integrated Disclosure: Refers to the Commission's integrated disclosure framework which simplifies registrant reporting by (1) making uniform the disclosure requirements under the Securities Act and the Exchange Act, (2) allowing periodic reporting under the Exchange Act to satisfy much of the Securities Act registration statement disclosure requirements, and (3) encouraging (but not requiring) the use of informal shareholder communications to satisfy certain of the Act's formal disclosure requirements.

Integration of Offerings: Doctrine by which seemingly separate offerings are construed as one integrated offering, thereby vitiating otherwise exempt offerings and frequently resulting in a violation of the Securities Act's registration requirements. The SEC has set forth criteria to determine when integration should apply as well as establishing certain safe harbor rules. *See Rules 147(b)(2) and 502(a).*

Investment Advisors Act of 1940: Requires registration of all non-exempt investment advisors and obligates such advisers to conform their conduct to statutory norms. The Act, *inter alia*, addresses fee arrangements between advisors and clients, prohibits fraudulent practices, precludes assignment of an investment advisory contract without the client's consent, requires advisors to maintain books and records consistent with rules that may be promulgated by the SEC, and authorizes the SEC to inspect such books and records.

Investment Company Act of 1940: Requires companies engaged primarily in the business of investing, reinvesting, and trading in securities and whose securities are offered to and held by the investing public to register with the SEC and to disclose their financial condition and investment policies. The Act contains antifraud provisions and private remedies. Investment companies also may be subject to the provisions of the 1933 and 1934 Acts.

"Investment Contract": Term used in § 2(a)(1) of the Securities Act and § 3(a)(10) of the Exchange Act as a type of instrument that constitutes a security. *See Howey Test.*

Justifiable Reliance: An objective or reasonable person test in determining whether a plaintiff's reliance on an alleged misrepresentation was justifiable in a cause of action under § 10(b) of the Exchange Act. Factors relevant to this determination include *(Myers v. Finkle*, 950 F.2d 165 (4th Cir. 1991)): "(1) the sophistication and expertise of the plaintiff in financial and securities matters; (2) the existence of long standing business or personal relationships; (3) access to the relevant information; (4) the existence of a fiduciary relationship (5) concealment of the fraud; (6) the opportunity to detect the fraud; (7) whether the plaintiff initiated the stock transaction or sought to expedite the transaction; and (8) the generality or specificity of the misrepresentations." *See Due Diligence; Statute of Limitations.*

Letter of Comments: *See Deficiency Letter.*

Letter of Intent: Signed letter between an issuer and its managing underwriter outlining the proposed terms of the offering as well as the underwriting compensation, but not binding either party, with certain exceptions (such as a provision concerning payment of expenses upon abandonment by one of the parties). *See Firm Commitment Underwriting; Market Out Clause.*

Leveraged Buyout (LBO):   Corporate control transaction frequently characterized by public shareholders of a corporation being cashed-out, with corporate insiders obtaining a substantial equity interest in the ongoing enterprise. The funds borrowed to finance the acquisition are collaterized by the corporation's assets, with repayment of the loans to be made out of the company's future revenue stream and the sale of certain divisions or subsidiaries. *See Going-Private.*

Lock-Up: An arrangement, made in connection with the contemplated acquisition of a publicly-held entity, that gives the prospective acquiror an advantage in acquiring the subject company over other potential acquirors.

Management Discussion and Analysis (MD&A):   Item 303 of Regulation S-K requires disclosure of Management's Discussion and Analysis of Financial Condition and Results of Operation (MD&A). In short, the MD&A disclosure requirements seek to provide investors with management's analysis of historical and prospective material events, trends, and uncertainties. Generally, disclosure is required where the subject event, trend or uncertainty is reasonably likely to occur and to have a material impact on the company's financial condition or results of operation. *See Regulation S-K.*

Market Information: Information about the market for a particular entity's securities as contrasted with information about the corporation or its business.

Market Maker: Refers to a broker-dealer in the over-the-counter market who buys and sells securities as a principal for its own account on a regular or continual basis. The market maker conducts "two-way" bids; *i.e.*, it stands willing to both buy and sell the securities for which it is making a market. Market makers are subject to regulation by FINRA and the SEC. *See FINRA.*

Market Out Clause: Permits an underwriter to avoid its commitment to acquire securities from the issuer prior to the closing of the offering if certain specified event(s) transpire. *See Firm Commitment Underwriting; Letter of Intent.*

Merit Regulation: Refers to state Blue Sky statutes that, in addition to requiring full and adequate disclosure, require that securities offerings be substantively fair, just, and equitable. *See "Blue Sky" Laws; Registration by Qualification.*

Misappropriation Theory: Generally extends liability for insider trading to persons who trade or tip material nonpublic information in breach of a duty owed to the source of the information (namely, to a source other than the subject corporation and its shareholders). *See "Disclose or Abstain" Rule.*

Model Accredited Investor Exemption: A model transactional exemption drafted by the North American Securities Administrators Association (NASAA) and adopted in full or in part by a number of states. The model exemption provides that issuers may avoid state registration requirements if the securities are sold only to "accredited" investors and certain other conditions are met. The model exemption allows the issuer to use a general advertisement to "test the waters" if such advertisement contains certain specified information. Similar to

Rules 505 and 506 of SEC Regulation D, limitations on resale apply. There is no federal exemption that entirely coordinates with NASAA's model exemption. *See Testing the Waters; Rule 1001; Regulation A.*

Money Penalties: Authorizes the SEC to impose administrative civil money penalties against regulated persons and to seek the levying of civil money penalties against all "persons" pursuant to order of a federal court. *See § 20(d) of the Securities Act; §§ 21(d), 21A, 21B of the Exchange Act.*

NASD (National Association of Securities Dealers, Inc.): Self-regulatory organization (SRO) of broker-dealers organized and governed under the supervision of the SEC pursuant to § 15 of the Exchange Act. The NASD's enforcement and inspection powers are now exercised by FINRA. *See FINRA.*

NASDAQ (National Association of Securities Dealers Automated Quotation System): Electronic means of publicizing buy and sell quotes to be used in the over-the-counter market. *See Market Maker; Over-The Counter Market.*

NASAA (North American Securities Administrators Association): A voluntary organization composed of securities regulatory authorities of the 50 states, the Commonwealth of Puerto Rico, Guam, as well as Mexico and the provinces of Canada.

National Market System Exemption: Preempts from state registration oversight, securities that are listed (or are authorized for listing) on the American Stock Exchange, the New York Stock Exchange, or the NASDAQ (National Market System). *See Covered Security; National Securities Markets Improvement Act (NSMIA); § 18 of the Securities Act.*

National Securities Markets Improvement Act of 1996 (NSMIA): 1996 federal legislation preempts state regulation of securities registration with respect to offerings of four classes of "covered" securities. The SEC has exclusive authority over the registration of these securities. Generally, these securities include: (1) securities offered by SEC registered investment companies; (2) securities offered to "qualified purchasers" as such term may be defined by SEC rule; (3) all securities listed (or authorized to be listed) on the American Stock Exchange, the New York Stock Exchange, or quoted in the NASDAQ National Market System (NMS); and (4) securities offered in specified transactions deemed exempt from Securities Act registration (*e.g.,* Rule 506 offerings). *See Covered Security; National Market System Exemption; § 18 of the Securities Act.*

New-Issue Markets: That part of the securities market which consists of initially issued securities. These securities are issued to the investing public through a network of underwriters and dealers. *See Trading Markets.*

New York Stock Exchange (NYSE): The dominant stock exchange in the United States. Most of this country's largest commercial and industrial companies have their securities listed and traded on the NYSE. *See Securities Exchanges.*

"No-Action" Letter: Letter issued by the SEC's staff, sought by a party prior to engaging in the contemplated conduct, in order to help ensure that such conduct will not raise the Commission's ire. After a staff no-action letter has been issued, the SEC is not precluded from subsequently bringing an enforcement action; however, as a practical matter, the chances of such an action being initiated are slim. Prospective plaintiffs are not precluded from bringing suit by the issuance of an SEC staff no-action letter.

Over-The-Counter Market (OTC Market): Generally, securities transactions in the secondary trading markets which do not take place on exchanges are said to be conducted over-the-counter. *See Market Maker; NASDAQ; Pink Sheets.*

Pac-Man Defense: A tender offer by the subject company for the securities of the bidder.

Penny Stock: Generally, penny stocks are highly speculative, low priced securities that are traded in the over-the-counter market (OTC). *See NASDAQ; Over-the-Counter Market; Pink Sheets.*

"Piggy-Back" Registration: Term used to refer to a manner in which a control person can register his/her stock in a public offering. If a control person has covenanted with the issuer for the right of "piggy-back" registration, he/she is authorized to "piggy-back" his/her stock or a portion thereof at the time that the issuer elects to file a Securities Act registration statement.

Pink Sheets: System used in the over-the-counter market to record quotes and reports of transactions of securities not traded on the NASDAQ System. *See Over-The-Counter Market.*

PIPEs (Private Investment in Public Equity): Generally, PIPEs involve the purchase of securities in an issuer private placement (such as pursuant to § 4(2) or Rule 506), the issuer's subsequent registration of the restricted stock with the SEC, and, upon effectiveness of the registration statement, the ability of the PIPE investors to resell immediately their stock into the public markets.

"Plain English" Disclosure: Refers to SEC requirements that are designed to make disclosure documents (primarily offering documents) easier for individual investors to understand by mandating that the documents be free of highly technical and legalistic language. Other requirements include the use of clear and concise paragraphs and sentences, prominent risk factor disclosure, limited use of glossaries to explain information in the prospectus, and the use of descriptive headings.

Pleading Requirements: Enacted as part of the PSLRA, Section 21D(b) of the Exchange Act requires that: a plaintiff in the complaint in any private securities fraud action alleging material misstatements and/or omissions "specify each statement alleged to have been misleading; the reason or reasons why the statement is misleading; and if an allegation regarding the statement or omission is made on information and belief, the complaint shall state with particularity all facts on which that belief is formed;" and (2) in any private action under the 1934 Act in which the plaintiff "may recover money damages only on proof that the defendant acted with a particular state of mind the complaint shall, with respect to each such act or omission alleged to violate the 1934 Act, state with particularity facts giving rise to a strong inference that the defendant acted with the required state of mind." Note that the pleading fraud with particularity requirement set forth in Rule 9(b) of the Federal Rules of Civil Procedure also applies in this context. *See Private Securities Litigation Reform Act (PSLRA).*

Poison Pill: Generally, an antitakeover provision (also called a "shareholder rights plan") whereby certain securities (such as rights or warrants) of the target company are triggered upon consummation of any enumerated transaction or event into the common stock or other security of the target or of the acquiror or cash.

PORTAL: A securities market established to allow trading of securities pursuant to Rule 144A. Purchasers of such securities must be qualified institutional buyers ("QIBs") as defined by Rule 144A. *See Qualified Institutional Buyer; Rule 144A.*

Post-Effective Period: Time period after the Securities Act registration statement filed with the SEC becomes effective. Sales of the subject securities can take place only in the post-effective period pursuant to § 5(a) of the Securities Act. *See § 5(a) of the Securities Act.*

Pre-Filing Period: Time period before a registration statement has been filed with the SEC. Subject to certain exceptions, offers to sell as well as offers to buy are prohibited; sales are prohibited; negotiations and agreements with underwriters who are or will be in privity with the issuer are permitted; Rule 135 announcements are permitted; certain broker-dealer published information is permitted pursuant to Rules 137–139. Note that pursuant to the SEC's 2005 amendments to its offering rules, well-known seasoned issuers may make offers to sell in the pre-filing period. *See Gun-Jumping, Well-Known Seasoned Issuer; Rules 163, 163A, 168, 169.*

Preliminary Prospectus: Prospectus used pursuant to Rule 430 in the waiting period as a written offer in satisfaction of § 10's prospectus delivery requirement. The preliminary prospectus contains substantially the same information as the § 10(a) statutory prospectus. A legend in red ink must be included, stating among other things, that the registration statement has yet to become effective. This document also has been called a "red herring" prospectus. *See Rule 430.*

Presumptive Underwriter Doctrine: Under this doctrine, one who purchases more than ten percent of the securities offered in a registered offering may be deemed an underwriter unless such person establishes sufficient investment intent. The SEC staff evidently has abandoned the presumptive underwriter doctrine. *See Underwriter; § 2(a)(11) of the Securities Act.*

Private Offering Exemption: Transactions by an issuer which are exempt from the registration requirements of § 5 of the Securities Act because they do not involve any public offering, and hence, fall within the § 4(2) exemption of the Securities Act. *See § 4(2) of the Securities Act; Rule 506.*

Private Securities Litigation Reform Act (PSLRA): Enacted by Congress in 1995, this comprehensive legislation, for example, provides for: securities class action reform, sanctions for abusive litigation, stays of discovery, auditor disclosure of corporate fraud or illegality, proportionate liability (and related issues), enhanced pleading requirements, SEC aiding and abetting authority, RICO reform, and a safe harbor from liability for certain forward-looking statements.

Proportionate Liability (& Related Issues): Enacted as part of the PSLRA in 1995, Congress circumscribed the former joint and several liability scheme. Except where actual knowledge of the falsity is shown, there now exists a proportionate liability framework for actions brought against multiple defendants under the Exchange Act or against outside directors of the issuer whose securities are the subject of an action under Section 11 of the Securities Act. The legislation also clarified several issues relating to partial settlements in federal securities actions. *See Private Securities Litigation Reform Act (PSLRA).*

Prospectus: Generally, as defined under § 2(a)(10) of the Securities Act, with certain exceptions, any written communication (or by radio or television) which offers any security for sale or confirms the sale of any security, including confirmations, letters, brochures, circulars, notices, and advertisements. Solely oral communications (if not by radio or television) do not constitute a prospectus. As construed by the U.S. Supreme Court (*Gustafson*, 513 U.S. 561 (1995)), the term "prospectus" as used in § 12(a)(2) of the Securities Act generally relates to a public offering by an issuer or its controlling shareholders.

Public Company Accounting Oversight Board (PCAOB): Created by the Sarbanes-Oxley Act, a five member board that oversees the auditing of public companies subject to the federal securities laws. The PCAOB has sweeping powers to establish quality control, ethical, and auditing standards for registered accounting firms. The Board also has the power and authority to inspect, investigate, and bring disciplinary proceedings against public auditing firms.

Public Notice: Pursuant to Rule 134, a communication concerning an offering, not deemed to be a prospectus under § 2(a)(10), which may be published or transmitted during the waiting period (and post-effective period). The public notice is used to ascertain what parties are interested in the securities and the extent of such interest. Mention of the price of the securities is permitted. *See Rule 134.*

Public Utility Holding Company Act of 1935: Statute regulating interstate holding companies which are engaged through their subsidiaries in the retail distribution of manufactured or natural gas or in the electric utility business. This Act requires such holding companies, unless exempted by the Act, to register with the SEC and to file initial and periodic reports detailing the financial structure, organization, and operations of such companies and their subsidiaries.

Qualified Institutional Buyer (QIB): Only QIBs can purchase securities in the Rule 144A market. A QIB generally must have at least $100 million invested in securities of issuers who are not affiliated with such QIB. Banks and savings and loan associations also must have a net worth of at least $25 million. Broker-dealers are subject to less rigorous standards. *See Regulation S; Rule 144A; PORTAL.*

Racketeer Influenced and Corrupt Organizations Act (RICO): RICO establishes criminal offenses and penalties as well as a civil private right of action for treble damages and attorneys' fees. Although enacted largely due to the concern of the extent to which organized crime had penetrated the national economy, controversy has arisen regarding the use of the private monetary right of action against accepted, legitimate businesses. In reaction to this concern, legislation enacted in 1995 precludes private parties from bringing RICO civil actions based on alleged violations of securities-related provisions, unless a criminal conviction has been procured.

Real-Time Disclosure: As mandated by the Sarbanes-Oxley Act and implemented by SEC rulemaking, requiring publicly-held companies to make rapid and current disclosure of their financial condition and operations. These disclosures normally are set forth in Form 8-K. *See § 409 of the Sarbanes-Oxley Act; Form 8-K.*

"Red Herring": *See Preliminary Prospectus; Rule 430.*

Refusal Order: Proceeding initiated by the SEC pursuant to § 8(b) of the Securities Act empowering the Commission, after providing an opportunity for a hearing, to declare a registration statement deficient on its face, and thereby issue a refusal order. To issue a refusal order, the SEC must act within ten days after the filing of such registration statement. The effect of the Commission's order is to prevent the registration statement from becoming effective until amended in accordance with such order. *See § 8(b) of the Securities Act.*

Regional Exchanges: The Boston (BSE), Philadelphia (Phix), Midwest (MSE), and Pacific (PSE) stock exchanges serve as examples of exchanges known as regional exchanges. The volume of trading conducted on such exchanges accounts for only a small percentage of all the trading done in the securities markets. *See Securities Exchanges; New York Stock Exchange; American Stock Exchange.*

Registration by Coordination: Type of state Blue Sky registration available to an issuer when a registered offering is being made under the U.S. Securities Act. This type of state registration requires only the filing of the 1933 Act registration statement as well as any additional information required by the state securities administrator. Note that many of these SEC registered offerings will have the effect of preempting state registration. *See National Securities Markets Improvement Act of 1986 (NSMIA).*

Registration by Notification: Type of state Blue Sky registration requiring the filing of a short-form registration statement. Such form of registration generally is available only when an issuer and its predecessors have had a seasoned business for at least five years (*e.g.*, no default and average net earnings).

Registration by Qualification: Type of state Blue Sky registration requiring, in addition to full and adequate disclosure, that the offering meet the strictures of merit regulation; *i.e.*, that the offering be substantively fair, just, and equitable. *See Merit Regulation.*

Registration Statement: The basic disclosure document which must be filed with the SEC pursuant to the 1933 Act's registration requirements for public offerings. The registration statement consists of the § 10(a) statutory prospectus, which must be accessible to prospective purchasers, and supplemental information which is placed on file and available for public inspection at the SEC's office.

Reporting Company: Generally refers to issuers subject to the periodic reporting requirements of the Exchange Act. With certain exceptions, these registrants include: (1) those which have had a public offering under the Securities Act (*see § 15(d) of the Exchange Act*), (2) those which have securities traded on a national stock exchange (*see § 12(b) of the Exchange Act*), and (3) those which have more than $10 million in total assets and a class of equity securities owned by at least 500 persons (*see § 12(g) of the Exchange Act; Rule 12g-1 of the Exchange Act*).

Repurchase Agreement: Financing arrangement whereby a person owning securities agrees to transfer the securities to another party for cash at a certain price. The original owner also simultaneously agrees to "repurchase" these securities at a fixed, higher price from the other, "lending" party, on a fixed date, the price differential being the return to the lender on the investment. Whether a "repo" is construed as a purchase and sale of a security or as a loan will determine how it will be scrutinized under the securities laws.

Restricted Security: Generally, securities acquired directly or indirectly from an issuer or its affiliate in a nonpublic offering, or securities subject to the Regulation D resale limitations. *See § 4(2) of the Securities Act; Rules 144*, 505, 506, 701.

"Risk Capital" Test: Under this test, an investment contract generally may be found if an investor invests money, property, or services in an enterprise or venture with the expectation of some pecuniary or non-pecuniary benefits to the investor to be derived essentially from the efforts of others; horizontal or vertical commonality need not be required. This important alternative to the *Howey* Test has been embraced by a number of states, although generally not by the federal courts. *See Howey Test.*

Safe Harbor for Certain Forward Looking Statements: This safe harbor extends only to private securities actions. Section 27A of the 1933 Act and Section 21E of the 1934 Act each provides a safe harbor provision for certain forward looking statements. Both written and oral statements are covered as long as certain requirements are met. These requirements generally are: (1) the statement must be identified as forward looking and accompanied by meaningful cautionary statements; (2) the statement lacks materiality; *or* (3) the plaintiff fails to prove that the statement was made with actual knowledge of the falsity. *See "Bespeaks Caution" Doctrine; Forward-Looking Statement; Private Securities Litigation Reform Act (PSLRA); "Soft" Information; § 27A of the Securities Act; § 21E of the Exchange Act.*

Sale of Business Doctrine: This doctrine, rejected by the Supreme Court in the companion cases of *Landreth Timber Co.*, 471 U.S. 681 (1985), and *Gould*, 471 U.S. 701 (1985), provides that the transfer of stock incidental to the sale of a business does not constitute a security.

Sarbanes-Oxley Act (SOX): Comprehensive federal legislation enacted in 2002. Among other provisions, SOX provides greater regulation of financial reporting for reporting companies under the Exchange Act, creates the Public Company Accounting Oversight Board, requires CEO and CFO certifications, sets forth audit committee functions and obligations, prohibits loans to directors and executive officers, bars insider buying or selling during blackout periods, and institutes attorney standards of conduct.

Scorched Earth Defense: Antitakeover device whereby the directors of the subject company take actions to sell off the subject company's assets, or failing this, to destroy the character of the company in an effort to defeat the bidder's tender offer.

Seasoned Issuer: Generally, an issuer that is eligible to use Form S-3 (or F-3) to register primary offerings of equity securities at-the-market.

Section "4(1-1/2)" Exemption: A hybrid exemption from registration, not enumerated in the Securities Act, yet ostensibly within its intent. This exemption, based largely on SEC no-action letters and other SEC pronouncements, seeks to fill the gap in the statutory exemptive scheme concerning sales of securities by affiliates, and sales of restricted securities by non-affiliates, who desire to sell such securities in a routine private transaction. Certain "established criteria" of the § 4(1) and § 4(2) exemptions must be met in order for a person to successfully invoke this exemption.

Securities Act of 1933: The first federal securities statute enacted, this "Truth in Securities" Act focuses on the initial offering context. It requires all securities offered for sale, unless otherwise exempted, to be registered with the SEC. The Act sets forth the requirements for registration of securities that are offered for sale to the public. The Act also contains exemptions from registration, private remedies, and antifraud provisions. Full disclosure, and not merit regulation, is the guiding principle.

Securities Exchange Act of 1934: Federal statute establishing the Securities and Exchange Commission (SEC) and setting forth provisions governing the public trading of securities. The Act, for example, contains antifraud provisions, extensive reporting as well as other requirements for certain issuers of securities, oversight of broker-dealers and national securities exchanges, requirements focusing on proxy solicitation, and provisions covering tender offers and going-private transactions.

Securities Exchanges: Forum with established rules and procedures where securities are traded by exchange members. The securities must be admitted to trading by the exchange and the members thereof trade for either their own accounts or for customers. By the provisions of the Exchange Act, the exchanges are subject to SEC oversight. *See American Stock Exchange; New York Stock Exchange; Regional Exchanges; § 6 of the Exchange Act.*

Securities Litigation Uniform Standards Act (SLUSA): With certain exceptions, SLUSA preempts state law with respect to securities class actions involving nationally traded securities. The authority of state securities commissioners is preserved. State actions also may be brought in individual actions, derivative suits and in going private actions, tender offers, and mergers.

SEC Aiding and Abetting Authority: The PSLRA added a new subsection (e) to Section 20 of the Exchange Act authorizing the SEC to seek injunctive relief and/or certain money penalties against aiders and abettors for knowing violation of the Exchange Act or any rule or regulation thereunder. *See Private Securities Litigation Reform Act; § 20(e) of the Exchange Act.*

"Shark Repellents": Amendments to a company's certificate of incorporation or by-laws that are devised to discourage unsolicited approaches from unwanted bidders.

"Shelf" Registration: Refers to Rule 415 which concerns Securities Act registration of securities to be offered or sold on a delayed or continuous basis in the future. Rule 415 allows, *inter alia,* Form S-3 (or F-3) issuers to file primary-at-the-market offerings of equity securities which they plan to offer in the future. *See Automatic Shelf Registration; Rule 415.*

Shell Corporation: A thinly capitalized entity normally consisting of few if any assets, little or no cash flow, and basically no business functions or operations. Shell corporations frequently are employed to shield promoters from personal liability and as a marketing tool in the securities law context.

Shingle Theory: Posits that broker-dealers are to be held to a fairly strict standard of conduct, because by hanging out its "shingle," a broker-dealer impliedly represents that its conduct and the behavior of its employees will be fair and will comport with professional norms. *See Suitability Theory.*

Short Sale: Practice where an investor places an order to sell at the current market price a security which he/she does not then own. By so doing, he/she incurs an obligation to sell which is to be fulfilled by purchasing the securities at a later date, hopefully for a lower price, and thereafter delivering such securities to the purchaser. Rules promulgated by the SEC regulate short sales. Moreover, § 16(c) of the 1934 Act prohibits short sales by insiders.

Short-Swing Profits: For purposes of § 16(b) of the 1934 Act, short-swing profits are profits realized by insiders (directors, officers, 10% shareholders) from the purchase and sale (or sale and purchase) of an equity security within a six-month period. Pursuant to § 16(b), such profits are subject to disgorgement to the corporation. Strict liability attaches in order to effectuate the remedial purpose of the statute. *See § 16(a), 16(b), 16(c) of the Exchange Act.*

Small Corporate Offering Registration Form (SCOR) Adopted by NASAA, SCOR provides a simplified state registration form for small offerings that are exempt from 1933 Act registration due to Rule 504 of Regulation D.

"Soft" Information: Refers to appraised asset valuations, projections, future earnings, and other less than "hard" information about an issuer which traditionally have not been required to be disclosed to investors and shareholders, but which today are frequently disclosed. *See "Bespeaks Caution" Doctrine; Forward-Looking Information; MD&A; Safe Harbor for Certain Forward-Looking Statements; § 27A of the Securities Act; § 21E of the Exchange Act; Rule 175.*

Specialist: A trader on a securities exchange who, pursuant to SEC and self-regulatory organization (SRO) regulations and for the purpose of maintaining "a fair and orderly market," purchases securities for his/her own account or executes orders for other broker-dealers, while specializing in the securities of particular issuers or companies.

Statute of Limitations: With respect to claims brought for alleged violations of §§ 11 and 12(a)(2) of the Securities Act, the statute of limitations is one year after the plaintiff knew or should have known of the facts constituting the violation and, in no event, more than three years after such violation. No equitable tolling applies. There is a one-year statute of limitations for § 12(a)(1) actions based on a violation of the § 5 registration provisions. Section 10(b) claims have a two year/five year statute of limitations. *See § 13 of the Securities Act; 28 U.S.C. § 1658.*

Statutory Prospectus: A § 10 preliminary or final prospectus. The statutory prospectus constitutes the first portion of the registration statement. *See § 10(a), (b) of the Securities Act.*

Stock: Type of corporate security, the purchase of which by an investor generally gives him/her the potential to share in the corporation's profits in the enterprise by way of dividends. Normally, holders of common stock have the right to elect the directors of the corporation and to vote on matters that will fundamentally change the structure or nature of the corporation. Stockholders, as equity owners of the corporation, can be said to own the corporation.

Stock Exchanges: *See Securities Exchanges.*

"Stop Order": Proceeding initiated by the SEC pursuant to § 8(d) of the Securities Act in response to materially false or misleading information in a registration statement. Once such a proceeding is initiated, and violations are found, the effectiveness of the registration statement becomes suspended until amended in accordance with the stop order. The Commission must provide notice and an opportunity for a hearing. *See § 8(d), (e) of the Securities Act.*

Strike Suit: A lawsuit of questionable merit initiated largely, if not solely, for its nuisance value and which seeks to induce the named defendants to settle the action. *See Private Securities Litigation Reform Act (PSLRA).*

Substantial Compliance: Although not a defense in SEC or state enforcement proceedings, Rule 508 of Regulation D generally provides that in private litigation minor and inadvertent errors in perfecting an exemption under Regulation D will not result in the loss of the exemption. To meet this standard, the person relying on the exemption must show: (1) that the term, condition or requirement was not "directly intended to protect that particular individual;" (2) that the failure to comply was "insignificant with respect to the offering as a whole;" and (3) that a "good faith and reasonable attempt was made to comply" with all of the Regulation's terms, conditions and requirements. Note that even in private litigation the substantial compliance defense cannot be invoked when: there is advertising or general solicitation; the amount of funds raised in a Rule 504 or Rule 505 offering is exceeded; or the number of nonaccredited purchasers in a Rule 505 or Rule 506 offering is greater than 35. *See Rule 508.*

Suitability Theory: As one aspect of the shingle theory, the suitability theory is premised on an implied representation by the broker that it will recommend only those securities suitable for each customer's investment objectives and economic status. *See Shingle Theory.*

Target Company: Refers to a company that is the subject (target) of a takeover bid.

Tender Offer: A means frequently used to acquire control of a corporation characterized by active solicitation to purchase a substantial percentage of the target's stock from the target's shareholders at a premium over the market price, offered for a limited period of time and that may be contingent upon the tender of a specific number of shares. Tender offers are governed by the Williams Act which was enacted by Congress as an amendment to the Exchange Act as well as state law. *See Williams Act; §§ 13(d), (e), 14(d), (e), and (f) of the 1934 Act.*

Testing the Waters: The ability of companies under Regulation A, Rule 1001, or the NASAA Model Accredited Investor Exemption to solicit potential investor interest in the company prior to the filing and delivery of the mandated offering statement. Testing the waters provisions are meant to provide developing companies with an opportunity to measure investor interest in the company before the company decides to undertake the substantial cost of compliance. In general, the test the waters document is a free writing subject to the inclusion of certain information, including that no funds are being solicited or will be accepted and that a detailed offering document will follow.

"Tombstone Ad": Advertisement of an offering, not deemed to be a prospectus under § 2(a)(10) of the 1933 Act, which may be published during the waiting period (and post-effective period). It provides basic information about the offering and identifies the members of the underwriting syndicate. Such an ad is used to ascertain what parties are interested in the securities and the extent of such interest. Mention of the price of the securities is permitted.

Trading Markets: Generally, consisting of securities that have been previously issued. These securities are bought and sold on stock exchanges and in the over-the-counter market.

Transactional Exemptions: Refers to transactions which are exempt from the registration requirements of § 5 of the Securities Act due to perfection of one of the Securities Act's statutory exemptions (or pursuant to an exemption prescribed by the SEC under its rulemaking authority). Usually, state securities law exemptions also must be perfected. *See Exempt Securities.*

Trust Indenture Act of 1939: Generally, federal legislation regulating the issuance of debentures, notes, bonds, and similar debt securities offered to the public pursuant to trust indentures. Often these securities also must be registered under the 1933 Act. The Trust Indenture Act regulates the conduct of the indenture trustee and the issuer and provides rights for security holders.

Two-Tier Offer: A two-step acquisition technique in which the first-step (front-end) is a cash tender offer and the second-step (back-end) often is a merger in which remaining shareholders of the subject company may receive securities of the bidder (and/or cash and securities from such bidder) which may be valued below the cash consideration offered in the first-step tender offer. This technique no longer is commonly used.

Underwriter: Any person who has purchased securities from an issuer (or from a controlling person) with a view to their distribution, offers or sells for an issuer (or for a controlling person) in connection with the distribution of securities, or directly or indirectly participates in any such undertaking, or the direct or indirect underwriting thereof. *See § 2(a)(11) of the 1933 Act; "Best Efforts" Underwriting; "Firm Commitment" Underwriting.*

Uniform Limited Offering Exemption (ULOE): Provides issuers with a uniform exemption from state registration and is intended to coordinate with SEC Regulation D. Most of the states have adopted some form of ULOE and it is the goal of the SEC and the North American Securities Administrators Association (NASAA) to achieve general uniformity in all the states. Note that state regulation of Rule 506 has been preempted by the National Securities Markets Improvement Act of 1996 (NSMIA).

Vertical Commonality: One of the two types of "common enterprise" for purposes of the *Howey* test. Vertical commonality generally requires that the fortunes of the investor(s) and promoter (or third party) rise or fall together or that the success of the venture depends essentially on promoter expertise. The lower federal courts widely disagree on whether vertical commonality satisfies the *Howey* common enterprise element. *See Horizontal Commonality; Howey Test.*

Waiting Period: Time period after a registration statement has been filed with the SEC but before it becomes effective. Oral offers and written offers by means of a § 10 prospectus are permitted; however, only in the post-effective period, may securities be sold and offers to buy be accepted; certain broker-dealer published information is permitted pursuant to Rules 137–139; the § 2(a)(10) "tombstone ad" and Rule 134 "limited public notice" may be used.

Well-Known Seasoned Issuer: An issuer that is required to file reports pursuant to § 13(a) or § 15(d) of the Exchange Act and, as of the date on which its status as a well-known seasoned issuer is determined, meets the requirements of Form S-3 (or F-3), is not an ineligible issuer, and either has a public float of at least $700 million as of the date within 60 days of its eligibility determination date or, as of the date within 60 days of its eligibility determination date, in the last three years, has issued at least $1 billion of registered non-convertible securities, other than common equity, in primary offerings for cash.

White Knight: The name given to a party sought out by a subject company in an attempt to fend off an unwanted bidder. Action taken by a white knight may include purchasing a large block of the target company's stock or making a competing tender offer.

Williams Act: Act adopted in 1968 as an amendment to the Exchange Act dealing generally with tender offers. Provisions of the Williams Act include §§ 13(d), (e), 14(d), (e) and (f) of the Exchange Act. *See Tender Offer.*

SECURITIES ACT OF 1933

Section 2: Provides the definitions of terms used throughout the Securities Act.

Section 3(a): Specifies and enumerates specific securities or categories of securities that are exempt from Securities Act (§ 5) registration, largely due to the intrinsic character or nature of the issuer itself. These exempt securities include, for example, certain short-term promissory notes or bills of exchange, securities issued or guaranteed by municipalities, state or federal governments, and securities issued by nonprofit, religious, educational or charitable organizations. Certain of the exempt securities, although not subject to 1933 Act registration, are regulated by other agencies (*e.g.*, securities issued by national banks are subject to regulation by the Comptroller of the Currency). Section 3(a)(2) through 3(a)(8) provides a listing of the exempt securities. Even an exempt security, however, is subject to the securities acts' antifraud provisions. *See Exempt Securities.*

Section 3(a)(9): Provides that securities exchanged by an issuer exclusively with its existing security holders, except those exchanged in a Title 11 bankruptcy proceeding, are exempt from Securities Act registration, provided that no commission or other remuneration is paid for soliciting such an exchange.

Section 3(a)(10): Generally exempts from Securities Act registration securities which are issued in exchange for bona fide legal claims, securities, or property interests when a court or other specified tribunal, after conducting an adversary proceeding on the transaction's fairness, grants such approval.

Section 3(a)(11): The "intrastate" exemption provides an exemption from Securities Act registration for securities offered and sold only to persons resident within the same state as the issuer is resident and doing business (or incorporated and doing business). *See Rule 147.*

Section 3(b): Empowers the SEC, through the promulgation of rules and regulations, to adopt additional exemptions from registration where, in the Commission's view, the public interest and the protection of investors does not require such securities to be registered either because of the limited character of the offering or the small amount involved. However, no offering of over $5,000,000 may be exempted under this subsection. *See Rules 504, 505, 701, 1001; Regulation A.*

Section 4(1): Exempts from the registration requirements of § 5 "transactions by any person other than an issuer, underwriter, or dealer." Hence, this provision generally permits investors to resell their securities without registration, provided such persons are not deemed underwriters and the resales are viewed as "transactions" rather than as part of a "distribution." *See Underwriter; Rule 144.*

Section 4(2): The private offering exemption provides that "transactions by an issuer not involving any public offering" are exempt from the registration requirements of § 5 of the Securities Act. The requirements for perfecting the § 4(2) exemption are detailed. There is no monetary limit to the amount of funds that can be raised under this exemption. *See General Solicitation; Private Offering Exemption; Rule 506.*

Section 4(3): This exemption concerns the prospectus delivery requirements of dealers. These requirements have been relaxed by the SEC. *See Rule 174.*

Section 4(4): Exempts from the registration requirements of § 5 "brokers' transactions executed upon customers' orders on any exchange or in the over-the-counter market but not the solicitation of such orders." *See Rule 144.*

Section 4(6): Provides an exemption for offerings not exceeding $5,000,000. Available to an unlimited number of accredited investors only. No general solicitation or advertising is permitted, there are no issuer qualifications, restrictions on resale apply, and no specific information need be furnished to investors. *See General Solicitation.*

Section 5(a): Prohibits the use of the mails or any instrument or means of interstate commerce to sell or to deliver a security for purposes of sale before the effective date of the registration statement. *See Pre-Filing Period; Waiting Period.*

Section 5(b): Prohibits the use of the mails or any other means of interstate commerce to transmit any prospectus, unless such prospectus meets the requirements of § 10. Also, the provision prohibits securities to be carried through the mails or in interstate commerce for purposes of sale or for delivery after sale unless accompanied or preceded by a § 10(a) prospectus. Note that access equals delivery. *See Post-Effective Period; Prospectus; Rules 172, 430 and 431.*

Section 5(c): Prohibits, subject to certain exceptions, the use of the mails or any means of interstate commerce to offer to sell or offer to buy the securities offered in the time period before a registration statement has been filed with the Commission or while the registration statement is the subject of a stop order, refusal order, or any public proceeding or examination under § 8. Note that well-known seasoned issuers may make offers to sell in the pre-filing period. *See "Gun-Jumping;" Pre-Filing Period.*

Section 6: Sets forth the filing requirements for registration statements including who must sign the statement, the effect of a signature affixed thereto, and the fee to be paid upon filing. This Section also states that a registration statement is deemed effective only as to the securities offered therein, that the registration statement or amendments thereto are considered to be filed as of the receipt thereof by the SEC (provided the proper fee accompanies the statement), and that the information contained in or filed with a registration statement shall be available for public inspection and copying.

Section 7: Generally provides that a registration statement shall contain the information and be accompanied by the documents specified in Schedule A. *See § 10(a) of the Securities Act; Schedule A.*

Section 8(a): Provides that the effective date of a registration statement is the twentieth day after it is filed or such earlier date as the SEC may determine (based upon factors stated therein). The statute also provides that the effective date of a registration statement begins to run anew if amendments are filed thereto (unless filed with the SEC's consent or pursuant to an SEC order). *See Rule 460.*

Section 8(b): Provides that if the Commission determines that a registration statement is deficient on its face, upon affording an opportunity to a hearing, the SEC can issue a refusal order, so long as it acts within ten days after the filing thereof, preventing the registration from becoming effective until amended in accordance thereto. *See "Refusal Order".*

Section 8(d): Provides that the SEC may initiate a stop order in response to materially false or misleading information in a registration statement, suspending the effectiveness of the registration statement until amended in accordance with the stop order. Notice and an opportunity for a hearing must be provided. *See Stop Order.*

Section 8(e): Empowers the SEC to make an investigation into whether a stop order under § 8(d) should issue. *See Stop Order.*

Section 8A: Empowers the SEC to issue cease and desist orders. *See Cease and Desist Order; § 21C of the Exchange Act.*

Section 10(a): Provides that a statutory prospectus must contain the information contained in the registration statement (see § 7) except the documents referred to in paragraphs (28) through (32) of Schedule A (or paragraphs (13) and (14) of Schedule B for foreign governmental issuers); however the SEC may by rules or regulations omit this required information from any prospectus if it determines that such information is not necessary or appropriate for the protection of investors and the public interest. Also provides under certain circumstances for the updating of information in a prospectus that is used more than nine months after the effective date of the registration statement. *See Statutory Prospectus; Schedule A.*

Section 10(b): Empowers the SEC to promulgate rules and regulations permitting the use of prospectuses that will satisfy § 5(b)(1). *See Free Writing Prospectus; Preliminary Prospectus; § 5(b) of the Securities Act; Rules 430 and 431.*

Section 11(a): Establishes a private right of action for damages on behalf of purchasers against an enumerated list of persons and entities who may be subject to civil liability for material misstatements or half-truths contained in the registration statement (including the prospectus which is part of the registration statement). The action may be brought by "any person acquiring such security" unless it can be shown that, at the time of the purchase, the purchaser knew of the misstatement or half-truth.

Section 11(b):   Provides defenses for subject parties other than the issuer for claims arising under § 11(a) of the Securities Act, the most important of which is the "due diligence" defense of § 11(b)(3). *See Due Diligence; Rule 176.*

Section 11(c):   States that the appropriate standard of reasonableness in determining what constitutes reasonable investigation and reasonable grounds for belief for purposes of the § 11(b)(3) "due diligence" defense is "that required of a prudent man in the management of his own property." *See Due Diligence; Rule 176.*

Section 11(e):   Provides for the measure of damages in suits brought under § 11(a) of the 1933 Act, as well as the payment of costs and attorney's fees. The provision also permits a defendant in a § 11(a) action to prove that the plaintiff's loss was due to factors other than the material misrepresentation(s) or nondisclosure(s) contained in the registration statement. The statute limits the damages of an underwriter to the dollar amount of the securities offered to the public by such underwriter.

Section 11(f):   With the exception of outside directors, provides for joint and several liability for the subject parties specified in § 11(a). Unless outside directors act with actual knowledge of the falsity, such directors are liable only in proportion to their fault. The statute also allows for contribution unless the parties who are liable were guilty of fraudulent misrepresentation and the others were not.

Section 11(g):   Prohibits recovery under § 11 of an amount exceeding the public offering price of the security.

Section 12(a)(1):   Provides the purchaser of securities with an express private right of action for rescission (or if he/she no longer owns the securities, for damages) against his/her seller if such seller offers or sells a security in violation of § 5. Generally, if a violation of § 5 has been committed by the seller, strict liability is imposed.

Section 12(a)(2):   Affords an express private right of action to a purchaser against his/her seller for rescission (or damages if the securities have been disposed of) where the purchaser acquired the securities by means of a prospectus or oral communication which contained a material misstatement or half-truth. The seller under § 12(a)(2) has a "reasonable care" defense. *See Due Diligence.*

Section 12(b):   Provides that in actions brought under Section 12(a)(2), a defendant may avoid all or part of the damages that otherwise would be incurred by proving that all or part of the depreciation in the value of the securities in question resulted from factors unrelated to the disclosure deficiency.

Section 13:   Provides the statute of limitations for actions brought under §§ 11, 12(a)(1), and 12(a)(2) of the 1933 Act.

Section 14:   Provides that any provision, condition, or stipulation that binds any person acquiring a security to waive compliance with any provision of the 1933 Act or the SEC's rules and regulations thereunder shall be void. *See § 29(a) of the Exchange Act.*

Section 15:   Provides that a person who controls a person held liable under § 11 or § 12 of the 1933 Act shall be jointly and severally liable with such controlled person, unless such controlling person did not have knowledge of the facts or reasonable grounds to believe in the existence of such facts upon which the controlled person's liability is predicated. *See Affiliate; Control Person; § 20(a) of the Exchange Act.*

Section 16: Provides that the rights and remedies provided by the 1933 Act shall be in addition to whatever rights or remedies exist at law or in equity.

Section 17(a): Makes it unlawful to engage in fraudulent or deceptive practices in the offer or sale of securities.

Section 17(c): Provides that the exemptions from registration contained in § 3 of the 1933 Act shall not apply to the provisions of § 17.

Section 18: Defines the classes of "covered" securities subject to exclusive SEC authority in regard to the registration of such securities, thereby preempting state regulation of such offerings. *See Covered Security; National Securities Markets Improvement Act of 1996.*

Section 19(a): Empowers the SEC to promulgate rules and regulations deemed necessary to carry out the provisions of the 1933 Act. Also states that good faith reliance on SEC rules or regulations will preclude 1933 Act liability.

Section 19(b): Empowers the SEC to subpoena witnesses, administer oaths and affirmations, take evidence, and request the production of documents for the purpose of enforcing the Securities Act.

Section 19(c): Authorizes the SEC to cooperate with state securities regulators in order to achieve greater uniformity and effectiveness of federal and state regulations and minimum interference with capital formation, particularly for small businesses.

Section 20(b): Empowers the SEC, when it appears that a person is engaged in or is about to engage in a practice or act violative of the 1933 Act or the rules or regulations promulgated thereunder, to bring an action in United States District Court to enjoin such practice or act, and upon a proper showing, an injunction or restraining order shall be granted. The statute also authorizes the SEC to transmit evidence concerning such practices or acts to the Attorney General who may bring the appropriate criminal proceedings.

Section 20(e): Authorizes the SEC to seek a court order barring a person from serving as an officer or director of a publicly-held company if such person violated § 17(a)(1) of the Securities Act and his/her conduct "demonstrates unfitness to serve as an officer or director of any such issuer." *See Director/ Officer Bar; § 21 of the Exchange Act.*

Section 22(a): Provides that the United States District Courts shall have jurisdiction over offenses and violations under the 1933 Act and the rules and regulations promulgated thereunder, and concurrent jurisdiction (consistent with the Securities Litigation Uniform Standards Act) with the states for suits at law or in equity brought to enforce any duty or liability created by the 1933 Act. The statute also provides for venue of suits; service of process, and judicial review. It prohibits the removal of properly instituted 1933 Act cases from state court to federal court. *See Securities Litigation Uniform Standards Act (SLUSA).*

Section 22(b):   Provides that, if a person refuses to obey a subpoena, a federal district court, upon application by the SEC, may issue an order to such person requiring him/her to appear before the SEC and produce evidence; failure to obey such order is punishable by contempt of court.

Section 23:   States that just because a registration statement has been filed or is in effect or no stop order has been issued in no way implies that the SEC represents that the registration statement is true and accurate and devoid of material misrepresentations or omissions or that the SEC has passed upon the merits of the security, and any representation to the contrary to any prospective purchaser shall be unlawful.

Section 24:   States that any person who willfully violates any provision of the 1933 Act or any rule or regulation promulgated thereunder, or who willfully makes a material misrepresentation or omission in a registration statement, shall upon conviction be subject to fines and/or imprisonment. *See § 32(a) of the Exchange Act.*

Section 27A: Enacted pursuant to the PSLRA, provides a safe harbor from liability for certain oral and written forward-looking statements made by 1934 Act reporting companies as well as certain persons acting on behalf of such issuers. *See Private Securities Litigation Reform Act (PSLRA); Safe Harbor for Forward-Looking Statements; § 21E of the Exchange Act.*

SECURITIES EXCHANGE ACT OF 1934

Section 2:   States the necessity for the Securities Exchange Act of 1934, and enumerates reasons in support thereof.

Section 3(a):   Provides the definition of terms used throughout the Exchange Act.

Section 4(a):   Establishes the SEC and sets forth the criteria and rules governing the appointment of its five commissioners and the terms of their office.

Section 4C: Authorizes the SEC to regulate persons appearing or practicing before it, including on the basis of competence, character, unethical behavior, "improper professional conduct," or willfully aiding and abetting a violation of the securities laws or the SEC's rules and regulations. Added by Sarbanes-Oxley § 602.

Section 6(a):   Permits an exchange to be registered as a national securities exchange pursuant to the terms and conditions of § 6 of the 1934 Act and the provisions of § 19(a) of the Act upon filing a registration application with the SEC in such form as the SEC may, by rule, prescribe containing the rules of such exchange and any other information or document as the SEC, by rule, may prescribe as germane for the public interest or the protection of investors.

Section 6(b):   Sets forth basic conditions that must, in the Commission's view, be satisfied in order for an exchange to be registered as a national securities exchange.

Section 7(a):   Provides that the Federal Reserve Board shall prescribe rules and regulations regarding the amount of credit which may be initially extended and subsequently maintained on a non-exempt security, and sets forth a standard upon which such rules and regulations shall be based for the initial extension of credit.

Section 7(b): States that notwithstanding the provisions of § 7(a), the Federal Reserve Board may from time to time raise or lower margin requirements for the initial extension of credit or the maintenance thereof.

Section 9: Provides an express private remedy for purchasers and sellers injured by those persons who engaged in the manipulation of securities which are traded on a national securities exchange.

Section 10(b): The basic antifraud provision of the securities laws makes it unlawful to employ deceptive or manipulative devices in connection with the purchase or sale of securities. *See Rule 10b-5.*

Section 10A: Sets forth requirements with respect to auditor disclosure of corporate fraud or illegality. The statute also enumerates certain mandated activities of the audit committee as well as the auditing firm. *See Auditor Disclosure of Corporate Fraud.*

Section 12(a): Makes it unlawful for any broker or dealer to conduct transactions in securities on a national securities exchange (other than for an exempted security) that have not been registered pursuant to the 1934 Act.

Section 12(b): Provides for 1934 Act registration of a security which is listed on a national securities exchange by filing an application with the exchange as well as with the SEC containing specified information.

Section 12(g): Requires registration of a security for 1934 Act purposes by the issuer filing specified information with the SEC. Pursuant to Rule 12g-1, this requirement occurs when the issuer has total assets of greater than $10 million and has a class of equity security held of record by at least 500 persons. *See Reporting Company.*

Section 13(a): Requires any issuer of a security registered pursuant to § 12 of the Exchange Act to file annual and other periodic reports as the Commission shall prescribe containing specified information. This periodic reporting obligation also is incurred by publicly-held issuers under § 15(d). *See § 15(d); Forms 8-K, 10-K, 10-Q.*

Section 13(b)(2): Generally requires publicly-held issuers to maintain reasonably accurate books and records and internal accounting controls. This statute was passed as part of the Foreign Corrupt Practices Act. *See Foreign Corrupt Practices Act (FCPA).*

Section 13(d): Requires any person (or group) who acquires, either directly or indirectly, a greater than five percent beneficial ownership interest in any equity security of a class subject to the 1934 Act's reporting requirements to file a Schedule 13D statement of ownership with the SEC within ten business days after attaining such percentage of ownership. *See Schedule 13D.*

Section 13(e): Makes it unlawful for any 1934 Act § 12 reporting company to purchase its own shares in contravention of SEC rules. *See Going-Private; Rules 13e-3, 13e-4; Schedule 13E-3.*

Section 13(k): Generally, prohibits personal loans made (or arranged) by a subject issuer to its executive officers or directors. Added by Sarbanes-Oxley § 402.

Section 13(j): Requires the SEC to adopt rules requiring Exchange Act reporting companies to disclose any material off-balance sheet transaction, arrangement, or obligation.

Section 13(l): Requires an Exchange Act reporting company, as the SEC directs by rule, to disclose "on a rapid and current basis . . . in plain English," "material changes in [its] financial condition or operations." Added by Sarbanes-Oxley § 409. *See Form 8-K.*

Section 14(a): Gives the SEC broad authority to regulate the solicitation of proxies with respect to securities registered under § 12 of the Exchange Act. The statute makes it unlawful for any person to violate SEC rules and regulations prescribed pursuant to § 14(a). *See Annual Reports to Security Holders; Rule 14a-9.*

Section 14(d): Requires any person making a tender offer for equity securities subject to the Exchange Act's reporting requirements and registered pursuant to § 12 of the Exchange Act to file with the SEC certain materials. Also, the statute sets forth procedural mandates, such as the offering period, pro rata rights, and the time within which tendered shares may be withdrawn. *See Tender Offer; Regulation M-A; Schedules TO, 14D-9.*

Section 14(e): Prohibits deceptive, manipulative, and fraudulent practices in connection with any tender offer, invitations or requests for tenders, or any solicitation of security holders for or against any such offer, invitation, or request. *See Tender Offer.*

Section 14(f): Requires a tender offeror to file with the Commission disclosures of the names and descriptions of individuals who are to be elected directors and other agreements affecting directors that will occur in connection with a change of management control pursuant to a tender offer for Exchange Act reporting equity securities.

Section 15(c)(1): Prohibits fraudulent, deceptive, or manipulative conduct by broker-dealers in the over-the-counter market (or on exchanges of which they are not members) in connection with the purchase or sale of securities.

Section 15(c)(4): Authorizes the Commission in an administrative proceeding, after providing notice and an opportunity for hearing, to order compliance by subject parties with the provisions of §§ 12, 13, 14, and 15(d) of the Exchange Act and SEC rules and regulations promulgated thereunder. The SEC also may proceed administratively against persons who are deemed to be a "cause" of a failure to comply with § 12, 13, 14, or 15(d).

Section 15(d): Generally obligates issuers of public offerings of securities made pursuant to the Securities Act to file annual, periodic, and other specified reports with the SEC. *See Forms 8-K, 10-K, 10-Q.*

Section 15D: Requires the SEC to adopt, or authorize rules to be adopted, by the self-regulatory organizations, addressing research analysts' conflicts of interest. *See Regulation AC.*

Section 16(a): Requires beneficial owners of over ten percent of any nonexempt security registered pursuant to § 12 of the 1934 Act and directors and officers of the issuer of such stock to file with the SEC (and with any national securities exchange that such stock is listed on) a statement specifying how much of the issuer's stock is owned by such person and changes in such ownership interest.

Section 16(b):   Provides that profits realized by insiders (as defined in § 16(a)) from the purchase and sale (or sale and purchase) of stock within a six-month period are subject to disgorgement to the corporation; strict liability attaches. If the corporation does not institute the action, a shareholder may bring the suit on behalf of the corporation. *See Short-Swing Profits.*

Section 16(c):   Generally prohibits short sales and sales against the box by insiders (as defined in § 16(a)). *See Short-Sale.*

Section 18(a):   Provides an express right of action for damages when an investor purchases or sells a security in reliance upon a materially false or misleading statement that is contained in a document filed with the SEC pursuant to the Exchange Act. Section 18(a) has strict reliance and causation requirements.

Section 20(a):   Imposes joint and several liability on persons directly or indirectly controlling one held liable under the Exchange Act (or rules or regulations promulgated thereunder), unless such controlling person acted in good faith and neither directly nor indirectly induced the violation. *See Affiliate; Control Person; § 15 of the Securities Act.*

Section 20(e):   Grants to the SEC the authority to bring suit and obtain relief against aiders and abettors of Exchange Act violations. *See SEC Aiding and Abetting Authority.*

Section 20A: Enacted as part of the Insider Trading and Securities Fraud Enforcement Act of 1988, this statute provides an express private right of action for those who traded securities contemporaneously with, and on the opposite side of, a transaction from the insider trader.

Section 21:   Gives the SEC broad authority to investigate possible violations, subpoena witnesses, require the production of memoranda and other records, initiate contempt proceedings, transmit evidence to the Attorney General (who may institute criminal proceedings), and bring actions for injunctive relief. Also, the statute permits the Commission to seek a treble monetary penalty against those engaged in insider trading. In addition, pursuant to the statute, the SEC may request a federal court to order director and officer bars in specified circumstances and to levy money penalties for violation of any provision of the Exchange Act or any rule or regulation prescribed thereunder. *See Director/ Officer Bar; Money Penalties; § 20(e) of the Securities Act.*

Section 21A: Enacted as part of the Insider Trading and Securities Fraud Enforcement Act of 1988, this statute imposes an affirmative duty upon broker-dealers and investment advisers to maintain and enforce reasonable supervisory mechanisms to prevent insider trading violations and imposes treble monetary penalties under specified conditions. The statute also addresses the amount of penalties that can be assessed against a controlling person, contains procedures for collection, and gives the SEC authority to award bounties to informants. *See Insider Trading and Securities Fraud Enforcement Act (ITSFEA).*

Section 21B: Provides the SEC with the authority to levy civil money penalties in administrative proceedings against regulated persons. *See Money Penalties.*

Section 21C: Empowers the SEC to issue cease and desist orders. *See Cease and Desist Order; § 8A of the Securities Act.*

Section 21D(b)(1)-(2): Sets forth strict pleading requirements for plaintiffs in private securities fraud suits. *See Pleading Requirements.*

Section 21D(b)(4): Requires that a plaintiff establish causation between the defendant's wrongful conduct and such plaintiff's loss. *See Express Causation Requirement.*

Section 21D(e): Places a limitation on damages in Exchange Act actions where a plaintiff attempts to establish damages by reference to the market price of a security. In this context, the award of damages is the difference between the purchase or sale price paid or received by the plaintiff, as applicable, and the mean trading price of the security during the 90-day period beginning on the date on which the information correcting the misstatement or omission that is the basis for the action is disseminated to the market.

Section 21E: Enacted pursuant to the PSLRA, provides a safe harbor from liability for certain oral and written forward-looking statements made by 1934 Act reporting companies as well as certain persons acting on behalf of such issuers. *See Private Securities Litigation Reform Act (PSLRA); Safe Harbor for Forward-Looking Statements; § 27A of the Securities Act.*

Section 24(d): Provides a basis for withholding disclosure under the Freedom of Information Act of certain records obtained from a foreign securities authority. Section 24(d) was enacted as part of the International Securities Enforcement Cooperation Act of 1990 and essentially enables the SEC to cooperate confidentially with foreign securities regulators.

Section 28(a): Provides that the rights and remedies contained in the Exchange Act shall be in addition to any other rights and remedies that may exist at law or in equity. The statute limits recovery in 1934 Act private damages actions to actual damages. It also states that nothing in the Exchange Act shall affect the jurisdiction of state securities commissions to the extent that the latter do not conflict with the Act or the rules and regulations promulgated thereunder.

Section 29(a): Provides that any condition, stipulation or provision binding a person to waive compliance with any provision of the 1934 Act or any SEC rule or regulation thereunder (or any stock exchange rule) shall be void. *See § 14 of the Securities Act.*

Section 29(b): Provides that every contract formed or performed in contravention of the 1934 Act or any rule or regulation prescribed thereunder "shall be void" as regards the rights of the violating party or his/her successor who takes with knowledge.

Section 30A: Enacted as part of the Foreign Corrupt Practices Act, the provision makes it unlawful for any publicly-held registrant or any person acting on behalf of such issuer to engage in bribery of any foreign official, foreign political party, or candidate for foreign political office. *See Foreign Corrupt Practices Act (FCPA).*

Section 32(a): Generally provides for fines and/or imprisonment for willful violation of any provision of the Exchange Act or any pertinent SEC rule or regulation thereunder. The provision states, however, that no person shall be subject to imprisonment for the violation of any rule or regulation if he/she proves that he/she had no knowledge of such rule or regulation. *See § 24 of the Securities Act.*

SARBANES-OXLEY ACT

Section 302: Requires the Commission to implement rules for CEO/CFO certifications in SEC periodic reports. Implemented in SEC Rules 13a-14 and 15d-14. *See Certifications; Rules 13a-14, 15d-14.*

Section 303: Prohibits attempts to "fraudulently influence" the registrant's auditors by a director or officer (or any person acting under the direction of any such director or officer) of a subject issuer. The statute grants the SEC authority to adopt implementing rules.

Section 304: Requires the CEO and CFO to reimburse the issuer for any incentive-based compensation and profits from the sale of such issuer's securities received during the twelve months after the issuance or filing of a financial statement that through misconduct was in material noncompliance with the securities laws and which requires an accounting restatement by the issuer.

Section 402: Generally, prohibits personal loans made (or arranged) by an issuer for its executive officers or directors. Adds Exchange Act § 13(k).

Section 404: Requires the SEC to adopt rules requiring a registrant's management to include an internal control report in such registrant's annual reports. The internal control report is to include a statement that management is responsible for internal control and financial reporting, an evaluation of effectiveness, and an attestation by a registered public accounting firm as to management's evaluation. *See Rule 13a-15.*

Section 406: Requires the SEC to adopt rules requiring issuers to disclose whether they have a code of ethics applicable to their senior financial officers, and if not, the reason(s) therefore.

Section 409: Requires Exchange Act reporting companies to "disclose to the public on a rapid and current basis such additional information concerning material changes in the financial condition or operations of the issuer, in plain English, which may include trend and qualitative information and graphic presentations, as the Commission determines, by rule, is necessary or useful for the protection of investors and in the public interest." Adds Exchange Act § 13(l). *See § 13(l) of the Exchange Act; Form 8-K.*

Section 501: Requires the SEC to adopt, or authorize for the self-regulatory organizations to promulgate, rules addressing analysts' conflicts of interest. *See Regulation AC.*

Section 602: Authorizes the Commission to regulate persons appearing or practicing before it, including on the basis of competence, character, unethical behavior, "improper professional conduct," or willfully aiding and abetting a violation of the securities laws or the SEC's rules and regulations. Adds Exchange Act § 4C.

Section 806: Creates a private remedy for an employee of an Exchange Act reporting company who suffers retaliation by providing information as a whistleblower.

Section 807: Creates a new crime, "securities fraud," punishable by imprisonment of up to 25 years.

Section 906: Requires the CEO and CFO to certify "that the periodic report containing the financial statements fully complies with the [Exchange Act periodic reporting] requirements and that information contained in the [subject] periodic report fairly presents, in all material respects, the financial condition and results of operations of the issuer." The statute imposes criminal liability on the certifying officers for knowing or willful violations. *See Certifications.*

SEC RULES
Securities Act Rules

Rule 134 Rule specifying what may be included in a "public notice." A "public notice" meeting the terms of Rule 134 is a communication not deemed to be a § 2(a)(10) prospectus and may be published or transmitted during the waiting period (and post-effective period). It is used to ascertain what parties are interested in the securities and the extent of such interest. *See Public Notice.*

Rule 135: Permits a pre-filing announcement by an issuer of a proposed registered offering that will not be deemed a violation of § 5. This rule provides that certain enumerated information may be publicly disseminated by the issuer as long as the notice contains only specified information. Communications under Rule 135 relating to business combination transactions must be filed with the SEC as required by Rule 425. *See Prospectus; § 5(c) of the Securities Act; Rule 425.*

Rule 137: With certain exceptions, permits a dealer not participating in a distribution to publish and distribute recommendations and opinions regarding securities of a reporting company that has filed or proposes to file a registration statement, provided that the dealer receives no remuneration from the issuer for such activities or from the ensuing distribution. The rule applies to the pre-filing, waiting, and post-effective periods.

Rule 138: With certain exceptions, permits dealers participating in a registered offering of non-convertible senior securities by a reporting company to publish recommendations and opinions concerning the issuer's common stock, and vice-versa. The rule applies to the pre-filing, waiting and post-effective periods.

Rule 139: Generally permits participating dealers to publish recommendations or opinions concerning securities of a publicly-held issuer that has filed or proposes to file a registration statement, provided that certain conditions are met. The rule applies to the pre-filing, waiting, and post-effective periods.

Rule 141: Excludes from underwriter status dealers who receive a commission from an underwriter or dealer not in excess of the usual and customary sellers' commissions. *See Dealer; Underwriter.*

Rule 142: Excludes from underwriter status those persons who, under the circumstances delineated in the rule, purchase for investment purposes all or a specified portion of the securities remaining unsold in a registered offering after the lapse of a defined period of time. *See Presumptive Underwriter Doctrine; Underwriter.*

Rule 144: Provides a safe harbor under the § 4(1) exemption for non-affiliated shareholders who are selling their restricted securities and for affiliates who are selling their unrestricted and/or restricted securities without registration. The rule also provides a safe harbor for brokers under the § 4(4) exemption who execute such transactions. If shareholders or brokers make a sale in compliance with the full set of objective conditions of Rule 144, they will not be deemed to be underwriters or involved in a distribution. *See §§ 4(1), 4(4) of the Securities Act.*

Rule 144A: Provides a non-exclusive safe harbor exemption from the Securities Act's registration requirements for resales to eligible institutions (QIBs) of certain restricted securities. *See Qualified Institutional Buyer (QIB); POR-TAL; Regulation S.*

Rule 145: Unless an exemption from registration is available, Rule 145 requires that securities issued in connection with mergers, consolidations and certain other recapitalizations must be registered under the Securities Act. The rule also addresses issuer communications in the pre-filing period, allowing communications that comply with Rules 135, 165 and 166 to be made prior to the filing of the registration statement. Applicable restrictions on resales by persons other than the issuer are also addressed. *See Form S-4.*

Rule 146: Former SEC safe harbor rule to the § 4(2) exemption from Securities Act registration. Rule 146 is no longer in effect and has been superseded by Rule 506 of Regulation D. *See § 4(2) of the Securities Act; Rule 506.*

Rule 147: Safe harbor to the § 3(a)(11) intrastate exemption. Generally, the rule includes an 80% "in state" business requirement upon the issuer, a nine-month out-of-state resale prohibition, a principal residence test for purchasers and offerees, and precautions against interstate offers and sales. The doctrine of integration applies. Unlike the § 3(a)(11) exemption, Rule 147 is only available for offerings by issuers. *See § 3(a)(11) of the Securities Act.*

Rule 152: Pursuant to the conditions set forth in the rule, provides a safe harbor from Securities Act integration of offerings when an issuer engages in a § 4(2) offering and shortly thereafter offers securities pursuant to a registered offering. *See Integration of Offerings; Rule 155.*

Rule 155: Pursuant to enumerated conditions, provides safe harbors from Securities Act integration of offerings (1) for a private offering that follows an abandoned registered offering; and (2) a registered offering that follows an abandoned private offering. *See Integration of Offerings; Rule 477.*

Rule 163: Acts as an exemption to § 5(c) of the Securities Act. Under Rule 163, well-known seasoned issuers can offer securities for sale before a registration statement is filed. Hence, Rule 163 serves as an exemption from § 5(c) for well-known seasoned issuers with respect to making offers to sell in the pre-filing period. *See Pre-Filing Period; Well-Known Seasoned Issuer; § 5(c) of the Securities Act.*

Rule 163A: Acts as an exemption for what is an offer to sell, offer for sale, and offer to buy under § 5(c). A communication is not an offer to sell, offer for sale, or offer to buy when it is made by or on behalf of an issuer more than thirty days prior to the issuer filing the registration statement and does not reference a securities offering. Hence, Rule 163A establishes a bright-line time period, terminating thirty days prior to the filing of the registration statement, during which subject issuers may communicate without risk of violating § 5's gun-jumping prohibition. *See Gun-Jumping; Pre-Filing Period; § 5(c) of the Securities Act.*

Rule 165: Permits offers in connection with a business combination transaction during the pre-filing, waiting, and post-effective periods. The rule defines a business combination transaction as any such transaction specified in Rule 145(a) or an exchange offer. To rely on Rule 165, a prospectus must be filed and applicable tender offer, proxy and information statement rules must be complied with. *See Rule 425.*

Rule 166: Provides that communications by participants in a registered offering involving a business combination transaction before the first public announcement of the offering are not in violation of § 5(c) of the Securities Act upon a showing that reasonable steps were taken to prevent further distribution of the communication until either the initial public announcement is made or the registration statement is filed with the Commission.

Rule 168: Provides a nonexclusive safe harbor for Exchange Act reporting companies from §§ 2(a)(10) and 5(c) for factual business information and forward looking information. If the conditions of the rule are met, the communication is deemed not to constitute an offer to sell for purposes of §§ 2(a)(10) and 5(c) of the Securities Act. *See Gun-Jumping; Pre-Filing Period; § 5(c) of the Securities Act.*

Rule 169: A safe harbor from the § 5 gun-jumping prohibition for continuing and ongoing business communications that allows a non-reporting issuer's continued publication or dissemination of regularly released factual business information that is intended for use by persons other than in their capacity as investors or potential investors. *See Gun-Jumping; § 5(c) of the Securities Act.*

Rule 172: The "access equals delivery" rule. Under the rule, a final prospectus will be deemed to precede or accompany a security for sale so long as the final prospectus meeting the requirements of Securities Act § 10(a) is filed with the SEC, or the issuer will make a good faith and reasonable effort to file it with the SEC as part of the registration statement by the prospectus filing date under Rule 424. Further, the rule allows written confirmations and notices of allocation to be sent after effectiveness of a registration statement without being accompanied or preceded by a final prospectus so long as the final prospectus meets the requirements of Securities Act § 10(a) and is filed with the SEC.

Rule 173: Generally permits an underwriter or dealer selling securities in a registered offering to satisfy the prospectus delivery requirements by providing, in lieu of a final prospectus, a notice to each purchaser stating that the sale was made pursuant to a registration statement. *See § 4(3) of the Securities Act; Rule 174.*

Rule 174: Provision, promulgated by the SEC pursuant to § 4(3) of the Securities Act, nullifying to a large degree, the prospectus delivery requirements of said statute.

Rule 175: Provides a safe harbor for forward-looking statements made by an issuer in a 1933 Act registration statement and in an SEC filed document pursuant to the Exchange Act by a reporting company if made with a reasonable basis and in good faith. The 1934 Act's counterpart to Rule 175 is Rule 3b-6. *See Forward-Looking Statement; "Soft" Information.*

Rule 176: Lists a number of factors for an adjudicator to take into account as "circumstances affecting the determination of what constitutes reasonable investigation" for purposes of the due diligence defense of § 11(b)(3). *See Due Diligence; § 11(b) of the Securities Act.*

Rule 405: Sets forth the definition of terms used throughout Regulation C. *See Regulation C.*

Rule 412: Provides, *inter alia*, that modification of disclosures made in previously filed SEC documents are not an admission that the earlier statements are materially misleading.

Rule 415: Concerns the Securities Act registration of securities to be offered or sold on a delayed or continuous basis in the future. Allows, *inter alia*, Form S-3 (or F-3) issuers to file primary-at-the-market offerings of equity securities which they plan to offer in the future. *See "Shelf" Registration.*

Rule 430: Authorizes the use of a preliminary prospectus or so-called "red herring" to be used in the waiting period as a written offer in satisfaction of the prospectus delivery requirements. *See Preliminary Prospectus; § 10(b) of the Securities Act.*

Rule 430A: Under this rule, issuers engaging in offerings of securities for cash are not required to file a pre-effective "pricing" amendment (*i.e.*, information relating to price and the underwriting syndicate). The information omitted in reliance on Rule 430A must be contained either in the final prospectus which will be deemed a part of the registration statement or in a post-effective amendment to the registration statement.

Rule 433: Contains the conditions which must be met in order for an eligible issuer to use a free writing prospectus, including the delivery or availability of the statutory prospectus at the time the free writing prospectus is used, the information contained in the free writing prospectus, the legend that is to be included, the filing of the free writing prospectus, and record retention for the free writing prospectus.

Rule 477: Provides conditions for an issuer's withdrawal of a Securities Act registration statement, including automatic effectiveness for a subject issuer's application to withdraw the entire registration statement prior to such registration statement becoming effective (unless the SEC objects within fifteen days after such issuer files the withdrawal application). *See Integration of Offerings; Rule 155.*

Rule 501: Sets forth the definitions of terms used throughout Regulation D.

Rule 502: Sets out four general conditions that are applicable to Regulation D offerings. The conditions concern the integration of offerings, with a safe harbor provided therefor; the information that must be disclosed by an issuer to purchasers under a Regulation D offering (except for offerings made pursuant to Rule 504 or solely to accredited investors); the prohibitions against advertising and general solicitation (with the exception of Rule 504(b)(1)); and the limitations on resale (except as provided in Rule 504(b)(1)).

Rule 503: Sets forth the requirements for filing a Form D with the SEC pursuant to a Regulation D offering.

Rule 504: Provides an exemption from Securities Act registration under § 3(b) for offerings not exceeding $1,000,000 in any twelve-month period. The number of investors is unlimited, there are no investor qualifications, and reporting companies and investment companies do not qualify for use of the exemption. Generally, if the securities are state registered or sold only to accredited investors in accordance with applicable state law, the prohibitions on general solicitation and advertising and the restrictions on resale do not apply. Otherwise, no advertising or general solicitation is allowed and restrictions on resale apply. Pursuant to federal law, no information need be specifically disclosed. Nonetheless, the federal antifraud provisions apply to Rule 504 offerings. *See § 3(b) of the Securities Act.*

Rule 505: Provides an exemption under § 3(b) for offerings not exceeding $5 million in any twelve-month period. The exemption is limited to 35 non-accredited purchasers plus an unlimited number of accredited investors. Specified information must be delivered to all non-accredited purchasers. The prohibitions on general solicitation and advertising apply, as well as the restrictions on resale. Investment companies may not use Rule 505. Moreover, issuers disqualified under Regulation A do not qualify for use of the exemption. Today, this exemption is not frequently used. *See § 3(b) of the Securities Act.*

Rule 506: Safe harbor to the § 4(2) exemption. The exemption permits sales to 35 non-accredited purchasers plus an unlimited number of accredited investors. Information supplying requirements (to non-accredited purchasers), investor sophistication requirements (unless the purchaser is accredited), resale limitations, and prohibitions on advertising and general solicitation apply. No dollar limitation applies to Rule 506 offerings. State regulation of Rule 506 offerings has been federally preempted. *See § 4(2) of the Securities Act.*

Rule 507: Eliminates the timely filing requirement of Form D as a condition to the Regulation D exemptions. However, Rule 507 serves as a disqualification to the use of Regulation D for future transactions by any issuer, if it, or a predecessor or affiliate, has been enjoined by a court for violating the filing obligation of Rule 503.

Rule 508: Provides that a failure to comply with one or more of the conditions of a Regulation D exemption will not make that exemption unavailable, provided that, the condition is not designed to protect specifically the complaining person; the failure to comply is insignificant to the offering as a whole; and there has been a good faith and reasonable attempt to comply with all requirements of the regulation. Rule 508 specifies that the provisions of Regulation D relating to advertising and general solicitation, the dollar limits of the Rules 504 and 505 exemptions, and the limits on non-accredited investors in Rules 505 and 506 are significant to every offering and thus are not subject to the Rule 508 defense. Further, Rule 508 does not apply to the SEC or to the state regulators. *See General Solicitation; Substantial Compliance.*

Rule 701: Adopted pursuant to § 3(b) of the Securities Act. The rule generally provides an exemption from registration according to a specified formula during any twelve-month period for offers and sales of securities for certain compensation benefit plans adopted for the participation of employees, officers, directors, consultants, and advisers of an eligible company. This amount may not exceed the greatest of (1) $1 million; (2) 15% of the outstanding securities of the applicable class; or (3) 15% of the issuer's total assets. If more than $5 million of securities are sold, specific disclosure is required. The exemption can only be used for compensatory purposes (rather than for capital raising purposes) and can be used only by nonreporting companies. Restrictions on resale apply to securities sold in Rule 701 offerings.

Rule 1001: Also called the California Exemption. The exemption provides a coordinating federal exemption under § 3(b) for offers not exceeding $5 million in any 12-month period that are exempt under paragraph (n) of Section 25102 of the California Corporations Code. This exemption is limited to issuers that are substantially connected to California and to investors who are determined to be "qualified" purchasers, as defined by the applicable California statutes and regulations. Rule 1001 allows an eligible issuer to "test the waters" by distributing a written general announcement that contains certain specified information. As a general rule, all offers are limited to qualified purchasers and all securities issued pursuant to the exemption are "restricted." *See Model Accredited Investor Exemption; Testing the Waters.*

SEC RULES
Exchange Act Rules

Rule 10b-5 Promulgated pursuant to § 10(b) of the 1934 Act, this rule makes it unlawful to employ any deceptive or manipulative device in connection with the purchase or sale of a security. *See § 10(b).*

Rule 10b5-1: Subject to certain affirmative defenses, this rule subjects a person to insider trading exposure if such person trades while "aware" of material nonpublic information concerning the company or the market for its securities. *See "Disclose or Abstain" Rule; Misappropriation Theory.*

Rule 10b5-2: Sets forth a non-exclusive list of three situations in which a person is deemed to have a relationship of trust and confidence for purposes of invoking the misappropriation theory under § 10(b). *See "Disclose or Abstain" Rule; Misappropriation Theory.*

Rule 13a-14/Rule 15d-14: Implements the CEO and CFO certification requirements set forth by §§ 302 and 906 of the Sarbanes-Oxley Act. *See Certification; §§ 302, 906 of the Sarbanes-Oxley Act.*

Rule 13a-15/Rule 15a-15: Implementing § 404 of the Sarbanes-Oxley Act, generally requires Exchange Act reporting companies to maintain adequate disclosure controls and procedures. *See § 404 of the Sarbanes-Oxley Act.*

Rule 13e-3: Generally, the rule prohibits fraudulent, deceptive, and manipulative acts or practices in connection with going-private transactions and prescribes filing, disclosure, and dissemination requirements as a means reasonably designed to prevent such acts or practices. *See Going-Private; § 13(e) of the Exchange Act.*

Rule 13e-4: Governs issuer tender offers for a company's own securities. The rule prohibits fraudulent, deceptive, and manipulative acts and practices and establishes filing, disclosure, and dissemination requirements. An issuer tender offer regulated by Rule 13e-4, that also constitutes a going-private transaction under Rule 13e-3, must comply with both rules. *See Going Private; Tender Offer; § 13(e) of the Exchange Act; Rule 13e-3; Schedule 13E-3.*

Rule 14a-8: The SEC shareholder proposal rule which sets forth the parameters (and exclusions) of this regimen.

Rule 14a-9: Prohibits the solicitation of proxies which contain any materially false or misleading statement. *See Annual Report to Security Holders; § 14(a) of the Exchange Act.*

Rule 14a-12: Permits management to solicit security holders in proxy contests before furnishing a proxy statement. However, a company is not allowed to secure promises to vote before a proxy statement is furnished to security holders.

Rule 14d-1: Sets forth the scope of Regulations 14D and 14E and the definitions applicable thereto.

Rule 14d-2: Provides when a tender offer is deemed to "commence." The rule also requires all written communications relating to a tender offer to be filed. The rule further provides that a legend is to be included on written communications advising security holders to read the tender offer statement when it is received.

Rule 14d-8: Extends the right of shareholders to receive proration of their shares in a tender offer that is oversubscribed from the previous ten-calendar-day period (as provided in § 14(d)(6)) to the entire period that the offer remains open.

Rule 14d-9: Allows target companies to communicate with security holders to the same degree bidders are permitted. The rule requires targets to file all written communications relating to the transaction on the date the communication is made and include a legend advising security holders to read the recommendation that is to be provided.

Rule 14d-10: Requires that a tender offer be open to all shareholders and that the best price paid to any security holder be paid to any other tendering security holder.

Rule 14d-11: Provides bidders the option to have a subsequent offering period in a third party cash or stock tender offer during which no withdrawal rights are available. The subsequent offering period may last from 3 to 20 business days at the bidder's discretion. The rule sets forth that the same consideration must be used for both offering periods but has no specific requirement that a minimum number of shares be tendered in the initial offering.

Rule 14e-3: Prohibits insider and tippee trading in the tender offer context by applying the disclose-or-abstain provision where an individual is in possession of material information relating to a tender offer when he/she knows or has reason to know that such information is nonpublic and was obtained directly or indirectly from the offeror, the subject corporation, any of their affiliated persons, or any person acting on behalf of either company. *See "Disclose or Abstain" Rule.*

Rule 14e-5: Provides that from the "public announcement" until the expiration of a cash tender offer or exchange offer, a person making the offer is prohibited from purchasing the security that is the subject of the offer other than as part of the offer.

Rule 14e-8: Antifraud rule intended to prevent fraudulent and misleading communications concerning proposed tender offers by prohibiting bidders from announcing an offer that the bidder does not have the intent and/or financing to complete or that is meant to manipulate the price of the bidder's or the target's securities.

Rule 15c2-11:   Generally prohibits broker-dealers from publishing a quotation for any security unless specified information is available with respect to the issuer and the security.

SEC REGULATIONS

Regulation A: Provides an exemption from Securities Act registration for offerings of securities not exceeding $5 million in any twelve-month period. Pursuant to this exemption, a Regulation A offering is available to an unlimited number of investors with no investor qualification requirements. No investment companies are permitted to use the exemption and issuers and underwriters subject to "bad boy" prohibitions are disqualified. The issuer is subject to certain disclosure and notification requirements that resemble a "mini registration." Restrictions on resale do not apply. Moreover, companies relying on the Regulation A exemption may "test the waters" for potential investor interest. *See Testing the Waters; § 3(b) of the Securities Act.*

Regulation AC — Analyst Certification: Requires securities research reports disseminated by broker-dealers to include two analyst certifications. First, the research analyst must certify that the views contained in the research report accurately reflect the analyst's personal views. Second, the analyst must certify whether or not the analyst received any compensation related to the specific recommendation. If any compensation was received, further disclosure as to the source, extent and purpose of the compensation is required as well as a statement that the recommendation could have been affected by that compensation. *See § 501 of the Sarbanes-Oxley Act.*

Regulation BTR — Blackout Trading Restriction: Prohibits directors and executive officers of a publicly-held issuer from trading equity securities they received as compensation from the issuer during a "blackout" period, generally defined as a period of three or more days with respect to which at least half of the plan participants in the issuer's pension plan(s) are barred from trading the company's equity securities.

Regulation C: Sets forth the procedural rules governing the registration of securities under the 1933 Act. *See Rule 405.*

Regulation FD: Prohibits issuers or individuals acting on their behalf from selectively disclosing material nonpublic information to certain enumerated persons (generally securities market professionals and holders of the issuer's securities who may well trade on the basis of the information) without disclosing the information publicly. If the selective disclosure is intentional, then the issuer must publicly disclose the information simultaneously by filing or furnishing a Form 8-K to the SEC or in a manner reasonably designed to provide broad distribution of the information. If the selective disclosure is unintentional, then the issuer must disclose the information to the public promptly, but in no event after the later of 24 hours or the opening of the next day's trading on the New York Stock Exchange. Violating Regulation FD exposes the issuer to SEC administrative and civil enforcement action, but does not by itself impose any Rule 10b-5 antifraud liability on the issuer or establish a private right of action.

Regulation G: Requires that a disclosure of non-GAAP financial measure be accompanied with the most analogous GAAP financial measure and a reconciliation of the two measures be provided.

Regulation M: Governs the activities of issuers, underwriters, and certain other participants in connection with securities offerings and is designed to prevent manipulative conduct by persons who have an interest in the subject offering.

Regulation M-A: Found in Regulation S-K, this regulation contains disclosure requirements for issuer tender offers, third-party tender offers, tender offer recommendation statements and going-private transactions, as well as certain requirements for cash merger proxy statements. The regulation also addresses the difficulty of understanding disclosure documents in business combination transactions by requiring a plain English summary sheet for all cash tender offers and mergers.

Regulation NMS: Sets forth substantive rules that seek to modernize and strengthen the regulatory framework of the U.S. equity markets. The regulation provides for a trade-through rule which requires that securities markets implement procedures entitling customers to have their orders executed at the best price posted that is available for automatic execution.

Regulation S-K: Sets forth the substantive disclosure requirements for filing forms under the 1933 and 1934 Acts.

Regulation S-X: Delineates the accounting rules and procedures to be followed in the preparation of the audited financial statements and SEC filings required by the 1933 and 1934 Acts.

Regulation S: Generally provides that § 5 of the 1933 Act does not apply to offers and sales outside of the United States and specifies the elements for determining whether an offer and sale is outside the United States. Regulation S is intended to clarify the extraterritorial reach of U.S. securities registration provisions and to enhance the U.S. position in international securities markets. Besides the general statement which is analyzed under all relevant facts and circumstances, Regulation S also provides several safe harbors for extraterritorial offers, sales, and resales of securities. *See Rule 144A.*

SEC FORMS

Form S-1: Used by first-time issuers for initial public offerings, this is the basic, long-form registration statement. Moreever, unseasoned Exchange Act reporting companies also use Form S-1 for their at-the-market offerings of common stock. With respect to such unseasoned issuers, generally incorporation by reference is permitted.

Form S-3: Generally available to a company reporting under the 1934 Act for a twelve month period and that is not a shell company — but, for issuer primary offerings of common stock, eligible issuers, prior to any such offering, also must have a class of equity security traded on a national securities exchange. Companies meeting these requirements are allowed the fullest incorporation by reference of 1934 Act documents into the registration statement. They need only include the transaction-specific description of the offering in the prospectus, as well as events that occurred after the filing of the most recent 1934 Act report incorporated by reference.

Form S-4: Form which may be used for the registration of securities issued in combinations, mergers, consolidations, recapitalizations, acquisitions of assets, and other transactions that require registration under Rule 145. *See Rule 145.*

Form S-8: Available to reporting companies offering securities to their employees or their subsidiaries' employees pursuant to a stock benefit plan.

Form 8-K: Form that requires disclosure of specified events that may arise in the period between 1934 Act periodic filings. Disclosure of events other than those called for by the form is permissive rather than mandatory. In view of the continuous reporting framework called for by § 409 of the Sarbanes-Oxley Act, the SEC has significantly expanded the scope of the Form 8-K. *See §§ 13(a), 15(d) of the Exchange Act; § 409 of the Sarbanes-Oxley Act.*

Form 10-K: The form used by issuers which are Exchange Act reporting companies for filing their annual reports pursuant to § 13 or § 15(d) of the Exchange Act. Information required to be included in the Form 10-K includes, for example, audited financial statements and a meaningful description of the issuer's business, operations, and financial condition. *See §§ 13(a), 15(d) of the Exchange Act.*

Form 10-Q: The form used by issuers which are Exchange Act reporting companies for the filing of quarterly reports pursuant to § 13 or § 15(d) of the 1934 Act. *See §§ 13(a), 15(d) of the Exchange Act.*

SEC SCHEDULES

Schedule A: Sets forth the information required to be contained in a statutory § 10(a) prospectus, which is filed as part of the registration statement. *See §§ 7 and 10(a) of the 1933 Act.*

Schedule 13D: Statement of ownership disclosure form which must be filed pursuant to § 13(d) of the 1934 Act when a person (or group) acquires over five percent beneficial ownership of a reporting class of equity security. The purpose is to alert investors, the marketplace, and the target company's management of a potential change in corporate control. *See § 13(d) of the Exchange Act.*

Schedule 13E-3: A comprehensive disclosure document which must be filed by an issuer (and its affiliates) pursuant to Rule 13e-3 in the event of a going private transaction. *See Going-Private; § 13(e) of the Exchange Act; Rules 13e-3 and 13e-4.*

Schedule 14A: Specifies the information that is required to be set forth in a proxy statement.

Schedule 14D-9: Statement which must be filed with the SEC by a subject (target) company of a tender offer, pursuant to Rule 14d-9, and containing information including, if material, a description of any arrangement or other understanding and conflicts of interest between, among others, the offeror, the subject corporation, and their affiliates. Certain negotiations and transactions undertaken by the target company in response to the tender offer and its position in regard to the tender offer (and the reasons therefor) must be disclosed. *See Tender Offer; § 14(d) of the Exchange Act; Rule 14d-9.*

Schedule TO: Refers to Regulation M-A for all substantive disclosure requirements and incorporates such requirements for, *inter alia*, issuer and third-party tender offers as well as going-private transactions. The Schedule must contain information regarding the tender offeror, including its identity and background, as well as its purpose for the tender offer and its proposals or plans.

TABLE OF CASES

[References are to pages.]

[References are to pages.]

C

[References are to pages.]

[References are to pages.]

G

H

[References are to pages.]

[References are to pages.]

[References are to pages.]

S

[References are to pages.]

TABLE OF STATUTES, RULES, AND REGULATIONS

[References are to pages and footnotes.]

[References are to pages and footnotes.]

[References are to pages and footnotes.]

[References are to pages and footnotes.]

[References are to pages and footnotes.]

[References are to pages and footnotes.]

[References are to pages and footnotes.]

[References are to pages and footnotes.]

[References are to pages and footnotes.]

INDEX

[References are to pages.]

[References are to pages.]

[References are to pages.]